# Electronic Devices and Circuits

**P. John Paul**
*Gurunanak Engineering College*
*Hyderabad*

PUBLISHING FOR ONE WORLD

**NEW AGE INTERNATIONAL (P) LIMITED, PUBLISHERS**
New Delhi • Bangalore • Chennai • Cochin • Guwahati • Hyderabad
Jalandhar • Kolkata • Lucknow • Mumbai • Ranchi
Visit us at **www.newagepublishers.com**

Published by New Age International (P) Ltd., Publishers
First Edition: 2003
Reprint: 2010



***Branches:***

- 36, Malikarjuna Temple Street, Opp. ICWA, Basavanagudi, **Bangalore**. © (080) 26677815
- 26, Damodaran Street, T. Nagar, **Chennai**. © (044) 24353401
- CC-39/1016,Carrier Station Road, Ernakulam South, **Cochin**. © (0484) 4051303
- Hemsen Complex, Mohd. Shah Road, Paltan Bazar, Near Starline Hotel, **Guwahati**. © (0361) 2543669
- No. 105, 1st Floor, Madhiray Kaveri Tower, 3-2-19, Azam Jahi Road, Nimboliadda, **Hyderabad**. © (040) 24652456
- RDB Chambers (Formerly Lotus Cinema ) 106A, Ist Floor, S.N. Banerjee Road, **Kolkata**. © (033) 22275247
- 16-A, Jopling Road, **Lucknow**. © (0522) 2209578
- 142C, Victor House, Ground Floor, N.M. Joshi Marg, Lower Parel, **Mumbai**. © (022) 24927869
- 22, Golden House, Daryaganj, **New Delhi**. © (011) 23262370, 23262368

**ISBN(10) : 81-224-1415-X**

**ISBN (13): 978-81-224-1415-8**

**Rs. 220.00**

**C-09-11-4170**

Printed in India at Mohanlal Printers, Delhi.

**PUBLISHING FOR ONE WORLD**
**NEW AGE INTERNATIONAL (P) LIMITED, PUBLISHERS**
4835/24, Ansari Road, Daryaganj, New Delhi-110002
Visit us at **www.newagepublishers.com**

*Dedicated to the*

***GOD ALMIGHTY***

*who gave me life and eternal life*

# PREFACE

In this postmodern world it is unable to imagine any application or any place without electronics, from domestic appliances to defence applications. Computation, automation, power generation, amplification and communication will always start from electronic devices and circuits. Therefore studying the basic subject like electronic devices and circuits is very essential for every engineer. Though there are many books on electronic devices and circuits every author has his own presentation and analysis. This book has evolved after teaching for about two decades for undergraduate students at engineering level and for competitive exams like GATE and IES. The book assumes elementary physics background though some links from physics to electronic devices and circuits are given. The book is written to make self sufficient and self-explanatory with thorough linking of the subject. The development of the subject is unique and original. The questions that are frequently asked by students and teachers are also incorporated while developing the subject. The book can be used for fresh B.Tech's, AMIE, AMIETE, GATE, IES and other competitive exams. Every chapter contains the concept, the required derivations, solved problems, objective questions, conventional questions, exercise problems and lab experiments. The answers are given for objective questions and exercise problems.

Chapter 1 is written with an intention of linking physics to electronic devices and circuits. The basics required for understanding the subject is provided. Chapter 2 deals with the first semiconductor device diode, its open circuit, DC and AC operations are dealt including rectifiers and filters. Chapter 3 contains special semiconductor diodes like zener, tunnel, light emitting diodes.

Chapter 4 introduces the semiconductor amplifier device called Bipolar Junction Transistor (BJT). Its OC and DC operation is dealt which includes biasing, stabilization and compensation of BJT. Chapter 5 deals with BJT amplifier, introduction, mid frequency and low frequency operations are dealt. Chapter 6 is emphasized on high frequency analysis of BJT, which includes the thorough discussion on gain bandwidth product.

Chapter 7 introduces the third important device, which is very popular in VLSI called Field Effect Transistor (FET). Its OC and DC operations are explained which includes the MOSFET's and biasing of all FET's. Chapter 8 is to explain the FET amplifier its mid frequency, low frequency and high frequency is dealt along with gain bandwidth product.

From chapter 9 to 11 BJT and FET are both together while explaining multistage amplifiers negative feedback amplifiers and sinusoidal oscillators.

In chapter 12 a slight deviation is taken in order to explain the power devices like thyristors and SCR's which includes UJT, their characteristics and applications are covered. In the last chapter the very important device for electronics engineer is covered, namely, cathode ray oscilloscope. Its operation and applications are discussed.

At the end of the book appendix A- physical constants, B- conversion factors and prefixes, C- useful properties of crystalline silicon, germanium and galium arsenide, D-PN junction diode, E- zener diode, F- tunnel diode, G- photo diode, H- BJT-NPN and PNP small signal transistor, I-N-channel and P-channel FET, J- power and small signal MOSFET.

I hope this book will be useful for students and teachers' suggestions for improvement and constructive criticism would be gratefully received and acknowledged.

**Author**

# ACKNOWLEDGEMENTS

First of all I thank GOD for giving this life and eternal life, to whom the book is dedicated. Secondly, I thank my parents who gave me birth and brought me up. Thirdly, my wife Kezia and children Danny and Shiny for their cooperation. I also thank Gurunanak Engineering College staff and in particular Sardar Tavinder Singh Kohli, the Chairman of Gurunanak Educational Society and H.S. Virk, the Principal of Gurunanak Engineering College who have given me time and encouragement to complete the book. And I also thank the staff of The Engineering Academy (TEA) Hyderabad and in particular K. Bindu Nischala who stood with me in taking the trouble and strain in completion of the book.

I thank publishers for printing and the inspiration given by them.

**Author**

# CONTENTS

# ‹1›

# SEMICONDUCTOR PHYSICS

## 1.1 INTRODUCTION

The concept of atom as a building block of matter dates back to the early Greek philosophers in 400 BC but detailed knowledge of atomic structure is new. The first experimental evidence of the existence of atom came from Dalton's law of combining weights in 1811. The electrical nature of atom was established later in the $19^{th}$ century owing to the discovery of electrolysis by Michael Faraday (1791-1867).

In 1897, electron was discovered by J.J. Thompson and was shown to be a universal constituent of matter. To that end many atomic models such as planetary (Rutherford), stationary-orbits model (Bohr) *etc*, were put forward in an attempt to unveil the mysteries behind the atomic debris.

The subsequent developments in that direction led to the genesis of *wave mechanics*; which is believed to be an adequate theory to fully describe the mechanics of the sub-atomic particles like electron, proton, neutron *etc*. For example, the Schrodinger wave equation, when written for a particle moving under the influence of a periodic potential (nearly free electron model), turns out to be a second order differential equation. And the solution of this wave equation aptly describes the band structure of solids, which allows us to distinguish between conductors, semiconductors and insulators.

Any material that supports a generous flow of charge when a voltage source of limited magnitude is applied across its terminals is called a *conductor*.

An *insulator* is a material that offers a very low level of conductivity under pressure for an applied voltage source.

A *semiconductor* therefore is a material whose conductivity level lies somewhere between the extremes of a conductor and an insulator.

## 1.2 ATOMIC NATURE

As we mentioned in the preceding section, many attempts were made to understand the nature of an atom. In 1911, Rutherford put forward his atomic model, based on the observations made from the x-ray scattering experiments. He found that an atom consists of a central core called *nucleus*, which is positively charged. And the negatively charged electrons orbit around it in various levels. As a specific illustration of this model, we consider hydrogen atom and study its atomic structure. This atom consists of one proton in nucleus and one single electron revolving round the nucleus. To account for the stability of the atom, he proposed that the Coulomb force of attraction:

$$F = \frac{Ze^2}{4\pi\varepsilon_0 r^2} \quad ...(1.1)$$

where, $Z$ is the atomic number (here $Z = 1$), $\varepsilon$ is the permittivity of the free space, $e$ is the charge of the electron and $r$ is the distance between the electron and the nucleus; is balanced by the centripetal force:

$$F = \frac{mv^2}{r} \quad ...(1.2)$$

From Eqs. (1.1) and (1.2), we get

$$mv^2 = \frac{e^2}{4\pi\varepsilon_0 r} \quad ...(1.3)$$

Now to arrive at an expression for the orbital energy, we have to calculate the potential energy at a distance '$r$' from the nucleus: P.E $= -\int_r^\infty F.dr$. Here, the negative sign indicates that the energy is spent on electron to bring it from $\infty$ to a radius $r$ against the force of attraction. Therefore

$$\text{P.E.} = \frac{-e^2}{4\pi\varepsilon_0 r} \quad ...(1.4)$$

and the total energy is given by:

$$W = \frac{1}{2}mv^2 + \left(-\frac{e^2}{4\pi\varepsilon_0 r}\right) \quad ...(1.5)$$

Thus, we can obtain the expression for the total orbital energy by combining Eqs (1.3) and (1.4) and substituting them in Eq. (1.5):

$$W = \frac{1}{2}\left(\frac{e^2}{4\pi\varepsilon_0 r}\right) - \frac{e^2}{4\pi\varepsilon_0 r} = \frac{-e^2}{8\pi\varepsilon_0 r}$$

Therefore, the orbital energy is:

$$W = \frac{-e^2}{8\pi\varepsilon_0 r} \quad ...(1.6)$$

The negative sign here reflects the fact that the atomic electron is bound to the nucleus.

## Drawbacks

Though, this model could successfully explain the nature of atom, it suffers from some serious drawbacks as listed below.

(i) It could not explain the stability of the atom. According to classical theory of electromagnetism, any accelerated charge which oscillates with a frequency *f*, will radiate energy of same frequency; and this emission of radiation, if it goes on and on the orbiting electron will lose energy and ultimately collapses into the nucleus and the whole atom would be obliterated.

(ii) Another serious drawback of this model is that it could not explain the discreteness of the spectrum.

## Bohr Atomic Model

In order to avert the aforementioned situation, the Danish physicist, Neils Bohr postulated the following three fundamental laws:

1. The atom cannot possess *continuum* of energies but it can possess certain discrete energies instead. As long as the electron orbits in one of these *descritized* energy states; it will not emit radiation and the electron is said to be in a *stationary* state.
2. During the transition from one stationary state of energy $W_2$, to another stationary state of energy $W_1$; radiation of definite frequency will be emitted. The frequency of this emitted radiation is given by

$$f = \frac{W_2 - W_1}{h} \quad ...(1.7)$$

   where *h* is Planck's constant.
3. the angular momentum of the electron in a stationary state is quantized and must be

   an integral multiple of $\frac{h}{2\pi}$ thus

$$mvr = n\frac{h}{2\pi} \quad ...(1.8)$$

   where *n* is an integer.

### *Expression to find out the energy of an atom*

Let $r_n$ : Radius of the orbit in which the electron is revolving

$v_n$ : Tangential velocity of electron

$h$ : Plank's constant = $6.626 \times 10^{-34}$ I – sec

$\varepsilon_0$ : absolute permittivity = $8.854 \times 10^{-18}$ F/m.

*From Coulomb's law*: The force of attraction between the nucleus and electron

$$F_e = \frac{e^2}{4\pi\varepsilon_o r^2} \quad ...(1.9)$$

The centrifugal force acting on the electron due to its motion along the circular path.

$$F_c = \frac{mv_n^2}{r_n} \quad ...(1.10)$$

According to Bohr, when the electron revolving in the orbit it will not lose energy.

$$\Rightarrow \quad F_e = F_c$$

$$\frac{e^2}{4\pi\varepsilon_0 r^2} = \frac{mv_n^2}{r_n}$$

$$\Rightarrow \quad mv_n^{\ 2} = \frac{e^2}{4\pi\varepsilon_0 r_n} \quad ...(1.11)$$

Kinetic energy $\quad \text{K.E} = \frac{1}{2}mv^2$

Potential energy $\cdot$ $\text{P.E} = \int_{rn}^{\infty} F_e dr.n. = -\int_{rn}^{\infty} \frac{e^2}{4\pi\varepsilon_0 r} dr_n$

$$= -\frac{e^2}{4\pi\varepsilon_0}\int_{rn}^{\infty}\frac{1}{r_n^2}\cdot dr_n = -\frac{e^2}{4\pi\varepsilon_0 r_n}$$

$$W = \text{K.E} + \text{P.E}$$

$$= \frac{1}{2}mv_n^2 + \left[-\frac{e^2}{4\pi\varepsilon_0 r_n}\right]$$

$$W = \frac{1}{2}\left\{\frac{e^2}{4\pi\varepsilon_0 r_n}\right\} - \frac{e^2}{4\pi\varepsilon_0 r_n} = -\frac{e^2}{8\pi\varepsilon_0 r_n} \quad ...(1.12)$$

From Bohr postulates

$$mvr = \frac{nh}{2\pi} \quad \Rightarrow \quad V_n^2 = \frac{n^2h^2}{4\pi^2 m^2 r_n^2} \quad ...(1.13)$$

Substitute eq. (1.13) in eq. (1.11)

$$\Rightarrow \qquad r_n = \frac{n^2 h^2 \varepsilon_0}{me^2 \pi} \qquad \text{...(1.14)}$$

Subsitute eq. (1.14) in eq. (1.12) we get

$$W_n = \frac{-me^4}{8h^2 {\varepsilon_0}^2}\left(\frac{1}{n^2}\right)$$

Thus upon combining Eq. (1.14) with Eq. (1.13) the exact frequencies of the emitted radiation are calculated. This is the remarkable achievement of Bohr's atomic model.

***Conclusions:***

1. All orbits are discrete
2. All orbits energies are negative.
3. As n increases, $W$ increases.

   $\therefore \quad W_3 > W_2 > W_1.$
4. $(W_3 - W_2) + (W_2 - W_1)$, orbits are not equidistant

***Atomic concentration:***

$$n = \left(\frac{A_0 d}{A}\right) \text{ atoms / cm}^{2\cdot}$$

Where $A$ is the atomic weight,
$d$ is the density.
$A_0$ is the Avogadro number,

for germanium.

$$A = 72.6$$
$$d = 5.32 \text{ g/cm}^3$$
$$A_o = 6.023 \times 10^{23} \text{ molecules/mole}$$
$$n = \frac{6.025 \times 10^{23} \times 5.32}{7.26}$$
$$n = 4.4 \times 10^{22} \text{ atoms/cm}^3.$$

for silicon.

$$A = 28/1$$
$$d = 2.33 \text{ g/cm}^3$$
$$A_o = 6.023 \times 010^{23} \text{ molecules/mole}$$
$$n = 5 \times 10^{22} \text{ atoms/cm}^3$$

$n_{si} > n_{Ge,}$ because atomic number of Si is less than atomic number of Ge.

### Advantages of Bhor's atomic model

1. There is no continuous radiation.
2. This model could explain the discreteness of the spectrum.

### *Energy diagram with orbits*

The experimentally determined energy-level diagram for mercury is shown in figure 1.1

The numbers to the left of the horizontal lines give the energy of these levels in electron volts, the arrows represent some of the transitions that have been found to exist in actual spectra, the attached numbers giving the wavelength of the emitter radiation expressed in angstrom units ($10^{-10}$m). The light emitted in these transitions gives rise to the luminous character of the gaseous discharge. It is customary to express the energy value of the stationary states in electron volts E rather than in joules W. Also it is more common to specify the emitted radiation by its wavelength λ in angstroms rather than by its frequency **f** in hertz. This may be rewritten in the form $\lambda = \dfrac{12400}{E_2 - E_1}$

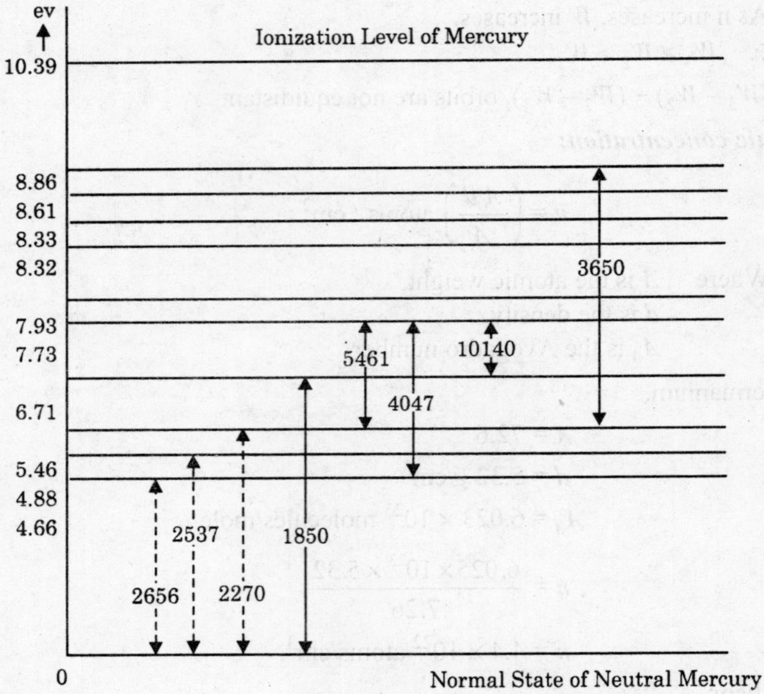


**Fig. 1.1** The lower energy levels of mercury.

The lowest energy state is called the normal level, and the other stationary states of the atom are called excited, radiating, critical, or resonance levels.

## 1.3 CRYSTALLINE NATURE

Most metals and semiconductors are crystalline in nature. A crystal is a systematic array of atoms or molecules built up by regular repetition in three dimensions of fundamental structural unit. The nature of crystal is nothing but atomic nature in the presence of other atoms. Electrostatic interaction will be negligible, if inter atomic spacing between two atoms increases. When atoms form crystal, the energy levels of the inner shell are not affected by the presence of neighboring atoms. The levels of the outer shells are changed since these electrons are shared by more than one atom in the crystal. The new energy levels of the outer electrons can be determined by means of Quantum Mechanics, and coupling between the outer shell electron of the atom results in a band of closely spaced energy instead of widely separated energy levels of the isolated atoms. The representation of atoms has shown in fig. 1.2.

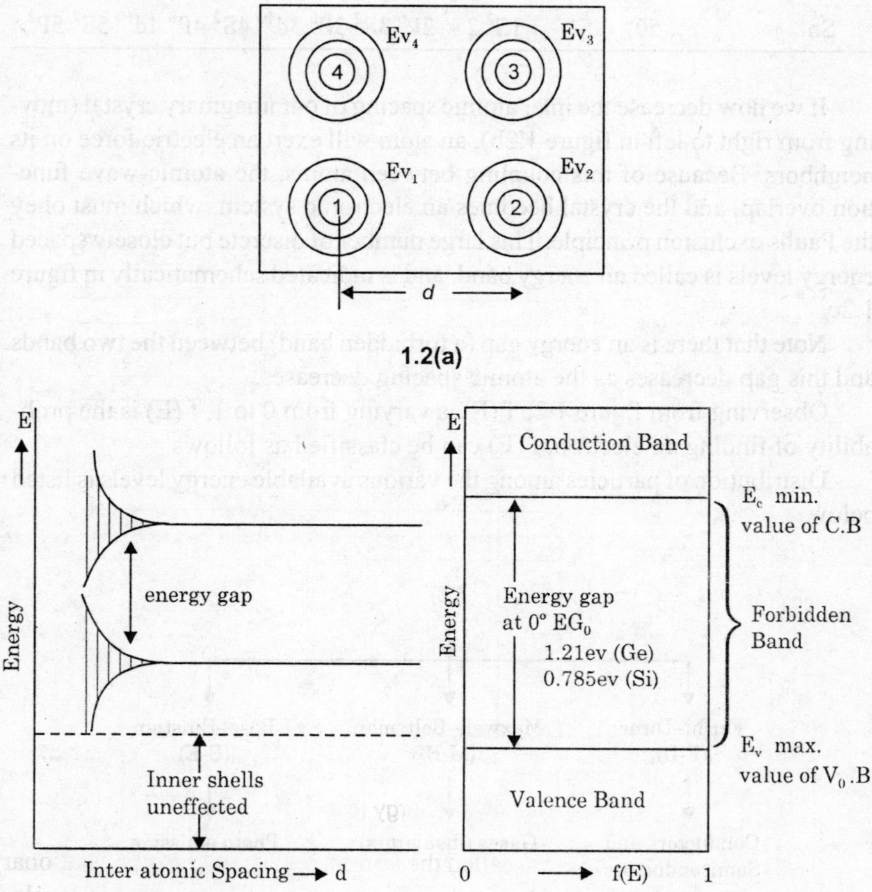


1.2(b) 1.2(c)

**Fig. 1.2** Representation of Atoms (a) atoms in a crystal (b) electrostatic interaction with inter atomic spacing (c) energy band diagram

Consider a crystal consisting of N atoms of one of the elements in Table 1-1. Imagine that it is possible to vary the spacing between atoms without altering the type of fundamental crystal structure. If the atoms are so far apart that the interaction between them is negligible, the energy levels will coincide with those of the isolated atom.

**Table 1.1** Electronic configuration in-group IVA.

| *Element* | *Atomic Number* | *Configuration* |
|---|---|---|
| C | 6 | $1S^2\ 2S^2\ 2P^2$ |
| Si | 14 | $1S^2\ 2S^2\ 2P^6\ 3S^2\ 3P^2$ |
| Ge | 32 | $1S^2\ 2S^2\ 2P^6\ 3S^2\ 3P^6\ 3d^{10}\ 4S^2\ 4P^2$ |
| Sn | 50 | $1S^2\ 2S^2\ 2P^6\ 3S^2\ 3P^6\ 3d^{10}\ 4S^2\ 4P^6\ 4d^{10}\ 5S^2\ 5P^2$ |

If we now decrease the inter atomic spacing of our imaginary crystal (moving from right to left in figure 1.2b), an atom will exert an electric force on its neighbors. Because of this coupling between atoms, the atomic-wave function overlap, and the crystal becomes an electronic system, which must obey the Paulis exclusion principle. This large number of discrete but closely spaced energy levels is called an energy band, and is indicated schematically in figure 1.2c.

Note that there is an energy gap (a forbidden band) between the two bands and this gap decreases as the atomic spacing decreases.

Observing from figure 1.2c f (E) is varying from 0 to 1, f (E) is the probability of finding an electron, f (E) can be classified as follows.

Distribution of particles among the various available energy levels is listed below

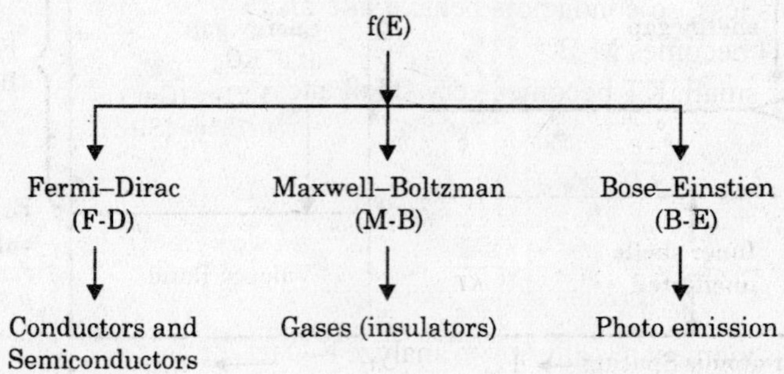


***Maxwell-Boltzman (M-B)*** M-B distribution is applicable to macroscopic (classical) particles and the probability and the probability distribution $f(E)$ is given by:

$$f(E) = \exp\left\{-\left(\frac{E - E_F}{KT}\right)\right\}$$

$$V_T = \frac{KT}{q} = \frac{T}{11600}$$

$$V_T = 26 \text{ mv}/300° \text{ k} \qquad KT = 26 \text{ meV}/300° \text{ K}$$

where k is Boltzmann constant, $E_0$ is the energy of the lowest level and T is the absolute temperature.The relationship between FD and MB is obtained at extremely low temperature where emmission is less.

## *Bose- Einstein (B-E)*

BE distribution is applicable to particles that are indistinguishable (i.e. microscopic particles) and the distribution can be written as:

$f(E) = \frac{1}{\left(e^{\frac{WF}{KT}} - 1\right)}$ it is called B-E distribution function. WF : Work Function

## *Fermi-Dirac (F-D)*

Particles were considered to be distinguishable and any number of them could occupy a given energy state, but F-D, which is applicable to electrons in solids, the particles are indistinguishable.

The distribution function of F-D is

$$F(E) = \frac{1}{1 + e^{\frac{E-E_F}{KT}}}$$

The relationship between F-D and M-B is at extremely low temperature, emission is less, so conductors behave like insulators.

∴ F-D becomes M-B.

If T is small, KT becomes very small and

$$e^{\frac{E-E_F}{KT}} >> 1$$

$$f(E) = e^{-\left(\frac{E-E_F}{KT}\right)}$$

At this moment it is alluring to analyze F-D function as various temperature.

## *Case (1)*

At $\qquad T = 0° \text{ K}$

$$f(E) = \frac{1}{1 + e^{\frac{(E-E_F)}{KT}}} = \frac{1}{1 + e^{\pm\alpha}}$$

(a) For $E > E_F$

$$f(E) = \frac{1}{1+e^{+\infty}} = \frac{1}{1+\infty} = 0$$

(b) For $E < E_F$

$$f(E) = \frac{1}{1+e^{-\infty}} = \frac{1}{1+0} = 1$$

$\therefore$ **At 0° K intrinsic semiconductor acts as an insulator.**

***Case (2)***

At $T = 300°$ k

$$f(E) = \frac{1}{1+e^{\pm l \arg e(E-E_F)}}$$

(a) $E >> E_F$

$$f(E) = \frac{1}{1+e^{(l \arg ex)\,(l \arg e\ value)}} = \frac{1}{1+e^{+\infty}}\ 0$$

(b) $E << E_F$

$$F(E) = \frac{1}{1+e^{(-l \arg ex)\,(l \arg e\ value)}} = \frac{1}{1+0} = 1$$

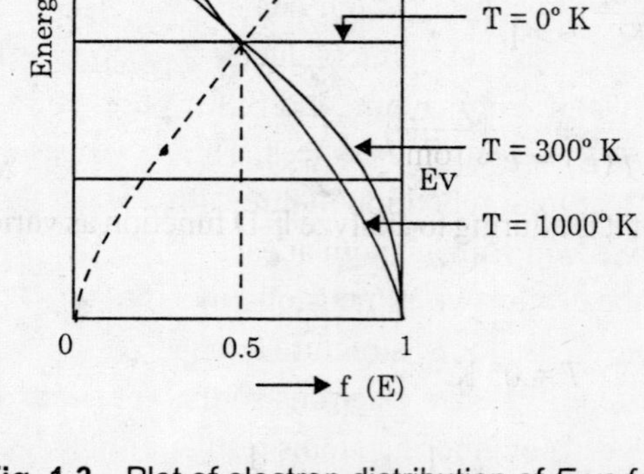


**Fig. 1.3** Plot of electron distribution of *E vs f (E)*

The equation $f(E)$ called Fermi-Dirac probability function, specifies the fraction of all states at energy E occupied under conditions of thermal equilibrium. From quantum statistics it is found that $f(E) = \frac{1}{1+e^{(E-E_F)/KT}}$ where $K$ is Boltzman constant $ev/o_k$ and $T$ is temperature 0°k. The Fermi level represents the energy state with 50% probability of being filled if no forbidden band exists because if $E = E_f$ then $f(E) = \frac{1}{2}$ for any temperature.

### *Conclusions*

1) $fe(F)$ is symmetrical around $E_F$
2) $fe(E) = f_h(E)$ above and below $E_F$
3) $fe(E) + f_h(E) = 1$ at same level
4) As temperature increases, conductivity increases
5) (a) $N_C$ = conduction constant.

$$= 4.82 \times 10^{15} \left(\frac{mn}{m}\right)^{3/2} + \frac{3}{2}$$

$mn$ = Effective mass of electron

$m$ = Rest mass of electron.

(b) $N_V$ = Valency constant

$$= 4.82 \times 10^{15} \left(\frac{mp}{m}\right)^{3/2} + \frac{3}{2}$$

$m_p$ = Effective mass of hole

$m$ = Rest mass of electron.

∴ In an intrinsic semiconductor, conductivity increases with temperature.

## 1.4 INTRINSIC SEMICONDUCTOR

A semiconductor is a material, which has a resistance in between that of a conductor and an insulator. A semiconductor in its purest form is known as intrinsic semiconductor. Germanium and Silicon are the two most important semiconductors used in electronic devices. The crystal structure of these materials consists of a regular repetition in three dimensions of a unit cell having the form of a tetrahedron with an atom at each vertex. This crystal structure is illustrated symbolically in two dimensions in figure 1.4. Germanium has a total of 32 electrons in its atomic structure arranged in shells. Each atom in Ge crystal contributes four valence electrons so that the atom is tetravalent. The binding force between neighboring atoms results from the fact that each of the valence electrons of Ge atom is shared by one of its nearest neighbors. This electron pair or covalent bond is shown in figure 1.4 by two dashed line, which join each atom to each of its neighbors. The valence electrons serve to bind one atom to the next this results in valence electrons being tightly bound to the nucleus. The crystal has low conductivity in spite of the availability of four valence electrons.

At a very low temperature (say 0°k) the ideal structure of figure 1.4 is approached and the crystal behaves as an insulator, since no free carriers are available. At room temperature, some of the covalent bonds will be broken because of thermal energy supplied to the crystal, and conduction is made possible.

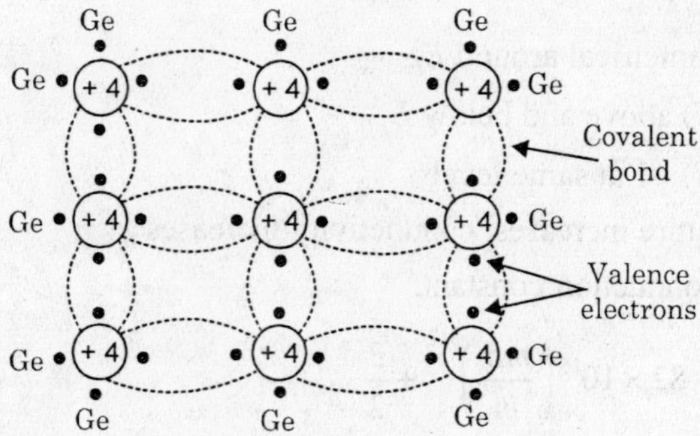


**Fig. 1.4** Crystal structure of Germanium, illustrated Symbolically in two dimensions

Here an electron, which for greater period of time forms part of covalent bond, is being dislodged and therefore free to wander in a random fashion through out the crystal. The energy required to break such a covalent bond is about 0.72ev for Ge and 1.1 ev for Si at room temperature. The absence of electron in covalent bond is represented by a small circle, and such an incomplete covalent bond is called a hole. The importance of the hole is that it may serve as a carrier of electricity comparable in effectiveness with the free electron.

When a bond is incomplete, so that a hole exists, it is relatively easy for a valence electron in a neighboring atom to leave its covalent bond to fill this hole. Hence the hole effectively moves in the direction opposite to that of the electronics. This hole in its new position may now be filled by an electron from another covalent bond and the hole will correspondingly move one more step in the direction opposite to the motion of the electron. This is the mechanism for the conduction of electricity, which does not involve free electron. The motion of hole in one direction actually means the transport of a negative charge an equal distance in the opposite direction. In a pure semi-conductor, the number of holes is equal to number of free electrons. Thermal agitation continues to produce new hole-electron pairs, whereas other hole electron pairs disappears as a result of recombination.

***Conductivity*** With each hole-electron pair created, two charge-carrying particles are found. One is negative that is free electron of mobility $\mu_n$ and the other is positive that is hole of mobility $\mu_p$. These particles move in opposite direction in electric field $\xi$, but since there are in opposite sign, the current of each is in the same direction. Hence the current density $J$ is given by

$$J = \rho v,\ \rho = nq. \text{ and } v = \mu\varepsilon.$$

$$\therefore \quad J = nq\mu\varepsilon$$

For semiconductor $J = (n\mu_n + p\mu_p)\, e\varepsilon = \sigma\varepsilon$ ...(1)

Where $n$ = magnitude of free electrons (negative) concentration

$P$ = magnitude of hole (positive) concentration

$\sigma$ = conductivity

Hence $\sigma = (n\mu_n + p\mu_p)\, e$ ...(2)

For the pure semiconductor called intrinsic

$$n = p = n_i$$

where $\mathbf{n_i}$ is intrinsic concentration.

With increasing temperature, the density of hole -electron pair increases and correspondingly the conductivity increases. The intrinsic concentration $\mathbf{n_i}$ varies with temperature in accordance with relationship

$$n_i^2 = A_0 T^3\, e^{\frac{-EG_0}{KT}} \quad ...(3)$$

where $EG_0$ is the energy gap at 0°k in electron volts

$k$ is Boltzman constant in eV/°K

### *Intrinsic concentration*

We know $n_i^2 = np$, mass action law

$$n_i^2 = \left\{N_C e^{-\frac{E_C(-EF)}{KT}}\right\}\left\{N_V e^{-\frac{(E_F-E_V)}{KT}}\right\}$$

$$= \left[4.82\times10^{15}\left(\frac{mn}{m}\right)^{3/2} T^{3/2}.e^{-\frac{(E_C-EF)}{KT}}\right]\times$$

$$\left[4.82\times10^{15}\left(\frac{m_p}{m}\right)^{3/2} T^{3/2}.e^{-\frac{(E_F-EV)}{KT}}\right]$$

$$= (2.32\times10^{31})\left(\frac{mp.mn}{m^2}\right)^{3/2} T^3\, e^{-\frac{EG(T)}{KT}}$$

$$EG(T) = EG_0 - \beta T,\ \beta = \text{Temperature Factor}$$

$$= 1.21 - (3.60\times10^{-4})\, T \to \text{Si}$$

$$= 0.785 - (2.23 \times 10^{-4})\, T \rightarrow \text{Ge}$$

$$n_i^2 = \left\{ 2.32 \times 10^{31} \left( \frac{m_n \cdot m_p}{m^2} \right)^{3/2} e^{+\frac{\beta}{K}} \right\} T^3 \, e^{-\frac{EG_0}{KT}}$$

$$n_i^2 = \text{A}_0 \, \text{T}^3 \, e^{-\frac{EG_0}{KT}}$$

$A_o$ is material constant,not avagadro number

$n_i$ is intrinsic carrier concentration

For Ge, $n_i$ is $2.5 \times 10^{13}$ carriers/cm$^3$ and

For Si, $n_i$ is $1.5 \times 10^{10}$ carrieres/cm$^3$ where $V_T = K_T/q$ at 300°k

$n_i$ gives number of covalent bands that are broken for the voltage developed at room temperature.

## 1.5 EXTRINSIC OR IMPURE SEMICONDUCTOR

A small percentage of trivalent or pentavalent atoms is added to the intrinsic Ge or Si to increase its conductivity. This process of adding impurity is called doping and the resulting semiconductor is called impure or extrinsic.

***Donor*** If the dopant has 5-valence electron the crystal structure of figure 1.5 is obtained. The impurity atom will displace some of the Ge atoms in crystal lattice. 4 or 5 valence electrons will occupy covalent bonds, and the 5$^{th}$ will be nominally unbound and will be available as a carrier of current. The energy required to detach this 5$^{th}$ electron from the atom is of the 0.01 ev for Ge and 0.05 ev for Si. The pentavalent impurities are antimony, phosphorous and arsenic. Such impurities donate excess electron carries, and are referred as donor, or n-type impurities

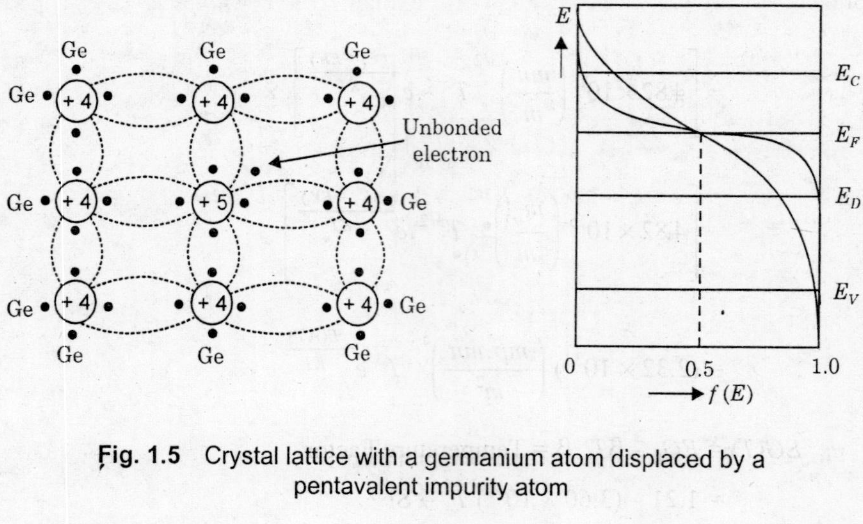


**Fig. 1.5** Crystal lattice with a germanium atom displaced by a pentavalent impurity atom

When donor impurities are added to a semiconductor, allowable energy levels are introduced a very small distance below the conduction band. These new allowable levels are essentially a discrete level because the added impurity atoms far apart in the crystal structure and their interaction are small. If intrinsic semiconductor material is doped with n-type impurities, the number of electrons increase and the number of holes decrease below that which would be available in the intrinsic semiconductor. The numbers of holes decrease because the larger number of electrons present increase the rate of recombination of electrons with holes.

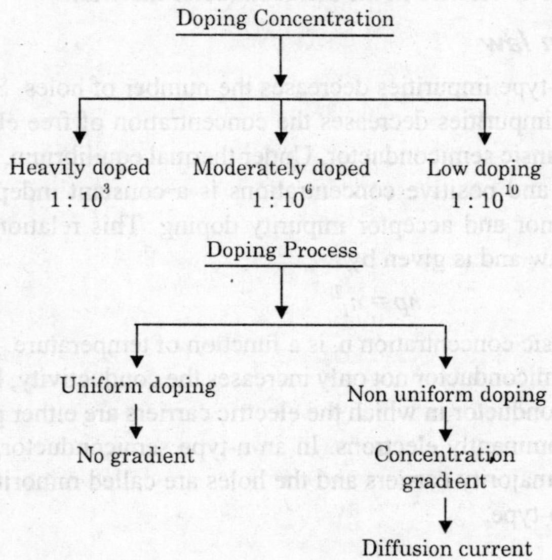


***Acceptors*** If a trivalent impurity is added to an intrinsic semiconductor only three of the covalent bonds can be filled and the vacancy that exists in the 4th bond constitutes a hole. This situation is explained in figure 1.6.

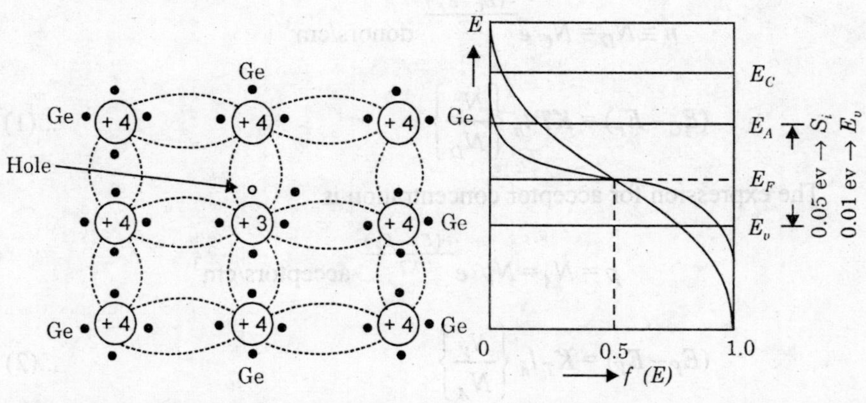


**Fig. 1.6** Crystal lattice with a germanium atom displaced by an atom of a trivalent impurity

Such impurities make available positive carriers because they create holes, which can accept electrons. These impurities are known as acceptor or p-type impurities. The amount of impurity which must be added to have an effect on the conductivity is very small.

When acceptor or p-type impurities are added to the intrinsic semiconductor, they produce an allowable discrete energy level which is just above the valence band. Since a very small amount of energy is required for an electron to leave the valence band and occupy the acceptor energy level, it follows that the holes generated in the valence band by these electrons constitute the largest number of carriers in the semiconductor material.

### *Mass-action law*

Addition of n-type impurities decreases the number of holes. Similarly, doping of p-type impurities decreases the concentration of free electrons below that in the intrinsic semiconductor. Under thermal equilibrium, the product of free negative and positive concentrations is a constant independent of the amount of donor and acceptor impurity doping. This relationship is called mass-action law and is given by

$$np = n_i^2$$

The intrinsic concentration $n_i$ is a function of temperature. The doping of an intrinsic semiconductor not only increases the conductivity, but also serves to produce a conductor in which the electric carriers are either predominantly holes or predominantly electrons. In an n-type semiconductor, the electrons are called the majority carriers and the holes are called minority carriers and vice versa in p-type.

## 1.6 VARIATION OF FERMI LEVEL

The expression for donor concentration is

$$n \cong N_D = N_C \, e^{\frac{-(E_C - E_F)}{KT}} \text{ donors/cm}^3$$

$$(E_C - E_F) = KT \, l_n \left\{ \frac{N_C}{N_D} \right\} \quad ...(1)$$

The expression for acceptor concentration is

$$p = N_A = N_V \, e^{\frac{-(E_F - E_V)}{KT}} \text{ acceptors/cm}^3$$

$$(E_F - E_V) = K_T \, l_n \left\{ \frac{N_V}{N_A} \right\} \quad ...(2)$$

Where $E_F$ = Fermi level or characteristic energy for the crystal , eV

$E_c$ = Energy level at the below the conduction band

$E_v$ = Energy level at the top of the valence band

$N_c$ and $N_D$ are Dimension of concentration (number per cubic meter)

$K$ = Boltzman constant

The only parameter which changes with impurities in equation (1) and (2) is fermi level $E_F$.

In case of no impurities $E_F$ lies in the middle of the energy gap, indicating equal concentrations of free electrons and holes. If a donor-type impurity is added to the crystal, then at a given temperature and assuming all donor atoms are ionized the first $N_D$ states in the conduction band will be filled. Hence it will be more difficult for the electrons from the valence band to bridge the energy gap by thermal agitation. Therefore the number of electron-hole pairs thermally generated for that temperature will be reduced.

Variation of Fermi levels depends on three cases these are 1) variation of doping concentration 2) temperature and 3) extremely high temperature.

***Case 1: Variation of doping concentration*** Intrinsic mean pure semiconductor, if we add a small percentage of trivalent or pentavalent atoms an extrinsic or impure or a doped (doping means adding), semiconductor is formed.

Energy levels are introduced a very small distance below the conduction band, when donor (if the dopant has five valence electrons)impurities are added to a semi conductor.

*Donor:* If pentavalent atoms like antimony phosphorus and arsenic (such impurities donates excess of (negative) electron carriers) are added to an intrinsic semiconductor, only four of the five valence electrons will occupy covalent band the covalent bonds can be filled, and fourth vacancy exists bonds and fifth will be unbounded and will be available as a carrier of current. These type of impurities are referred as n-type or donor, impurities.

Let us consider if increase in Concentration of donor atoms $N_D$ positive charge per cubic meter, keeping temperature and $N_c$ constant (i.e. $N_D > N_C$) then $(E_C - E_F) < 0$

$$\therefore \qquad E_C < E_F$$

even if $E_F$ goes beyond $E_C$, it does not becomes a conductor .In n type semiconductor , the fermi level goes up as depending concentration increases. The energy band diagram shown in figure 1.7. The distance of new discrete allowable energy level is 0.01 eV in Ge, and 0.05 in Si below the conduction band, therefore at room temperature almost all the 5 th electrons of the donor materials are raised in to the conduction band. Intrinsic semiconductors Si or Ge is doped with n-type impurities.

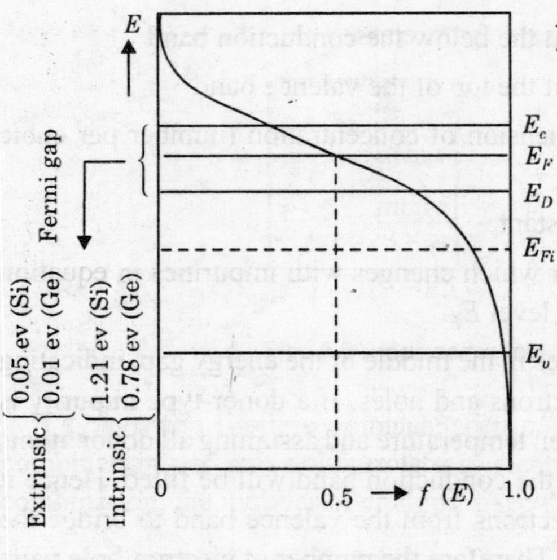


**Fig. 1.7a** n- type semiconductor Energy band diagram

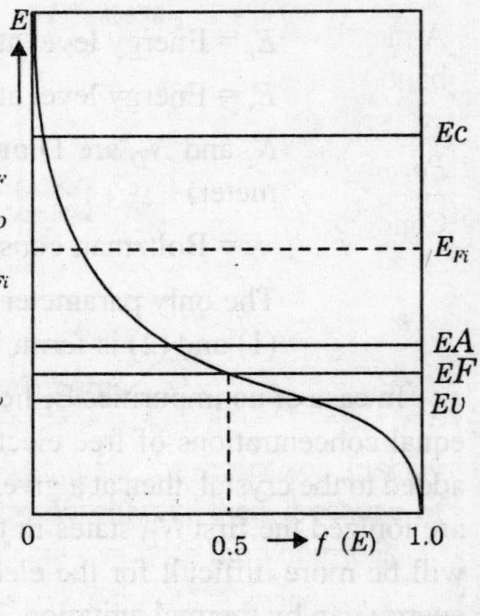


**Fig 1.7b** p- type semiconductor Energy band diagram

*Acceptors:* If a trivalent impurities like boron, gallium, or indium is added to an intrinsic semiconductor, only three of the covalent bonds can be filled, and fourth vacancy exists bond constitute a hole. Such type of impurities makes available positive carriers because they create holes, which can accept electrons. These types of impurities are known as acceptor or *p*- type impurities.

When these type of impurities are added to intrinsic semiconductor they produce an allowable energy level which is just above the valence band shown in figure 1.7b.

***Case 2: Increase in temperature*** For increased temperature $N_C$ will be increases, it means $N_C$ become more compare with $N_D$ i.e. $N_C > N_D$ only after a critical temperature , but not in the normal case.$(E_C - E_F) > 0$

$$\therefore \quad E_C > E_F$$

As temperature increases, the Fermi levels goes down there fore conductivity decreases. It may, because of collision of electrons in the conduction band, which leads to mesh formation

***Case 3: Extremely high temperature*** If we increase the temperature extremely high *i.e.* greater than critical temperature fermi level comes down very close to $E_{Fi}$, then the extrinsic semi conductor essentially acts as intrinsic semiconductor.

At initial temperatures all the extrinsic carrier takes conduction and at extremely high temperature even intrinsic takes carrier conduction that is number of electrons is approximately equal to number of holes.

## Comparison of conductors, semiconductors and insulators

Already at the introduction level we discussed the properties of these three classes.

A metal, which is placed in on these three, classes depending up on its energy band structure

| *Parameter* | *Conductor* | *Semiconductors* | *Insulators* |
|---|---|---|---|
| Conductivity | More (Coper $5.8 \times 10^7$ S/M Aluminium $3.8 \times 10^7$ S/M)<br>Excellent conductors | Medium (Ge $2.2 \times$ S/M Si$4.35 \times 10^{-4}$ S/M)<br>Conductivity lies in between conductors and insulators | Low (Glass $5.88 \times 10^{-12}$ Porcelain $3.33 \times 10^{-10}$ S/M)<br>very poor conductors |
| Energy bands | 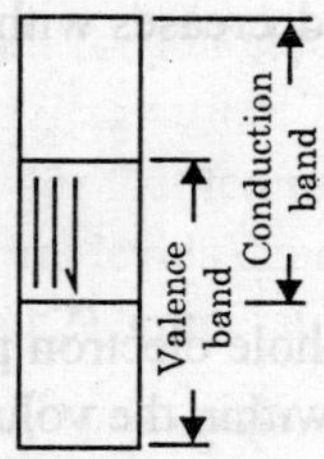 | 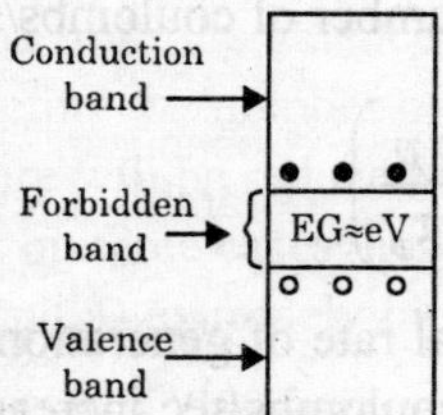 | 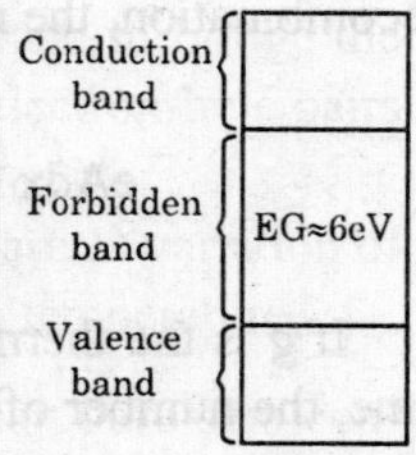 |
| Temperature | Increasing in temperature conductivity decreases (mesh formations), it means positive temperature coefficient i.e increase in temperature resistivity also increases | Increasing in temperature conductivity increases then *energy gap* will be reduces, then it becomes as a Conductor, it means negative temperature coefficient i.e. increase in temperature resistivity will decreases. | Increasing in temperature conductivity increases. |

## 1.7 CONTINUITY EQUATION

The continuity equation gives the condition of dynamic equilibrium for the density of charge carriers in an elementary volume of the semiconductor. The holes in $n$-type material diffuse exponentially. Thus, carrier concentration in a semiconductor is function of both time and distance. The differential equation governing this functional relationship is called continuity equation and is based on the factor that charge can neither be created nor destroyed. Consider the infinite terminal elementary volume semiconductor of cross sectional area $A$ and length $dx$ within which the average hole concentration is $p$.

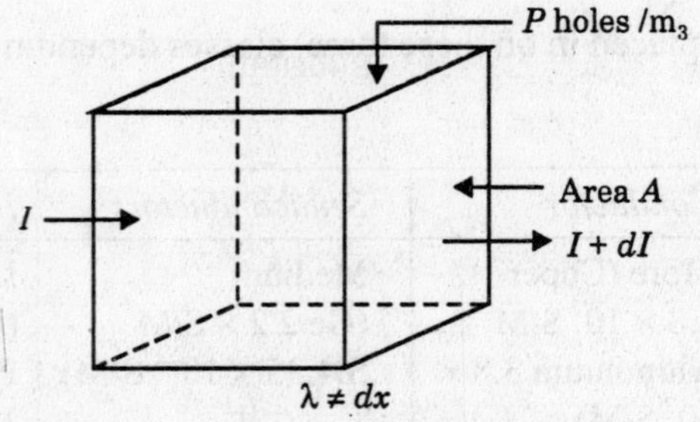


**Fig. 1.8** Conservation of charge

If $\tau_p$ is mean lifetime of holes, then $p/\tau_p$ equals the holes/sec lost by recombination per unit volume. If $e$ is electronic charge, then, because of recombination, the number of coulombs/sec decreases with the volume is

$$eAdx\left(\frac{p}{\tau_p}\right) \quad ...(1)$$

If $g$ is the thermal rate of generation of hole electron pairs per unit volume, the number of coulombs/sec increases within the volume

$$= e\,Adx\,g \quad ...(2)$$

As indicated in figure 1.8 the current entering the volume at $x$ is $I$ and leaving at $x + dx$ is $I + dI$. The number of coulombs/sec decreases within the volume $= dI$ ...(3)

Because of the above effects, the hole density must change with time, and the total number of coulombs per second increases within the volume

$$= e\,A\,dx\,\frac{dp}{dt} \quad ...(4)$$

since charge must be conserved,

$$e\,A\,dx\,\frac{dp}{dt} = -\,e\,A\,dx\,\frac{p}{\tau_p} + e\,A\,dx\,g - dI \quad ...(5)$$

the hole current is the sum of diffusion current and the drift current, or

$$I = -A\,e\,D_p\frac{dp}{dx} + A_p\,e\,\mu p\varepsilon \quad ...(6)$$

Where $\varepsilon$ is the electric field intensity within volume. Equilibrium is the status at which the concentration is independent of time and distance. Under equilibrium conditions $p$ becomes $p_o$ and $dp/dt = 0$, so that from equation (5)

$$g = \frac{p_0}{\tau_p} \quad ...(7)$$

Where $p_o$ = no of holes after equilibrium

$\tau_p$ = carrier lifetime.

Combining equations (5), (6) and (7) we get the equation of conservation of charge, or the continuity equation that is $p(tx)$ which is function of time and distance

$$\frac{dp}{dt} = -\frac{p_i}{\tau_p} + D_P \frac{d^2 p}{dx^2} - \mu_p \frac{d}{dx}(\rho\varepsilon)$$

where $p_i = (p - p_0)$

we consider two special cases of continuity equation.

***Case (1): Concentration independent of x and with zero electric field***

Consider a situation in which $\varepsilon = 0$ and the concentration is independent of $x$.

At $t = 0$ the equation (8) reduces to

$$\frac{dp}{dt} = \frac{-p_i}{\tau_p} \qquad \text{...(9)}$$

The solution is $p(t) = ke^{-\frac{t}{\tau_p}}$

$K$ is calculated from initial conditions

If $t = 0, p = p_i$

$\therefore \quad k = p_i$

$$\therefore \quad p(t) = p_i\, e^{-\frac{t}{\tau_p}}$$

$p(t)$ is drawn with t and shown in fig 1.9

From above relation, the mean lifetime of holes $\tau_p$ may be defined as time it takes for the concentration to fall 1/e of its initial value.

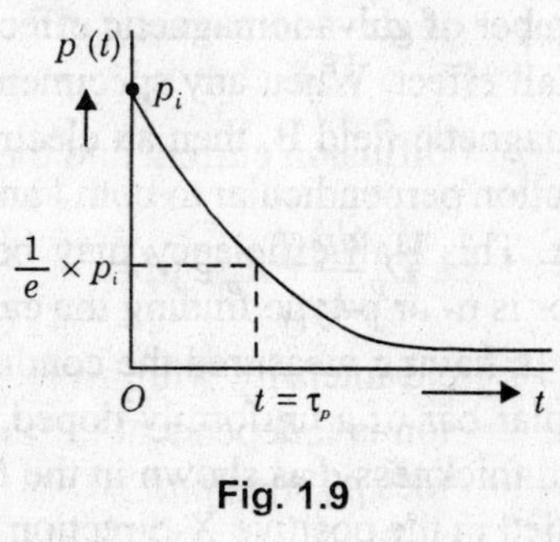


**Fig. 1.9**

***Case (2): concentration independent of t with zero electric field***

Consider a situation in which $\varepsilon = 0$ and concentration is independent of $t$ that is

$$-\frac{p_i}{\tau_p} + D_P \frac{d^2 p}{dx^2} = 0$$

$$\therefore \quad \frac{d^2 p}{dx^2} + \frac{1}{D_P \tau_P} p_i = 0$$

The solution of this equation is of the form

$$P_N - P_{NO} = Ae^{-\frac{x}{Lp}} + Be^{-\frac{x}{Lp}} \qquad \text{...(12)}$$

Where A and B are constants of integration to be determined by boundary conditions and $L_P = \sqrt{D_P \tau_P}$

The concentration approaches zero as $x \to \infty$, the constant $B = 0$. Hence equation (12) must reduce to

$$P(x) = Ae^{\left(-\frac{x}{L_P}\right)} \qquad \text{...(13)}$$

If $x = 0$ then $p(x) = p_i$

$$\therefore \quad A = p_i$$

i.e.

$$p(x) = p_i e^{\frac{-x}{L_P}} \qquad \text{...(14)}$$

$L_P$ is called diffusion length of the holes, represents at the distance into the semiconductor at which the injected concentration falls to $1/e$ of its value at $x = 0$, at zero frequency, this equation reduces to

## 1.8 HALL EFFECT

The motion of electrons and holes in the presence of electric and magnetic fields gives rise to a number of galvanomagnetic effects. The most important of these effects is the Hall effect. When any specimen carrying a current I is placed in a transverse magnetic field B, then an electric field ε is induced in the specimen in the direction perpendicular to both I and B. This phenomenon is called the Hall effect. This Hall efficiency may be used for determining whether a semiconductor is n- or p-type finding the carrier concentration and calculating the mobility μ, having measured the conductivity σ.

Consider a rectangular bar of a uniformly doped, n-type semiconductor of length *L*, width *W* and thickness *d* as shown in the figure 1.10 below.

If a current I is applied in the positive X-direction and a magnetic field B is applied in the positive Z-direction, a force will be exerted in the negative Y-direction of the current carrier. The current is carried by electron from side

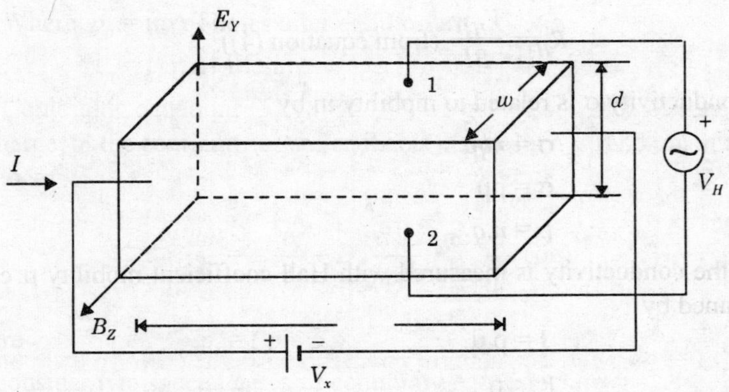


**Fig. 1.10** Representation of Hall effect. The carriers (electrons or holes) are subjected to a magnetic force in the negative Y-direction.

1 to side 2, if the semiconductor is n-type. Therefore Hall voltage $V_H$ appears between surfaces 1 and 2. The electric field developed in Y- direction is

$$V_H/d = \varepsilon_y \quad \text{...(1)}$$

Where *d* is the distance between surfaces 1 and 2. In the equilibrium state the electric field intensity ε due to Hall effect must exert a force on the carrier which just balances the magnetic force that is

$$e\varepsilon_y = Bev \quad \text{...(2)}$$

where *e* is the magnitude of the charge on carrier,

*v* is the drift speed.

$$J = \rho v = \frac{I}{Wd} \quad \text{...(3)}$$

Where *J* is the current density

ρ is the charge density

and W is the width of the specimen in the direction of the magnetic field

Combining the equation (1), (2), and (3) we find

$$V_H = \varepsilon_y \ d = Bvd = BJd/\rho = BI/\rho W \quad \text{...(4)}$$

If $V_H$, *B*, *I* and *W* are measured, the charge density ρ can be measured from equation (4).

If the polarity of $V_H$ is positive at terminal 1 then the carrier must be electron and $\rho = ne$ where n is the electron concentration.

If the terminal *2* becomes charged positive with respect to terminal 1 the semiconductor must be of p-type and $\rho = pe$ where p is the hole concentration.

$$R_H = 1/\rho \quad \text{...(5)}$$

Where $R_H$ is the Hall coefficient

$$R_H = \frac{V_H w}{BI} \text{ (from equation (4))} \qquad ...(6)$$

Conductivity σ is related to mobility m by

$$\sigma = nq\mu$$

$$\therefore \qquad \sigma = \rho\mu \qquad ...(7)$$

where $\rho = n.q$

If the conductivity is measured with Hall coefficient mobility μ can be determined by

$$J = \rho.\mu.$$

$$\frac{1}{\rho} = \frac{\mu}{\sigma} = R_H \qquad ...(8)$$

From equation (5) and equation (8) we get

$$R_H = \frac{\mu}{\sigma}$$

$$\Rightarrow \qquad \mu = \sigma R_H . \qquad ...(9)$$

Due to randomness of the drift speed, it is found that instead of equation (9) the actual mobility is given by

$$\mu = \left(\frac{8}{3\pi}\right). \sigma R_H$$

*Applications of Hall effect:*

1. By using Hall effect,we can know the type of semiconductor (p- type or n- type).
2. Determine the value of mobility $\mu = [\sigma R_H]$ theoretically
   $\mu = [8\sigma/3\pi]\ R_H$ practically
3. Semiconductor or metal carrying a current $I$, since $V_H$ is proportional to B then the Hall effect has been introduced in to a magnetic field meter. Hall effect multiplier, is available to give an output proportional to the product of two signals. If $I$ is proportional to one of the inputs and if B is linearly related to the second signal, then, from equation (4), $V_H$ is proportional to the two inputs.

## 1.9 SOLVED PROBLEMS

**1. In a semiconductor at room temperature (300°k) the intrinsic carrier concentration and resistivity are $1.5 \times 10^{16}$ m$^3$ and $2 \times 10^3$ σ–m respectively. It is converted into an extrinsic semiconductor with a doping concentration of $10^{20}$ m. For the extrinsic semiconductor, calculate the**

**(a) Minority carrier concentration**

**(b) Minority carrier concentration when its temperature is increased to a value at which the intrinsic carrier concentration n doubles.**

**Assume: (1) The mobility of minority and majority carriers to be the same, (2) kT = 26m ev at room temperature.**

**Solution:**

$$\text{Carrier concentration } n_i = 1.5 \times 10^{16}/\text{m}^2$$

$$\text{Resistivity p} = 2 \times 10^3$$

$$\text{Extrinsic doping} = 10^{20}$$

(a) $$np = n_i^2$$

$$\text{majority} \times \text{minority} = n_i^2$$

$$10^{20} \times \text{minority concentration} = 2.25 \times 10^{32}$$

$$\text{minority concentration} = 2.25 \times 10^{12}/\text{m}^2$$

(b) $n_i^2 = np$

$\therefore\ p = n$

$= n_i^2 = 9 \times 10^{32}$

$$\text{minority concentration} = \frac{n_i^2}{majorityconc} = \frac{9 \times 10^{32}}{10^{20}} = 9 \times 10^{12}/\text{m}^3$$

**2. A specimen of metal has 7.87 × 10^28 free electrons per cubic meter. The mobility of electrons in the metal is 34.8 cm²/v-s (a) Compute the conductivity of the metal (b) If an electric field of 30 V/cm is applied across the specimen, find the drift velocity of free electrons and the current density.**

**Solution:**

(a) Mobility $\mu = 34.8 \text{ cm}^2/\text{v-s}$

$= 34.8 \times 10^{-4} \text{ m}^2/\text{v-s}$

$$\text{conductivity } \sigma = n\, q\, \mu$$

$= 7.87 \times 10^{28} \times 1.6 \times 10^{-19} \times 34.8 \times 10^{-4}$

$= 438.2 \times 10^5 \text{ s/m}$

(b) electric field intensity $\varepsilon = 30 \text{ V/cm}$

$= 30 \times 10^2 \text{ V/m}$

Hence drift velocity of free electrons is $V = \mu\, \varepsilon$

$= 34.8 \times 10^{-4} \times 30 \times 10^2 \text{ m/s}$

$= 10.44 \text{ m/s}$

$$\text{currentdensity } J = \sigma\, \varepsilon = 438.2 \times 30 \times 10^2$$

$= 13.15 \times 10^{10} \text{ A/m}^3$

**3. (a) Find the conductivity of intrinsic Ge at 300°k**

**(b) If donor type impurity is added to the extent of 1 impurity atom in $10^7$ Ge atoms, find conductivity (c) If acceptor impurity is added to the extent of 1 impurity atom in $10^7$ Ge atoms, find the conductivity. Given that $n_i$ at 300°k is $2.5 \times 10^{13}/cm^3$, $\mu_n$ and $\mu_p$ in Ge are 3800 and 1800 $cm^2$/v-s respectively and number of Ge atoms/$cm^3$ $= 4.41 \times 10^{22}$.**

**Solution:**

(a) $n = p = n_i$

$$\sigma = n_i\, q(\mu_n + \mu_p)$$

$$= (2.5 \times 10^{13}\ cm^{-3})(1.6 \times 10^{-19}\ c)\ (3800 + 1800)\ cm^2/v\text{-}s$$

$$= 0.0224\ s/cm$$

(b) Number of Ge atoms/$cm^3$ $= 4.41 \times 10^{22}$

Hence with the given donor impurity of 1 donor atom per $10^7$ Ge atoms.

$$N_D = 4.41 \times 10^{15}\ atoms/cm^3$$

Further $\quad n \approx N_D$

$$\text{Hence } p = \frac{n_i^2}{N_D} = \frac{(1.5\times10^{13})^2}{4.41\times10^{15}} = 1.42 \times 10^{11}\ holes/cm^3$$

Since $n >> p$, we may neglect p in calculating the conductivity

$$\sigma = n\, q\, \mu_n = 5 \times 10^{14} \times 1.6 \times 10^{-19} \times 3800$$

$$= 3.04\ s/cm$$

(c) With the given acceptor impurity of 1 acceptor atom per $10^7$ Ge atoms

$$N_A = 4.41 \times 10^{15}\ atoms/cm^3$$

Further $\quad p \approx N_A$

$$\text{Hence } n = \frac{n_i^2}{N_A} = \frac{(2.5\times10^{13})^2}{4.41\times10^{15}} = 1.42 \times 10^{11}\ negative/cm^3$$

Since $p >> n$, we may neglect n in calculating the conductivity. Then

$$\sigma = p\, q\, \mu_p = 4.41 \times 10^{15} \times 1.6 \times 10^{-19} \times 1800$$

$$= 1.275\ s/cm$$

**4. (a) Find the conductivity of intrinsic Si at 300°k. It is given that $n_i$ at 300°k in Si is $1.5 \times 10^{10}/cm^3$, the mobilities of electrons and holes is Si are 1300 $cm^2$/v-s and 500 $cm^2$/v-s respectively and number of Si atoms/$cm^3$ $= 5 \times 10^{22}$.**

**(b) If donor type impurity is added to the extent of 1 impurity atom is $10^8$ Si atoms, find the conductivity**

**(c) If acceptor type impurity is added to the extent of 1 impurity atom is $10^8$ Si atoms, find the conductivity.**

**Solution:**

(a) $n = p = n_i$

Hence $\sigma = n_i\, q\, (\mu_p + \mu_n)$

$= (1.5 \times 10^{10}\ cm^{-3})\ (1.6 \times 10^{-19} c)\ (500 + 1300)\ cm^2/v\text{-}s$

$= 4.32 \times 10^{-6}\ s/cm$

(b) If there is 1 donor atom per $10^8$ Si atoms, then $N_D = 5 \times 10^{14}$ atoms/cm$^3$

Further $n \approx N_D$

$$\text{Hence } p = \frac{n_i^2}{N_D} = \frac{(2.5\times10^{10})^2}{5\times10^{14}} = 4.5 \times 10^5 \text{ holes/cm}^3$$

Since $n >> p$, we may neglect p in calculating the conductivity.

Thus $\sigma = n\, q\, \mu_n = 5 \times 10^{14} \times 1.6 \times 10^{-19} \times 1300$

$= 0.104$ s/m

(c) With 1 acceptor atom per $10^8$ Si atoms $N_A = 5 \times 10^{14}$ atoms/cm$^3$

Further $p \approx N_D$

$$\text{Hence } n = \frac{n_i^2}{N_A} = \frac{(1.5\times10^{10})^2}{5\times10^{14}} = 4.5 \times 10^5 \text{ electrons/cm}^3$$

Since $p >> n$, we may neglect n in calculating the conductivity. Then

$\sigma = p\, q\, \mu_p = 5 \times 10^{14} \times 1.6 \times 10^{-19} \times 500$

$= 0.04$ s/cm

**5. Find the conductivity of Ge (a) intrinsic condition at 300°k (b) with donor impurity of 1 part in $10^6$ (c) with acceptor impurity of 1 part in $10^7$ (d) when both the above impurities are present simultaneously. Given that $n_i$ for Ge at 300°k is $2.5 \times 10^{13}$/cm$^3$. $m_n$ and $m_p$ for Ge are 3800 and 1800 cm$^2$/v-s respectively and the number of Ge atoms/cm$^3$ $= 4.4 \times 10^{22}$**

**Solution:**

(a) $n = p = n_i = 2.5 \times 10^{13}$/cm$^3$

$\sigma = n_i\, q\, (\mu_n + \mu_p)$

$= (2.5 \times 10^{13})\ (1.6 \times 10^{-19})\ (3800 + 1800)$ s/cm

$= 0.0224$ s/cm

(b) Number of Ge atoms/cm$^3$ $= 4.4 \times 10^{22}$

Hence number of donor atoms/cm$^3$ is

$$N_D = \frac{4.4\times10^{22}}{10^6} = 4.4 \times 10^{16}/\text{cm}^3$$

Further $n \approx N_D$

$$\text{Hence} \quad p = \frac{n_i^2}{N_D} = \frac{\left(2.5\times10^{13}\right)^2}{4.4\times10^{16}} = 1.4210^{10} \text{ holes/cm}^2$$

Thus $n >> p$. Hence we may neglect $p$ in calculating the conductivity

$$\sigma = n\, q\, \mu_n = (4.4 \times 10^{16}\ \text{cm}^{-3})(1.6 \times 10^{-19}\ \text{c})\ (3800\ \text{cm}^2/\text{v-s})$$

$$= 26.57\ \text{s/m}$$

(c) Number of acceptor atoms/cm is

$$N_A = \frac{4.4 \times 10^{22}}{10^7} = 4.4 \times 10^{15}/\text{cm}^3$$

Further $p \approx N_A$

$$n = \frac{n_i^2}{N_A} = \frac{(2.5 \times 10^{13})^2}{4.4 \times 10^{15}} = 1.42 \times 10^{11}\ \text{electrons/cm}^3$$

Thus $p>>n$. hence we may neglect $p$ in calculation the conductivity

$$\sigma = p\, q\, \mu_p = (4.4 \times 10^{15}\ \text{cm}^{-3})\ (1.6 \times 10^{-19} c)\ (1800\ \text{cm}^2/v\text{-}s)$$

$$= 1.2675/\text{cm}$$

(d) With both $p$ and $n$ type impurities present simultaneously $N_D = 4.4 \times 10^{16}/\text{cm}^3$ and $N_A = 4.4 \times 10^{15}/\text{cm}^3$

Then $N_A$ holes combine with equal number of free electrons leaving the material $n$-type with net concentration

$$N = (N_D - N_A) = 0.9 \times 4.4 \times 10^{16}/\text{cm}^3 = 3.96 \times 10^{16}/\text{cm}^3$$

$$N = N_D = 3.96 \times 10^{16}/\text{cm}^3$$

Here again $p$ being equal to is very small compared with $N$ and may be neglected in calculating the effective conductivity

Hence $\sigma = N_D\, q\, \mu_n = (3.96 \times 10^{16})\ (1.6 \times 10^{-19})\ (3800)$ s/cm

$$= 24.08\ \text{s/cm}$$

**6. In an $n$-type semiconductor, the Fermi level lies 0.3 ev below the conduction band at 300°k. If the temperature is increased to 330°k .Find the new position of Fermi level.**

**Solution:**

$$N_D = N_C\, e^{\frac{-(E_C - E_F)}{KT}}$$

$$E_F = E_C - KT \ln \frac{N_C}{N_D}$$

$$(E_F - E_C) = KT \ln \frac{N_C}{N_D}$$

$$0.3\ \text{ev} = 330\ \text{K} \ln \frac{N_C}{N_D}$$

$$0.3 \text{ ev} = 300 \text{ K} \ln \frac{N_C}{N_D}$$

$$(E_C - E_F) = \frac{330 \times 0.3}{300} = 0.33 \text{ ev}$$

Thus fermi level lies 0.33ev below the conduction band

**7. In an *n*-type semiconductor, the Fermi level lies 0.02 ev below the conduction band. If the concentration of donor atoms is increased by a factor 4 times , find the new position of the Fermi level. Assume *KT* = 0.025 eV.**

**Solution:**

Concentration of donor atoms in n-type material

$$N_D = N_C e^{\frac{-(E_C - E_F)}{KT}}$$

Let initially $N_D = N_{D0}$ and $E_F = E_{F0}$

$$Ec - E_{F0} = 0.2 \text{ eV}$$

Therefore $N_{D0} = N_c e^{-0.2/0.025} = N_c e^{-8}$

When $N_D = 4N_{D0}$ and $E_F = E_{F1}$

$$4N_{D0} = N_c e^{-(Ec - E_{F1})/0.025}$$

$$= N_c e^{-40(Ec - E_{F1})}$$

$$4 \times N_c e^{-8} = N_c e^{-40(Ec - E_{F1})}$$

$$4 = e^{-40(Ec - E_{F1}) + 8}$$

taking natural logarithm on both sides, we get

$$l_n 4 = -40 (E_c - E_{F1}) + 8$$

$$1.384 = -40(E_c - E_{F1}) + 8$$

therefore $(E_c - E_{F1}) = 0.165$ eV

**8. An *n*-type Ge bar has cross-sectional area of 1.5 mm², length of 1.6cm, resistivity of 20 Ω-cm and carrier lifetime of 60ms. One end of the bar is continuously irradiated with $8 \times 10^{15}$ photons/second. Find the resistance of the bar under continuous excitation at room temperature assuming that (i) each incident photon generates one negative-hole pair and (ii) these electrons and holes are uniformly distributed throughout the bar. Given that $n_i$ at 300 k = $2.5 \times 10^{13}$/cm³, $m_n$ = 3800 cm²/v–s**

$$\mu_p = 1800 \text{ cm}^2/\text{v–s}, q = 1.6 \times 10^{-19} c$$

**Solution:**

In the absence of radiation $\sigma = 1/\rho = 1/20 = 0.05$ s/cm

$$\sigma = q(n\mu_n + p\mu_p) = q(n\,\mu_n + n_i^2/n\,\mu_p) \text{ since } p\,n = n_i^2$$

substituting the values $0.05 = 1.6 \times 10^{-19}\left(n \times 3800 + \dfrac{6.25 \times 10^{26}}{n} \times 1800\right)$

Solution of quadratic equation yields:

$$n = 7.847 \times 10^{13}/\text{cm}^3 \text{ and } 0.3775 \times 10^{13}/\text{cm}^3$$

But $n_i = 2.5 \times 10^{13}/\text{cm}^3$.

Hence in $n$-type Ge, value of $n = 0.3775 \times 10^{13}/\text{cm}^3$ is in admissible.

Hence we accept $n = 7.847 \times 10^{13}/\text{cm}^3$

Hence $$p = \frac{n_i^2}{n} = \frac{(2.5 \times 10^{13})^2}{7.847 \times 10^{13}} = 0.796 \times 10^{13}/\text{cm}^3$$

Volume of Ge bar is

$$v = 1.6 \times 1.5 \times 10^{-2} \text{ cm}^3 = 0.024 \text{ cm}^3$$

Incidence of light on the bar adds $\Delta n$ electrons/cm$^3$ and $\Delta p$ holes/cm$^3$

where $\Delta p = \Delta n$

Lifetime of carriers is $\tau = 60 \times 10^{-6}$ seconds

Number of electron-hole pair added/second $= 8 \times 10^{15}$

Hence $$8 \times 10^{15} = \frac{\Delta n \times v}{\tau}$$

$$\Delta n = \frac{8 \times 10^{15} \times \tau}{v} = \frac{8 \times 10^{15} \times 60 \times 10^{-6}}{0.024} = 2 \times 10^{13}/\text{cm}^3 \text{ and}$$

$$\Delta p = \Delta n = 2 \times 10^{13}/\text{cm}^3$$

Hence under radiated condition, conductivity of the bar is

$$\sigma = q\,[(n + \Delta n)\,\mu_n + (p + \Delta p)\,\mu_p]$$

$$= 1.6 \times 10^{19}[(7.847+2)10^{13} \times 3800 + (0.796 + 2)10^{13} \times 1800]$$

$$= 6.792 \times 10^{-2} \text{ s/cm}$$

Hence resistivity $= \rho = 1/\sigma = \dfrac{100}{6.792} = 14.72\ \Omega$-cm

Resistance $R = \rho L/A = \dfrac{14.72 \times 1.6}{0.015} = 1570\ \Omega$

**9. Show that the minimum conductivity of extrinsic Si sample occurs when it is slightly p-type. Calculate the electron and hole concentration when the conductivity is minimum given that $\mu_n$ = 1350cm$^2$/v-sec $\mu_p$ = 450cm$^2$/v-sec and the intrinsic carrier concentration $n_i$ = 1.5 × 100$^{100}$ cm$^{-3}$**

**Solution:**

For an extrinsic semiconductor

$$\sigma = q(\mu_n n_o + \mu_p p_o)$$

$$n_i^2 = n_o p_o$$

$$\sigma = \left[\mu_n (n_o) + \mu_p \left(\frac{n_i^2}{n_o}\right)\right]$$

For minimum conductivity $\dfrac{d\sigma}{dn_0} = 0$

$$\frac{d\sigma}{dn_0} = q\left[\mu_n - \mu_p \left(\frac{n_i^2}{n_0}\right)\right] = 0$$

$$\mu_n = \mu_p \frac{n_i^2}{n_0^2} = \mu_p \frac{p_0}{n_0}$$

$$p_o = n_i \sqrt{\frac{\mu_n}{\mu_p}} \text{ and } n_o = n_i \sqrt{\frac{\mu_p}{\mu_n}}$$

$$\mu_n > \mu_p \therefore p_o > n_o$$

Hence sample is p-type

$$p_o = n_i \sqrt{\frac{\mu_p}{\mu_n}} = 1.5 \times 10^{10} \sqrt{\frac{450}{1350}} = 866 \times 10^7 \text{ cm}^{-3}$$

$$p_o = \frac{n_i^2}{n_o} = 2.6 \times 10^{10} \text{ cm}^{-3}$$

**10. The resistivity of p-type Si specimen is 0.12 Ωm. Find electron and hole concentration.**

**Solution:**

$$\sigma = q\,(n_p \mu_n + p_p \mu_p) \cong N_A \mu_p q$$

$$N_A = \frac{\sigma}{\mu_p q} = \frac{\frac{1}{0.12}}{0.048 \times 1.6 \times 10^{-19}} = 1.69 \times 10^{21}/\text{cm}^3$$

$$N_D = \frac{n_i^2}{N_A} = 2.06 \times 10^{11}/\text{cm}^3$$

**11. 1 kΩ resistor is to be fabricated as a narrow strip of p-type Si 4mm thick. If the strip is 20 μm wide and 400 μm long, what concentration of acceptor atoms is required?**

**Solution:**

$$\rho = \frac{RA}{l} = \frac{1000 \times 20 \times 10^{-6} \times 4 \times 10^{-6}}{400 \times 10^{-6}} = 2 \times 10^{-4}\ \Omega$$

$$\sigma = \frac{1}{\rho} = N_A\, \mu_p\, q$$

$$N_A = \frac{1}{p\mu_p q} = \frac{1}{2 \times 10^{-4} \times 500 \times 1.6 \times 10^{-19}}.$$

$$= 6.5 \times 10^{23}/\text{m}^3$$

**12. Calculate the diffusion constants $D_n$ and $D_p$ for *Si* at room temperature**

**Solution:**

$$\frac{KT}{q} = 0.0259$$

$$D_n = \mu_n \frac{KT}{q} = (3800)\ (0.0259) = 3.5 \times 10^3\ \text{m}^2/\text{s}$$

$$D_p = \mu_p \frac{KT}{q} = 1300 \times (0.0259) = 1.2 \times 10^3\ \text{m}^2/\text{s}$$

**13. If the effective mass of an electron is equal to thrice the effective mass of an hole, find the distance (in ev) of the Fermi level in an intrinsic semiconductor from the center of the forbidden band at room temperature.**

**Solution:**

$$m_n = 2\, m_p$$

$$E_F = \frac{E_C + E_V}{2} - KT/2\ ln\ (N_C/N_V)$$

$$N_c = 4.81 \times 10^{15} \left(\frac{m_n}{m}\right)^{3/2} (T)^{3/2}$$

$$N_V = 4.81 \times 10^{15} \left(\frac{m_n}{m}\right)^{3/2} (T)^{3/2}$$

Therefore $N_C/N_V = \left(\frac{m_n}{m_p}\right)^{3/2}$

$$\Rightarrow \frac{KT}{2}\ ln\ N_C/N_V = \frac{KT}{2}\ \ln \left(\frac{m_n}{m_p}\right)^{3/2}$$

$$= \left(\frac{m_n}{m_p}\right)^{3/2} ln\left(3\frac{m_n}{m_p}\right)^{3/2}$$

$$= \frac{KT}{2}\left(\frac{3}{2}\right)\ln 3$$

$$= \frac{3}{2}\times\frac{26}{2}\times(0.693)\ 10^{-3} = 21.42 \text{ mev}$$

**14. (a) Prove that the resistivity of intrinsic Ge at 300°k is 45 Ω-cm**
**(b) If a donor-type impurity is added to the extent of 1 atom per $10^9$ Ge atoms, prove that the resistivity drops to 32.4 Ω-cm**

**Solution:**

(a) $\sigma = (\mu_n + \mu_p)\, q\, n_i;$

$= (3800 + 1800)\,(1.6 \times 10^{-19})\,(2.5 \times 10^{13})$

$= 0.0224\ (\Omega\text{-cm})^{-1}$

$\rho = 1/\sigma = 44.64\ \Omega\text{–cm} \cong 45\ \Omega\text{–cm}$

(b) Atomic concentration $n = 4.4 \times 10^{22}$

If 1 impurity per $10^9$ atoms added, then $n = 4.4 \times 10^{22} \times \frac{1}{10^9} = 4.4 \times 10^{13}$ atoms/cm$^3$

We know that $n\, p = n_i^2$

$$p = \frac{n_i^2}{n} = \frac{\left(2.5\times10^{13}\right)^{12}}{4.4\times10^{13}} = 1.42 \times 10^{13} \text{ atoms/cm}^3$$

Therefore $\sigma = (n\mu_n + p\mu_p)q$

$= 0.0308(\Omega\text{-cm})^{-1}$ $(\therefore \mu_n = 3800 \text{ v-cm}^2\text{/sec}$

$\mu_p = 1800 \text{ v-cm}^2\text{/sec})$

Therefore $\rho = \frac{1}{\sigma} = 32.4\ (\Omega\text{-cm})$

**15. (a) Determine the concentration of free electron and holes in a sample Ge at 300°k which has a concentration of donor atoms equal to 4 × $10^{14}$ atoms/cm$^3$ and a concentration of acceptor atoms equal to 5 × $10^{14}$atoms/cm$^3$. Is this p or n type Ge? In other words, is the conductivity primarily due to holes or due to electrons?**
**(b) Repeat part for a equal donor and acceptor concentration of $10^{14}$ atoms/cm$^3$. Is this *p* or *n*-type Ge?**
**(c) Repeat part a for a temperature of 400° k, and show that the sample is essentially intrinsic.**

**Solution:**

(a) Given $N_D = 4 \times 10^{14}$ atoms/cm$^3$

$N_A = 5 \times 10^{14}$ atoms /cm$^3$

Using charge neutrality $n + N_A = p + N_D$

$$n\text{-}p = N_D - N_A = 10^{14}$$

$$\Rightarrow \quad n = p - 10^{14}$$

$$\Rightarrow \quad p = n + 10^{14}$$

The mass action law $n\,p = n_i^2$

$$\Rightarrow \quad n\,p = (2.5 \times 10^{13})^2$$

$$\Rightarrow \quad n(n + 10^{14}) = (2.5 \times 10^{13})^2$$

$$n^2 + 10^{14}n - (2.5 \times 10^{13})^2 = 0$$

$$n = \frac{-10^{14} \pm \sqrt{\left(10^{14}\right)^2 + 4\left(2.5 \times 10^{13}\right)^2}}{2} = 5.9 \times 10^{12} \text{ (or) } -1.05 \times 10^4$$

Therefore $p = n + 10^{14} = 1.05 \times 10^{14}$ acceptor/cm$^3$

Therefore $p > n \Rightarrow$ the sample is *p*-type

(b) $n = N_D = 10^{14}$ atoms/cm$^3$

$$p = N_A = 10^{14} \text{ atoms/cm}^3$$

$$n + N_A = p + N_D$$

$$\Rightarrow \quad n - p = N_D - N_A = 0$$

$$\Rightarrow \quad n = p$$

Therefore sample is intrinsic

(c) We know that $n_i^2 = A_o T^3 e^{-E_{GO}/KT}$

$$= A_o (300)^3\, e^{-0.785/0.026}$$

$$A_o = 2.79 \times 10^{32}$$

At $T = 400°$ k, $n_i^2 = A_o T^3 e^{-E_{GO}/KT}$

$$= (2.79 \times 10^{32})\,(400)^3\, e^{\frac{-0.785}{8.62 \times 10^{-5} \times 400}}$$

$$= 2.31 \times 10^{30}$$

Therefore $\quad n\,p = n_i^2$

$$\Rightarrow \quad n_i^2 = n\,(n + 10^{14})\; n_i = 1.61 \times 10^{15}$$

so $\quad n = 1.61 \times 10^{15} - 0.05 \times 10^{15}$

$$= 1.56 \times 10^{15} \text{ electrons/cm}^3$$

$$p = n + 10^{14}$$

$$= 1.56 \times 10^{15} + 0.1 \times 10^{15}$$

$$= 1.66 \times 10^{15} \text{ holes/cm}^3$$

Hence, the sample at $T = 400°$k is essentially intrinsic, since $p \approx n \approx n_i$

**16. Find the concentration of holes and of electrons in *p*-type Ge at 300°k, if the conductivity is 300 $(\Omega cm)^{-1}$**

**Solution:**

In *p*-type $p_p >> n_p$

Therefore $\sigma = p_p \mu_p q$

$$\Rightarrow \quad p = \frac{\sigma}{\mu_p q} = \frac{300}{1800 \times 1.6 \times 10^{-19}} = 1.04 \times 10^{18} \text{ holes/cm}^3$$

$$n_p = \frac{n_i^2}{p_p} = \frac{(2.5 \times 10^{13})^2}{1.04 \times 10^{18}}$$

$$= 0.6 \times 10^9 \text{ electrons/cm}^3$$

**17. A sample of Ge is doped to the extent of $10^{14}$ donor atoms/cm$^3$ and $5 \times 10^{13}$ acceptor atoms/cm$^3$. At temperature of the sample the resistivity of pure (intrinsic) Ge is 80 Ω-cm. If the applied electric field is 5 v/cm. Find the total conduction current density.**

**Solution:**

Given that $N_D = 10^{14}$ donor atoms/cm$^3$

$N_A = 5 \times 10^{13}$ acceptor atoms/cm$^3$

$\rho_i = 80$ Ω-cm, $\varepsilon = 5$ V/m J = ?

From charge neutrality $n + N_A = p + N_D$

$$\Rightarrow \quad n - p = N_D - N_A = 5 \times 10^{13}$$

$$n = p + 5 \times 10^{13}$$

$$\sigma_i = \frac{1}{\rho_i} = (\mu_n + \mu_p)\, q\, n_i$$

$$n_i = (\mu_n + \mu_p)\, q\, \rho_i$$

$$= (3800 + 1800)(1.6 \times 10^{-19})(80)$$

$$= 1.4 \times 10^{13}$$

From mass action law $n\,p = n_i^2$

$$= (1.4 \times 10^{13})^2$$

therefore $p\,(p + 5 \times 10^{13}) = (1.4 \times 10^{13})^2$

$p^2 + 5 \times 10^{13}\, p - (1.4 \times 10^{13})^2 = 0$

$$\Rightarrow \quad p = \frac{-5 \times 10^{13} \pm \sqrt{(5 \times 10^{13})^2 + 4(1.4 \times 10^{13})^2}}{2}$$

$$= 3.65 \times 10^{12} \text{ acceptor/cm}^3$$

$$\Rightarrow \quad n = p + 5 \times 10^{13}$$

$$= 5.36 \times 10^{13} \text{ donor/cm}^3$$

Therefore $J = (n\,\mu_n + p\,\mu_p)\,q\,\varepsilon$

$= [\,5.36 \times 10^{13}(3800) + 3.65 \times 10^{12}(1800)](1.6 \times 10^{-19})5$

$= 0.168\ \text{A/cm}^2$

**18. A p-type material has an acceptor ion concentration of $1 \times 10^{16}$ per cm$^3$. Its intrinsic carrier concentration is $1.48 \times 10^{10}$/cm. The hole and electron mobilities are 0.05 m$^2$/v-s and 0.13 m$^2$/v-s respectively. Calculate the resistivity of the material.**

**Solution:**

$N_A = 1 \times 10^{10}/\text{cm}^3 \quad n_i = 1.48 \times 10^{10}/\text{cm}^3$

$\mu_p = 0.05\ \text{m}^2/\text{v-sec} = 0.05 \times 10^4\ \text{cm}^2/\text{v-sec}$

$\mu_n = 0.13\ \text{m}^2/\text{v-sec} = 0.13 \times 10^4\ \text{cm}^2/\text{v-sec}$

Since the given material is of *p*-type $p >> n$ and $N_D \approx 0$

The neutrality equation is given as $p + N_D = n + N_A$

Hence $p \approx N_A = 1 \times 10^{16}/\text{cm}^3$

Also $pn = n_i^2$ Hence $n = \dfrac{n_i^2}{p}$

$$n = \frac{\left(1.48 \times 10^{10}\right)^2}{1 \times 10^{16}} = 2.19 \times 10^4/\text{cm}^3$$

Now conductivity is given as $\sigma = q\,(\mu n_n + \mu p_p)$

$$= \frac{1}{1.6 \times 10^{-19}\left(0.13 \times 2.9 \times 10^4 + 0.05 \times 1 \times 10^{16}\right) \times 10^4}$$

$= 1.25$ ohm/cm

**19. A p-type Si sample is placed in a magnetic field as shown in figure. The applied electric field is 750 v/m, $B = 0.005\text{m}^2/\text{V-s}$. The electron and hole mobilities are 0.14 and 0.05 m$^2$/v-s respectively at the operating temperature. Find the magnitudes of**

**(i) the voltage across the sample length**
**(ii) the drift velocity**
**(iii) the transverse force per coulomb of moving charge due to B**
**(iv) the transverse electric field intensity**
**(v) the Hall voltage**

**Solution:**

Given $\mu_n = 0.05\ \text{m}^2/\text{V-s}$

$\mu_p = 0.14\ \text{m}^2/\text{V-s}$

$|E| = 750\ \text{V/m}$

$|B| = 0.05\text{T}$

(a) voltage across samplelength $V = ExL$

$= 750 \times 1.25 \text{ cm} \times 10^{-2}$

$= 9.375$ Volts

(b) drift velocity $Vd = \mu_n E$

$= 0.05 \times 750 = 37.5$ m/sec

(c) transverse force $F = Q \times (v \times B)$

$|F| = Q\, v\, B$

transverse force per cuoulomb is

$|(F|)/Q = VB$

$= 37.5 \times 0.05$

$= 1.875$ N/C

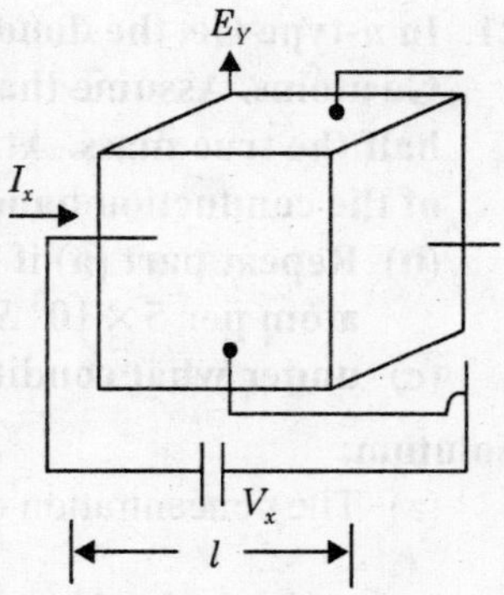


Fig 1.13

(d) transverse electric field intensity

$E = |(F|)/Q$ because $|(F|) = QE$

$= 1.875$ V/m

(e) Hall voltage $V_H = E.\text{d}$

$= 1.875 \times 0.9 \times 10^{-2}$

$V_H = 16.875$ mV

**20. Find the resistivity of intrinsic Si at 300 °k (b) If a donor-type impurity is added to the extent of 1 atom per $10^5$ Si atoms, find the resistivity**

**Solution:**

(a) Using CGS units From equation $\sigma = (\mu_n + \mu_p)\, q\, n_i$

$\mu_n = 1300\text{V-cm}^2/\text{sec}$

$\mu_p = 500 \text{ V-cm}^2/\text{sec}$

$\sigma = (1.5 \times 10^{10})\,(1.6 \times 10^{-19})\,(1300 + 500)$

$= 4.32 \times 10^{-6} (\Omega\text{-cm})^{-1}$

Therefore $\rho = 1/\sigma = 231481.4\ (\Omega\text{-cm})$

(b) Donor type impurity is added 1 atom per $10^8$ Si atoms

$$n = 5 \times 10^{22} \times \frac{1}{10^5} = 5 \times 10^{17} \text{ donor atoms/cm}^3$$

Since $n \approx N_D$, $p = \dfrac{n_i^2}{n} = \dfrac{n_i^2}{N_D} = \dfrac{\left(1.5 \times 10^{10}\right)^2}{5 \times 10^{17}}$

$= 450$ acceptor atoms/cm$^3$

Therefore $\sigma_n = (n\mu_n + p\mu_p)$

$= [5 \times 10^{17}(1300) + (450)(500)]\ 1.6 \times 10^{-19}$

$= 104\ (\Omega\text{–cm})^{-1}$

$p = 1/\sigma = 9.61 \times 10^{-3}\ \Omega\text{–cm}$

**21. In $n$-type Ge, the donor concentration corresponds to 1 atom per $10^7$ Ge atoms. Assume that the effective mass to the electron equals one-half the true mass. At room temperature, (a) how far from the edge of the conduction band is the Fermi level? Is $E_F$ above or below $E_c$?**

**(b) Repeat part (a) if impurities are added in the ratio of 1 acceptor atom per $5 \times 10^3$ *Si* atoms**

**(c) under what condition will $E_F$ coincide with $E_V$**

**Solution:**

(a) The concentration of *Ge* atom is

$$N = 6.02 \times 10^{23} \frac{\text{atom}}{\text{mole}} \times \frac{1 \text{ mole}}{72.6 \text{ g}} \times \frac{5.32 \text{ g}}{\text{cm}^2} = 4.41 \times 10^{22} \text{ atoms/cm}^3$$

Therefore $N_D = 4.4 \times 10^{22} \times 1/10^7 = 4.41 \times 10^5$ atoms/cm$^3$

$$N_C = 4.82 \times 10^{15} \left(\frac{m_n}{n}\right)^{3/2} T^{3/2}/\text{cm}^3$$

If $m_n = ½$ m and $T = 300°$ k

$$N_C = 4.82 \times 10^{15} \times 1/\sqrt{8} \times (300)^{3/2}$$

$$N_C = 8.87 \times 10^{18}/\text{cm}^3$$

$$E_C - E_F = KT \ln \frac{N_C}{N_D}$$

$$= -8.62 \times 10^{-5} \times 300 \ln \left(\frac{8.87 \times 10^{18}}{4.41 \times 10^{19}}\right)$$

$$= -0.1967$$

$(E_C - E_F) > 0$ Hence $E_C > E_F$

(b) If 1:$10^3$ Si atoms are added $N_D = 4.4 \times 10^{22} \times 1/10^3 = 4.4 \times 10^{19}$/cm$^3$

Therefore $E_F - E_C = -0.026 \ln \left(\frac{8.87 \times 10^{18}}{4 + 1 \times 10^{19}}\right) ev$

$$= (0.026)(-1.6)$$

$$= +0.0415 \text{ ev}$$

Therefore $E_F$ is above $E_C$

(c) To coincide $E_F$ with $Ec$

If $N_D = N_C$

When $E_F - E_C = 0$

Thus $4.4 \times 10^{22} \times \frac{1}{10^x} = 8.87 \times 10$

$$x = 4.41 \times 10^{22}$$

or Donor concentration per Ge atoms $= 20 \times 10^{-5}$

Therefore the doping level should be 20 donor atoms per $10^5$Ge atoms.

**22. In *p*-type Si the acceptor concentration corresponds to 1 atom per $10^6$ Si atoms. Assume that $m_p$ = 0.8 m at room temperature how far from the edge of the valence band is the Fermi level? (a) Is $E_F$ above or below $E_V$?**

**(b) Repeat part a if impurities are added in the ratio of 1 acceptor atom per $10 \times 10^3$ *Si* atoms**

**(c) Under what condition will $E_F$ coincide with $E_V$?**

**Solution:**

(a) The concentration of *Si* atoms is

$$N = 6.023 \times 10^{23} \frac{\text{atoms cm}^3}{\text{mole}} \times \frac{1 \text{ mole}}{28.1 \text{ g}} \times \frac{2.33 \text{ g}}{\text{cm}^3}$$

$$= 5 \times 10^{22} \text{ atoms/cm}^3$$

$$N_A = 5 \times 10^{22} \times 1/10^6 = 5 \times 10^{16} \text{ acceptor/cm}^3$$

$$N_V = 4.82 \times 10^{15} \left(\frac{m_p}{m}\right)^{3/2} T^{3/2} \text{ where } m_p = 0.8 \text{ m and } T = 300°\text{k}$$

$$N_V = 4.82 \times 10^{15} (0.8)^{3/2} (300)^{3/2}$$

$$= 1.79 \times 10^{19}/\text{cm}^3$$

$$E_F - E_C = KT \ln \frac{N_V}{N_A}$$

$$= 0.026 \ln \left(\frac{1.79 \times 10^{19}}{5 \times 10^{16}}\right)$$

$$= 0.153 \text{ ev}$$

or $E_F - E_V = 0.26$ ev

Therefore $E_F$ is above $E_V$

(b) $1:10^3$ *Si* atoms

$$N_A = 5 \times 10^{22} \times \frac{1}{10 \times 10^3} = 5 \times 10^{18} \text{ acceptor atoms/cm}^3$$

$$N_V = 1.79 \times 10^{19}/\text{cm}^3$$

Therefore $$E_F - E_V = KT \ln \frac{N_V}{N_A}$$

$$= 0.026 \ln \left(\frac{(1.79 \times 10^{19})}{5 \times 10^{16}}\right) \text{ ev}$$

$$= 0.033 \text{ ev}$$

Therefore $E_F$ will be above $E_V$

(c) $E_F = E_V$ only when $N_A = N_V$

Therefore concentration of acceptor = $3.58 \times 10^{-4}$

The doping level should be 3.58 acceptor atoms per $10^4$ *Si* atoms

∴ To coincide $E_C$ with $E_F$

$$E_C = E_F \text{ if } N_C = N_D\, m_n = n$$

Therefore $4.81 \times 10^{15}(T)^{3/2} = 1.79 \times 10^{19}$

Therefore $T = 246.8^{\circ}\text{k}$

**23. (a) Find the magnitude of the hall voltage $V_H$ in an *n*-type Ge bar used in figure having majority carrier concentration $N_D = 10^7/\text{cm}^3$**

**(b) What happens to $V_H$ if an identical *p*-type Ge bar having $N_A = 10^{17}/\text{cm}^3$ is used in part?**

**Solution:**

(a) $$V_H = \frac{BI}{\rho\omega} = \frac{BJD}{\rho} \quad ...(1)$$

And $$J = \sigma\, e \quad ...(2)$$

And $$\sigma = \rho\, \mu \quad ...(3)$$

Substituting equation (2) and (3) in equation (1)

$$V_H = \frac{BJD}{\rho} = \frac{B(\sigma\varepsilon)\, d}{\rho} = B\mu\varepsilon d$$

Using MKS units

$$V_H = 0.1 \times 3800 \times 10^{-4} \times 1500 \times 3 \times 10^{-3}$$

$$= 171 \text{ mv}$$

(b) $V_H$ retains the same value but changes polarity.

**24. The Hall effect is used to determine the mobility of holes in a p-type Si bar used in figure. Assume the bar resistivity is 300,000 Ω-cm, the magnetic field**

**$B_z = 0.1$ wb/m² and $d = w = 6$ mm. The measured values of the current and Hall voltge are 10 μA and 60 mv respectivity. Find $m_p$.**

**Solution:**

$$R_H = \frac{V_H\omega}{BI}$$

$$= \frac{60 \times 10^{-3} \times 6 \times 10^{-3}}{0.1 \times 10 \times 10^{-6}}$$

$$= 360 \text{ (A-s/m}^3)^{-1}$$

$$\mu = \sigma R_H = R_H/\rho = \frac{300}{3000}$$

$$= 120 \times 10^{-3} \text{ m}^2/\text{v-sec}$$

or $$\mu_p = 1200 \text{ cm}^2/\text{v-sec.}$$

## 1.10 OBJECTIVE QUESTIONS

1. A silicon sample is uniformly doped with $10^{16}$ phosphorus atoms/cm$^3$ and 2 × $10^{16}$ boron atoms/cm$^3$. If all the dopants are fully ionized, the material is
(a) n-type with carrier concentration of $10^{16}$/cm$^3$
(b) p-type with carrier concentration of $10^{16}$/cm$^3$
(c) p-type with carrier concentration of 2 × $10^{16}$/cm$^3$
(d) $T_2$-will get damaged and $T_1$ will be safe
**Ans:** (b)

2. A semiconductor is irradiated with light such that carriers are uniformly generated throughout its volume. The semiconductor is n-type with $N_D$ = $10^{19}$ per cm$^3$. If the excess electron concentration in the steady state is $\Delta n$ = $10^{15}$ per cm$^3$ and if $\tau_P$ = 10μ sec. (minority carrier life time) the generation rate due to irradiation
(a) is $10^{20}$ e-h pairs /cm$^3$/s
(b) is $10^{24}$ e-h pairs/cm$^3$/s
(d) is $10^{10}$ e-h pairs /cm$^3$/s
(d) cannot be determined as the given data is insufficient.
**Ans:** (a)

3. A small concentration of minority carriers is injected into a homogeneous semiconductor crystal at one point. An electric field of 10 v.cm is applied across the crystal and this moves the minority carriers a distance of 1 cm is 20μ sec. The mobility (in cm$^2$/volt.sec).
(a) 1,000
(b) 2,000
(c) 5,000
(d) 500,000
**Ans:** (c)

4. In a p-type silicon sample, the hole concentration is 2.25 × $10^{15}$/cm$^3$. If the intrinsic carrier concentration 1.5 × $10^{10}$/cm$^3$, the electron concentration is
(a) zero
(b) $10^{10}$/cm$^3$
(c) $10^5$/cm$^3$
(d) 1.5 × $10^{25}$/cm$^3$
**Ans:** (c)

5. The intrinsic carrier density at 300K is 1.5 × $10^{10}$/cm$^3$ is silicon. For n-type silicon doped to 2.25 × $10^{15}$ atoms/cm$^3$, the equilibrium electron and hole densities are
(a) $n = 1.5 \times 10^{15}/\text{cm}^3, p = 1.5 \times 10^{10}/\text{cm}^3$
(b) $n = 1.5 \times 10^{10}/\text{cm}^3, p = 2.25 \times 10^{15}/\text{cm}^3$
(c) $n = 2.25 \times 10^{15}/\text{cm}^3, p = 1.0 \times 10^{5}/\text{cm}^3$
(d) $n = 1.5 \times 10^{10}/\text{cm}^3, p = 1.5 \times 10^{10}/\text{cm}^3$
**Ans:** (c)

6. The electron and hole concentrations in a intrinsic semiconductor are $n_i$ and $p_i$ respectively, when doped with a p-type material, these change to $n$ and $p$, respectively then,

(a) $n + p = n_i + p_i$  (b) $n + n_i = p + p_i$
(c) $np_i = n_ip$  (d) $np = n_ip_i$
**Ans:** (d)

7. A long specimen of p-type semiconductor material
(a) is positively charged
(b) is electrically neutral
(c) has an electric field directed along its length
(d) acts as a dipole
**Ans:** (b)

8. The probability that an electron in a metal occupies the fermi-level, at any temperature (>0K)
(a) 0  (b) 1  (c) 0.5  (d) 1.0
**Ans:** (c)

9. When $n_e$ and $n_h$ are electron and hole densities, and $\mu_e$ and $\mu_n$ are the carrier mobilities, the Hall coefficient is positive when
(a) $n_h \mu_h > n_e\mu_e$  (b) $n_h\mu_h^2 > n_e\mu_e^2$
(c) $n_h\mu_h < n_e\mu_h$  (d) $n_h\mu_h^2 > n_e \mu_e^2$
**Ans:** (b)

10. n-type semiconductors are
(a) negatively charged
(b) produced when Indium is added as an impurity to Germanium
(c) produced when phosphorous added as an impurity to silicon
(d) none
**Ans:** (c)

11. If the temperature of an extrinsic semiconductor is increased so that the intrinsic carrier concentration is doubled, then
(a) the majority carrier density doubles
(b) the minority carrier density doubles
(c) the minority carrier density becomes 4 times the original value
(d) both majority and minority carrier densities double
**Ans:** (d)

12. At room temperature, the current in an intrinsic semiconductor is due to
(a) holes  (b) electrons
(c) ions  (d) holes and electrons
**Ans:** (d)

13. Measurement of Hall coefficient enables the determination of
(a) mobility of charge carriers
(b) type of conductivity and concentration of charge carriers
(c) temperature coefficient and thermal conductivity
(d) fermi level and forbidden energy gap
**Ans:** (b)

**14.** For a photo conductor with equal electron and hole mobilities and perfect ohmic contacts at the ends, an increase in the intensity of optical illumination results

(a) a change in open-circuit voltage (b) a change short-circuit current
(b) a reduction of resistance (d) an increase of resistance

**Ans:** (c)

**15.** Consider the following statements about condrtions that make a metal-semiconductor contact rectifying:

(a) N-type semiconductor with its work function $\phi_S$, greater than the work function $\phi_M$ of the metal
(b) N-type semiconductor with its work function $\phi_S$ small than the work function $\phi_M$ of the metal
(c) P-type semiconductor with its work function $\phi_S$, greater than the work function $\phi_M$ of the metal
(d) P-type semiconductor with its work function $\phi_S$, smaller than the work function $\phi_M$ of the metal.

Of these statements:

(a) 1 and 3 are correct (b) 2 and 3 are correct
(c) 1 and 4 are correct (d) 2 and 4 are correct

**Ans:** (a)

**16.** A sample of N-type semiconductor has electron density of $6.25 \times 10^{18}/\text{cm}^3$ at 300K. If the intrinsic concentration of carriers in this sample is $2.5 \times 10^{13}/\text{cm}^3$, at this temperature, the hole density works out to be

(a) $10^6/\text{cm}^3$ (b) $10^3/\text{cm}^3$
(b) $10^{10}/\text{cm}^3$ (d) $10^{12}/\text{cm}^3$

**Ans:** (b)

**17.** Consider the following statements: compared to Silicon, Gallium Arsenide (GaAs) has

1. higher signal speed since electron mobility is higher
2. poorer crystal quality since stoichiometric growth difficult
3. easier to grow crystals since the vapor pressure Arsenic is high
4. higher optoelectronic conversion efficiency

Of these statements:

(a) 1, 2, 3 and 4 are correct (b) 1, 2 and 3 are correct
(c) 3 and 4 are correct (d) 1, 2 and 4 are correct

**Ans:** (c)

**18.** A good ohmic contact on a p-type semiconductor chip is formed by introducing

(a) gold as an impurity below the contact
(b) a high concentration of acceptors below the contact
(c) a high concentration of donors below the contact
(d) a thin insulator layer between the metal and semiconductor

**Ans:** (c)

**19.** If the drift velocity of holes under a field gradient of 100 v/m is 5 m/s their mobility (in the same SI units is)

(a) 0.05 (b) 0.5

(c) 50 (d) 500

**Ans:** (a)

**20.** Hall effect is observed in a specimen when it (metal or a semiconductor) is carrying current and is placed in a magnetic field. The resultant electric field inside the specimen will be in

(a) a direction normal to both current and magnetic field

(b) the direction of current

(c) a direction anti parallel to magnetic field

(d) an arbitrary direction depending upon the conductivity of the specimen.

**Ans:** (a)

**21.** In a p-type semiconductor, the conductivity due to holes ($= \sigma_P$) is equal to ($e$ = charge of hole, $\mu_P$-hole mobility, $p$ = hole concentration)

(a) $p.e/\mu_P$ (b) $\mu_P/p.e$

(c) $p.e.\ \mu_P$ (d) $1/p.e.\ \mu_P$

**Ans:** (c)

**22.** The conductivity of an intrinsic semiconductor is (symbols have the usual meanings).

(a) generally lesser than that of a doped semiconductor

(b) given by $\sigma_i = en_i\ (\mu_n - \mu_p)$

(c) given by $\sigma_i = en_i\ (\mu_n + \mu_p)$

(d) given by $\sigma_i = n_i\ (\mu_n + \mu_p)$

**Ans:** (c)

**23.** The difference between the electron and hole $I_m$ refs of a semiconductor laser is 1.5eV and the band gap of the semiconductor is 1.43eV. The upper and lower frequency limits of the laser will be respectively

(a) $3.3 \times 10^{14}$ and $9.9 \times 10^{13}$ Hz (b) $3.7 \times 10^{14}$ and $3.5 \times 10^{14}$ Hz

(c) $6.28 \times 10^{14}$ and $3.1 \times 10^{14}$ Hz (d) $1.16 \times 10^{15}$ and $8.97 \times 10^{14}$ Hz

**Ans:** (c)

**24.** Measurement of Hall coefficient in a semiconductor provides information on the

(a) sign and mass of charge carriers

(b) mass and concentration of charge carriers

(c) sign of charge carriers alone

(d) sign and concentration of charge carriers

**Ans:** (d)

**25.** If the energy gap of a semiconductor is 1.1eV it would be

(a) opaque to the visible light

(b) transparent to the visible light

(c) transparent to the ultraviolet radiation

**Ans:** (a)

**26.** Some ceramic superconductors become super conducting
(a) below liquid helium temperature
(b) between and liquid nitrogen temperatures
(c) above liquid nitrogen temperature but below room temperature
(d) above room temperature
**Ans:** (a)

**27.** At very high temperature the extrinsic semiconductors become intrinsic because
(a) of drive-in diffusion of dopants and carriers
(b) band to band transition dominates over impurity ionization
(c) impurity ionization dominates over band to band transition
(d) band to band transition is balanced by impurity ionization
**Ans:** (d)

**28.** Consider the following statements regarding a semiconductor:
1. acceptor level lies close to the valence band
2. donor level lies close to the valance band
3. n-type semiconductor behaves as conductor at zero Kelvin
4. p-type semiconductor behaves as an insulator at zero Kelvin
Of these statements:
(a) 2 and 3 are correct (b) 1 and 3 are correct
(c) 1 and 4 are correct (d) 3 and 4 are correct
**Ans:** (c)

**29.** The Hall effect voltage in intrinsic silicon
(a) is positive (b) is zero
(c) is negative (d) changes sign as application of magnetic field
**Ans:** (c)

**30.** If the drift velocity of holes under a field gradient of 100v/m is 5m/p, the mobility (in the same SI units) is
(a) 0.05 (b) 0.5 (c) 50 (d) 500
**Ans:** (a)

**31.** In a semiconductor, $J$, $J_p$ and $J_n$ indicate total diffusion current density, hole current density and electron current density respectively, $\frac{\partial n}{\partial x}$ and $\frac{\partial p}{\partial x}$ are the electron and hole concentration gradient respectively is x-direction and $D_p$ and $D_n$ are the hole and electron diffusion constants respectively. Which one of the following equations is correct? ($q$ denotes charge of electron)

(a) $J_n = -q\, D_n \frac{\partial n}{\partial x}$ for electrons (b) $J = -q\, D_p \frac{\partial p}{\partial x}$ for holes

(c) $J_p = -q\, D_p \frac{\partial p}{\partial x} - q\, D_n \frac{\partial n}{\partial x}$ (d) $J = q\, D_p \frac{\partial p}{\partial x} + D_n \frac{\partial n}{\partial x}$

**Ans:** (b)

**32.** The Hall coefficient of sample (A) of a semiconductor is measured at room temperature. The Hall coefficient of A at room temperature is $4 \times 10^{-4}$ $m^3$ $coulomb^{-1}$. The carrier concentration in sample A at room temperature is

(a) $\approx 10^{-14}$ $m^{-3}$ (b) $\approx -10^{+24}$ $m^{-3}$

(c) $\approx 10^{4}$ $m^{-3}$ (d) $\approx 10^{22}$ $m^{-3}$

**Ans:** (d)

**33.** In an intrinsic semiconductor, the mobility of electrons in the conduction band is:

(a) zero

(b) less than the mobility of holes in the valence band

(c) equal to the mobility of holes in the valence band

(d) greater than the mobility of holes in the valence band.

**Ans:** (d)

**34.** Assuming carrier mobility to be temperature independent it can be shown that pure Si ($E_g$ = 1.1eV) and Ge ($E_g$ = 0.7eV) have the same conductivity at a temperature of

(a) 191 K (b) 3000 K

(c) 471 K (d) 1470 K

**Ans:** (d)

**35.** The Hall coefficient of an intrinsic semiconductor is:

(a) positive under all conditions (b) negative under all conditions

(c) zero under all conditions (d) Zero at 0 K

**Ans:** (b)

**36.** If the lattice temperature is increased, then the coefficient of a semiconductor will:

(a) decrease (b) increase

(c) first increase to a peak and then decrease (d) remain constant

**Ans:** (b)

**37.** Consider the following statements: pure germanium and pure silicon are examples of

1. direct band-gap semiconductors
2. indirect band-gap semiconductors
3. degenerate semiconductors

Of these statements:

(a) 1 alone is correct (b) 2 alone is correct

(c) 3 alone is correct (d) 1 and 3 are correct

**Ans:** (a)

**38.** The room temperature resistivity (in Ω-m) of pure silicon is:

(a) 3000 (b) 300

(c) 30 (d) 3

**Ans:** (a)

**39.** In a semiconductor, the electron and hole concentrations are comparable, which one of the following conditions must be satisfied for the Hall-coefficient to be positive?

(a) (Hole concentration) × (hole mobility)$^2$ should be less than (electron concentration) × (electron mobility)$^2$
(b) (Hole concentration) × (hole mobility)$^2$ should be more than (electron concentration) × (electron mobility)$^2$
(c) (Hole concentration) × (electron mobility)$^2$ should be greater than (electron concentration) × (hole mobility)$^2$
(d) (Hole concentration) × (electron mobility)$^2$ should be less than (electron concentration) × (hole mobility)$^2$

**Ans:** (b)

**40.** Light is incident on a long open circuited n-type semiconductor bar. The diffusion current varies as:

(a) $\varepsilon^{-x/\sqrt{L_p}}$ (b) $\varepsilon\sqrt{\dfrac{x}{L_p}}$

(c) $\varepsilon^{-x/Lp}$ (d) $\varepsilon^{(x/Lp)^2}$

**Ans:** (a)

**41.** Light is incident on along open circuited n-type semiconductor bar. The hole diffusion current is proportional to

(a) $D_p/L_p$ (b) $L_p/D_p$

(c) $(D_p/L_p)^2$ (d) $\sqrt{\dfrac{D_p}{L_p}}$

**Ans:** (a)

**42.** Light is incident on a long open n-type semiconductor bar. The ratio of electron diffusion current to hole diffusion current is

(a) $D_n/D_p$ (b) $-D_n/D_p$

(c) $(D_n/D_p) - 1$ (d) $(D_p/D_n) - 1$

**Ans:** (b)

**43.** Light is incident on a long open n-type semiconductor bar. The ratio of electron drift current to hole diffusion current equals.

(a) $D_n/D_p$ (b) $-D_n/D_p$

(c) $(D_n/D_p) - 1$ (d) $(D_p/D_n) - 1$

**Ans:** (c)

**44.** Light is incident on a long open n-type semiconductor bar. The ratio of hole drift current to hole diffusion current equals.

(a) $(p/n)(\mu_p/\mu_n)(D_n/D_p) - 1$ (b) $(p/n)(\mu_p/\mu_n)(D_n/D_p)$

(c) $(p/n)(\mu_p/\mu_n)(D_p/D_n) - 1$ (d) $(p/n)(\mu_p/\mu_n)(D_p/D_n)$

**Ans:** (a)

**45.** In an open circuited step graded $p$–$n$ junction having donor concentration $N_D$. acceptor concentration $N_A$ the contact difference of potential developed is:

(a) $V_T \ln \dfrac{N_A N_D}{n_i^2}$ (b) $V_T \ln \dfrac{n_i^2}{N_A N_D}$

(c) $1/V_T \ln \dfrac{N_A N_D}{n_i^2}$ (d) $1/V_T \ln \dfrac{n_i^2}{N_A N_D}$

**Ans:** (a)

**46.** A p-type silicon sample has a higher conductivity compared to an n-type sample having the same dopant concentration (True/False).
**Ans:** False

**47.** If a semiconductor is placed in a transverse magnetic field B, and an electric field E is applied across its other two faces, then it would produce an electric current 'I' in the direction perpendicular to both B and E (True/False).
**Ans:** True.

**48.** Considering two p-n-p and n-p-n transistors of identical construction as far as shape, size and doping are concerned, the n-p-n transistor will have a better frequency response (True/False).
**Ans:** True.

**49.** The electron mobility is higher than that of the hole mobility.
**Ans:** True.

## 1.11 CONVENTIONAL QUESTIONS

1. What is the drawback of Rutherford model? What is the remedy for it?
2. Explain crystalline nature of semiconductor materials.
3. What is difference between extrinsic and intrinsic semiconductors?
4. Define a hole in a semiconductor? Indicate how a hole contributes to conduction pictorially?
5. Define (a) conductivity (b) mobility (c) donor (d) acceptor.
6. Define intrinsic concentration, what is the relationship between this density and intrinsic concentration for electrons? What do these equal at 0°k?
7. Derive the condition of dynamic equilibrium for the density of charge carriers for Continuity equation.
8. What is Hall effect? Derive the relation between mobility (μ) and Hall coefficient $R_H$?

## 1.12 EXERCISE PROBLEMS

1. A specimen of metal has $1.808 \times 10^{30}$ free electrons per cubic meter. The mobility of free electrons in the metal is 1 cm²/v-s (a) calculate the conductivity of the metal and (b) if an electric field of 50 V/cm is applied across the specimen, find the drift velocity of free electrons and the current density.
   **Ans:** $\sigma = 2.9 \times 10^7$ s/m ; v = 0.5 m/s; $J = 14.5 \times 10^{10}$ A/m³

**2.** (a) Find the resistivity of intrinsic Ge at 300deg k. It is given that $n_i$ at 300deg k is $2.5 \times 10^{13}$ $cm^3$ and $\sigma_n$ and $\mu_p$ are 3800 and 1800 $cm^2$/v-s respectively.

(b) If donor impurity is added to the extent of 1 impurity atom per $5 \times 10^7$ Ge atoms. Find the resistivity.

(c) If acceptor impurity is added to pure Ge to the extent of 1 impurity atom per $2 \times 10^7$ Ge atoms. Find the resistivity.

**Ans:** 4.46 Ω-cm; 1.86 Ω-cm; 1.575 Ω-cm

**3.** (a) Find the resistivity of intrinsic Si at 300°k. It is given that $n_i$ at 300°k in Si is $1.5 \times 10^{10}$ /$cm^3$ and the mobilities of electrons and holes in Si are 1300 $cm^2$/v-s and 500 $cm^2$/v-s respectively.

(b) If donor type impurity is added to the extent of 1 impurity atom in $5 \times 10^7$ Si atoms. Find the resistivity.

(c) If acceptor type impurity is added to the extent of 1 impurity atom in $2 \times 10^8$ Si atoms, find the resistivity.

**Ans:** $2.38 \times 10^5$ Ω-cm; 4.8 Ω-cm; 50 Ω-cm

**4.** Find the conductivity of Si

(a) in intrinsic condition at 300°k

(b) with donor impurity of 1 part in $10^7$

(c) with acceptor impurity of 5 parts in $10^7$

(d) with both the above impurities present simultaneously. Given that $n_i$ for Si at 300°k is $1.5 \times 10^{10}$/$cm^3$, $\mu_n$ and $\mu_p$ is Si are 1300 $cm^2$/v-s and 500 $cm^2$/v-s respectively and the number of Si atoms/$cm^3$ is $5 \times 10^{22}$

**Ans:** $4.32 \times 10^{-6}$ s/cm; 1.04 s/cm; 0.08 s/cm; 0.832 s/cm

**5.** A p-type Ge bar has cross-sectional area of 2 $mm^2$, length of 2 cm, resistivity of 25 Ω-cm and carrier life time of 100 μs. One end of the bar is continuously irradiated with $3 \times 10^6$ photons/sec. Find the resistance of the bar under continuous excitation at room temperature assuming that

(i) each incident photon generates 2 electron-hole pairs and

(ii) these electrons and holes are uniformly distributed throughout the bar. Given that $n_i$ at 300°k is $2.5 \times 10^{13}$/$cm^3$ $\mu_n = 3800$ $cm^2$/v-s; $\mu_p = 1800$ $cm^2$/v-s $q = 1.6 \times 10^{-19}$ c.

**Ans:** 573.4 Ω

**6.** A Si bar 0.1 cm long and 100 $\mu m^2$ in cross-sectional area is doped with $10^{17}$ $cm^{-3}$ Antimony. Find the current at 300°k with applied voltage 10v applied.

**Ans:** 1.12 mA

**7.** Calculate effective densities of states $N_c$ and $N_v$ for Si at 300°k. Also find its intrinsic carrier concentration.

**Ans:** $2.89 \times 10^{19}$ $cm^3$; $1.05 \times 10^{19}$ $cm^3$; $8.6 \times 10^9$ $cm^{-3}$

**8.** In an n-type semiconductor, if the concentration of donor atoms is increased by a factor of 4, find the shift in the position of Fermi level. Assume $KT$ = 0.03 ev.

**Ans:** Upward shift of 0.0416 ev

9. In a p-type semiconductor, if the concentration of acceptor atoms is increased by a factor ten, find the shift in the position of Fermi level. Assume $KT = 0.03$ ev.

   **Ans:** Downward shift of 0.069 ev

10. Show that a semiconductor has minimum conductivity at a given temperature when $n = n_i \sqrt{\frac{\mu_n}{\mu_e}}$ and $p = n_i \sqrt{\frac{\mu_e}{\mu_n}}$

# ❮ 2 ❯

# SEMICONDUCTOR DIODES

## 2.1 INTRODUCTION

Before the invention of semiconductor diode there was vacuum tube diode which is bulky, costly and noisy. It takes more power and it takes more time to start conducting because of the thermionic emission and these limitations were solved by semiconductor junction diode.

## 2.2 JUNCTION FORMATION

When $p$ and $n$ regions are brought together at extremely high temperatures, the majority carriers move towards the opposite side because of the concentration gradient and such a process is called diffusion process and some of the carriers get recombined making atoms as ions and because of these ions potential is developed across the junction which can stop the further flow of diffusion. The potential thus formed will enable the minority carriers to flow in the opposite direction.

### *Open circuited p-n junction:*

The junction formation and voltage development is shown in Fig 2.1(a). The charge density (ρ) outside the junction is zero and the extrinsic semiconductor is neutral. The charge distribution within the junction can be explained with the help of Poisson's equation.

$$\frac{d^2v}{dx^2} = \frac{-\rho\vartheta}{\varepsilon} \qquad \text{....(1)}$$

$\vartheta$ = electrostatic potential,
$\varepsilon$ = permitivity of the medium.
$x$ = distance from the junction.

By integrating we get electric field and once again by integrating we get voltage against holes and voltage against electrons. Therefore Poissons equation is satisfied within the junction and the Laplace equation is satisfied outside the junction. The voltage against holes starts from as if $-\frac{w}{2}$ cannot start

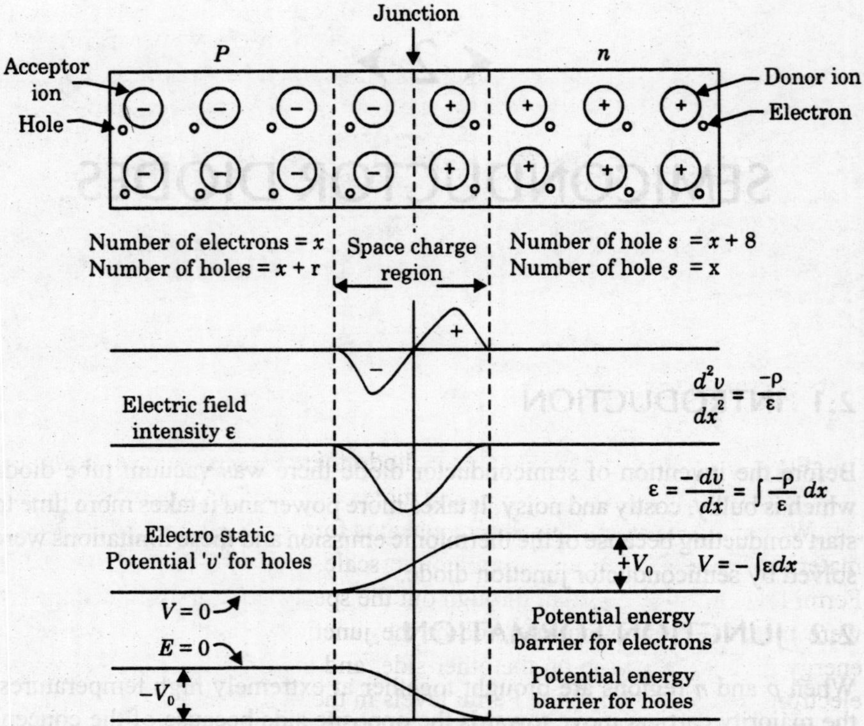


**Fig. 2.1** A *p–n* junction schematic diagram, shows charge density electric field intensity, and potential (a) general shape of charge density ρ (b) negative field intensity (c) potential against holes (d) potential against electrons.

below that is because of the electrostatic influence and it becomes maximum at $+\frac{w}{2}$. The potential raised will retain outside the junction because nothing is added or subtracted outside the junction.

The junction potential neither depends on ions in the junction nor on the doping concentration but it depends on the ratio of carriers in the opposite regions at equilibrium as derived in the next section.

## 2.3 EXPRESSION FOR $V_o$.

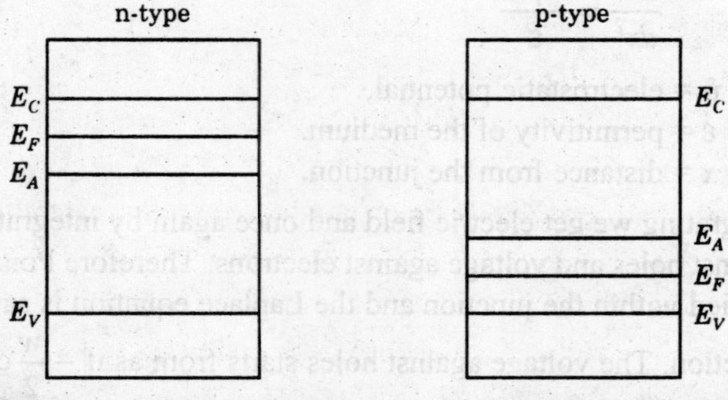


**Fig. 2.2** (a) energy band d iagram of n-type (b) energy band diagram of p-type

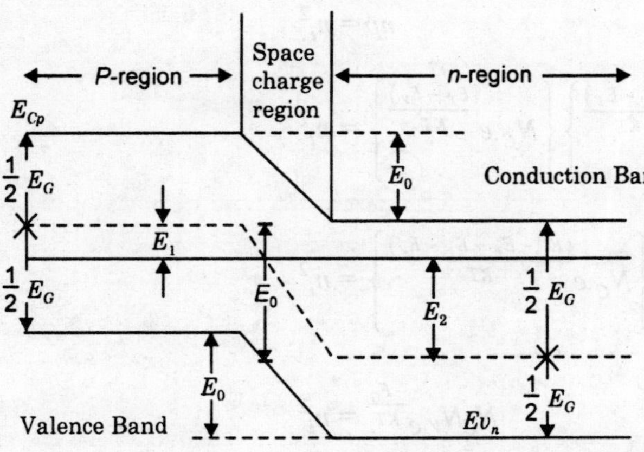


**Fig. 2.2** (c) Band diagram of p-n junction under open circuit conditions.

We consider here a *PN* junction, which is formed by placing *p* and *n*-type materials in initiate contact on an atomic scale. Under these conditions the Fermi level must be constant through out the specimen at equilibrium. If this were not so, electrons on one side of the junction would have an average energy higher than those on the other side, and there would be a transfer of electrons and energy until the Fermi levels in the two sides did line up.

The Fermi level $E_F$ is closer to the condition band edge $E_{Cn}$ in the *n-type* material, and closer to the valence band in $E_{VP}$ the *p-side.* Clearly, then, the conduction band edge $E_{Cp}$ in the *p-type* cannot be at the same level as, nor can be the valence band edge $E_{Vn}$ in the *n* sideline up with $E_{VP}$. Hence the energy band diagram for a junction appear as shown in figure 2.2, where a shift in energy levels *Eo* is indicated.

$$E_0 = E_{Cn} - E_{Cp} = E_{VP} - E_{Vn} = E_1 + E_2 \quad ...(4)$$

In equation (4) 'o' represents thermal equilibrium conditions. This energy Eo represents the *potential energy* of the electrons at the junction.

$$\text{For } n\text{-type: } Ec - E_F = KT \ln\left(\frac{N_C}{N_D}\right)$$

$$\text{For } p\text{-type: } E_F - Ev = KT \ln\left(\frac{N_V}{N_A}\right)$$

$$E_{Cn} - E_F = ½\, E_G - E_2 \quad ...(5)$$

$$E_F - E_{VP} = ½\, E_G - E_1 \quad ...(6)$$

Addition of (5) and (6) gives

$$(E_{Cn} - E_F) + (E_F - E_{VP}) = E_G - (E_1 + E_2)$$

$$KT \ln \frac{N_C}{N_D} + KT \ln\left(\frac{N_V}{N_A}\right) = \{E_G\} - Eo \quad ...(7)$$

$$np = n_i^2$$

$$\left\{N_C.e^{\frac{(E_C - E_F)}{KT}}\right\}\left\{N_C.e^{\frac{(E_F - E_V)}{KT}}\right\} = n_i^2.$$

$$\left\{N_C.e^{\frac{(E_C - E_F + E_F - E_V)}{KT}}\right\} = n_i^2$$

$$N_C N_V\, e^{\frac{-F_G}{KT}} = n_i^2$$

$$E_G = KT \ln\left(\frac{N_C N_V}{n_i^2}\right) \qquad ...(8)$$

$$KT \ln\left(\frac{N_C}{N_D}\right)\cdot\left(\frac{N_V}{N_A}\right) = KT \ln\left(\frac{N_C N_V}{n_i^2}\right) - \mathrm{E_o}$$

$$\mathrm{E_o} = KT \ln\left(\frac{N_C N_V}{n_i^2\left(\frac{N_C N_V}{N_D N_A}\right)}\right)$$

$$\therefore \qquad \mathrm{E_o} = KT \ln\left(\frac{N_A N_D}{n_i^2}\right) \qquad ...(9)$$

**This shows the contact energy depends on doping concentration. But this cannot be true because there occurs recombination's to form-junction.**

**The contact potential depends only upon equilibrium concentrations and not at all upon charge density in the transition region.**

According to charge neutrality of semiconductors:

Total positive charge = Total negative charge

$$p + N_D = n + N_A.$$

*For n-type :* $\qquad N_A = 0.$

$$\therefore \qquad P_{no} + N_D = n_{no} + 0.$$

But normally in *n*-type materials $n_{no} >> p_{no}$.

$$\therefore \qquad n_{no} \approx N_D$$

from mass-action law

$$n_{no} \times p_{no} = n_i^2$$

$$n_{no} = \frac{n_i^2}{N_D} \qquad ...(10)$$

Similarly in *p*-type materials

$$Ppo \approx N_A$$

$$n_{po} = \frac{n_i^2}{N_A} \qquad ...(11)$$

Substituting (10) and (11) in (9) we get

$$Eo = KT \ln \left( \frac{P_{Po}}{P_{no}} \right) \qquad ...(12)$$

Similarly $$Eo = KT \ln \left[ \frac{N_{no}}{n_{Po}} \right] \qquad ...(13)$$

Conversion from *Vo* (volts) to $E_o$ (electron volts) is $Vo = \frac{E_O}{q}$

$$\therefore \quad V_O = \frac{KT}{q} \ln \left\{ \frac{P_{po}}{P_{no}} \right\} = \frac{KT}{q} \ln \left\{ \frac{n_{no}}{n_{po}} \right\} \qquad ...(14)$$

For Ge Vo = 0.2 V and for *Si Vo* = 0.6 V

## 2.4 V-I CHARACTERISTICS

***Forward Bias:*** The applied voltage is in opposite to the internal junction potential. So in order to overcome the barrier then only current can flow in the diode and the characteristics are shown in fig. 2.3.

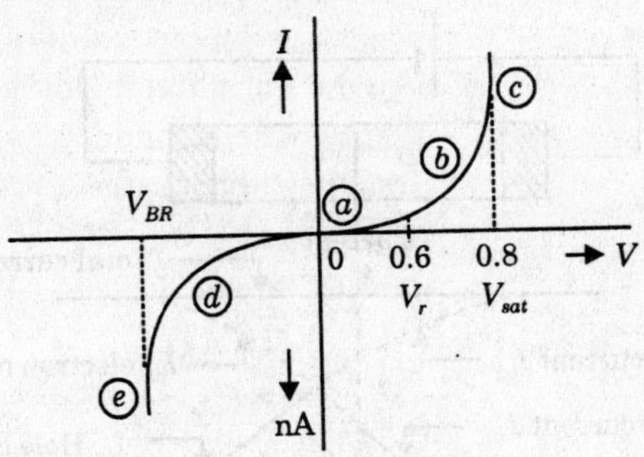


**Fig. 2.3** *V-I* characteristics

(a) $V_a < V_r$: As the applied potential is not sufficient to overcome the barrier, no current flows.

(b) $V_r < V_a < V_{sat}$ : For every increase in junction voltage the current also equally increases so it is almost a exponential relationship between $V$ and $I$.

(c) $V_a < V_{sat}$ : The carriers that are emitted due to external supply will collide with one another and create temperature. That temperature breaks the covalent bonds and gives the emission called secondary emission and the secondary emission starts right at small voltage because the carriers are majority and the dynamic resistance in the forward direction of the diode is very low at the order of ohms.

***Reverse Bias:*** According to the figure the applied voltage is added to internal voltage. Therefore there is no cutin voltage existing.

(a) $V_a < V_{BR}$ : The electric field gives the e mission but it is very small because it is due to minority carriers at the order of micro amperes for germanium and nano amperes for silicon.

(a) $V_a < V_{BR}$ : The carriers that are emitted due to electric field will collide and create secondary emission but that happens at very high voltage because the carriers are very less and the junction diode will spoil in the breakdown region. The dynamic reverse resistance is very high at the order of mega ohms.

## 2.5 V-I EQUATION AND CHARACTERISTICS

### *Current Components*

When a voltage is applied to a *p-n* junction diode the electron and hole distributions in the space charge and neutral regions are changed from their equilibrium values. Holes are injected to *n*-side and electrons to *p*-side when a forward bias is applied to diode. The number of these injected minority carriers fall of exponentially with distance from the junction indicated in figure 2.4 are two minority carriers *Ipn* and *Inp*.

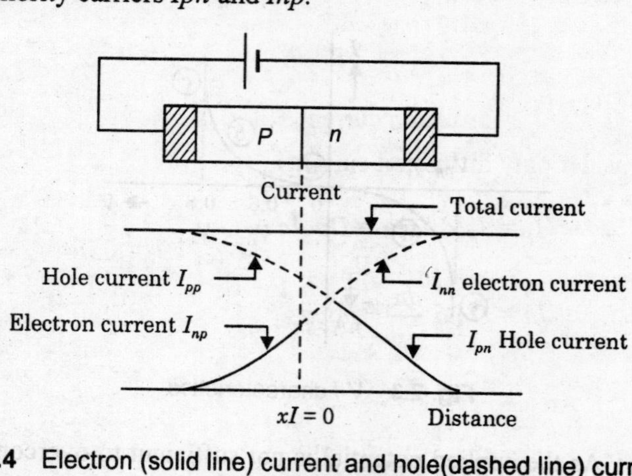


**Fig. 2.4** Electron (solid line) current and hole(dashed line) current vs distance in PN junction diode.

*Ipn* (*x*) – hole diffusion current in the *n* material and *Inp* (*x*) – electron diffusion current in *p* material as a function of *x*. The electrons crossing the junction at $x = 0$ from right to left constitute a current in same direction as holes crossing from left to right. The total current is algebraic sum of holes and electron currents *i.e* $I = Ipn\ (0) + Inp\ (0)$

The current is plotted as a function of distance in *PN* junction diode. The space-charge region is assumed to be negligible. This figure is drawn for an unsymmetrical doped diode, so that $Ipn \neq Inp$ assume to be negligible, because the doping on the two sides of the junction need not be identical.

*Assumptions in VI equation:*

(1) Junction width is neglected

(2) Low injection is assumed.

(3) Minority concentration << majority concentration.

∴ Recombination within the junction is neglected

## Current Calculations

$P_{n(o)}$ = holes in to *n* type at $x = 0$

$P_{(no)}$ = holes in to *n* type at $x = L_p$

$n_{p(o)}$ = electrons in to *p* type at $x = 0$

$n_{po}$ = electrons in to *p* type at $x = L_n$

$L_n$ = diffusion length of electrons

$L_p$ = diffusion length of holes

Figure 2.4 assumed that the acceptor concentration is much greater than the donor density, so $P_{no} > n_{po}$ and $L_p > L_n$ because *p* side is heavily doped .The total current *I* is denoted as $I = Ipn(o) + Inp(o)$

Diffusion current decreases the amount of current where as drift current supplies it

$$Ip = JpA.$$

$$\therefore \quad Jp = -Dp\, q\, \frac{dp}{dx} + p\mu_p q\varepsilon$$

$J_P$ = diffusion current + drift current

But we consider only diffussion currents.

$$I_P = J_P \times \text{Area} = Dp\, Aq\, \frac{dp}{dx} \qquad ...(1)$$

Similarly $$Jn = Dn\, q\, \frac{dn}{dx} + n\mu_n q\varepsilon$$

$$I_n = J_n \times \text{Area} = -D_n A\, q\, \frac{dn}{dx} \qquad ...(2)$$

$$\therefore \quad I = Ipno + Inpo$$

$$= -Dp\,q\,\frac{dp}{dx} + D_n A\,q\,\frac{dn}{dx}$$

$$Ip = -DpqA\left\{\frac{P_n(0) - Pno}{0 - Lp}\right\}$$

$$Ipn(o) = \frac{AqDp}{Lp}\{P_n(0) - P_{no}\} \quad ...(3)$$

Similarly $$Inp(0) = \left\{\frac{DnqA}{Ln}\right\}\{n_p(0) - n_{p0}\} \quad ...(4)$$

The holes emitted by the junction into the *n* region diffuse away from the junction, and there concentration reduces steadily because of recombination with electrons. Similarly electrons emitted by the junction into *p*- region diffuse away from the junction producing a gradient in the concentration.

In a forward biased *p-n* diode, the current enters the *p* side as a hole current and leaves the *n* side as an electron current of same magnitude. The current in a *PN* junction is bipolar since it is made up of both positive and negative carriers of electricity.

***Law of Junction:*** Consider that the junction is forward biased by an applied voltage *V*,then the barrier voltage $V_B$ is decreased from its equilibrium value *Vo* by the amount *V* or $V = (\vartheta_o - V)$. The hole and equal to thermal equilibrium value $Pp = Ppo$.

The hole concentration values vs distance shown in figure 2.5.

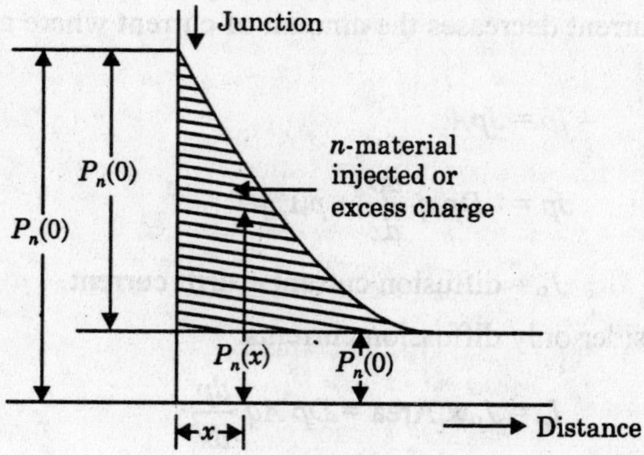


**Fig. 2.5** $P_{n(0)}$ (holes in to *n* type at $x = L_p$) vs distance in pn junction

$$P_{n0} = P_n(0)\,e^{\frac{-V}{\eta V_T}} \quad ...(5)$$

$$Pn(0) = Pno\,e^{V/VT} \quad ...(6)$$

Similarly $$n_p(0) = n_p e^{\frac{-V}{\eta V_T}} \qquad ...(7)$$

This boundary condition is called the *law of the junction*. It states that, for a forward bias the hole concentration $Pn(0)$ at the junction is much greater than the thermal equilibrium value $Pno$. In terms of thermal equilibrium $p_{no}$ and applied voltage $v$, is called *law of junction.* Substituting the value $Pno$ from equation (6) into equation (3) the we can get the *total diode current* $I_{Pn(o)}$.

$$I_{Pn(o)} = \frac{AqDpPno}{Lp}(e^{v/vT} - 1) \qquad ...(8)$$

This expression for electron current $I_{Pn(o)}$ crossing the junction in to $p$ side is obtained from equation (8) by inter changing $p$ and $n$. At $x = 0$ the total diode current

$I = I_{Pn(o)} + I_{np(o)}$, because electrons crossing the junction at $x$=0 from right to left constitute a current in the same direction as hole crossing the junction from left to right.

Similarly $$n_p(0) = n_{po}e^{V/VT}$$

$$I_{np}(0) = \frac{D_n qA}{L_n} n_{po}\left\{e^{V/V_T} - 1\right\}$$

$$I = \left[\frac{D_p qA}{L_P} P_{no} + \frac{D_n qA}{L_n} n_{po}\right]\left\{e^{V/V_T} - 1\right\}$$

$$I = I_0\left\{e^{V/V_T} - 1\right\}$$

If the minority carriers and the junction width is consider then we should consider the recombination with in the junction. And therefore, the net current I at horizontal line in above figure (same throughout the series circuit) becomes as

$$I = I_o\left(e^{V/\eta V_T} - 1\right) \qquad ...(9)$$

Where $\eta \geq 1$ if majority concentration >> minority carrier concentration like *Si*

$\eta = 1$ if majority carrier concentration >> minority carrier concentration like Ge

$I_o$ is reverse saturation current

$\eta$ cannot be calculated theoretically but experimentally it is found to be $\eta = 2$.

$$\eta = \left\{V/V_T \ln\left(\frac{I}{Io} + 1\right)\right\} \qquad ...(10)$$

if $$V = V_T$$

$$\eta \approx \left\{1/\ln\left(\frac{I}{Io}+1\right)\right\} \quad ...(11)$$

Similarly $\quad n_p(0) = n_{po}e^{V/VT}$

$$I_{np}(0) = \frac{D_n qA}{L_n} n_{Po}\left\{e^{V/V_T}-1\right\}$$

$$I = \left[\frac{D_n qA}{L_P} P_{no} + \frac{D_n qA}{L_n} P_{no}\right]\left\{e^{V/V_T}-1\right\}$$

$$I = I_0\left\{e^{V/V_T}-1\right\}$$

$\eta = 1$ for Ge and 2 for *Si*

$V_T$ = volt equivalent of temperature, is given by

$$V_T = \frac{T}{11{,}600} \quad ...(12)$$

At room temp ($T = 300°K$) $V_T = 0.026V$

(a) When the voltage $V$ is positive and several times $V_T$, the unity in the parentheses of equation (1) may be neglected i.e $e^{V/\eta VT} >> 1$

$$I = I_0\, e^{V/\eta VT}$$

(b) When $V$ is negative i.e diode is reverse biased and $|V|$ is several times $V_T$, $I \approx -I_0$. $I_0$ is referred to as the reverse saturation current. This is represented by a straight line (in 3rd quadrant)

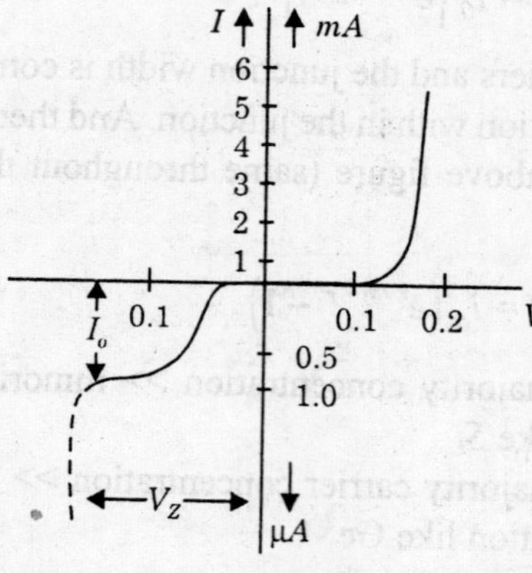


**Fig. 2.6** Ge Characteristics

(c) When the applied voltage is zero $V = 0$ equation (1) becomes $I = I_0\,(e^0 - 1) = 0$ so the curve passes through $V = 0$, $I = 0$ i.e the origin.

(d) For small values of voltage $V$ (both positive and negative) charges view is shown in figure 2.6 b near the origin.

***Cutin voltage $V_r$ :*** Cutin voltage is the voltage below which the current is very small (say less than 1% of max rated value). Beyond $V_r$ the current rises very rapidly. In practical terms, this is the voltage at which the diode may be considered to start the conduction.

For Ge $V_r = 0.2\text{V}$
For Si $V_r = 0.6\text{V}$

***Different forms of $I_0$ :***

$$I_0 = \left[\frac{D_p qA}{L_p} P_{no} + \frac{D_n qA}{L_n} n_{po}\right] \quad ...(1)$$

$I_0$ = reverse saturation current

$I_0$ depends on doping concentration. Therefore no external parameters can change this $I_0$ i.e this cannot be varied at user level.

$$n_{no} \approx N_D,\ p_{no} \approx N_A$$

$$p_{no} \approx \frac{n_i^2}{N_D} \text{ and } n_{p0} \approx \frac{n_i^2}{N_A}$$

$$I_0 = \frac{D_p qA n_i^2}{L_p N_D} + \frac{D_n qA n_i^2}{L_n N_A}$$

$$I_0 = qAn_i^2\left[\frac{D_p}{L_p N_D} + \frac{D_n}{L_n N_A}\right] \quad ...(2)$$

$$\frac{D_p}{\mu_p} = \frac{D_n}{\mu_p} = \text{V}_\text{T} \longrightarrow \text{Einstein Relation}$$

$$\therefore \quad I_0 = qA\, n_i V_T^2\left[\frac{\mu_p}{L_p N_D} + \frac{\mu_n}{L_n N_A}\right] \quad ...(3)$$

Multiply & Divide with $\mu_{nq} + \mu_{pq}$

$$I_0 = qA\, n_p^2\, V_T\left[\frac{\mu_p \mu_n q}{L_p N_D \mu_n q} + \frac{\mu_n \mu_p q}{L_n N_A \mu_p q}\right]$$

$$\sigma = N_D \mu_n q$$

$$I_0 = Aq^2 n_p^2 V_T \mu_n \mu_p \left\{\frac{1}{\mu_p \sigma_n} + \frac{1}{L_n \sigma_p}\right\} \quad ...(4)$$

Divide & multiply with $(\mu_n + \mu_p)^2$

$$I_0 = \frac{Aq^2 n_i^2 V_T \mu_n \mu_p}{(\mu_n + \mu_p)^2}\left\{\frac{1}{\mu_p \sigma_n} + \frac{1}{L_n \sigma_p}\right\}(\mu_n + \mu_p)^2$$

$$\sigma = (n\mu_n + p\mu_p)q;$$

for intrinsic $n = p = n_i$

$$\sigma_i = (\mu_n + \mu_p)qn_i$$

$$\sigma_i^2 = (\mu_n + \mu_p)^2 q^2 n^2$$

$$\therefore \quad I_0 = \frac{A\sigma_i^2 V_T \mu_n \mu_p}{(\mu_n + \mu_p)^2}\left\{\frac{1}{\mu_p \sigma_n} + \frac{1}{L_n \sigma_p}\right\} \quad ...(5)$$

$$I_0 = \frac{A\sigma_i^2 V_T \mu_n \mu_p}{\mu_p^2\left(1 + \frac{\mu_n}{\mu_p}\right)^2}\left\{\frac{1}{\mu_p \sigma_n} + \frac{1}{L_n \sigma_p}\right\}$$

$$\therefore \quad I_0 = \frac{A\sigma_i^2 b V_T}{(1 + b^2)}\left\{\frac{1}{\mu_p \sigma_n} + \frac{1}{L_n \sigma_p}\right\} - \text{VI}$$

Where $\quad b = \frac{\mu_n}{\mu_p}$

## 2.6 JUNCTION CAPACITANCE

If the voltage applied to a junction is changed, the charge distribution near the transition region must also change. There is an additional current is developed due to rate of change of applied voltage, which is capacitive in nature. Hence we have attributed a certain capacitance to the pn junction. This depends on separation of charges and not upon the amount of charges actually present. Both majority and minority carriers contribute a transition capacitance. The majority carriers contribute a transition capacitance and is considered in reverse-bias case. This is also called as space-charges capacitance.

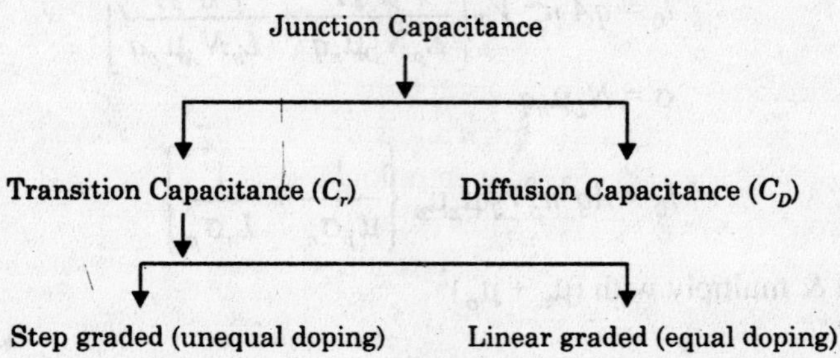

***Transition capacitance:*** majority carriers move away from the junction when a *pn* junction is placed in the Reverse Biased (*RB*),in this case uncovered mobile charge is more. There fore when *RB* is applied to the *pn* junction the thickness of the space charge layer at the junction is increases, it is due to a capacitive effect, this capacitance is called $C_T$ (Transition capacitance) is defined as

$$C_T = \frac{dQ_\vartheta}{dV_j}$$ Where $dq$ = increase in charge caused by a change $dV$ voltage.

From this equation that the change in voltage $dV$ with time $dt$ result in a current

$$i = dQ/dt$$

***Step graded or abrupt or alloy or fusion or barrier capacitance(unequal doping):*** When a junction is in *RB*, the junction width increases this increase is more in the lightly doped.

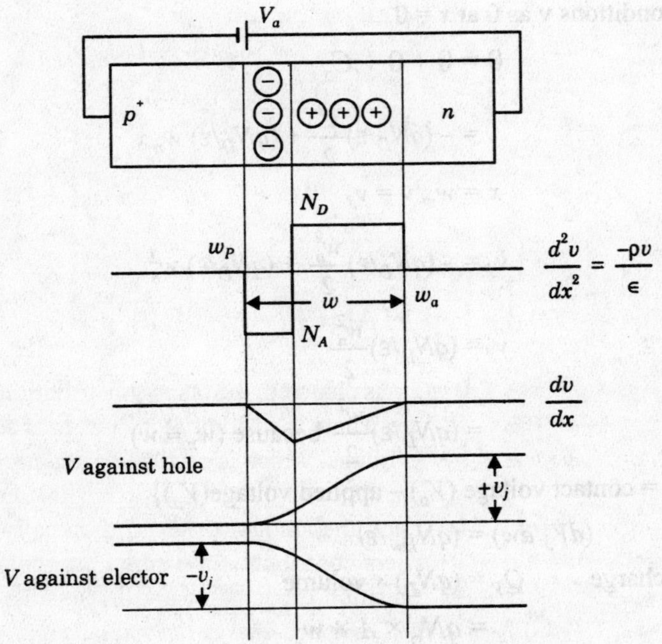


**Fig. 2.7** Representation of step graded capacitance

A junction in which there an abrupt change from acceptor ions from one side to donor ions on other side such a junction is called fusion or alloy junction, it is not necessary that the concentration of $N_A$ of acceptor ions equal the concentration $N_D$ of donor impurities shown in figure 2.8.

The junction width should be different to maintain equal number of ions with unequal doping. In the analysis, we consider voltage against holes because the boundary conditions are simple.

From figure At $x = 0$, $v \approx 0$, $w \approx w_n$

$$d^2v/dx^2 = \rho v/\varepsilon \quad \text{...(1)}$$

Here $\rho v = q\,N_D$ 0r $qN_A$

$$\therefore \quad d^2v/dx^2 = -\,q\,N_D/\varepsilon \quad \text{...(2)}$$

integrating w. r .t $x$

$$dv/dx = -\,(qN_D/\varepsilon)\,w_n + C_1 \quad \text{...(3)}$$

initial conditions $dv/dx = 0$ at $x = w_p, w_n$

$$0 = -\,(qN_D/\varepsilon)\,w_n + C_1$$

$$\therefore \quad C_1 = (qN_D/\varepsilon)\,w_n$$

$$\therefore \quad (dv/dx) = -\,(qN_D/\varepsilon)x + (qN_D/\varepsilon)\,w_n \quad \text{...(4)}$$

integrating

$$v = -\,(qN_D/\varepsilon)\,\frac{x^2}{2} + (qN_D/\varepsilon)\,w_n\,x + C_2$$

initial conditions $v$ as 0 at $x = 0$

$$0 = 0 + 0 + C_2$$

$$\therefore \quad v = -\,(qN_D/\varepsilon)\frac{x^2}{2} + (qN_D/\varepsilon)\,w_n\,x \quad \text{...(5)}$$

at $x = w_n$, $v = v_J$

$$v_J = -\,(qN_D/\varepsilon)\frac{w_n^2}{2} + (qN_D/\varepsilon)\,w_n^2$$

$$\therefore \quad v_J = (qN_D/\varepsilon)\frac{w_n^2}{2} \quad \text{...(6)}$$

$$= (qN_D/\varepsilon)\frac{w^2}{2} \text{ because } (w_n \approx w)$$

$\{V_J$ = contact voltage $(V_o)$ – applied voltage$(V_a)\}$

$$(dV_J/dw) = (qN_{Dw}/\varepsilon) \quad \text{...(7)}$$

volume charge $Q_V = (qN_D) \times \text{volume}$

$$= qN_D \times A \times w_n$$

$$= q\,N_D\,A\,w$$

$$\frac{dQv}{dw} = q\,N_D\,A \quad \text{...(8)}$$

$$C_T = \frac{dQv}{dV_j} \quad \text{...(9)}$$

$$= \left(\frac{dQv}{dV_w}\right)\left(\frac{dQv}{dV_j}\right)$$

$$= (qN_D A / q N_D w).\varepsilon = (\varepsilon A/w)$$

$$\therefore \quad C_T = (\varepsilon A/w) \quad \text{...(10)}$$

Juinction capacitance behaves like a parallel plate capacitor, with the dielectric constant as Silicon material which is $\varepsilon_{r=}$ 12.

***Linear graded (equal doping) or grown junction capacitance:*** A second form of transition capacitance is grown junction capacitance is obtained by adding *p*-type and *n*-type impurities to a single crystal from a melt of Ge whose type is changed during the drawing process. Here we can consider either side, unlike the previous, show in figure 2.8 below.

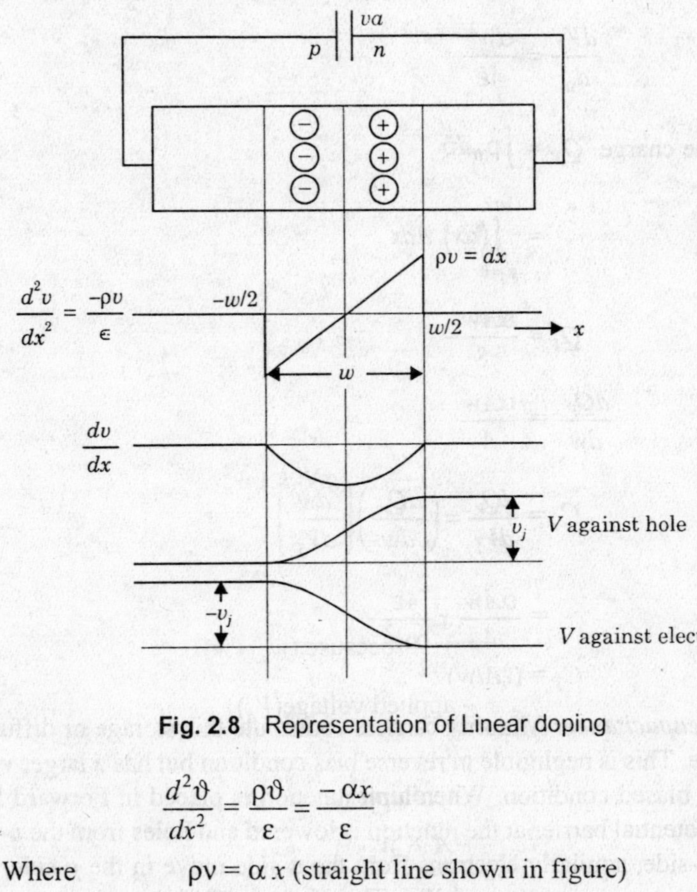


**Fig. 2.8** Representation of Linear doping

$$\frac{d^2\vartheta}{dx^2} = \frac{\rho\vartheta}{\varepsilon} = \frac{-\alpha x}{\varepsilon}$$

Where $\rho v = \alpha\, x$ (straight line shown in figure)

$$dv/dx = 0 \text{ at } x = + w/2 \text{ or } - w/2$$

$$0 = -[\alpha(w/2)^2 / 2\varepsilon] + C_1$$

$$C_1 = \alpha w^2 / 8\varepsilon$$

$$\therefore \quad dv/dx = (\alpha x^2/2\varepsilon) + (\alpha w^2/8\varepsilon)$$

$$V = -(\alpha x^3/6\varepsilon) + (\alpha w^2 x/8\varepsilon) + C_2$$

$$V = 0 \text{ at } x = (-w/2) \text{ and}$$

$$V = V_J \text{ at } x = (+ w/2)$$

$$0 = \{-\alpha[(-w/2)^3]/6\varepsilon\} + \{\alpha[(w^3/2)]/8\varepsilon\} + C_2 \quad ...(2)$$

$$C_2 = \frac{\alpha w^3}{24\varepsilon}$$

$$V = \frac{-\alpha w^3}{6\varepsilon} + \frac{\alpha w^2}{8\varepsilon} + \frac{\alpha w^3}{24\varepsilon}$$

At $x = +w/2 \; V = V_J$

$$V_J = \frac{-\alpha w^3}{6\varepsilon} + \frac{\alpha w^2}{8\varepsilon} + \frac{\alpha w^3}{24\varepsilon} = \frac{\alpha w^3}{12\varepsilon} \quad ...(3)$$

$$\therefore \quad \frac{dV_J}{d_w} = \frac{\alpha w^2}{4\varepsilon} \quad ...(4)$$

volume charge $Q_V = \int \rho_\vartheta d\vartheta$ ...(5)

$$= \int_{x=0}^{w/2} (ax)\, A dx$$

$$Q_V = \frac{\alpha A w^2}{8} \quad ...(6)$$

$$\frac{dQ_V}{dw} = \frac{\alpha A w}{4}$$

$$C_T = \frac{dQ_V}{dV_j} = \left(\frac{dQ_V}{dw}\right)\left(\frac{dw}{dV_j}\right) \quad ...(7)$$

$$= \frac{\alpha A w}{4} x \frac{4\varepsilon}{\alpha w^2}$$

$$\therefore \quad C_T = (\varepsilon A/w) \quad ...(8)$$

***Diffusion capacitance:*** Minority carriers contribute this storage or diffusion capacitance. This is negligible in reverse bias condition but has a larger value in forward biased condition. When a *pn* junction is placed in Forward Bias (*FB*), the potential barrier at the junction is lowered and holes from the *p*-side enter the *n*-side, similarly electrons from the n side move in the *p*-side, this process of minority carriers injection .The of change of injected charge with applied voltage is called as *diffusion or storage capacitance*

$$C_D = d_q/d_v \quad ...(1)$$

As the density of the carriers is high near the junction and decays exponentially with distance. In *FB* the junction width is negligible, therefore the capacitance no more depends on the junction width, but it depends on current only. *$C_T$ depends in Reverse voltage and $C_D$ depends on Forward current.*

*Expressions for Diffusion capaciytance $C_D$:*

$$C_D = \frac{dQv}{dv} \quad \text{...(1)}$$

The hole current $I = \frac{Q}{T}$

$$dI = dQ/\tau$$

$$\therefore \quad dQ = \tau\,(dI) \quad \text{...(2)}$$

substitute eq. (2)) in eq.(1), we get

$$C_D = \tau\left(\frac{dI}{dV}\right) \quad \text{...(3)}$$

$$I = I_o(e^{v/v}{}_T - 1) \quad \text{...(4)}$$

$$\frac{dI}{dV} = \frac{I_o e^{v/\eta v_T}}{\eta V_\Gamma} \rightarrow \text{Dynamic conductance}(g)$$

$$\frac{dI}{dV} = \frac{I_o e^{v/\eta v_T}}{\eta V_\Gamma} - \frac{I_o}{V_T\eta} + \frac{I_o}{V_T\eta}$$

$$= \frac{I_o\left(e^{v/\eta v_T} - 1\right) + I_o}{\eta v_T}$$

$$g = \frac{dI}{dV} = \frac{I + I_o}{\eta V_T} \quad \text{...(5)}$$

$$\approx I/\eta V_T = \text{resistance 'r'}$$

$$C_D = \tau\,(I/\eta V_T) \quad \text{...(6)}$$

$$\therefore \quad C_D \propto I$$

## 2.7 INTERCONNECTION OF DIODES

Diodes can be interconnected in many ways such as series and parallel. In series, diodes are connected as in same direction as well as opposite direction. And in series same direction both forwards biased and both reverse biased.

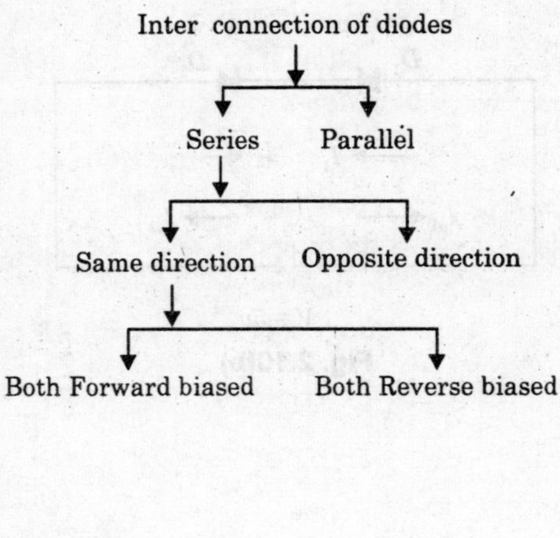

The different ways of calculating voltage and current is illustrated in the examples below.

**P1:** For the circuit shown in figure show that $e^{\frac{qV_1}{k_T}} + e^{\frac{-qV_1}{k_T}} = 2$ for two identical Ge diodes $\eta = 1$.

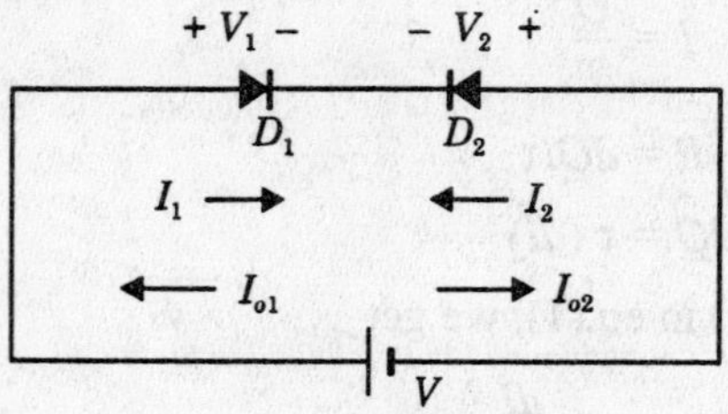

**Fig. 10(a)**

$D_1$ is forward biased and the current flowing is $I_1$,

$D_2$ is reverse biased and the current flowing is $I_{o2}$

In a series connection there can't be two currents and the overall current is the least i,e $I_{o2}$.

$$\therefore \quad I_1 = I_{o2}$$

$$I_2 = I_{o_2}\left(e^{\frac{V_1}{\eta V_T}} - 1\right) = -I_{o2}$$

In a reverse biased diode the reverse current is the overall current itself.

$$I_1 = -I_2$$

$$I_{o_1}\left(e^{\frac{V_1}{\eta V_T}} - 1\right) = -I_{o_2}\left(e^{\frac{V_2}{\eta V_T}} - 1\right)$$

Since $I_{01} = I_{02}$ as they an identical diode currents $V_T = \dfrac{kT}{q} = \eta = 1$

$$\therefore \quad \left(e^{\frac{qV_1}{k_T}} + e^{\frac{-qV_2}{k_T}} = 2\right)$$

**P2:** For the circuit shown in figure calculate current through each diode and voltage across each diode if $v = 5$V and zener breakdown is more than 5V, Si diodes used are identical.

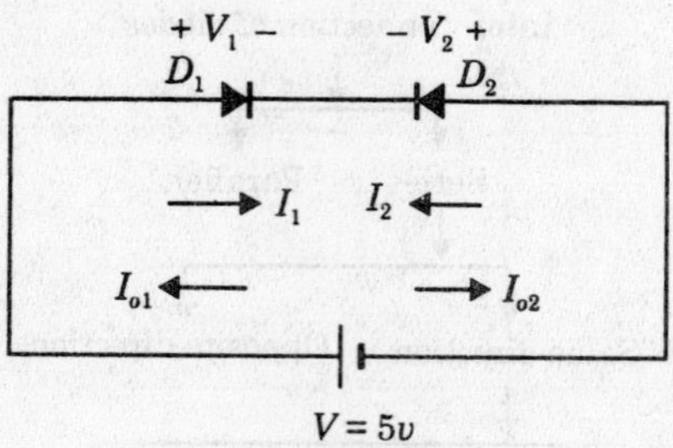

**Fig. 2.10(b)**

**Sol:** $D_1$ is forward biased and the current flowing in it is $I_1$. Zener effect is due to electric field and avalanche effect is due to thermal field.

Zener effect exists everywhere, wherever current is due to the electric fields. Junction diode can never operate in a break down region.

$$V_1 = \eta V_T \text{ in}\left\{1+\frac{I_1}{I_{01}}\right\}$$

$$I_1 = I_{02} \text{ and } I_2 = -I_{02}$$

$$V_1 = 2 \times 26 \times 10^{-3} \ln\left\{1+\frac{I_1}{I_{01}}\right\} \text{ But } I_{02} = I_{01}$$

$$\therefore \quad V_1 = 52 \times 10^{-3} \ln(2) = 0.036\text{V}.$$

If series opposing we cannot calculate voltage across the reverse biased diode directly

∴ *KVL* is applied

$$V - V_1 + V_2 = 0$$

$$\therefore \quad -V_2 = V - V_1 \Rightarrow V_2 = V_1 - V$$

$$= 0.036 - 5 = -4.96 \text{ V}.$$

**P3:** Repeat the above problem if a series resistance of 5KΩ is added with $I_0 = 5\mu\text{A}$.

**Sol:** $V_1 = \eta V_T \ln\left\{1+\frac{I_2}{I_{01}}\right\}$

$$= \eta V_T \ln(2) = 0.036 \text{ V}$$

$$-V_2 = (V - V_1 - RI_0)$$

$$-V_2 = 5 - 0.036 - 5 \times 10^3 \times 5 \times 10^{-6}$$

$$-V_2 = 4.96 - 0.025 = -4.935$$

$$V_2 = 4.935 \text{ V}.$$

**P4:** Calculate the voltage across the diode and current through each diode shown in figure. Diodes are not identical but made up of Ge.

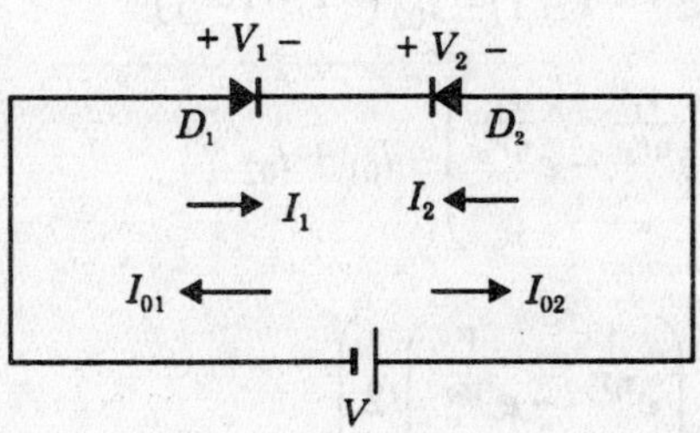


**Fig. 2.10(c)**

**Sol:**

$$I_{01} = 1\mu A$$
$$I_{02} = 2\mu A$$
$$\eta G_e = 1$$

$D_1$ is reverse biased and the current flowing is $I_1$ i.e $- I_{01}$
$D_2$ is reverse biased and the current flowing is $I_2$ is $- I_{02}$
Overall current is $I_1 = I_2 = - I_{01} = 1\ \mu A$

$$V_2 = \eta V_T \ln\left\{1 + \frac{I_2}{I_{02}}\right\} = \eta V_T \ln\left\{1 - \frac{I_{01}}{I_{02}}\right\}$$

$$= 1 \times 26 \times 10^{-3} \ln\left[1 - \frac{1}{2}\right] = 26 \times 10^{-3} \ln(0.5) = -0.018\ V$$

In series opposing same direction we cannot calculate the voltage across the reverse bias diode with least $I_0$ directly. There fore KVL is applied.

$$V + V_2 + V_1 = 0$$
$$-V_1 = (V + V_2)$$
$$-V_1 = 5 - 0.018 = 4.98$$
$$V_1 = -4.98\ V.$$

**P5:** For the circuit shown in figure and obtain the expression for $V$ in terms of $I$. Diodes are identical.

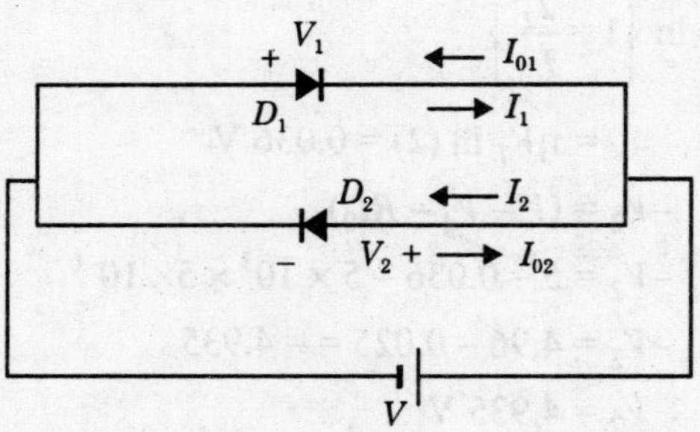


**Fig. 2.10(d)**

**Sol:** $I_1 = I_{01}\,(e^{v_1/\eta V_T} - 1) - I_{02}\,(e^{v_2/\eta V_T} - 1)$

$$I = I_o\left(e^{\frac{V_1}{\eta V_T}} - e^{\frac{V_2}{\eta V_T}}\right) - I_{01} + I_{02}$$

$$I = 2I_0\left(\left(e^{\frac{V}{\eta V_T}} - e^{\frac{V}{\eta V_T}}\right)/2\right)$$

$$\frac{I}{2I_0} = \sin h\left(\frac{V}{\eta V_T}\right)$$

$$V = \eta V_T \sin h^{-1}\left[\frac{I}{2I_0}\right]$$

## 2.8 EFFECT OF TEMPERATURE ON DIODES

The relationship between the voltage applied to the diode and current passing through it is expressed by the eq $I = I_0\left(e^{V/\eta V_T} - 1\right)$ ...(1)

The dependence of $I_0$ on temperature $T$ is given approx by

$$I_0 = KT^m e^{-VGo/\eta V_T} \quad ...(2)$$

Where $K$ is a constant and $eV_{GO}$ is the forbidden – gap energy in joules

For $Si$ : $\eta = 2$ m = 1.5 $V_{Go} = 1.21$V

For $G_e$ : $\eta = 1$ m = 2 $V_{GO} = 0.785$V

Taking the derivative of the logarithm of eq (2) we get

$$\frac{1}{I_0} \times \frac{dI_0}{dT} = \frac{d(\ln I_0)}{dT} = \frac{m}{T} + \frac{V_{GO}}{\eta T V_T} \quad ...(3)$$

At room, temperature, $d(\ln Io)/dT = 0.11°C^{-1}$ for $Ge$

$= 0.08°C^{-1}$ for Si

From experimental data we find that the reverse saturation current increases approximately 7 percent/C° for both Ge & Si, Since $(1.07)^{10} \approx 2.0$, the reverse saturation current approximately doubles for every 10°C rise in temperature.

It is uncommon for S Ge with an reverse saturation current in the order of $I$ or 2 μA at 25°C to have a leakage current of 100 μA = 0.1 mA at a temperature of 100°C.Tipical values of reverse saturation current for Si are much lower than that of Ge for similar values of current and power values. As the temperature increases the forewarned characteristics are actually becoming more ideal, in the reverse bias region the break down voltage is increasIng with temperature .

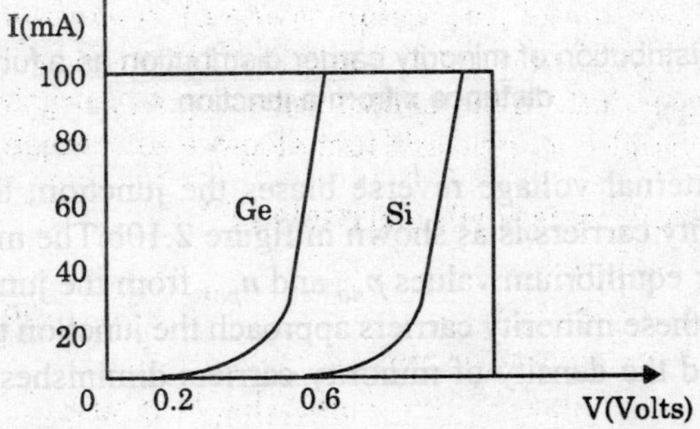


**Fig. 2.11** Variation of diode characteristics due to temperature changes

Consider a diode operating at room temperature (300°K) and just beyond threshold voltage $V_r$ (say 0.2V for Ge and 0.6 for S*I*) then dV/dT = –2.5 mV/ c° for Ge and Si.

## 2.9 SWITCHING CHARACTERISTICS OF A DIODE

A semiconductor diode works as an electronic switch it is in ON state when forwards biased and in OFF state when reverse biased . In both cases the diode response is a accompanied by transient, an interval of time elapses before the diode recover to its steady state. When a diode is switched to forward bias condition from existing reverse bias condition, it takes certain time interval $t_{fr}$ i.e forward recovery time, $t_{fr}$ is the time difference between the 10% point of the diode voltage and the time when this voltage reaches and remains within 10% of its final value. However $t_{fr}$ usually does not pose a serious practical problem.

***Reverse recovery time:*** When an external voltage forward biases a P-N junction the steady state density of minority carries is as shown in figure 2.10a. The number of minority carrIes becomes very large. These mInorIty carries have, in each case, been supplied from the other side of the junction, when being majority carriers, they are in plentiful.

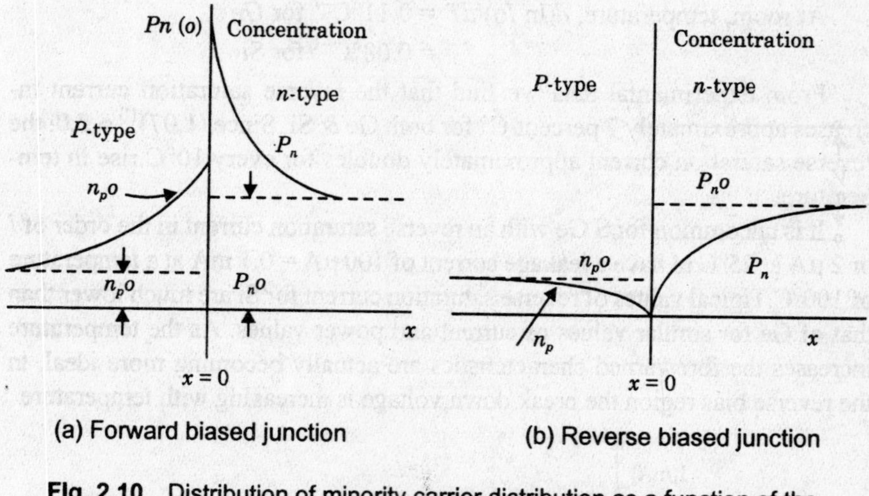


**Fig. 2.10** Distribution of minority carrier distribution as a function of the distance x from a junction.

When an external voltage reverse biases the junction, the steady state density of minority carriers is as shown in figure 2.10b.The minority carriers are equal to their equilibrium values $p_{no}$ and $n_{po}$, from the junction shown in figure 2.10a. As these minority carriers approach the junction they are rapidly swept across, and the density of minority carriers diminishes to zero at this junction, the diode will conduct easily and the current will be let by the external resistance in the diode circuit. The diode current will not immediately fall to its steady state reverse voltage value, if the external voltage bis suddenly reversed in a diode circuit which has been carrying current in the forward direction. Until the minority carrier distribution, the current can not attain its study state value, which at the moment of voltage reversal had the form in fig. 2.10a reduces the distribution in fig. 2.10b.

***Storage Time:*** When a conducting diode is reversed biased, a series of events take place as shown in figure. Let us consider a time instant *t*, the input voltage *Vi* is applied to the diode-resistance circuit of fig. 2.11a is reversed abruptly. For a long time, and up to time *t*, the voltage $V_i = V_F$ has been in the direction to forward bias the diode The resistance $R_L$ is assumed to be large in comparison to the forward biased diode resistance.

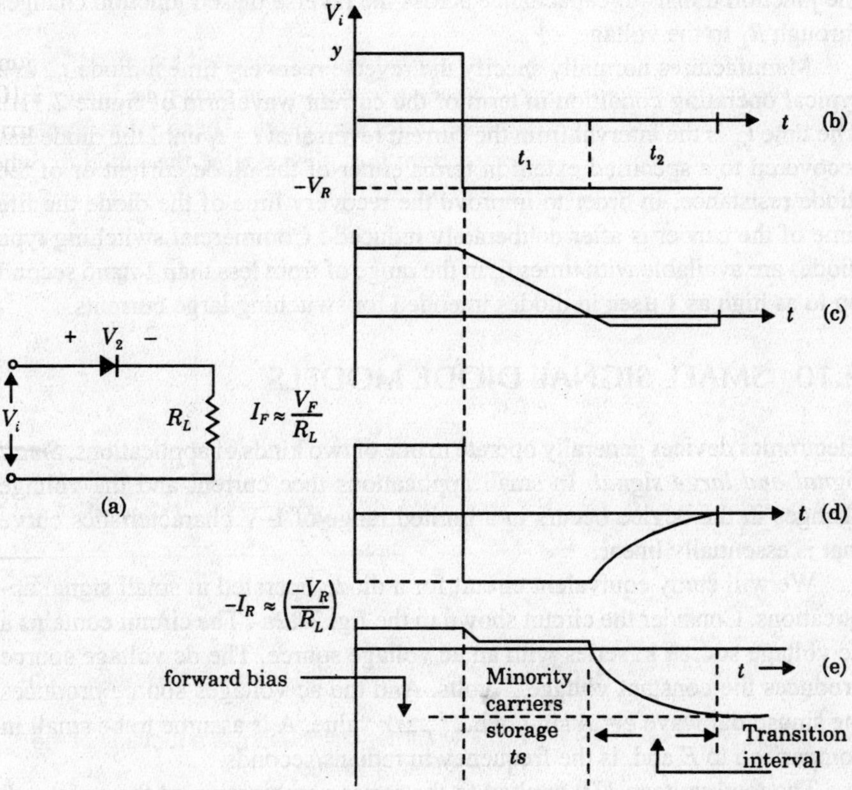


**Fig. 2.11** (a) A diode connected in series with resistor (b) Voltage applied to the diode series with resistor (a) (c) representation of carriers at the junction (d) the diode current (e) the diode voltage.

So, that almost whole of the voltage drop across $R_L$. Thus the current is $I \cong \frac{V_F}{R_L} \cong I_F$. Even after $t = t_1$ the current does not drop to zero, but instead reverse and remains at the value $I \cong \frac{-V_R}{R_L} = -I_R$ until the time $t = t_2$. At $t = t_2$ as seen in figure 2.11c. The minority carrier density $p_n$ at $x = 0$ has reached its equilibrium state $p_{no}$. Since these minority carriers can disappears only as a result of recombination with majority carriers moving into the junction, by diffusion of the minority carriers away from the junction, time is required for $p_n$ to reduce to zero. This time interval $t = (t_2 - t_1)$ during which the stored minority change reduce to zero, is called storage time $t_s$. At the time $t_2$, the diode voltage $V$ falls slightly but does not reverse.

***Transition time:*** The time which claps between $t_2$ and the time when the diode as normally recovered is called the transition time $t_1$. This recovery time interval is required for the minority carrier which are at same distance from the junction, to diffuse to the junction and cross it. Also during this interval the junction transistor capacitance across the reverse biased junction changes through $R_L$ to the voltage $- V_R$.

Manufactures normally specify the reverse recovery time a diode $t_{rr}$ in a typical operating condition in term of the current waveform of figure 2.11d. The time $t_{rr}$ is the interval from the current reversal at $t = t_1$ until the diode has recovered to a specified extent in terms either of the diode current or of the diode resistance. In order to improve the recovery time of the diode the life time of the carrier is after deliberately reduced . Commercial switching type diodes are available with times $t_{rr}$ in the range of from less than 1 nano second up to as high as 1 μsec in diodes intended for switching large currents.

## 2.10 SMALL SIGNAL DIODE MODELS

Electronics devices generally operate in one of two kinds of applications, *Small signal and large signal.* In small applications thee current and the voltage changes in the device occurs in a limited range of I–V characteristics curve that is essentially linear.

We will study equivalent circuit for a diode operated in small signal applications. Consider the circuit shown in the fig. 2.12a . The circuit contains a dc voltage source in series with an ac voltage source. The dc voltage source produces the constant voltage E volts. And the ac voltages source produces the sinusoidal wave $e = A \sin t$, where peak value. A is assume to be small in comparison to $E$ and, is the frequency in radians/seconds.

The total voltage $V(t)$ applied to the series combination of the resistor $R$ and diode is the of dc and ac voltages.

$$V(t) = E + A \sin \omega t,$$

The total voltage $V(t)$ called an ac voltage with a dc level of $e$ volts. This is shown in figure 2.12b. $V(t)$ has maximum value $(E + A)$ and a minimum value $E = A$. Assuming that the voltage and current changes are small enough to you be considered in small signal operation. We can determine current and voltage across the diode.

By using superposition theorem. Containing two voltage sources, we can determine the current in the circuit due to each source acting alone and then add these results to find the actual current when both sources are present.

To calculate ac resistance $r_d$ we need to determine the dc diode current in the fig. 2.12a Eliminating the ac voltage source in fig. 2.12a we obtain a circuit that in fig. 2.12b.

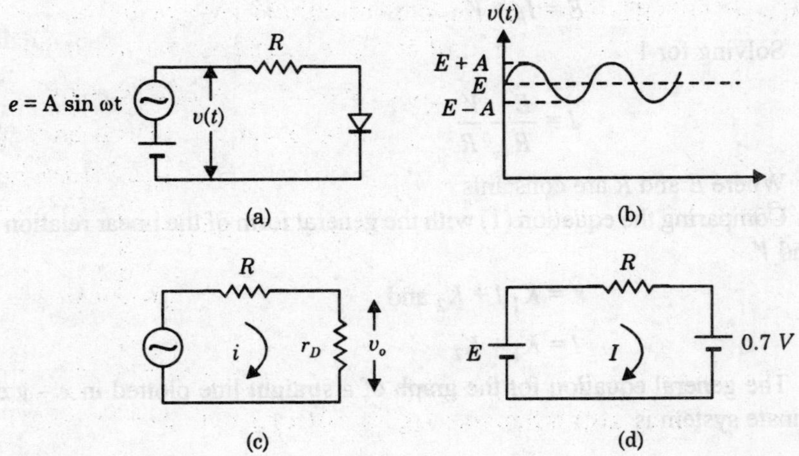


**Fig. 2.12** Circuit diagram of (a) Diode operating at small signal applications (b) AC voltage with DC level (c) equivalent circuit. (d) DC equivalent circuit.

$I = (E - 0.7)/R$ assuming a Si diode. The ac resistance $r_D$ of the diode can be found using the equation $r_D = 0.026/I$

Eliminating the dc voltage source, the ac equivalent circuit is as shown in fig. 2.12c. The ac equivalent circuit represents the diode by a single equivalent resistance equal to $r_D$ ohms. AC current in fig. 2.12c can be calculated by applying ohms law.

$$I = \frac{e}{R + r_D} = \frac{A}{R + r_D} \sin wt$$

The ac diode voltage $V_D$ can be calculated from $V_D = I\, r_D$ or by applying voltage divide rule

$$V_D = \frac{r_D\, A \sin wt}{R + r_d}$$

Combing the results of 0V dc and ac analysis, the total current and voltage in the diode is

$$i\,(t) = I + i$$

$$i(t) = [(E - 0.7)/R] + [A/R + r_D] \sin wt$$

And $$V_D(t) = 0.7 + \frac{r_D A \sin wt}{R + r_d}$$

***Load line:*** Consider the circuit shown in fig. 2.12d . Here the equivalent circuit that the result when ac is stored. Except instead of treating the dc diode voltage as a constant. We consider it to be variable quantity $V$.

By Kirchhoffs voltage law.

$$E = I_R + V$$

Solving for 1

$$I = \frac{E}{R} - \frac{V}{R} \qquad \text{...(1)}$$

Where $E$ and $R$ are constants

Comparing the equation (1) with the general form of the linear relation let $I$ and $V$.

i.e. $$V = K_1 I + K_2 \text{ and}$$

$$I = K_1 + K_2$$

The general equation for the graph of a straight line plotted in $x - y$ coordinate system is

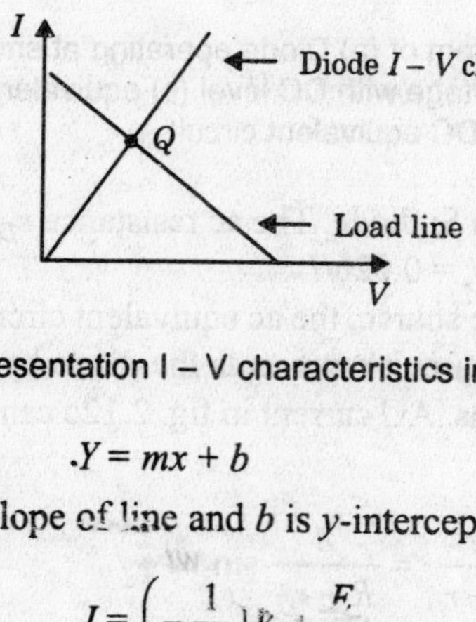


**Fig. 2.13** Representation I – V characteristics in terms of coordinate system.

$$.Y = mx + b \qquad \text{...(2)}$$

Where $m$ is slope of line and $b$ is $y$-intercept.

$$I = \left(-\frac{1}{R}\right)V + \frac{E}{R}$$

$$y = 1, m = -1/R, V = x, b = E/R$$

The graph of equation (1) is a straight line on I-V axes and has slope $\frac{-1}{R}$ and I-intercept $\frac{E}{r}$, this line is called dc *load line.*

The significance of dc load line is that every possible combination of the current and voltage $V$ in the circuit of figure 2.12c is a point that lies some where on the line. The current-voltage combination of that diode can be found by plotting the dc load line on same I – V axes,that contains the diode characteristics curve. The intersection of the dc load line and characteristic curve gives us the actual diode current and voltage that result when diode is used in the circuit.

$$I = \left(-\frac{1}{R}\right)V + \frac{E}{R} \text{ .....load line}$$

$$I = I_s\left(e^{V/\eta V_T} - 1\right) \text{ ........characteristic wave.}$$

This point of intersection $Q$ is called quiescent point or $Q$-point or operating point of diode.

## 2.11 RECTIFIERS

The process of converting the alternating voltages and current to pulsating direct currents is called *rectification.* The pulsating direct current must be filtered so, that output voltage is constant. An electrical device which offers a low resistance to the current in one direction, but a high resistance to the current in the opposite direction is called a *rectifier.* Such a device is capable of converting a sinusoidal input wave form,whose average value is zero, into a unidirectional though not constant wave form with a non zero average component .Both vacuum diodes (directly and indirectly heated cathode) and semiconductor diodes can be used for the rectifier circuit.

Rectifiers can be classified into the following

1. Half Wave Rectifier
2. Full wave Rectifier
3. Bridge wave Rectifier

### 1. Half wave Rectifier

The basic circuit for half wave rectifier is shown in figure 3.14. The piece wise linear approximation for the diode indicates that the device has essentially infinite resistance in the reverse direction (for voltage $V < V_\gamma$ offset voltage) and a small and constant resistance $R_f$ in the forward direction (for $V > V_\gamma$). Since in a rectifier circuit the input $V_i = V_m \sin \omega t$ has a peak value $V_m$ which is very large compared with the offset voltage.

Assume in the following discussion that $V_\gamma = 0$. Subject to this idealization of the diode character, the current in the diode or load $R_L$ is given by

$I = I_m \sin \omega t$ where $0 \le \omega t \le \pi$

$I = 0$ where $\pi \le \omega t \le 2\pi$

$$I_m = \frac{V_m}{R_f + R_L}$$ the transformer secondary wave form $V_i$ is given by

$$V_i = V_m \sin \omega t$$

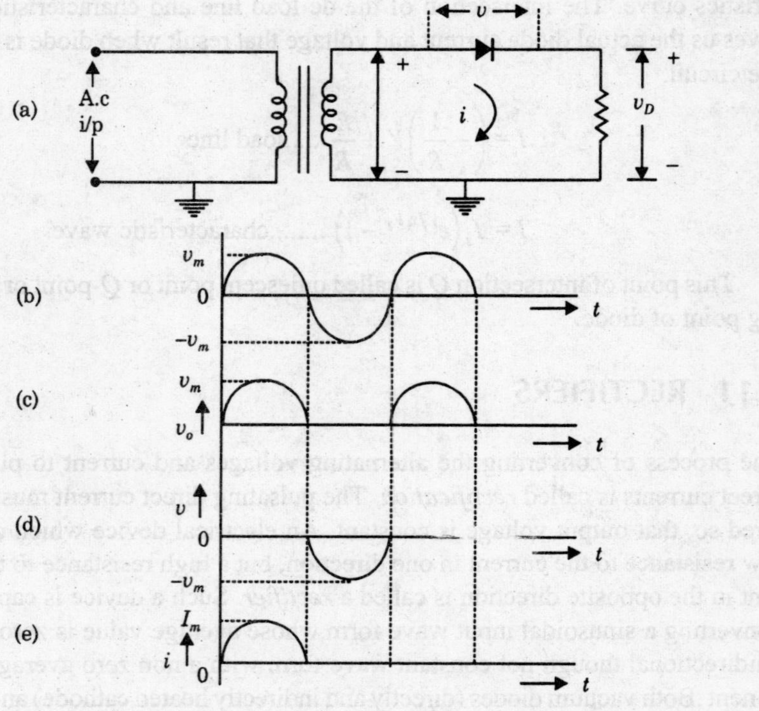


**Fig. 2.14** (a) Basic half wave rectifiers circuit (b)Voltage across the transformers secondary (c) Output voltage (d) Voltage across the diode (e) Current through the diode

***D.C. current or Average Current ($I_{dc}$)(Moving Coil armature Reading):*** The dc value of the current at the output is given by

$$I_{dc} = \frac{1}{2\pi} \int i(\alpha)\, d\alpha \qquad \text{...(1a)}$$

Where $\alpha = \omega_o t$

$$i(\alpha) = I_m \sin \alpha,\ 0 \le \alpha \le \pi$$

$$= 0,\ \pi \le \alpha \le 2\pi$$

$$V_i(\alpha) = I_m \sin \alpha,\ 0 \le \alpha \le 2\pi$$

$$I_{dc} = \frac{1}{2\pi} \int_{\alpha=0}^{2\pi} I_m \sin \alpha d\alpha + \frac{1}{2\pi} \int_{\pi}^{2\pi} 0.d\alpha$$

$$I_{dc} = \frac{-I_m}{2\pi} |\cos \alpha|_0^\pi = \frac{-I_m}{2\pi} |-1-1| = \frac{I_m}{\pi} \qquad \text{...(1b)}$$

$$I_{dc} = \frac{I_m}{\pi}$$

on substitute the value of $I_m$ we get

$$I_{dc} = \frac{V_m}{\pi\left(R_f + R_L\right)} \quad ...(2)$$

***RMS Value of Current ($I_{rms}$):*** The *rms* value of current is given by

$$I_{ms} = \sqrt{\frac{1}{2\pi \int_0^{2\pi} i^2(\alpha)\, d\alpha}}$$

$$I^2{}_{rms} = \frac{1}{2\pi}\left[\int_0^{2\pi} (I_m \sin\alpha)^2\, d\alpha + \int_0^{2\pi} 0\, d\alpha\right]$$

$$= \frac{I_m^2}{2\pi} + \frac{\pi}{2} = \frac{I_m^2}{4}$$

$$I_{rms} = \frac{I_m}{2} \quad ...(3)$$

***D.C. Output Voltage ($V_{dc}$):*** The dc output voltage appearing across $R_L$ is

$$V_{dc} = I_{dc}.R_L \quad ...(4)$$

Substitute (2) in (4)

$$V_{dc} = \frac{V_m}{\pi\left(R_f + R_L\right)} R_L$$

$$V_{dc} = \frac{V_m}{1 + \frac{R_f}{R_L}} \quad ...(5)$$

***Ripple Factor:*** A measure of the fluctuating components is given by ripple factor $R$, which is defined as

$$R = \frac{\text{rms value of alternting components of wave}}{\text{Average value of wave}}$$

$$R = \frac{I_{rms}}{I_{dc}} = \frac{V_{rms}}{V_{dc}} \quad ...(6)$$

Where I and V denote the instantaneous *ac* component of the current and voltage respectively, currnt is given by

$$I = I - I_{dc}$$

Then $$I^1_{rms} = \sqrt{\frac{1}{2\pi}\int_0^{2\pi} (I - I_{dc})^2 \, d\alpha}$$

$$= \sqrt{\frac{1}{2\pi}\int_0^{2\pi} (I - 2I_{dc}I + I_{dc})^2 \, d\alpha}$$

The first term of the integral becomes simply of the total wave.

Since $\frac{1}{2\pi}\int_0^{2x} I d\alpha = I_{dc}$ by definition the second term under the integral sign is

$$(-2I_{dc})\,(I_{dc}) = -2I_{dc}^2$$

$$I^1_{rms} = \sqrt{I_{rms}^2 - 2I_{dc}^2 + I_{dc}^2} = \sqrt{I_{rms}^2 - I_{dc}^2} \quad \text{...(7)}$$

On substuting (7) in (6) we get

$$R = \sqrt{\frac{I_{rms}^2 - I_{dc}^2}{I_{dc}}} = \sqrt{\left(\frac{I_{rms}}{I_{dc}}\right)^2 - 1} \quad \text{...(8)}$$

In case of half wave rectifier, the ratio $(I_{rms}/I_m) = (I_m/2) / (I_m/\pi)$

Hence $$r = \sqrt{(1.57)^2 - 1} = 1.21 \quad \text{...(9)}$$

this result indicates that the rms ripple voltage exceeds the *DC* out put voltage and shows that the half wave rectifier is a relatively poor for converting *AC* to *DC*.

***Efficiency:*** Efficiency is defined as

$$\eta = \frac{\text{depower deliver edit the load}}{\text{a.c. input power}} \times 100\%$$

$$= P_{dc}$$

$$\eta = \frac{P_{dc}}{P_{ac}} \times 100\% \quad \text{...(10)}$$

$$P_{dc} = I_{dc}^2 . RL \quad \text{...(11)}$$

$$P_{ac} = I_{rms}^2 \, (R_L + R_f) \quad \text{...(12)}$$

$$\eta = \frac{I_{dc}^2\, R_L}{I_{rms}^2 \left(R_L + R_f\right)} = \frac{I_{dc}^2}{I_{rms}^2} \frac{1}{\left\{1 + \dfrac{R_f}{R_L}\right\}}$$

$$\eta = \frac{1}{F^2\left(1 + \dfrac{R_f}{R_L}\right)} = \frac{0.48}{\left(1 + \dfrac{R_f}{R_L}\right)} \text{ on neglecting } R_f \text{ we get}$$

$$\eta = (1/F^2) = 0.408 \times 100\ \% = 48\ \% \qquad ...(13)$$

if $R_f << R_L$ then $\eta = 40.8\ \%$ which means that only 40.6 % of AC input power is converted in to DC power in the load, rest exists as AC power in the load.

***Transformer Utility Factor (TUF):*** In any power supply it is necessary to determine the rating of Transformer. For this knowledge of power to be delivered to the load and the type of rectifying circuit used is a must.

$$\text{TUF} = \frac{\text{DC power delivered to the load}}{\text{AC rating of the transformer sec ondery}}$$

$$= [P_{dc}/P_{ac(\text{rating})}] \qquad ...(14)$$

Since the rating of transformer secondary is different from actual power delivered by the secondary, TUF is different from the rectifier efficiency. The power rating of secondary is given by

$$P_{ac(\text{rated})} = V_{ac(\text{rms})} \times I_{rms} \qquad ...(15)$$

Using equation (10) for $P_{dc}$ and equation for $P_{ac(\text{rated})}$

$$\text{TUF} = \frac{P_{dc}}{P_{ac(rated)}} = \frac{\left(I_{ac}\right)^2 R_L}{V_{ac(rms)}\, X\, I_{rms}}$$

For Half Wave Rectifier $V_{ac(rms)} = \dfrac{V_m}{\sqrt{2}}$ and

$$I_{rms} = \frac{I_m}{2}\; I_{dc} = \frac{I_m}{\pi}$$

$$\text{TUF} = \frac{I_{dc}^2\, R_L}{\left(\dfrac{V_m}{\sqrt{2}}\right) X \left(\dfrac{I_m}{2}\right)} \qquad ...(16)$$

But $\quad V_m = I_m\,(R_f + R_L)$

$$\text{TUF} = \frac{\left(\frac{I_m}{\pi}\right)^2 R_L}{\frac{I_m^2 \left(R_f + R_L\right)}{2\sqrt{2}}}$$

$$= \frac{0.286}{1 + \left(\frac{R_f}{R_L}\right)}$$

$$\text{TUF} = 28.6\%$$

***Regulation:*** It is a measure of deviation in the nominal value of the output voltage with respect to variation in the load current. It is defined as the ratio of variation in the output voltage under variation of load current to the full load voltage i.e. open circuit voltage. It is expressed as

$$\text{Regulation} = \frac{V_{dc\,(\text{no load})} - V_{dc\,(\text{full load})}}{V_{dc\,(\text{full load})}} \quad ...(17)$$

***For Half wave Rectifier:***

$$I_{dc} = \frac{I_m}{\pi} = \frac{V_m/\pi}{\left(R_f + R_s + R_L\right)}.$$

or

$$I_{dc}\,(R_f + R_S) + I_{dc}\,R_L = \frac{V_m}{\pi}$$

As

$$I_{dc}\,R_L = V_{dc(full\ load)}$$

$$\frac{V_m}{\pi} = V_{dc(no\ load)}$$

$$I_{dc}\,(R_f + R_S) + V_{dcFL} = V_{dcNL}$$

$$V_{dcFL} = -\,I_{dc}\,(R_f + R_S)$$

Also

$$V_{dcNL} - V_{dcFL} = I_{dc}\,(R_f + R_S) = \frac{I_{dc}\left(R_f + R_s\right)}{\frac{V_m}{\pi} - I_{dc}\left(R_f + R_s\right)} \quad ...(18)$$

***Peak Inverse voltage (PIV):*** PIV is the maximum voltage to which the diode is subjected to. This potential is called the peak inverse voltage. It occurs during half cycle when the diode is non-conducting consequently PIV for a diode in a half wave rectifier is $V_m$ is to be considered when selecting a diode for a power.

## 2. Full Wave Rectifier

The full wave rectifier circuit shown in the fig. 2.15 comprise of two half-wave circuits which are so connected that conduction takes place through one diode during one half of the power cycle and through other diode during second of the power cycle.

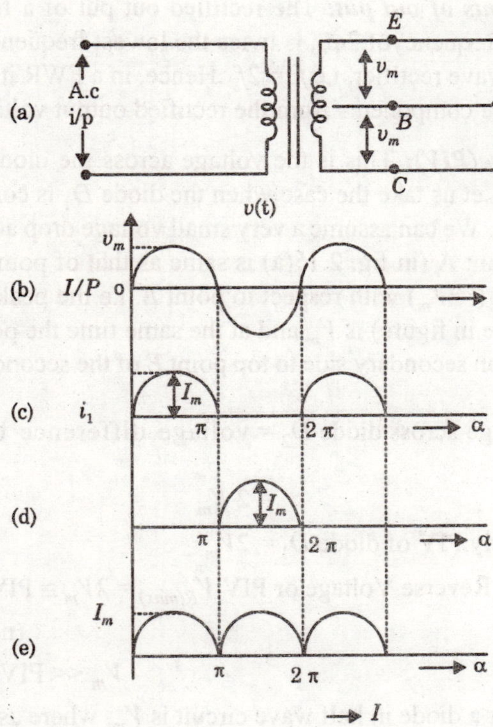


**Fig. 2.15** (a) A schematic of the centre tapped transformer type of full wave rectifier circuit.(b) input voltage (c), (d) and e are current wave forms.

Let us discuss how the circuit behaves. From figure shown above, the top of the transformer secondary is positive w.r.t the center tap, while the bottom of the transformer secondary is negative w.r.t the center tap. When this happens, current will flow in $D_1$ but not through $D_2$ during upper(positive part) half of the input signal, then $D_1$ acting as a closed switch, the lower part of the transformer is disconnected from the load because the lower diode $D_2$ acting as open switch. When the polarity of the input is changes, making the top of the transformer is negative w.r.t the bottom of the transformer, in this case $D_2$ conducts, connecting the bottom half of the transformer to the load, and $D_1$ is acting as an open switch, because it disconnected from the load.

$$0 - \pi : D_1 \text{ ON}, D_2 \text{ OFF}$$

$$\pi - 2\pi : D_1 \text{ OFF}, D_2 \text{ ON}$$

$$I(\alpha) = I_m \sin \alpha$$
$$= -I_m \sin \alpha$$

Figure 2.15(c) and (d) shows the wave form of currents $i_1$, and $i_2$. Since $i_1$ and $i_2$ flow through the load $R_L$, the total current $i$ through $R_L$ is $i = i_1 + i_2$ which is obtained by adding two wave form and is shown in fig. 2.15(e).

***1. Frequency components of out put:*** The rectified out put of a full wave rectifier has an angular frequencyof $2\omega_0$, is twice the lowest frequency in the ripple voltage of a half wave rectifier, i.e $f_r = 2f_s$ .Hence, in a FWR it is easier to filter the ripple voltage components from the rectified output voltage.

***2. Peak Inverse Vontage(PIV):*** This is the voltage across the diode during non conduction period. Let us take the case when the diode $D_1$ is conducting and $D_2$ is not conducting. We can assume a very small voltage drop across $D_1$. So the voltage of the point A (in fig. 2.15(a) is same as that of point $E$. The voltage of the point $C$ is $(-2V_m)$ with respect to point $E$. i.e the peak voltage that occurs across $R_L$ (see in figure) is $V_m$ and at the same time the peak voltage from centre point $B$ on secondary side to top point $E$ of the secondary also $V_m$.

The maximum voltage across diode $D_2$ = voltage difference between point $A$ and point $C$

$$= 2\,V_m$$

Similarly PIV of diode $D_1 = 2V_m$

Then the Maximum Reverse Voltage or PIV $V_{R(max)} = 2V_m \cong$ PIV

(not good)

$V_m <<$ PIV (safety)

We note that PIV for a diode in half wave circuit is $V_m$, where as PIV for diode in full wave circuit is $2V_m$.

***3. Average current $I_{dc}$: PIV*** The average current $I_{dc}$ is given by

$$I_{dc} = \frac{1}{2\pi}\int_0^{2\pi} i d\alpha \quad \text{Where} = \omega_0 t$$

$$= \frac{1}{2\pi}\int_0^{2\pi} I_m \sin \alpha d\alpha$$

$$= \frac{I_m}{2\pi}\left[\int_0^{\pi} \sin \alpha d\alpha + \int_0^{2\pi} \sin \alpha d\alpha\right]$$

$$I_{dc} = \frac{I_m}{2\pi}\left[[-\cos \alpha]_0^{\pi} + [-\cos \alpha]_{\pi}^{2\pi}\right]$$

$$I_{dc} = \frac{2I_m}{\pi} = \frac{2V_m}{\pi(R_f + R_L)} \qquad \text{...(19)}$$

For full-wave rectifier, the waveform of $i$ in the period $\pi \leq \alpha \leq 2\pi$ is same as the period $0 \leq \alpha \leq 2\pi$, therefore the area under the curve will twice that of the half wave case.

***4. RMS Load current ($I_{rms}$):*** The load current flows in both half cycles. In the period $\pi \leq \alpha \leq 2\pi$, the wave form is sinusoidal, except that it is inverted in polarity. Since for rms value the polarity is immaterial, the wave form of fig. 2.15(d) has same rms value as that of normal sinusoid.

Hence $$I_{rms} = \frac{I_m}{\sqrt{2}} \qquad ...(20)$$

***5. Form Factor (F):*** Form Factor $F$ is given by $F = \dfrac{I_{rms}}{I_{dc}} = 1.11$

***6. Ripple factor:*** The ripple factor $\boldsymbol{r}$ is given by

$$r = \sqrt{\left(\frac{I_{rms}}{I_{dc}}\right)^2 - 1}$$

For full wave rectifier,

$$I_{rms} = I_m/\sqrt{2} \text{ from equation} \qquad ...(20)$$

$$I_{dc} = \frac{2I_m}{\pi} \text{ from equation} \qquad ...(19)$$

$$r = \sqrt{\frac{\left(\dfrac{I_m}{2}\right)^2}{\left(\dfrac{2I_m}{\pi}\right)} - 1}$$

$$r = \sqrt{\left(\frac{\pi}{2\sqrt{2}}\right)^2 - 1} = 0.482$$

A comparative value with the value given by equation (9), it shows that ripple factor has dropped from 1.21 in the half wave rectifier to 0.482 in full wave rectifier. i.e $r_{(FWR)} < r_{(HWR)}$, therefore output of full wave rectifier is a better dc than that of half wave.

***7. Rectification efficiency:*** The rectification efficiency is given by

$$\eta = \frac{P_{dc}}{P_{ac}} \times 100\%$$

for a full-wave rectifier circuit

$$P_{dc} = (I_{dc})^2 R_L = \left(\frac{2I_m}{\pi}\right)^2 \frac{1}{\left(R_f + R_L\right)^2} = \frac{4V_m^2 R_L}{\pi^2 \left(R_f + R_L\right)^2}$$

$$P_{ac} = I_{rms}^2 (R_f + R_L) = \frac{V_m^2}{2\left(R_f + R_L\right)}$$

$$\therefore \quad \eta = \frac{P_{dc}}{P_{ac}} \times 100\% = \frac{0.812}{\left(1 + \frac{R_f}{R_L}\right)} \times 100\%$$

$\therefore$ efficiency $\quad \eta = 81.6\ \%$

***9. Transformer Utilization Factor (TUF):*** Since current flows in the secondary side of FWR in opposite directions. Therefore there is no problem due to DC saturation of flux in the core of the transformer. In a FWR the average TUF is found by considering the primary and secondary windings separately.

This value is $\quad \text{TUF} = \dfrac{\left(\dfrac{2I_m}{\pi}\right)^2 R_L}{\left(\dfrac{V_m}{\sqrt{2}}\right)\left(\dfrac{I_m}{\sqrt{2}}\right)}$

$$= \frac{\left(\frac{2I_m}{\pi}\right)^2 R_L}{\left(\frac{I_m}{\sqrt{2}}\right)\left(R_L + R_f\right)} = \frac{8}{\pi^2} \times \frac{1}{\left[1 + \frac{R_f}{R_L}\right]}$$

$$= \frac{0.689}{\left(1 + \frac{R_f}{R_L}\right)}$$

$\therefore \quad \text{TUF} = 68.9\%$

***10. Regulation:*** The % of voltage regulation is given by

$$\text{\% of voltage regulation} = \frac{V_{dcNL} - V_{dcFL}}{V_{dcFL}} \times 100\%$$

For full wave rectifier

$$I_{dc} = \frac{2I_m}{\pi} = \frac{\frac{2V_m}{\pi}}{\left(R_f + R_S + R_L\right)}$$

$$I_{dc}(R_f + R_S) + I_{dc} R_L = \frac{2V_m}{\pi}$$

or $$I_{dc}(R_f + R_S) + V_{dcFL} = V_{dcNL}$$

$$V_{dcFL} = \frac{2V_m}{\pi} - I_{dc}(R_f + R_S)$$

$$V_{dcNL} - V_{dcFL} = I_{dc}(R_f + R_S)$$

## 3. Bridge Rectifier

However in full wave rectifier the transformer is needed to provide the necessary centre tap. It is possible to design a *FWR* circuit in which the can be fed directly from the line and also does not require so large a *PIV* rating for the diodes, such a circuit is called Bridge Rectifier. Figure 2.16 shows the bridge rectifier circuit.

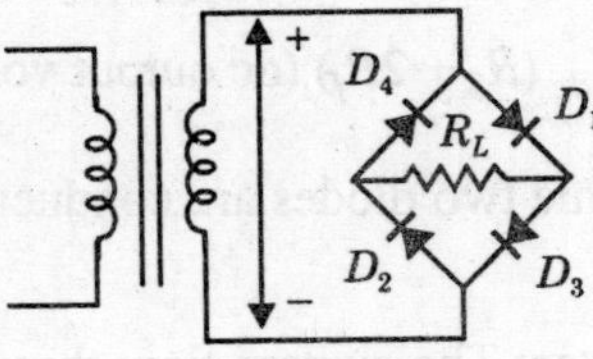

(a)

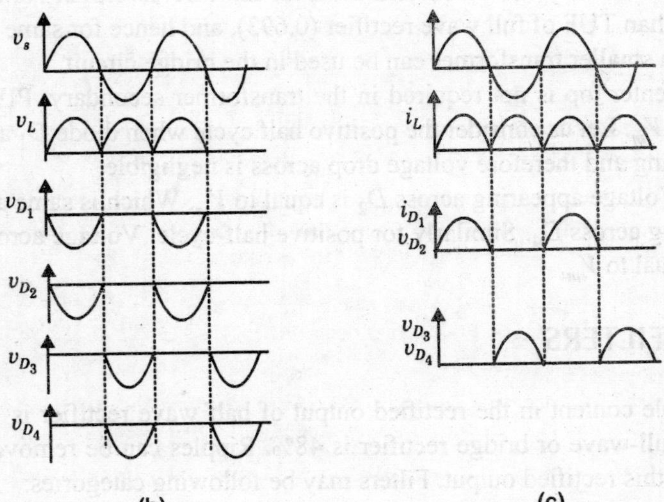

(b) (c)

**Fig. 2.16** (a) Full wave Bridge Rectifier circuit (b) voltage wave form (c) Diode current wave form.

Using four diodes $D_1$ to $D_4$ connected in the form of a bridge circuit and hence the name bridge rectifier. 0 _ π: $D_1$, $D_3$ ON and $D_2$, $D_4$ OFF

$\pi\_2\pi : D_1, D_3$ OFF and $D_2, D_4$ ON

The a.c from the secondary of the transformer is fed to the two corners and the load resistance $R_L$ is connected to the other two corners.

During positive half cycle, the point $A$ is more positive than the point $B$. The current path is point $A$, through $D_1, R_L, D_3$ and back to point $B$. during this time, diodes $D_2$ and $D_4$ are reverse-biased.

In negative half-cycle, the point $B$ is more positive than point $A$. the current path is point $B$ through $D_2, R_L, D_4$ and back to point $A$. during this time, diodes $D_1$ and $D_3$ are reverse biased.

The direction of the current flows through $R_L$ is the same in both the half-cycles. Thus we obtain full wave rectification, the wave form begin same as for full wave rectifier. Because of this, it has same expressions for $I_{dc}$, $I_{rms}$, $V_{dc}$, ripple factor, rectification efficiency ($\eta$) as those of full wave rectifier circuit.

$$V_{dcNL} = \frac{2V_m}{\pi} \text{ (no load dc output voltage)}$$

$$V_{dcFL} = \frac{2V_m}{\pi} - I_{dc}\,(R_S + 2R_f) \text{ (dc output voltage at full load)}$$

The term $2R_f$ is become two diodes are conducting in series at any given time.

***Transformer Utility Factor:*** The current flow through both primary and the secondary windings are sinusoidal. Due to this TUF of the both the primary and the secondary are 0.812 and the over all TUF is 0.812. As this value greater than TUF of full wave rectifier (0.693), and hence for same dc output power, a smaller transformer can be used in the bridge circuit.

A center top is not required in the transformer secondary. PIV of each diode is $V_m$. Let us consider the positive half cycle when diode $D_1$ and $D_3$ are conducting and therefore voltage drop across is negligible.

∴ Voltage appearing across $D_2$ is equal to $V_m$, Which is same as voltage appearing across $D_4$. Similarly for positive half-cycle. Voltage across $D_1$ and $D_3$ is equal to $V_m$.

## 2.12 FILTERS

The ripple content in the rectified output of half wave rectifier is 121%and that of full-wave or bridge rectifier is 48%. Ripples can be removed by the filtering this rectified output. Filters may be following categories:

(a) Capacitor filters
(b) Series indicator filter
(c) L-c filters

Filters are employed to reduce the rectifier output ripple. This is achieved bypassing the AC output components around the load by a shunt capacitance, or limiting their magnitude to allow value in the load by a series inductor or a combination of these two for more efficient circuits. The purpose of a filter is to reduce AC and to retain DC so that the ripple factor is reduced $r = \frac{V_{rms}}{V_{dc}}$

***(a) Capacitor Filter With Half Wave Rectifier:*** Figure gives the circuit diagram of half wave rectifier in which filter capacitor $C$ is placed in the parallel with the load resistance $R_L$. The capacitor stores energy during the conduction period and delivers energy to the load during the non conducting period. Through this mechanism, time interval of conduction current through the load gets prolonged and the ripple component gets appreciably reduced.

Let us first assume that $R_L$ has infinite resistance.

Let the sinusoidal input voltage to the rectifier diode be $V_i$ given by

$$V_i = V_m \sin \omega t \qquad ...(1)$$

Let switch $S$ be closed at time $t = 0$. Then the current $i_c$ through diode $D$ and capacitor $C$ is given by

$$i_c = \frac{CdV_c}{dt} = \omega_c V_m \cos \omega t \qquad ...(2)$$

This current $i_c$ leads the applied current $V_i$ by 90 degrees. At phase angle /2 radians, capacitor $C$ gets charged to the voltage $V_m$ and current $i_c$ becomes zero. Subsequently $V_i$ reduces below $V_m$ and the current tends to reverse in direction but diode $D$ prevents any such reverse current. Hence capacitor $C$ cannot discharge and voltage $V_c$ across capacitor $C$ remains constant at value $V_m$. The diode voltage is always negative and has peak inverse voltage of $2V_m$.

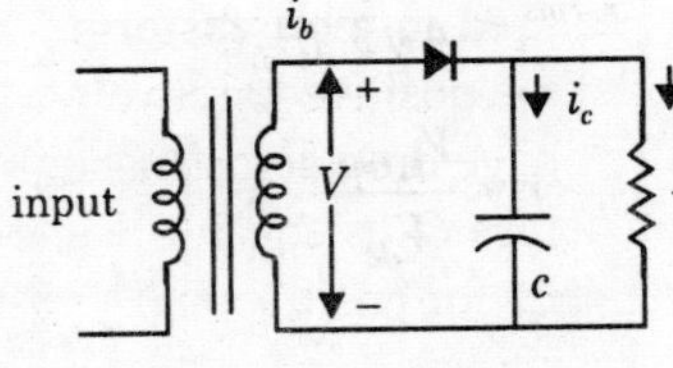


**Fig. 2.17** Capacitor filter with half wave rectifier

***Approximate method:*** The average value of the load current Idc is the average value of the capacitor discharge current over an interval of $T_2$. The amount of the charge lost by capacitor during this interval is

$$Q_{discharge} = I_{dc} \times T_2$$

This charge is replaced during a short interval $T_1$ during which is voltage across the capacitor changes by an amount equal to the peak to peak voltage of the ripple, $V_r$, $p$-$p$ using the relation $Q = VC$, the change in charge is

$$Q_{charge} = V_{r,p\text{-}p} \times C$$

But

$$Q_{charge} = Q_{discharge}$$

$$V_{r,p\text{-}p} \times C = I_{dc} \times T_2$$

and $$V_{r,p\text{-}p} \times C = \frac{I_{dc}}{C} \times T_2$$

**Now let us assume the load is light, the ripple is small, and time for re-charging the capacitor small compared with the time for which it discharges. In other words,**

$$T_1 << T_2$$

and $$T_2 \approx \frac{T}{2} = \frac{1}{2f}$$

then $$V_{r,\,p\text{-}p} \times C = \frac{I_{dc}}{2\,fc}$$

*rms* value is

$$V_{r,\,rms} = \frac{Vr\,,p-p}{2\sqrt{3}}$$

Thus using $I_{dc} = \dfrac{V_{dc}}{R_L}$ we obtain

$$V_{r,\,rms} = \frac{I_{dc}}{4\sqrt{3}\;fC}$$

$$V_{r,\,rms} = \frac{V_{dc}}{4\sqrt{3}\;fR_LC}$$

and since ripple factor $$r = \frac{V_{r,rms}}{V_{dc}}$$

We have

$$r = \frac{1}{4\sqrt{3}\;fR_LC}$$

$$= \frac{2410}{CR_L}$$

**for $f$ = 60 Hz, $C$ in $F$, and $R_L$ in ohms with these approximations the dc output voltage is**

$$V_{dc} = V_m - \frac{V_{r,p-p}}{2}$$

But $$V_{r,\,p-p} = \frac{I_{dc}}{2\,fc} \text{ and } I_{dc} = \frac{V_{dc}}{R_L}$$

from which
$$V_{ac} = V_m - \frac{I_{dc}}{4fc}$$

$$= \left(\frac{4fR_LC}{4fR_LC+1}\right)V_m$$

Thus the ripple may be decreased by increasing $R_L$ or $C$ (or both) with a resulting increase in dc output voltage. The wave form has a peak of $V_m$ and peak to peak ripple magnitude of $V_r$. The average or dc of output voltage is

$$V_{dc} = V_m \frac{V_R}{2}$$

During the capacitor discharge interval, $\theta_2$ to $\pi + \theta_1$, the capacitor is assumed to lose charge at a constant rate $\frac{dq}{dt} = I_{dc}$.

The rate of loss of capacitor potential then is

$$\frac{dv_c}{dt} = \frac{V_R}{\pi - (\theta_2 - \theta 1)} = \frac{1}{\omega c}\frac{dq}{dt}$$

***For Full Wave rectifier or Bridge rectifier:*** In this case, the capacitor discharge interval is $\theta_2$ to $\pi + \theta_1$, The rate of loss of capacitor potential is

$$I_{dc} = I_m - \frac{I_R}{2}$$

$$V_{dc} = I_{dc} R_L$$

$$= V_m - \frac{I_R}{2}$$

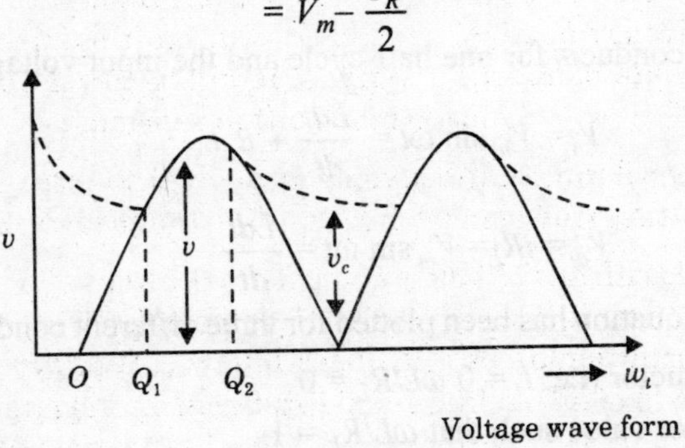


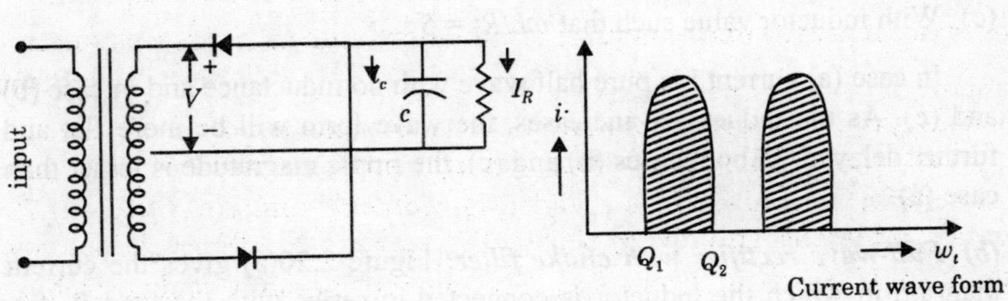


Fig. 2.18 Capacitor Filter with Full Wave Rectifier

Where ω is the supply frequency. The effective of the ripple component is

$$V_R = I_R R_L$$

So $$V_{rms} = \frac{I_R R_L}{2\sqrt{3}}$$

$V_{dc} = I_{dc}R$, the ripple factor is given by

$$r = \frac{V_{rms}}{V_{dc}} = \frac{V_R}{2\sqrt{3}\,I_{dc}R_L} = \frac{1}{4\sqrt{3}\,CR_L f}$$

(a) ***Series Inductor Filters:*** Inductor filter has an inductor (choke) connected in series with the load. The operation of this filter depends on the fundamental property of an inductor to oppose any change current. This filter tries to smoothen the ripples of the current as any sudden changes are smoothed out in the presence of inductor in the circuit.

***Half Wave Rectifier with Choke filter:*** Current *i* flow through the choke and the load as shown in the fig. 2.19.

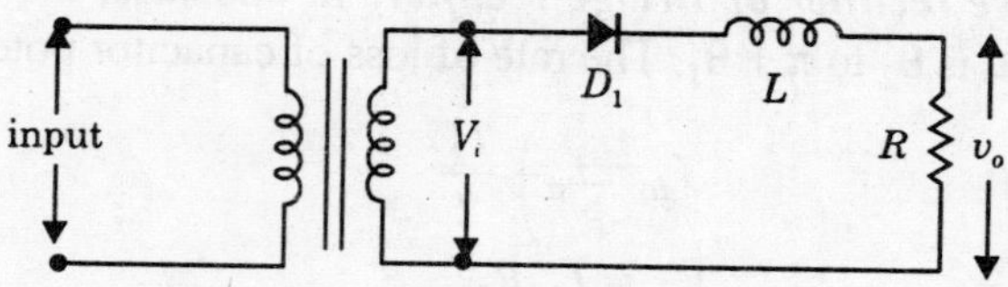


**Fig. 2.19** Half wave inductor Filter

The circuit conducts for one half-cycle and the input voltage is given by

$$V_i = V_m \sin \omega t = \frac{Ldi}{dt} + R_L i$$

$$V_o = iR_L = V_m \sin \omega t = \frac{Ldi}{dt}$$

The above equation has been plotted for three different conditions namely

(a) With no inductor (i.e. $L = 0\ \omega L/R_L = 0$

(b) With inductor value such that $\omega L/R_L = 1$

(c) With inductor value such that $\omega L/R_L = 5$

In case (a) current i is pure half wave with no inductance and in case (b) and (c). As the inductance increases, the wave form will be more flat and further delayed. In both cases (b) and (c), the ripple magnitude is lesser than case (a)

***(b) Full-wave rectifier with choke filter:*** Figure 2.20(a) gives the current diagram in which the inductor is connected in series with the load $R_L$ fig. 3.19(b) gives the current wave forms.

Case (a) with out choke filter

Case (b) with choke in the circuit. The current has much less ripples around the average value $I_{dc}$

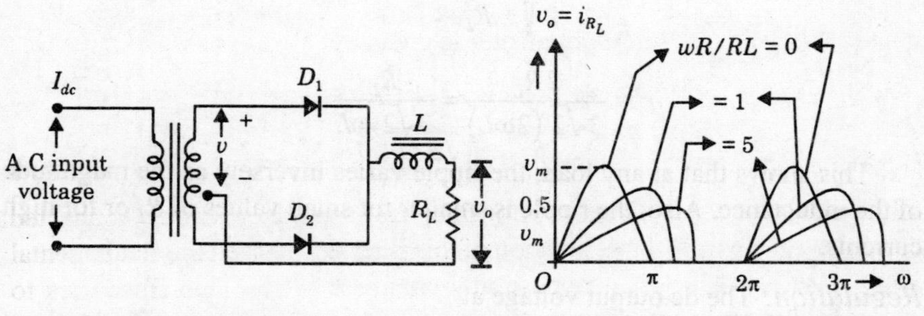


**Fig. 2.20** (a) Full wave rectifier with chock filter (b) current wave forms

*Analysis:* The load current is given by

$$i = \frac{2V_m}{\pi R_L} - \frac{4V_m}{3\pi\sqrt{R_L^2 + 4\omega^2 L^2}} \cos(2\omega t - \theta)$$

where $$\theta = \tan^{-1}\left(\frac{2\omega L}{R}\right)$$

The *rms* current $I_{rms}$ is given by $I_{rms} = \dfrac{4V_m}{3\pi\sqrt{2}} \dfrac{1}{\sqrt{R_L^2 + 4\omega^2 L^2}}$

$$\text{DC current } I_{dc} = \frac{2V_m}{\pi R_L}$$

$$\text{So ripple factor } (r) = \frac{I_{rms}}{I_{dc}} = \frac{2R_L}{3\sqrt{2}} \frac{1}{\sqrt{R_L^2 + 4\omega^2 L^2}}$$

$$r = \frac{2}{3\sqrt{2}} \frac{1}{\sqrt{R_L^2 + \dfrac{4\omega^2 L^2}{R_L^2}}}$$

(i) At no load i.e. $R_L = \infty$ the filtering is poorest and ripple factor reduced to

$$r = \frac{2}{3\sqrt{3}} = 0.482$$

(ii) If $\dfrac{4\omega^2 L^2}{R_L^2} >> 1$ then

$$r = \frac{2}{3\sqrt{2}\,\dfrac{1}{\sqrt{\dfrac{4\omega^2 L^2}{R_L^2}}}}$$

$$r = \frac{2R_L}{3\sqrt{2}\,(2\omega L)} = \frac{R_L}{3\sqrt{2}\,\omega L}$$

This shows that at any load, the ripple varies inversely as the magnitude of the inductance. Also, the ripple is smaller for small values of $R_L$ or for high currents.

*Regulation:* The dc output voltage at

$$V_{dc} = I_{dc} R_L$$

***(c) LC Filters (L-Section Filter):*** This filter combines the decreasing ripple with increasing load' of the series inductor with increasing ripple with increasing load of the shunt capacitor such filter is called LC filter or choke-input filter. The inductance offers a high series impedance to the harmonic terms and the capacitors offers low shunt impedance to them so that resulting current through the load is smoothed out much more effectively.

If $L$ is small, then the capacitor $C$ will get charged to peak voltage $V_m$ and diodes will conduct only for short periods in each half cycle. If $L$ is large, the diode wills conduct for longer period due to smoothening effect of the inductor. If the value of $L$ is more than certain min value (called critical inductance), each diode will conduct for complete half-cycle.

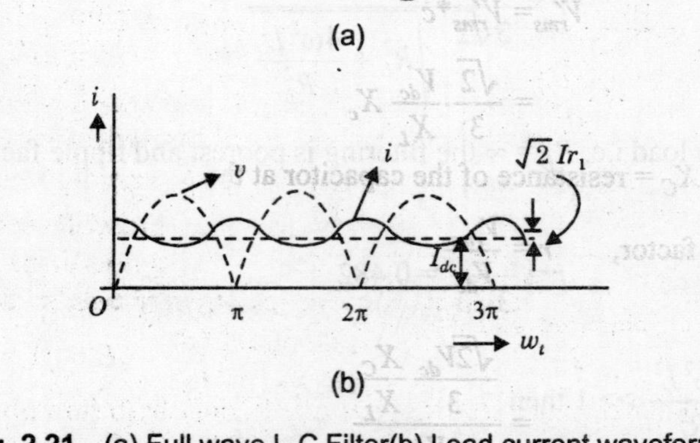


**Fig. 2.21** (a) Full wave L-C Filter(b) Load current waveforms

***Regulation:*** The d.c. voltage at no load condition is

$$V_{acNL} = \frac{2V_m}{\pi}$$

The output dc voltage on load is

$$V_{dcFL} = \frac{2V_m}{\pi} - I_{dc}\,(R_f + R_c + R_s)$$

where $R_f$, $R_c$, $R_s$ are resistances of diode, choke and secondary winding.

***Ripple factor:*** Since the object of the filter is to suppress the harmonic components in the system the reactance of the inductor must be large compared with combined parallel impedance of capacitor and resistor. Thus, we can assume that entire a.c. current across $AB$ is approximately $X_L = 2\omega L$. since ripple frequency = $2\omega$

The ripple voltage has the magnitude $\frac{4V_m}{3\pi}$ and

Ripple current $I' = \frac{4V_m}{3\pi}.\frac{1}{X_L}$

The *rms* value of ripple current is $I'/\sqrt{2}$. So,

$$I_{rms} = \frac{4V_m}{\sqrt{2}\,3\,\pi}\frac{1}{X_L}$$

$$= \frac{\sqrt{2}}{3}\frac{2V_m}{\pi}\frac{1}{X_L}$$

$$= \frac{\sqrt{2}}{3}\frac{V_{dc}}{X_L}\left(V_{dc} = \frac{2V_m}{\pi}\right)$$

The a.c ripple voltage is

$$V'_{rms} = V'_{rms} * c$$

$$= \frac{\sqrt{2}}{3}.\frac{V_{dc}}{X_L}X_c$$

Where $X_C$ = resistance of the capacitor at the ripple frequency

Ripple factor, $\quad r = \frac{V_{rms}}{V_{dc}}$

$$= \frac{\frac{\sqrt{2}V_{dc}}{3}\frac{X_C}{X_L}}{V_{dc}}$$

$$= \frac{\sqrt{2}\, X_C}{3X_L}$$

$$= \frac{\sqrt{2}}{3} \frac{1}{2\omega C} \frac{1}{2\omega L} = \frac{\sqrt{2}}{12\omega^2 LC} = \frac{1}{6\sqrt{2}\omega^2 LC}$$

We note that the ripple factor is dependant on the value of $L$ and $C$ but is independent of load.

***Critical Inductance:*** In the previous analysis, we have assumed that the current flows through the circuit at all times. For this, the value of inductance $L$ must be kept above certain minimum value which is called critical inductance. This value of inductance depends on load resistance $R_L$ and supply frequency $w$.

For the current to flow through the circuit, the value of $I_{dc}$ must be more than the peak value of the ac (ripple) component,

or $$I_{dc} > I_m$$

$$I_{rms} = \frac{\sqrt{2}}{3} \frac{V_{dc}}{X_L}$$

$$\frac{V_{dc}}{R_L} \geq \sqrt{2} \cdot \frac{\sqrt{2}}{3X_L} V_{dc}$$

or $$XL \geq \frac{2R_L}{3}$$

Let the critical of inductance be $L_C$

$$2\omega L_C \geq \frac{2R_L}{3}$$

or $$L_C \geq \frac{R_L}{3}$$

Which gives the required value of critical inductance for 50 Hz supply frequency

$$L_C \geq \frac{R_L}{3x314} \quad i.e. \frac{R_L}{942}$$

***Bleeder Resistance:*** Since the inductor depends upon current for its operation and for optimum functioning the inductor should have at least a certain minimum current flowing through it at all times. In order to provide this minimum current, a bleeder resistance $R_b$ is usually included in the circuit. The function of the bleeder is to maintain the minimum current necessary for optimum inductor operation. A bleeder resistor $R_b$ being used to maintain minimum current in $L$, discharge $C$ (shown in below figure) and vary output voltage. This bleeder resistance $R_b$ is connected in parallel to $R_L$, so that a current of $I_{min}$ bleeds (i.e., flows) through $R_b$. Making use of previous equation.

$$R_b \leq 942\, L_C$$

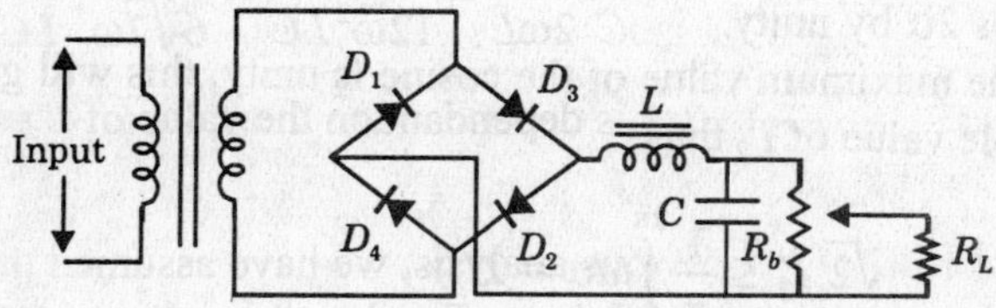


**Fig. 2.22** A Bleeder resistor

***π-Section Filter:*** A very smooth output may be obtained by using a filter that consists of two capacitors separated by an inductor as shown in the figure. Such filters are characterized by highly peaked tube currents and by poor regulation.

The action of a π-section filter can be understood by considering the inductor and the second capacitor as an $L$-section filter that acts upon the triangular output voltage wave from the first capacitor. The output potential is then approximately that from the input capacitor decreased by the dc voltage drop in the inductor. The ripple contained in this output is reduced by the $L$-section filter. The ripple voltage can be calculated by analyzing the triangular wave into a fewer series and then multiplying each component by $X_{C1}/X_{L1i}$ for this harmonic. The Fourier analysis of this wave form is given by

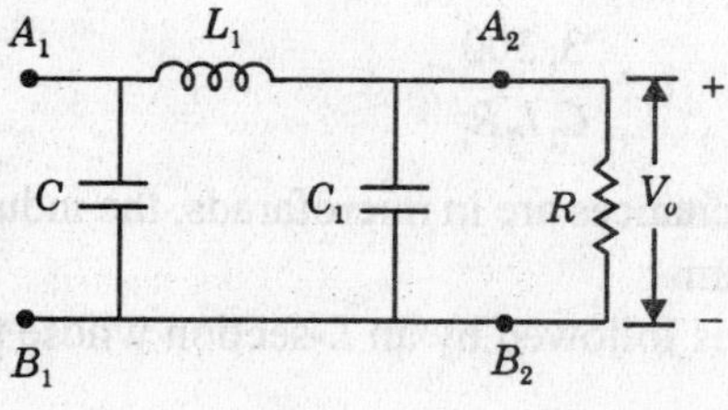


**Fig. 2.23** Section Filter

$$v = V_{dc} - \frac{V_r}{\pi}\left(\sin 2\omega t - \sin\frac{4\omega t}{2} + \sin\frac{6\omega t}{3} \ldots\right)$$

and
$$V_r = \frac{I_{dc}}{2fC}$$

The *rms* second harmonic voltage is

$$V_2' = \frac{V_r}{\pi\sqrt{2}} = \frac{I_{dc}}{2\pi fC\sqrt{2}} = \sqrt{2}\, I_{dc} X_C$$

where $X_C$ is the resistance of $C$ at the second harmonic frequency.

If the instantaneous current to the filter is $I$, then the *rms* second harmonic current $I_2'$ is given by the Fourier component.

$$\sqrt{2}\, I_2' = \frac{1}{\pi}\int_0^{2\pi} i \cos 2\alpha d\alpha$$

replacing cos 2α by unity.

Since the maximum value of the cosine is unity, this will give the maximum possible value of $I^1{}_2$ thus

$$\sqrt{2}\, I_2' \le \frac{1}{\pi}\int_0^{2\pi} i d\alpha = 2I_{dc}$$

because, by definition

$$I_{dc} \equiv \frac{1}{2\pi}\int_0^{2\pi} i d\alpha$$

Hence the upper limit of the rms second harmonic voltage is

$$V_2' = I_2' X_C = \sqrt{2}\, I_{dc}\, X_c$$

The output ripple $r$ when voltage $V_2^1$ is impressed on an $L$-section is $V_2'$ $X_{C1}/X_1$. Hence the ripple factor is

$$r = \frac{V_{rms}}{V_{dc}} = \frac{\sqrt{2}\, I_{dc} X_C}{V_{dc}} \frac{X_{C1}}{X_{L1}} = \sqrt{2}\frac{X_c}{R_L}\frac{X_{C1}}{X_{L1}}$$

Where all reactants are calculated at the second harmonic frequency.

For 60 Hz the above equation reduces to

$$r = \frac{3,300}{C_1 L_1 R_1}$$

Where the capacitances are in microfarads, the inductances in henrys and the resistances in ohms.

If the π-section is followed by an $L$-section whose parameters are $L_2$ and $C_2$, then

$$r = \sqrt{2}\,\frac{X_C X_{C1} X_{C2}}{R_L X_{L1} X_{L2}}$$

This analysis can be extended in an obvious fashion to include any number of sections. Thus, for a single π-section, the half wave ripple is eight times that for a full wave circuit.

π-section filter with a resistor replacing the inductor.

The ripple factor is given by replacing $X_L$ by R for a single section,

$$r = \sqrt{2}\,\frac{X_C X_{C1}}{R_L R}$$

Thus for example, if in a full wave circuit with an output current of 100 mA a 20 H choke is to be replaced by a resistor to give the same ripple, its value must be

$$R = X_L = 4f_L = 15000\ \Omega$$

The voltage drop in this resistor would be

$$(15000)\ (0.1) = 1500\text{V}.$$

The dc power dissipated would be

$$I_{dc}{}^2 R = (0.1)^2\ (150000) = 150\ \text{W}.$$

## 2.13 SOLVED PROBLEMS

**1. Find the ratio of reverse saturation current in Ge to that in *Si*, Assume $L_n = L_p = 0.01$ cm and $\sigma_n = \sigma_p = 1.0$ for Ge, where as the corresponding values are 0.01 cm 0.01 $(\Omega - \text{cm})^{-1}$ for Si.**

**Solution:**

$$\frac{I_{0(Ge)}}{I_{0(Si)}} = \frac{\dfrac{Av_T\sigma_i^2 b}{(1+b)^2}\left[\dfrac{1}{L_p\sigma_n} + \dfrac{1}{L_n\sigma_p}\right]}{\dfrac{Av_T\sigma^2 b}{(1+b)^2}\left[\dfrac{1}{L_p\sigma_n} + \dfrac{1}{L_n\sigma_p}\right]}$$

$$= \frac{(0.0224)^2\,(2.11)\,(20)}{(3.11)^1} \times \frac{(3.6)^2}{\left((4.3)^2 \times 10^{-6}\right)^2 (2.6)\left(20 \times 10^3\right)}$$

$$= 2.9 \times 10^4$$

For *Ge*: – where $b = \dfrac{\mu_n}{\mu_p} = \dfrac{3800}{1500} = 2.11$

$$\sigma_i = (\mu_n + \mu_p) n_i q$$

$$= (3800 + 1500)\ 2.5 \times 10 \times 1.6 \times 10^{-19}$$

$$= 0.0224\ (\Omega - cm)^{-1}$$

For *Si*: – $b = \dfrac{\mu_n}{\mu_p} = \dfrac{1300}{500} = 2.6$

$$\sigma_i = (1300 + 500)\ 1.5 \times 10 \times 1.6 \times 10$$

$$= 4.32 \times 10$$

**2. Find the reverse saturation point of current for a *Si p-n* junction diode at room temperature, 300° K. The cross-sectional area is 4.0 mm² and**

$$\boldsymbol{\sigma_n = \sigma_p = 0.01\ (\Omega - cm)^{-1},\ L_n = L_p = 0.01\ \text{cm}}$$

**Solution:**

$$b = \frac{\mu_n}{\mu_p} = \frac{1300}{500} = 2.6$$

$$n_i = 1.5 \times 10^{1\circ}/\text{cm}^3$$

$$= 4.32 \times 10^{-6} (\Omega - \text{cm})^{-1}$$

$$L_n\sigma_p = L_p\sigma_n = 10^{-4}$$

$$I_O = Av_T\sigma_i^2 \frac{b}{(1+b)^2}\left(\frac{1}{L_p\sigma_n} + \frac{1}{L_n\sigma_p}\right)$$

$$= \frac{(4\times10^{-10})(0.026)(4.32x10^{-6})^2(2.6)}{(3.6)^2}\left[\frac{1}{1\times10^{-4}} + \frac{1}{1\times10^{-4}}\right]$$

$$= 7078\ \mu\text{A}.$$

**3. Find the reverse saturation point of current for a Si *p-n* junction diode at room temperature, 300° K. The cross-sectional area is 4.0 mm and**

$$\sigma_p = 1.0\ (\Omega - \text{cm})^{-1};\ \sigma_n = 0.1(\Omega - \text{cm});\ L_n = L_p = 0.15\ \text{cm}$$

**Solution:**

$$I_O = Av_T \frac{b - \sigma^2}{(1+b)^2}\left(\frac{1}{L_p\sigma_m} + \frac{1}{L_n\sigma_p}\right)$$

$$= \frac{(4x10^{-4})(26x10^{-3})(2.11)(0.0224)}{(3.22)^2}\left[\frac{1}{0.015} + \frac{1}{0.15}\right]$$

$$= 8.34\ \mu\text{A}$$

**4. (a) For what voltage will the reverse current in *p-n* junction Ge diode reach 90% of its saturation point of the room temperature?**

**(b) What is the ratio of the current for a forward bias of 0.05V to the current for same magnitude reverse bias?**

**(c) If the reverse saturation current is 10mA, calculate the forward currents for voltages of 0.1, 0.2 and 0.3V respectively.**

**Solution:**

(a) $$I = I_O\left(e^{V/\eta V_T} - 1\right)$$

$$V = \eta V_T \ln\left(\frac{I}{I_0} + 1\right)$$

$$= 1\ (0.026)\ \ln\left(\frac{-0.9\ I_0}{I_0} + 1\right)$$

$$= 0.026 \ln(-2.3)$$

$$= -0.059\text{V} \cong -0.06\text{V}$$

(b) $$0.06 = I_O\left(e^{\frac{0.05}{\eta V_T}} - 1\right) \quad ...(1)$$

$$-0.06 = I_O\left(e^{\frac{-0.05}{\eta V_T}} - 1\right) \quad ...(2)$$

$$\frac{(1)}{(2)} \Rightarrow \frac{0.06}{-0.06} = \frac{e^{\frac{0.05}{\eta V_T}} - 1}{e^{\frac{-0.05}{\eta V_T}} - 1}$$

$$\Rightarrow \quad \frac{e^{\frac{0.05}{\eta V_T}} - 1}{e^{\frac{-0.05}{\eta V_T}} - 1} = \frac{e^{\frac{0.05}{0.026}} - 1}{e^{\frac{-0.05}{0.026}} - 1}$$

$$\Rightarrow \quad \frac{e^{1.92} - 1}{e^{-1.92} - 1} = \frac{6.84 - 1}{0.146 - 1} = \frac{5.84}{-0.85} = -6.87$$

(c) For $I_O = 10\ \mu\text{A}$

$$\Rightarrow V = 0.1\ \text{V}$$

$$I = I_O\left(e^{\frac{V}{\eta V_T}} - 1\right)$$

$$I = 10 \times 10^{-6}\left(e^{\frac{0.1}{0.026}} - 1\right) = 0.45 mA$$

$$\Rightarrow \quad V = 0.2\text{V}$$

$$I = 10 \times 10^{-6}\left(e^{\frac{0.2}{0.026}} - 1\right) = 21.9 mA$$

$$\Rightarrow \quad V = 0.3\text{V}$$

$$I = 10 \times 10^{-6}\left(e^{\frac{0.3}{0.026}} - 1\right) = 1.02 A$$

**5. (a) Prove that, for an alloy Si *p-n* junction (with $N_A << N_D$), the depletion-layer capacitance in Pico farads per square-cm is given by**

$$C_T = 2.9 \times 10^{-4} \left(\frac{N_A}{N_B}\right)^{\frac{1}{2}}.$$

**(b) If the resistivity of the *p*-material is 3.5 W–cm, the barrier height $V_O$ is 0.35 V, the applied reverse voltage is 5 V, and the cross-sectional area is circular of 40 miles diameter, find $C_T$.**

**Solution:**

With $N_A << N_D$

The depletion layer $W$ capacitance in Pico farads per square cm is given by

$$C_T = 2.9 \times 10^{-4} \left(\frac{N_A}{N_B}\right)^{\frac{1}{2}}$$

$$V_i = \frac{qN_A W^2}{2\varepsilon}$$

$$W = \left[\frac{2\varepsilon V_j}{qN_A}\right]^{\frac{1}{2}}$$

$$C_T = \frac{\varepsilon A}{W} = \frac{\varepsilon_A (qN_A)^{\frac{1}{2}}}{(2\varepsilon V_j)^{\frac{1}{2}}}$$

$$\Rightarrow \quad \frac{C_T}{A} = \sqrt{\frac{q\varepsilon}{2}} \left(\frac{N_A}{V_i}\right)^{\frac{1}{2}}$$

$$V_i = V_B \Rightarrow \sqrt{\frac{q\varepsilon}{2}} \left(\frac{N_A}{V_i}\right)^{\frac{1}{2}}$$

$f = f_o f_r$ taken $\varepsilon_r = 12$, $A = 1\text{cm}^2$

$$= \sqrt{\frac{1.6 x 10^{-19} \dfrac{1}{36\pi x 10^{11}} x\, 12}{2}} \left[\frac{N_A}{N_B}\right]^{\frac{1}{2}}$$

$$\therefore \quad C_T = 2.91 \times 10^{-16} \left[\frac{N_A}{N_B}\right]^{\frac{1}{2}} \text{PF/cm}^2$$

$$C_T = 2.9 \times 10^{-4} \left[\frac{N_A}{N_B}\right]^{\frac{1}{2}} \text{PF/cm}^2.$$

**6. Calculate the barrier capacitance of a Ge *p-n* junction whose area is 1 by 1mm and space-charge thickness is 2*10$^{-4}$ cm. The dielectric constant of Ge is 16 (relative to free space)**

**Solution:**

$$A = 1\text{mm} \times 1\text{mm},\ \omega = 2 \times 10^{-4}\text{cm},\ \varepsilon_r = 16$$

$$C_T = \frac{\varepsilon A}{W} = \frac{\varepsilon_0 \varepsilon_r A}{W}$$

$$= \frac{\frac{1}{36\pi \times 10^9} \times 16 \times 1 \times 10^{-3} \times 10^{-3}}{2 \times 10^{-4} \times 10^{-2}}$$

$$= \frac{16 \times 1 \times 10^{-6}}{2 \times 3 \times \pi \times 10^{-6} \times 10^{8}}$$

$$= 70.7 \text{ PF}$$

**7. The zero-voltage barrier height at an alloy Ge *p-n* junction is 0.2 V. The cone $N_A$ of acceptor atoms in the *p*-side is much smaller than the donor atom in the n material and $N_A$ = 3*10$^{2}$°atoms/m. Calculate the width of the depletion layer for an applied reverse voltage of (a) 10 V (b) 0.1V and (c) for a forward bias of 0.1V (d) if the cross sectional area of the diode is 1mm, evaluate the space-charge capacitance corresponding to the values of applied voltage in (a) and (b)**

**Solution:**

Given at $V_a = 0.2\ (N_A << N_D)$

$$N_A = 3 \times 10^{20} \text{ atom/m}$$

$$\therefore \quad W = \left[\frac{2\varepsilon V_j}{qN_A}\right]^{\frac{1}{2}}$$

$$W^2 = 2 \times \frac{1}{36\pi \times 10^9} \times 16 \times \frac{1}{1.6 \times 10^{-91}} \times \frac{1}{3 \times 10^{40}}(0.2 - V_a)$$

$$= 5.9 \times 10^{-12}\ (0.2 - V_a)$$

$$\Rightarrow \quad W = 2.42 \times 10^{-6}\sqrt{(0.2 - V_a)}$$

(a) $V_a = -10$ V

$$W^2 = 5.9 \times 10^{-12}\ (0.2 - (-10))$$

$$= 5.9 \times 10^{-12}\ (10.2)$$

$$W = 7.75\ \mu\text{m}$$

(b) $V_a = -0.1$ V

$$W^2 = (5.9 \times 10)\ (0.2 - (-10))$$

$$\Rightarrow W = 1.33 \text{ mm}$$

(c) $r_a = 0.1$ V

$$W^2 = (5.9 \times 10^{-12})\,(0.2 - 0.1)$$

$$W = 0.76\ \mu\text{m}$$

(d) $C_T = \dfrac{\varepsilon A}{W}$ where $\varepsilon = \varepsilon_o \varepsilon_T$

$$= 1.6 \times \frac{1}{36\pi \times 10^9} = 0.14 \times 10^{-9}$$

$$A = 1\ (\text{m.m}) = 10^{-6}\ \text{m}^2$$

$$W = 5.9 \times 10^{-12} \left[(0.2 - V_a)\right]^{\frac{1}{2}}$$

$$= 2.42 \times 10^{-6} \left[(0.2 - V_a)\right]^{\frac{1}{2}}$$

$$C_T = \frac{0.14 \times 10^{-9} \times 10^{-6}}{2.42 \times 10^{-6}\,(0.2\ _-\ V_a)^{\frac{1}{2}}} = \frac{0.05 \times 10^{-9}}{(0.2 - V_a)^{1/2}}$$

(i) $V_a = -\ 10a$

$$C_T = \frac{0.05 \times 10^{-9}}{(10.2)^{\frac{1}{2}}} = 15.7\ Pf$$

(ii) $V_a = -0.1$ V

$$C_T = \frac{0.05 \times 10^{-9}}{(0.3)^{\frac{1}{2}}} = 91.2\ Pf$$

**8. A diode reaches its maximum power rating of 2 W when operating in the forward mode at the forward voltage of 900 mv.Calculate (a) the maximum allowable forward current $I_{f(\max)}$ (b) The forward diode resistance $R_f$**

**Solution:**

(a) $I_{f(\max)} = \dfrac{P_{\max}}{v_f}$

$$= \frac{2W}{0.9V} = 2.2\text{A}$$

(b) $R_f = \dfrac{P_{\max}}{I^2_{\max}} = \dfrac{2}{(2.2)^2} = 0.405\ \Omega$

**9. Prove that for an alloy *p-n* junction (with $N_A << N_D$), the width *W* of the depletion is given by**

$$W = \left( \frac{2e\,\mu_p V_0}{\sigma_p} \right)^{\frac{1}{2}}$$

**Where $V_O$ is the contact junction potential**

**Solution:**

$$\frac{d^2 v}{dx^2} = \frac{-p}{\varepsilon} \qquad \text{...(1)}$$

$$\frac{dv}{dx} = \frac{-qN_D}{\varepsilon} = \frac{-(-qN_A)}{\varepsilon} = \frac{qN_A}{\varepsilon}$$

$$\frac{dv}{dx} = \frac{qN_A x}{\varepsilon} + C_1$$

$$\frac{dv}{dx} = 0,\ N = W_n,\ N = W_P$$

$$0 = \frac{qN_A}{\varepsilon} W_p + C_1 \Rightarrow C_1 = \frac{-qN_A}{\varepsilon} W_p$$

$$\therefore \quad \frac{dv}{dx} = \frac{qN_A x}{\varepsilon} - \frac{qN_A}{\varepsilon} W_p$$

Integrating with respect to '$x$'

$$V = \frac{qN_A}{\varepsilon}\frac{x^2}{2} - \frac{qN_A}{\varepsilon} W_p \cdot x + C_2$$

At $N = 0$, $V = 0$ if potential against electrons is considered

$$0 = 0 - 0 + C_2 \Rightarrow C_2 = 0$$

$$V = \frac{qN_A}{\varepsilon}\frac{x^2}{2} - \frac{qN_A}{\varepsilon} W_p \cdot x$$

Also $\quad V = V_i = W_P$

$$V_i = \frac{qN_A}{\varepsilon}\frac{W_p^2}{2} - \frac{qN_A}{\varepsilon} W_p \cdot W_p$$

$$V_i = \frac{-qN_A W_p^2}{2}$$

$$\Rightarrow \qquad W_p{}^2 = \left[\frac{2\varepsilon V_j}{qN_A}\right]$$

Here $W_P >> W_n$ and $W = W_P + W_n$

$$\therefore \qquad W \cong W_P$$

Also $\qquad V_i = V_O - V_a \cong V_0$

$$W^2 = \frac{2\varepsilon V_0}{qN_A} = \frac{2\varepsilon V_0 \mu_p}{qN_A \mu_p} = \frac{2\varepsilon V_0 \mu_p}{\sigma_p}$$

**10. For an alloy junction fore which $N_A$ is not negligible compared with $N_D$, verify that VB = $\frac{eN_A}{26} W^2$ remains valid. Provided that W is interrupted as the total space charge width and $1/N_A$ is replaced by $\frac{1}{N_A} + \frac{1}{N_D}$.**

**Solution:**

$$W = W_n + W_P$$

$$N_A W_P = N_D + W_n$$

$$\Rightarrow \qquad W_n = \left[\frac{N_A}{N_D}\right] W_p$$

$$W = \left[\frac{N_A}{N_D}\right] W_P + W_P$$

$$\Rightarrow \qquad W_P = \left[\frac{N_D}{N_A + N_D}\right] W \qquad \text{...(1)}$$

$$\Rightarrow \qquad W_n = \left[\frac{N_D}{N_A + N_D}\right] W \qquad \text{...(2)}$$

$$\therefore \qquad V = -\frac{qN_D}{2\varepsilon} x^2 = \frac{qN_A W_p}{\varepsilon} + \frac{qN_A W_p^2}{2\varepsilon}$$

At $x = W_m$, $V = V_O$

$$\frac{2\varepsilon}{q} V_0 = -N_D W_n^2 + 2N_A W_p W_n + N_a W_p^2$$

From the (1) and (2)

$$V_O = \frac{q}{2\varepsilon} W^2 \left[\frac{N_A N_D}{N_A + N_D}\right]$$

$$V_O = \left[\frac{\dfrac{2\varepsilon V_0 (N_A + N_D)}{N_A + N_D}}{q}\right]^{\frac{1}{2}} = W$$

$$V_O = \left[\frac{2\varepsilon V_0}{\dfrac{1}{N_A} + \dfrac{1}{N_D}}\right]^{\frac{1}{2}} W$$

$$\frac{dV}{dX} = \frac{-ax^2}{2\varepsilon} + \frac{aW^2}{8\varepsilon}$$

Integrating

$$V = \frac{-ax^3}{2\varepsilon \times 3} + \frac{-aW^2}{8\varepsilon} \times x + C_2$$

$$V = 0 \text{ at } x = -W/2$$

$$0 = \frac{-a.\left(\dfrac{-W}{2}\right)^3}{2\varepsilon \times 3} + \frac{a.W^2}{8\varepsilon}.\left(\frac{-W}{2}\right) + C_2$$

$$0 = \frac{aW^3}{48\varepsilon} - \frac{a.W^3}{16\varepsilon} + C_2$$

$$\therefore \qquad C_2 = \frac{aW^3}{48\varepsilon} - \frac{a.W^3}{16\varepsilon}$$

$$C_2 = \frac{2aW^3}{48\varepsilon} = \frac{a.W^3}{24\varepsilon}$$

$$V = \frac{-ax^3}{6\varepsilon} + \frac{aW^2}{8\varepsilon} \cdot x + \frac{aW^3}{24\varepsilon}$$

$$V = V_j \text{ at } x = \frac{W}{2}$$

$$V_j = \frac{-a\left(\dfrac{W}{2}\right)^3}{6\varepsilon} + \frac{aW^2 \cdot \left(\dfrac{W}{2}\right)}{8\varepsilon} + \frac{aW^3}{24\varepsilon}$$

$$V_j = \frac{-aW^3}{48\varepsilon} + \frac{aW^3}{16\varepsilon} + \frac{aW^3}{24\varepsilon}$$

$$V_j = \frac{-aW^3 + 3aW^3 + 2aW^3}{48\varepsilon} = \frac{4aW^3}{48\varepsilon} = \frac{aW^3}{12\varepsilon}$$

$$V_j = \frac{aW^3}{12\varepsilon}$$

$$\frac{dV_j}{dW} = \frac{3aW^2}{12\varepsilon} = \frac{aW^2}{4\varepsilon}$$

(b) $$C_T = \frac{\varepsilon A}{W}$$

$$C_T = \frac{d\partial_V}{dV_j} = \left(\frac{d\partial_V}{dW}\right)\left(\frac{dW}{dV_j}\right)$$

$\partial V$ = volume charge = volume charge density * volume

$$\partial V = \rho_q \,.\, A.\, dx$$

$$\partial V = \int \rho_V .A.dx$$

$$\therefore \quad \partial V = \int_0^{\omega/2} \rho_V .A.d_x = \int_0^{\omega/2} \rho\, a_x .A.dx$$

$$= aA.\frac{x^2}{2}\int_0^{\omega/2} = \frac{aA}{2}\frac{W^2}{4} = \frac{aAW^2}{8}$$

$$\therefore \quad \frac{d\partial V}{dV_j} = \frac{aAW}{4}$$

$$C_T = \frac{aAW}{4}\left(\frac{4\varepsilon}{aW^2}\right)$$

$$C_T = \frac{\varepsilon A}{W}$$

**11. A single-phase full wave rectifier uses a semiconductor diode. The transformer voltage 35 *V* rms to center tap. The load consists of a 40 μF capacitance in parallel with a 250-Ω resistor. The diode and the transformer resistances and leakage resistance may be neglected. Calculate the cut out angle.**

**Solution:**

$$Wt_1 = \alpha_1 = \pi - \psi$$

$$= 180^\circ - \tan^{-1}(377 \times 250 \times 40 \times 10^{-6})$$

$$= 180^\circ - 75^\circ = 105^\circ$$

**12. The output of a FWR is fed from a 40 – 0 – 40 V transformer. The load current is 0.1 A. Two 40 μF capacitors are available. The circuit resistance exclusive of the load is 50 Ω. (a)Calculate the value of inductance for a two stage L-section filter. The inductances are to be equal. The ripple factor is to be 0.0001 (b) Calculate the output voltage.**

**Solution:**

$$LC = 1.76\left(\frac{0.472}{r}\right)^{\frac{1}{n}}$$

$$L = \frac{1.76}{40 \times 10^{-6}}\left(\frac{0.471}{0.0001}\right)^{\frac{1}{2}}$$

$$= 3.02 \text{ H}$$

(b) $$V_{dc} = \frac{2V_m}{\pi} - I_{dc}R = \frac{(2\sqrt{2})40}{\pi} - 0.1 \times 50$$

$$36 - 5 = 31\text{V}$$

**13. The output of a FWR is fed from a 40 – 0 – 40 V transformer. The load current is 0.1 A. Two 40 μF capacitors are available. The circuit resistance exclusive of the load is 50 Ω. (a) Calculate the value of inductance for a two stage *L*-section filter. The inductances are to be equal. The ripple factor is to be 0.0001**

**Solution:**

$$LC = 1.76\left(\frac{0.471}{r}\right)^{\frac{1}{n}}$$

$$L = \frac{1.76}{40 \times 10^{-6}}\left(\frac{0.471}{0.0001}\right)^{\frac{1}{2}}$$

$$= 3.02 \text{ H}$$

$$V_{dc} = \frac{2V_m}{\pi} - I_{dc}R = \frac{(2\sqrt{2})40}{\pi} - 0.1 \times 50$$

$$= 36 - 5 = 31\text{V}$$

**14. An *L*-section filter is used in the output of a FWR that fed from a 40 – 0 – 40 – V transformer. The load current is 0.2 A. Two 40 μF capacitances and two 2 – *H* chokes are available. The diodes used are ideal.**

**(a) Calculate the 120 Hz ripple voltage if a single section on filter is used with the two chokes in series and the two capacitors in parallel**

**(b) Repeat part a for a two section filter.**

**(c) Calculate the 240 Hz ripple voltage if a single-section filter is used.**

**Solution:**

(a)
$$V_{dc} = \frac{2V_m}{\pi}$$

$$= \frac{2\sqrt{2} \times 40}{\pi} = 36 \text{ V}$$

$$V_{dc} = I_{dc} R_L = 0.2 R_L = 36$$

$$\Rightarrow \quad R_L = 180\ \Omega$$

$$L_C = \frac{R_L}{1130} = \frac{180}{1130} = 0.16 \text{ H}$$

$$V = \frac{2V_m}{\pi}\left[1 - \frac{2}{3}\cos\omega t - \frac{2}{15}\cos 4\omega t + \ldots\right]$$

$$V'_{120} = \frac{4V_m}{3\pi\sqrt{2}}\left(\frac{X_C}{X_L}\right)$$

$$= \frac{4V_{rms}}{3\pi}\,\frac{1}{4\pi^2 f^2 LC}$$

$$= \frac{40}{3\pi^3(120)^2 \times 4 \times 80 \times 10^{-6}} = 0.0935\text{V}$$

$$= 93.5 \text{ mV}$$

(b)
$$V'_{120} = \frac{4V_m}{3\pi\sqrt{2}}\left(\frac{X_C}{X_L}\right)^2$$

$$= \frac{4V_{rms}}{3\pi\left(4\pi^2 f^2 LC\right)^2}$$

$$= \frac{4 \times 40 \times 10^{12}}{3\pi^5\,(120)^2\,16(4)(1600)}$$

or $\quad V'_{120} = 0.008125 \text{ V} = 8.25 \text{ mV}$

(c) For $\quad f = 240$ Hz

$$V'_{240} = \frac{4V_m}{5\pi\sqrt{2}}\left(\frac{X_C}{X_L}\right)$$

$$= \frac{4 \times 40}{15\pi} \frac{1}{2\,(\pi f_C)(2\pi f_L)}$$

This voltage is $\left(\frac{1}{5}\right)\left(\frac{1}{4}\right) = \frac{1}{20}$ of that in part

(a) or $$V'_{240} = \frac{93.5}{20} = 4.67 mV$$

**15. Given a FWR circuit a 375 – 0 – 375 V transformer, $R_L$ = 2000 Ω, each diode has a forward resistance of 100 W, two 20-H chokes and two 16 – μF capacitors. The transformer resistance to center tap and each choke resistance are 200W. Calculate the approximate output voltage and ripple factor under the following filter arrangements.**

**(a) The two chokes are connected in series with the load.**
**(b) The two capacitors are connected in parallel across the load.**
**(c) A single section L-filter consisting of the two inductors in series and the two capacitors in parallel.**
**(d) A two-section L filter**
**(e) A π-section filter, using both inductors.**

**Solution:**

(a) $$V_{de} = \frac{2V_m}{\pi} - I_{dc}\,R$$

$$R = 200 + 100 + 400 = 700\ \Omega$$

and $$I_{dc} = \frac{V_{dc}}{R_L}$$

or $$V_{dc} = \frac{2\sqrt{2}V_{rms}}{\pi} - V_{dc}\left(\frac{R}{R_L}\right)$$

∴ $$V_{dc} = \frac{2\sqrt{2}\,(375)}{\pi}/(1.35) = 250V$$

Since $$\frac{4\omega^2 L^2}{R_L^2} = \frac{4 \times (377)^2\ 40^2}{(2000)^2} = 225 >> 1$$

$$r = \frac{1}{3\sqrt{2}} \cdot \frac{R_L}{\omega_L} = \frac{1}{3\sqrt{2}}\left(\frac{2000}{377 \times 40}\right) = 0.031$$

(b) $$V_{dc} = V_m - \frac{I_{dc}}{4f_C} = \mathrm{V_m} - \frac{V_{dc}}{4\,fR_LC}$$

$$V_{dc} = \frac{V_m}{1+\dfrac{1}{4f\,R_LC}}$$

$$V_{dc} = \frac{\sqrt{2}\times 375}{1+10^6/(4\times 60\times 2000\times 32)} = \frac{531}{1.065} = 500V$$

$$r = \frac{1}{4\sqrt{3}\,f\ fR_LC} = \frac{10^6}{\left(4\sqrt{3}\right)60\times 2\times 10^3\times 32} = 0.0376$$

(c) $V_{dc} = 250$ V

$$r = \frac{0.83}{LC} = \frac{0.83}{40\times 32} = 6.5\times 10^{-4}$$

(d) $V_{dc} = 250$ V

$$r = \frac{\sqrt{2}}{3}\times\frac{10^{12}}{[16\pi^2\times 3600\times 20\times 16]^2} = 1.42\times 10^{-5}$$

(e) $$V_{dc} = V_m - \frac{4170}{C}\cdot\frac{V_{dc}}{R_L} - 700\frac{V_{dc}}{R_L}$$

$$V_{dc} = \frac{\sqrt{2}\times 375}{1+\dfrac{4170}{2000\times 16}+\dfrac{700}{2000}}$$

$$V_{dc} = 360\mathrm{V}$$

$$\Rightarrow \quad r = \frac{3300}{16\times 16\times 40\times 2000} = 1.6\times 10^{-4}$$

**16. A full wave signal-phase rectifier employs a π-section filter consisting of two 4 μF capacitances and a 20 H choke. The load current is 50 μA. Calculate the dc output voltage and ripple voltage. The resistance of the choke is 200 Ω.**

**Solution:**

$$V_{dc} = V_m - \frac{4170}{C}I_{dc} - I_{dc}\,R$$

$$= 300\sqrt{2} - \frac{4170}{4}(0.05) - (0.05)\times 200$$

$$= 424.26 - 52.125 - 10$$

$$= 362.13\ \mathrm{V}$$

$$r = \frac{3300}{CC_l\, L_l\, R_L}$$

$$= \frac{3300 \times 0.05}{4 \times 4 \times 20 \times 353}$$

$$= 1.46 \times 10^{-3}$$

$$V_{rms} = r\, V_{dc} = 0.015 \text{ V}$$

**17. The voltage at the input capacitor of a p-section filter is given to the close approximation by $V(t) = 525 - 40 \sin 745t$. The output capacitance of the filter is 10 μF. If the filter dc output voltage is 500 V for a 100 μA load with a ripple factor of 0.001, determine the inductance and dc resistance of the filter choke.**

**Solution:**

$$V = 525 - 40 \sin 745t$$

$$V = I_{dc}\, R = 0.1 \times R$$

$$= 0.1 \times R = 25.$$

$$R = 250\ \Omega$$

The ripple voltage is $rV_{dc} = \dfrac{40}{\sqrt{2}}$

$$\frac{X_C}{X_L} = \frac{40}{\sqrt{2}} \times \frac{1}{(754)^2\, LC} = 0.001 \times 200$$

$$\therefore \quad L = \frac{1}{(754)^2 \times 10^{-5} \times 0.5} = 10 \text{ H}$$

**18. A Si diode has a saturation current of 0.1 pA at 20°C. Find its current when it is forward biased by 0.55 V. Find the current in the same diode when the temperature rises to 100°C**

**Solution:**

$$V_T = \frac{KT}{q} \text{ volts}$$

At $\quad T = 20°\text{C}\ V_T = \dfrac{KT}{q} = \dfrac{1.38 \times 10^{-23}(273 + 20)}{1.6 \times 10^{-19}}$

$$= 0.02527 \text{ V}$$

Assuming $\eta = 1$

$$I = I_s\left(e^{V/\eta V_T}\right)$$

$$= 10^{-13}(e^{0.55/0.02527} - 1)$$

$$= 0.283 \text{ mA}$$

At $T = 100°C\ V_T = \frac{KT}{q} = \frac{1.38 \times 10^{-23}(273 + 100)}{1.6 \times 10^{-19}}$

$= 0.03127$

On going from 20°C to 100°C, the temperature increases of 10°C each

100 – 20 = 80

80/10 = 8

Therefore $I_s$ doubles 8 times that is increase by a factor $2^8 = 256$.

So at 100°C

$$I_s = 256 \times 10^{-13} A$$
$$I = 256 \times 10^{13} (e^{0.55/0.032} - 1)$$
$$I = 0.681 \text{ mA}$$

**19. A Si PN junction is formed from p material doped with $10^{22}$ acceptors/m³ and n material doped with $1.2 \times 10^{21}$ donors/m³. Find the thermal voltage and barrier voltage at 25°C**

**Solution:**

$$T = 273 + 25 = 298 \text{ k}$$

$$V_T = \frac{KT}{q} = \frac{1.38 \times 10^{-23}(273 + 298)}{1.6 \times 10^{-19}}$$

$$= 25.7 \text{ mV}$$

$$n_i^2 = (1.5 \times 10^{16})^2$$
$$= 2.25 \times 10^{32}$$

$$Vo = V_T \ln\left(\frac{N_A N_D}{n_i^2}\right)$$

$$= 0.0257 \ln\left(\frac{10^{22} \times 1.2 \times 10^{21}}{2.25 \times 10^{32}}\right)$$

$$= 0.257\ (24.699)$$
$$= 0.635 \text{ V}$$

**20. The current flowing in a certain PN junction at room temperature is $2 \times 10^{-7}$A, when a large reverse bias voltage is applied. Calculate the current flowing when 0.1 V is applied?**

**Solution:**

The volt-ampere relation for a junction diode is $I = Io\left(e^{V/V_T} - 1\right)$

Where $V_T$ is volt equivalent of temperature $V_T = 0.026$ v at room temperature (300°k)

For large reverse bias

$$I \cong I_o = 2 \times 10^{-7} \text{A}$$

$$I = 2 \times 10^{-7} \{\exp(0.1/0.026) - 1\}$$

$$= 2 \times (46.814 - 1) \times 10^{-7}$$

$$= 91.625 \times 10^{-7} = 9.1625 \ \mu\text{A}$$

**21. The reverse bias saturation current for a p-n junction diode is 1 μA at 300°k. Determine its a.c resistance at 150 mv forward bias.**

**Solution:**

$$r_{ac} = dV/dI = \frac{1}{\dfrac{dI}{dV}}$$

$$= \frac{1}{(I_O/KT)\exp(V/V_T)}$$

but at temperature of 300°k

$$KT = 8.62 \times 10^{-5} \times 300$$

$$= 25.86 \times 10^{-3} \text{ V}$$

$$r_{ac} = \frac{25.86 \times 10^{-3}}{10^{-6} \times \exp(0.15/0.02586)}$$

$$= \frac{25.86 \times 10^{3}}{332.66} = 77.65 \text{W}$$

**22. What is the change in barrier height of a p-n junction at 300°k when the doping on the n-side is changed by a factor of 1000 and the doping on the p-side remains unchanged.**

**Solution:**

Relating the semiconductor *p-n* junction built-in voltage to the impurity level on each side of the junction

$$(\Delta Vo)_1 = \frac{KT}{q} \ln \frac{(N_a)_1 (N_a)_1}{n_i^2}$$

and

$$(\Delta Vo)_2 = \frac{KT}{q} \ln \frac{(N_a)_2 (N_a)_2}{n_i^2}$$

where the subscript 1 refer to lightly doped case the
where the subscript 2 refer to heavily doped case
Subtracting the first equation from the second gives

$$(\Delta Vo)_2 - (\Delta Vo)_1 = \frac{KT}{q} \ln \frac{(N_a)_2 (N_a)_2}{(N_a)_1 (N_a)_1}$$

$$= 0.026 \ln (1000) = 0.18 \text{ V}$$

Hence thousand fold change in doping alters the barrier height by only 180 mv

**23. The capacitance of an abrupt *p-n* junction $1.0 \times 10^{-8}$ m² in area measured at –1.0 V reverse bias is 5.0 *pf*. The built-in voltage $\Delta V_o$ of this device is 0.9 v. When the diode is forward biased with 0.5 V, a current of 10 mA flows. The *n*-region minority hole lifetime is known to be 1.0 μ sec at 300°k. Calculate (a) the depletion layer capacitance of this junction at 0.5 v forward bias and (b) the diffusion capacitance of the diode operating as in part (a) at 300°k**

**Solution:**

(a) The depletion layer capacitance of a *p-n* junction is given by

$$C_j = A\left[\frac{\varepsilon_0 \varepsilon_r q}{2\left(\frac{1}{N_a}+\frac{1}{N_d}\right)(\Delta V_o - V_0)}\right]^{1/2}$$

where $V$ is the applied voltage. Hence in the forward direction at 0.5v, the depletion layer capacitance is

$$C_j = 5.0 \text{ pF}\left|\frac{-1.0-0.9}{0.5-0.9}\right|^{1/2} = 11 \text{ pF}$$

(b) $$C_D = \frac{I\tau_p}{KT/q} = \frac{10\times10^{-3} A\left(1.0\times10^{-6}\text{ sec}\right)}{0.026V}$$

$$= 39 \times 10^{-8} \text{ F}$$

$$= 390{,}000 \text{ pF}$$

**24. (a) A step graded Ge pn junction has $N_D = 500\ N_A$ where $N_A$ corresponds to 2 acceptor atoms per $10^8$ Ge atoms. Calculate the contact potential at room temperature (b) Repeat part (a) for Si *pn* junction. It is given that the number of atoms/cm³ in Ge is $4.4 \times 10^{22}$ and that in Si is $5 \times 10^{22}$ = $1.381 \times 10^{-23}$ J/deg *k*, $q = 1.6 \times 10^{-19}$ c, $n_i$ for Ge is $2.5 \times 10^{13}$/cm³ and $n_i$ for Si is $1.5 \times 10^{10}$/cm³**

**Solution:**

$$V_o = V_T \ln p_1/p_2 = V_T \ln \frac{p_{po}}{p_{no}} = \text{V}_\text{T} \ln \frac{N_A N_D}{n_i^2}$$

$$V_T = \frac{KT}{q} = \frac{1.38\times10^{-23}\times300}{1.6\times10^{-19}} = 0.02589 \text{ volts.}$$

$$N_A = \frac{2 \times 4.4 \times 10^{22}}{10^8} = 8.810^{14}/\text{cm}^3$$

$$N_D = 500\ N_A = 500 \times 8.8 \times 10^{14} = 4.4 \times 10^{17}/\text{cm}^3$$

$$n_i = 2.5 \times 10^{13}/\text{cm}^3$$

$$V_o = V_T \ln \frac{N_A\ N_D}{n_i^2} = 0.02589 \ln \frac{8.8 \times 10^{14} \times 4.4 \times 10^{17}}{\left(2.5 \times 10^{13}\right)^2}$$

$$= 0.405 \text{ V}$$

$$V_T = 0.02589\text{V}; \quad N_A = \frac{2 \times 5 \times 10^{22}}{10^8} = 10^{15}/\text{cm}^3$$

$$N_D = 500\ N_A = 5 \times 10^{17}/\text{cm}^3$$

$$n_i = 1.5 \times 10^{10}/\text{cm}^3$$

$$V_D = V_T \ln \frac{N_A\ N_D}{n_i^2} = 0.02589 \ln \frac{10^{15} \times 5 \times 10^{17}}{\left(1.5 \times 10^{10}\right)^2}$$

$$= 0.736 \text{ volts.}$$

**25. For the *P* and *N* regions of silicon diode, the conductivities are 1000 s/m and 20 s/m and the minority carrier lifetimes are 5 μs and 1 μs respectively. Calculate the ratio of hole current to electron current in the depletion layer, the reverse-bias saturation current density and the total current density flowing through the junction with a forward bias of 0.3v. Assume room temperature $T = 300°k$ $n_i = 1.5 \times 10^{16}$ m$^{-3}$, $m_n = 0.13$ m$^2$/v– s and $\mu_p = 0.005$ m$^2$/v–s**

**Solution:**

The reverse saturation current across the *PN* junction is

$$Io = e\left(\frac{n_{po} L_n}{\tau_n} + \frac{P_{no} L_p}{\tau_p}\right)$$

The first term and second term represents the current conducted by electrons and holes respectively. The majority carrier densities are calculated as

$$P_{po} = \frac{\sigma_p}{e\mu_p} = \frac{1000}{1.6 \times 10^{-19} \times 0.05}$$

$$P_{po} = 1.248 \times 10^{23}/\text{m}^3$$

$$n_{No} = \frac{\sigma_N}{e\mu_n} = \frac{20}{1.6 \times 10^{-19} \times 0.13}$$

$$n_{No} = 9.603 \times 10^{20}/\text{m}^3$$

Then from mass-action law, the minority carrier density

## 2.14 OBJECTIVE QUESTIONS

1. In a forward biased photo diode with increase in incident light intensity, the diode current
   (a) increases (b) remains constant
   (c) decreases
   (d) remaining constant, the voltage drop across the diode increases.
   **Ans:** (a)
2. In a junction diode,
   (a) the depletion capacitance increases with increase in the reverse bias.
   (b) the depletion capacitance decreases with increase in the reverse bias.
   (c) the diffusion capacitance increases with increase in the forward bias.
   (d) the diffusion capacitance is much higher than the depletion capacitance when it is forward biased.
   **Ans:** (b), (c), and (d).
3. A *P-N* Junction in series with a 100 ohms resistor is forward biased so that a current of 100 mA flows. If the voltage across this combination is instantaneously reversed to 10 volt at $t = 0$ the reverse current that flows through the diode at $t = 0$ is approximately given by
   (a) 0 mA (b) 100 mA (c) 200 mA (d) 50 mA
   **Ans:** (b)
4. The built-in potential (diffusion potential) in a *p-n* junction
   (a) is equal to the difference in the Fermi level of the two sides, expressed in volts.
   (b) increases with the increases in the doping levels of the two sides.
   (c) increases with the increase in temperature.
   (d) is equal to the average of the fermilevel of the two sides.
   **Ans:** (a), (b), (c).
5. The diffusion potential across a *P-N* junction
   (a) decreases with increasing doping concentration
   (b) increases with decreasing band gap
   (c) does not depend on doping concentration
   (d) increases with increase in doping concentrations
   **Ans:** (d)
6. The depletion capacitance, $C_J$ of an abrupt *P-N* junction with constant doping on either side varies with reverse bias, $V_R$, as
   (a) $C_J \propto V_R$ (b) $C_J \mu V_R^{-1}$ (c) $C_J \propto V_R^{-½}$ (d) $C_J \mu V_R^{-1/3}$
   **Ans:** (c)
7. As compared to a full-wave rectifier using two diodes, the four diode bridge rectifier has the dominant advantage of
   (a) higher current carrying
   (b) lower peak incerse voltage requirement
   (c) lower ripple factor (d) higher efficiency
   **Ans:** (b)

8. If $V_m$ is the peak value of an applied voltage in half-wave rectifier with a large capacitor across the load, then the peak inverse voltage will be

(a) $V_m/2$ (b) $V_m$ (c) $\sqrt{2}\,V_m$ (d) $2V_m$

**Ans:** (d)

9. If $V_r$ is the reverse voltage across a graded $P-N$ junction, then the junction capacitance $C_j$ is proportional to

(a) $(V_r)^2$ (b) $(V_r)^n$ (c) $(V_r)^{-n}$ (d) $(V_r)^{3/2}$

**Ans:** (b)

10. In a uniformly doped abrupt *p-n* junction, the doping level of the *n*-side is four (4) times doping level of the *p*-side: the ratio of the depletion layer width is

(a) 1.25 (b) 0.5 (c) 1.0 (d) 2.0

**Ans:** (a)

11. Gold is often diffused into silicon *PN* junction devices to
(a) increase the recombination rate
(b) reduce the recombination rate
(c) make silicon a direct gap semiconductor
(d) make silicon semi-metal

**Ans:** (b)

12. The current through a *PN* junction diode with *V* volts applied to the *P* region relative to the *N* region (where $I_o$ is the reverse saturation current of the diode, the ideality factor, *K* the Boltzmann constant, *T* the absolute temperature and *q* the magnitude of charge on an electron) is

(a) $I_o\left(\dfrac{-qv}{e^{mKT}-1}\right)$ (b) $I_o\, e^{\frac{-qv}{mKT}}$

(c) $I_o\left(1-e\dfrac{+qv}{mKT}\right)$ (d) $I_o\left(\dfrac{-qv}{e^{mkt}-1}\right)$

**Ans:** (d)

13. Of the various capacitances associated with a junction transistor, the gain-bandwidth product is affected to a maximum extent by
(a) base-collector parasitic capacitance
(b) base-collector space charge layer capacitance.
(c) base-emitter space charge layer capacitance
(d) base-emitter diffusion capacitance

**Ans:** (d)

14. When compared with germanium diodes, silicon diodes show a lower degree of temperature dependence under reverse bias conditions.
Select the correct answer using the codes given below:
Codes:

(a) 1 and 2 (b) 1, 2, 3 and 4 (c) 2, 3 and 4 (d) 1 and 3

**Ans:** (b)

**15.** In a *P-N* junction, the space charge capacitance is proportional to $V^{-n}$ where $V$ is the applied bias voltage and '$n$' is a constant. The value of '$n$' for step, linearly graded and diffused junctions would be respectively

(a) 1/2, 1/3 and 1/2.5 (b) 1/3, 1/2 and 1/2.5

(c) 1/2, 1/2.5 and 1/3 (d) 1/3, 1/2.5 and ½

**Ans:** (a)

**16.** In an *LC* filter, the ripple factor

(a) increases with the load current

(b) increases with the load resistance

(c) remains constant with the load current

(d) has the lowest value

**Ans:** (d)

**17.** The ripple factor of power supply is given by (symbols have the usual meaning).

(a) $\dfrac{P_{dc}}{P_{ac}}$ (b) $\sqrt{\left(\dfrac{I_{rms}}{I_{dc}}\right)^2 - 1}$ (c) $\sqrt{\left(\dfrac{I_{dc}}{I_{rms}}\right)^2}$ (d) $\dfrac{I_{dc}}{I_{rms}}$

**Ans:** (b)

**18.** A *PN* junction which is produced by recrystallisation on a base crystal from a liquid phase of one or more components and the semiconductor is called:

(a) doped junction (b) alloy junction

(c) fused junction (d) none of these

**Ans:** (c)

**19.** In an open circuit *PN* junction, the energy band diagram of *n*-region shifts elative to that of *p*-diagram :

(a) downward by $E_o$ (b) upward by $E_o$

(c) downward by $E_o/4$ (d) upward by $E_o/4$

**Ans:** (a)

**20.** The contact potential $V_o$ in a *PN* diode equals:

(a) $V_T \ln \dfrac{N_A N_D}{n_i^2}$ (b) $V_T \ln \dfrac{n_i^2}{N_A N_D}$

(c) $V_T \ln N_A/N_D$ (d) $V_T \ln N_D/N_A$

**Ans:** (a)

**21.** The output of a half-wave rectifier is suitable only for

(a) charging batteries (b) running car radios

(c) running a.c motors (d) running tape-recorders

**Ans:** (a)

**22.** Larger the value of filter capacitor

(a) smaller the d.c. voltage across the load

(b) longer the time that current pulse flows through the diode

(c) larger the peak current in the rectifying diode
(c) larger the *p-p* value of ripple voltage
**Ans:** (c)

**23.** A bridge rectifier is preferable to an ordinary two-diode full ware rectifier because
(a) it needs much smaller transformer for the same output
(b) its transformer has no center tap
(c) it uses four diodes
(d) it has higher safety factor
**Ans:** (a)

**24.** Each diode of full wave center-tapped rectifier conducts for
(a) 90° only (b) 180° only
(c) 270° only (d) 360° complete period
**Ans:** (b)

**25.** Bulk resistance of a diode is
(a) the sum of resistance values of *n*-material and *p*-material
(b) the sum of half the resistance value of *n*-material and *p*-material
(c) equivalent resistance of the resistance value of *p* and *n*-material is parallel
(d) none of the above
**Ans:** (a)

**26.** In unbiased *PN* junction, thickness of depletion layer is of the order of
(a) $10^{-12}$ m (b) 15 μm (c) 0.5 μm (d) 0.005 μm
**Ans:** (c)

**27.** In a power supply, the point where the diode stops conducting is known as
(a) cut in point (b) cut out point (c) knee point (d) cut off point
**Ans:** (b)

**28.** Operation of series inductor filter
(a) depends on the magnitude of current throughout it
(b) is independent of current
(c) depends on voltage through it
(d) none
**Ans:** (a)

**29.** The disadvantages of capacitor input LC filter
(a) high cost, more weight and external field produce by series inductor
(b) high cost, less weight
(c) low cost., more weight
(d) none
**Ans:** (a)

**30.** For low voltage rectification
(a) two diode full wave rectifier is suitable
(b) bridge rectifier is suitable
(c) both bridge and two diode rectifiers are equal suitable D)none
**Ans:** (a)

**31.** The induction filter is mostly used for rectifiers
(a) light loads (b) high loads
(c) only half wave rectifiers (d) only full wave rectifiers
**Ans:** (b)

**32.** In a center-tap full wave rectifier, 100 v is the peak voltage between the center tap and one end of the secondary. The maximum voltage across the reverse-biased diode is.
(a) 200V (b) 141.1V (c) 100V (d) 86V
**Ans:** (a)

**33.** When a diode is forward biased, the recombination of free electron and holes may produce.
(a) heat (b) light (c) radiation (d) all of the above
**Ans:** (d)

**34.** Which rectifier requires four diodes?
(a) half-wave voltage doublers (b) full-wave voltage doublers
(c) full-wave bridge circuit (d) voltage quadrupler
**Ans:** (c)

**35.** In a step graded junction, the width w of the depletion layer varies as:
(a) $V_j$ (b) $V_j^2$ (c) $\sqrt{V_j}$ (d) $1/V_j$
**Ans:** (c)

**36.** In a reverse biased *PN* diode, the concentration of minority carrier holes in the *n*-region at the junction boundary equals:
(a) $P_{no}$ (b) $P_{no}\, e^{V/V_T}$ (c) $P_{no}\, e^{-V/V_T}$ (d) zero
**Ans:** (d)

**37.** The law of junction gives that in *PN* diode, the concentration of holes injected to *n*–region at the junction is given by:
(a) $n_{po}\, \varepsilon^{V/V_T}$ (b) $n_{po}\, \varepsilon^{-V/V_T}$ (c) $p_{no}\, \varepsilon^{V/V_T}$ (d) $p_{no}\, \varepsilon^{-V/V_T}$
Where *v* is voltage applied at *p* terminal relative to *n* terminal, $n_{po}$ and $p_{no}$ are the thermal equilibrium concentration of electrons and holes in *p* and *n* regions respectively.
**Ans:** (c)

**38.** In a forward biased diode, with $N_A >> N_D$, product of the diffusion capacitance $C_D$ and the dynamic diode resistance *r* equals:
(a) $1/Tp$ (b) $Tp$ (c) $Tp2$ (d) $1/Tp2$
where *Tp* is the life time of injected minority carrier holes.
**Ans:** (b)

**39.** In a forward biased diode, with $N_A >> N_D$, the following equation relates the diffusion current *I*, the injected excess minority carrier charge *Q* and the file time of hole $T_p$:
(a) $I = QT_P$ (b) $I = Q_2/T_P$ (c) $I = Q/T_P$ (d) $I = T_P^2$
**Ans:** (c)

**40.** In a *pn* diode, for constant value of current at room temperature, $d_v/d_t$ varies approximately at the rate of

(a) –2.5 mV/deg c (b) –25 mV/deg c
(c) 2.5 mV/deg c (d) 25 mV/deg c

**Ans:** (a)

**41.** The most significant component of a ripple voltage in a half-wave rectifier is contained in

(a) fundamental frequency (b) second harmonics.
(c) DC component (d) none

**Ans:** (a)

## 2.15 CONVENTIONAL QUESTIONS

1. Explain different types of biasing?
2. Drwa the Band diagram of *p-n* junction? Define Law of junction?
3. How many types of junction capacitances are there? Explain with neat diagrams?
4. Explain switching characteristics of diode? what is load line?
5. Explain (a) storage time (b) transition time?
6. Explain, how temperature effects on *p-n* junction diode?
7. Explain the variation of fermi level, in *p-n* junction diode?
8. Explain about junction capacitance?
9. Sketch neat diagram of I-V characteristics of *p-n* junction diode, and explain? give the relation between current I and voltage V ?
10. What is rectifier? How many types are there? Explain about Full Wave Bridge rectifier?
11. Explain (a) peak inverse volytage (b) ripple factor (c) Transformer utilization factor (d) rectifier efficiency. (e) form factor.
12. Explain the operation of FWR, and sketch different waveforms?
13. Define Critical inductance? What is its value?
14. What is the Bleeder resistor $R_b$ used in *LC* filter?
15. Draw the circuit diagram of a series inductor filter with a FWR .What is (a) the regulation (b) the ripple factor for such a circuit?
16. Draw the circuit diagram of half wave capacitive filter and explain?

## 2.16 EXERCISE PROBLEMS

**1.** The blk *N*-type and *p* type materials of a perticular Ge junction have conductivities of $10^4$ S/m and $10^2$ S/m respectivly at 300 K. Find the constant difference of potential across the junction at 300 K assuming $n_i = 2.5 \times 10^{19}\ m^{-3}$, $\mu_n = 0.38\ m^2/Vs$ and $\mu_p = 0.18\ m^2/Vs$.

**Ans:** $V_B = 0.3568$ V

2. Half wave rectifier has an input voltage of 240 V rms.If the step down treansformer has a turns rati of 8:1 what is the peak load voltage?
   **Ans:** 42.5 V
3. A bridge rectifier has a DC load current of 10 mA and a filter capacitance of 470 μF.What is the peak to peak ripple out of a capacitor input filter? (**Hint:** frequencu $f = 60$ Hz)
   **Ans:** $V_R = 0.177$ V
4. For the *P* and *N* regions of a Si dide the conductivities are 1000 S/m and 20 S/m respectivly and the minority cartrierlife times are 5 μs and 1 μs respectivrely. Calculate the ratio of hole current to electron current in the depletion layer, the reverse bias saturation current density and the total current density flowing through the junction with a forward bias of 0.3 V. Assume temperature $t = 300$ K, $n_I = 1.5 \times 10^{16}$ m$^{-3}$ $\mu_n = 0.31$ m$^2$/Vs and $\mu_p = 0.05$ m$^2$/Vs.

   **Ans:** 0.6 μA, 36.12, 67 mA

## 2.17 LAB EXPERIMENTS

### Exp No: 1

### *A. V-I characteristics of diode*

**AIM:** To obtain and study the volt ampere characteristics of a junction diode

**Equipment**

1. DC power supply
2. DC Ammeter/Multimeter having current range in micro amperes
3. DC voltmeter
4. Oscilloscope

**Components**

1. One pn junction diode IN914
2. One 1k resistor

**Circuit Diagram**

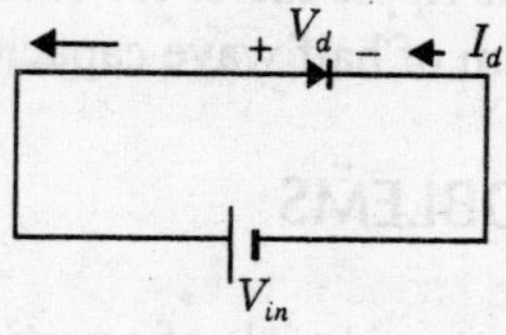


**Fig. 2L1**

**Procedure**

1. Connect the circuit as shown below in figure (1)
2. Apply the power supply and vary the input voltage between –10 to 2 Vdc

3. Observe the current flowing through the diode for each voltage set with a milliammeter.
4. Plot a V-I graph.

| *S.No.* | *Vd(V)* | $I_d(A)$ |
|---|---|---|
| 1 | 2 | |
| ⋮ | ⋮ | |
| • | –10 | |

**Procedure for obtaining VI characteristic on oscilloscope:**

1. Set up the circuit as shown below
2. Connect the oscilloscope in the *X-Y* mode of operation as illustrated in fig. 2.
3. The voltage across the diode ($V_d$) is applied to the horizontal input of the scope. The current passing through the diode $I_d$ is displayed as a vertical deflection. This is because $I_D = \frac{V_{RI}}{R_1}$. For $R_1 = 1\text{k}\Omega$, $I_d = V_{RI}$ mA. $V_{R1}$ is fed to the vertical input of the oscilloscope. The vertical sensitivity control V/div is converted to mA/div.
4. Trace out the VI curve as seen on the scope, either by observation or by tracing on a special, ridiculed transparent paper which can stick on the display.

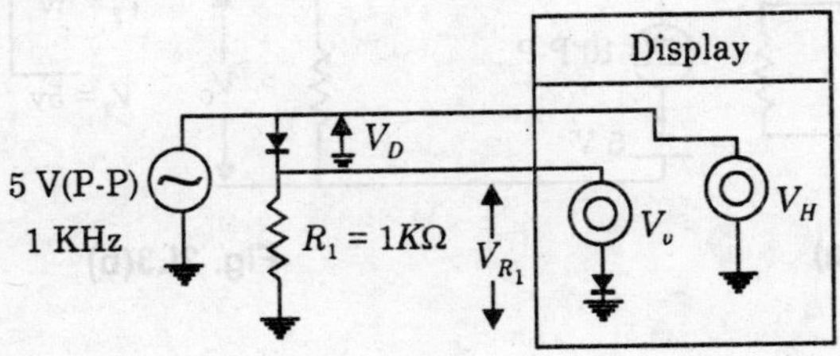


**Fig. 2L2**

**Precautions:**

1. Proper triggering of the scope is necessary for a stationary display.
2. There should be zero phase difference between $V_H$ and $V_V$ input for proper display. This phase difference may be caused due to:
   (i) Stray capacitance and inductance of the diode
   (ii) Oscilloscope differences in the horizontal and vertical circuits.

   A non-zero phase difference can cause loops. To test whether this phase difference is contributed by oscilloscope amplifiers, just replace the diode by a carbon resistor. If the display is still a loop and not a straight line, the scope error is confirmer.

## Exp No: 2

### *Switching charecteristics of juncton diode*

**AIM:**

1. To observe and understand the delay involved when a diode is made to undergo a transition from ON or forward biased state OFF or reverse-biased state.
2. To understand the various components of this delay and their causes.
3. To measure the storage time and transition time of the diode by subjecting it to a square wave input.

**Components:**

1. Diode (IN 3071) (or any other switching diode)
2. Resistance 1 kΩ

**Equipment:**

1. Dual channel oscilloscope
2. AF signal generator
3. 5V dc power supply

**Circuit Diagram**

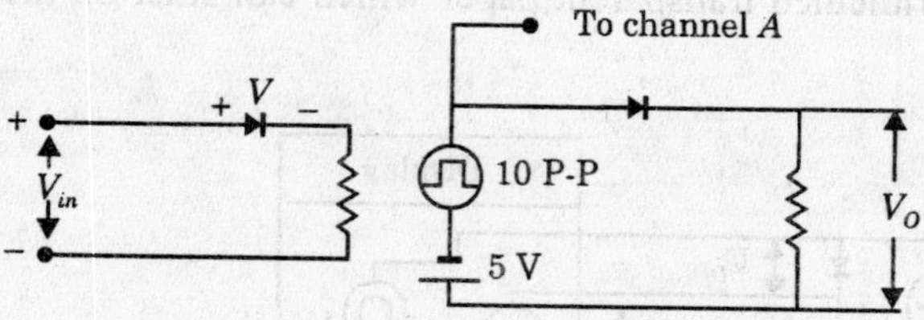


Fig. 2L3(a)

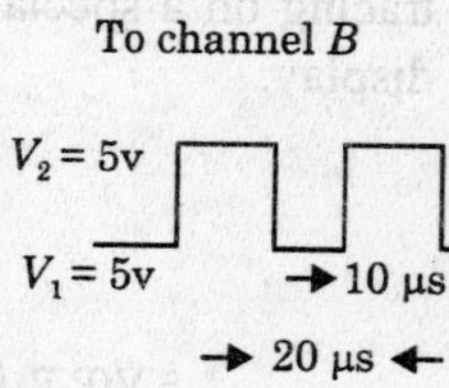


Fig. 2L3(b)

**Procedure:**

1. Set up the circuit as shown in figure with $R = 1$ kΩ
2. Apply a −5V to +5V (10*Vp-p*) square wave of 5 KHz, 5% duty cycle to the circuit.
3. Adjust the time/div horizontal sensitivity of both channels *A* and *B* of the dual scope oscilloscope with the square wave applied to the vertical input, such the only one or two cycles are observed on the CRO.
4. Observe the input and output waveform of channel A and B respectively. Measure the storage and transition times refer figure.

**Observations:**

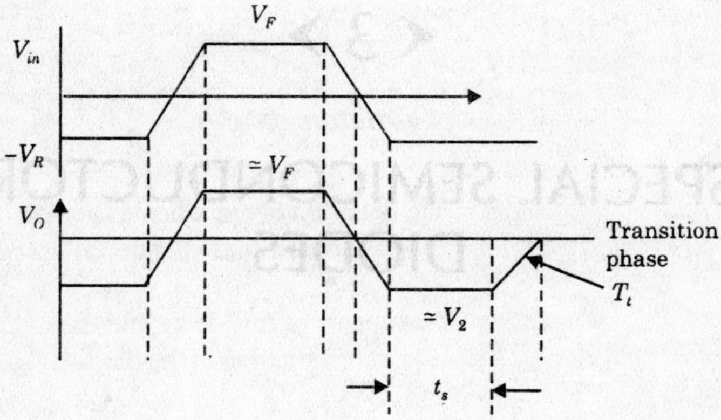


**Fig. 2L4** Response of the diode circuit across when a square-wave input is applied. The finite non-zero rise and fall times at the input are shown.

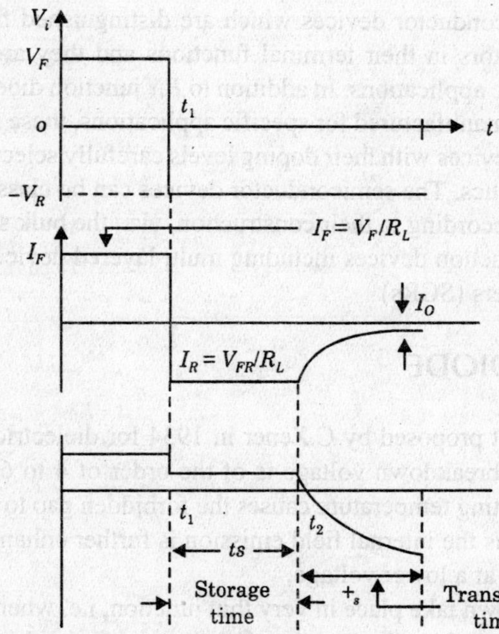


**Fig. 2L5** The applied voltage, diode current IF and diode voltage $V_D$

# ❮ 3 ❯

# SPECIAL SEMICONDUCTOR DIODES

## 3.1 INTRODUCTION

Some of the semiconductor devices which are distinguished from the usual diodes and transistors in their terminal functions and they are found to be suitable for specific applications. In addition to *PN* junction diode, other types of diodes are also manufactured for specific applications, these special diodes are two terminal devices with their doping levels carefully selected to give the desired characteristics. The semiconductor devices can be classified into two broad categories according to their construction, viz., the bulk semiconductor devices and the junction devices including multi layered devices like Silicon Controlled Rectifiers (SCRs)

## 3.2 ZENER DIODE

Zener diode is first proposed by C.Zener in 1934 for dielectric break down. The typical zener breakdown voltage is of the order of 4 to 6 volts. An increase in the operating temperature causes the forbidden gap to become some what narrower, thus the internal field emission is further enhanced and zener breakdown occurs at a lower voltage.

Zener breakdown take place in very thin junction, i.e. when both sides of the junctions are very heavily doped and consequently the depletion layer is narrow. In a very thin (less than 100°A) depletion layer width, the electric field becomes as high as $10^7$ V/m with small applied reverse bias voltages (of order 4 Volts or so), and the bands in the transition region are steeply tilted as shown in fig. 3.1. It then becomes possible for some electrons to jump across the barrier from the valence band in *P* material to some of the unfilled conductive levels in *N* material. This processing is known as tunneling through the barrier and is purely a quantum mechanical effect attributed to the wavelike properties of the electrons. This is also some times known as the *internal field emission or Zener break down.*

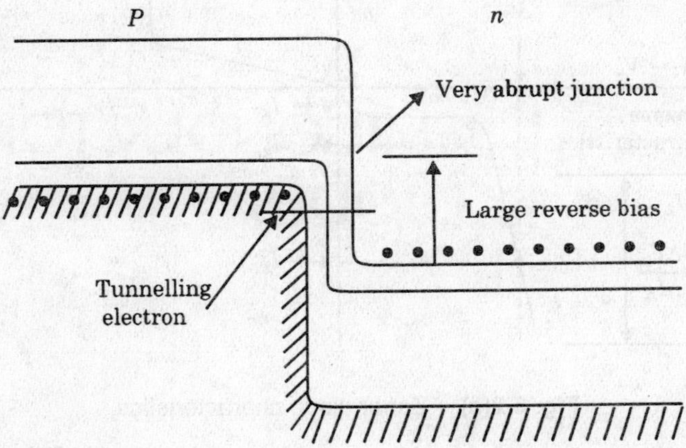


**Fig. 3.1** Zener effect

Zener diode is a heavily doped (*P*-side as well as *N*-side) *PN* junction semiconductor diode, its circuit symbol is shown in fig 3.2(a) and its equivalent circuit is fig. (b).

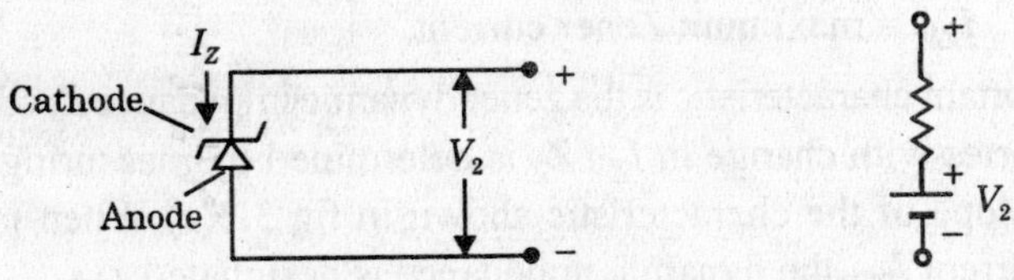


(a) Zener diode symbol (b) Equivalent circuit diagram

**Fig. 3.2**

## Zener Diode Characteristics

The zener breakdown level is quite stable and choice of material conductivity permits design of diode units with varying breakdown levels. Such units, known as Zener diodes are used to accurately regulate dc voltage sources. The VI characteristics of Zener diode are shown in fig. 3.2(c). When the breakdown voltage is reached in these diodes the current increases rapidly with additional voltage. As a result, a diode in breakdown maintains an almost constant voltage across itself over a wide current range. Thus Zener diodes are ideally suited for voltage regulation and can be easily tailored to specific voltages by changing the doping levels.

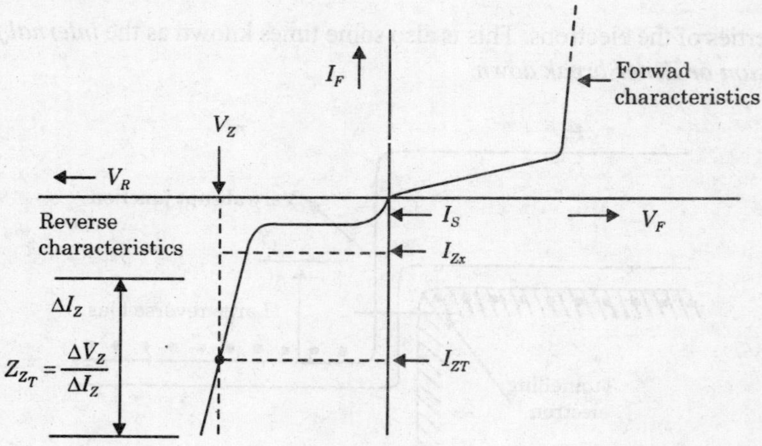


**Fig. 3.2(c)** Zener diode characteristics

The forward characteristic is similar to that of an ordinary forward-biased junction diode. In the reverse characteristics are:

$V_Z$ = Zener breakdown voltage.

$I_{ZT}$ = Test current at which *VZ* is measured.

$I_{ZK}$ = Zener current near the knee of the characteristic.

$I_{ZM}$ = maximum Zener current.

The most important characteristic is the zener dynamic impedance *Z*, which defines how $V_Z$ varies with change in $I_Z$ . $Z_Z$ is determined by measuring the reciprocal of the slope of the characteristic shown in fig 3.2(c) When measured at the test current $I_{ZT}$, the dynamic impedance is designated $Z_{ZT}$.

$$Z_{ZT} = \frac{\Delta V_Z}{\Delta I_Z}$$

## *Zener Diode as Voltage Regulator*

Figure 3.3(a) shows the regulator circuit. The Zener current may be set to just beyond the knee of the reverse characteristic.

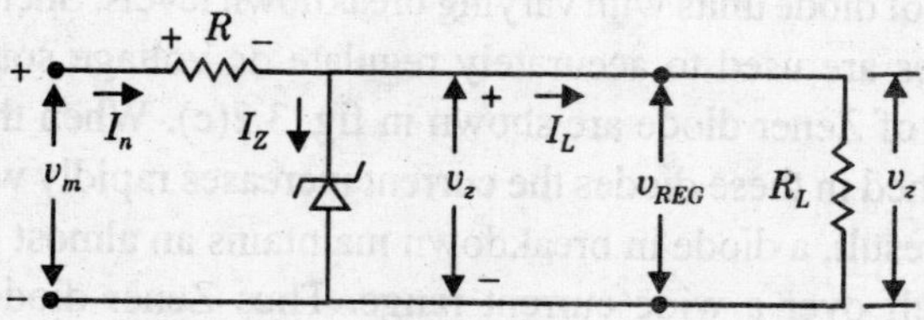


(a) Regulator circuit

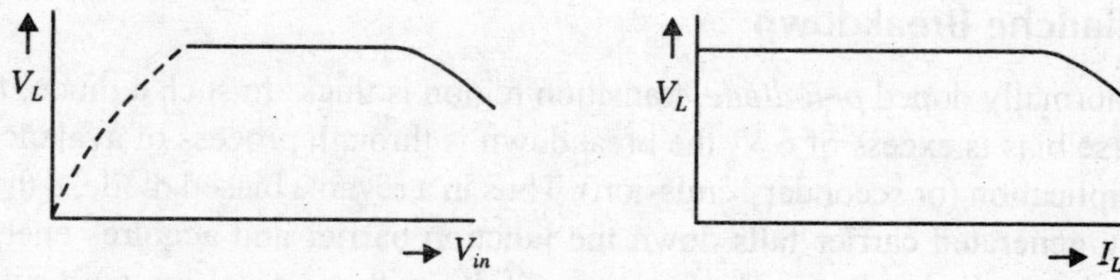


(b) Line Regulator (c) Load Regulator

**Fig. 3.3**

A zener diode is sometimes called a voltage regulator diode because it maintains a constant output voltage even though the current through it changes.

The current through the resistor $R$ is given by $I_{in} = \dfrac{V_{in} - V_Z}{R}$.

## 3.3 BREAK DOWN DIODES

When an ordinary Si junction diode is reverse biased, only a very small reverse saturation current flows. If the reverse voltage is increased sufficiently, the junction breaks down and a large reverse current flows. This current could be large enough to destroy the junction. If the reverse current is limited by means of a suitable series resistor, the power dissipation at the junction will not be excessive, and the device may be operated continuously in its break down condition. When the reverse bias is reduced to the breakdown voltage, the current returns to its normal level. There are two mechanisms by which breakdown can occurs at a reverse-biased *p-n junction (i) Zener break down (ii) Avalanche break down.* Either of the two may occur independently, or they may both occur at once.

### Zener Breakdown

This usually occurs in silicon *pn*-junctions at reverse bias of less than 5V. In zener breakdown, using heavily doped *p* and *n* regions, direct rupture of covalent bonds takes place because of the strong electric field at the junctions of *p-n* diode. The new electron-hole pairs so created increase the reverse current in a reverse biased *p-n* diode. The increase in current takes place at an almost constant value of reverse bias typically below 6v for heavily doped diodes. Due to heavy doping of *p* and *n* regions, the depletion region width becomes very small and for an applied reverse bias of 6V lies, the field across the depletion region becomes high, of the order of $2 \times 10^7$ V/M. For lightly doped diodes, zener breakdown voltage become high and breakdown in this predominant by avalanche multiplication.

## Avalanche Breakdown

For normally doped *p–n diode*, transition region is thick. In such a diode, for reverse bias is excess of 6 V, the breakdown is through process of avalanche multiplication (or secondary emission). Thus in a reverse biased diode, a thermally generated carrier falls down the junction barrier and acquires energy from the applied voltage. Thus carrier collides with a crystal ion with sufficient kinetic energy to disrupt a covalent bond. This is known as impact ionization.Thus in addition to the original carrier, a new electron-hole pair gets created. These new carriers in their turn, may also acquire enough energy from the applied field, collide with another crystal ion and create still another electron-hole pair. This is a circulative process and is known as avalanche multiplication. The net result is a large reverse current at an almost constant voltage drop and avalanche breakdown is said to take place.

## 3.4 TUNNEL DIODE

Tunnel diode is also referred to as ESAKI diode. In the conventional $p-n$ junction, the impurity concentration is about 1 part in $10^8$. The width of the depletion layer across the junction is of the order of 5 microns (i.e. $5 \times 10^{-4}$ cm). This potential barrier restrains the flow of carriers from the region where they constitute majority carriers into the region where they are minority carrier. If the concentration of impurity atoms is greatly increased, say to 1 part in $10^3$ (corresponding to a density in excess of $10^{19}$ $cm^{-3}$). This barrier width allows charge carriers to penetrate through the barrier. This phenomenon is termed as *tunneling* and hence the diodes formed with such impurity concentration densities are termed as Tunnel diode.

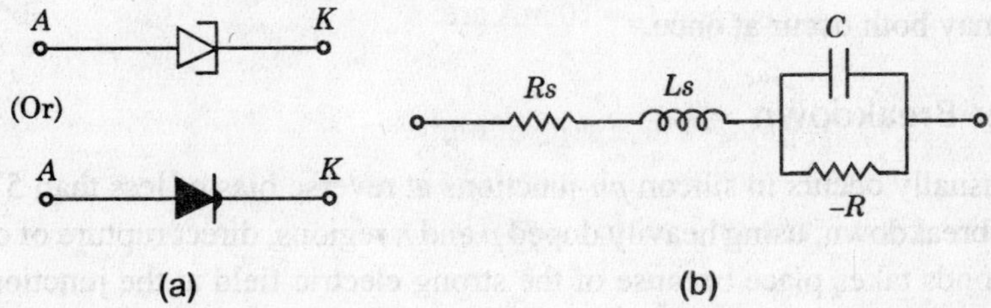


**Fig. 3.4** (a) Symbolic representation of Tunnel diode
(b) Small signal model of a Tunnel diode.

## Volt-ampere Characteristics of Tunnel Diode

The V-I characteristics of Tunnel diode is as shown in fig. 3.5. The Tunnel diode has excellent conduction in the reverse direction. For small forward voltage i.e. unto point *P*, the forward resistance remains small. At point *P*, the current is at maximum level. The current and voltage at this peak point *P* are shown as $I_P$ and $V_P$. At pt $P$, the slope $dI/dv$ is zero. In the section $PV$ to the right of the point $P$, diode exhibits negative resistance. At pt $V$, current is minimum. The current and voltage at this valley point $P$ are shown as $I_V$ and $V_V$. At the valley point $V$, the slop $di/dv$ is again zero.

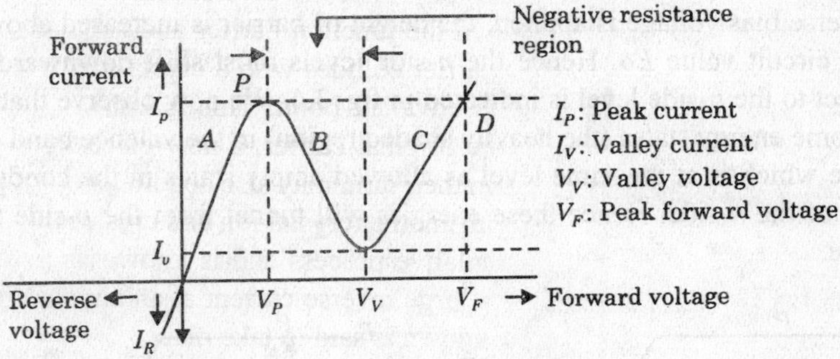


**Fig. 3.5** Volt-ampere characteristics of Tunnel diode

Beyond point $V$, the current contribution is mostly the injected current. The current reaches the value $I_P$ called peak forward voltage $V_F$.

The interval between $I_V$ and $I_P$, as seen in the curve is triple valued i.e. any forward current > $I_V$ but < $I_P$ can be obtained for three different applied voltages. This multi valued feature of the I-V characteristics of the device makes it useful in pulse and digital circuits.

A tunnel diode is symbolically represented as shown in the fig. 3.4(a). And the equivalent circuit of tunnel diode in negative resistance region is shown in fig. 3.4 (b). $R$ denotes the negative resistance of the diode. $R_S$ is the diode resistance and $C$ is the junction capacitance. Also $L_S$ represents the inductance of lead wires. Typical values of these parameters for a tunnel diode with peak forward current $I_P = 10$ mA are: $R = 30\ \Omega$; $R_S = 1\ \Omega$; $L_S = 5\ nH$ and $C = 20$ pF.

*Merits of Tunnel diode:* The merits of tunnel diode are its low cost, low noise, simplicity of construction, high speed of switching, low power drain, environmental immunity, high linearity and rehability.

*Drawback:*

1. Low output voltage swing.
2. It being a two terminal device, there is no isolation between input and output causing serious circuit design difficulties.
3. Practical tunnel diodes are manufactured from either Ge or GaAs semiconductor material. GaAs is preferred, since it gives maximum voltage swing and has largest peak forward current $I_P$ for a given valley current $I_V$.

## Tunnel Diode and Backward Diodes

With the aid of energy-band picture of fig. 3.6. and the concept of quantum mechanical tunneling, the tunnel diode characteristics may be explained. Let us consider that the *p*-material is grounded and that a voltage applied across the diode shifts the *n*-side potential with respect to the *p*-side. For example if a reverse bias voltage is applied, the height of barrier is increased above the open circuit value *Eo*. Hence the *n*-side levels must shift downward with respect to the *p*-side level is indicated in fig. 3.6. We now observe that there are some energy states (the heavily shaded region) in the valence band of the *p*-side which is at the same level as allowed empty states in the conduction band of the *n*-side. Hence these energies will tunnel from the *p*-side to the *n*-side.

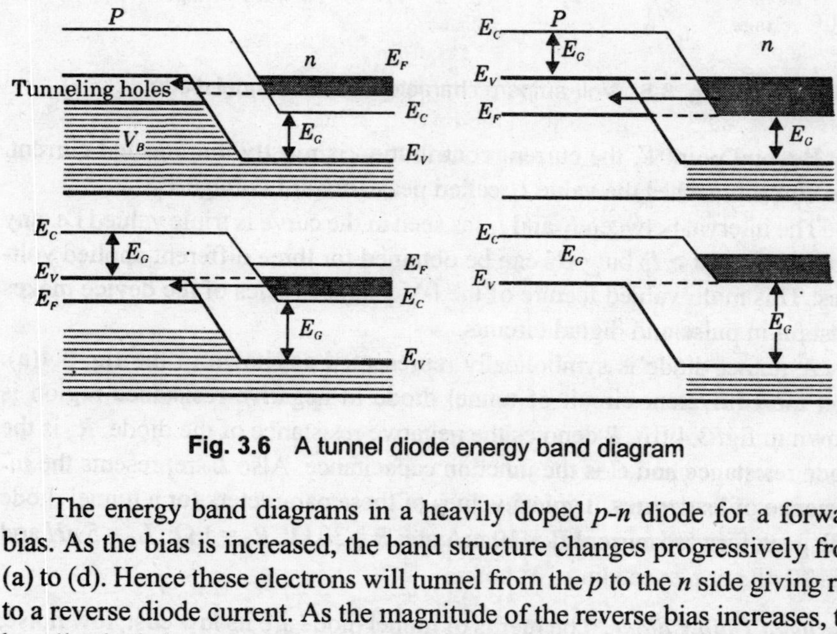


**Fig. 3.6** A tunnel diode energy band diagram

The energy band diagrams in a heavily doped *p-n* diode for a forward bias. As the bias is increased, the band structure changes progressively from (a) to (d). Hence these electrons will tunnel from the *p* to the *n* side giving rise to a reverse diode current. As the magnitude of the reverse bias increases, the heavily shaded area grows in size, causing the reverse current to increase.

Consider now that a forward bias is applied to the diode so that the potential barrier is decreased below *Eo*. Hence the *n*-side level must shift upward with respect to those on the *p*-side and the energy band picture for this situation is indicated in fig. 3.6. It is now evident that there are occupied states in the conduction band of the *n* material (the heavily shaded levels) which is at the same energy as allowed empty states (holes) in the valence band of the *p*-side. Hence electron will tunnel from the *n* to the *p* material, giving rise to the forward currents.The increased condition of the forward bias is shown in fig. 3.6. Now the maximum no. of electrons can leave occupied states on the right of the junction, and tunnel through the barrier to empty slates on the left side, giving rise to the peak current $I_P$ in fig. 3.6. If still more forward bias is applied, the situation in fig 3.6 is obtained and the tunneling current decreases. Finally at an even larger forward bias, the band structure of fig. 3.6 is valid. Since now there are no empty allowed states on one side of the junction at the same energy as occupied states on the other side, the tunneling current must drop to zero.

## 3.5 LIGHT EMITTING DIODE

Charge carriers' recombination takes place at *pn*-junction as electron crosses from the *n*-side and recombines with holes on the *p*-side. When the junction is forward biased the free electron is in the conduction band and is at a higher energy level than hole located at valence band. The recombination process involves radiation of energy in the form of photons or leaf. If the semiconductor material is translucent, the light will be emitted and the junction becomes a light source i.e. a Light Emitting Diode (LED).

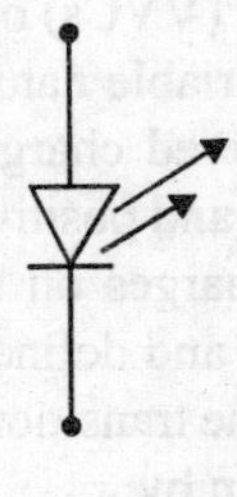

**Fig. 3.7** LED symbol

In other words LED is a diode which gives *OH* visible light from the region of the depletion layer when it is forward biased. Typical LED uses GaAsP *pn*-junction. In Si and Ge, greater % of released energy is given up in the far of heat and the emitting light is insignificant. The efficiency of light generation increases with the increase of injected current and with decrease in temperature. Since LED is a *pn*-junction device, it has forward current vs forward voltage characteristics similar to that of a diode. Numbers 0 to 9 may be created by segments using LEDs. LEDs are available in different colors. LEDs have fast response and offers good contrast ratios of visibility. Life line of LEDs is high, exceeding $10^6$ hours.

*Advantages of LEDs*

1. Low operating voltage, current and power consumption makes LEDs compatible with electronic drive circuits.
2. LEDs exhibit high resistance to mechanical shock and vibration and allow LEDs to be used in severe environment conditions.
3. LEDs ensure a longer operating life line, thereby improving overall rehability and lowering maintenance costs of equipment.
4. LEDs have low inherent noise levels and also high immunity to externally generated noise.
5. LEDs exhibit linearity of radiant power output with forward current over a wide range.

*LEDs have certain limitations such as*

Temperature dependence of radiant output power and wavelength.

Sensitivity to damages by over voltage or over current.

Theoretical overall efficiency is not achieved except in special cooled or pulsed conditions.

## 3.6 VARACTOR DIODE

Varactor diode also known as varicap diode or voltage variable capacitor diodes (VVCs) or volta cap diode is a semiconductor diode utilizing the voltage variable nature of the transition capacitance $C_T$ under reverse regions of uncovered charges on either side of the junction, negative charges on the *p*-side and positive charges on the *n*-side. These regions of positive and negative charges on two sides of the junction together constitute the depletion region and define the total width *W* of the depletion region.

The transition capacitance $C_T$ caused by these isolated uncovered charges is given by:

$$C_T = \frac{\varepsilon A}{W} \qquad \text{...(1)}$$

where ε is permitivity of the semiconductor device

$A \rightarrow$ *pn* junction area

$W \rightarrow$ depletion region width.

As the magnitude of the reverse bias increases, the width *W* of the depletion region increases and the transition capacitance *CT* reduces.

In an alloy (step graded) junction, the width *W* of the depletion layer is given by:

$$W^2 = \frac{2\varepsilon V_j}{qN_D} \qquad \text{...(2)}$$

Where *Vj* is the junction voltage

$$Vj = Vo + Vd \qquad \text{...(3)}$$

Where *Vo* is the contact potential *Vd* is magnitude of applied reverse bias.

For linearly graded (diffused) junction diode, width W of depletion layer is given by

$$W^2 = \frac{2\varepsilon V_j}{qN_D} \qquad \text{... (4)}$$

Combining (1) & (4) we get

$$C_T = \frac{K_1}{(V_0 - V_d)^{1/2}}$$

For zero bias ($Vd = 0$), transition capacitance $C_{TD}$ is

$$C_{TD} = \frac{K_1}{\sqrt{V_0}} \text{ then } C_T = \frac{C_{TO}}{\left(1 + \left|\frac{V_d}{V_0}\right|\right)^{1/2}}$$

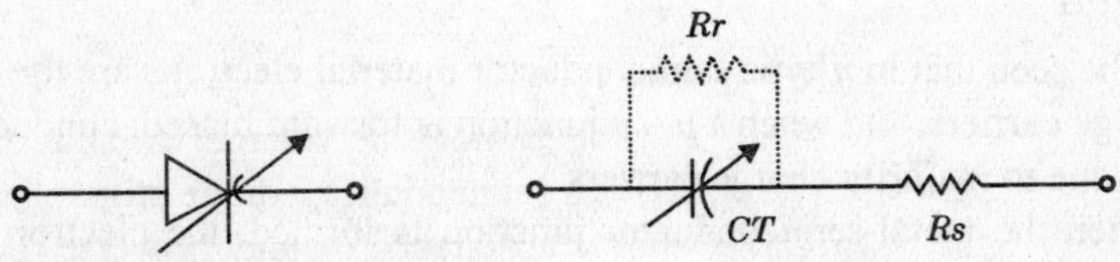


**Fig. 3.8** (a) Varactor diode circuit symbol (b) Circuit model

$R_S$: Ohmic or body series resistance of the diode

$L_S$: is at order of few nano-henrys.

*Uses of Varactor diode:*

1. In frequency modulation system
2. In AFC circuits.
3. In a adjustable B.P.F.
4. In parametric amplifiers.
5. In self-adjusting bridge circuits.

## 3.7 SCHOTTKY DIODE

Schottky diode for surface barrier or hot-carrier diode is a special purpose diode used extensively in very high frequency applications. The reverse recovery line (trr) of Schottky diode is very much lower than conventional junction which finds use as a very fast-acting switch.

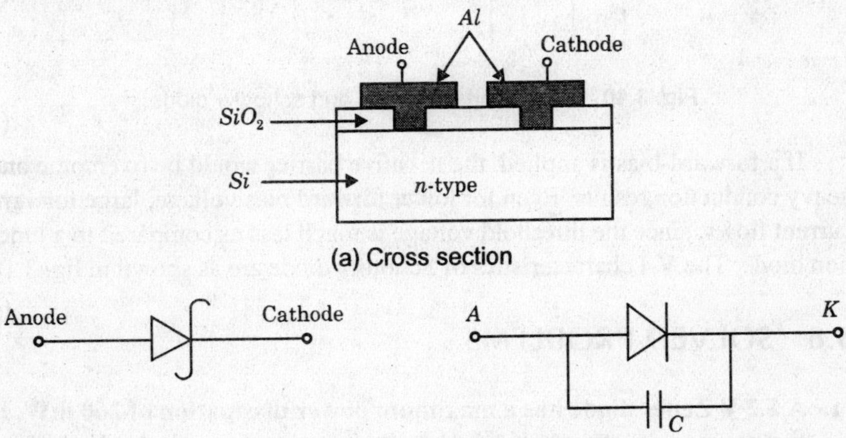


(a) Cross section

(b) Schottk circuit symbol (c) Equivalent circuit of schottky diode

**Fig. 3.9**

## Construction

Schottky diode uses metal-semiconductor junction instead of semiconductor junction used in conventional *pn* diode. Usually *n*-type Si and a metal like Al (or, platinum or tungsten or molybdenum) is formed by a suitable process.

## Working

It may be seen that in *n*-type semiconductor material electrons are the majority charge carriers, and when a $p-n$ junction is forward biased, conduction is mainly due to majority charge carriers.

When the metal-semiconductor junction is formed, the electron in the *n*-type semiconductor such towards the junction with high K.E. and move into the metal, where diode, since these injection electrons have high K.E. compared to the electron of the metal, they are referred to as hot carriers and the diode is called hot carrier diode. These hot carrier diodes thus form an entirely new type of diodes wherein conduction is entirely by majority carriers.

This heavy injection of electron into the metal region results in a region in the Si close to the junction depleted of electronic charge wall or surface barrier in the metal at the interface b/w and the Si. This barrier prevents any further current.

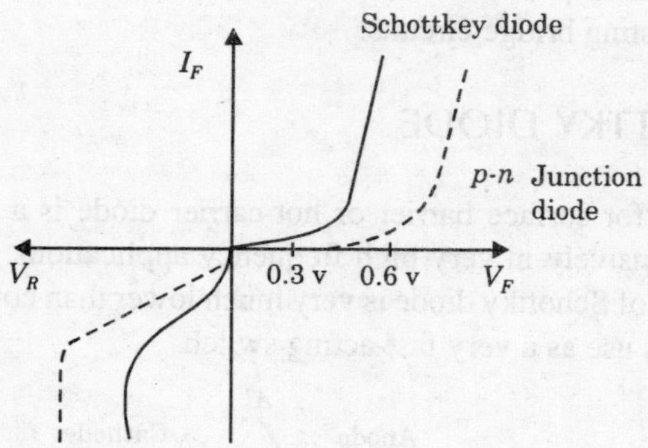


**Fig. 3.10** Characteristics of pn and schottky diode.

If a forward-bias is applied, the negative barrier would be overcome and heavy conduction results. Even for lower forward bias voltage, large forward current flows, since the threshold voltage is much less as compared to a junction diode. The V-I characteristics of Schottky diode are as shown in fig. 3.10

## 3.8 SOLVED PROBLEMS

1. **A 5.2 V Zener diode has a maximum power dissipation of 260 mW. It maintains a constant voltage when the current through the diode does not fall below 10% of the maximum permissible current. A 15V**

**supply is given to the Zener through a series resistor *R*. Find the range for *R* so that Zener maintains its constant voltage. Find the new range when the diode is loaded by 50W loads.**

**Solution:**

$$\text{Maximum permissible current} = \frac{260 \times 10^{-3}}{5.2} = 50 \text{ mA}$$

$$10\% \text{ of } 50 \text{ mA} = 5 \text{ mA}$$

Maximum current through the diode to maintain constant voltage

$$= (50 - 5) \text{ mA i.e.} 45 \text{ mA}$$

Now $$R_{min} = \frac{15 - 5.2}{50 \times 10^{-3}} = 196\,\Omega$$

and $$R_{max} = \frac{15 - 5.2}{45 \times 10^{-3}} = 217.7\,\Omega \approx 218\,\Omega$$

$$R + R_L = \frac{15 - 5.2}{1} = \frac{9.8}{1}$$

Or $$R^1 = \frac{9.8}{1} - R_L = \frac{9.8}{1} - 50$$

Now $$R^1_{minimum} = \frac{9.8}{I^1_{maximum}} - 50 = \frac{9.8}{50 \times 10^{-3}} - 50$$

And $$R^1_{maximum} = \frac{9.8}{I^1_{minimum}} - 50 = \frac{9.8}{45 \times 10^{-3}} - 50$$

$$= 218 - 50 = 168\,\Omega$$

**2. When the current through a Zener diode increase from 20 mA to 30mA, the voltage across it changes from 5.6 V to 5.65 V. What is the voltage across the Zener when the current is 35 mA?**

**Solution:**

Characteristics of Zener diode can be assumed linear

$$V = 5i + 5.5$$

$$= 5 \times 35 \times 10^{-3} + 5.5 = 5.675\text{V}$$

**3. A Schottky barrier is formed between a metal having $f_m$ = 4.3 V and *p*-type Si ($x$ = 4 V). The acceptor doping in the Si is $N_a = 10^{17}$ cm$^{-3}$.**

**(a) Draw the equilibrium band diagram showing a numerical value for $qV_0$**

**(b) Draw the band diagram with 0.3 V forward bias. Repeat for 2 V reverse bias.**

**Solution**

$$E_i - E_F = KT \ln \frac{p_o}{n_i}$$

$$= 0.254 \ln \frac{10^{17}}{1.5 \times 10^{10}} = 0.047\text{eV}$$

$$\phi_0 = 4 + 0.55 + 0.407 = 4.957 \text{ V}$$

**4. The Zener diode can be used to prevent over loading of sensitive meter movements without affecting meter linearity. The circuit shown represents a *dc* voltmeter which reads 20 V full scale. The meter resistance is 1kW and $R_1 + R_2 = 200$k. If the diode is a 16 V zener, find $R_1$ and $R_2$, so that, when $V_i > 20$ V, the zener diode conducts and the overload current is shunted away from the meter.**

**Solution:**

With $V_i = 20$V the zener diode does not conduct.

Hence $$Z_0 = (R_1 + R_2 + R_m)$$

$$V_i = (200 + 1) \times 10^3 \text{ I}$$

Or $$I = \frac{20}{201k} = 99.5\mu\ A\left[\text{full scale}\right]$$

With $V_i > 20$ V, the voltage across $R_1$ and $R_m$ (meter) must be equal to the zener voltage $V_Z = 16$ V

Or $$R_1 + R_m = \frac{V_z}{I} = \frac{16}{99.5\mu\ A} = 160.8k\Omega$$

$$R_1 \approx 159.8 \text{ KW}$$

$$R_2 \approx 40.2 \text{ KW}$$

**5. A series combination of a 5V avalanche diode and a forward biased Si diode is to be used to construct a zero temperature co-efficient voltage reference. The temperature co-efficient of the Si diode is –1.7 mV/°C. Express in percentage per degree centigrade the required temperature co-efficient of the zener diode.**

**Solution:**

For the Si diode, the temperature co-efficient = –1.7 mV/°C. If the series combination is to have a zero temperature co-efficient, then the temperature co-efficient of the avalanche diode must be at the biasing current +1.7 mV/°C.

In percent, temperature co-efficient $= \dfrac{1.7 \times 10^{-3} V}{5V}(100\%) = 0.034\%/°\text{C}.$

**6. The avalanche diode regulates at 150 V over a range of diode current from 5 to 40mA. The supply voltage V = 300 V. Calculate $R$ to allow voltage regulation from a load current $I_L = 0$ up to $I_{maximum}$, the maximum possible value of $I_L$.**

**(a) What is $I_{maximum}$?**

**(b) If $R$ is set as in part (a) and the load current is set at $I_L = 25$ mA, what are the limit between which $V$ may vary without loss of regulation in the circuit?**

**Solution:**

(a) For $I_L = 0$ and $V_0 = 50$ we have

$$I_D = I_T = \frac{300 - 150}{R} \le 40mA$$

or $$R \ge \frac{150}{40} \times 10^3 = 3.75K$$

For $I_L = I_{maximum}$; $I_D \ge 5$ mA

But for $R = 3.75$ k; $I_T = 40$ mA

Hence $I_{maximum} = 40 - 5 = 35$mA

(b) Minimum current $I_D$ for good regulation is 5 mA

Hence $I_T = 25+5 = 30$mA

And $V_{minimum} = 30 \times 3.75 + 150 = 262.5$ V

Maximum current $I_D$ for good regulation is 40 mA,

Hence $I_T = 25 + 40 = 65$mA

$V_{maximum} = 65 \times 3.75 + 150 = 393.75$

**7. Consider a tunnel diode with $N_D = N_A$ and with the impurity concentration corresponding to 1 atom per $10^4$ Ge atoms. At room temperature, calculate (a) the height of the potential-energy barrier under open-circuit conditions (the contact potential energy) (b) The width of the space charge region.**

**Solution:**

$$N = 6.02 \times 10^{23} \frac{\text{atoms}}{\text{mole}} \frac{1 \text{ mole}}{72.6g} \times 5.32 g/^3$$

$$N = 4.41 \times 10^{22} \text{ atoms/cm}^3$$

$$N_A = N_D = 10^{-3}\, N = 4.41 \times 10^{22} \times \frac{1}{10^{-4}} = 4.41 \times 10^{18}/\text{cm}^3$$

As $$E_0 = KT \ln \frac{N_A N_D}{n_i^2}$$

$$= (2.3) \log_{10}$$

or $$E_0 = 0.026 \times (24.16) = 0.628$$

From the equation $V_B = \dfrac{eN_A}{2\varepsilon} W^2$

$$W^2 = \frac{2\varepsilon V_0}{eN_A}$$

Replace $1/N_A$ with $\dfrac{1}{N_A} + \dfrac{1}{N_D} = \dfrac{2}{N_A}$ we have

$$W^2 = \frac{4\varepsilon V_0}{eN_A}$$

$$= \frac{4 \times 16 \times 0.628}{36\pi \times 10^9 \times 4.41 \times 10^{18} \times 10^6 \times 1.6 \times 10^{-19}}$$

$$= 5 \times 10^{-16}\ \text{m}^2$$

or $$W = 22.4 \times 10^{-10}\text{m} = 224\ \text{A}^\circ$$

## 3.9 OBJECTIVE QUESTIONS

**1.** A Zener diode works on the principle of
(a) Tunneling of charge carriers across the junction
(b) thermionic emission
(c) Diffusion of charge carriers across the junction
(d) doping of charge carriers across the junction
**Ans:** (a)

**2.** In Gunn diodes electrons are transferred from
(a) High to low mobility energy bands
(b) low to high mobility energy bands
(c) Valley to domain formation
(d) domain to valley formation
Ans: (a)

**3.** If $P_r$ is the rate at which carriers are produced by light in a photo diode, $\tau$ is the average life time for the newly created carriers, $T_t$ is the average transit time for carriers to reach the holmic contacts of the diode and '*e*' is the electronic charge, then the steady state photo current will be given by
(a) $i = (2eP_r\tau)/Tt$ (b) $i = (eP_r\tau)/2T_t$
(c) $I = (eP_r\tau)/T_t$ (d) $i = (eP_r\tau)/3T_t$
**Ans:** (a)

**4.** Schottky diodes, also called hot carrier diode, are used in wave shaping circuit because.
(a) They have a small recovery time
(b) they have a large reverse resistance

(c) They have large forward current
(d) their peak inverse voltage is small.
**Ans:** (a)

**5.** Silicon diode is less suited for low voltage rectifier operation because of
(a) it can withstand high temperatures
(b) its reverse saturation current is low
(c) its cut-in voltage is high
(d) its breakdown voltage is high
**Ans:** (d)

**6.** Silicon is not suitable for fabrication of light emitting diodes because it is
(a) an indirect band gap semiconductor
(b) a direct band gap semiconductor
(c) a wide band gap semiconductor
(d) a narrow band gap semiconductor
**Ans:** (b)

**7.** For an abrupt junction Varactor diode, the dependence of the device capacitance (C) an applied reverse bias (V) is given by
(a) $C \propto V^{1/3}$ (b) $C \propto V^{-1/3}$ (c) $C \propto V^{1/2}$ (d) $C \propto V^{-1/2}$
**Ans:** (b)

**8.** A general propose diode is more likely to suffer avalanche breakdown rather than Zener breakdown because
(a) it is lightly doped (b) its leakage current is small
(c) it has weak covalent bonds (d) it has low reverse resistance
**Ans:** (a)

**9.** A Zener diode
(a) Has a high forward voltage rating
(b) has a sharp breakdown at low reverse voltage
(c) is useful as an Amplifier
(d) has a negative resistance.
**Ans:** (b)

**10.** Avalanche breakdown in a semiconductor diode occurs when
(a) Reverse bias exceeds a certain value
(b) forward bias exceeds a certain value
(c) Forward current exceeds a certain value
(d) the potential barrier is reduced to zero
**Ans:** (a)

**11.** Zener breakdown results from
(a) Strong electric field (b) high applied potential
(c) any other cause
**Ans:** (a)

**12.** The important advantage of tunnel diode is
(a) it is less sensitive to nuclear radiation
(b) it is less noisy

(c) it can be operated safely at high temperatures
(d) none
**Ans:** (b)

**13.** The temperature coefficient of a breakdown diode based on Avalanche break down is
(a) Positive (b) negative (c) Zero (d) none
**Ans:** (a)

**14.** Which of these is a best description of a Zener diode.
(a) it operates in the reverse region (b) it is a constant voltage device
(c) it is a constant current device (d) it works in forward region
**Ans:** (b)

**15.** When two Zener diodes of each 10v and 15v are connected in series aiding, the overall voltage between them when they are in conduction is
(a) 10.6 v (b) 15.6 v (c) 25 v (d) zero
**Ans:** (c)

**16.** In a standard regulator circuit using Zener diode 10 v the input voltage varies from 25 to 40v and load current is 10 mA to 20 mA, the minimum Zener current is 5 mA, the value of the series resistance in ohms.
(a) 1500 (b) 1200 (c) 600 (d) 1000
**Ans:** (c)

**17.** The LED's are usually made of materials like
(a) Ga and As (b) *C* and Si (c) Ge and As (d) *P* and Si
**Ans:** (a)

**18.** Varactor diodes are used in FM receivers to obtain
(a) Automatic frequency control (b) Automatic gain control
(c) Automatic volume control (d) Automatic noise control.
**Ans:** (a)

**17.** No load voltage of power supply is 100v and full load voltage is 80 v, the percentage of regulation is
(a) 0 (b) 25 (c) 20 (d) 2.5
**Ans:** (b)

**20.** Both Avalanche and Zener breakdown are commonly known as
(a) Zener break down (b) Avalanche breakdown
(c) Current breakdown
**Ans:** (a)

**21.** Zener diodes are used as
(a) Reference voltage elements (b) reference current elements
(c) Reference resistance.
**Ans:** (a)

**22.** Zener diodes are
(a) specially doped *P-N* junction (b) normally doped *P-N* junction
(c) lightly doped *P-N* junction
**Ans:** (a)

**23.** The diode in which impurities are heavily doped is
(a) Varactor diode (b) PIN diode
(c) Tunnel diode (d) Zener diode
**Ans:** (c)

**24.** The frequency limit of Tunnel diode is
(a) $10^4$ Hz (b) $10^8$ Hz (c) $10^{12}$ Hz
**Ans:** (b)

**25.** The doping densities required in Tunnel diode is of the order of
(a) $10^6$ atoms/m$^3$ (b) $10^{10}$ atoms /m$^3$
(c) $10^{16}$ atoms/m$^3$ (d) $10^{26}$ atoms/m$^3$
**Ans:** (d)

**26.** The efficiency of an LED for generating light is directly proportional to the
(a) Temperature (b) voltage applied
(c) Level of doping (d) current injected
**Ans:** (d)

**27.** If the junction temperature of LED is increased the radiant output power
(a) Decreases (b) increases (c) Remains the same
**Ans:** (a)

**28.** The output colour of the GaAs P LED is
(a) Yellow (b) green (c) Amber (d) red
**Ans:** (d)

**29.** The breakdown voltage for LED is approximately
(a) 1.6 v (b) 0.72 (c) 1.12 v (d) 9 v
**Ans:** (a)

**30.** When thermally generated holes and electrons gain enough energy from the reversed biased source of a Zener diode to produce new current carriers it is called.
(a) Avalanche breakdown (b) reverse breakdown
(c) Zener breakdown (d) low voltage breakdown
**Ans:** (a)

**31.** The Zener effect is valid
(a) Below 5 v (b) above 5 v (c) Equal to 5 v (c) none of these
**Ans:** (a)

**32.** The Avalanche effect is valid
(a) Below 5 v (b) above 5 v (c) Equal to 5 v (d) none of these
**Ans:** (b)

**33.** In a Zener diode with high breakdown voltage
(a) both *P* and *N* are heavily doped (b) both *P* and *N* are lightly doped
(c) either *P* or *N* is lightly doped. (d) None
**Ans:** (b)

**34.** The cut in voltage of a diode is also known as
(a) off-set voltage (b) threshold voltage
(c) Knee voltage (d) all the above
**Ans:** (d)

**35.** The Varactor is usually
(a) Forward biased (b) reverse biased
(c) Un biased (d) in the breakdown region.
**Ans:** (b)

**36.** In a Gunn diode, negative resistance results from:
(a) Avalanche breakdown due to high voltage gradient
(b) Electron transfer to an energy level with less mobility
(c) Tunneling across the junction
(d) electron domains forming at the junction
**Ans:** (b)

**37.** LED's fabricated from GaAs permit radiation in the:
(a) Ultraviolet region (b) infrared region
(c) Visible range (d) none of these
**Ans:** (c)

**38.** The most important application of tunnel diode is:
(a) as rectifier (b) as switching device in digital circuits
(c) as voltage controllable device (d) as oscillator
**Ans:** (b)

**39.** Avalanche breakdown results basically due to:
(a) Impact ionization (b) strong electric field across the junction
(c) Emission of electrons (d) rise in temperature
**Ans:** (a)

**40.** In a Varactor diode using alloy junction, the transition capacitance is proportional to
(a) $V^2_J$ (b) $1/V_J$ (c) $1/\sqrt{V_J}$ (d) $1/V^2_J$
**Ans:** (c)

## 3.10 CONVENTIONAL QUESTIONS

1. "The Zener diode is a misnomer .Actually zener diodes used in voltage regulator circuits operate in the avalanche breakdown region." Explain
2. Explain Zener breakdown is in fact tunneling mechanism only?
3. Breafly explain the Tunnel diode operation? Sketch the characteristic curve of Tunnel diode?
4. Explain about Schottky diode? Explain its construction and working principle?
5. What is Varactor diode?
6. Explain about LED?
7. Define (a) Zener break down and (b) Avalanche breakdown

## 3.11 EXERCISE PROBLEMS

1. A 7.2 V Zener diode is used in the circuit of fig. 1 and the load current is to vary from 12 to 100mA. Find the value of $r_i$ required to maintain this load current if the supply voltage $V_{dc}$ = 12 V

(**Answer:** $r_i$: 13.5 Ω; $I_C$: 12 mA to 100 mA; $R_L \approx 72$ Ω)

2. The 7.2 V Zener diode is used in a circuit similar to that shown in the fig. 1. An *ac* ripple voltage $V_r$ is added to the unregulated *dc* voltage. The load draws a current of 100 mA. The output of the unregulated supply $V_T$ can be represented as $V_T = 12 + 1 \cos wt$. Find the source resistance $r_i$ for proper operation and the peak to peak value of the ripple voltage present across the load. (**Answer:** $r_i = 32\Omega$; $V_{ripple} = 0.118$ Vp-p)
3. (a) Sketch the $V_Z I_Z$ characteristics for $n = 4$ and $n = 1$
   **Hint:** Plot $I_z/I_o$ versus $V_z/V_0$ to obtain normalized characteristics
   (b) Obtain the knee of the curve.
   (c) Sketch a piece wise-linear approximation to the curve using two straight lines.
   (d) The slope of the straight line curve below the knee is called the zener resistance $r_z$. Calculate $r_z$. Note that $r_z$ continually changes.

## 3.12 LAB EXPERIMENTS

### Exp No: 1 Zener Diode

*Part (A)*

**AIM:** To obtain the characteristics of a Zener diode.

**Apparatus:**

1. Zener diode FZ 9.1
2. Resistance 1 K-Ohm
3. Voltmeter 0-10 V
4. Multi-meter
5. Connecting wires, Bread board and DC Power supply.

**Circuit Diagram:**

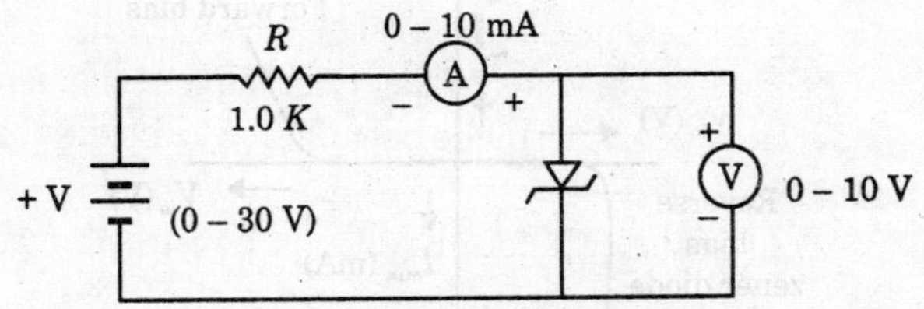


**Fig. 3.11** Forward Biased Circuit

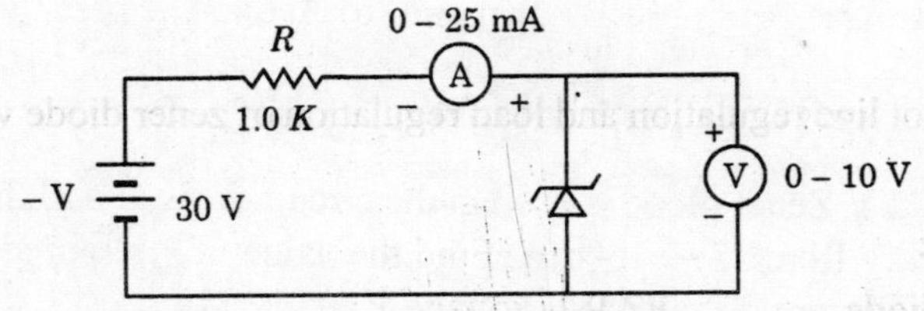


**Fig. 3.12** Reverse Biased Circuit

***Theory:*** Zener diode is an ordinary *P-N* Junction diode except that it is properly doped (1 in $10^6$) to have a very sharp and almost vertical breakdown. They are exclusively operated under reverse biased condition and designed to operate in breakdown region without damage. Zener diode primarily depends for their working on Zener effect. One of the prime applications of Zener diode is in regulation of line voltage.

***Procedure:*** To obtain the forward characteristic, the connections are made as per the circuit diagram. The diode voltage is varied from 0 to 1 colt in steps of 0.1 volt and the corresponding diode currents are noted down. A graph is plotted taking voltage on *X*-axis and current on *T*-axis. For the reverse characteristics the direction of the diode is reversed and the procedure is repeated. From the plot of the reverse characteristics, note down the breakdown voltage

***Tabular column:***

| *Voltage (Volts)* | *Current(mA)* |
|---|---|
| | |

| *Voltage (Volts)* | *Current(mA)* |
|---|---|
| | |

***Result:*** The characteristics of Zener diode are determined and graph is drawn.

The Zener breakdown voltage is _______________ volts.

**Nature of Graph:**

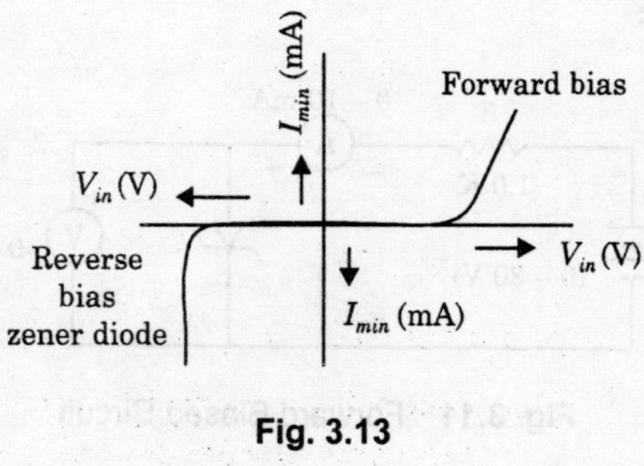


**Fig. 3.13**

## *Part (B)*

**AIM:** To plot line regulation and load regulation of zener diode voltage regulate.

**Apparatus:**

1. Zener diode FZ 9.1
2. Resistance 1 K-Ohm

3. Ammeter 0-10 mA
4. Voltmeter 0-10 V
5. Dc power supply
6. Connecting wires and Bread board

**Circuit Diagram:**

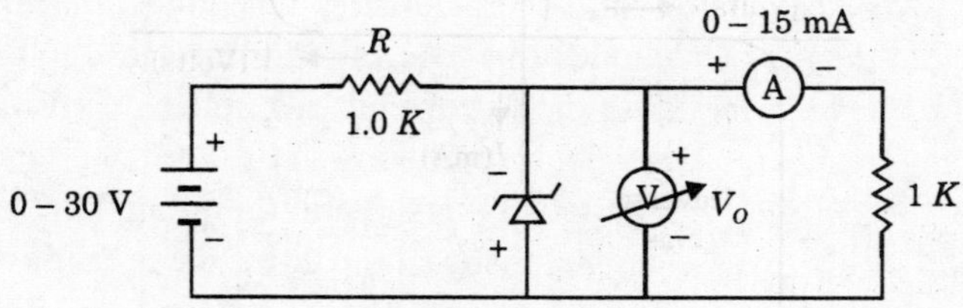


**Fig. 3.14**

**Procedure:**

1. Connect the circuit as shown in the circuit diagram.
2. To plot the line regulation graph, select $R_L$ so that $R_L$ = 1 k-Ohm.
3. Now vary *Vs* in steps of 1V from 0 to 15 V. For each value of $V_s$ note down the corresponding value of $V_o$.
4. For load regulation characteristics, keep *Vs* as constant ($V_s$ = 3 V). Now vary $R_L$ such that $I_L$ is increased in steps of 1mA from 0 to10 mA. For each value of $I_L$ note down the corresponding output voltage *Vo*.
5. Plot a graph between $V_o$ versus *Vs* taking *Vs* on the *X*-axis. This gives the line regulation characteristics. Similarly plot a graph between $V_o$ versus $I_L$ taking $I_L$ on the *X*-axis which gives the load regulation characteristics.

## *Tabular Column*

Line Regulation $I_L$ = 1 mA

| *S. No.* | $V_S$ *(Volts)* | $V_L$ *(Volts)* |
|---|---|---|
| | | |

Load Regulation $V_S$ = 25 VA

| *S. No.* | $I_L$ *(mA)* | $V_L$ *(V)* |
|---|---|---|
| | | |

### *Nature of Graph*

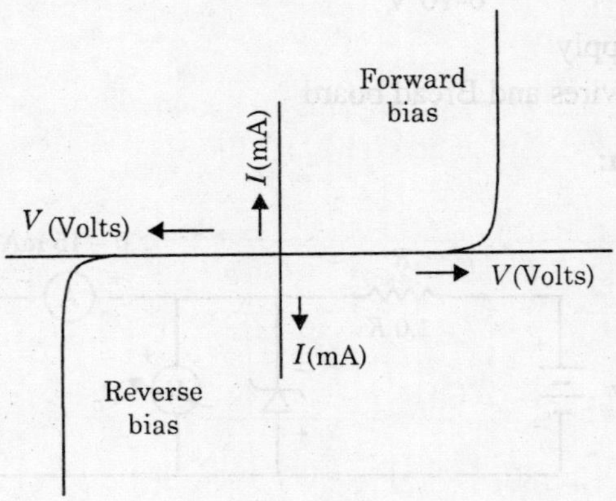


**Fig. 3.15**

## Questions

1. Explain the mechanism of Avalanche breakdown and Zener breakdown.
2. Explain the working of Zener breakdown voltage regulator.
3. How a Zener diode is differ from an ordinary diode.

## Exp No: 2

## LED (Light Emitting Diode)

**AIM:** (1) To obtain the LED voltages of both Red LED and green LED.
(2) To study seven-segment display

**Materials Required**

(1) Two power supplies: One at 15 V, another adjustable from at least 1 to 15 V.

**Equipment**

1. Digital Multimeter, VOM
2. Resistors: Two 270 Ω 1- Ω
3. Diode: IN914
4. Red LED: TIL221
5. Green LED: TIL222
6. Seven-segment display: TIL312

### *Data for Red LED*

1. Connect the circuit of fig. 1 using a red LED. The $V_{OM}$ is connected as an ammeter that measure the current through the LED. The electronic voltmeter measures the voltage across the LED. The IN914 protects the LED against accidentally applying a reverse voltage.
2. Adjust source voltage Vs to get 10 mA through the LED. Record the corresponding LED voltage in Table 1.

3. Adjust the source voltage to set up the remaining currents listed in tanle1. Record each LED voltage.

### *Date for a Green LED*

1. Replace the red LED by a green LED in the circuit of fig. 1.
2. Repeat steps 2 & 3 for the green LED.

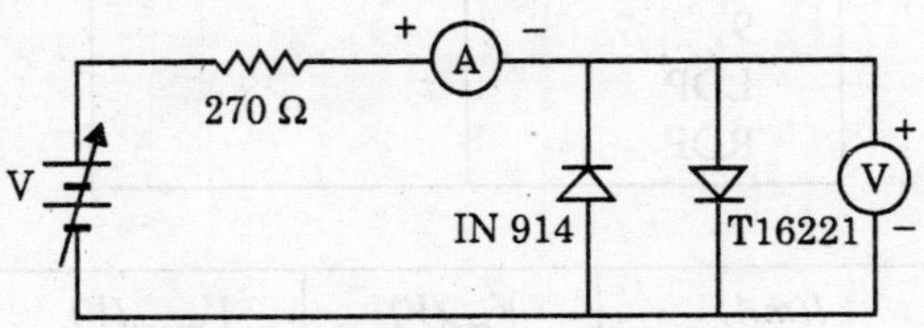


**Fig. 3.16** Circuit for LED data

### *Using a Seven-segment Display*

1. Figure (a) shows the pin out for the seven segment display used in this experiment. It includes a left decimal point (LDP) and a right decimal point (RDP). Connect the circuit of fig. (b)
2. Figure (c) shows the schematic diagram for a TIL312. Ground pins 1, 10 and 13. if the circuit is working correctly, digit 7 will be displayed.
3. Disconnect the grounds on pins 1, 10 and 13
4. Ground correctly, enter the pin numbers in table.
5. Repeat step 4 for the remaining digits 1 to 9 and the decimal points.

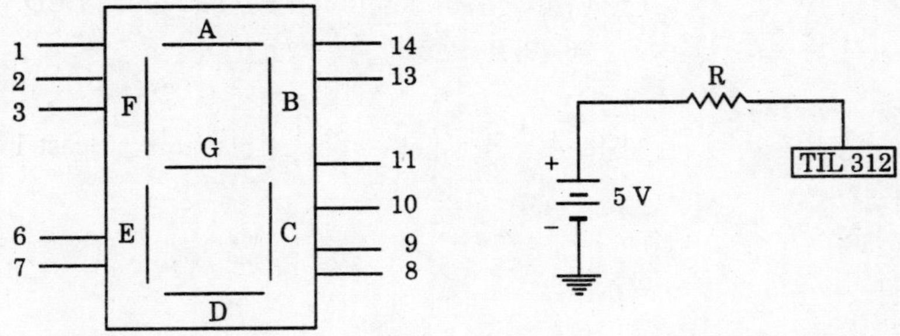


(a) Pin out of TIL 312 (b) Circuit for TIL 312.

**Fig. 3.17**

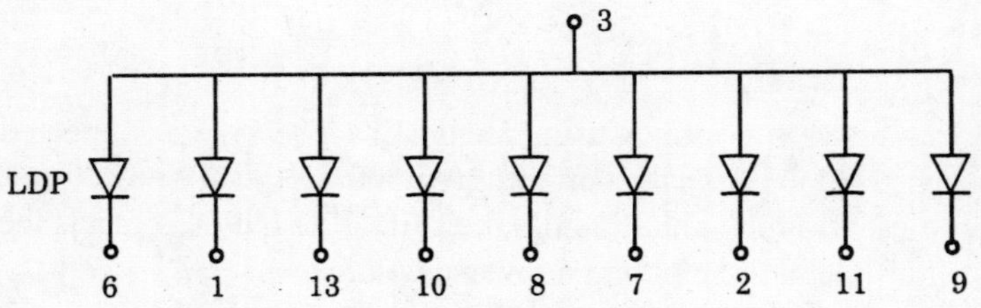


**Fig. 3.17** (c) Schematic diagram.

**Table** Seven-segment indicator

| *Display* | *Pins Grounded* |
|---|---|
| 0 | |
| 1 | |
| . | |
| . | |
| 9 | |
| LDP | |
| RDP | |

| *I(mA)* | $V_{red}(V)$ | $V_{green}(V)$ |
|---|---|---|
| 10 | | |
| 20 | | |
| . | | |
| . | | |

# ❮ 4 ❯

# BIPOLAR JUNCTION TRANSISTOR

## 4.1 INTRODUCTION

In 1904, the vacuum tube diode was introduced by J.A Fleming, there after in 1906, Lee De Forest added a third element called control grid, to the vacuum diode. In the yearly 1930s the four-element tetrode and five-element pentode gained prominence in the electron tube industry. The amplifying action of the first Transistor is demonstrated by William schockley, Walter H. Brattain and John Bardeen at the Bell Telephone Laboratories on December 23, 1947. A Bipolar Junction Transistor (BJT) is a three layer active device consisting of two *p-n* junctions connected back to back as shown in fig. 4.1. In BJT, the operation depends on the interconnection of both majority and minority carriers and hence the name Bipolar.

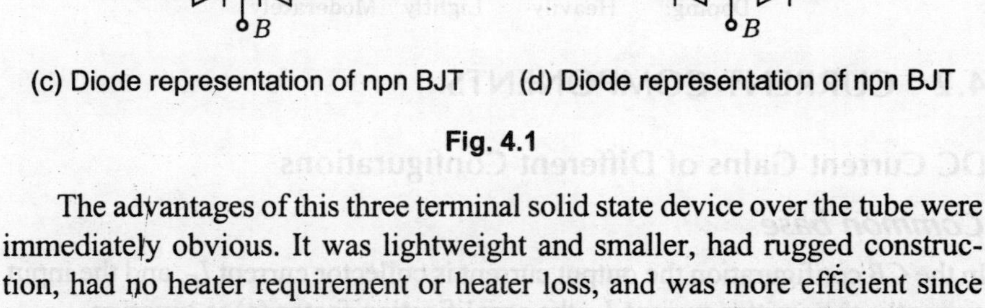


(c) Diode representation of npn BJT (d) Diode representation of npn BJT

**Fig. 4.1**

The advantages of this three terminal solid state device over the tube were immediately obvious. It was lightweight and smaller, had rugged construction, had no heater requirement or heater loss, and was more efficient since less power was absorbed by the device itself, it was instantly available for use, requiring no warm-up period, and lower operating voltages were possible.

Transistors are used as amplifiers, oscillators, switching circuits etc.The principal use of a transistor is as an amplifier.

An amplifier increases the magnitude of a given signal applied at its input and the signal may be periodic. A periodic signal may be sinusoidal. Signals mostly used in communication systems are sinusoidal. *In any active device, the arrow shows conventional current direction if the junction is forward biased.*

A Bipolar Junction Transistor (BJT) is a solid state device, which is mainly used as an amplifier. There are three distinct terminals in a transistor: *emitter, base and collector.*

The physical behavior of BJT is given below.

### *Emitter*

(a) is a heavily doped extrinsic semiconductor to emit more carriers.

(b) moderate in size to maintain, heavy doping without diluting it or mesh formation in it. Function is to supply charge carriers necessary for conduction, when an external voltage is applied.

### *Base*

(a) Lightly doped to reduce the recombination, within the base so as to increase collector current.

(b) Small in size to facilitate the carriers in reaching the collector before its lifetime elapses.

### *Collector*

(a) Moderately doped to avoid the chances of mesh formation even after taking the carriers from the emitter.

(b) Large in size to withstand the temperature generated at the collector.

- BJT acts as a current controlled voltage source.

| | E | B | C |
|---|---|---|---|
| Size: | Moderate | Small | Large |
| Doping: | Heavily | Lightly | Moderately |

## 4.2 CURRENT COMPONENTS

### DC Current Gains of Different Configurations

#### *Common base*

In the *CB* configuration the output current is collector current $I_C$, and the input current is the emitter current $I_E$, the amplification factor (a) is given as

$$\alpha = \frac{I_C}{I_E}, \alpha = 0.95 \rightarrow 0.98$$

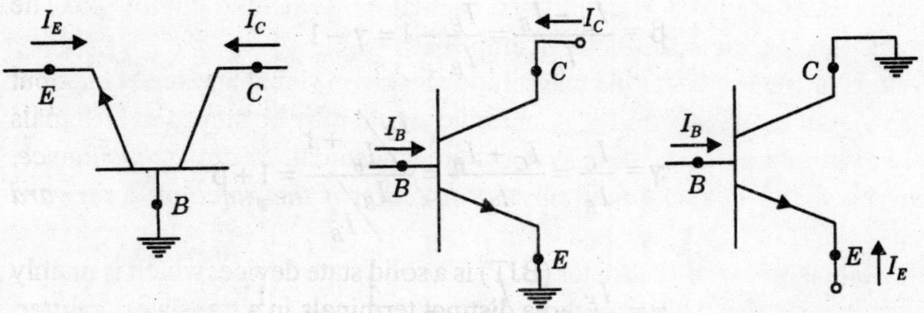


(a) Common base (b) Common emitter (c) Common collector

**Fig. 4.2**

### *Common emitter*

In the *CE* configuration the output current is collector current $I_C$, and the input current is the base current $I_B$.

$$\beta = I_C / I_B,$$

$$\beta = 50 \text{ to } 500.$$

### *Common collector*

In the *CC* configuration the output current is emitter current $I_E$, and the input current is the base current $I_B$, the amplification factor (γ) is given as

$$\gamma = \frac{I_E}{I_B}.$$

$$\gamma = 51 \text{ to } 501.$$

### *Conversion of α, β, γ*

$$I_E = I_C + I_B$$

$$\alpha = \frac{I_C}{I_E} = \frac{I_C}{I_C + I_B} = \frac{I_C/I_B}{I_C/I_B + 1} = \frac{\beta}{1+\beta}$$

$$\alpha = \frac{I_E - I_B}{I_E} = \frac{I_E/I_B - 1}{I_E/I_B} = \frac{\gamma - 1}{\gamma}$$

$$\beta = \frac{I_C}{I_B} = \frac{I_C}{I_E + I_C} = \frac{I_C/I_E}{1 - I_C/I_E} = \frac{\alpha}{1-\alpha}$$

$$\beta = \frac{I_E - I_B}{I_E} = \frac{I_E}{I_B} - 1 = \gamma - 1$$

$$\gamma = \frac{I_C}{I_E} = \frac{I_C + I_B}{I_B} = \frac{I_C/I_B + 1}{I_B/I_B} = 1 + \beta$$

$$\gamma = \frac{I_E}{I_B} = \frac{I_E}{I_E - I_C} = \frac{1}{1 - \frac{I_C}{I_E}} = \frac{1}{1 - \alpha}$$

Figure 4.3 shows the biasing arrangement and the result in current components in a *p-n-p* transistor under normal operation. The electron-hole pair generation and recombination in the two junction depletion regions is ignored.

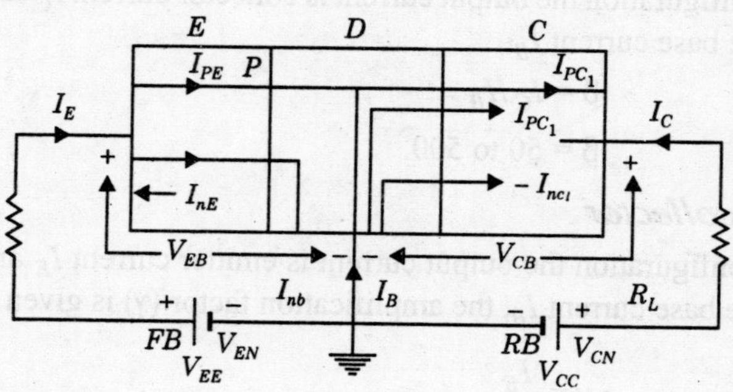


**Fig. 4.3** Current Components of BJT. Emitter junction is forward biased, and collector junction is reversed biased.

*Assumptions in current components*

1. All terminal currents are considered as flowing inside. is also considered as flowing inside so as to make the transistor analysis as two port analysis.
2. All current directions are assumed to be same as hole or conventional direction .

*Majority carriers in forward biased*

1. Holes are attracted by positive and repelled by negative of and negative of $V_{CC}$
2. Electrons flow from base to emitter and not from base to collector.

*Minority carriers in revere biased*

1. Electrons flow from collector and then to base because base is more positive when compared to emitter and even if some electrons enter the emitter, they will be simply recombined.
2. Holes flow from base to collector but not from base to emitter.

$$I_E = I_{P_E} + I_{N_E}$$
$$I_{C0} = -(I_{N_{C0}} + I_{P_{C0}})$$
$$I_C = -I_{P_{C1}} + I_{C0}$$

$I_{P_{C1}}$ is hole current in collector.

$I_{N_E}$ is hole current in emitter.

Transportation factor $\alpha_T = \dfrac{I_{P_{C_1}}}{I_E} \alpha$

$$\therefore \quad -I_{P_{C1}} = -\alpha I_E = \alpha(I_C + I_B)$$
$$I_E + I_B + I_C = 0 \Rightarrow I_E = -(I_C + I_B)$$
$$\therefore \quad I_C = \alpha(I_C + I_B) + I_{C0}$$
$$I_C(1+\alpha) = \alpha I_B + I_{C0}$$
$$I_C = \left(\frac{\alpha}{1-\alpha}\right) I_B + \left(\frac{1}{1-\alpha}\right) I_{C_0}$$
$$I_C = \beta I_B + (1+\beta) I_{C0}$$

## *Early effect or Base-width Modulation*

An increase in magnitude of collector voltage increases the *space-charge width* at the output junction diode as indicated by the equation.

$$V_B = \frac{eN_A}{2\varepsilon} w^2$$

$\varepsilon \rightarrow$ permittivity

$w \rightarrow$ total space-charge width

$N_A \rightarrow$ Acceptor ion concentration

$e \rightarrow$ charge

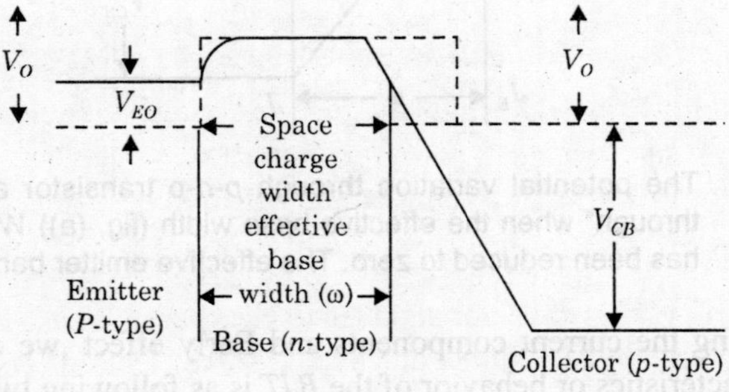


**Fig. 4.4 (a)** The potential variation through the transistor under biased. (Representation of Early effect)

From fig. 4.4 (a) we see that such action causes the effective base width *w* to decrease this is a phénomenon known as the early effect. This decrease in *w* has two consequences: *first* there is less chance for recombination within the base region. Hence the transport factor β, and also a, increase with an increase in magnitude of the collector junction voltage.

*Second* the charge gradient is increased with in the base and consequently, the current of minority carriers injected across the emitter junction increases.

As the Reverse bias collector junction voltage ($V_{CB}$) is increased, the effective base width w decreases.

## Punch through

The mechanism by which a transistor usefulness may be terminated as the collector voltage is increased is called *punch-through (or) reach-through,* and results from the increased width of the collector-junction transition region with increased collector-junction voltage (the early-effect).

The transition region at a junction is the region of uncovered charges on both sides of the junction at the positions occupied by the impurity atoms as the voltage applied across the junction increases, the transition region penetrates deeper into the collector and base. Because neutrality of charge must be maintained, the number of uncovered charges on each side remains equal. Since the doping of the base is ordinarily substantially smaller than that of collector, the penetration of transition region into the base is larger then into the collector. Since the base is very thin it is possible that, at moderated voltage, the transition region will have spread completely across the base to reach the emitter junction. At this point normal transition action ceases, since emitter and collector are effectively shorted.

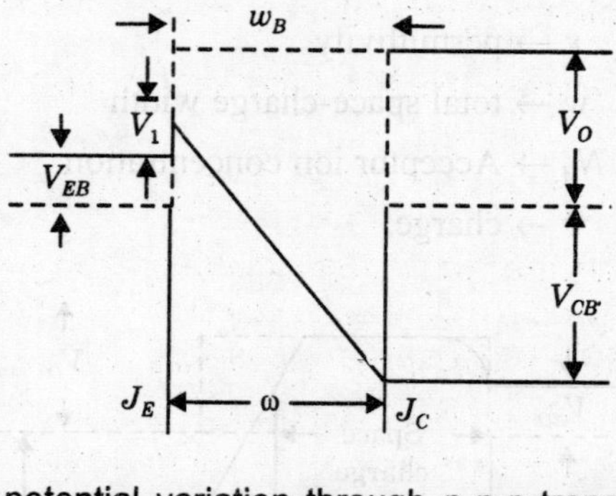


**Fig. 4.4(b)** The potential variation through *p-n-p* transistor after "reach-through" when the effective base width (fig. (a)) $W_{B'} = W_B - W$ has been reduced to zero. The effective emitter barrier is $V'$.

Combining the current components and Early effect ,we can conclude that the characteristics or behavior of the *BJT* is as following two equations.

Input voltage = *f*(Input current, output voltage)

Output current = *f*(Input current, output voltage)

For CB configuration $V_E = f(I_E + V_{CB})$

$$I = f(I_E + V_{CB})$$

## 4.3 BJT CHARACTERISTICS

A transistor can be used as a two-port network; an input port and an output port. *The output current is varied by the output voltage at constant input current. Similarly at constant output voltage the input current is varied by the input voltage.*

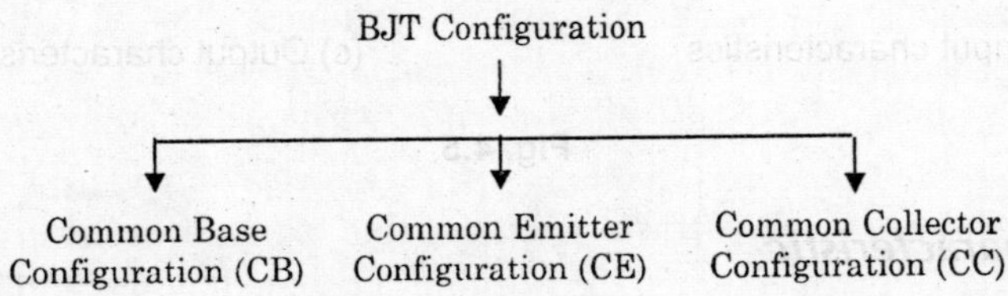


Now the input and output characteristics of a transistor in CB, CE and CC modes are discussed in detail.

### 1. Common Base (CB)

The configuration where the emitter is the input electrode and the base is common to both the input and output circuits, is called the common base (CB) configuration as shown in the circuit symbol in fig. 4.5(a) for an npn transistor. The circuit also shows the positive directions of electrode currents (conventional) and the positive directions of inter electrode voltages, $V_{EB}$ and $V_{CB}$ for normal operation of the device that is active region $V_{EB}$ is negative causing the emitter-base junction to be forward biased and $V_{CB}$ is positive so that the collector-base junction is reverse biased.

$V_{EE}$ or $V_{EN}$ $\rightarrow$ supply voltage

$V_{EB}$ $\rightarrow$ terminal voltage

$$V_{EB} = f(I_E, VCB)$$

$$I_C = f(I_E, VCB)$$

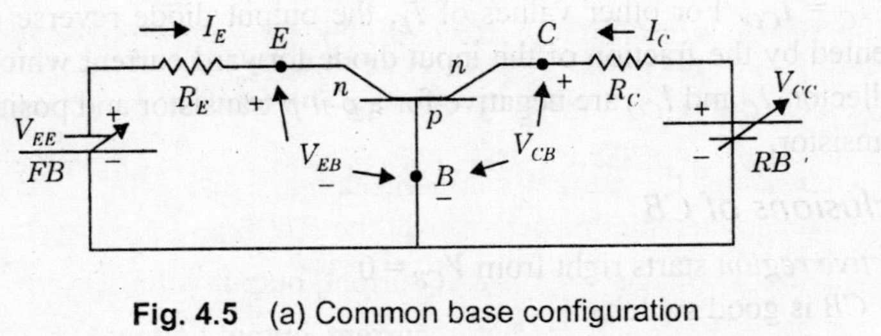


**Fig. 4.5** (a) Common base configuration

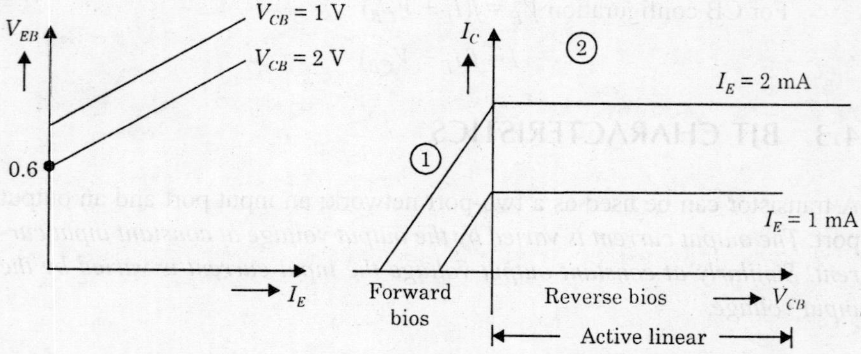


(b) input characteristics (c) Output characteristics

**Fig. 4.5**

### *Input characteristic*

The input Characteristics shown in fig. 4.5(b) are the forward characteristics of the emitter to base diode for various collector voltages. A noteworthy feature of the input characteristics of *CB* configuration is that there exists a cutin, offset or threshold voltage $V\gamma$ bellow which the emitter voltage is very small. In general, $V\gamma \cong 0.1$ for Ge $V\gamma \cong 0.5$ for Si. In the active region the input diode (emitter-to-base) is biased in forward direction.

An increase in magnitude of collector voltage will, by Early effect, cause the $I_E$ to increase, with $V_{BE}$ held constant. The curve with the collector open represents the characteristic of the forward biased emitter diode.

Take independent variable on *x*-axis. As $V_{CB}$ increases the curve comes down because of the early effect

$$R_{iCB} = \frac{\Delta V_{EB}}{\Delta I_E} \text{ is very small.}$$

In *CB* the input changes drastically with output voltage because of early effects and so much because input resistance is very low. Therefore loading effect should also be considered.

### *Output characteristics*

The output characteristics of *CB* configuration is shown in fig. 4.5(c). If $I_E = 0$, the $I_C = I_{CO}$. For other values of $I_E$, the output diode reverse current is augmented by the fraction of the input diode forward current which reaches the collector. $I_C$ and $I_{CO}$ are negative for a *p-n-p* transistor and positive for *p-n-p* transistor.

### *Conclusions of CB*

1. *Active region* starts right from $V_{CB} = 0$
   $\therefore$ *CB* is good switch.
2. *CB* has largest voltage gain because $R_i$ is very low

$$A_V = \frac{V_0}{V_i} = \frac{I_0 R_L}{I_i R_i} = A_I \frac{R_L}{R_i}$$

3. $R_L$ should be taking as very small otherwise voltage gain indefinitely increases and Bandwidth decreases

$$R_{LCB} < R_{LCE} < R_{LCC}$$

4. Current gain is the least that is $A_I \leq 1$, $\alpha = \frac{I_C}{I_B} \leq 1$

5. *Input resistance $R_i$ small and output resistance $R_o$ is high*
6. *CB* is used for radio frequency amplifiers because its upper cut off is very high

$$f_2 = \frac{1}{2\pi R_i C_i} \quad \therefore R_i \text{ is less, } f_2 \text{ is more}$$

*CB* is for radio frequency voltage amplifier
*CE* is of audio frequency voltage amplifier
7. *CB* is used of avoiding direct feed through in superhetrodyne receiver. Though *CB* is a very good switch , it is never used because of low input impedance.

## 2. Common Emitter (CE)

When a large current gain is required, *BJT* is used with the base as the input electrode and the emitter as the common node between the input and output circuits as shown in fig. 4.6. Such a configuration is called the *Common Emitter (CE)* configuration. This is the most important and frequently encountered transistor configuration because it is desirable to use the small base current rather than the large emitter current as the control quantity.

As we already know $IC = \left(\frac{\alpha}{1-\alpha}\right) I_B + \frac{I_{CBO}}{1-\alpha}$

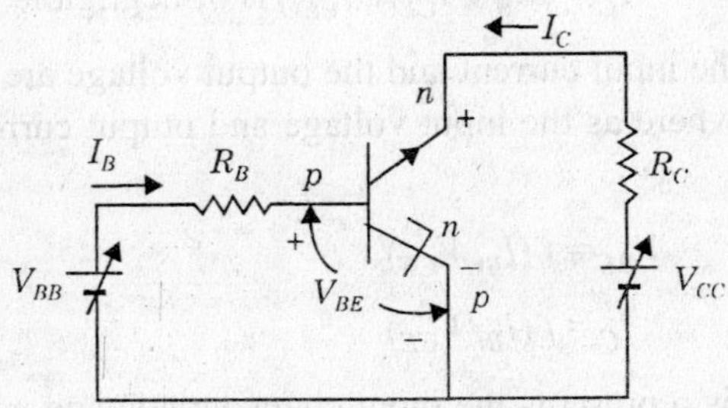


**Fig. 4.6** (a) Common emitter configuration

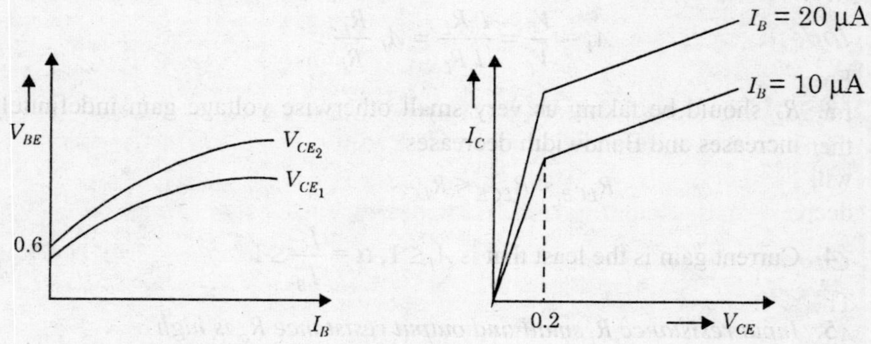


(b) Input characteristics (c) Output characteristics

**Fig. 4.6**

We define $\beta = \left(\frac{\alpha}{1-\alpha}\right)$ as the common emitter *dc* forward current gain of the transistor. The collector current then can be written as

$$I_C = \beta I_B + (1+\beta) I_{CBO}$$

As reverse saturation current $I_{CBO}$ is of negligible order

$$I_C \approx \beta I_B \text{ (or)} \beta = \frac{I_C}{I_B}$$

Also; if $I_B = 0$ $I_{CEO} = \frac{I_{CBO}}{1-\alpha} = (1+\beta) I_{CBO}$/

Where $I_{CEO}$ is the emitter collector current with the base open circuited that is collector cut-off current(*CE* configuration).

Collector current then can be written as

$$I_C = \beta I_B + I_{CEO};\ I_{CEO} \text{ is of negligible order.}$$

In the *CE*, the input current and the output voltage are taken as independent variables, where as the input voltage and output current are the dependent variables.

$$V_{BE} = f(I_B, V_{CE}) \qquad ...(1)$$

$$I_C = f(I_B, V_{CE}) \qquad ...(2)$$

Equation 1 is represents the input characteristic and equation 2 is represents the output characteristic for a fixed value of $I_B$ ,the collector current is not a very sensitive value of $V_{CE}$. The base current is much smaller than the emitter current.

### *Input characteristics*

From equation (1) $V_{BE}$ is a function of $I_B$ and $V_{CE}$, the fig. is plotted $V_{BE}$ vs $I_B$ for various values of collector to emitter voltage $V_{CE}$. If $V_{BE}$ becomes zero, then $I_B$ will be zero under these condition both emitter and collector junctions will be shot circuited. In general, increase $V_{CE}$ with constant $V_{BE}$ causes a decrease in base width and results in a decreasing recombination base current.

### *Output characteristics*

The common emitter output characteristic is the family of curves show in fig. 4.6 (c) in which $I_C$ vs $V_{CE}$ is plotted for varying values of $I_B$ while $I_B$ vs $V_{BE}$ is that of forward biased diode characteristic. From the graph of output characteristics, the output current $I_C$ increases with increase in $V_{CE}$ up to about 1v. Below this voltage, there is no increase in $I_C$, even though $V_{CE}$ is increased. The graph is almost horizontal and below which remains practically constant is termed as knee voltage.

The output current below the knee region is given as $I_C = \beta I_B$ where β = current gain. The output resistance of the transistor in the CE mode is quite high (about 50 kW).

Output characteristics of *CE* configuration is divided into three regions , as an active region, cut off region and saturation region. is plotted in figure. In *active region*: the collector junction is reverse biased, and emitter junction is forward biased. In this region the transistor output current responds most sensitively to an input signal. If a transistor is to be used as an amplifier ,it must be restricted to operate in this active region.

### *Conclusions*

$$R_{OCE} = \frac{\Delta V_{CE}}{\Delta I_{IC}} = \text{medium} = 10\ \text{k}\Omega$$

$$R_{iCE} = \frac{\Delta V_{BE}}{\Delta I_{IB}} = \text{medium} = 1\ \text{k}\Omega$$

1. $R_i = 1\text{k}\Omega$, $R_o = 10\ \text{k}\Omega$
2. Audio frequency voltage amplifier
3. Saturation approaches into active
4. Voltage gain is medium
5. Current gain is medium: β = 50/500

In *CC* Base collector is forward and emitter junction is reverse therefore *CC* always acts as an alternate and hence gain is ≤ 1.

## 3. Common Collector (CC)

When a transistor is operated in the common collector mode, base current $I_B$ is the input current, emitter current $I_E$ is the output current and $V_{CE}$ (collector-emitter voltage) is the output voltage. *CC* configuration is shown in fig. 4.7.

### *Input Characteristics*

Base current $I_B$ is varied by varying the input voltage $V_{CB}$ at constant output voltage $V_{CE}$. $V_{CE}$ changes and for this $V_{CE}$, $I_B$ and $V_{CB}$ are noted. From this the input characteristics are plotted fig. 4.7 (b) from the shape of the input characteristic it can be observed that CC configuration differs basically from $C_B$ and $C_E$ modes of operation. Since the levels of $V_{CE}$ is fixed, $V_{CB}$ cannot be varied over a wide range.

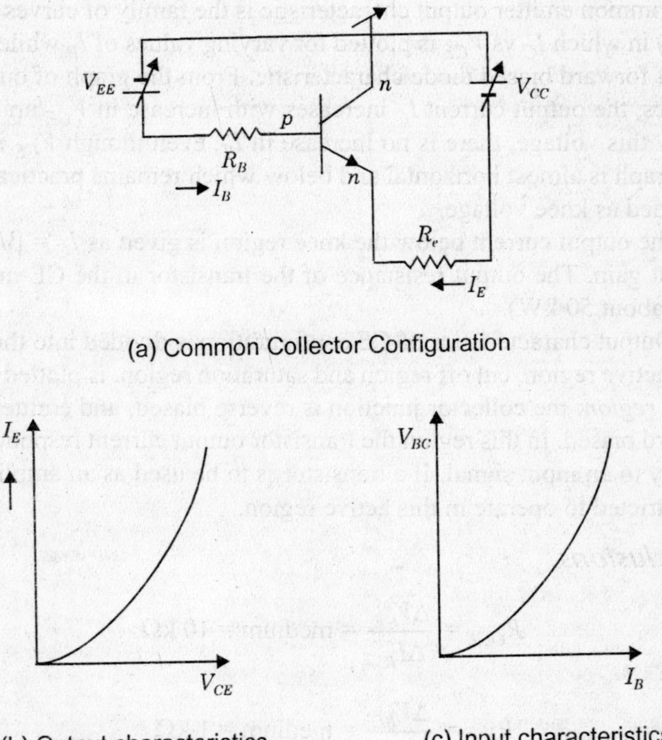


(a) Common Collector Configuration

(b) Output characteristics (c) Input characteristics

**Fig. 4.7**

### *Output Characteristics*

Now for the output characteristic, $I_B$ must be kept constant and $I_E$ is varied by varying $V_{CE}$. The family of curves is as shown in fig. 4.7(c). The output characteristic for the *CC* configuration is seen to be resemble that for *CE* configuration. This is so because $I_E$ and $I_C$ are almost equal.

Output: $I_E = f(I_B, V_{CE})$ $\quad R_{OCC} = \dfrac{\Delta V_{EC}}{\Delta F_C}$

Input : $V_{BC} = f(I_B, V_{CE})$ $\quad R_{ICC} = \dfrac{\Delta V_{BC}}{\Delta I_B}$ = very large.

## Conclusions for CB, CE and CC Configurations

### *1. Common base configuration*

(a) Active region starts from $V_{CB} = 0$,
$\therefore$ *CB* is the best configuration of switching but it is never used for switching because of its input impedance is very less. *CB*: $-\infty \le V_{CB} \le 0 \rightarrow$ saturation.

(b) Has largest voltage gain because of less input impedance.

$$A_o = \frac{V_o}{V_i} = \frac{I_o R_L}{I_i R_i} = A_1 = \frac{R_L}{R_i}$$

(c) $R_L$ should be taken as very small otherwise voltage gain indefinitely increases and Band width decreases

(d) Current gain is the least. that is $A_I \le 1$.

$$\alpha = \frac{I_C}{I_B} \le 1.$$

(e) $R_i$ is small and $R_O$ is high

(f) Is used in $R_F$ amplifier because of its upper cut off is very high.

$$f_2 = \frac{1}{2\pi R_i C_i}.$$

$\therefore$ $R_i$ is less, $f_2$ is more

(g) *CB* is used for avoiding direct feed through in superhetrodyne receiver.

*Applications:*

1. Used in $R_F$ amplifier.
2. Best unilateral amplifier for cascade amplifier.

### *2. Common emitter configuration*

(a) Active region starts from 0.2 $C_E$: $-\infty \le V_{CE} \le 0.2$ _______saturation.

(b) Voltage gain medium.

(c) Current gain is medium that is $\beta = \dfrac{I_C}{I_B}$: 50 – 500

(d) Saturation approaches into active.

*Application:* Audio frequency voltage amplifier.

### *3. Common collector configuration*

(a) $R_O$ is very small

(b) Current gain $\gamma = \dfrac{I_E}{I_B}$: 51 – 501

*Application:*
Impedance matching.
Comparison of *CB*, *CE* and *CC* parameters:

| *Parameter* | *CB* | *CE* | *CC* |
|---|---|---|---|
| 1. *DC* current gain | $\alpha = \frac{I_C}{I_E} < 1$ | $\beta = \frac{I_C}{I_B}$:50 to 500 | $\gamma = \frac{I_E}{I_B}$:51 to 501 $= 1 + \beta$ |
| 2. $R_i$ | Low: 10 Ω | 1.1 kΩ to 1 kΩ | High: 100 kΩ |
| 3. $R_o$ | High: 100 kΩ | 10 kΩ | 10 kΩ |
| 4. *AC* current gain | α | $\beta\ h_{fe} \leq \beta$ | γ |
| 5. *AC* Voltage gain | very large | medium | ≅ 1 |
| 6. Application | $R_F$ voltage amp | $A_f$ voltage amp | impedance matching |

## 4.4 OPERATION MODES

A BJT can operate in cut-off, active and saturation modes. If both the collector and emitter junction *are reverse biased, the transistor is in the cut-off mode.* If the *collector-base junction is reverse biased and the emitter-base junction forward biased, then the transistor is operating in the active region.* If *both the junctions are forward biased, the transistor is said to be in saturation.*

Operating modes of BJT are given in table below.

| | Junction bias | | |
|---|---|---|---|
| *Operating mode* | *Emitter-Base* | *Collector-Base* | *application* |
| Forward-active | Forward | Reverse | controlled current source; amplification |
| Cut-off | Reverse | Reverse | switch "OFF" |
| Saturation | Forward | Forward | switch "ON" |
| Reverse-active (inverted) | Reverse | Forward | attenuator |

From the above table, if the input is forward the transistor is either in *active or saturation* region. If the output voltage is minimum and has maximum output current then it is *saturation* whereas output voltage is maximum and with a minimum of output current it is *cut off.*

*Testing the region of operating is only to test the output junction.* The input junction forward biased is mainly of two, that is output Reverse biased in active and the other output forward biased in saturation and for this we define two methods of testing mainly active method and the other saturation method.

### *Testing method 1: Active*

Consider the CE configuration circuit shown fig. 4.8 (a).

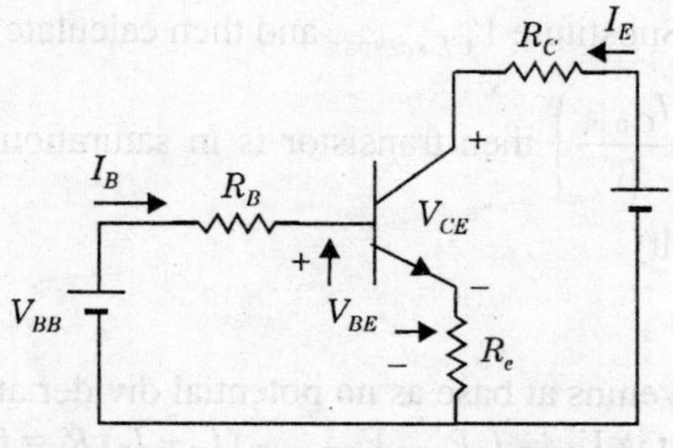


**Fig. 4.8** (a) Testing the operation mode of CE configuration. (Method 1)

*Steps to follow through:*

$S_1$: Apply Thevenins theorem if required at the base that is input.

$S_2$: Apply Kirchoff's voltage law (KVL) to the input.

$S_3$: Substitute $V_{BE}$ active = 0.7 in case of silicon ,
= 0.2 in case of Germanium and then solve for
$I_B$ and $I_C$ $I_C = \beta\ (I_B)$

$S_4$: Apply again Kirchoff's voltage law now to the output and substitute $I_C$ and $I_B$ then solve for $V_{CB}$.

**Verification (check)**

If $V_{CB}$ is positive given to n leads to reverse bias it is in active region.

If $V_{CB}$ is negative given to n leads to forward bias it is in saturation region.

## *Method 2: Saturation*

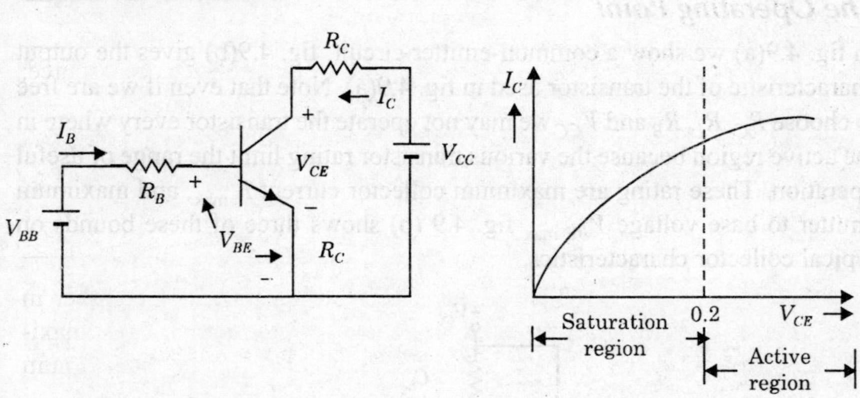


(a) (b)

**Fig. 4.8.2** (a) Testing the operation mode of CE configuration (Method 2)
(b) Output Characteristics of the transistor.

*Steps to follow through:*

$S_1$: Apply Thevenins at the input if required

$S_2$: *KVL* to input and the substitute $V_{BE\ sat} = 0.8$ and get $I_B$

$S_3$: *KVL* to output, Substitute $V_{CE\,sat/max}$ and then calculate $I_{C\,min}$.

$S_4$: check if $I_B > \left(\frac{I_{C\,min}}{\beta}\right)$ then transistor is in saturation otherwise it is active (by default)

**Check (Verification)**

$S_1$: No need of Thevenins at base as no potential divider at base

$S_2$: *KVL* to input that is $V_{BB} - I_B R_B - V_{BE\,sat} - (I_C + I_B) R_e = 0$ where $I_C = \beta I_B$

$S_3$: $V_{CC} - I_C R_C - V_{CE} - (I_C + I_B) R_e = 0$ for $V_{CE\,sat} = 0.2$. $I_C = \frac{V_C - V_{CE\,sat}}{R_C}$ then $I_{c\,min} = \frac{12 - 0.2}{R_C}$ check for $I_B > \frac{I_{c\,min}}{\beta}$. The saturation and active regions are plotted below. The voltage ratings for both Germanium and silicon are listed in table below.

| | *Max* $V_{BE}$ *cut off* | $V_{BE}$ *cutin* | $V_{BE}$ *active* | $V_{BE}$ *sat* | $V_{CE}$ *sat.max* |
|---|---|---|---|---|---|
| Ge | − 0.1 | 0.1 | 0.2 | 0.3 | 0.1 |
| Si | 0.0 | 0.6 | 0.7 | 0.8 | 0.2 |

- This is for an npn transistor at room temperature of npn about 300°k. For pnp transistor the operation is charge of sign that is the opposite sign.

## The Operating Point

In fig. 4.9(a) we show a common-emitter circuit, fig. 4.9(b) gives the output characteristic of the transistor used in fig. 4.9(a). Note that even if we are free to choose $R_C$, $R_L$, $R_B$ and $V_{CC}$ we may not operate the transistor every where in the active region because the various transistor rating limit the range of useful operation. These rating are maximum collector current $I_{c\,max}$, and maximum emitter to base voltage $V_{BE\,max}$ fig. 4.9 (b) shows three of these bounds on typical collector characteristics.

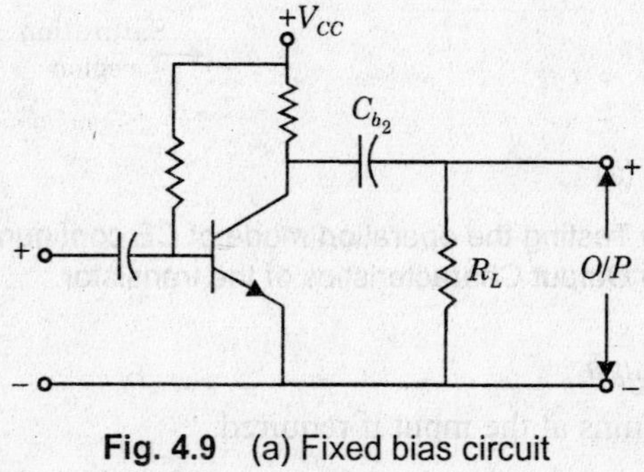


**Fig. 4.9** (a) Fixed bias circuit

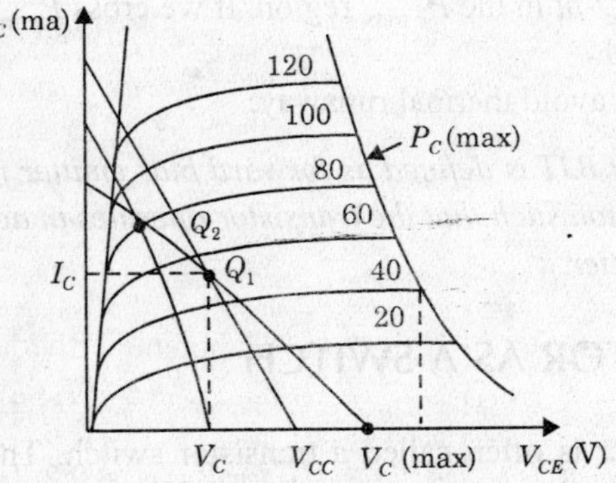


**Fig. 4.9** (b) Characteristics of CE and representation of AC and DC load lines.

## Transistor biasing and Thermal Stabilization

*"It is defined as forward biasing input junction and reverse biasing output junction such that transistor operates in active region, so to act as an amplifier".*

### *Condition for biasing for faithful amplifier*

1. $V_{BE}$ should be $\geq$ 0.7 for *Si* / $\geq$ 0.2 for Ge } to ensure active region.
2. $i_C \leq I_C$ to avoid negative clipping.

   small signal collector current $\leq$ zero signal collector current.

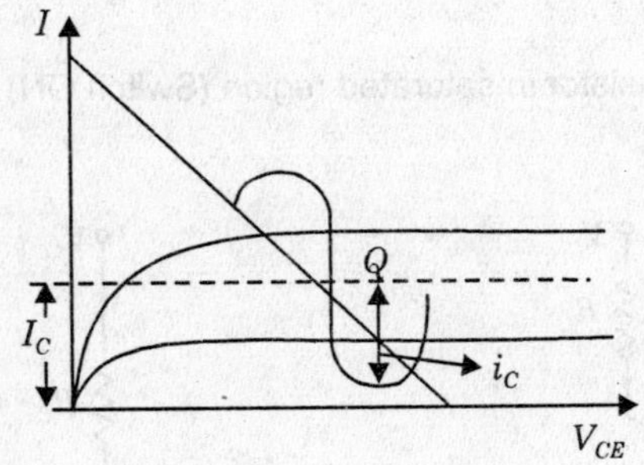


**Fig. 4.10**

3. $I_c \leq \dfrac{V_{CC}}{2(R_c + R_e)}$ to stabilize the *Q* point (to ensure thermal stability)
4. $V_{CE} \geq$ 1v for $S_i$ / $\geq$ 0.5v for Ge } to ensure potential difference at collector

5. Never choose *Q-pt* in the $P_{c\,max}$ region, if we cross $P_{c\,max}$, transistor will become spoiled.
6. $V_{CE} \le V_{CC}/2$ to avoid thermal runaway.

**Biasing:** *Biasing of BJT is defined as forward bias emitter junction, Reverse bias collector junction such that the transistor operates in active region so as to acts as an amplifier.*

## 4.5 TRANSISTOR AS A SWITCH

A transistor inverter is often called a transistor switch. This is appropriate because the ON and OFF states of the transistor correspond closely to the closing and opening of a switch connected between the collector and emitter. When the transistor is ON, or saturated, the voltage between collector and emitter is nearly zero, as it would be across a closed switch, and the current is the maximum possible, $V_{CC}/R_c$.

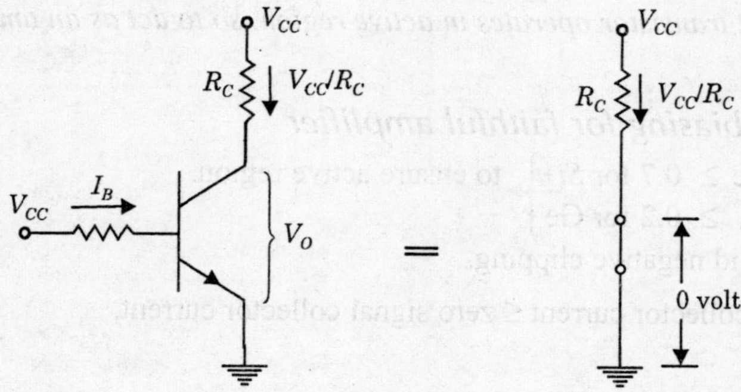


**Fig. 4.11** (a) Transistor in saturated region (Switch ON) closed circuit,

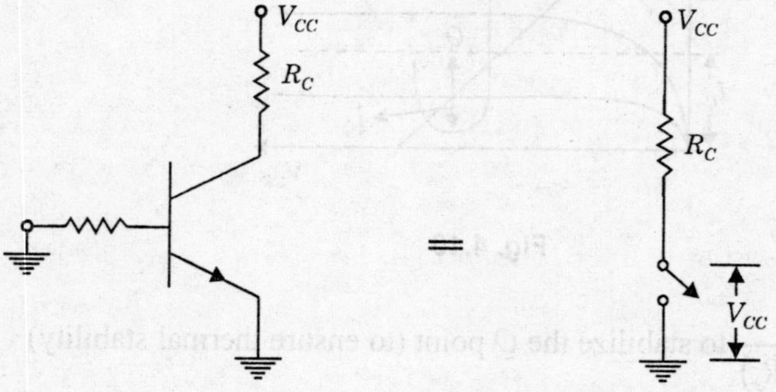


**Fig. 4.11** (b) Transistor in cut off region (Switch OFF) open circuit

When the transistor is OFF, zero current flows from collector to emitter and the voltage is maximum, as it would be across an open switch. The switch is opened or closed by the input voltage a high input closes it and a low input open it. The transistor as a voltage-controlled switch. A high input closes the switch and a low input opens it.

### *Switching action of a transistor*

The circuit in fig. 4.11 (a) shows the use of BJT as a switch. Assume that the input voltage has the waveform as in fig. 4.11 (b). When the supply voltage $V_s = -V_1$, the emitter base diode is reverse biased. The BJT is cut-off and no current exists any where in the circuit. Similarly, when $V_0 = V_{CC}$ and $I_C = 0$ refers to an open switch. Now when $V_S = V_2$, the transistor is driven into saturation that $V_o$= 0.2V and $I_C$ is large this refers to a closed switch. The output waveform is shown in fig. 4.11 (c). Testing the region of operation

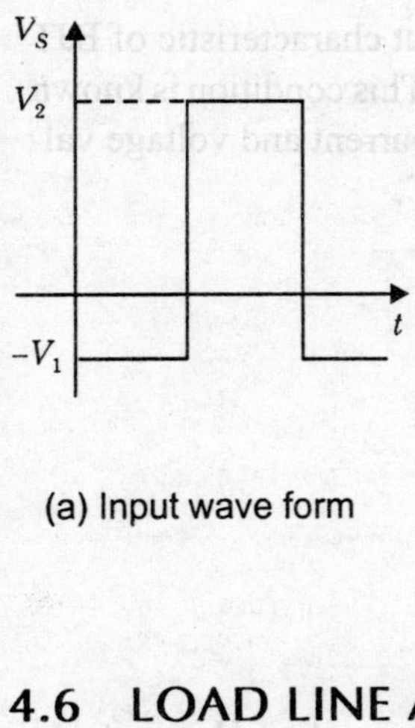


(a) Input wave form

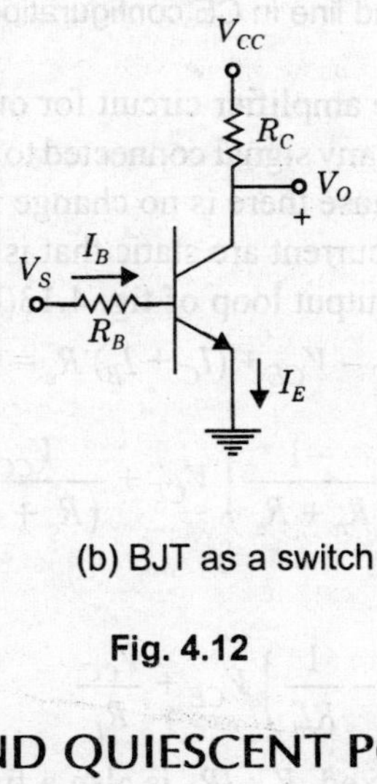


(b) BJT as a switch

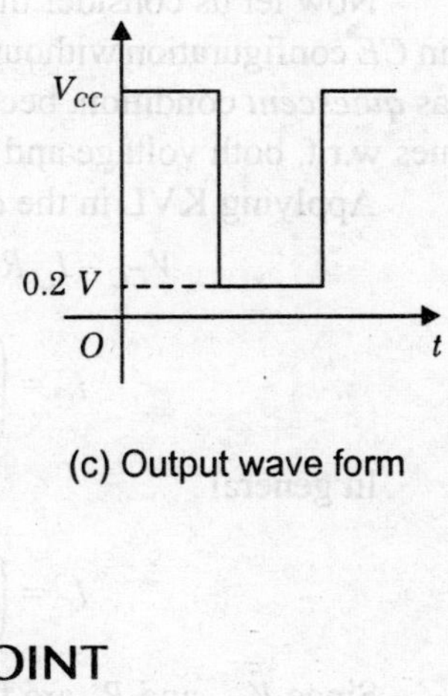


(c) Output wave form

**Fig. 4.12**

## 4.6 LOAD LINE AND QUIESCENT POINT

In order to develop a useful output, the BJT must have a load resistance. The distribution of the DC voltage $V_{CC}$ across the load resistance and across the transistor can be obtained graphically by plotting the DC load line on the output V-I characteristics of the BJT as indicated in fig. 4.13 (a).

The output characteristics can't give the direct relation between output voltage and output current. Therefore, we need a DC load line which is a straight line on the output characteristics with a DC slope such that there would be direct relation between output voltage and output current.

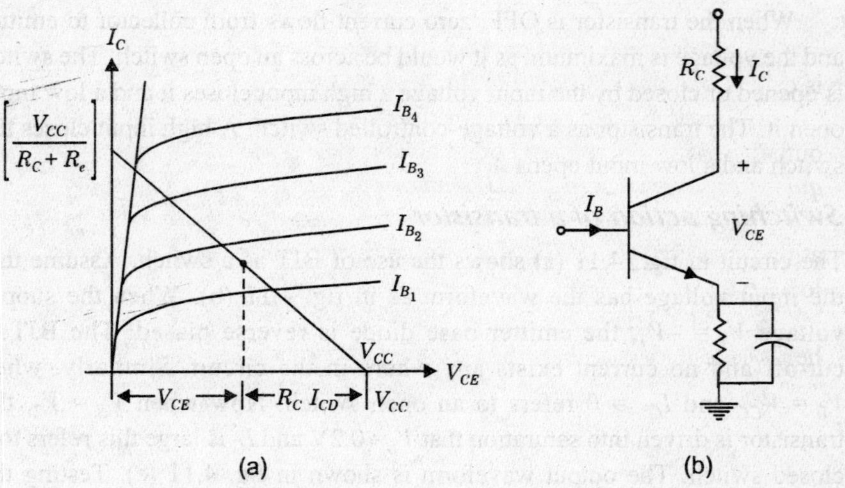


**Fig. 4.13** (a) Representation opf D.C (b) Representation of CE configuration load line in CE configuration

Now let us consider the amplifier circuit for output characteristic of BJT in *CE* configuration without any signal connected to it. This condition is known as *quiescent* condition, because there is no change in current and voltage values w.r.t. both voltage and current are static that is DC.

Applying KVL in the output loop of fig. 4.13(b)

$$V_{CC} - I_C R_C - V_{CE} + (I_C + I_B) R_e = 0$$

$$I_C = \left(\frac{-1}{R_c + R_e}\right) V_{CE} + \frac{V_{CC}}{(R_c + R_e)}$$

In general

$$I_C = \left(-\frac{1}{RL}\right) V_{CE} + \frac{V_{CC}}{R_L}$$

Since $V_{CC}$ and $R_L$ are fixed, $V_{CC}/R_L$ is also a fixed quantity. Hence it can be simplified as an equation of a straight line and is also know as load line also.

That is $y = mx + c$ where $y = I_C$, $x = V_{CE}$

$M = \dfrac{-1}{R_L}$ = slope of the line $C$ = intercept at *Y*-axis

The load line can be plotted on the static V-I characteristics shown in fig. 4.13 (a) obtaining the intercepts on both current (*Y*-axis) and voltage (*x*-axis) axes as:

1. for $I_C = 0$, $V_{CE} = V_{CC}$ this is a point on the *X*-axis
2. for $V_{CE} = 0$, $I_C = V_{CC}/R_L = \dfrac{V_{CC}}{(R_c + R_e)}$

This indicates a point on the y-axis. Combining these two points by a line is called load line as shown in fig. 4.13 (a).

Assume DC load line gives a direct relation between output voltage and output current. Therefore $Q$ point always lies as the DC load line. The *'Q' is quiescent point or zero signal point or operating point.*

Zero point means operating signal frequency is zero so therefore the operating point is $Q$ ($V_{CE}$, $IC$). Now we come to another load line that is the AC load line.

A.C. load line also passes through the *Q-point* but with AC slope which helps us to understand the AC. swing without distortion.

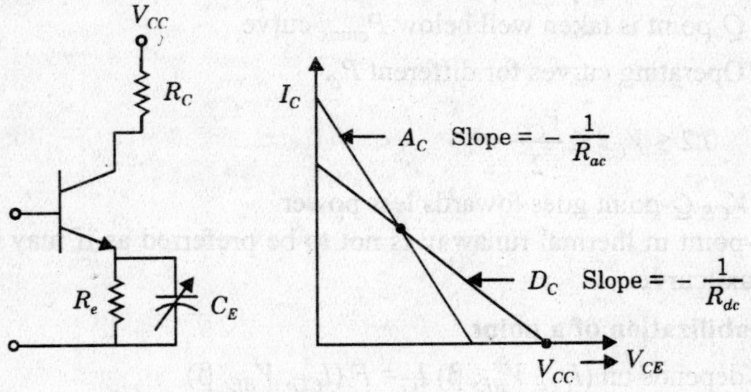


**Fig. 4.14** Representation of AC load line

To provide a short circuit even for audio frequency the capacitor should be large enough about $\mu F$. $X_{ce} = \dfrac{1}{2\pi f_c}$ where $f$ is the audio frequency. $C$ is the capacitor that should be large enough to make $X_c$ to zero.

$$\text{DC Slope} = -\left(\frac{1}{R_c + R_e}\right)$$

$$\therefore \quad R_{ac} = R_c$$

$$\text{AC slope} = -\frac{-1}{R_{QC}}$$

$\therefore$ AC slope $= \left(\dfrac{-1}{R_C}\right)$. AC slope is lesser than DC slope, in this the capacitor has very low impedance, so $R_L$ comes in parallel with the collector resistance $R_C$.

1. **Quiescent Point Produce:** The operating point shifts with changes in temperature $T$, because of transistor parameters ($\beta$, $I_{CO}$, $V_{BE}$) are functions

of $T$. A criterion is established for comparing the stability of different biasing circuits. Compensation techniques are also presented for quiescent point stabilization.

2. **Steps to be followed to calculate Q-point**

$S_1$ : Apply Thevenins at input if required

$S_2$ : $KVL$ to support

$S_3$ : substitute $V_{BE} = 0.7$(Ge) or 0.2 (Si) and get $I_B$ and then $I_C$

$S_4$ : $KVL$ to output

$S_5$ : substitute $I_C$ and $I_B$ then solve for $V_{CE}$. $Q$ ($V_{CE}$, $I_C$).

3. **Location of Q-point**

1. $Q$-point is taken well below $P_{cmax}$ curve
2. Operating curves for different $P_c$.

$$0.2 \leq V_{CE} \leq \frac{V_{CC}}{2}$$

if $V_{CE}$ $Q$-point goes towards less power.

$Q$-point in thermal runaway is not to be preferred as if may goes to $Pc$ max. curve.

4. **Stabilization of a point**

$I_C$ depends on ($I_{CO}$, $V_{BE}$, β) $I_C = F$ ($I_{CO}$, $V_{BE}$, β)

By applying taylor's series to the above equation,

$$\Delta I_C = \frac{\partial I_C}{\partial I_{CO}} \Delta I_{CO} + \frac{\partial I_C}{\partial I_{BE}} + \frac{\partial I_C}{\partial F} \Delta\beta - 1/2\, \frac{\partial^2 I_C}{\partial I_{CO}^2} (\Delta I_{CO})^2$$

higher order terms are neglected as change is small

$$\therefore \quad \Delta I_C = S\Delta I_{CO} + S'\Delta V_{BE} + S''\,\Delta\beta$$

In reality there are instability factors because they were defined w.r.t change, but they are used stability of it. So they are called stability factors.

$$S = \frac{\Delta I_C}{\Delta I_{CO}}\ |V_{BE} \rightarrow \beta \text{ constant} = \frac{\partial I_C}{\partial I_{CO}}$$

$$I_C = \beta I_B + (1+\beta)\, I_{CO}$$

Partially differentiate w.r.t $I_C$

$$1 = \beta \frac{\partial I_B}{\partial I_C} + (1+\beta)\frac{\partial I_{CO}}{\partial I_C}$$

$$\therefore \quad S = \frac{1+\beta}{1-\beta\left(\dfrac{\partial I_B}{\partial I_C}\right)}$$

**5. Steps to be followed to calculate S**

$S_1$ : Apply Thevenins at the base that is at the input if required.

$S_2$ : Apply *KVL* to input that is to support and get $\frac{\partial I_B}{\partial I_C}$.

## 4.7 THERMAL STABILITY

We know, the collector current for the *CE* circuit is $I_C = \beta I_B + (1 + \beta) I_{CO}$. Here β, $I_B$, and $I_{CO}$ increases with increase in temperature. In particular, the reverse saturation current or leakage current $I_{CO}$ changes greatly with temperature. Specifically, it doubles for every 10° C rise in temperature. The $I_C$ causes the collector base junction temperature to rise which, in turn, increase $I_{CO}$, as a result $I_C$ will increase still further, which will further rise the temperature at the collector base junction. This process will become cumulative leading to "*thermal runaway*".

1. Power dissipated from collected $P_D$:

   $(T_J - T_A) \propto P_D$

   where $T_j$: Junction temperature. $T_A$: Ambient/room temperature

   Proportionality constant Θ is called thermal resistance °C/watt

   $$(T_J - T_A) = \Theta P_D$$

   Partial differentiation .w.r.t, $T_j$

   $$1 - 0 = \frac{\Theta \partial P_D}{\partial T_j}$$

   $$\frac{\partial P_D}{\partial T_j} = \frac{1}{\Theta} \qquad \text{...(1)}$$

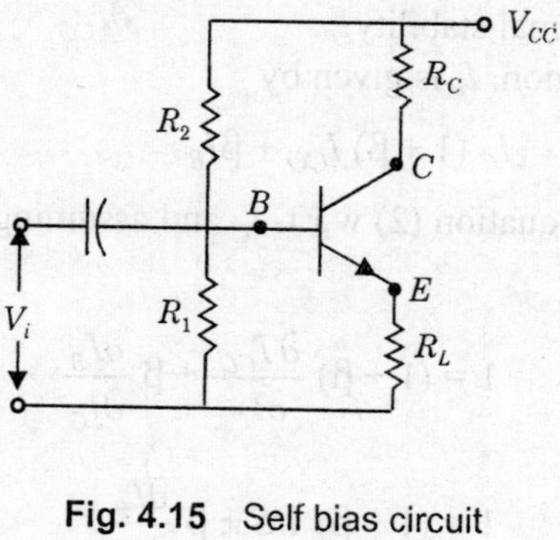


**Fig. 4.15** Self bias circuit

2. Power collected at the collector $P_C$

$$P_C = I_C V_{CB} \cong I_C V_{CE}$$

Applying *KVL* to the output loop of the self bias circuit in fig 4.15

$$V_{CC} - I_C R_C - V_{CE} - I_C R_e = 0$$

$$V_{CE} = V_{CC} - I_c (R_c + R_e)$$

$$P_c = V_{CC} I_C - Ic^2 (R_C + R_e)$$

$$\frac{\partial P_c}{\partial T_j} = \left(\frac{\partial P_c}{\partial T_c}\right)\left(\frac{\partial I_{co}}{\partial I_{co}}\right)\left(\frac{\partial I_{co}}{\partial T_J}\right)$$

$$= \{V_{CC} - 2I_C (R_C + R_e)\} \{S\} \{0.07 I_{CO}\} \leq \frac{1}{\Theta}$$

In order to satisfy the above condition $\{V_{CC} - 2I_C (R_C + R_e)\}$ should be negative

$$I_C \geq \frac{V_{CC}}{2(R_C + R_e)} \quad \text{...(4)}$$

Eq. (3) is Exact condition for thermal stability whereas equation (4) is a simplified condition

## 4.8 VARIATION OF COLLECTOR CURRENT

### *1. Stability factor S*

The stability factor of a circuit is defined as the ratio of change of collector current to the change in collector-base leakage current:

$$\frac{\partial I_C}{\partial I_{CO}} = \frac{\Delta I_C}{\Delta I_{CO}} \quad \text{...(1)}$$

The above equation is the mathematical representation. Smaller the value of $S$ better is the thermal stability...

In the Active region, $I_c$ is given by

$$I_C (1 + \beta) I_{CO} + \beta I_B \quad \text{...(2)}$$

Differentiating equation (2) w.r.t. $I_C$ and assuming β to be constant with *IC*, we get

$$1 = (1 + \beta) \frac{\partial I_{CO}}{\partial I_C} + \beta \frac{\partial I_B}{\partial I_C} \quad \text{...(3)}$$

or

$$1 = (1 + \beta) 1/S + \beta \frac{\partial I_B}{\partial I_C} \quad \text{...(4)}$$

Hence $$S = \frac{1+\beta}{1-\beta\dfrac{\partial I_B}{\partial I_C}} \quad ...(5)$$

The value of differential $\dfrac{\partial I_B}{\partial I_C}$ depends on the method of biasing circuit.

## *2. Biasing and Stabilization*

$$I_C = f(I_{CO}, V_{BE}, \beta)$$

As temperature increases the following happens: (1) $I_{CO2} = I_{CO1} \times 2 \times \dfrac{t_2 - t_1}{10}$

(3) $V_{BE} = -2.3$ mv/°c (4) β doubles ⟶ 100°C → $S_i$
⟶ 50°C → $G_e$

*Note*: $I_{CO}$ doubles approximately every 10°C and $V_{BE}$ decreases by approximately 2.5 mV/°C. The effect due to $V_{BE}$ and β almost called in efficiency the $I_C$.

∴ *S* is very important factor, $S = \dfrac{\partial I_c}{\partial I_{co}}$

## 4.9 DIFFERENT BIASING CIRCUITS

### Different Biasing Methods

Various possible Methods are as given below:

(i) Two battery bias
(ii) fixed bias
(iii) Emitter bias
(iv) collector-to-base bias
(v) self bias.

There are additional biasing circuits.

### Requirements of Biasing Circuits

1. Single battery to bias both junctions.
2. Negative feedback for AC to stabilize the Q-point.
3. Easy way of reducing loss of AC gain
   ∴ we want negative feed back for DC not for AC
4. Slow variation of *Q*-point:
   (a) *Do not touch the load, if so gain may be disturbed.*
   (b) *Do not touch feedback resistance if zero amount of stability disturbed.*
   (c) *Do not vary large value of resistance at input.*

5. Simple. If we vary $R_B$ which vary β and $I_C = \beta I$ so $Q$ varies fastly. It must be coated that:
   - *In the active region, emitter-base junction is forward biased, and collector-base is reverse biased.*
   - In the saturation region, both junctions are forward biased.
   - In the cut-off region, both junctions are reverse biased.

   Different types of biasing circuits by using biasing methods are discussed below

### *1. Two-battery Biasing Circuit*

The bias arrangement is shown in fig. 4.16 is general biasing circuit.

Applying *KVL* to the input we get

$$V_{BB} - I_B R_B - V_{BE} = 0$$

$$\therefore \qquad I_B = \frac{V_{BB} - V_{BE}}{R_B}$$

Now Apply *KVL* to the output

$$V_{CC} - I_O R_C - V_{CE} = 0$$

$$\therefore \qquad I_C = \frac{V_{CC} - V_{CE}}{R_B}$$

$$\therefore \qquad \frac{\Delta I_B}{\Delta I_C} = 0$$

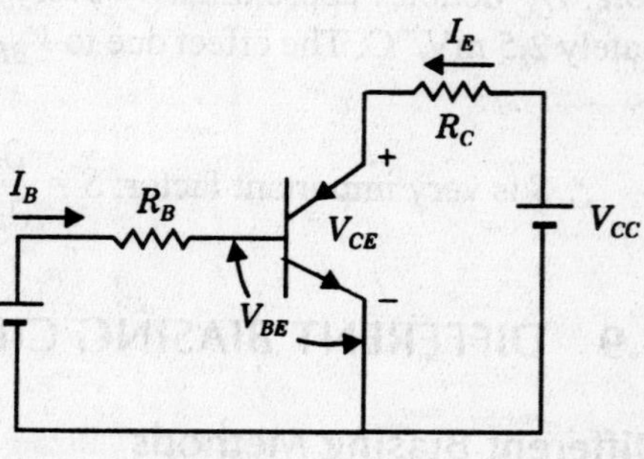


**Fig. 4.16** General biasing circuit

$$S = \frac{1+\beta}{1 - \left(\dfrac{\Delta I_B}{\Delta I_C}\right)}$$

Hence $\qquad S = 1 + \beta$

Stability factor $S'$: The variation of $I_C$ with $V_{BE}$ is given by the stability factor $s^1$ defined by $S' = \dfrac{\partial I_C}{\partial V_{BE}} \cong \dfrac{\Delta I_C}{\Delta V_{BE}}$ at fixed $I_{CBO}$ and β

Since $\qquad I_C = \beta\left(\dfrac{V_{BB} - V_{BE}}{R_E}\right)$

change in $I_C$ w.r.t change in β is $\dfrac{\Delta I_C}{\Delta \beta} = \dfrac{V_{BB} - V_{BE}}{R_E}$

$$\therefore \qquad S'' = \frac{V_{BB} - V_{BE}}{R_E}$$

*Advantage:* we can reduce loss of gain easily.

*Disadvantages:* two batteries are used to bias both junctions.

## 2. Fixed Bias Circuit

The bias arrangement shown in fig. 4.17 is known as fixed current bias or base resistor biasing circuit. The base current $I_B$ is fixed by the bias voltage $V_{CC}$ and the resistor $R_B$. The circuit is a *CE* amplifier using fixed bias with only one battery $V_{CC}$. Apply *KVL* to the base emitter loop that is to input.

$$V_{CC} - I_B R_B - V_{BE} = 0$$

$$\therefore \quad I_B = \frac{V_{BB} - V_{BE}}{R_B} \quad \text{...(1)}$$

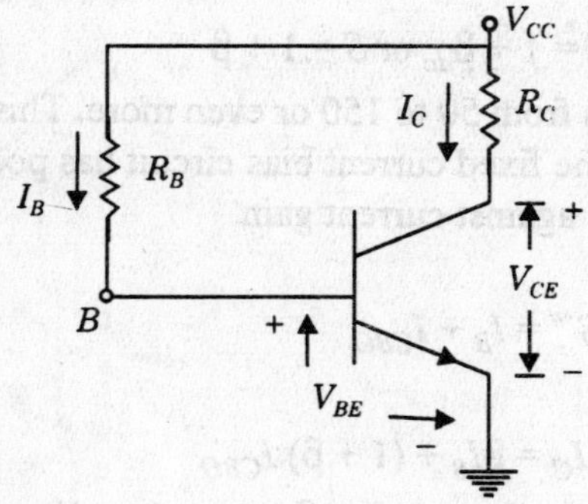


**Fig. 4.17** Fixed Bias Circuit

As $V_{CC}$, $V_{BE}$ and $R_B$ are constant quantities, $I_B$ remains fixed at a particular level. In this circuit $I_B$ is not affected by the transistor value. For a fixed value of $R_B$, the base current $I_B$ remains fixed in magnitude. Resistance $R_B$ is selected to obtain in the desired level of $I_B$.

Collector current $I_C$ is given as

$$I_C = \beta_{dc} I_B \quad \text{...(2)}$$

where $\beta_{dc}$ is the current gain in the active region. Biasing supply is normally fixed because variable supply is costly. (for clearance, if an equation contains $V_{BE}$ that is called input *KVL* and $V_{CE}$ its output *KVL*)

Now Apply $K_{VL}$ to output:

$$V_{CC} - I_C R_C - V_{CE} = 0$$

$$V_{CE} = V_{CC} - I_C R_C \quad \text{...(3)}$$

From the above all expressions for $I_B$, $I_C$ and $V_{CE}$, the data necessary for plotting the *Q*-point and drawing the load line is computed.

Cut-off point = $(V_{CC}, 0)$ $V_{CE} = V_{CC}$ for $I_C = 0$, and saturation point = $(0, V_{CC}/R)$ for $V_{CE} = 0$.

$\therefore$ The coordinates of *Q*-point are $(V_{CE}, I_C)$.

**Stability factor *S*, for fixed Bias:** For the fixed bias configuration as mentioned earlier, we have: $I_B = \frac{V_{CC} - V_{BE}}{R_B}$. When $I_B$ changes by a small amount $\Delta I_B$ as $V_{CC}$ and $V_{BE}$ are constant and are not affected by any change in $I_B$ and also as $I_C$ is not in the equation,

$$\frac{\Delta I_B}{\Delta_c} = 0 \quad ...(4)$$

(i) As $S(I_{CBO})$ or $S = \frac{1 + \beta_{dc}}{1 - \beta_{dc}\left(\frac{\Delta I_B}{\Delta I_C}\right)}$ substituting (4) in $S$ we get

$$S = 1 + \beta_{dc} \text{ or } S = 1 + \beta$$

In practice β ranges from 50 to 150 or even more. This gives a value of $S$ from 51 to 151. Thus, the fixed current bias circuit has poor thermal stability as well as poor stability against current gain.

For fixed bias ckt;

$$S'' = I_B + I_{CBO}$$

As, we have:

$$I_C = \beta I_B + (1 + \beta) I_{CBO}$$

Let β change by a small amount, Δβ at constant $V_{BE}$ and $I_{CBO}$. It is clear that $I_B$ remains constant, $I_C$ changes by a small amount $\Delta I_C$.

$$\therefore \quad \Delta I_C = (\Delta \beta) I_B + I_{CBO} + (\Delta\beta) I_{CBO}$$

or

$$\frac{\Delta I_C}{\Delta \beta} = I_B + I_{CBO}.$$

where $I_{CBO}$ become zero, since it is not affected by the changes in β. If $I_{CBO}$ is neglected, we have

$$S'' = I_B.$$

or

$$S'' = \frac{V_{CC} - V_{BE}}{R_B}$$

from this expression also, it is obvious that, for a fixed bias circuit to be stable, $R_B$ must be quite large.

### 3. Fixed Bias with Emitter Resistor

Applying *KVL* to input $V_{CC} - R_B I_B - V_{BE} - R_E(I_C + I_B) = 0 \quad ...(1)$

$$I_B = \frac{V_{CC} - V_{BE} - I_C R_E}{R_B + R_E}$$

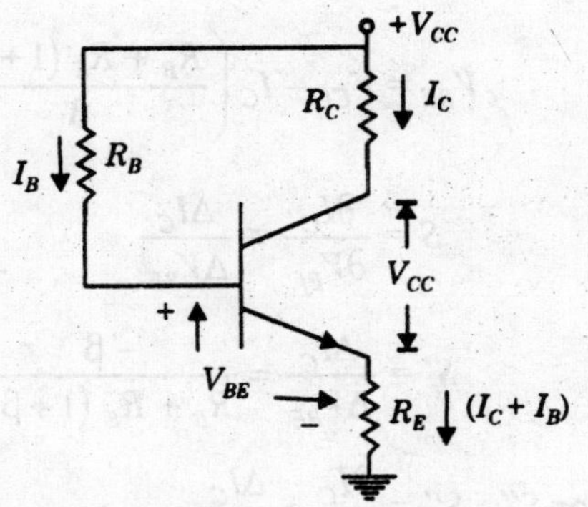


**Fig. 4.18** Fixed Bias with Emitter Resistor

Applying *KVL* to output $V_{CC} - R_C I_C - V_{CE} - R_E(I_C + I_B) = 0$ ...(2)

$$I_C = \frac{V_{CC} - V_{BE} - I_B R_E}{R_C + R_E}$$

$$V_{CC} = I_C R_E + (R_B + R_E) + V_{BE}.$$

When $I_{CBO}$ change by $\Delta$, $\Delta I_{CBO}$, $I_B$ changes by $\Delta I_B$ and $I_C$ changes by $\Delta I_C$. There is no effect upon $V_{CC}$ and $V_{BE}$ then the equation becomes

$$0 = \Delta I_C R_e + \Delta I_B (R_B + R_E)$$

$$-\Delta I_C R_e = \Delta I_B (R_B + R_E)$$

$$\frac{\Delta I_B}{\Delta I_C} = \frac{-R_E}{R_B + R_E}$$

$$S = \frac{1+\beta}{1-\beta\left(\dfrac{\Delta I_B}{\Delta I_C}\right)}$$

$$S = \frac{1+\beta}{1+\beta\left(\dfrac{R_E}{R_B + R_E}\right)}$$

$$S' = \frac{\partial I_C}{\partial V_{BC}} = \frac{\Delta I_C}{\Delta V_{BE}}$$

From equation (1)

$$V_{CC} - R_B I_B - V_{BE} - R_E(I_C + I_B) = 0$$

$$V_{CC} - R_B.(I_C/\beta) - V_{BE} - R_E.I_C - R_E.(I_C/\beta) = 0$$

$$V_{BE} = V_{CC} - I_C\left(\frac{R_B}{\beta} + R_E + \frac{R_E}{\beta}\right)$$

$$V_{BE} = V_{CC} - I_C\left(\frac{R_B + R_E\,(1+\beta)}{\beta}\right)$$

$$S = \frac{\partial I_C}{\partial V_{Bf}} = \frac{\Delta I_C}{\Delta V_{BE}}$$

$$S' = \frac{\Delta I_C}{\Delta V_{BE}} = \frac{-\beta}{R_B + R_E\,(1+\beta)}.$$

Stability factor $S''$ : $S'' = \dfrac{\partial I_C}{\partial \beta} \approx \dfrac{\Delta I_C}{\Delta \beta}$

From equation (1) $\quad I_B = \dfrac{V_{CC} - V_{BE} - I_C R_E}{R_B + R_E}$

$$I_C/\beta\,(R_B + R_E) = V_{CC} - V_{BE} - I_C R_E$$

$$I_C\left[\frac{R_B + R_E}{\beta} + R_E\right] = V_{CC} - V_{BE}$$

$$I_C/\beta = \frac{1}{R_B + R_E} \quad \therefore S'' = \frac{1}{R_B + R_E}$$

For any value of $S > 10$, the circuit may be considered as thermally not stable.

Hence the fixed-bias circuit is very sensitive to changes of $I_{CBO}$. Fixed bias is worst kind of biasing, as it can't compensate or causal variations.

*Advantages:*

1. Single battery.
2. No need of reducing loss of gain.

*Disadvantages:*

1. No feed back

### 4. Collector-to-base Bias

This bias configuration is a remedy over the fixed current bias current studied earlier. The below fig. 4.19 gives the circuit of a *CE* amplifier with collector-to-base bias. In this circuit, the base resistor $R_B$ is connected to the collector of the transistor. This gives the circuit design a little more complicated, but improves the DC bias stability. To know clearly how the bias stability is improved, observe that the voltage across $R_B$ is dependent upon $V_{CE}$. If $I_C$ becomes larger than the design value, it causes an increased voltage drop across $R_C$.

This results in a smaller level of $V_{CE}$, which in turn causes $I_B$ to be smaller than its design level. But since $I_C \cong \beta\, I_B$, $I_C$ will also tend to be reduced. Thus, an increase in $I_C$ produces a feedback effect, which tends to return $I_C$ towards its original level. From fig. 4.19 then.

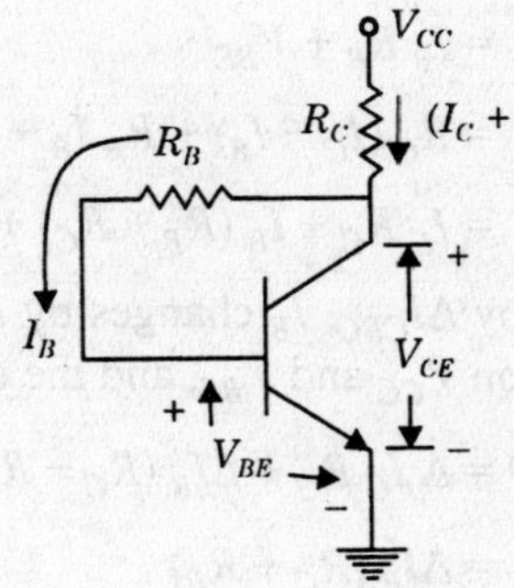


**Fig. 4.19**

Apply *KVL* to output loop which, is collector-emitter loop:

$$V_{CC} = R_C\,(I_C + I_B) + V_{CE} \qquad ...(1)$$

Since $I_B$ is quite small in the active region, it may be ignored.

$$\therefore \qquad V_{CC} = I_C\,R_C + V_{CE}$$

or

$$I_C = \frac{V_{CC} - V_{CE}}{R_C}$$

Now applying *KVL* input with collector-base, we have,:

$$V_{CC} = R_C\,(I_C + I_B) + I_B\,R_B + V_{BE}$$

Ignoring, $I_B\,R_C$ since $R_C$ is very small as compared to $R_B$ and $I_B$ also is negligibly small, we get:

$$V_{CC} = I_C\,R_C + I_B\,R_B + V_{BE}$$

or

$$V_{CC} = I_C\,R_C + \left(\frac{I_C}{\beta_{dc}}\right) R_B + V_{BE}, \text{ (as } I_C = \beta_{dc}\,I_B)$$

or

$$I_C\left(R_C + \frac{R_B}{\beta_{dc}}\right) = V_{CC} - V_{BE}$$

$$\therefore \qquad I_C = \frac{V_{CC} - V_{BE}}{R_C + \dfrac{R_B}{\beta_{dc}}}$$

Also

$$V_{CE} = I_B\,R_B + V_{BE} \text{ from the circuit} \qquad ...(2)$$

$$I_B = \frac{V_{CC} - V_{BE}}{R_C + R_B}$$

***S* for collector-to-base bias:** From the equation 1 and 2 that is

$$V_{CC} = R_C\,(I_B + I_C) + V_{CE}$$

and $$V_{CE} = I_B R_B + V_{BE}$$

$$V_{CC} = R_C (I_C + I_B) + R_B I_B + V_{BE}$$

$$= I_C R_C + I_B (R_B + R_C) + V_{BE} \quad ...(3)$$

When $I_{CBO}$ changes by $\Delta I_{CBO}$, $I_B$ changes by $\Delta I_B$ and and $I_C$ changes by $\Delta I_C$ There is no effect upon $V_{CC}$ and $V_{BE}$, and the equation becomes

$$O = \Delta I_C R_C + \Delta I_B (R_C + R_B)$$

$$-\Delta I_C R_C = \Delta I_B (R_C + R_B)$$

$$\frac{\Delta I_B}{\Delta I_C} = \frac{-R_C}{R_C + R_B}$$

Substituting this expression into the equation which is

$$S = \frac{1+\beta}{1-\beta\left(\frac{\Delta I_B}{\Delta I_C}\right)}$$ gives for collector-to-base bias $$S = \frac{1+\beta}{1-\beta\left(\frac{R_c}{R_c + R_B}\right)}$$

Using the current gain, β and resistance values in practice it is seen that $S$ ranges 24 to 35. This is an improvement over the fixed current bias stability factor, but in many cases it may be unacceptable. From the expression for $S$, it is seen that for a small value of $S$, $R_B$ must be as small as possible.

$$S' = \frac{\partial I_C}{\partial V_{BE}} = \frac{\Delta I_C}{\Delta V_{BE}}$$

From equation 3

$$V_{CC} = R_C I_C + (R_B + R_C) I_B + V_{BE}$$

$$V_{CC} = R_C I_C + (R_B + R_C) \frac{I_C}{\beta} + V_{BE}$$

$$V_{CC} - V_{BE} = I_C \left( R_C + \frac{R_B}{\beta} + \frac{R_C}{\beta} \right)$$

$$V_{CC} - V_{BE} = \frac{I_C}{\beta} [R_C (1+\beta) + R_B]$$

$$\frac{\Delta I_C}{\Delta V_{BE}} = \frac{-\beta}{R_B + R_C (1+\beta)}$$

$$S' = \frac{-\beta}{R_B + R_C (1+\beta)}$$

## 5. Collector to base Bias with Emitter Resistor

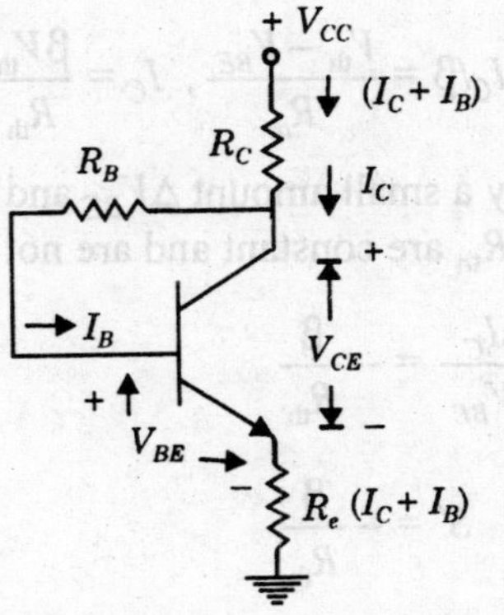


**Fig. 4.20**

Applying $K_{VL}$ to the input

$$V_{CC} - R_C\,(I_C + I_B) - I_B R_B - V_{BE} - (I_C + I_B)\,R_E = 0 \qquad ...(1)$$

Applying $K_{VL}$ to the output

$$V_{CC} - R_C(I_C + \mathrm{I}_B) - V_{CE} - (I_C I_B) R_E = 0 \qquad ...(2)$$

From equation (1)

$$V_{CC} - I_B\,(R_C + R_B + R_E) - I_C\,(R_C + R_E) - V_{BR} = 0$$

$$V_{CE} - V_{BE} = I_B(R_C + R_B + R_E) + I_C\,(R_C + R_E)$$

When $I_{CBO}$ changes by $\Delta I_{CB}$, and $I_B$ changes by $\Delta I_B$ and $I_C$ change by $\Delta I_C$. There is no effect upon $V_{CC}$ and $V_{BE}$ and the equation becomes.

$$0 = \Delta I_C\,(R_C + R_E) + \Delta I_B(R_C + R_E + R_B)$$

$$\therefore \quad -\Delta I_C\,(R_C + R_E) = \Delta I_B(R_C + R_E + R_B)$$

$$\therefore \quad \frac{\Delta I_B}{\Delta I_C} = \frac{-R_C + R_E}{R_B + R_C + R_E}$$

Substitute this expression into the equation which is

$$S = \frac{1+\beta}{1-\beta\left(\dfrac{\Delta I_B}{\Delta I_C}\right)} \text{ gives}$$

$$S = \frac{1+\beta}{1+\beta\left(\dfrac{R_c + R_\varepsilon}{R_c + R_\varepsilon + R_B}\right)}$$

We have from equation 2

$$V_{th} - R_{th} I_B - V_{BE} = 0$$

On substitution $I_B = I_C/\beta$ we get

$$I_C/\beta = \frac{V_{th} - V_{BE}}{R_{th}}, \; I_C = \frac{\beta V_{th}}{R_{th}} - \frac{\beta V_{BE}}{R_{th}} = eI_C$$

Let $V_{BE}$ change by a small amount $\Delta V_{BE}$ and as a result but $I_C$ change by $\Delta I_C$. Since $\beta$. $V_{th}$ and $R_{th}$ are constant and are not affected $y$ a change of $V_{BE}$.

$$\therefore \quad \frac{\Delta I_C}{\Delta V_{BE}} = -\frac{\beta}{R_{th}}$$

$$\therefore \quad S' = -\frac{\beta}{R_{th}}$$

We have from equation 1

$$I_B = \frac{V_{BB} - V_{BE}}{R_E}$$

Substituting $\quad I_B = \frac{I_C}{\beta} = \frac{V_{BB} - V_{BE}}{R_E}$

$$I_C = \frac{\beta (V_{BB} - V_{BE})}{R_E}$$

$$I_C = \frac{\beta V_{BB}}{R_E} - \beta \frac{V_{BE}}{R_E}$$

Let $V_{BE}$ change by a small amount $\Delta V_{BE}$ and as a result let $I_C$ change by $\Delta I_C$. Since $\beta$, $V_{BB}$ and $R_E$ are constant and are not affected by change of $V_{BE}$

$$\therefore \quad \frac{\Delta I_C}{\Delta V_{BE}} = -\frac{\beta}{R_E}$$

$$\therefore \quad S' = -\frac{\beta}{R_E}$$

**Stability factor $S''$:** The variation of $I_C$ w.r.t $\beta$ is given by the stability factor

$S''$ defined by $\quad S'' = \frac{\partial I_C}{\partial V_{BE}} = \frac{\Delta I_C}{\Delta \beta}.$

$$S'' = \frac{\Delta I_C}{\Delta \beta}.$$

The variation of $I_C$ w.r.t $\beta$ is given by the stability factor $S''$ defined by

$$S'' = \frac{\partial I_C}{\partial \beta} = \frac{\Delta I_C}{\Delta \beta}.$$

From equation (2)$R_{th} I_b = V_{th} - V_{BE}$. But $I_B = \frac{I_C}{\beta}$

$$\therefore \quad I_C = \beta\left(\frac{V_{th} - V_{BE}}{R_{th}}\right)$$

change in $I_C$ w.r.t change in β is $\frac{\Delta I_C}{\Delta \beta} = \frac{V_{th} - V_{BE}}{R_{th}}$

$$\therefore \quad S'' = \frac{V_{th} - V_{BE}}{R_{th}} \beta$$

## 6. Circuit 6

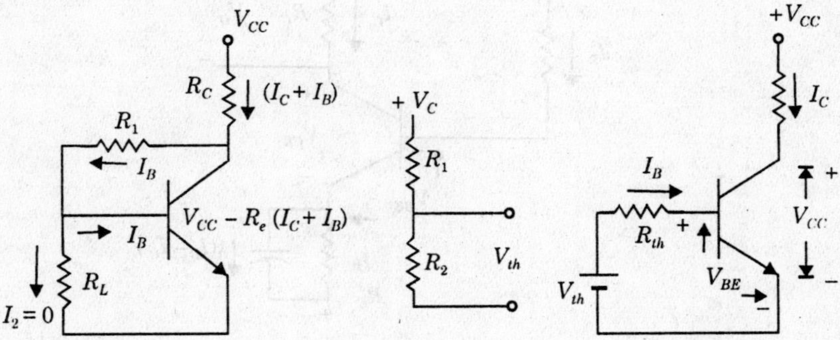


(a) (b) Thevenin's equivalent circuit

**Fig. 4.21**

Here $$V_C = V_{CC} - R_C(I_C + I_B)$$

$$R_2 >> R_1 => I = 0$$

$V_{th} = \left[\frac{V_C}{R_1 + R_2}\right] R_2$; $R_2$ should be large enough to make $V_{th}$ substantial even for a very small $V_C$.

$$R_{th} = R_1 || R_2$$

Applying *KVL* to the input

$$V_{th} - I_B R_{th} - V_{BE} = 0$$

Applying *KVL* to the output

$$V_{CC} - I_C R_C - V_{CE} = 0$$

## 7. Emitter Bias Circuit

The bias configuration is an improvement over the fixed-bias configuration studied earlier. This is nothing but fixed bias with emitter circuit resistor. The circuit uses an additional resistor $R_E$ in series with the emitter terminal, as shown in fig. 4.22.

The voltage drop across $R_E$ is $V_E = R_E \times I_E$ and $V_E = R_E \times I_E$

$$\therefore \quad I_E = \frac{V_B - V_{BE}}{R_E} \text{ if } V_B >> V_{BE}, I_E \approx \frac{V_B}{R_E}$$

In this, $I_E$ is a very stable quantity not depending on the value of β. Since $I_C \cong I_E$, the collector current is also a stable quantity.

The resistance $R_E$ tends to stabilize the operating point in spite of temperature change or transistor replacement. This results because of current feedback action through resistor $R_E$.

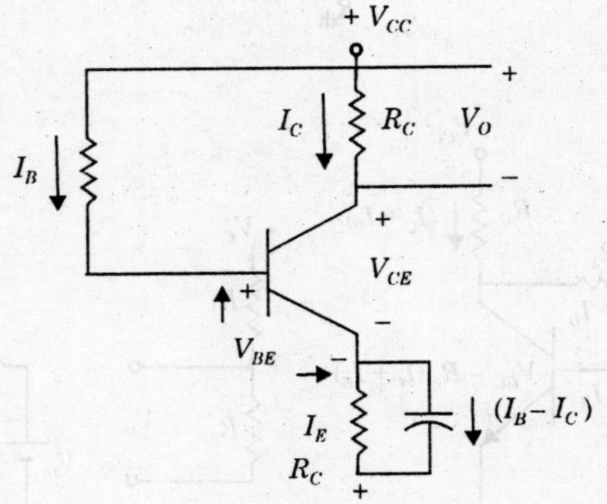


**Fig. 4.22** Emitter Bias Circuit

Applying *KVL* to the base-emitter loop that is input we have,

$V_{CC} - I_B R_B - V_{BE} + (I_B + I_C) R_E = 0$

As $\quad I_E = I_B + I_C = I_B + \beta I_B$

$$I_E = (1 + \beta) I_B$$

Substituting this value of $I_E$ in equation above;

$$V_{CC} = I_B R_B + V_{BE} + (1 + \beta) I_B R_E$$

On rearranging the terms, $I_B (R_B + (1 + \beta) R_E) = V_{CC} - V_{BE}$

$$\therefore \quad I_B = \frac{V_{CC} - V_{BE}}{R_B + (1 + \beta) R_E} \quad ...(1)$$

If $R_E$ is removed and a resistor $(1 + \beta) R_E$ is included in the base circuit, in addition to $R_B$, we get the same expression for current $I_B$.

For the fixed-bias circuit earlier, we have obtained the expression for $I_B$ as,

$$I_B = \frac{V_{CC} - V_{BE}}{R_B} \quad ...(2)$$

On comparing the equations 1 and 2, it is obvious that for the same values of $V_{CC}$ and $R_B$, the base current level for the emitter-bias circuit is lower than for the fixed-bias circuit. Also, any increase in β has the effect of decreasing the level of $I_B$, and hence of $I_C$. Thus any tendency for $I_C$ to increase due to increase in β is effectively offset. The final result is that there is improvement of stability.

Applying *KVL* to the collector-emitter loop which is at output; we have:

$V_{CC} - I_C R_C - V_{CE} - (I_C + I_B) R_E = 0$ or $V_{CC} = I_C R_C + V_{CE} + I_E R_E$

Since $I_B$ is quite small, $I_E \cong I_C$ as mentioned earlier, with this approximation

$$V_{CC} = V_{CE} + I_C (R_C + R_E)$$

or

$$V_{CE} = V_{CC} - I_C (R_C + R_E)$$

Also, $I_C = I_E$, $V_E = I_E R_E$, $V_C = V_{CE} + I_E R_E$ and $V_B = V_{BE} + V_E$ or $V_B = V_{CC} - I_B R_B$.

Note $V_C$, $V_E$ and $V_B$ are the potentials of collector, emitter and base terminals respectively w.r.t. ground.

**S for Emitter Bias:**

$$S = \frac{\Delta I_C}{\Delta I_{CBO}}$$

By analyzing the emitter-bias circuit, it can be shown that stability factor *S* is given as:

$$S = \frac{\Delta I_C}{\Delta I_{CBO}} = (1 + \beta) \frac{1 + R_B / R_E}{(1 + \beta) + R_B / R_E}$$

If the ration $(R_B/R_E)$ is for greater than $(1 + \beta)$, the above expression for *S* reduces top $S = 1 + \beta$.

If $R_E >> R_B$ that is the ratio $R_B/R_E << 1$, it is seen that $s \to 1$, which is its minimum possible value. Hence the circuit is quite stable when $R_E >> R_B$. It is necessary that $R_B > R_E$. Hence a compromise is generally mode. The ckt would be quite stable when $R_B/R_E$ is quite small.

**Stability factor $S'$:** The variation of $I_C$ with $V_{BE}$ is given by the stability factor $S'$ defined by.

$$S' = \frac{\partial I_C}{\partial V_{BE}} \cong \frac{\Delta I_C}{\Delta V_{BE}}$$

$$S' = \frac{\Delta I_C}{\Delta V} = \frac{-\beta}{R_B + (1 + \beta) R_E}$$

Dividing both $N_r$ and $D_r$ by $R_E$, we get $S^1 = \dfrac{-\beta / R_E}{(R_B / R_E)(1 + \beta)}$

If the ratio $(R_B/R_E) << (1 + \beta)$; the expression for $S'$ reduces to

$$S' = \frac{-\beta/R_E}{1+\beta} = \frac{-\beta}{R_E\beta}, \text{ substituting } 1 + \beta = \beta \text{ or } S' = -1/R_E$$

From this expression it is clear that $R_E$ must quite large, for the system to be quite stable

**Stability factor $S''$:** The variation of $I_C$ w.r.t b is given by the stability factor $S''$ defined by

$$S'' = \frac{\partial I_C}{\partial \beta} \approx \frac{\Delta I_C}{\Delta \beta}$$ where both $I_{CO}$ and $V_{BE}$ are considered constant let $I_C$,

denote the collector current for $\beta = \beta$, as temperature changes, changes and hence $I_C$ changes. Let $\beta$ change to $\beta_2$. It can now be shown that

$$S'' = \frac{I(1+R_B/R_E)}{\beta_1(1+\beta_2+R_B/R_E)}$$

The change in $\beta$ may also be due to transistor replacement.

## 8. Transformer Coupled Biasing Circuit

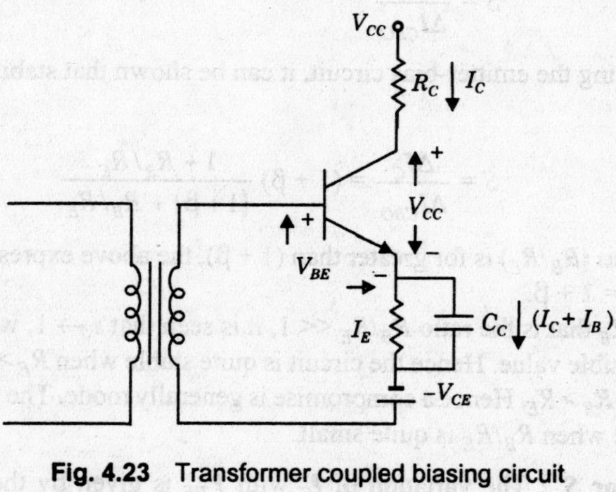


**Fig. 4.23** Transformer coupled biasing circuit

Applying $KVL$ to the input

$$R_{dc} - V_{BE} - R_E(I_C + I_B) + V_{EE} = 0 \quad ...(1)$$

But $R_{dc} = 0$ then $V_{BE} + R_E(I_C + I_B) - V_{EE} = 0$

Applying $KVL$ to the output

$$V_{CC} - I_C R_C - V_{CE} - R_E(I_C + I_B) + V_{EE} = 0 \quad ...(2)$$

When $I_{CBO}$ changes by $\Delta I_{CBO}$, $I_B$ changes by $\Delta I_C$. There is no effect upon $V_{CE}$ and $V_{BE}$ then the equation (2)

Becomes $I_C(R_C + R_E) + I_B R_E = 0$

$$I_B R_E = -(R_C + R_E) I_C$$

$$\frac{\Delta I_B}{\Delta I_C} = -\frac{R_C + R_E}{R_E}$$

$$S = \frac{1+\beta}{(1-\beta)\frac{\Delta I_B}{\Delta I_C}}$$

$$\therefore \quad S = \frac{1+\beta}{1+\beta\left(\frac{R_C + R_E}{R_E}\right)}$$

*Stability factor S′ :*

$$S' = \frac{\partial I_C}{\partial V_{BE}} = \frac{\Delta I_C}{\Delta V_{BE}}$$

From equation (1)

$$V_{BE} + R_E (I_C + I_B) - V_{EE} = 0$$
$$V_{BE} + R_E (I_C + I_C/\beta) - V_{EE} = 0$$
$$V_{BE} + I_C (R_E + R_E/\beta) - V_{EE} = 0$$

$$I_C = \frac{R_E\,(1+\beta)}{\beta} = V_{EE} - V_{BE}$$

$$\frac{\partial I_C}{\partial V_{Be}} = \frac{\Delta I_C}{\Delta V_{BE}}$$

$$\therefore \quad S' = \frac{\Delta I_C}{\Delta V_{BE}} = \frac{-\beta}{R_E\,(1+\beta)}$$

$$S'' = \frac{\partial I_C}{\partial \beta} \cong \frac{\Delta I_C}{\Delta \beta}$$

### 9. Self-bias Circuit

This circuit is also called as potential-divider bias with emitter circuit resistor also known as emitter current bias circuit. This is the most widely used of all bias configurations because if produces excellent operating point stability.

Bias stabilization is achieved by the potential divider biasing circuit of fig. 4.24 (a) where in the transistor base is connected to a potential divider circuit across $V_{CC}$. This biasing circuit is redrawn in fig. 4.24 (b) with the potential divider replaced by its thieving requirement, where,

$$V_{BB} = V_{CC}\,(R_2 // R_1 + R_2) = V_{CC}\,(R_B / R_1) \quad ...(1)$$

$$R_B = R_{th} = R_1 // R_2 \quad ...(2)$$

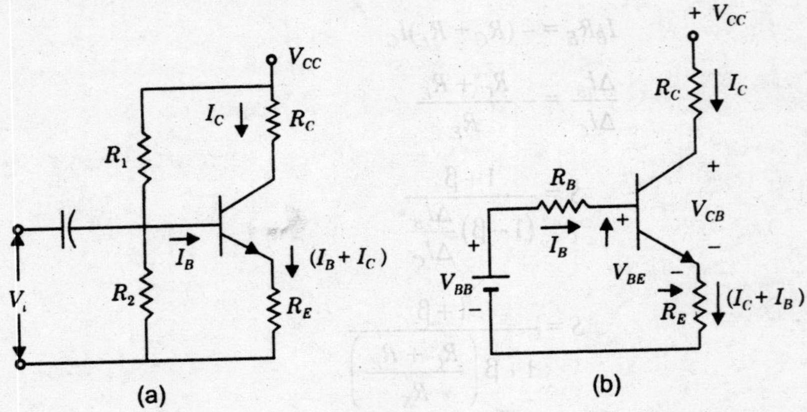


**Fig. 4.24** (a) Potential divider biasing circuit (b) Self-Bias Circuit

From fig. 4.24 (b) the *KVL* equation for the base emitter loop is written as

$$V_{BB} = I_B R_B + V_{BE} + (I_B + I_C)\, R_E$$

$$V_{BB} = (R_E + R_B)\, I_B + V_{BE} + R_E I_C \qquad \text{...(3)}$$

or

$$I_B = \frac{V_{BB} - V_{BE}}{R_B + R_E} - \left(\frac{R_E}{R_B + R_E}\right) I_C \qquad \text{...(4)}$$

We know that the collector current

$$I_C = \beta I_B + (\beta + 1)\, I_{CBO} \qquad \text{...(5)}$$

Substituting for $I_B$ from equation 4

we get

$$I_C = \frac{\beta (V_{BB} - V_{BE})}{R_B + R_E} - \left(\frac{R_E}{R_B + R_E}\right) \beta I_C + (\beta + 1) I_{CBO} \qquad \text{...(6)}$$

On rearranging the terms we get

$$I_C = \frac{(V_{BB} - V_{BE}) + \left(\frac{\beta + 1}{\beta}\right) I_{CBO}\, (R_B + R_E)}{R_E + \frac{R_B + R_E}{\beta}} \qquad \text{...(7)}$$

Before going to the expression for stability factor, let us consider the bias stabilizing action of the circuit.

Assume that β increases with rise in temperature resulting in increased $I_C$. This in turn causes the voltage drop across emitter resistance to increases from equation (4) it is known that this would tend to decreases $I_B$ ($V_{BE}$ decreases accordingly) thereby counting the increase in $I_C$ of equation (5). So the negative feedback effect of $R_E$ the emitter resistance keeps the bias currents stabilized.

For $\beta \geq 20, \frac{\beta+1}{\beta} \approx 1.$

Chose $R_B \geq 5R_E$. for making $I_C$ to become independent of β choose

$$\frac{R_B + R_E}{\beta} \approx \frac{R_B}{\beta} << R_E$$

Equation (7) for $I_C$ then simplifies to

$$I_C = \frac{(V_{BB} - V_{BE}) + I_{CBO}(R_B + R_E)}{R_E} \quad ...(8)$$

As long as we choose $V_{BB} >> V_{BE}$, the effect of change in $V_{BE}$ with temperature on $I_C$ can be neglected.

($V_{BE}$ = –2.5 mv/°C × 50 = 0.1 V for 50°C temperature rise)

we shall now assume $V_{BE}$ in active region to remain constant at 0.7 V.

$$\therefore \quad I_C = \frac{V_{BB} + (R_B + R_E)\, I_{CBO}}{R_E} \quad ...(9)$$

∴ $S(\beta) = 0$ , that is $I_C$ is independent of β

$$\therefore \quad S(I_{CBO}) = (1 + R_B/R_E) \quad ...(10)$$

In Si transistor $I_{CBO}$ is in nanoamperes and its variations with temperature contribute in significantly to changes in $I_C$. where as in Ge transistor $I_{CBO}$ being in microampers, $Ic$ is sensitive to temperature caused changes in $I_{CBO}$

*Advantages:*

single battery

loss of gain

$Q$ variation

*Analysis of the self-bias circuit:* If the circuit component values in fig. 4.24 (a) above, are specified the quiescent pt. is found as follows *KVL* around the collector circuit yields

$$-V_{CC} + I_C(R_C + R_E) + I_B R_E + V_{CE} = 0 \quad ...(1)$$

if the circuit to the left between the base B and ground N terminals in fig. 4.24 (a) above is replaced by its thevenins equivalent, the two -mesh circuit of fig. 4.24(b) above is obtained by where

$$V = R_2 \frac{V_{CC}}{R_2 + R_1};\ R_B = \frac{R_2 R_1}{R_2 + R_1} \quad ...(2)$$

*KVL* around the base circuit yields

$$V = I_B R_B + V_{BE} + (I_B + I_C) R_E \quad ...(3)$$

**The stabilization factor $S$:** We define $S$ as the rate of change of collector current w.r.t . the reverse saturation current keeping b and $V_{BE}$ constant,

or $$S = \frac{\partial I_C}{\partial I_{CO}} \approx \frac{\Delta I_C}{\Delta I_{CO}} \quad ...(1)$$

$$S = (1+\beta)\frac{1+\dfrac{R_B}{R_E}}{1+\beta+\dfrac{R_B}{R_E}} \quad ...(2)$$

Note that $S$ varies between 1 for small $R_B/R_E$ and $(1 + \beta)$ for $R_B/R_E \to \infty$ If $\beta + 1 >> R_B/R_E$, equation (2) reduces to

$$S \approx 1 + \frac{R_B}{R_E} \quad ...(3)$$

Thus, for constant $\beta$, $V_{BE}$ and small $S$, we have

$$\frac{\Delta I_C}{I_C} \approx S\frac{\Delta I_{CO}}{I_C} \approx \frac{\Delta I_{CO}}{I_C} + \frac{R_B}{R_E} + \frac{\Delta I_{CO}}{I_C} \quad ...(4)$$

$$\frac{\Delta I_{CO}}{I_C} = \text{DC Voltage drop across } R_e$$

For the typical design, $R_B/R_E > 1$ making the second term in equation (4) larger than first.

**The stability factor $S'$:** The variation of $I_C$ with $V_{BE}$ is given by the stability factor $S'$

Defined by $$S' = \frac{\partial I_C}{\partial V_{BE}} \approx \frac{\Delta I_C}{\Delta V_{BE}} \quad ...(5)$$

Where both $I_{CO}$ and b are considered constant.

We defined already $V_{BE} = V + (R_B + R_E)\, I_{CO} - I_C \dfrac{R_B + R_E(1+\beta)}{\beta}$ ...(6)

From equation (6) we find $$S' = \frac{-\beta}{R_B + R_E(1+\beta)} = \frac{\dfrac{-\beta}{R_E}}{1+\beta+\dfrac{R_B}{R_E}} \quad ...(7)$$

If we again assume that $\beta + 1 >> \dfrac{R_B}{R_E}$, and also that $\beta >> 1$, then equation (7) reduces to

$$S' \approx \frac{\Delta I_C}{\Delta V_{BE}} \approx -\frac{1}{R_e} \quad ...(8)$$

or

$$\frac{\Delta I_C}{I_C} \approx S' \frac{\Delta V_{BE}}{I_C} \approx -\frac{\Delta V_{BE}}{I_C R_E} \quad ...(9)$$

$$S' = \frac{-\beta}{R_{th} + (1+\beta) R_E}$$

**The stability factor $S''$ :** The variation of $I_C$ with respect to b is given by the stability factor $S^{11}$ defined by

$$S'' = \frac{\partial I_C}{\partial I_B} = \frac{\Delta I_C}{\Delta \beta} \quad ...(10)$$

Where both $I_{CO}$ and $V_{BE}$ are considered constant

$$I_C = \frac{\beta \left(V + V^1 - V_{BE}\right)}{R_B + R_E (1+\beta)} \quad ...(11)$$

$$S'' = \frac{\partial I_C}{\partial I_B} = \frac{I_C S}{\beta (1+\beta)} \quad ...(12)$$

The change in collector current due to change in β is

$$\Delta I_C \approx S'' \Delta \beta = \frac{I_C S}{\beta (1+\beta)} \Delta \beta \quad ...(13)$$

Where $\Delta\beta = (\beta_2 - \beta_1)$ may represent a large change in β. Hence it is not clear whether to use $\beta_1$, $\beta_2$ or perhaps some average value of β in the expressions for $S''$. Thus difficulty is avoided if $S''$ is obtained by taking finite difference rather by evaluating a derivative thus:

$$S'' \approx \frac{I_{C2} - I_{C1}}{(\beta_2 - \beta_1)} = \frac{\Delta I_C}{\Delta \beta} \quad ...(14)$$

From equation (11) we have

$$\frac{I_{C2}}{I_{C1}} = \frac{\beta_2}{\beta_1} = \frac{R_B + R_E (1+\beta_1)}{(R_B + R_E)(1+\beta_2)} \quad ...(15)$$

Subtracting unity for both side of equation (15) yields

$$\frac{I_{C2}}{I_{C1}} - 1 = \left(\frac{\beta_2}{\beta_1} - 1\right) \frac{R_B + R_E}{R_B + R_E (1+\beta_2)} \quad ...(16)$$

$$S'' = \frac{\Delta I_C}{\Delta \beta} = \frac{\Delta I_{C1} S_2}{\beta_1 (1+\beta_2)} \quad ...(17)$$

from equation (17) $\dfrac{\Delta I_C}{I_{C1}} \approx \left(1+\dfrac{R_B}{R_c}\right)\dfrac{\Delta\beta}{\beta_1\beta_2} = \left(1+\dfrac{R_B}{R_c}\right)\dfrac{\dfrac{\beta_2}{\beta_1}-1}{\beta_2}$ ...(18)

## 10. Self Bias with Base Spreading

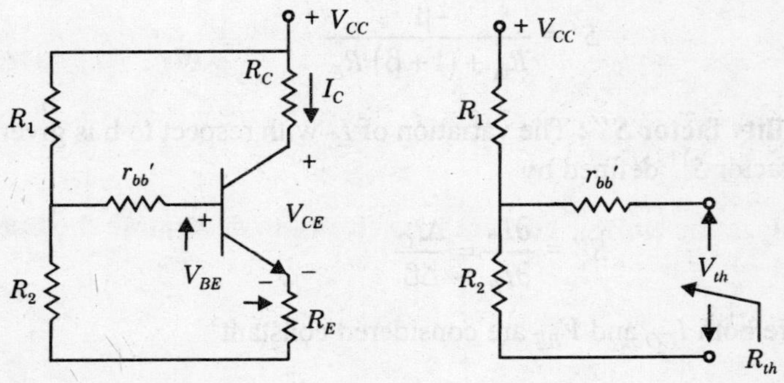


**Fig. 4.25** Self bias with base spreading

Where $V_{\text{th}} = \left(\dfrac{V_{CC}}{R_1+R_2}\right)R_2$

$$R_{\text{th}} = (R_1 \parallel R_2) + r_{bb}^1$$

Applying *KVL* to the input

$$V_{\text{th}} - R_{\text{th}}\, I_B - V_{BE} - R_E\,(I_C + I_B) = 0 \qquad ...(1)$$

Applying *KVL* to the output, we get

$$V_{CC} = I_C R_C - V_{CE} - R_E\,(I_C + I_B) = 0 \qquad ...(2)$$

$$V_{CC} - V_{CE} - I_C\,(R_C + R_E) - I_B R_E = 0$$

When $I_{CBO}$ changes by $\Delta I_{CBO}$, $I_B$ change by $\Delta I_B$ and $I_C$ changes by $\Delta I_C$. There is no effect upon $V_{CC}$ and $V_{CE}$, then the equation (2) becomes

$$0 = \Delta I_C\,(R_C + R_E) + \Delta I_B R_E$$

$$-\Delta I_B R_E = \Delta I_C\,(R_C + R_E)$$

$$\therefore \qquad \frac{\Delta I_B}{\Delta I_C} = -\frac{(R_C + R_E)}{R_E}$$

$$S = \frac{1+\beta}{1-\beta\left(\dfrac{\Delta I_B}{\Delta I_C}\right)}$$

$$S = \frac{1+\beta}{1+\beta\left(\frac{R_C + R_E}{R_E}\right)} \text{ on substituting } \frac{\Delta I_B}{\Delta I_C}$$

$$S' = \frac{\partial I_C}{\partial V_{BE}} = \frac{\Delta I_C}{\Delta V_{BE}}$$

From equation (1):

$$V_{th} - R_{th}\, I_B - V_{BE} - R_E(I_C + I_B) = 0$$

On substituting $I_B = \frac{I_C}{\beta}$, we get

$$V_{th} - V_{BE} = I_C\left(\frac{R_{th}}{\beta} + R_E + \frac{R_E}{\beta}\right)$$

Let $V_{BE}$ change by a small amount $\Delta V_{BE}$ and as a result let $I_C$ change by $\Delta I_C$. Since $V_{th}$ is constant, it is not affected by change, of $V_{BE}$.

$$\therefore \qquad \frac{\Delta I_C}{\Delta V_{BE}} = \frac{-\beta}{R_{th} + R_E\,(1+\beta)}$$

$$\therefore \qquad S' = \frac{-\beta}{R_{th} + R_E\,(1+\beta)}$$

## 4.10 BIAS COMPENSATION

So far we have seen several biasing techniques. The purpose mainly of proper biasing is to render the operating point stable that is. to make $I_C$ and $V_{CE}$ as much independent as practicable, of variations in β, $I_{CBO}$ and $V_{BE}$. Inspite of best design $V_{CE}$ and $I_C$ tend to change with changes of temperature, with the result that there is a drift of the Q-point.Thus the bias stabilization techniques discussed earlier proved to be inadequate

The bias compensation methods discussed are as below:

(a) Diode compensation fui $V_{BE}$
(b) Diode compensation for $I_{CBO}$
(c) Thermistor compensation
(d) Sensistor compensation.

(a) *Diode compensation for $V_{BE}$* A self-bias circuit employing diode compensation technique is shown in fig. 4.26. Diode and transistor should be made of the same material. Thus the effect of temperature is of the same order as both the diode and the transistor. If it is always forward-biased by means of battery $V_{DD}$ and resistor $R_d$. If there is an increase in temperature, the $I_{CO}$ and in turn, the $I_C$ of the transistor will increase. Also the leakage current *Io* through the diode *D* will increase, due to temperature change.

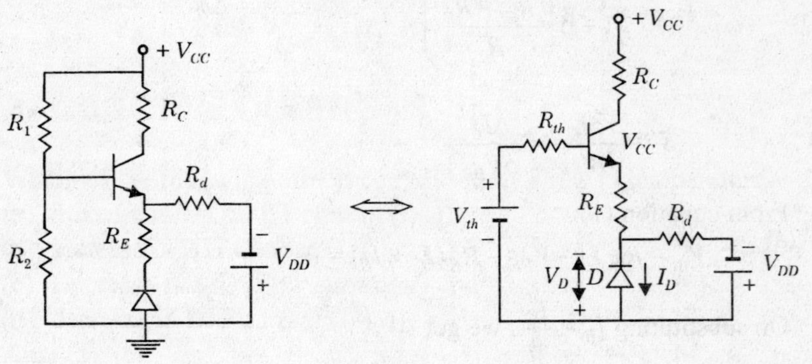


**Fig. 4.26** (a) Stabilization by means of self bias add diode compensation technique

Since $I_O$ will increase, the base current $I_B$ will decrease. This decrease in $I_B$ will lead to decrease in $I_C$, thereby trying to keep $I_C$ constant in spite of change in temperature. An external supply (voltage) is added to negative diode to give forward bias for a diode.

Applying *KVL* to the base-emitter diode loop, we get:

That is $-V_{th} + I_B R_{th} + I_E R_E + V_{BE} - V_O = 0$

Substituting in $I_E = I_B + I_C$ and $I_B = \dfrac{I_C - (1+\beta) I_{CBO}}{\beta}$. And simplifying, we get:

$$I_C = \frac{(V_{th} - V_{BE} + V_O) + (1+\beta)(R_{th} + R_e) I_{CBO}}{R_{th} + (1+\beta) R_E}$$

From the above equation it is that for every change in $V_{BE}$ there is an equal change in $V_O$. Since both have the same temperature coefficient. Hence the collector current $I_C$ remains practically constant, irrespective of change of temperature. Thus $I_C$ is insensitive to changes in $V_{BE}$, which may be caused due to changes of temperature.

(b) *Diode compensation for $I_{CBO}$* As the change of $V_{BE}$ with temperature contribute significantly to changes in collector current of Silicon transistors and for the germanium transistors, change in $I_{CO}$ with temperature playing the more important role in collector-current stability. The diode compensation circuit shown in fig. 4.27. offers the stabilization against variations in $I_{CO}$, and is therefore useful for stabilizing germanium transistors.

If the diode and the transistor are of the same type and the material, the reverse saturation current $I_O$ of the diode will increase with temperature at the same rate as the transistor collector saturation current $I_{CO}$.

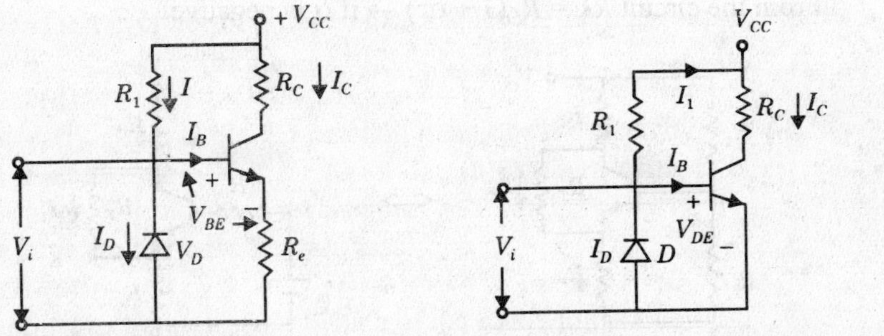

(a) Diode compensation for $I_{CBO}$ (b) diode compensation for a Ge diode.

**Fig. 4.27**

This phenomenon is especially marked in germanium transistors. A compensation technique adopted to offset the effect of temperature changes on $I_{CBO}$ is shown in fig. 4.27 is a diode which works in the reverse-bias mode. $I_O$ is the reverse saturation current of the diode. Diode is of the same material and type as the transistor.

*For $I_{CBO}$*: From the circuit:

$$I_1 = \frac{V_{CC} - V_{BE}}{R_1};\ V_{BE} << V_{CC}$$

Hence $$I_1 = \frac{V_{CC}}{R_1} = \text{constant.}$$

Since the diode is reverse biased by an amount $V_{BE} = 0.2$ V for germanium devices, if follows that the current through $D$ is $Io$.

The base current is, $I_B = I - I_O$

Where as in the active region the base current and collector current are related as:

$$I_C = (1 + \beta)\, I_{CO} + \beta I_B$$

$$= (1 + \beta)\, I_{CO} + \beta\, (I - I_O);\ \beta >> L$$

$$I_C = \beta I + \beta\, (I_{CO} - I_O)$$

$$\therefore \quad I_C = \beta I + \beta\, (I_{CO} - \dot{I}_O)$$

if $\beta >> 1$, and if Io of $D$ and $I_{CO}$ of $Q$ cancell each other over the desired temperature range, then $I_C$ remains essentially constant.

(c) *Thermistor compensation:* Thermistor is a temperature sensitive resistive element having negative temperature coefficient of resistance decreasing exponentially with increase of temperature $T$.

The circuit of fig. 4.28 gives a self biased $C_E$ amplifier with Thermistor $R_T$ connected from $V_{CC}$ supply to the emitter terminal. Thermistor $R_T$ uses to minimize the increase in collector current due to changes in $I_{CO}$, $V_{BE}$, or $\beta$ with $T$.

From the circuit $R_{th} = R_O(1 + \alpha t) \rightarrow$ if $\alpha$ is negative

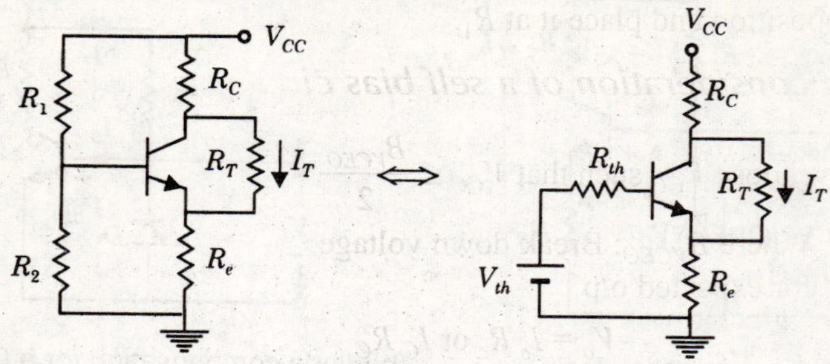


**Fig. 4.28** Thermistor compensation

As $T$ rises, $R_T$ decreases, and the current fed through $R_T$ into $R_e$ increase. Since the voltage drop across $R_e$ is in the direction to reverse-bias the transistor, the temperature sensitivity of $R_T$ acts so as to tend to compensate the increase in $I_C$ due to $T$. There is an other configuration using thermistor configuration which is an alternative that is to move $R_T$ from its position in fig. and place it across $R_2$. As T increase, the drop across $R_T$ decreases, and hence the forward-biasing base voltage is reduced. This behavior will tend to off set the increase in collector current with temperature. For stabilization, negative feedback should be increased. (Thermistor is connected in series or in the place of $R_2$).

(b) *Sensistor compensation:* Sensistor is a heavily doped bulk semiconductor device and has positive temperature coefficient of resistance of 0.7 percent/deg $C$ over the temperature range from –60°C to 150°C. Sensistor resistor is more sensitive than the ordinary resistor. The circuit of fig. gives the clean description of compensation of sensistor. From the circuit: $R_S = R_O(1 + \alpha t)$

$$S = \frac{1+\beta}{1-\beta\left(\dfrac{\partial I_B}{\partial I_C}\right)}; \; I_C \text{ should always be negative.}$$

As $T$ rises, $R_S$ increases, and the current fed to $R_S$ through $R_E$ increases. $\therefore I_E R_E$ increases with the decrease of $I_B$ and $I_C$ with the inclusion of $V_{BE}$.

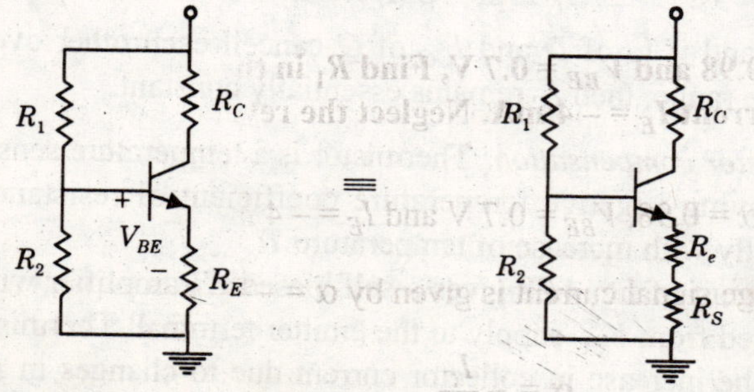


**Fig. 4.29** Representation of sensistor compensation.

An alternative configuration using sensistor compensation is to move $R_S$ from its position and place it at $R_1$.

### *Design consideration of a self bias circuit*

$S_1$ : choose $V_{CC}$ such that $V_{CC} \leq \frac{B_{VCEO}}{2}$

Where $B_{VCEO}$: Break down voltage

$S_2$ : for expected o/p

$$V_o = I_c R_c \text{ or } I_C R_C$$

$$\therefore \qquad R_C = \frac{V_0}{I_C}$$

$S_3$ : Calculate $R_E$ from $Q$–$pt$

$$V_{CC} - I_C R_C - V_{CE} - (I_C + I_B) R_E = 0$$

$S_4$ : (a) Calculate $R_{th}$ from Stability factor $S = \dfrac{1+\beta}{1+\beta\left(\dfrac{R_E}{R_E + R_{th}}\right)}$

(b) by default $R_{th} = \dfrac{\beta R_E}{\omega}$

$S_5$ : Calculate $V_{th} = I_B R_{th} + V_{BE} + (I_C + I_B) R_E$

$S_6$ : Calculate $R_1$ from

$$R_1 = \left(\frac{V_{cc}}{V_{th}}\right) R_{th}, \; V_{th} = \left(\frac{V_{CC}}{R_1 + R_2}\right)\frac{R_2 \cdot R_1}{R_1} = \frac{V_{CC}}{R_1} R_{th}$$

$S_7$ : Calculate $R_2$ from $R_{th}$ and $R_1$

$$\frac{1}{R_2} = \frac{1}{R_{th}} - \frac{1}{R_1}$$

## 4.11 SOLVED PROBLEMS

**1. If $\alpha = 0.98$ and $V_{BE} = 0.7$ V, Find $R_1$ in the circuit shown for an emitter current $I_E = -4$ mA. Neglect the reverse saturation current.**

**Solution:**

Given $\alpha = 0.98$, $V_{BE} = 0.7$ V and $I_E = -4$ mA, $R_1 = ?$

The large signal current is given by $\alpha = -\dfrac{I_C - I_{CO}}{I_E}$ on neglecting $I_{CO}$,

i.e. $$\alpha = -\frac{I_C}{I_E}$$

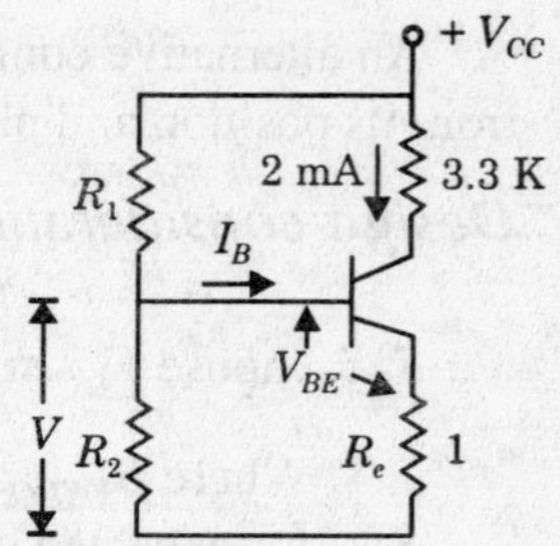


$$I_C = -\alpha I_E = 3.92 \text{ mA.}$$

But $$I_B = -I_C - I_E = -(1-\alpha)I_E$$

$$= -(1-0.98)I_E$$

$$I_B = 0.02 \times 4 \text{ mA} = 80 \text{ µA}$$

Taking *KVL* in loop 1:

$$V_{BN} = V_{BE} + I_E + I_E R_E$$

$$= 0.7 + (-4 \times 10^{-3})(100)$$

$$= -3.3 \text{ V.}$$

Here $$I_{R1} = I_B + I_{R2} \text{ and}$$

$$I_{R2} = \frac{V_{BN}}{R_2} = \frac{3.3}{10 \times 10^3} = 330 \text{ µA}$$

$\therefore$ $$I_{R1} = 80 \text{ µA} + 330 \text{ µA} = 110 \text{ µA.}$$

From the circuit, $V_{CN} = V_{CC} - (I_C + I_{R1}) R_c$

$$= 12 - (3.92 \times 10^{-3} + 110 \times 10^{-6})(3.3 \times 10^3)$$

$$= 12 - (1.96 + 0.085 + 10^{-3})(3.3 \times 10^3)$$

$$= -1.299\text{V}$$

$\therefore$ The Voltage across

$$R_1 = V_{CN} - V_{BN} = -1.299 - 0.9$$

$$= -2.199 \text{ V}$$

$\therefore$ $$R = \frac{V_{RI}}{I_{RI}} = -\frac{2.199}{110 \times 10^{-6}} = 20 \text{ K}$$

**2. (a) Find $R_C$ and $R_b$ in the circuit of fig. If $V_{CC} = 12$ V and $V_{BB} = 5$ V, so that $I_C = 10$ mA and $V_{CE} = 5$ V. A silicon transistor with $\beta = 50$, $V_{BE} = 0.7$ V, and negligible reverse saturation current is under consideration.**

**(b) Repeat part (a), if a 100 Ω emitter resistor is added to the circuit.**

**Solution:**

Given $V_{CC} = 12$ V, $V_{BB} = 5$ V, $I_C = 10$ mA, $V_{CE} = 5$ V, $\beta = 50$, $V_{BE} = 0.7$ V.

(a) Since $V_{CE} = 5\text{V} < \text{V}_{CC}$, the transistor cannot be at cut off or in saturation, hence it is in the active region. On neglecting $I_{CO}$ from equation we have $I_C = \beta I_B$

$\therefore$ $$I_B = \frac{10\, mA}{50} = 0.2 \text{ mA}$$

from the base circuit ie. *KVL* to input:

$$V_{BB} - I_B R_B - V_{BE} = 0$$

$$5 - 0.2 \times 10^{-3} R_B - 0.7 = 0$$

$$R_B = 21.5 \text{ K.}$$

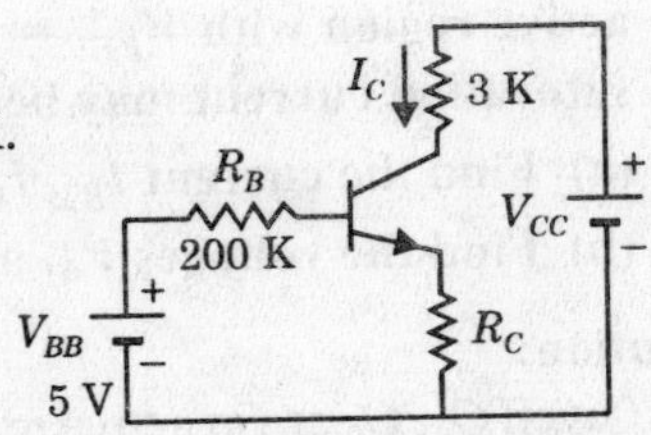


From the collector circuit; ie. *KVL* to output:

$$V_{CC} - I_C R_C - V_{CE} = 0$$

$$2 - 10 \times 10^{-3} R_C - 5 = 0$$

$$R_C = 700\ \Omega$$

Since $I_B = 100\ \mu A$ and for Si transistors $I_{CO}$ is of the order of magnitude of *nA*.

(b) In this from the collector circuit ie. *KVL* to input:

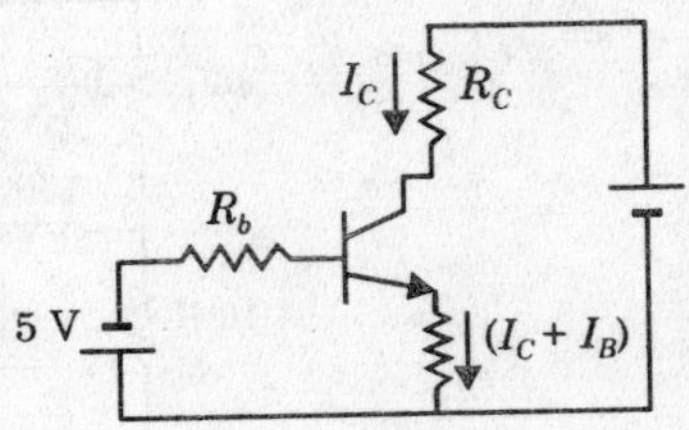


$$V_{BB} = I_B R_B + V_{BE} + (I_C + I_B)\ \beta$$

$$5 = R_B\ 0.2 \times 10^{-3} + 0.7$$

$$+ 10.2 \times 10^{-3} \times 50$$

$$R_B = 21.245\ \text{K}\Omega$$

**3. In the circuit shown, $V_{CC}$ = 20 V, $R_C$ = 10 K, and $R_e$ = 200 Ω. If a silicon transistor is used with β = 50 and if $V_{CE}$ = 5 V, find *R*. Neglect the reverse saturation current.**

**Solution:**

Given $V_{CC}$ = 20 V, $R_C$ = 10 K, $R_E$ = 200 Ω; β = 50 and $V_{CE}$ = 5 V, *R* = ?

Applying *KVL* in the collector emitter circuit gives: i.e., *KVL* to output

$$V_{CC} - (I_C + I_B)\ R_C - (I_C + I_B)\ R_E - V_{CE} = 0$$

$$\Rightarrow \quad V_{CC} - (I_C + I_B)\ (R_E + R_C) - V_{CE} = 0$$

$$20 - (1 + \beta)\ I_B\ (10200) - 5 = 0$$

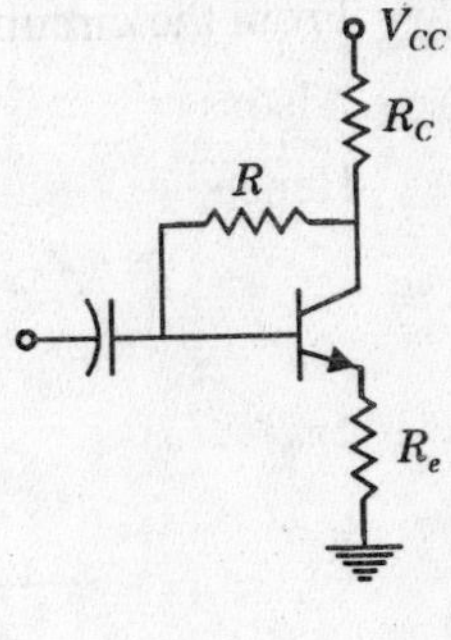


$$I_B = \frac{15}{51 \times 10200} = 28.8 \text{ mA}$$

$$\Rightarrow \quad I_C = \beta I_B = 1.44 \text{ mA.}$$

$$\therefore \quad V_{CE} = V_{CB} + V_{BE}$$

$$V_{CB} = 5 - 0.7 = 4.3 \text{ V.}$$

Applying *KVL* to input,

$$-I_B R = V_{CE} - V_{BE} = 0 \Rightarrow -I_B R + V_{CB} = 0$$

$$R = \frac{4.3}{28.8 \times 10^{-6}}$$

$$\therefore \quad R = 149\ \text{k}\Omega$$

**4. For the circuit shown in the fig , transistors $Q_1$ and $Q_2$ operate in the active region with $V_{BE1} = V_{BE2} = 0.7$, $\beta_1 = 100$, $\beta_2 = 50$. The reverse saturation current may be neglected.**

**(a) Find the current $I_{B2}$, $I_1$, $I_2$, $I_{C2}$, $I_{B1}$, $I_{C1}$ and $I_{E1}$.**

**(b) Find the voltages $V_{01}$ and $V_{02}$.**

**Solution:**

Given $Q_1$, $Q_2$ are in active region. $V_{BE1} = V_{BE2} = 0.7$ V, $\beta_1 = 100$, $\beta_2 = 50$. Applying Thevenin's theorem to the left of Point $B'$, we obtain the equivalent circuit shown below where

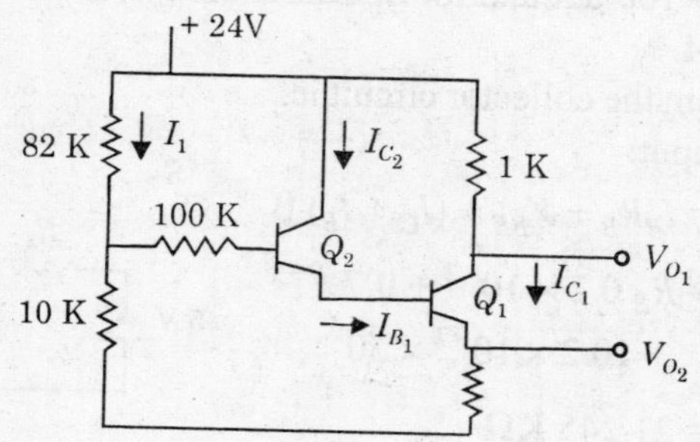


$$V_{\text{th}} = V_{eq} = 24\left(\frac{10k}{82k + 10k}\right) = 2.608 \text{ V}$$

$$R_{\text{th}} = R_{eq} = 82 \text{ k} \parallel 10\text{k} = 8.91 \text{ k}$$

$\therefore$ $R_{\text{th}} + 100 \text{ k} = 108.9 \text{ k}.$

Applying *KVL* to input:

$$2.608 = (108.9 \text{ k})\, I_{B2} + 1.4 + (I_{B1} + I_{C1})\, 100\ \Omega \qquad ...(1)$$

From the circuit, $I_{B1} = I_{B2} = I_{C2} + I_{B2} = (1 + \beta_2)\, I_{B2}$

Also $I_{C1} = \beta_1 I_{B1} = \beta_1(1 + \beta_1)\, I_{B2}$

Hence $I_{B1} = 51\, I_{B2}$, $I_{C1} = 5100\, I_{B2}$ ...(2)

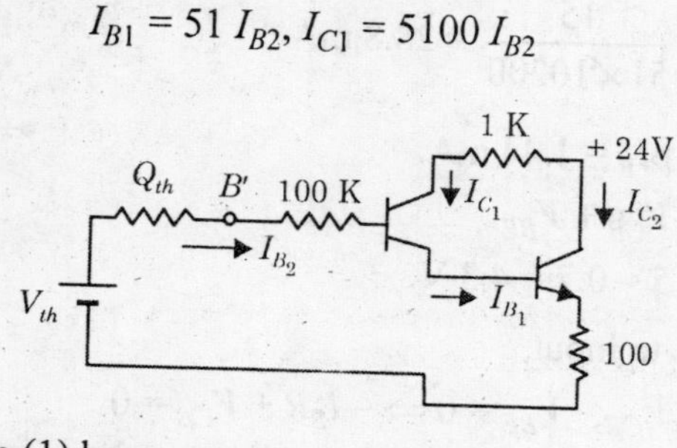


Then equation (1) becomes

$$2.608 = (108.92)\, I_{B2} + 1.4 + (51.51)\, 0.1\, I_{B2}$$

$$I_{B2} = \frac{1.21}{624.02} = 0.194 \times 10^{-5} = 1.94\ \mu\text{A}$$

Hence $I_{C2} = 50, I_{B2} = 97\ \mu A, I_{B1} = 51\ I_{B2} = 99\ \mu A$

$I_{C1} = 100, I_{B1} = 9.9\ \mu A.$

From the circuit, $V_{01} = 24 - I_{C1} \times 10^3 = 24 - 9.9 = 14.1$ V.

and $V_{02} = 100\ (I_{B1} + I_{C1}) = 0.999$V.

also $V_{BN} = (100\ k)\ I_{B2} + 0.7 + 0.7 + 0.999 = 2.399$ V

$$\therefore \quad I_1 = \frac{24 - V_{BN}}{82k} = 0.26 \text{ mA}$$

$$I_1 = I_2 + I_{B2} \Rightarrow I_2 = I_1 - I_{B2} = 0.261 \text{ mA}$$

**5. (a) The reverse saturation current of the germanium transistor in fig. is 2 μA at room temperature (25°C) and increases by a factor of 2 for each temperature increase of 10°C. The bias $V_{BB} = 4$ V. Find the maximum allowable value for $R_B$ if the transistor is to remain cut off at a temperature of 75° C.**

**(b) If $V_{BB} = 1.0$ V and $R_B = 100$ k, how high may the temperature increase before the transistor comes out of cut off?**

**Solution:**

(a) Given $I_{CBO}$ at 25°C = 2 μA.

$I_{CBO}$ at 75° C = $I_{CB}$ (at 25° C)2 = $(2 \times 10^{-6})2^5 = 64\ \mu A$.

Applying *KVL* in the basic circuit, we have:

$$-V_{BB} - (-I_{CBO})\ R_B - V_{BE} = 0 \qquad ...(1)$$

i.e. $-V_{BB} + (R_B)_{\max}\ I_{CBO}(\text{at } 75°\text{ C}) = V_{BE}(\text{cut off}) = -0.1$ V

i.e. $-5 + R_{B\max} \times 64 \times 10^{-6} = -0.1$

$\therefore\ R_{B\max} = 75.38.$

(b) If $V_{BB} = 1$ V, and $R_B = 100$ k,

We have: $-V_{BB} + I_{CBO}\ R_B = -V_{BE\text{cut off}}$

$-1 + 100 \times 10^3\ I_{CBO} = -0.1$

or $I_{CBO} = \dfrac{1 - 0.1}{50} = 9\ \mu A$

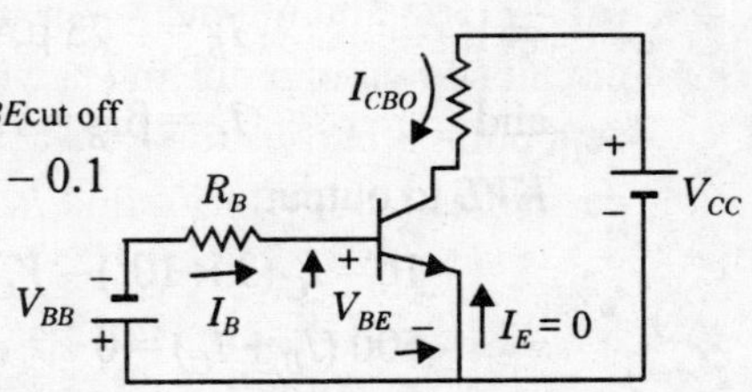


$\therefore\ 9 \times 10^{-6} = I_{CBO}\ (\text{at } 25°\text{C})\ 2^{\Delta t/10}$

$= 2 \times 10^{-6}\ 2^{\Delta t/10}$

$\Rightarrow \quad 2^{\Delta t/10} = 4.5 \Rightarrow \Delta t = 21.7$

$\therefore \quad T = 25 + 21.7 = 46.7$°C.

**6. A silicon transistor with $V_{BEsat} = 0.8$ V, $\beta = h_{fe} = 100$, $V_{CEsat} = 0.2$ V is used in the circuit shown. Find the minimum value of $R_C$ for which the transistor remains in saturation.**

**Solution:**

Given $V_{BEsat} = 0.8$ V, $\beta = h_{fe} = 100$, $V_{CEsat} = 0.2$ V, $Rc_{min} = ?$

Apply *KVL* to input:

$$6 - 200 \times 10^3 I_B - V_{BEsat} = 0$$

$$6 - 200 \times 10^3 I_B - 0.8 = 0$$

$$I_B = \frac{5.2}{200 \times 10^3} = 0.026 \text{ mA.}$$

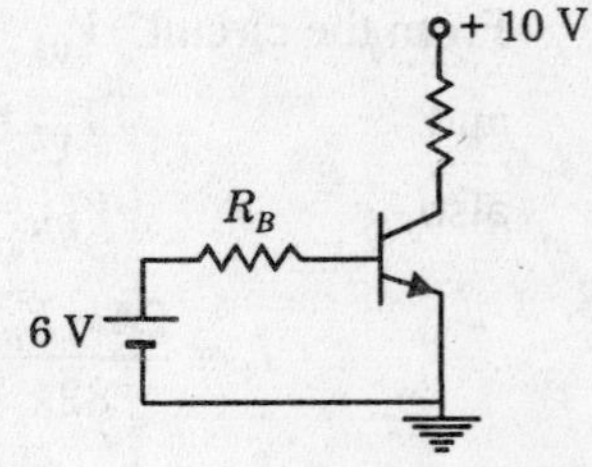


Now apply *KVL* to output:

$$10 - \beta I_B R_C - V_{CEmax} = 0 \qquad (\because I_C = \beta I_B)$$

$$10 - (100)(0.026 \times 10^{-3}) Rc_{min} - 0.2 = 0$$

$$\therefore \quad R_{Cmin} = \frac{9.8}{2.6 \times 10^{-3}} = 3.769 \text{ K}$$

$$R_{Cmin} = 3.769 \text{ K}$$

**7. For the circuit shown assume $\beta = h_{fe} = 100$.**

**(a) Find if the silicon transistor is in cut off, saturation, or in the active region. Find $V_o$.**

**(b) Find the minimum value for the emitter resistor $R_e$ for which the transistor operates in the active region.**

**Solution:**

(a) $\beta = 100$.

Assuming transistor is in active region *KVL* to input

$$-5 - (8 \times 10^3) I_B + 0.7 - 500 (I_B + I_C) = 0$$

As $\quad I_C = \beta I_B$

$\Rightarrow \quad I_B = -73\ \mu$A

and $\quad I_C = \beta I_B = 7.3$ mA,

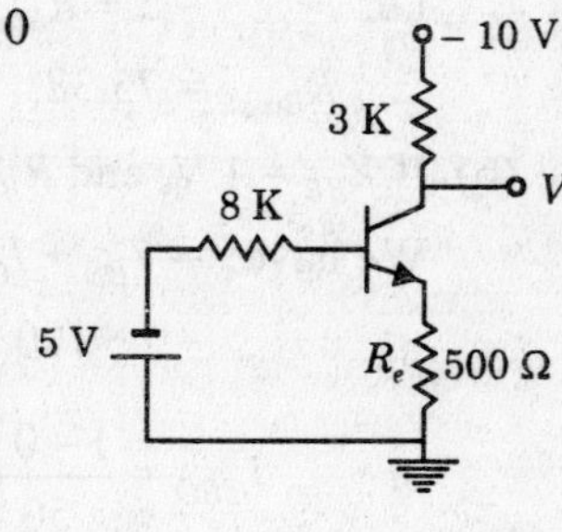


*KVL* to output:

$$-10 - I_C(3 \times 10^3) - V_{CEactive}$$
$$-500 (I_B + I_C) = 0$$

$$\therefore \Rightarrow \quad V_{CEactive} = -10 - I_B\{100 (3 \times 10^3) + 500 (101)\} = 4.02$$

$$\Rightarrow \quad V_{CB} + V_{BEactive} = 4.02 \Rightarrow V_{CB} = 4.02 - (-0.7) = 4.9 \text{ V.}$$

i.e. output is forward bias with input forward bias.

$\therefore$ Transistor is in saturation.

(b) $V_o = V_{CE} + (I_C + I_B)\, 500 = -0.2 + (2.02) = 2$ V

(c) *KVL* at input is:

$$-5 - 8 \times 10^3 (I_B) - V_{BEwt} - (I_B + I_C) R_E = 0$$

$V_{BEwt} = -5 - 8 \times 10^3 (-73 \times 10^{-6}) - 101(-73)(10^{-6}) R_E < 0.8$ to be in active

$\Rightarrow \quad 7.73 \times 10^{-3} Re < 5.216$

$\Rightarrow \quad Re < 674\ \Omega$

$\therefore \quad R_{C\min} = 674.7\ \Omega$

**8. If the Silicon transistor used in the circuit shown has a minimum value of $\beta = h_{fe}$ of 30 and if $I_{CBO} = 10$ mA at 25° C,**

**(a) Find $V_o$ for $V_i = 12$ V and in which region is $Q$.**

**(b) Find the minimum value of $R_1$ for which the transistor in part (a) is in active region.**

**(c) If $R_1 = 15$ k and $V_i = 0.7$ V find $Vo$ and show that $Q$ is at cut off.**

**(d) Find the maximum temperature at which the transistor in part (c) remains at cut off.**

**Solution:**

(a) From input:

$I_B = I_1 - I_2$

$$= \frac{12 - 0.8}{10k} - \frac{0.8 - (-12)}{120k} = \frac{11.2}{15} - \frac{12.8}{100}$$

$I_B = 1.01$ mA

$\therefore \quad I_C = \beta I_B = 30\,(1.01 \text{ mA}) = 30.4$ mA.

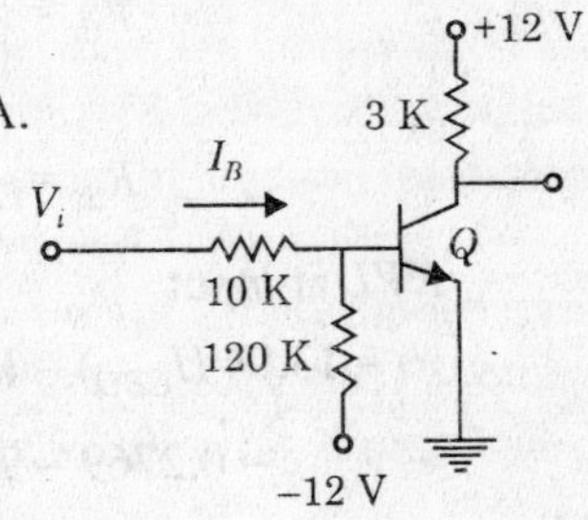


From output:

$12 - I_C R_C - V_{CE} = 0$

$$\Rightarrow \quad I_{C\min} = \frac{12 - 0.2}{3k} = 3.93 \text{ mA}$$

$\therefore \quad I_C > I_{C\min}$

It is clear that transistor is in saturation and $V_o = V_{CEsat} = 0.2$ V

$$V_{BEactive} = 0.7 \text{ V}, I_B = \frac{12 - 0.7}{R_1} - \frac{0.7 - (-12)}{120k}$$

$$= \frac{11.3}{R_1} - 0.1058 \text{ mA}$$

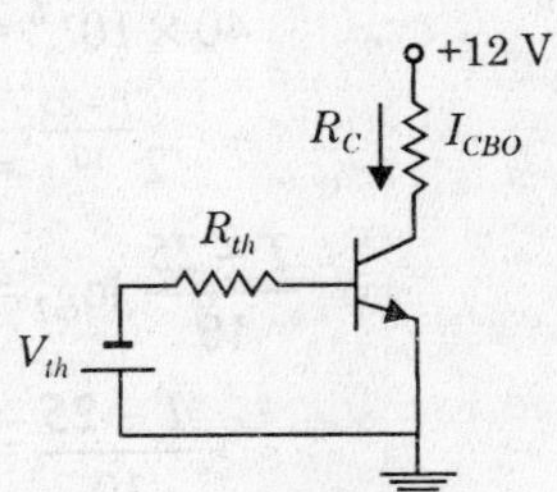


$$\Rightarrow \quad I_C = \beta I_B = 30\left(\frac{11.3}{R_1} - 0.1058\right)$$

$$= \frac{339}{R_1} - 3.175 \text{ mA}$$

*KVL* at output:

$12 - I_C R_C - V_{CE} = 0$

$$V_{CE} = 12 - I_C R_C$$

For transistor to be in active, $V_{CE} > 0.2$

$$\Rightarrow \quad 12 - I_C R_C > 0.2$$

$$\Rightarrow \quad 12 - 3\text{ k}\left(\frac{339}{R_1} - 3.175mA\right) > 0.2$$

$$\Rightarrow \quad 12 - \frac{1017k\Omega}{R_1} + 9.525 \geq 0.2$$

$$\Rightarrow \quad 21.525 - 0.2 \geq \frac{1017\,k}{R_1}$$

$$\Rightarrow \quad R_1 \geq \frac{1017}{21.325} \Rightarrow R_1 \geq 47.69\text{ k.}$$

i.e, $\quad R_{min} = 47.69$ k.

(c) for $V_i = 1$ V; $V_{BE} = \dfrac{12k \times 2}{130k} - \dfrac{10k}{130k} \times 12 = \dfrac{240 - 120}{130} < 0 - 0.3 < 0$

i.e. transistor is in cut off $\Rightarrow V_o = 12$

(d) For the Thevenin's equivalent circuit.

$$V_{th} = \left(\frac{120\,(0.7)}{120 + 10} - \frac{10 \times 12}{120 + 10}\right) = -0.2769$$

$$R_{th} = \frac{10 \times 12}{120 + 10} = 9.23\text{ k}\,\Omega$$

*KVL* at input:

$$-13.04\,(I_{CBO}) - V_{BE} = 0$$

$$-0.2769 - 9.23\text{ k}\,(-I_{CBO}) - V_{BE} = 0$$

$$\Rightarrow \quad I_{CBO} = 53.29\text{ mA}$$

$$V_{BE} \leq -0.2769 + 9.23\,I_{CBO} \leq 0$$

$$I_{CBO} = 40\ \mu\text{A.}$$

Given $\quad I_{CBO} = 10$ mA at 25° C

$$\therefore \quad 40 \times 10^{-6} = 10 \times 10^{-9}\, 2^{\frac{T-25}{10}}$$

$$2^{\frac{T-25}{10}} = 4000$$

$$\frac{T - 25}{10} \log_2 = \log\,(4000)$$

$$\frac{T - 25}{10} = \frac{3.6}{0.3010} = 11.96$$

$$T - 25 = 119.6$$

$$\therefore \quad T = 144.6°\text{ C}$$

**9. Consider the circuit of fig. shown with $V_{CC} = 12$ V, $R_B = 12$ kΩ, and $R_C = 2$k. The transistor with $\beta = 100$, $V_{BE} = +0.7$ V and a saturation voltage $V_{CEsat} = 0.1$ V. Find the operating conditions when (a) $V_{BB} = 1$ V and (b) 12 V.**

**Solution:**

(a) for $V_{BB} = 1.0$ V

Applying *KVL* at the base-emitter loop:

$$-V_{BB} + I_B R_B + V_{BE} = 0$$

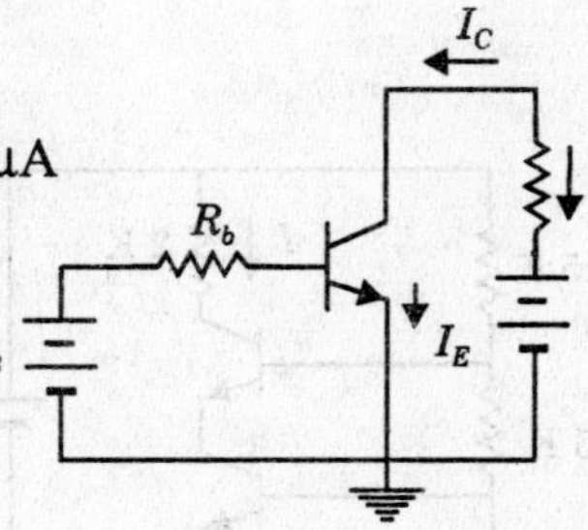


$$I_B = \frac{V_{BB} - V_{BE}}{R_B} = \frac{1.0 - 0.7}{12 \times 10^3} = 25\ \mu\text{A}$$

$$I_C = \beta I_B$$

$$= 10 \times 25\ \mu\text{A} = 2.5\ \text{mA}$$

$$I_E \approx I_C = 2.5\ \text{mA}$$

$$V_{CE} = V_{CC} - I_C R_C = 12 - (2.5 \times 10^{-3})(2 \times 10^3) = 7\ \text{V}$$

Thus the transistor is operating within the active region i.e.($V_{CE} > V_{CEsat}$) as shown on the load line of fig. b.

(b) For $V_{BB} = 12$ V

$$I_B = \frac{12 - 0.7}{12 \times 10^3} = 0.94\ \text{mA}$$

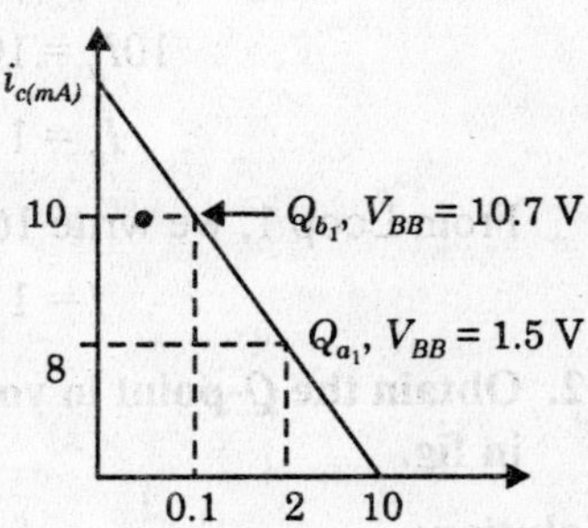


$$I_C = \beta I_B = 94\ \text{mA}$$

And $V_{CE} = 12 - (94 \times 10^{-3})(2\ \text{k})$

$$= -176\ \text{V}$$

∴ the transistor is in saturation, and

$$V_{CE} = V_{CEsat} \approx 0.1\ \text{V}.$$

The collector current is:

$$I_C = \frac{V_{CC} - V_{CEsat}}{R_C} = \frac{12 - 0.1}{2\,k\Omega} = 5.95\ \text{mA}$$

And $I_E = I_C + I_B = 5.95 + 0.94 = 6.89$ mA

Hence β in saturation condition is $\frac{I_C}{I_B} = 6.33$

**10. For good stabilized biasing of the transistor of the *CE* amplifier of fig, the condition is to be:**

**Solution:**

Biasing stability:

$$R_1 \| R_2 = R_B$$

$$S = \frac{(\beta+1)R_B/R_e}{\beta+1+R_B/R_e}$$

$$S = 1 \quad \text{i.e. } R_b/R_e << 1$$

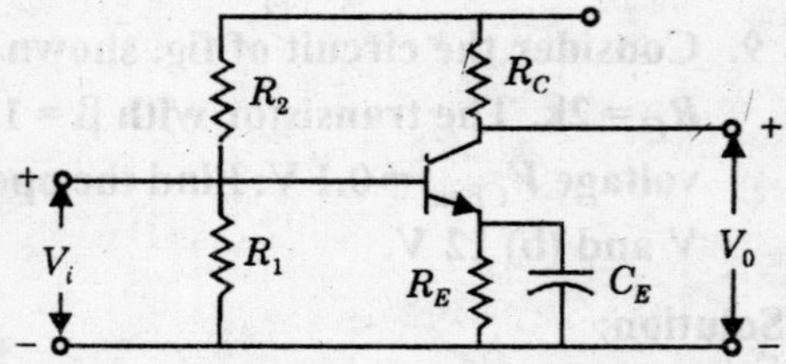


**11. If the transistor in fig. have high values of β and a $V_{BE}$ of 0.65 V. The current flowing through the 2 kΩ resistance will be:**

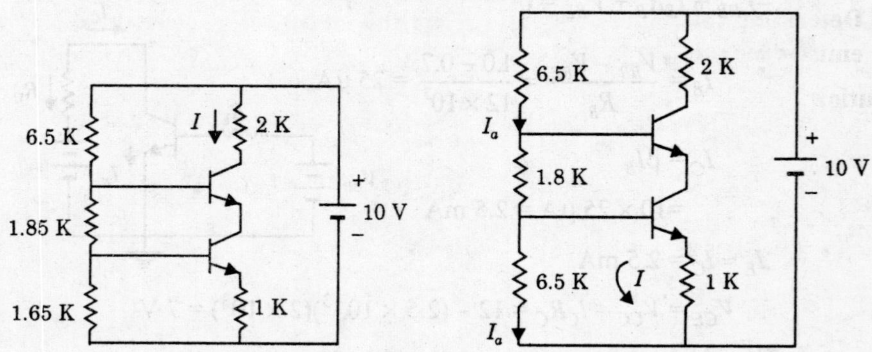


(a) (b)

**Solution:**

Neglecting $I_B$

$$10I_a = 10 \text{ V}$$

$$I_a = 1 \text{ mA}$$

From Loop 1, we write $16.5 - 65 = 1kI_d$

$$\therefore \qquad I = 1 \text{ mA.}$$

**12. Obtain the *Q*-point in voltage divider with emitter bias circuit shown in fig.**

**Solution:**

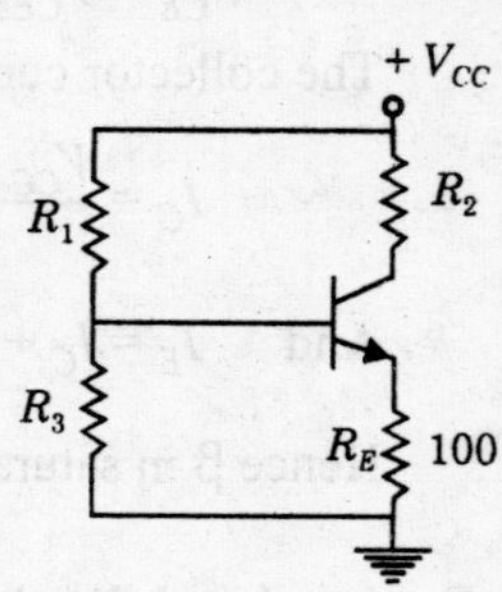


Given $V_{CC} = 12$ V; $R_1 = R_2 = 10$ k, $R_C = 1$ k.

$R_E = 5$ k, $\beta = 100$, $V_{BE} = 0.7$ k

$$V_B = \frac{12 \times 10}{20} = 6 \text{ V}, R_B = 5 \text{ k}$$

$$V_B = R_B I_B + V_{BE} + R_B \beta I_B$$

$$= 5 \text{ k} \times I_B + 0.7 + 5 \text{ k} \times \beta \times I_B$$

$$= 505 \text{ k } I_B + 0.7$$

$$I_B = \frac{5.3}{505k} = 0.010 \text{ mA}$$

$$I_C = \beta I_B = 100 \times 00.0105 \text{ mA} = 1.05 \text{ mA}$$

$$V_{CE} = V_{CC} - I_C (R_C + R_E)$$

$$= 12 - 6\text{k} \times 1.05 \text{ mA}$$

$$= 12 - 6.3$$

$$V_{CE} = 5.7 \text{ V}.$$

**13. Determine the value of $R_1$ and $R_2$ in the circuit of voltage divider emitter bias shown in fig.**

**Solution:**

$$V_{CC} = 12 \text{ V}, V_{CE} = 0.2 \text{ V}, I_{CQ} = 18 \text{ mA},$$

$$I_{BQ} = 0.3 \text{ mA}, S = 10, \beta = 100$$

$$V_{CEQ} = 4.25 \text{ V}, R_C = 0.330 \text{ k}, R_E = 0.1 \text{ k},$$

$$V_{BE} = 0.2 \text{ V}$$

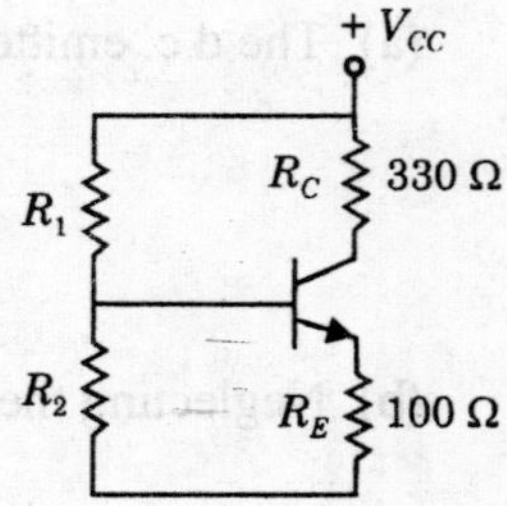


$$V_{BB} = R_B I_B + V_{BE} + R_E I_E$$

$$= 0.3 \text{ mA } R_B + 0.2 + 0.1\text{k} \times 10 \text{ mA}$$

$$= 2.0 + 0.3 \times 10^{-3} R_B$$

$$S = 10 = \frac{(1+\beta)(R_B + R_E)}{R_B + (1+\beta) R_E}$$

$$= \frac{101(R_B + 0.1k)}{R_B + (101 \times 0.1k)}$$

$$R_B + 10.1 \text{ k} = 10.1 R_B + 1.01 \text{ k}$$

$$9.1 R_B = 9.09 \text{ k}$$

$$R_B = 1\text{k}$$

$$V_{BB} = 2 + 3 \times 10^{-3} \times 1 \text{k} = 2.3 \text{ V}$$

$$= \frac{V_{CC} R_2}{R_1 + R_2} = \frac{12 R_2}{R_1 + R_2}$$

$$R_1 + R_2 = 5.22 R_2$$

$$R_1 = 4.22 R_2$$

If $R_2 = 1.2 \text{ k}$

$\therefore$ $R_1 = 5 \text{ k}$

**14. A *BJT* has $\alpha = 0.99$, $i_B = I_B = 25$ mA and $I_{CBO} = 200$ *nA*. Find (a) the *dc* collector current, (b) the dc emitter current, and (c) the percentage error in emitter current when leakage current is neglected.**

**Solution:**

As $\alpha = \dfrac{I_C - I_{CBO}}{I_E} \Rightarrow \beta = \dfrac{\alpha}{1-\alpha} = \dfrac{I_C - I_{CEO}}{I_B}$ ...(1)

Leakage currents are related by

$$I_{CEO} = (\beta + 1)\, I_{CBO} \quad \text{...(2)}$$

Given $\alpha = 0.99$,

$$\beta = \frac{\alpha}{1-\alpha} = \frac{0.99}{1-0.99} = 99$$

using equation (2) in (1) gives

$$I_C = \beta I_B + (\beta + 1)\, I_{CBO}$$
$$= 99\,(25 \times 10^{-6}) + (99 + 1)\,(200 \times 10^{-9})$$
$$= 2.495 \text{ mA},$$

(a) The d.c. emitter current is

$$I_E = \frac{I_C - I_{CBO}}{\alpha} = \frac{2.495 \times 10^{-3} - 200 \times 10^{-9}}{0.99}$$
$$= 2.518 \text{ mA}$$

(b) Neglecting the leakage current, we have

$$I_C = \beta I_B$$
$$= 99(25 \times 10^{-6})$$
$$= 2.475 \text{ mA}$$

and $$I_E = \frac{I_C}{\alpha} = \frac{2.475}{0.99} = 2.5 \text{ mA}$$

with an emitter-current error of $\dfrac{2.518 - 2.5}{2.518} = 0.71$

$\therefore$ Percentage error in $I_E$ when leakage current is neglected is 0.71%.

**15. In the circuit shown, $V_{CC}$ = 26 V, $R_C$ = 20 k and $R_E$ = 470 Ω . If a Silicon transistor is used with β = 45 and if under quiescent conditions $V_{CE}$ = 8 V, determine (a) *R* (b) the stability factor *S*.**

**Solution:**

Given $V_{CC} = 26$ V, $R_C = 20$ k and $R_E = 470\ \Omega$ $\beta = 45$ $V_{CE} = 8$ V

*KVL* to input:

$$V_{CC} - (I_C + I_B)\, R_C - V_{CE} - R_E(I_C + I_B) = 0 \quad \text{...(1)}$$

$$V_{CC} - (1 + \beta)\, I_B R_C - V_{CE} - R_E\,(1 + \beta)\, I_B = 0.$$

$$V_{CC} - (1 + \beta)\, I_B\,(R_C + R_E) - V_{CE} = 0$$

$$26 - (1 + 45)\, I_B\,(20 \times 10^3 + 470) - 8 = 0$$

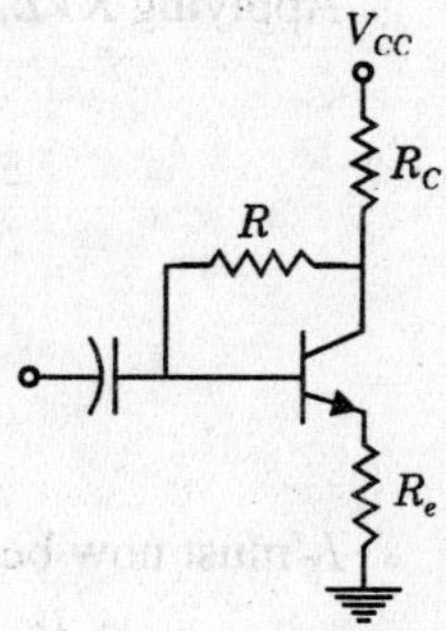


$$\Rightarrow \qquad I_B = \frac{26-8}{46\left(20\times10^3+470\right)} = 19.1\ \mu\text{A}$$

as $\qquad I_C = \beta I_B$

$$= 45\times19.1\times10^{-6}$$

$\therefore \qquad I_C = 860.2\ \mu\text{A}.$

*KVL* to input:

$$V_{CC} - R_C\,(I_C + I_B) - RI_B - R_E(I_C + I_B)\,V_{BE} = 0 \qquad \text{...(2)}$$

$$\therefore \qquad R = \frac{V_{CC} - R_C\,(I_C + I_B) - R_E\,(I_L + I_B)\,V_{BE}}{I_B}$$

$$R = \frac{26 - \left(20\times10^3\right)(860.2+19.1)\,10^{-6} - 470\,(860.2+19.1)\,10^{-6} - 0.7}{19.1\times10^{-6}}$$

$\therefore R = 382\ \text{k}\Omega$

**Differentiating equation (2) partially with respect to $I_C$. We get:**

$$\frac{\partial I_B}{\partial I_C} = -\frac{R_C + R_E}{R_C + R_E + R}$$

$$\therefore \qquad S = \frac{1+\beta}{1+\left(\dfrac{\beta\,(R_E)}{R_E + R_B}\right)}$$

$$S = \frac{1+45}{1-45\,(-0.0853)} = 29.74$$

$$\therefore \qquad S = 29.74$$

**16. A *p-n-p* Ge transistors is used in the self-biasing arrangement of fig. the circuit component values are $V_{CC} = 4.5$ V, $R_c = 1.5$ K, $R_e = 0.27$ K, $R_2 = 2.7$ K and $P_1 = 2.7$ K, If $\beta = 44$ (a) find the quiescent point (b) Recalculate these values if the base spreading Resistance of 690 Ω is taken into account.**

**Solution:**

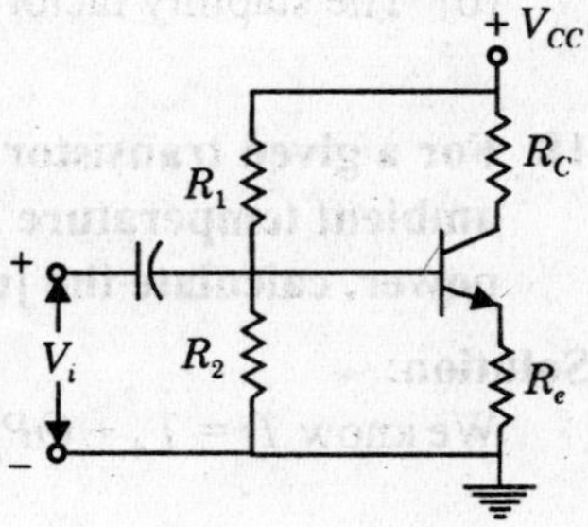


$$V = \frac{R_1 V_{CC}}{R_1 + R_2} = \frac{2.7\times1.5}{2.7\times2.7} = 0.409\ \text{V}$$

$$R_b = \frac{R_1 R_2}{R_1 + R_2} = \frac{2.7\times2.7}{2.7+2.7}\ K = 2.46\ \text{K}.$$

For Germanium, $|V_{BE}| = 0.2$

Applying *KVL*, we get

$$-V = I_B R_B + V_{BE} + (1+\beta) I_B R_C$$

$$-0.409 = I_B (2.46 + 45\ 0.27) - 0.2$$

$$I_B = -14.3 \text{ mA}$$

$$I_C = \beta I_B = -0.63 \text{ mA}$$

$$V_{CE} = -V_{CC} - I_C R_C - (I_B + I_C) R_e = -3.38 \text{ V.}$$

$I_B$ must now be inversed by 690 Ω

$$2.49 + 0.69 = 3.15 \text{ K}$$

$$-4.09 = I_B (15.29) - 0.2$$

$$I_B = -13.7\ \mu\text{A}$$

$$I_C = -0.6 \text{ mA.}$$

$$V_{CE} = -4.5 + 0.6 \times 1.5 + 0.602 \times 0.27 = -3.43 \text{ V.}$$

**17. A *PNP* transistors type 2N464 with β = 25 is used in a *CE* amplifiers with collector-to-base bias. The collector circuit resistance $R_c$ = 2.5 KΩ and $V_{CC}$ = 10 V. Assuming $V_{BE}$ = 0. Find (a) suitable value of $R_b$ so as to make quiescent collector- to-emitter voltage $V_{CE}$ = – 5 V, (b) the stability factor *S*.**

**Solution:**

$$I_L = \frac{-V_{CC} - V_{CE}}{R_C} = \frac{-10-(-5)}{2.5 \times 10^3} = -2 \text{ mA}$$

If the current $I_{co}$ is assumed to be negligibly small, the quiescent base current is given by

$$I_B = \frac{I_C}{\beta} = \frac{-2}{25} = -80 \text{ mA.}$$

Since the voltage $V_{BE}$ is assumed to be zero, the resistance $R_D$ can be determined by the relation.

$$R_B = \frac{V_{CE} - V_{BE}}{I_B} = \frac{-5-0}{-8.0 \times 10^{-6}} = 62.5 \text{ k}\Omega$$

(b) The stability factor $S = \dfrac{1+\beta}{1+\beta\left[R_c/\{R_c + R_b\}\right]} = 13.32.$

**18. For a given transistor , the thermal resistance is 8° C/W and for the ambient temperature $T_A$ is 27° C . If the transistor dissipater 3 W of power, calculate the junction temperature $T_j$.**

**Solution:**

We know $Tj = T_A + \Theta P_D = 27 + (8° \text{ C/W}) \times 3\text{W} = 27 + 24 = 51° \text{ C}$

**19. Determine the power dissipation capability of a transistor which has been mounted with a heat sink having thermal resistance $Q_{HS-A} = 8°C/W$,**
**$T_A = 40°C$, $T_j = 160°C$, $\Theta_{J-C} = 5°C/W$ and $\Theta_{C-A} = 85°C/W$**

**Solution:**

$$\Theta_{J-A} = \Theta_{J-C} + \Theta_{C-A} // \Theta_{J-A} = 5 + 85//8$$

$$= 5 + \frac{85 \times 8}{85 + 8} = 5 + 7.31 = 12.35 \text{ C/W}$$

$$P_D = \frac{T_J - T_A}{\Theta_{J-A}} = \frac{160 - 40}{12.31} = 9.75 \text{ W}$$

**20. For the o/p characteristic shown in figure,if the base current $I_{BQ}$ = 20 mA, the $Q$-point collector current, $I_{CQ}$ = 1.2 mA for $R_L$ = 3 KW and $V_{cc}$ = 10 V. Obtain in the maximum permissible swing**

**Solution:**

The quiescent point in figure is defined as $I_{CQ}$ = 1.2 mA and

$I_{BQ}$ = 20 mA.

Hence the drop across the load line

$= R_L I_{CQ} = 3 \times 12 = 3.6$ V

thus $V_{CE} = 9.36 = 5.4$ V.

For equal distribution of $V_{CC}$ across the load resistance and the transistor, the $Q$-point should be selected such that $I_{BQ}$ fills between 20 mA to 30 mA which will yield maximum swing in the corresponding maximum of $I_C$ and $V_{CE.}$

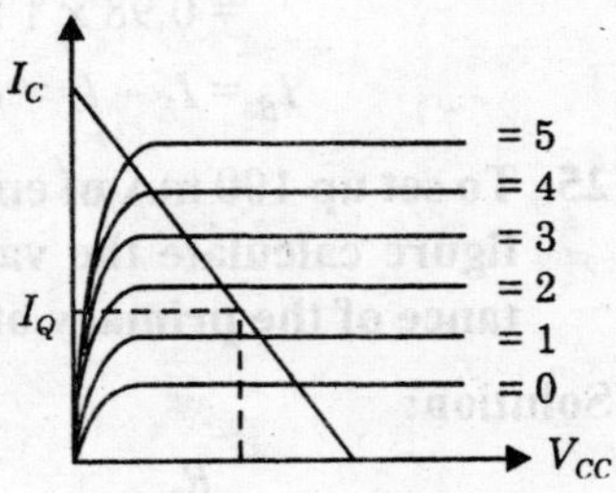


**21. When the current of transistor is changed by 1mA its collector current changes by 0.995 mA. Calculate (a) its common-base short circuit gain α, (b) its common-emitter short circuit current gain β**

**Solution:**

$$\alpha = \frac{\nabla i_C}{\nabla i_E} = \frac{0.995 \times 10^{-3}}{1 \times 10^{-3}} = 0.995.$$

$$\beta = \frac{\alpha}{1 - \alpha} = \frac{0.995}{1 \times 0.995} = 199$$

**22. The *dc* current gain of a transistor in *CE* configuration is 100. Find its *dc* current gain in *CB* configuration.**

**Solution:**

$$\alpha_{dc} = \frac{\beta_{dc}}{\beta_{dc}+1} = \frac{100}{100+1} = 0.99.$$

**23. Calculate the maximum collector current in figure, if the 50 < β < 200, $R_B$ = 200 KΩ, $R_C$ = 2 kΩ, $V_{CC}$ = 20 V.**

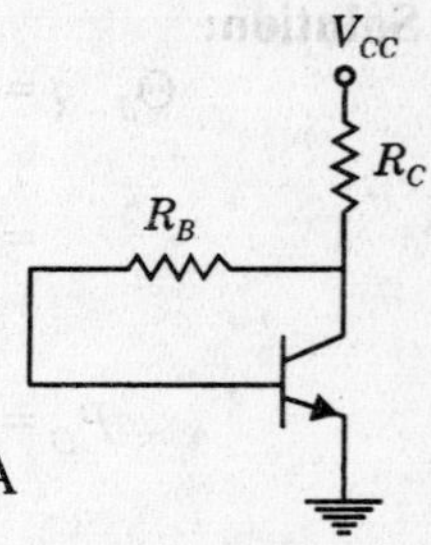


**Solution:**

$$I_B = \frac{V_{CC}}{R_B + \beta R_C}$$

for maximum value of β, i.e., β = 200

$$I_B = \frac{20}{200\times10^{-3} + 200\times2\times10^{-3}} = \frac{10^{-4}}{3} = 33.3 \text{ mA}$$

$$I_c = \beta I_B = 200 \times 33.3 \times 10^{-6} = 6.6 \ \mu\text{A}.$$

**24. A certain transistor has $\alpha_{dc}$ of 0.98 and a collector current $I_{CO}$ of 1 μA. Calculate the collector and base current when $I_E$ = 1mA.**

**Solution:**

With $I_E$ = 1 mA

$$I_c = \alpha_{dc}\, I_E + I_{CO}$$

$$= 0.98 \times 1 \times 10^{-3} + 110^{-6} = 0.981 \times 10^{-3} = 0.981 \text{ mA}$$

$$I_B = I_E - I_L = (1-0.9821)\, 10^{-3} = 0.019 \text{ mA} = 19 \ \mu\text{A}$$

**25. To set up 100 mA of emitter current in the Power amplifier circuit of figure calculate the value of the resistor $R_E$ and $V_{CE}$. The *dc* resistance of the primary of the o/p transformer is 20 Ω.**

**Solution:**

$$V_B = \frac{R_2}{R_1 + R_2} \times V_{CC}$$

$$= \frac{100}{200+100} \times 15 = 5 \text{ V}$$

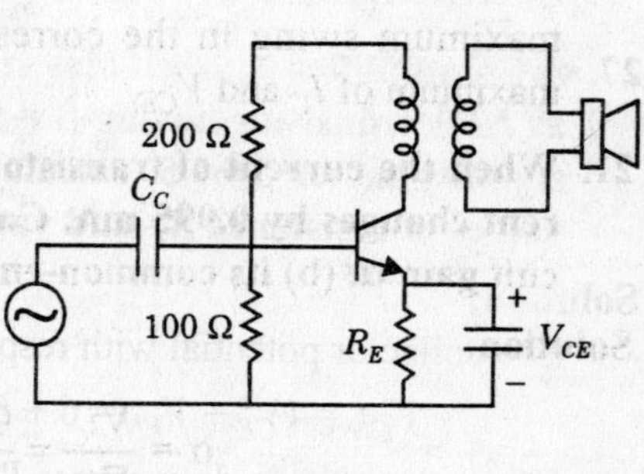


Substitute

$V_{BE}$, $V_E = V_B = 5$ V

$$R_E = \frac{V_E}{I_E} = \frac{5}{0.1} = 50 \ \Omega$$

$$V_{CE} = V_{CC} - (R_C + R_E)\, I_c = 15 - (20 + 50)\ 0.1 = 8 \text{ V}$$

**26. Calculate the minimum value of emitter current for the biasing circuit of figure. Also calculate the corresponding values of collector-to-emitter voltage.The transistor used in the circuit is a Ge transistor. If the collector resistance, $R_C$ is changed to 1 KΩ. Determine the new Q-points for the minimum values of β.**

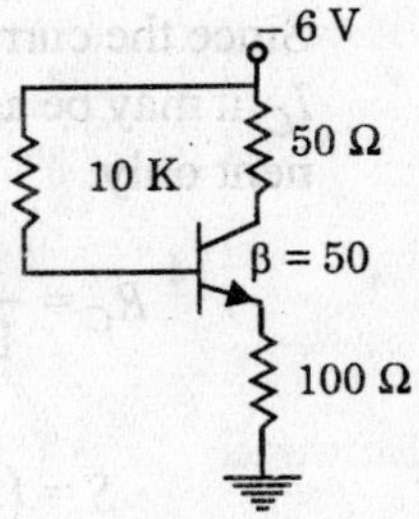


**Solution:**

Since for Ge transistor $V_{BE} = 0.3$

$$I_B = \frac{V_{CC} - V_{BE}}{R_B + (\beta + 1)\, R_E}$$

Multiplying by (β + 1) on both sides

$$(\beta + 1)\, I_B = \frac{(V_{CC} - V_{BE})\, \beta + 1}{R_B + (\beta + 1)\, R_E}$$

$$I_E = (\beta + 1)\, I_B$$

$$I_E = \frac{(V_{CC} - V_{BE})\, \beta + 1}{R_B + (\beta + 1)\, R_E} = \frac{(6 - 0.3)\,(50 + 1)}{10 \times 10^{-3} + (50 + 1)\, 100} = 19.25 \text{ mA.}$$

$$V_{CE} = V_{CC} - (R_C + R_B)\, I_E = 6\text{-}(50 + 100)\ 19.2910^{-3} = 3.1 \text{ V.}$$

Since the value of emitter current does not depend upon the value of $R_c$, the emitter current $I_E$ remains the same.

$$\text{For } \beta = 50,\ I_E = 19.25 \text{ mA}$$

$$V_{CE} = V_{CC} - (R_C + R_E)\, I_E$$

$$= 6\text{-}(1000 + 100)\ 19.2510^{-3} = -15.17 \text{ V.}$$

The above result is observed. We face such difficulties when the transistor is in saturation. The maximum possible current that can be supplied by $V_{CC}$ to o/p section is

$$I_{C(sat)} = \frac{V_{cc}}{R_C + R_E} = \frac{6}{1000 + 100} = 5.45 \text{ mA}$$

Under saturation, the collector-to-emitter voltage is $V_{CE(sat)} = 0$ V.

**27. A CE amplifier with self bias arrangement as shown in figure employs as *NPN* transistor having β = 99. If the circuit is required to have a stability factor *S* of 5, calculate the values of $R_1$, $R_2$ and $R_c$, if the values of resistance $R_C$ and various voltages are as shown in figure.**

**Solution:**

The collector potential with respect to the ground terminal *N* in given as

$$V_{CN} = V_{CE} + V_{EN} = 6 + 5.5 = 11.5 \text{ V}$$

Hence the voltage drop across $R_C = 15 - 11.5 = 3.5$ V the collector current,

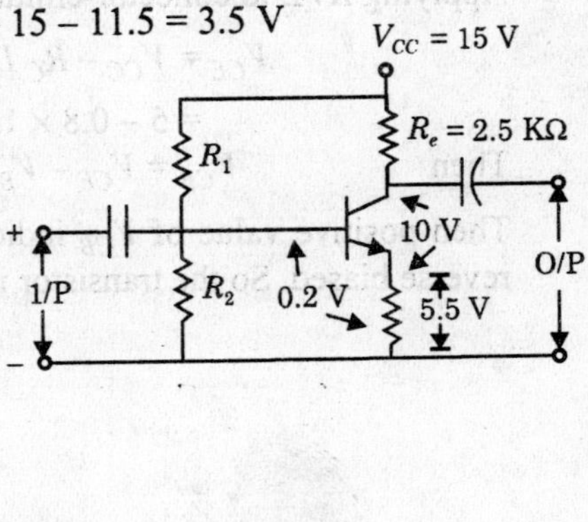


$$I_C = \frac{3.5}{2.5 \times 10^3} = 1.4 \text{ mA.}$$

$$I_B = \frac{I_C}{\beta} = \frac{1.4}{99} = 14 \text{ mA}$$

Since the current $I_B$ is very small as compared with the collector current, $I_C$, it may be assumed that the emitter consists of collector current component only.

$$R_C = \frac{5.5}{1.4 \times 10^{-3}} = 3.13\ \text{k}\Omega$$

$$S = (1+\beta) \times \frac{1 + R_b/R_C}{1+\beta + R_b/R_C};\ R_b/R_C = 4.167$$

$$R_b = 4.167 \times R_C = 4.167 \times 3.93 = 16.376\ \text{mA}.$$

$$R_1 = R_b \frac{V_{CC}}{V} \text{ and } R_2 = \frac{R_1 V}{V_{CC} - V}$$

$$V = I_B R_B + V_{BE} + (I_B + I_C) R_C$$

$$= 0.014 \times 16.376 + 0.2 + (0.014 + 1.4)\ 3.93 = 6\ \text{V}$$

$$\text{Hence } R_1 = \frac{16.373 \times 15}{6} = 40.94\ \text{K}\Omega$$

$$R_2 = \frac{40.94 \times 6}{15 - 6} = 27.29\ \text{K}\Omega.$$

**28. Consider the transistor in figure which has a resistance included between emitter and ground. Show that the transistor is operating in active mode. Calculate $I_C$, $I_E$ and $I_B$. Given $\beta = 50$.**

**Solution:**

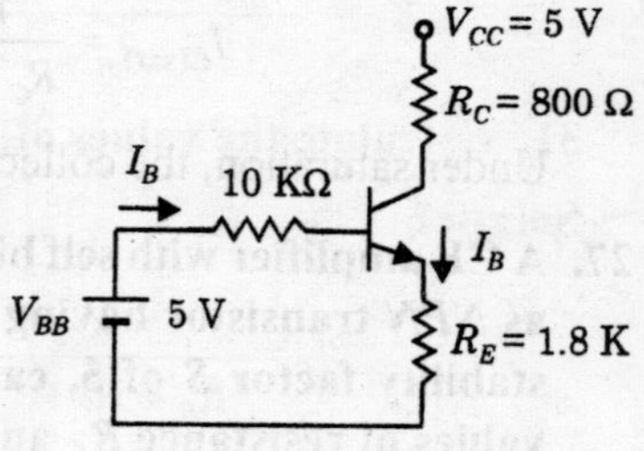


$$I_C = \beta I_B$$

$$I_E = I_B + I_C = (\beta + 1)\ I_B$$

Applying *KVL* in the base-emitter loop

$$V_{BB} - R_B I_B - V_{BE} - R_E I_E = 0$$

$$5 - 50\ I_B - 0.7 - 1.8\ (50 + 1)\ I_B = 0$$

$\Rightarrow$ $$I_B = 0.03\ \text{mA}$$

then $$I_C = 50 \times 0.03 = 1.5\ \text{mA}$$

$$I_E = I_B + I_C = 1.53\ \text{mA}$$

Applying *KVL* to collector-emitter loop

$$V_{CE} = V_{CC} - R_C I_C - R_E I_E$$

$$= 5 - 0.8 \times 1.5 - 1.8 \times 1.53 = 1.05\ \text{V}.$$

Then $$V_{CB} = V_{CE} - V_{BE} = 1.05 - 0.7 = 0.35\ \text{V}$$

Then positive value of $V_{CB}$ indicates that the collector-base junction is reverse biased. So the transistor is operating in active region.

**29. Make use of Thevenin's theorem to find accurate values of collector current and collector-to-emitter voltage in figure.**

**Solution:**

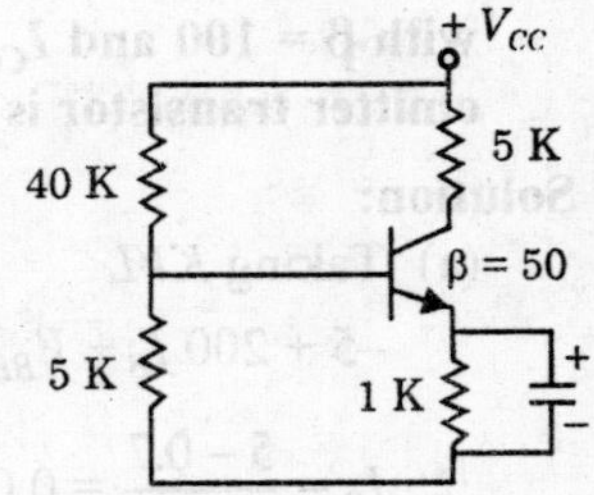


$$R_{TH} = \frac{R_2}{R_1 + R_2} \times V_{CC} = \frac{5 \times 10^3}{(40+5)\,10^3} \times 12 = 1.3 \text{ V.}$$

$$R_{TH} = \frac{R_1 R_2}{R_1 + R_2} = 4.4 \text{ k}\Omega$$

$$I_B = \frac{V_{TH} - V_{BE}}{R_{TH} + \beta\, R_E} = \frac{13 - 0.3}{4.4 \times 10^{-3} + 60 \times 10^{-3}}$$

$$= 15.52 \times 10^{-6} \text{ A}$$

$$I_C = \beta I_B = 0.93 \text{ mA}$$

$$V_{CE} = V_{CC} - (R_C + R_E)\, I_C = 6.42 \text{ V.}$$

**30. Calculate $R_B$ in the biasing circuit of figure so that the $Q$ point is fixed at $I_C = 8$ mA and $V_{CE} = 3$ V.**

**Solution:**

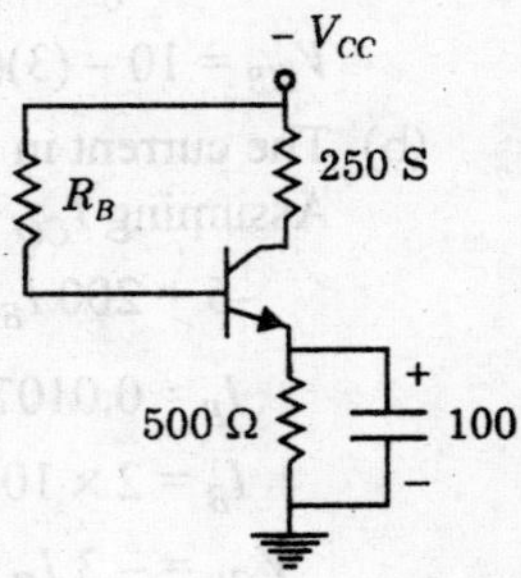


$$I_B = \frac{I_C}{\beta} = \frac{8 \times 10^{-3}}{80} = 1 \times 10^{-4} \text{ A.}$$

$$I_B R_B + (\beta + 1)\, I_B R_E = V_{CC} - V_{BE} \approx V_{CC}.$$

$$R_B = \frac{V_{CC} - (\beta + 1)\, I_B R_E}{R_B} = 49.5 \text{ K}\Omega.$$

**31. Calculate the values of the three currents in figure.**

**Solution:**

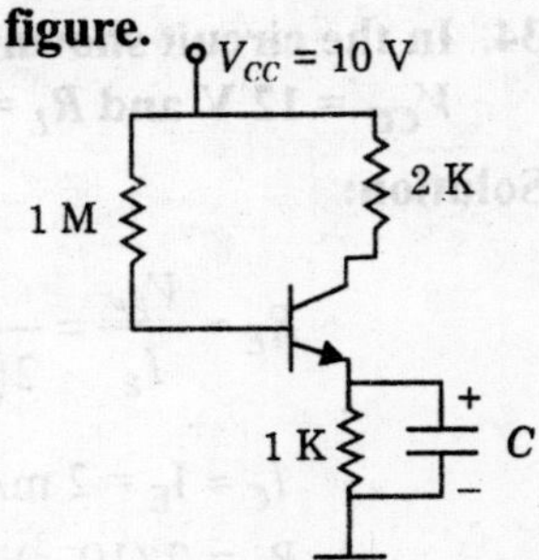


$$I_B = \frac{V_{CC}}{R_B + (\beta + 1)\, R_E} = 9.09 \text{ µA.}$$

$$I_C = \beta I_B = 0.909 \text{ µA}$$

$$I_E = I_C + I_B \approx I_C = 0.909 \text{ µA.}$$

**32. A Si npn transistor with $\alpha = 0.99$ and $I_{CBO} = 10^{-11}$ A is connected as shown in figure. Find $I_C$, $I_E$ and $V_{CE}$.**

**Solution:**

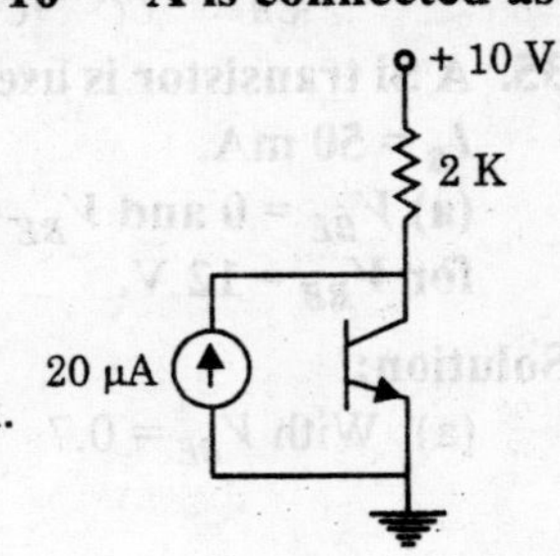


$$\beta = \frac{\alpha}{1 - \alpha} = 99$$

$$I_{CEO} = (1 + \beta)\, I_{CBO} = (1 + 99)\, 10^{-11} = 10^{-9} \text{A.}$$

$$I_C = \beta I_B + I_{CEO} = 1.98 \text{ mA}$$
$$I_E = -(I_B + I_C) = -(0.02 + 1.98) \times 10^{-3} = -2 \text{ mA.}$$
$$V_{CE} = 10 - I_C R_C = 10 - 2 \text{ mA} \times 2 \text{ K} = 6 \text{ V}$$
$$V'_{CE} = V_{CE} - V_{BE} = 6 - 0.7 = 5.3 \text{ V.}$$

**33. Find the transistor current in the circuit of the figure. A Si transistor with $\beta = 100$ and $I_{CO} = 20$ nA is used (b) Repeat point (a) if a 2 KΩ emitter transistor is added to the circuit.**

**Solution:**

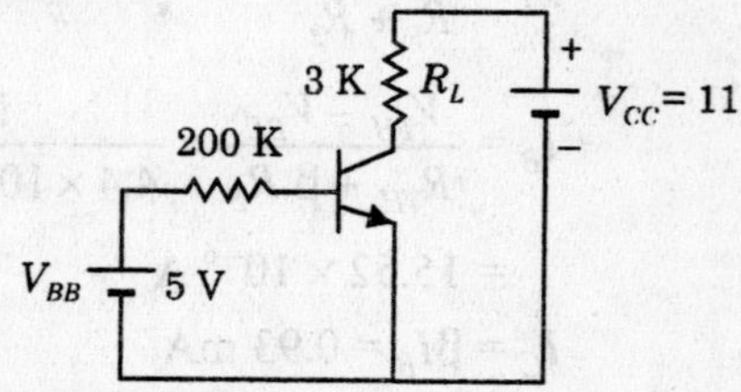


(a) Taking *KVL*

$$-5 + 200\, I_B + V_{BE} = 0$$

$$I_B = \frac{5 - 0.7}{200} = 0.0215 \text{ mA.}$$

Since $I_{CO} << I_B$, then $I_C \approx \beta I_B = 2.15$ mA.

Taking *KVL* to collector

$$-10 + 3\, I_C + V_{CB} + V_{BE} = 0$$
$$V_{CB} = 10 - (3)(2.15) - 0.7 = 2.85 \text{ V.}$$

(b) The current in the emitter resistor is $I_B + I_C \approx I_B + \beta I_B = 101\, I_B$

Assuming $I_{CO} << I_B$

$$-5 + 200\, I_B + 0.7 + (0.2)\,(101\, I_B) = 0$$
$$I_B = 0.0107 \text{ mA}, I_C = 100\, I_B = 1.07 \text{ mA}$$
$$I_B = 2 \times 10^{-5} \text{ mA} << I_B.$$
$$V_{CB} = -3\, I_C + 10 - (2)\,(101\, I_B) - 0.7 = 3.93 \text{ V.}$$

**34. In the circuit shown in fig., $I_E$ is chosen to be 2.0 mA. If $V_{EE} = 12$ V, $V_{CC} = 12$ V and $R_L = 5$ KΩ. Determine $R_E$, $I_C$, $I_C R_L$ and $V_{CB}$.**

**Solution:**

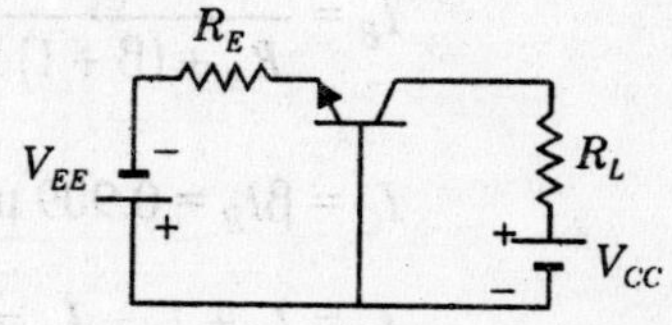


$$R_E \approx \frac{V_{EE}}{I_E} = \frac{12}{2(10^{-3})} = 6 \text{ K}\Omega.$$

$$I_C \approx I_E = 2 \text{ mA}$$
$$I_C R_L = 2\,(10^{-3})\,(5)\,(10^3) = 10 \text{ V.}$$
$$V_{CB} = V_{CC} - I_C R_L = 12 - 10 = 2 \text{ V.}$$

**35. A Si transistor is used in the circuit shown in figure. If $V_{BB}$ is 4 V and $I_B = 50$ mA.**

**(a) $V_{BE} = 0$ and $V_{BE} = 0.7$. Determine $R_B$ for $V_{BB} = 4$ V (b) Repeat (a) for $V_{BB} = 12$ V.**

**Solution:**

(a) With $V_{BE} = 0.7$

$$R_B = \frac{V_{BB} - V_{BE}}{I_B} = \frac{4 - 0.7}{50 \times 10^{-6}} = 66 \text{ KW.}$$

With $\quad V_{BE} = 0$

$$R_B = \frac{V_{BB}}{I_B} = \frac{4}{50 \times 10^{-6}} = 80 \text{ k}\Omega.$$

(b) $\quad V_{BE} = 0.7 \text{ V}.$

$$R_B = \frac{12 - (0.7)}{50\left(10^{-6}\right)} = 226 \text{ K}\Omega$$

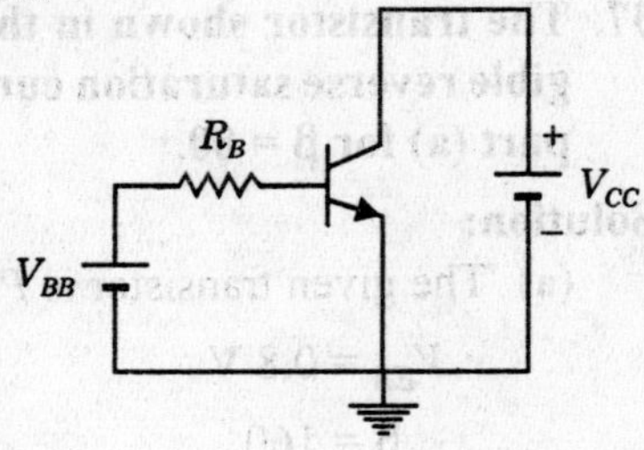


With $V_{BE} = 0$ V

$$R_B = \frac{12}{50\left(10^{-6}\right)} = 240 \text{ k}\Omega$$

**36. The measured collector and base currents of a certain transistor are $I_C = 5.202$ mA, $I_B = 50$ µA. $I_{CBO} = 2$ µA., (a) Calculate $\alpha_{dc}$ & $\beta_{dc}$ and $I_E$ (b) Find the new level of $I_B$ required to make $I_C = 10$ mA.**

**Solution:**

$$I_C = \alpha_{dc} I_E + I_{CBO}$$

$$I_E = I_B + I_C$$

(a) Solving for $I_C$

$$I_C = \frac{\alpha_{dc}}{1 - \alpha_{dc}} I_B + \frac{1}{1 - \alpha_{dc}} I_{CBO}$$

Since $\beta_{dc} = \dfrac{\alpha_{dc}}{1 - \alpha_{dc}}$

$$I_C = \beta_{dc} I_B + (1 + \beta_{dc}) I_{CBO}$$

$$5.202 \times 10^{-3} = (\beta_{dc}) [50 \times 10^{-6} + 2 \times 10^{-6}] + 2 \times 10^{-6}$$

$$\beta_{dc} = \frac{5.202 \times 10^{-3} - 2 \times 10^{-6}}{50 \times 10^{-6} + 2 \times 10^{-6}}$$

$$\beta_{dc} = 100$$

$$I_E = I_C + I_B$$

$$I_E = 5.202 \text{ mA} + 50 \text{ mA} = 5.252 \text{ mA.}$$

$$I_C = \alpha_{dc} I_E + I_{CBO}$$

$$\alpha_{dc} = \frac{5.202 mA - 2\mu\, A}{5.252} = 0.99$$

(b) $I_C = \beta_{dc} I_B + (\beta_{dc} + 1) I_{CBO}$

$$10 \times 10^{-3} = (100 \times I_B) + 101 \times 2 \times 10^{-6}$$

$$I_B = \frac{10 \times 10^{-3} - 202 \times 10^{-6}}{100} = 97.98 \text{ mA.}$$

**37. The transistor shown in the circuit of figure has $\beta = 160$ and negligible reverse saturation current. (a) Determine $I_C$ and $V_{CE}$ (b) Repeat part (a) for $\beta = 80$.**

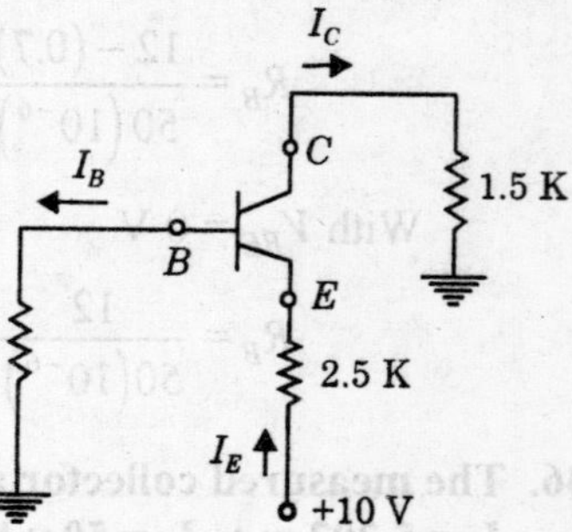


**Solution:**

(a) The given transistor is *PNP*

$\therefore V_{EB} = 0.8$ V

$\beta = 160$

$I_C = 160\, I_B;\ I_E = I_C + I_B = 161\, I_B$

For base-emitter loop

$$10 = 2.5\, I_E + V_{EB} + 400\, I_B$$

Substituting the numerical values we get

$$I_B = \frac{10 \times 0.8}{2.5 \times 161 \times 400} \times 10^3 = 11.5 \text{ μA.}$$

$$I_C = \beta I_B = 160 \times 11.5\ \mu = 1.85 \text{ mA.}$$

For collection-emitter loop

$$10 = 2.5\, I_E + V_{CE} + 1.5\, I_C$$

$$10 = 2.5 \times 1.85 + V_{CE} + 1.5 \times 1.84$$

$$V_{EC} = 2.6 \text{ V} \Rightarrow V_{CE} = -2.6 \text{ V}$$

(b) $\beta = 80$

$I_C = 80\, I_B,\ I_E = 81\, I_B$

$$I_B = \frac{10 - 0.8}{2.5 \times 81 + 400} \times 10^3 = 15.3 \text{ μA.}$$

$$I_C = 80 \times 15.3 = 1.23 \text{ mA.}$$

$$I_E = 81 \times 15.3 = 1.24 \text{ mA.,}$$

For collector emitter loop

$$10 = 2.5 \times 1.24 + V_{CE} + 1.5 \times 1.23$$

$$V_{CE} = 5.08 \text{ V or } V_{CE} = -5.08 \text{ V.}$$

**38. In the biasing with feedback resistor method, a Si transistor with feedback transistor is used .The operating point is at 7 V, 1 mA and $V_{CC}$ = 12 V. Assume $\beta = 100$. Determine (a) the value of $R_B$, (b) stability**

**factor and (c) what will be new operating point it β = 50 with all other circuit values are same.**

**Solution:**

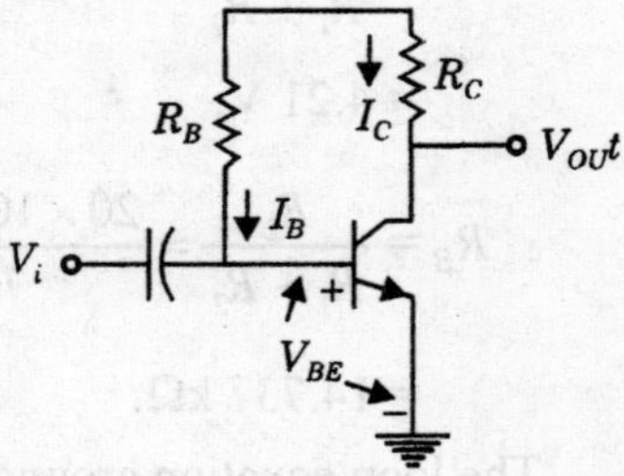


$V_{BE} = 0.7$ V.

The operating point is at

$V_{CE} = 7$ V and $I_C = 1$ mA

$$R_C = \frac{V_{CC} - V_{CE}}{I_L} = \frac{12 - 7}{1 \times 10^{-3}} = 5 \text{ K}\Omega$$

$$I_E = \frac{I_C}{\beta} = \frac{1 \times 10^{-3}}{100} = 10 \text{ μA}$$

$$R_B = \frac{V_{CC} - V_{BE} - I_C R_C}{I_B} = \frac{12 - 0.7 - 1.10^{-3} \times 5 \times 10^{-3}}{10 \times 10^{-6}} = 630 \text{ K}\Omega.$$

$$S = \frac{1+\beta}{1+\beta\left[\frac{R_c}{R_c + R_B}\right]} = \frac{1+100}{1+100\left[\frac{5 \times 10^3}{(5+630)\,10^3}\right]} = 56.5.$$

when β = 50

$$V_{CC} = \beta I_B R_C + I_B R_B + V_{BE}$$
$$= I_B(\beta R_C + R_B) + V_{BE}$$
$$12 = I_B(50 \times 5 \times 10^3 + 630 \times 10^3) + 0.7$$
$$I_B = \frac{11.3}{880 \times 10^3} = 12.84 \text{ μA}.$$
$$I_c = \beta I_B = 50 \times 12.84 \times 10^{-6} = 0.642 \text{ mA}$$
$$V_{CE} = V_{CC} - I_C R_C$$
$$= 12 - 0.642 \times 10^{-3} \times 5 \times 10^3 = 8.79 \text{ V}.$$

The coordinates of the new operating point are $V_{CEQ} = 8.79$ V and

$I_{CQ} = 0.642$ mA.

**39. In a CE Germanium transistor amplifier circuit, the bias is provided by self bias.for the emitter resistor and potential divide arrangement refer to figure. The various parameters are $V_{CC} = 16$ V, $R_C = 3$ KΩ, $R_E = 2$ KΩ, $R_1 = 56$ kΩ, $R_2 = 20$ KΩ and α = 0.985. Determine (a) the co-ordinate of the operating point and (b) stability factor *S*.**

**Solution:**

For Ge Transistor, $V_{BE} = 0.3$ V.

$$\alpha = 0.985,\ \beta = \frac{\alpha}{1-\alpha} = \frac{0.985}{1-0.985} = 66$$

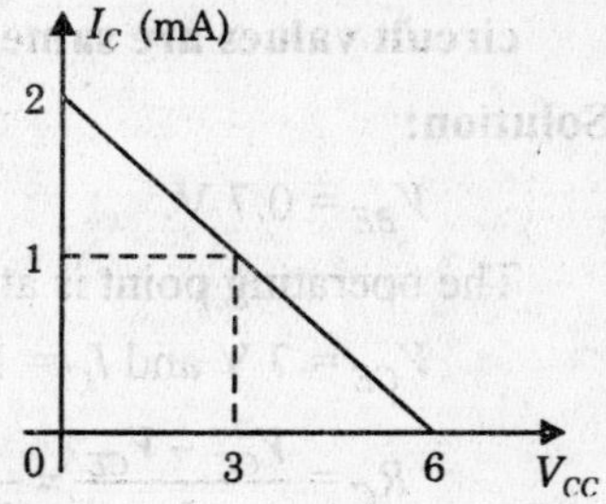


$$V_T = \frac{R_2}{R_1 + R_2} \times V_{CC} = \frac{20 \times 10^3}{76 \times 10^3} \times 16$$

$$= 4.21 \text{ V.}$$

$$R_B = \frac{R_2}{R_1 + R_2} = \frac{20 \times 10^3 \times 56 \times 10^3}{76 \times 10^3}$$

$$= 14.737 \text{ k}\Omega.$$

The loop equation around the base circuit is

$$V_T = I_B R_B + V_{BE} + (I_B + I_C) R_E$$

$$= \frac{I_C}{\beta} R_B + V_{BE} + \left(\frac{I_C}{\beta} + I_C\right) R_E$$

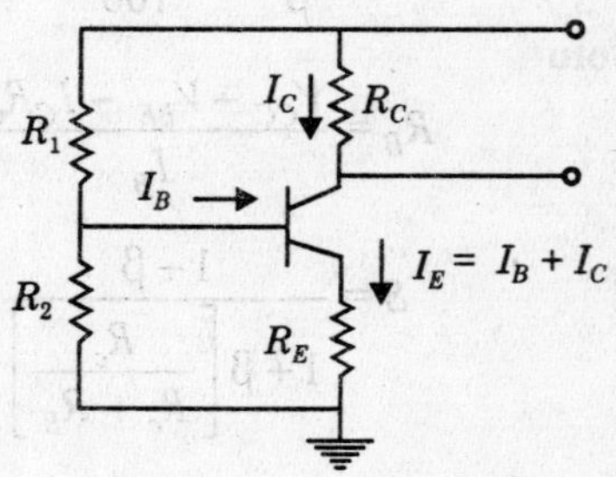


$$4.21 = \frac{I_C}{66} \times 14.737 \times 10^3 + 0.3$$

$$+ I_C\left(\frac{1}{68} + 1\right) \times 2 \times 10^3$$

$$3.91 = I_C\,(0.223 + 2.03) \times 10^3$$

$$I_C = \frac{3.91}{2.253 \times 10^{-3}} = 1.73 \text{ mA.}$$

**40. A *CE* transistor amplifier with voltage divider bias circuits of figure is designed to establish the quiescent point at $V_{CE}$ = 12 V, $I_C$ = 2 mA and stability factor < 5.1. If $V_{CC}$ = 24 V, $V_{BE}$ = 0.7 V, β = 50 and $R_c$ = 4.7 KΩ, determine the values of resistor $R_E$, $R_1$ and $R_2$.**

**Solution:**

(a) To determine $R_E$

$$V_{CE} = V_{CC} - I_C R_C - I_E R_E = V_{CC} - I_C (R_C + R_E)$$

$$12 = 24 - 2 \times 10^{-3}\,[4.7 \times 10^3 + R_E]$$

$$R_E = 1.3 \text{ k}\Omega.$$

(b) To determine $R_1$, $R_2$

$$S = \frac{1 + \beta}{1 + \beta\left(\frac{R_E}{R_E + R_B}\right)}$$

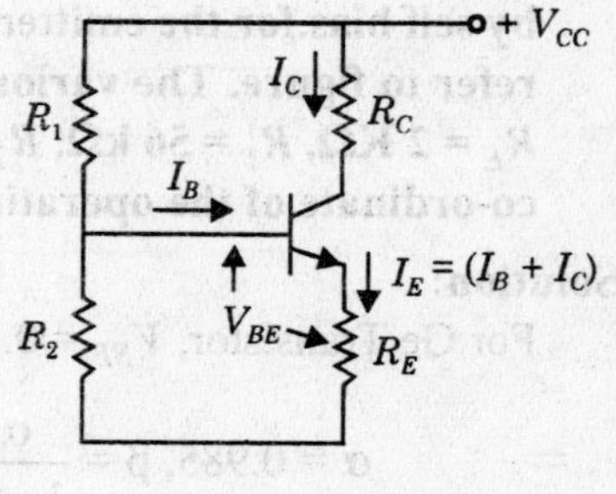


where $\quad R_B = \dfrac{R_1 R_2}{(R_1 + R_2)}$

The base current $I_B$ is given by

$$I_B = \frac{I_C}{\beta} = \frac{1.5}{50} mA = 30\ \mu A$$

$$V = 0.03 \times 3.25 + 0.6 + (0.03 + 1.5) \times 1.0 = 2.23\ V$$

$$R_1 = \frac{3.25 \times 18}{2.23} K\Omega = 26.23\ k\Omega$$

$$R_2 = \frac{26.23 \times 2.23}{18 - 2.3} = 3.7\ k\Omega.$$

**41. For the transistor circuit of figure, find the transistor currents Given $\beta = 125$.**

**Solution:**

Since base is forward biased,the transistor is not in cutoff, let us assume, it is in the active region.

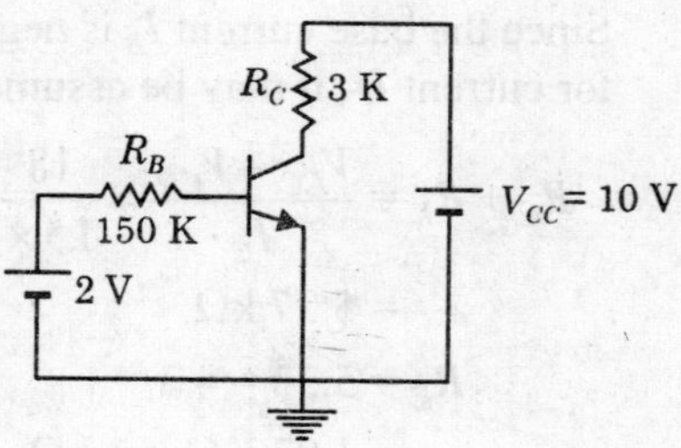


$$I_B = \frac{5 - 0.7}{150k} = 28.67 \times 10^{-3}\ mA.$$

$$I_C = \beta I_B = 125 \times 28.\ 67 \times 10^{-3}$$

$$= 3.583\ mA.$$

Applying *KVL* to the collector circuit

$$-10 + 3\ K\ I_C + V_{CB} - V_{BE} = 0$$

$$\Rightarrow V_{CB} = -1.45\ V.$$

For an *NPN* transistor this value of $V_{CB}$ represented a forward biased collector junction and hence the transistor is not in the active region but in the saturation region.

$$V_{CE} = 0.2V.$$

Applying *KVL* to the collector circuit

$$-10 + 3\ K\ I_C + V_{CE} = 0$$

$$\Rightarrow \qquad I_C = 3.27\ mA.$$

Also in saturation $V_{BE} = 0.8$ V

$$I_B = \frac{5 - 0.8}{150 \times 10^3} = 28 \times 10^{-3}\ mA.$$

$$5.1 = \frac{5.1}{1 + 50\left(\frac{1.3 \times 10^3}{1.3 \times 10^3 + R_B}\right)}$$

$$\Rightarrow \qquad R_B = 5.9\ K\Omega$$

for a good voltage divider, the value of resistor $R_2 = 0.1 \times \beta\, R_E = 0.1 \times 50 \times 1.3\ \times 10^3$

$$R_2 = 6.5\ \text{K}\Omega$$

$$R_B = \frac{R_1 R_2}{R_1 + R_2}$$

$$5.910^3 = \frac{R_1 \times 6.5 \times 10^3}{R_1 + 6.5 \times 10^3}$$

$$R_1 = 64\ \text{K}\Omega.$$

**42. In a self-bias circuit of figure, a Si transistor is used with $\beta = 50$, $V_{BE} = 0.6$ V, $V_{CC} = 18$ V and $R_C = 4.3$ KΩ. It is desired to establish a quiescent point at $I_C = 1.5$ mA, $V_{CE} = 10$ V and a stability factor $S = 4$. Find $R_C$, $R_1$ and $R_2$.**

**Solution:**

Since the base current $I_B$ is negligibly small as compared with the collector current $I_C$, it may be assumed that he current in $R_e$ is $I_c + I_B = I_C$

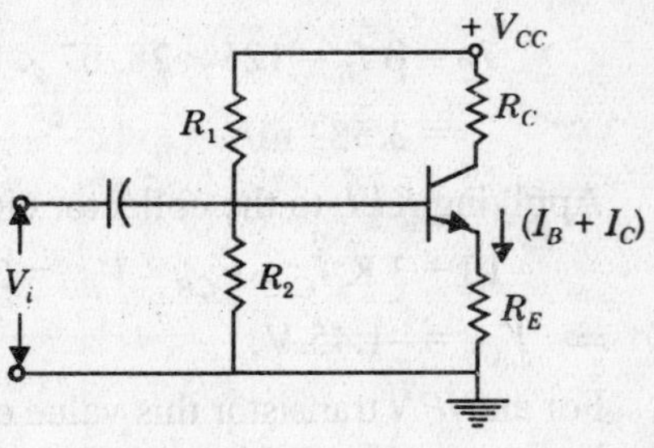


$$R_C + R_E = \frac{V_{CC} - V_{CE}}{I_C} = \frac{18 - 10}{1.5 \times 10^{-3}}$$

$$= 5.37\ \text{k}\Omega$$

$$R_E = 5.33 - 4.3$$

$$= 1.03\ \text{K}\Omega = 1\ \text{k}\Omega$$

$$R_B/R_E = \frac{(50+1)(4-1)}{1+50-4} = 3.25.$$

Observe that $\beta\, I_B = 125 \times 28 \times 10^{-3} = 3.5\ \text{mA} > I_C = 3.27\ \text{mA}$

This will always be two for a transistor in saturation the maximum base current to cause the transistor to go into saturation is given as

$$I_{B\,(\text{min})} = \frac{I_C}{\beta};\ I_C\ (\text{collector current in saturation}) = \frac{3.27}{1.25} = 0.026\ \text{mA}.$$

**43. Obtain the value of $R_1$ and $R_2$ to provide the following bias conditions to a Ge transistor arranged as in circuit of**

**Solution:**

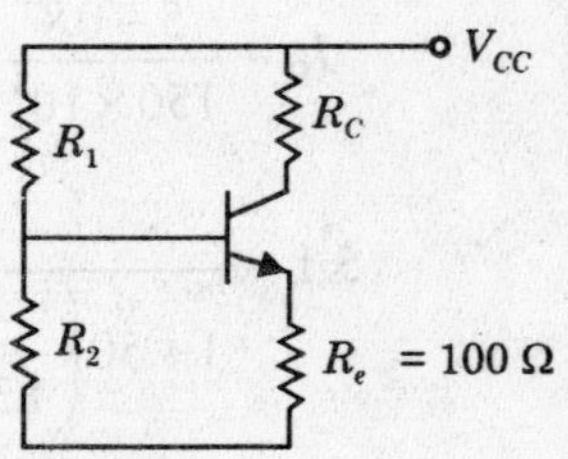


Stability factor

$$S_I = \frac{1+\beta}{1 + \dfrac{\beta R_E}{R_B + R_E}}$$

$$1 = \frac{1+100}{1 + \dfrac{100 \times 100}{100 + R_B}},\ 1 + \frac{100 \times 100}{100 + R_B} = 10$$

$\therefore \qquad R_B = 9$

$R_B = 1\text{ K} - 100\ \Omega = 1\text{ K}$

$V_B = 2.2 + 0.3 \times 1 = 2.5\text{ V}$

$$= \frac{V_{CC}R_2}{R_1 + R_2} = \frac{12 \times R_2}{R_1 + R_2}$$

$$R_1 + R_2 = \frac{12R_2}{2.5} = 4.8\ R_2$$

$R_1 = 3.8\ R_2.$

**44. Analyze the emitter current bias circuit to determine the bias conditions when β = 50**

**Solution:**

$$V_T = V_{CC} \times \frac{R_2}{R_1 + R_2}$$

$$= 15 \times \frac{11.4K}{18.6K + 11.4K} = 5.7\text{ V}$$

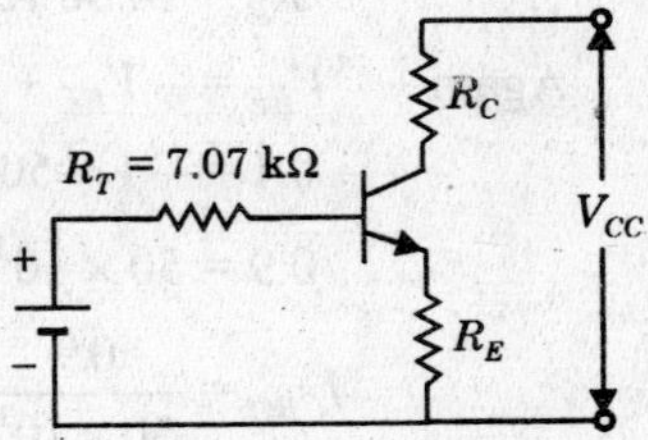


$R_T = R_1 // R_2 = 7.07\text{ k}\Omega$

$V_T = I_B\, R_T + V_{BE} + R_E\ (I_B + I_C)$

$$I_B = \frac{I_C}{\beta},\ V_T = \frac{I_C}{\beta}\, R_T + V_{BE} + \text{R}_\text{E}\left(\frac{I_C}{\beta} + I_C\right)$$

Which gives $V_T - V_{BE} = I_C\left[\frac{R_T}{\beta} + R_E\left(\frac{1}{\beta} + 1\right)\right]$

$$I_C = \frac{V_T - V_{BE}}{\frac{R_T}{R} + R_E\left(\frac{1}{\beta} + 1\right)}$$

For $\quad \beta = 50$

$$I_C = \frac{5.7 - 0.7}{\frac{7.07K}{50} + 1K\left(\frac{1}{50} + 1\right)} = 4.31\text{ mA}$$

$V_{CE} = 15\text{ V} - (4.31 \times 10^{-3}\ 1\text{ k}) - 1\text{ k}$

$$\left(\frac{4.31 \times 10^{-3}}{50} + 4.31 \times 10^{-3}\right) = 6.29\text{ V.}$$

**45. In the transistor circuit shown below $I_{CBO}$ = 2 μA at 25° C and doubles for every 10°C increase in temperature**

**(a) Find the maximum allowable value of $R_B$, if the transistor is to remain in cut off at 75°C**

**(b) If $V_{BB}$ = 1V and $R_B$ = 50 KΩ, how high may the temperature increase before the transistor comes out of cutoff?**

**Solution:**

Given, $I_{CBO}$ = 2 μA at 25°C and doubles for every 10°C increase in temperature.

At 75° C, $I_{CBO} = 2^6 = 64$ μA

At cutoff $\quad I_b = I_{CBO}$ and $V_B = -0.1$ V

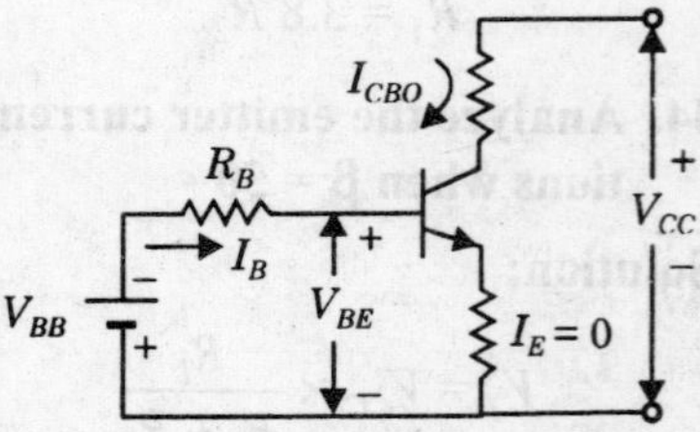


Then $\quad V_{BE} = -V_{BB} + R_B I_{CBO} \leq 0.1$ V

$$-0.1 = -1 + R_B \times 64 \times 10^{-6}$$

∴ $\quad R_B = 14.06$ KΩ

Again $\quad V_{BE} = -V_{BE} + R_B I_{CBO}$

$$-0.1 = -1 + 50 \times 10^3\, I_{CBO}$$

$$0.9 = 50 \times 10^3\, I_{CBO}$$

$$I_{CBO} = \frac{0.9}{50 \times 10^3} = 1.8 \times 10^{-5} = 18\ \mu A$$

For temperature rise we have

$$18 = 2 \times 2^{(T-25)/10}$$

$$\frac{T-25}{20} \log^9_2 = 3.1$$

$$T = 56°\ C$$

**46. A silicon transistor with $V_{BE(sat)}$ = 0.8 V, β = $h_{fe}$ = 100, $V_{CE(sat)}$ = 0.2 V is used in the circuit shown. Find the minimum value of $R_C$ for which the transistor remains in saturation.**

**Solution:**

Let $\quad V_{BE} = 0.7$ for Si transistor

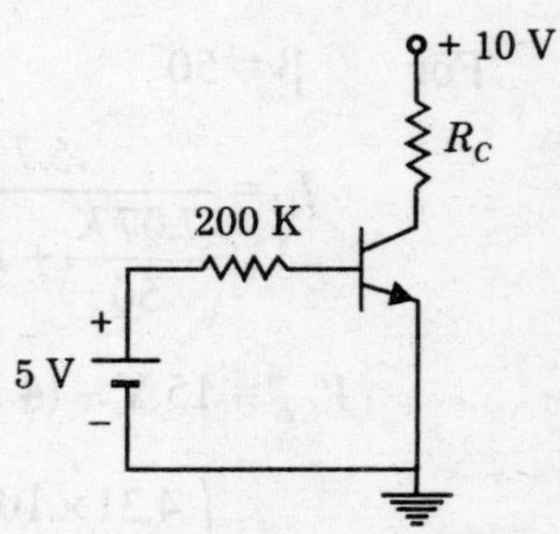


$$I_B = \frac{5 - V_{BE}}{200K} = \frac{5 - 0.7}{200 \times 10^3} = 21.5$$

A transistor is said to be in saturation region

$$I_B \geq \frac{I_{CS}}{h_{fe}}$$

where $\quad I_{CS} = \dfrac{V_{CC} - V_{CE(sat)}}{R_C}$

Putting in equation (1) we get

$$I_B \geq \frac{V_{CC} - V_{CE(sat)}}{R_C h_{fe}}$$

Hence for saturation,

$$R_C \geq \frac{V_{CC} - V_{CE(sat)}}{h_{fe}\, I_B}$$

$$= \frac{10 - 0.2}{100 \times 21.5 \times 10^{-6}}$$

$$R_C \geq 4558.14\ \Omega$$

$$R_{\min} = 4.558\ \text{k}\Omega$$

**47. For the circuit shown in figure $\alpha_1 = 0.98$, $\alpha_2 = 0.96$, $V_{CC} = 24$ V, $R_C$ = 120 Ω and $I_E = -100$ mA. Calculate the currents $I_{C1}$, $I_{B1}$, $I_{B2}$, $I_{C2}$, $I_{E1}$ and $I_C$, the voltage $V_{CE}$, and the ratios $I_C/I_B$ and $I_C/I_E$. Neglect reverse saturation currents.**

**Solution:**

For the given circuit:

$$\alpha_1 = 0.98,\ \alpha_2 = 0.96,\ V_{CC} = 24\ \text{V}$$

$$R_C = 120\ \Omega \text{ and } I_E = -100\ \text{mA}$$

$$\beta_1 = \frac{\alpha_1}{1 - \alpha_1} = \frac{0.98}{1 - 0.98} = 49$$

$$\beta_2 = \frac{\alpha_2}{1 - \alpha_2} = \frac{0.96}{1 - 0.96} = 24$$

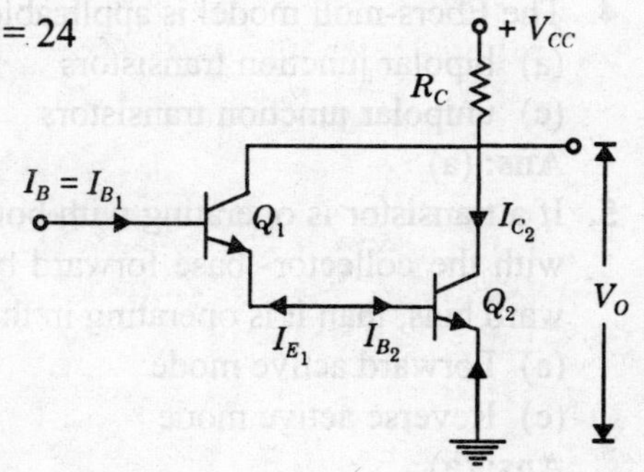


$$I_E = -100\ \text{mA}$$

$$(1 + \beta_2)\, I_{B2} = 100\ \text{mA}$$

$$I_{B2} = \frac{100}{25}$$

$$I_{E1} = -I_{B2} = -4\ \text{mA}$$

$$I_{C2} = \beta_2\, I_{B2}$$

$$= 24 \times 4 = 96\ \text{mA}$$

$$I_{B1} = \frac{4}{1 + \beta_1} = \frac{4}{50} = 0.08\ \text{mA}$$

$$I_B = I_{B1} = 0.08\ \text{mA}$$

$$I_{C1} = \beta_1\, I_{B1} = 49 \times 0.08 = 3.92\ \text{mA}$$

$$I_C = I_{C1} + I_{C2} = 3.92 + 96 = 99.92\ \text{mA}$$

$$V_{CE} = V_{CC} - I_C R_C = 24 - 99.92 \times 10^{-3} \times 120 = 12 \text{ V}$$

$$\frac{I_C}{I_B} = \frac{99.92}{0.08} = 1249; \frac{I_C}{I_E} = \frac{99.92}{-100} = -0.099$$

## 4.12 OBJECTIVE QUESTIONS

**1.** Which of the following effects can caused by a rise in temperature
(a) increase in MOSFET current ($I_{DS}$)
(b) increase in BJT current ($I_C$)
(c) Decrease in MOSFET current ($I_{DS}$)
(d) decrease in BJT current ($I_C$)
**Ans:** (a), (c).

**2.** The break down voltage of a transistor with its base open is $BV_{CEO}$ and with emitter open is $BV_{CBO}$, then
(a) $B\,V_{CEO} = B\,V_{CBO}$ (b) $B\,V_{CEO} > B\,V_{CBO}$
(c) $B\,V_{CEO} < B\,V_{CBO}$ (d) is not related to $B\,V_{CBO}$
**Ans:** (c).

**3.** A BJT is said to be operation in the saturation region if
(a) both the junctions are reverse biased.
(b) Base-emitter junction is reverse biased and base-collector junction is forward biased.
(c) Base-emitter junction is forward biased and base-collector junction is reverse-biased.
(d) Both the junction are forward biased
**Ans:** (d)

**4.** The Ebers-moll model is applicable to
(a) bipolar junction transistors (b) N MOS transistors
(c) unipolar junction transistors (d) junction field-effect transistors
**Ans:** (a)

**5.** If a transistor is operating with both of its junctions forward biased, but with the collector- base forward bias greater than the emitter-base forward bias, than it is operating in the
(a) Forward active mode (b) reverse saturation mode
(c) Reverse active mode (d) forward saturation mode
**Ans:** (a)

**6.** In a bipolar transistor at room temperature, if the emitter current is doubled, the voltage across its base-emitter junction.
(a) Doubles (b) halves
(c) Increases by about 20 mv (d) decrease by about 20v
**Ans:** (a)

**7.** The emitter coupled pair of BJT gives a linear transfer relation between the differential output voltage and the differential input voltage $v_{id}$ only when the magnitude of $v_{id}$ is less then a times the thermal voltage, wherea is

(a) 4 (b) 3 (c) 2 (d) 1

**Ans:** (d)

**8.** The early-effect in bipolar junction transistor is caused by

(a) Fast turn-on (b) fast turn-off

(c) large collector-base reverse bias

(d) large emitter-base forward bias.

**Ans:** (c)

**9.** For the junction transistor, which of the following is true

(a) $\alpha = \frac{\beta}{1-\beta}$ (b) $\alpha = \beta(1+\beta)$ (c) $\beta = \frac{\alpha}{1-\alpha}$ (d) $\beta = \frac{\alpha}{1+\alpha}$

**Ans:** (c)

**10.** In an idea; junction transistor, the impurity concentration in the emitter (E) base (B) and collector (C) are such that

(a) $E > B > C$ (b) $B > C > E$ (c) $C > E > B$ (d) $C = E = B$

**Ans:** (a)

**11.** When a junction transistor is operated under saturated conditions

(a) both the *CB* and *EB* junctions are forward biased

(b) the *CB* junctions is forward biased but the *EB* junction is reverse biased

(c) the *CB* junction is reverse biased but the *EB* junction is forward biased

(d) both the *CB* and *EB* junctions are reverse biased

**Ans:** (a)

**12.** The collector to emitter cut-off current ($I_{CEO}$) of a transistor is related to collector to base cut-off current ($I_{CBO}$) AS (α is the *CB* current gain of the transistor).

(a) $I_{CEO} = I_{CBO}$ (b) $I_{CEO} = \alpha I_{CBO}$ (c) $I_{CEO} = \frac{I_{CBO}}{1-\alpha}$ (d) $I_{CEO} = \frac{I_{CBO}}{1+\alpha}$

**Ans:** (c)

**13.** Which one of the following is correct for the biasing of a bipolar junction transistor in its active region?

| *Biasing* *Emitter junction* | *Collector junction* |
|---|---|
| (a) Forward | Forward |
| (b) Forward | Reverse |
| (c) Reverse | Forward |
| (d) Reverse | Reverse |

**Ans:** (b)

**14.** The Ebers-Moll equation for $I_E$ in *CB* configuration is given by

(a) $I_E = \alpha n + I_{CEO}$ (b) $I_E = \alpha,\ I_C + I_{CO}$

(c) $I_E = \alpha n\ I_C + I_{CO}\,(e^{qVEB/KT} - 1)$ (d) $I_E = \alpha,\ I_C = I_{CEO}\,(e^{qV_{EB}/KT} - 1)$

**Ans:** (d)

**15.** For BJT, under saturation condition,

(a) $I_C = \beta IB$ (b) $I_C > \beta IB$

(c) $I_C$ is independent of all other parameters

(d) $I_C < \beta I_B$

**Ans:** (d)

**16.** If both the emitter-base and the collector-base junctions of a bipolar transistor are forward biased, the transistor is in the

(a) Active region (b) saturated region

(c) Cut-off region (d) inverse mode

**Ans:** (b)

**17.** Which of the following circuits realizes self-bias with compensation? Select the correct answer using the code give below:

(a) 2 and 3 (b) 1 and 2 (c) 1 and 3 (d) 1,2 and 3

**Ans:** (b)

**18.** For the circuit shown in figure the quiescent point is

(a) 12 v, 5 mA (b) 12 v, 2 mA (c) 10 v, 2 mA (d) 10 v, 5 mA

**Ans:** (c).

**19.** The modulation of effective base width by collector voltage is known as early effect, Hence reverse collector voltage

(a) increases both alpha and beta

(b) decreases both alpha and beta

(c) Increases alpha but decreases beta

(d) Decreases beta but increases alpha

**Ans:** (c)

**20.** For a bipolar junction transistor, if the current amplification factor and cut-off frequency in the *CB* mode are $\propto CB$ and $f \propto CB$ respectively, then the cut off frequency in the *CE* mode is equal to

(a) $f \propto CB/\alpha CB$ (b) $f \propto CB(1 - \alpha CB)$

(c) $f \propto CB/(1 - \alpha CB)$ (d) $\alpha CB f \alpha CB$

**Ans:** (c)

**21.** If $\propto = 0.995$, $I_E = 10$ mA and $I_{CO} = 0.5$ mA, then $I_{CEO}$ will be

(a) 100 μA (b) 25 μA (c) 10.1 ma (d) 10.5 mA

**Ans:** (a)

**22.** Match list-I (Transistor parameter) with list-2 (typical value) and select the correct answer using the codes given below the lest:

| *List-1* | *List-2* |
|---|---|
| (a) $r_{bb}$ | 1. 80 kΩ |
| (b) $r_{be}$ | 2. 1 kΩ |
| (c) $r_{ce}$ | 3. 100 Ω |
| (d) $c_{be}$ | 4. 100 pF |
| | 5. 3 pF |

Codes:

(a) A B C D
3 2 1 4

(b) A B C D
3 2 1 5

(c) A B C D
1 3 2 4

(d) A B C D
1 3 2 5

**Ans:** (b)

**23.** For a transistor amplifier with self-biasing network, the following components are used: $R_1 = 4$ k, $R_2 = 4$ k and $R_e = 1$ k. The approximate value of the stability factor 's' will be

(a) 4 (b) 3 (c) 2 (d) 1.5

**Ans:** (b)

**24.** In a transistor amplifier, the reverse saturation current $I_{CO}$

(a) doubles for every 10º C rise in temperature
(b) doubles for every 1º rise in temperature
(c) increases linearly with temperature
(d) doubles for every 5º rise in temperature

**Ans:** (a)

**25.** To avoid thermal runaway in the design of an analog circuit, the operating point of the BJT should be such that it satisfies the condition.

(a) $V_{CE} = ½ V_{CC}$ (b) $V_{CE} \leq 1/2\ V_{CC}$
(c) $V_{CE} \geq 1/2\ V_{CC}$ (d) $V_{CE} \leq 0.78\ V_{CC}$

**Ans:** (b)

**26.** The input resistance of common emitter stage can be increased by

(1) run bypassing emitter resistance
(2) bootstrapping ]
(3) biasing it at low quiescent current
(4) using compounded BJTs

the correct sequence in descending order of the effectiveness of these methods is

(a) 2, 4, 1, 3 (b) 4, 3, 2, 1 (b) 2, 4, 3, 1 (d) 4, 2, 3,1

**Ans:** (d)

**27** Thermal runaway will take place if the quiescent point is such that

(a) $V_{CE} > \frac{1}{2} V_{CC}$ (b) $V_{CE} \leq V_{CC}$
(c) $V_{CE} > 2\ V_{CC}$ (d) $V_{CE} < \frac{1}{2} V_{CC}$

**Ans:** (d)

**28.** A transistor is said to be in quiescent state when:

(a) it is unbiased
(b) no signal is applied to it
(c) no current is flowing in it
(d) emitter junction bias is equal to collector junction bias

**Ans:** (b)

29. Base-to-emitter voltage $V_{BE}$ is forward biased transistor decreases with increase of temperature at the following rate:
(a) 25 mv/deg c (b) 0.25 mv/deg c
(c) 2.5 mv/deg c (d) 0.6 mv/deg c
**Ans:** (c)
30. Which one of the following bipolar transistors has the highest current gain, bandwidth product ($f_T$) for similar geometry
(a) NPN Ge transistor (b) NPN Si transistor
(c) PNP Ge transistor (d) PNP Si transistor
**Ans:** (b)
31. the output voltage of the circuit shown in the given figure is
(a) −10.2 v (b) −8.8 v (c) zero (d) 0.2 v
**Ans:** (d)

## 4.13 CONVENTIONAL QUESTIONS

1. Define BJT? How many types of Configurations are there.
2. How is collector current $I_C$ related to the emitter current $I_E$?
3. Why does $I_{CBO}$ differ from $I_{CO}$?
4. Explain the Early effect.
5. By which principal mechanism the carriers are transported across the base region of a transistor?
6. Why is an orduinory junction transistor called bipolar?
7. Sketch a family of *CB* input and output characteristics for a transistor. Explain the shape of the curve quantitatively.
9. Sketch a family of *CE* input and output characteristics for a transistor? Explain the shape of the curve quantitatively? Indicate the cutoff ,active and saturation regions.
10. Draw the circuit of a transistor in *CC* configuration.
11. (a) Define *DC* current gain for a *CE* transistor in *CE* configuration (b) give its order of merits.
12. Collector current variation with temperature? Explain Stability factors *S*, *S′* and *S″*.
13. What is biasing? What is necessity of biasing circuits?
14. Explain different types of biasing methods? Draw ten types of biasing circuits.
15. Draw the circuit diagram of self bias Derive the expressions of stability factors *S*, *S′* and *S″*.
16. What is need of bias compensation? Explain different types of bias compensation circuits.
17. Draw the circuit diagram of fixed bias circuit? Derive the expression of Stability factor?
18. Define (a) Thermal runaway (b) Thermal resistance.
19. What is the condition for Thermal stability? Explain with self bias Circuit?
20. Define and explain (a) Load line and (b) Quiescent Point?

21. Draw the circuit diagram of Transistor in saturated region when Switch is ON position and explain its working phenomenon?
22. Draw the circuit diagram of Transistor in Cut off region when Switch is OFF position and explain its working phenomenon?

## 4.14 EXERCISE PROBLEMS

1. Determine the quiescent level of $I_{cQ}$ and $V_{CEQ}$ for the circuit given bellow.
   **Ans:** 1.07 mA, 3.69 V

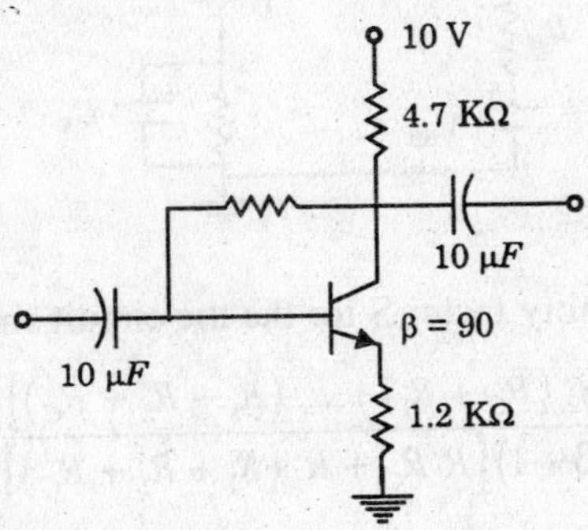


2. Determine the necessary value of $R_B$ for the circuit shown in below.
   **Ans:** 51.85 k ohm

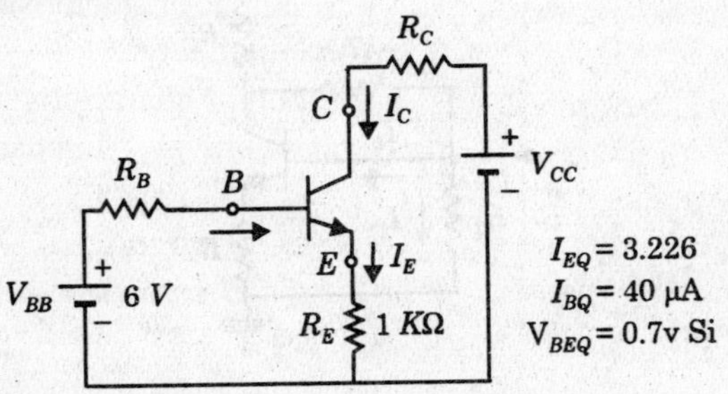


3. Determine $V_C$ and $V_B$ for the network shown in the figure below.
   **Ans:** 8.53 V, –11.59 V

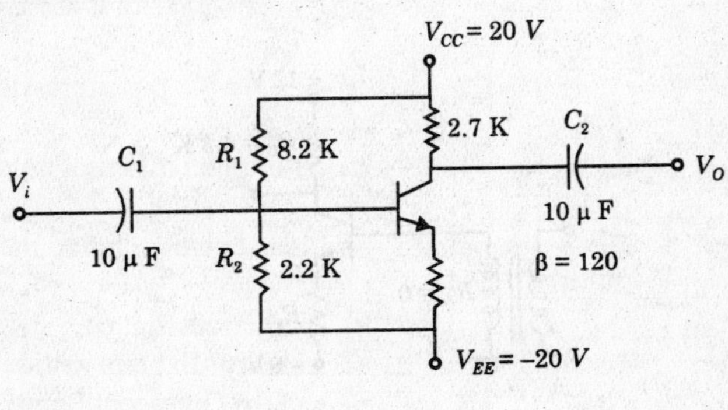

**4.** For the *CE* amplifier given below ,use stability factor to find an expresson for the change in $I_{CQ}$ due to variations in, $I_{CBO}$, and $V_{BEQ}$.

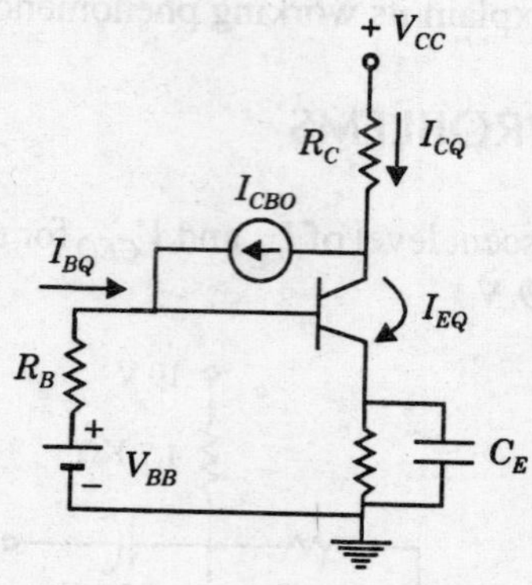


**5.** Determine the stability factor S for the the circuit shown in the figure.

**Ans:** $$S = \frac{(\beta+1)\left[R_2\left(R_C+R_1\right)+R_e\left(R_1+R_2+R_C\right)\right]}{R_1 R_2+(\beta+1)\left[R_2 R_C+R_e\left(R_1+R_2+R_C\right)\right]}$$

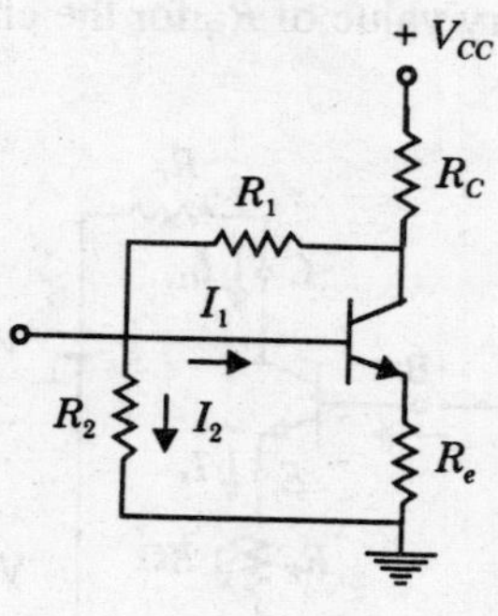


**6.** The figure shown in below determine $R_e$, if $V_{BE} = 0.7$ V, $I_C = 2$ mA, $\beta = 50$.

**Ans:** 2.74 K

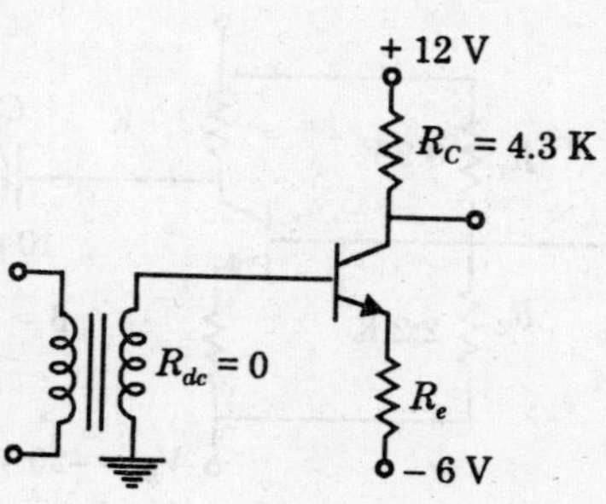

**7.** Find the $Q$-point and stability factor of the circuit shown in fig. for $V_{BB} = 2$ V, 100 K, $V_{BE} = 0.7$ V, $V_{CC} = 12$ V, $R_C = 5$ K and $\beta = 50$.
**Ans:** 51

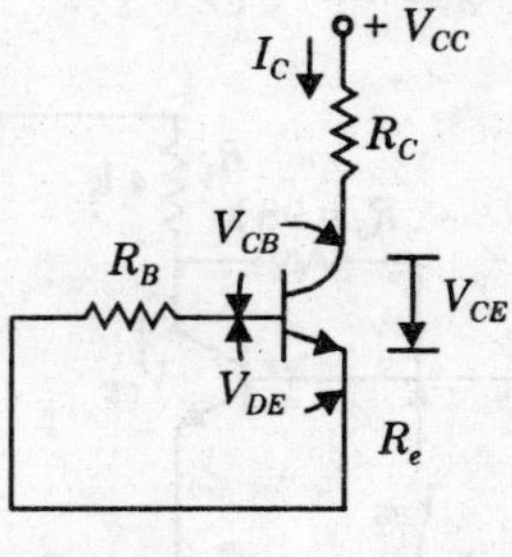


**8.** (a) Determine the quiescent currents and the collector-to-emitter voltage for a Silicon transistor with $\beta = 50$ in the self-biasing arrangement of fig. The circuit component values are $V_{CC} = 20$ V, $R_C = 2.5$ k, $R_e = 0.1$ k, $R_1 =$ 80 k, and $R_2 = 6$ k. (b) Repeat (d) for a germanium transistor.

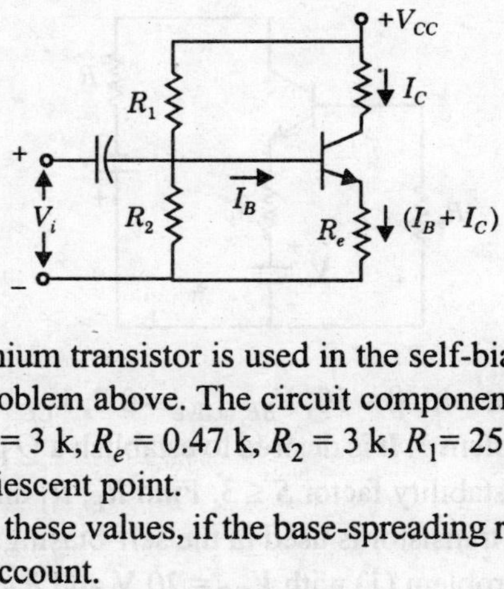


**9.** A *p-n-p* Germanium transistor is used in the self-biasing arrangement of fig. shown in problem above. The circuit component values are $V_{CC} = 12$ V, $R_C = 3$ k, $R_e = 0.47$ k, $R_2 = 3$ k, $R_1 = 25$ k. If $\beta = 44$.
   (a) Find the quiescent point.
   (b) Recalculate these values, if the base-spreading resistance of 690 Ω is taken into account.

**10.** A *p–n–p* Silicon transistor is used in a common collector circuit (with $R_C = 0$). The circuit component values are $V_{CC} = 12$ V, $R_C = 1.1$ k, $R_1 = R_2$ $= 6$ k. if $\beta = 44$
   (a) Find the quiescent point.
   (b) Recalculate these values, taking the base-spreading resistance of 690 Ω into account.

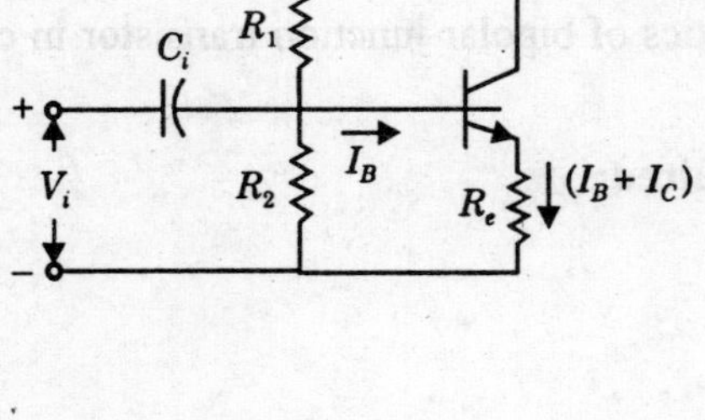


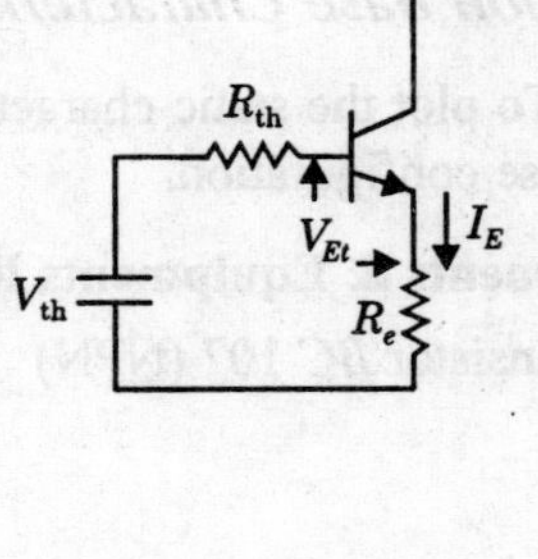

11. For the circuit shown:
    (a) Calculate $I_B$, $I_C$ and $V_{CE}$ if a Silicon transistor is used with $\beta = 50$
    (b) Specify a value for $R_b$ so that $V_{CE} = 7$ V.

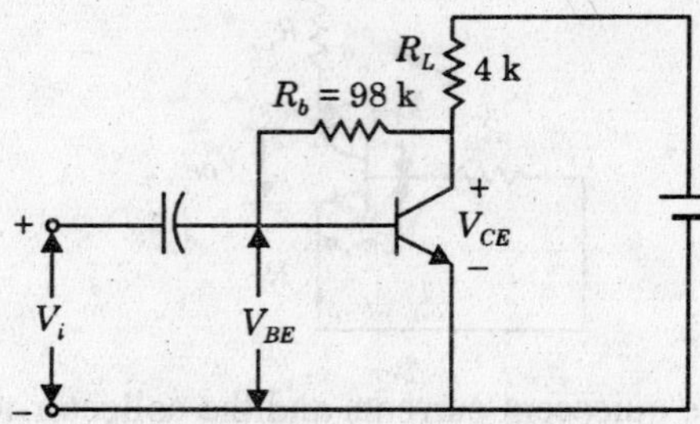


12. For the two-battery transistor circuit shown in figure, find the stabilization factor S.

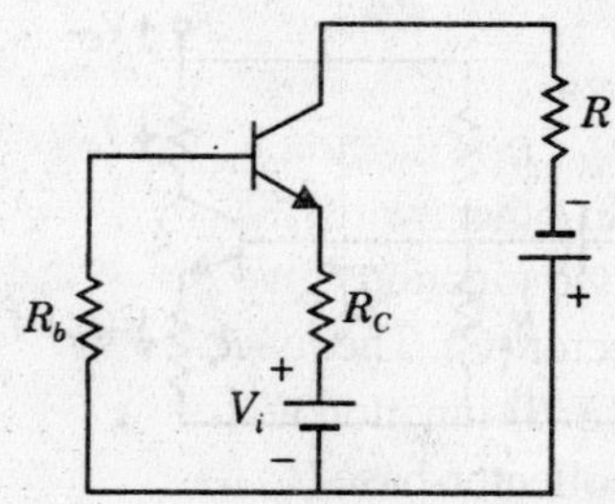


13. A Silicon transistor with $\beta = 50$, $V_{BE,\text{ active}} = 0.7$, $V_{CC} = 20$ V and $R_C = 2.6$ K is shown in problem 1. It is desired to establish a $Q$ point at $V_{CE} = 12$ V, $I_C = 2.0$ mA, and stability factor $S \le 3$. Find $R_E$, $R_1$ and $R_2$.
14. (a) A Germanium transistor is used in the self-biasing arrangement of the circuit shown in problem (1) with $V_{CC} = 20$ V and $R_C = 2.5$ k. The quiescent point is chosen to be $V_{CE} = 10$ V and $I_C = 7$ mA. A stability factor $S$ is desired as 12. If $\beta = 50$, find $R_1$, $R_2$ and Re. (b) Repeat part (c) for $S = 3$

## 4.15 LAB EXPERIMENTS

### EXP No: 1

### *Common Base Characteristics of BJT*

**AIM:** To plot the static characteristics of bipolar junction transistor in common base configuration.

**Components & Equipments Required:**

1. Transistor *BC* 107 (NPN)

2. Resistor 4.7 K-Ohm
3. DC Ammeter 0-25mA
4. DC Voltmeter 0-1 V and 0-25 V
5. Dual Power Supply 0-30 V
6. Connecting wires, bread board etc.

**Circuit Diagram:**

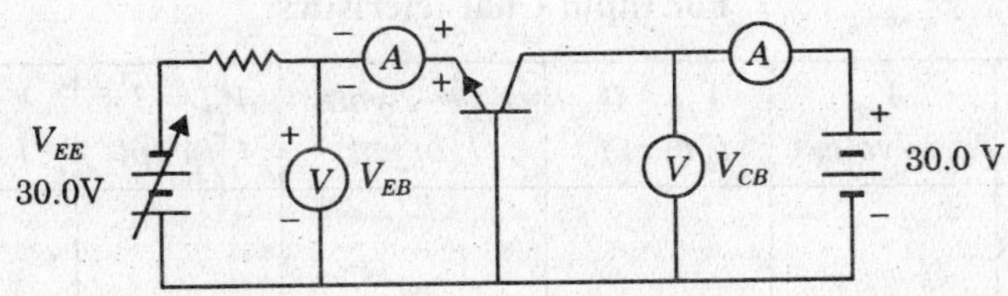


**Fig. 4L1**

**Theory:** When a third doped element is added to a diode in such a way that two *PN*-junctions are formed, the resulting device is known as a transistor. It consists of two-back- to back *P-N* junctions manufactured in a single piece of a semiconductor crystal. In other words, it has three layers, three terminals and two junctions. These two junctions give rise to three regions called Emitter (E), Base (B) and Collector (C). The junction between the emitter and base is called the emitter-base (*E/B*) junction and the junction between the collector and base is called the collector-base (*C/B*) junction. In junction transistors both majority and minority charge carriers are involved.

Therefore they are called bipolar junction transistors or simply bipolar transistor. There are two types of transistors, namely *NPN* transistor and *PNP* transistor. A transistor can be connected in a circuit in the following three ways.

1. Common Base Configuration (*CB* Configuration)
2. Common Emitter Configuration (*CE* Configuration)
3. Common Collector Configuration (*CC* Configuration)

In the arrangement for common base configuration, the input is fed between the emitter and base and the output is taken from the collector and base. Here the base of the transistor is common to both input and output circuit. So it is called the common base configuration.

**Procedure:**

1. Connect the circuit as shown in the circuit diagram.
2. Keep the collector voltage $V_{cb}$ constant at 0 v, 2 v 3 v and $V_{cb}$ open. For each value of $V_{cb}$, vary $V_{ee}$ such that $V_{eb}$ is increased in steps of 0.1 v from 0 to 1 volt and note down the corresponding emitter current $I_e$. From these readings, draw the graph $V_{eb}$ versus $I_e$ for each fixed value of $V_{cb}$. This will give input characteristics of BJT in *CB* configuration.

Keep the emitter current $I_e$ constant 0 mA, 1 mA, 2mA, 5 mA etc. For each fixed value of $I_e$, vary $V_{cc}$ such that $V_{cb}$ is increased in steps of 1 volt from 0 to 10 volt and note down the corresponding value of $I_c$.

From the above readings, draw the graph $I_c$ versus $V_{cb}$ for ieach fixed value of $I_e$. This will give output characteristics of BJT in *CB* configuration.

**Tabular Column:**

**1. For Input Characteristics**

| *S. No.* | $V_{eb}$ *in volts* | $V_{cb} = 0$ $I_e$ *in mA* | $V_{cb} = 2$ *volts* $I_e$ *in mA* | $V_{cb} = 3$ $I_e$ *in mA* | $V_{cb}$ *open* $I_e$ *in mA* |
|---|---|---|---|---|---|
| | | | | | |

**2. For Output Characteristics**

| *S. No.* | $V_{eb}$ *in volts* | $I_E = 0$ *mA* $I_c$ *in mA* | $I_e = 1$ *mA* $I_c$ *in mA* | $I_c = 2$ *mA* $I_c$ *in mA* | $I_e = 5$ *mA* $I_c$ *in mA* |
|---|---|---|---|---|---|
| | | | | | |

**Nature of Graph:**

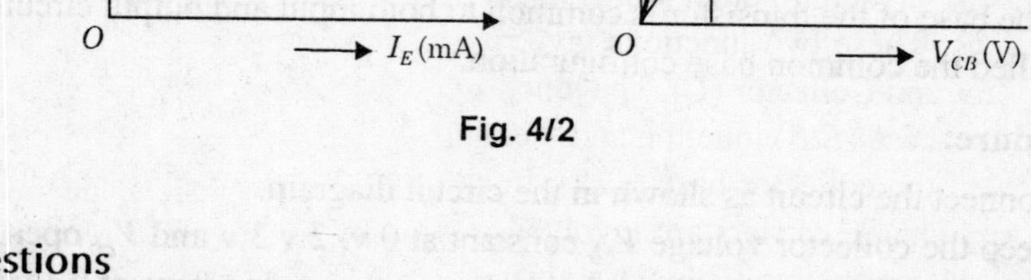


**Fig. 4/2**

## Questions

1. Define alpha of a transistor.
2. What is the order of input resistance, output resistance, voltage gain and current gain when a BJT is used as an amplifier in a *CB* Configuration

**3.** If alpha of a transistor is 0.99 and the base current is 100 micro amperes, estimate the collector current.

**4.** Identify the three different operating regions of a transistor on the output characteristics.

## EXP. No: 2

### *Common Emitter Characteristics of BJT*

**AIM:** To plot the static characteristics of bipolar transistor in common emitter configuration.

**Equipment and components required:**

| | |
|---|---|
| 1. Transistor | *BC* 107 (*NPN*) |
| 2. Resistor | 4.7 k? |
| 3. Ammeter | 0 – 25 mA |
| 4. Voltmeter | 0 – 25 volt |
| 5. Power supply | 0 – 30volt |

6. Breadboard and connecting wires.

**Circuit Diagram:**

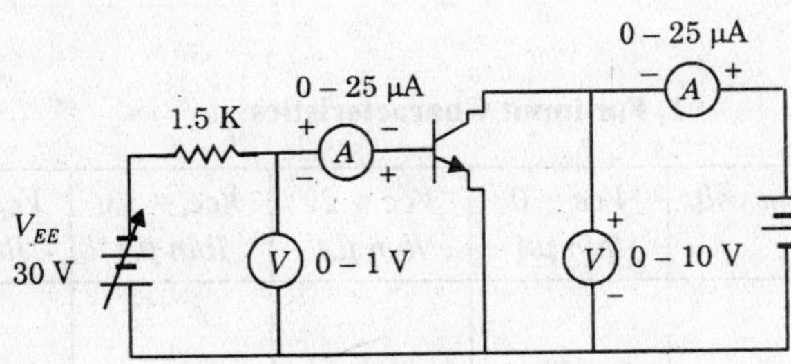


**Fig. L/3**

**Theory:** When a doped third element is added to a diode in such a way that two *PN* – junctions are formed, the resulting device is known as transistor. It consists of two back to back *PN*- junctions manufactured in a single piece of a semiconductor crystal. In other words, is has three layers, three terminals and two junctions. These two junctions give rise to three regions called Emitter (*E*), Base (*B*), and Collector (*C*). The junction between the emitter and base is called emitter-base (*E*/*B*) junction and the junction between the collector and base is called the collector-base (*C*/*B*). In junction transistors both majority and minority charge carriers are involved. Therefore they are called bipolar junction transistor or simply bipolar transistor. There are two types of transistors namely NPN transistor and PNP transistor. A transistor can be connected in a circuit in the following ways.

1. Common base configuration (*CB* configuration)
2. Common Emitter configuration (*CE* configuration)
3. Common collector configuration(*CC* configuration)

In the arrangement for common emitter configuration, the input is fed between the emitter and base and the out put is taken from the collector and Emitter. Here the emitter of the transistor is common to both input and out put circuit. So it is called common emitter configuration.

**Procedure:**

1. Connect the circuit as shown in the circuit diagram.
2. Keep the collector voltage *Vce* constant at 0 v, 2 v, 3 v and *Vce* open. For each value of *Vce*, vary *Vbb* such that Vbe increase in steps of 0.1 v from 0 to 1 volt and note down the corresponding base current *Ib*.
3. From these readings draw the graph *Vbe Vs Ib* for each fixed value of *Vce*. This will give input characteristics of *CE*
4. keep Ib constant at 50mA, 80mA,100mA etc. for each fixed value of Ib vary Vcc such that Vce is increased in steps of 1v from 0 to 10 volt and note down the corresponding values of Ic.
5. from the above readings, draw the graph *Ic Vs Vce* for each fixed value of *Ib*. This will give output characteristics of BJT in *CE* configuration.

**Tabular Form:**

**1. For input Characteristics**

| *S.No* | *Vbe in volts* | *Vce = 0*<br>*Ibin μA* | *Vce = 2v*<br>*Ibin μA* | *Vce = 3 v*<br>*Ibin μA* | *Vce open*<br>*Ibin μA* |
|---|---|---|---|---|---|
| | | | | | |

**2. For output Characteristics**

| *S. No* | *Vce (volts)* | *Ib = 50 mA*<br>*Ic in mA* | *Ib = 80 mA*<br>*Ic in mA* | *Ib =100 A*<br>*Ic in mA* | *Ib=120A*<br>*Ic in mA* |
|---|---|---|---|---|---|
| | | | | | |

**Nature of Graph:**

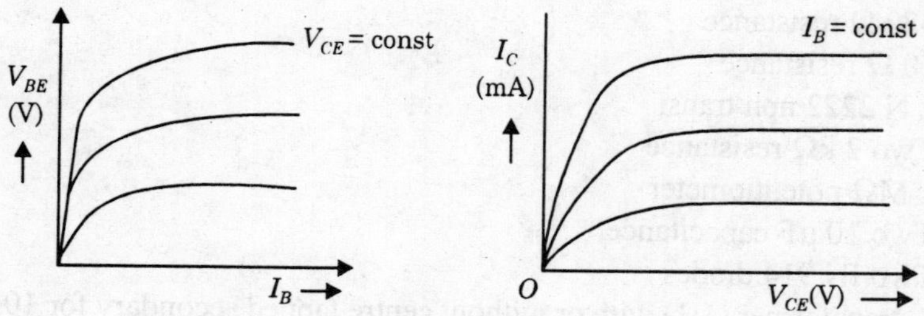


**Fig. 4L4**

## EXP. No: 3

### *Transistor Characteristics*

**Objectives:** At the end of this experiment, you will be able to

1. Display the *CE* transistor output characteristics family of curves on the oscilloscope.
2. Find out the small signal current gain $h_{FE}$ of the transistor from the output characteristic curves.
3. Operate the transistor in the *CE* node to drive a resistive load coupled in d.c and a.c modes.
4. Display the corresponding *dc* and ac load lines for each load on the CRO.
5. Determine the quiescent operating point of the collector circuit for a given load and biasing conditions.

**Equipment:**

1. Oscilloscope
2. AF signal generator
3. Variable power supply 0-5 volts
4. 10 V power supply
5. digital Multimeter

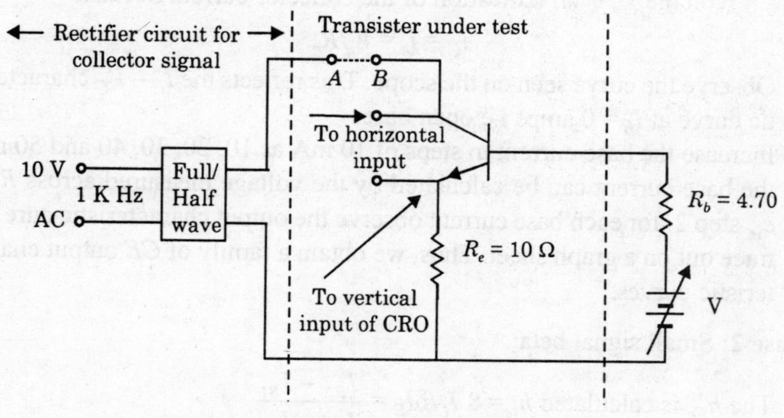


**Fig. 4L5** Step up the CE output

**Materials:**

1. 470 Ω resistance
2. 10 Ω resistance
3. 2 N 2222 npn transi
4. Two 2 kΩ resistance
5. 1 MΩ potentiometer
6. Two 10 μF capacitance
7. Two IN 914 diodes
8. A transformer (1:1) with or without centre tapped secondary for 10 V a.c input.

**Procedure:** 1. Oscilloscope calculation: Connect the 1 *Vp-p* voltage available at the *CRO* terminal to its own vertical input and calibrate the scale.

**Phase1:**

1. The *CE* output characteristics observed on the oscilloscope in the $X - Y$ mode of operation.
2. Set up the circuit shown in the figure 1 connect a 10 V ac signal of 1 KHz frequency (or any frequency that is comfortably observed) to the full wave rectifier circuit.
3. Observe the voltage across resistor $R_b$ on the scope or measure it with a multimeter. The base current is $I_B = \frac{V_{Rb}}{R_b}$, Initially set $V_{BB}$ at zero, so that $I_b = 0$ amps. This is the open-base condition.
   (i) Now connect the collector terminal of the transistor to the horizontal input of the *CRO*. This fixed up the horizontal amplifier drive to be the collector voltage $V_C$. The periodically varying collector-voltage $V_c(t)$ provides a sweep signal to the horizontal amplifier. Connect the emitter terminal to the vertical input. This causes the vertical amplifier drive to be the voltage $V_e$. $V_e$ and $V_c$ are related. Hence a stable display on the scope is assured with internal triggering. The emitter ground voltage $V_e$ is an indication of the collector current because

   $$i_C = i_e = V_e/R_e.$$

   Observe the curve seen on the scope. This reflects the $I_C - V_C$ characteristic curve at $I_b = 0$ amps i.e open base.
4. Increase the base current in steps of 10 mA as 10, 20, 30, 40 and 50 mA. the base current can be calculated by the voltage measured across $R_b$ as $c_{in}$ step 2. for each base current observe the output characteristic cure and trace out on a graph sheet. Thus, we obtain a family of *CE* output characteristic curves.

**Phase 2:** Small signal beta:

The $h_{Fe}$ is calculated $h_{fe} = 8\ I_C/\delta I_B = \frac{I_{B2} - I_{B1}}{I_{C2} - I_{C1}}$

***Figure 2:*** *A family of output characteristic curves*

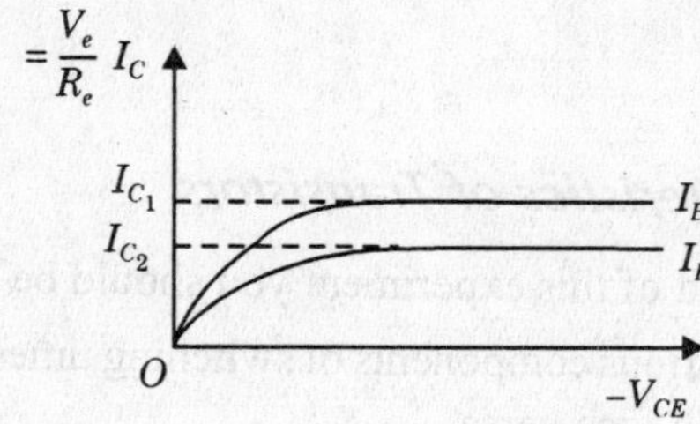


**Fig. 4L6**

**Phase 3:** *DC* and *AC* load lines:

1. Set up the circuit as shown below. Here the base signal voltage is varies sinusoidal and superimposed on the base bias voltage. $R_c$ is the dc load of the circuit. The oscilloscope horizontal and vertical inputs are connected to the collector and emitter terminal a respectively to get the $I_C - V_C$ relationship with the load connected, as explained earlier.

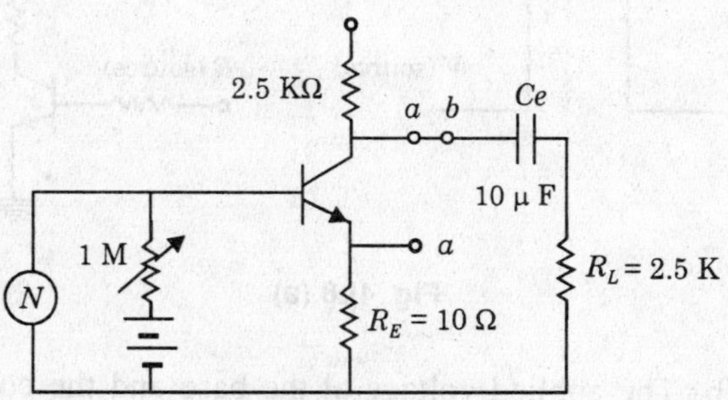


**Fig. 4L7**

2. Remove the short *a* – *b*. Observe the curve as seen on the scope. It is the dc load line. As the base current is increased from zero to its maximum value $i_b$ (max), the characteristic curves shift upwards. The right tip of the characteristic curve traces out the load line. This is because the intersections of the upward shifting $I_C - V_C$ curve with the load line are actually the operating points of the collector circuit, which appear on the *CRO* screen (see Q4). Trace out this dc load line on the output characteristics obtained in phase 1.
3. Connect the capacitively coupled load the collector to the transistor by shorting a and *b*.
   Set the frequency of the base signal such that the capacitances offers a low resistance. If this frequency is 1 KHz. The capacitive reactance is 100 ohms, which can taken to be a short.
4. Observe the $I_C V_C$ relationship on the scope as before. The load line that is observed corresponds to a parallel combination of $R_C$ and $R_L$. Trace out

the ac load line on the same graph as the characteristics curve set obtained in phase 1.

## EXP. No: 4

### *Switching Characteristics of Transistors*

**Objectives:** At the end of this experiment you should be able to

1. Understand the various components of switching times of a transistor from off to on states and vice versa.
2. Measure these timing components by applying a square wave input, and observing the output at the collector node of a *CE* transistor evaluate the total turn-on and turn-off time of the transistor from this data.

Figure 1(a) Pulse waveform at the input of a CE transistor causing transition from OFF and ON and back to OFF state.

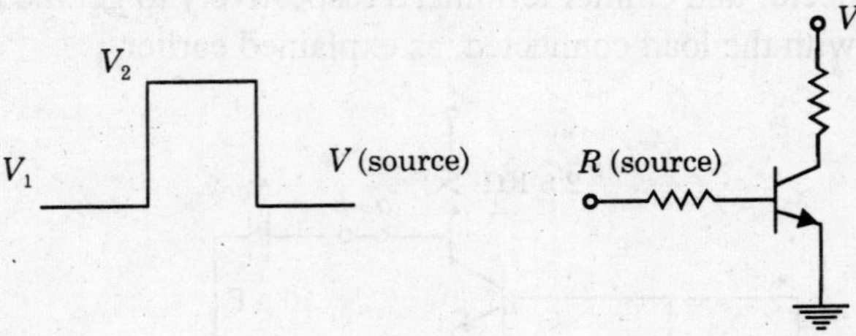


**Fig. 4L8 (a)**

Figure 1(b) The applied voltage at the base and the collector current response of the amplifier.

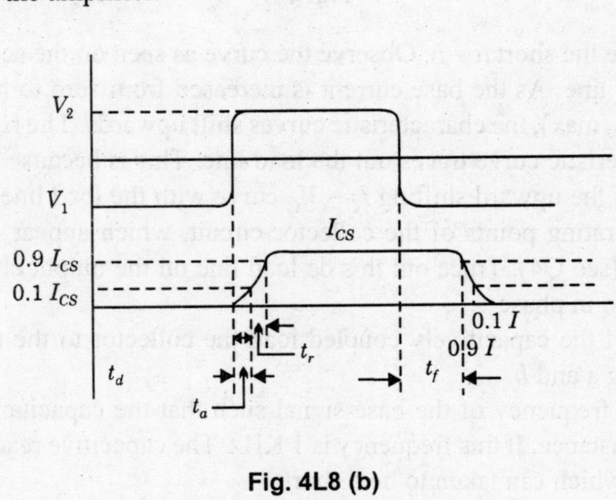


**Fig. 4L8 (b)**

**Components:**

(1) Resistances 3 kΩ one
10 kΩ one
1 kΩ one
(2) Capacitor 0.5 μF one
(3) Transistor – 2 N 2222 A.

**Equipment:**

(1) Dual channel oscilloscope
(2) AF function generator
(3) DC power supply 0-5 V

**Procedure:**

1. Connect the circuit as shown below figure 2
2. Input excitation:
   (i) the input is a square wave signal applied through a 50 Ω cable. The voltage levels *V*1and *V*2 at point *P* are changed by the d.c voltage of 3 V superimposed at the base

   Hnce: $V_1 = -3$ V
   $V_2 = (10 - 3) = 7$ V

   (ii) The duty cycle of the waveform is made equal to 5%, this allows a fair time for all transients to settle down before thenext pulse arrives causing another OFF to ON transition and back. Thus,

   $f = 5$ KHz
   $T = 200$ μS
   $T_{ON} = 0.05 \times T = 10$ μs.

   (iii) The coupling capacitor $C_C = 0.5$ μF offers a low impedance path to the a.c. signal and can be considered to be an a.c. short since $\frac{1}{2\pi f_x C_c}$ = 65 Ω, at the given frequency

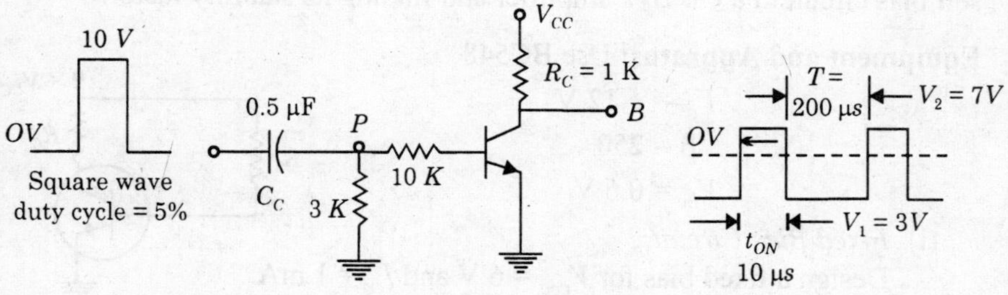


**Fig. 4L8** (c) Circuit for determining switching timer characteristics at transistor 2N2222A

3. Set the horizontal (time-base) sensitivity of both channels of the oscilloscope to the same value such that only one or twopulses are seen on the *CRO* when the input square wave is observed on each channel. Observe the input at *P* on the channel *A* and the collector voltage at *C* on channel *B*.
4. Measure the various switching times as illustrated in figure 4 Record all observations as:

Delay time $t_d =$

Rise time $t_r =$

Storage time $t_s =$

Fall time $t_f =$

Turn-on time $T_{ON} = t_d + t_r =$

Turn-off time $T_{OFF} = t_s + t_f =$

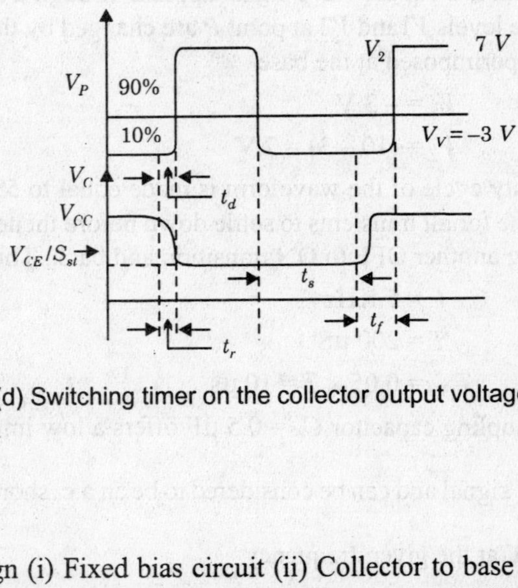


**Fig. 4L8** (d) Switching timer on the collector output voltage waveform.

## EXP. No: 5

## *BJT Biasing*

**AIM:** To design (i) Fixed bias circuit (ii) Collector to base bias circuit (iii) self bias circuit to a *CE* BJT amplifier and finding its stability factor.

**Equipment and Appratus:** Use BC548

$V_{cc} = +12$ V

$\beta = 250$

$V_{be} = 0.6$ V

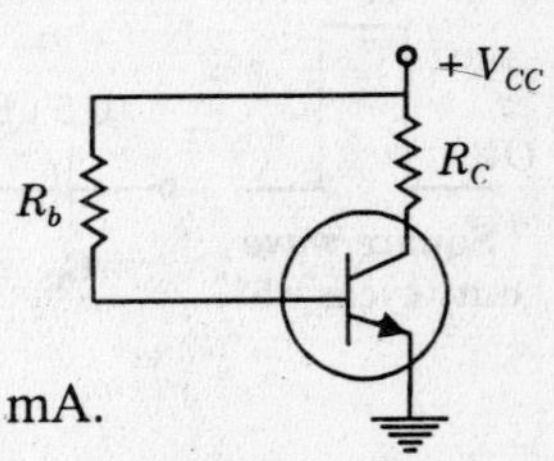


**Fig. 4L9 (a)**

(i) *Fixed Bias Circuit:*

Design a fixed bias for $V_{ceq} = 6$ V and $I_{cq} = 1$ mA.

$$V_{cc} = I_c R_c + V_{ce} \quad \text{...(1)}$$

$$R_c = 6 \text{ kohm}$$

$$R_b = (V_{cc} - V_{be})/I_b$$

(ii) *Collector to base bias circuit:* Design a collector to base bias circuit for $V_{ceq} = 6$ V and $I_{cq} = 1$ mA

$$V_{cc} = (I_c + I_b) + V_{ce}$$

$$R_c = 5.98 \text{ kohm} = 6 \text{ kohm}$$

$$V_{ce} = I_b R_b + V_{be}$$

$$R_b = 1.35 \text{ M}$$

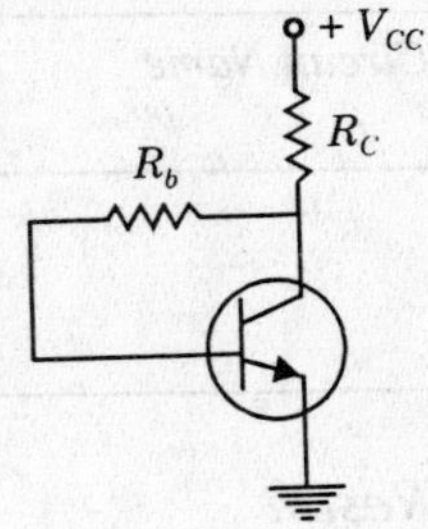


**Fig. 4L9 (b)**

(iii) *Self Bias Circuit:* Design Self bias circuit for $V_{ceq} = 6$ V, $I_{cq} = 1$ mA, $S <= 20$ and Select $R_c = 1/5 * R_c$

$$R_c = 5 \text{ K}$$

$$R_e = 1 \text{ K}$$

$$R_1 = 147 \text{ K}$$

$$R_2 = 23.93 \text{ K}$$

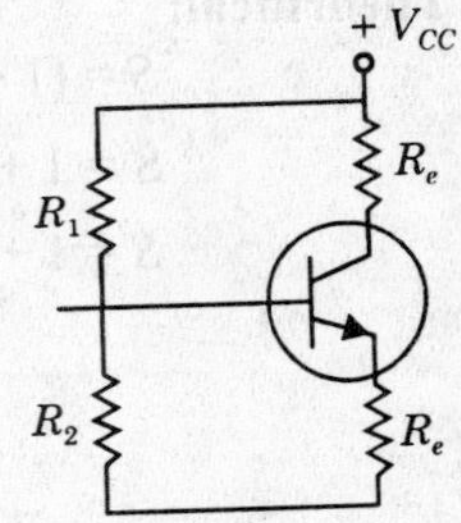


**Fig. 4L9 (c)**

**Components and Equipment:**

1. Transistor *BC* 548
2. Regulated Power Supply 0-30 V
3. Bread Board
4. Multimeter
5. Resistors as mentioned in the design
6. Connecting wires.

**Procedure:**

1. Make circuit connections as for the circuit diagrams.
2. Measure dc operating conditions (i.e $I_c$, $I_b$, $V_{ce}$, $V_{be}$).
3. Heat the transistor and measure $I_c$ and $I_b$ values at different interval of time.
4. From the above readings Calculate Stability Factor Value S.

$$S = (1 + \beta)\ 1 - \beta\ (d\, I_b / d\, I_c)$$

5. Repeat the above procedure for the biasing circuits.

## *Observations*

**Before Heating**

| *Circuit Name* | $I_b$ *(mA)* | $I_c$ *(mA)* | $V_{ce}$ *(V)* | $V_{be}$ *(V)* |
|---|---|---|---|---|
| 1. Fixed bias | | | | |
| 2. Collector-Base Bias | | | | |
| 3. Self bias | | | | |

**After Heating**

| *Circuit Name* | $I_b$ *(mA)* | $I_c$ *Ma* $I_{c1}$ $I_{c2}$ | $(I_{b2} - I_{b1})/(I_{c2} - I_{c1})$ | *S* |
|---|---|---|---|---|
| | | | | |

### *Result*

**Practical:** *S* for fixed bias
*S* for fixed Collector base bias
*S* for Self Bias

**Theoritical:**

$S = (1 + \beta) \longrightarrow$ fixed Bias

$S = 1 + \beta/(1 + \beta\ (R_e/R_e + R + G) \longrightarrow$ Self Bias

$S = 1 + \beta/(1 + \beta\ (R_c/R_e + R_c)$

# 《 5 》

# BJT AMPLIFIER

## 5.1 INTRODUCTION

The major application of the transistors and vacuum tubes in the field of electronics is as amplifiers. Both types of these devices may be used to amplify signal voltages of different characteristics. An amplifier constitutes of an essential part of radio, television and communication systems. As we have seen that a transistor can be need as an amplifier and that there are possible configurations in which a transistor can be used.

Amplification is the process of strengthening a weak signal without any change in the general shape of a signal. During the process of amplification, the original characteristics of the signal must be maintained. But, since neither the transistor nor the vacuum tube is a perfect linear device, distortion of the signal takes place during the process of amplification.

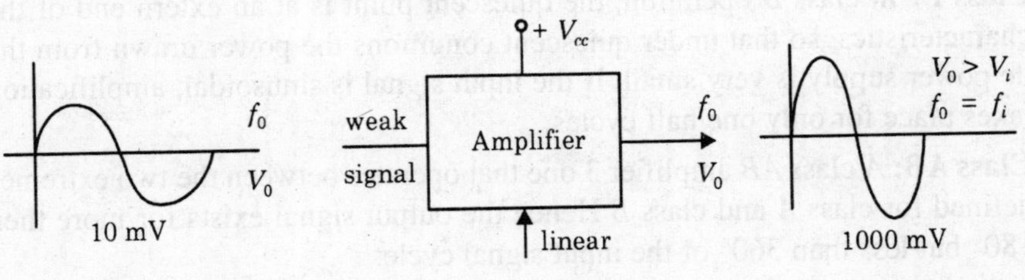


**Fig. 5.1**

## 5.2 CLASSIFICATION OF AMPLIFIER

1. *According to transistor configuration*
   (a) Common Emitter Configuration (*CE*)
   (b) Common Base Configuration (*CB*)
   (c) Common Collector Configuration (*CC*)
2. *Based on active devices*
   (a) BJT amplifiers
   (b) FET amplifiers

3. *According to operating condition (Q-point)*
   (a) Class *A* amplifiers
   (b) Class *B* amplifiers
   (c) Class *C* amplifiers
4. *According to number of stages*
   (a) Single stage amplifier
   (b) Multi stage amplifier
5. *According to frequency response*
   (a) Audio frequency (*AF*) amplifier
   (b) Intermediate frequency (*IF*) Amplifier
   (c) Radio frequency (*RF*) Amplifier
6. *According to bandwidth*
   (a) Narrow band amplifier (*RF* amplifier)
   (b) Wide band amplifier
7. *According to out put*
   (a) Voltage amplifier
   (b) Power amplifier

The position of the quiescent point and the extent of the characteristics that is being used determine the method of operation. Four classes of operation for either transistor or vacuum tube amplifiers are thus defined as follows and are graphically illustrated by means of dynamic transfer characteristic curves in figure.

**Class A:** In class *A* operation, the quiescent point and the input signal are such that the current in output circuit (in the collector, drain, or plate electrode) flows for all times. Thus operates essentially over a linear portion of its characteristics there by giving rise to minimum of distortion.

**Class B:** In class *B* operation, the quiescent point is at an extern end of the characteristics, so that under quiescent conditions the power drawn from the dc power supply is very small. If the input signal is sinusoidal, amplification takes place for only one half cycles.

**Class AB:** *A* class *AB* amplifier 3 one that operates between the two extremes defined for class *A* and class *B* Hence the output signal exists for more then 180° but less than 360° of the input signal cycle.

**Class C:** In class *C* operation the quiescent point is chosen such that the output signals (voltage or current) is zero for more than one-half of an input sinusoidal signal cycle.

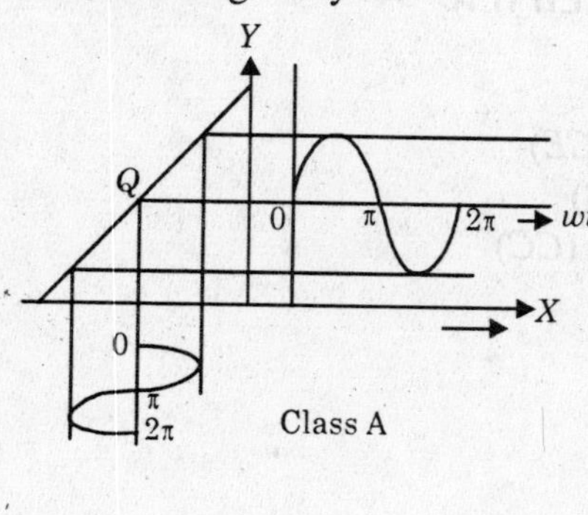

Class A

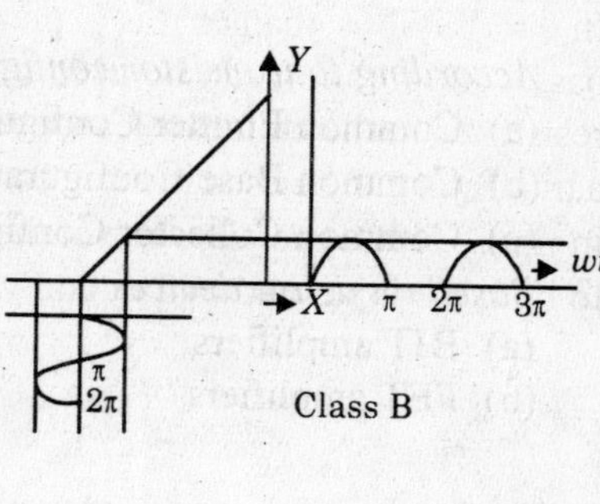

Class B

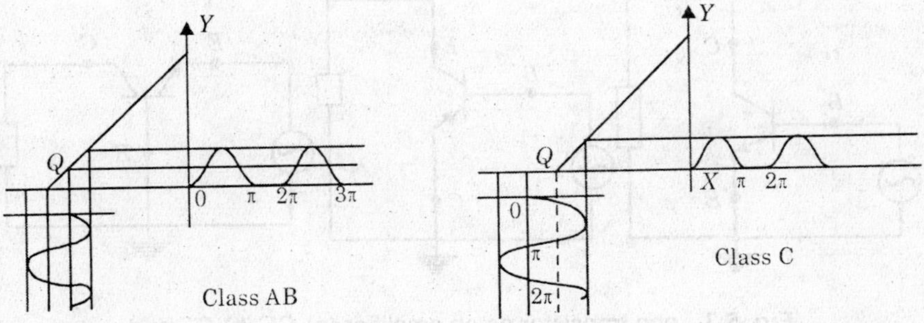


**Fig. 5.2** Classification of amplifiers in terms of the conditions of operation Means of dynamic transfer characteristics curves.

| *Parameter* | *Class A* | *Class AB* | *Class B* | *Class C* |
|---|---|---|---|---|
| Angle (θ) | 0° – 360° | 180° ≤ θ ≤ 360 | 180° | θ < 180° |
| Distortion | Least | *b/w A* and *B* | Medium | More |
| Power Efficiency | 25% 50% (transformer coupled) | | 78.5% | >80% |
| Linearing | Always linear | | Can be made as linear | Always non linear |
| Application | Linear voltage Amplifier | | Linear power amplifier | Non-linear power amplifier |

The above classification is valid for both power and voltage amplifiers but it is not required to have class *C* and class *B* in voltage amplifiers.

*A linear amplifier is the one which retain the shape of input at the output i.e., without distortion*

A single stage of an amplifier is not sufficient to boost up the voltage or power of the signal to the designed level. A number of stages may then be required to be connected in cascade. There are different methods by which the next amplifier stage or the load may be connected to the preceding stage. Thus there exist direct-coupled resistance capacitance coupled, Inductance-capacitance coupled, transformer coupled amplifiers.

## 5.3 BJT AS AN AMPLIFIER

In our previous chapter it is explained how a junction transistor in a common base configuration can be used to amplify signal voltages by placing a high resistance in the collector lead, even its current gain is less then unity. In fact, a transistor can be used in three configurations or modes of operation as shown in figure 5.3. Generally, one of the terminals in an amplifier is made common to both the input and output and very often this terminal is grounded.

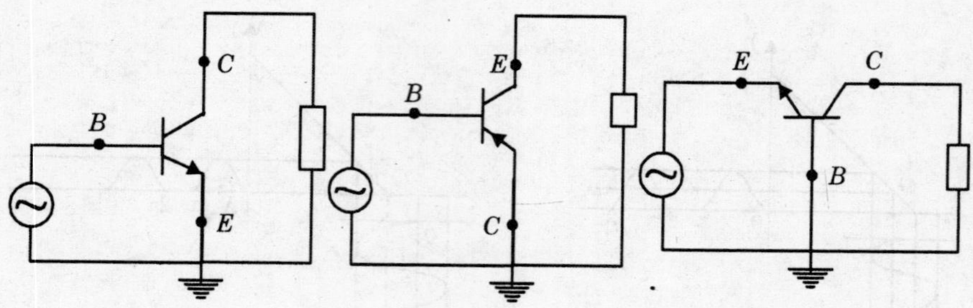


**Fig. 5.3** pnp transistor as an amplifier (a) *CE* (b) *CC* and (c) *CC* configurations.

When the emitter lead of the transistor is made common to the input and output circuits, the transistor is said to be working in common-emitter (*CE*) configuration Similarly, in the common- collector (*CC*) and common-Base (*CB*) configuration, the collector lead and the base load is common to the input and the output, respectively as shown in figure 5.3 (*b*) and (*c*) . In figure the biasing to voltage have not been shown for the sake of simplicity. According to signal strength we have small signal and large signal amplifiers.

| *S.No.* | *Small signal* | *Large signal* |
|---|---|---|
| 1 | Variation of signal from Q-point is small | Variation is largePower |
| 2 | Voltage Amplifiers | Power Amplifiers |
| 3 | Always operate in Class A | Operates in Class A,AB, B and C |
| 4 | Voltage amplifiers drives Power amplifiers | Power amplifiers drives the load |
| 5 | By models<br>(a) *h*-parameters(*LF*, *MF*)<br>(b) models (*RF*) | Very complex model .(Always analysis is by graphical) |

## 5.4 BJT AS A CE AMPLIFIER RC COUPLED AMPLIFIER

Function of each component:

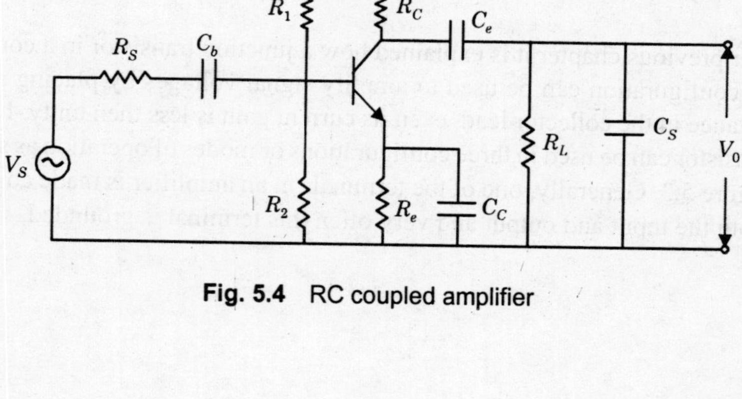


**Fig. 5.4** RC coupled amplifier

***Resistors:***

$R_1$, $R_2$ are used to bias the input and output with a single battery.

*Rc* is used to control *Vce* and also acts as a load.

*Re* is used for *Q*-point stability.

*RS* is used as a signal source resisitor.

*RL* is used as load.

The basic requirements of amplifier are

(i) Variable voltage gain without disturbing *Q* -point.

(ii) Variable bandwidth without disturbing the gain.

1. If $R_C$ is load then both *d.c* and *a.c* are varied

$$R_{dc} = R_{ac} = R_c$$

2. If $R_L$ is load then both *d.c* and *a.c* are varied

$$Rac = \frac{R_C R_L}{R_C + R_L}, R_{dc} = R_C \text{ and } R_L \text{ which is not better.}$$

3. $R_{dc} = R_c$ when $C_C$ is open circuited.

$$R_{ac} = \frac{R_C R_L}{R_C + R_L} \text{ when } C_C \text{ is short circuited.}$$

To act as a short circuit even for audio frequencies capacitor must be large enough (as large as microfarads)

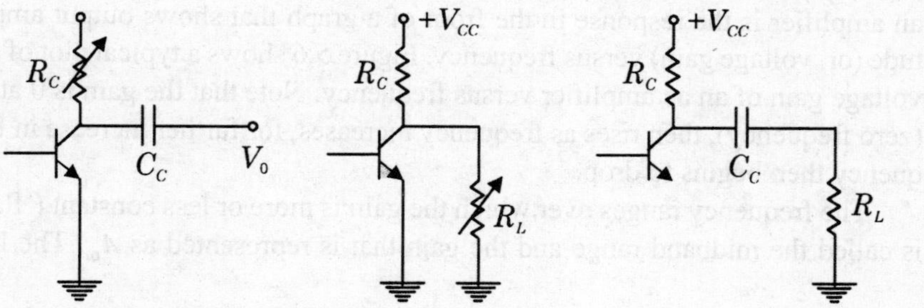


**Fig. 5.5**

Among all the above circuits shown in fig only the circuit in the fig 5.5 (c) can have variable voltage gain without disturbing *Q* point.

***Capacitors:***

$C_b$ is used to block d.c components and to allow a.c

$C_e$ is used to reduce loss of gain.

$C_c$ is used to make $V_0$ free from d.c,it connects $R_L$ for a.c and disconnects for d.c,it also isolates different stages for d.c and couples for a.c.

$C_{sh}$ or $C_L$ is used as shunt or load capacitor. This is used to vary the bandwidth without changing the voltage gain. It gives good fidelity (reproducibility).

Gain bandwidth product need not be constant for a loaded amplifier whereas it is always constant for a given device in the case of short circuit amplifier.

$C_{be}$ is a forward biased capacitor and an internal capacitor.

$C_{bc}$ is a reverse biased capacitor and an internal capacitor.

They act as open circuited for low and mid frequecies and reacts at high frquencies.

## 5.5 FREQUENCY RESPONSE OF AN AMPLIFIER

### *Frequency Response*

*Definition:* The frequency response of an electronic device or system is, the variation it causes if any, in the level of its output signal when the frequency of the signal is changes otherwise, it is the manner in which the device responds to changes in signal frequency. Figure 5.6 shows an amplifier whose frequency response causes small output amplitudes at both low and high frequencies .Also that the input signal amplitude is the same at each frequency, but the output signal amplitude changes with frequency. Thus the gain of the amplifier is a function of frequency. In this the gain is small at the low frequency and small at the high frequency.

An amplifier whose frequency response is such that the output signal amplitude is small at both low and high frequencies. The frequency response of an amplifier is the response in the from of a graph that shows output amplitude (or, voltage gain) versus frequency. Figure 5.6 shows a typical plot of the voltage gain of an ac amplifier versus frequency. Note that the gain is 0 at dc (zero frequency), then rises as frequency increases, for further increase in frequency then begins to drop.

The frequency ranges over which the gain is more or less constant ('flat') is called the midband range and the gain that is represented as $A_m$. The low frequency at which the gain equals $\left(\frac{1}{\sqrt{2}}\right) A_m = 0.707\ A_m$ is called the lower cutoff frequency and is denoted as f1. The high frequency at which the gain once again drops to 0.707 $A_m$ is called the upper cutoff frequency and is designated $f_2$. The bandwidth of the amplifier is defined to the difference between the upper and lower cutoff frequencies.

$$\text{Bandwidth} = BW = f_2 - f_1$$

At each cutoff frequencies Re o/p voltage is $v$, so the power is

$$P\ (\text{at cut off}) = \frac{\left(\frac{\upsilon}{\sqrt{2}}\right)^2}{R} = \frac{0.5v^2}{R} = 0.5\text{P(mid band)}$$

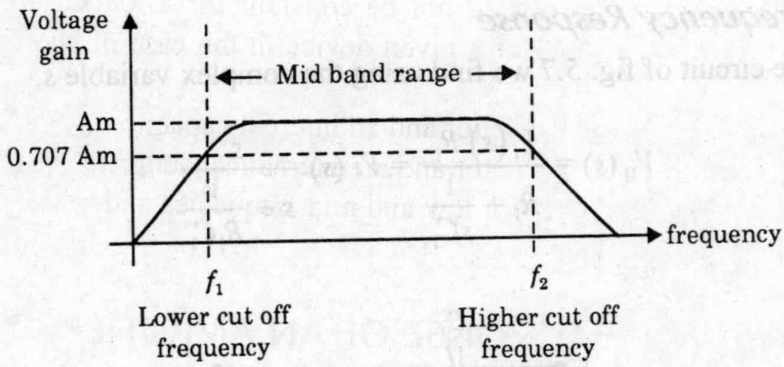


**Fig. 5.6** A typical amplifiers frequency response with gain vs frequency this is frequency response of an amplifier in general.

Now the frequency response of an amplifier on fidelity consideration experimentally is as follows

*Fidelity consideration:* Considering a sinusoidal signal of angular frequency '*w*' represented by $Vm = \sin(wt + \phi)$. If the voltage gain of the amplifier has a magnitude *A* and if the signal suffers a phase change that is lead angle θ then the output will be

$$AV_m \sin(wt + \phi + \theta) = AV_m \sin\left[w\left(t + \frac{\theta}{w}\right) + \phi\right]$$

If the amplification *A* is independent of frequency and if the phase shift q is proportional to frequency (or is zero), then the amplifier will preserve the form of the input signal, although the signal being shifted in time by an amount

$D = \dfrac{\theta}{w}$.

This suggests that the extent to which an amplifier amplitude response is not uniform and its time delay is not constant with frequency, is a measure of the lack of fidelity to be anticipated in it. For an amplifier stage the frequency characteristic are to be divided into three regions there is a range called the *mid band* frequency one which the amplification is reasonably constant and equal to $A_0$, and over which the delay is also quite constant, let us assume that the mid band gain is normalized to unity i.e $A_0 = 1$. In the second which is low-frequency region, below mid band an amplifier stage may behave like the simple high-pass circuit of fig 5.7. The response decreases with decreasing frequency and the output usually approaches zero at *dc* ($f = 0$), in the third that is the *high-frequency region* above mid band, the circuit after behaves like the simple *low-pass* network of fig 5.14 (a), and the response decreases with increasing frequency.

The total frequency characteristics for all the three regions are detailed below.

## *Low Frequency Response*

From the circuit of fig. 5.7 we find using the complex variable *s*,

$$V_0(s) = \frac{V_i(s)\,R_1}{R_1 + \dfrac{1}{sC_1}} = Vi(s)\,\frac{s}{s + \dfrac{1}{R_1C_1}} \qquad \ldots(1)$$

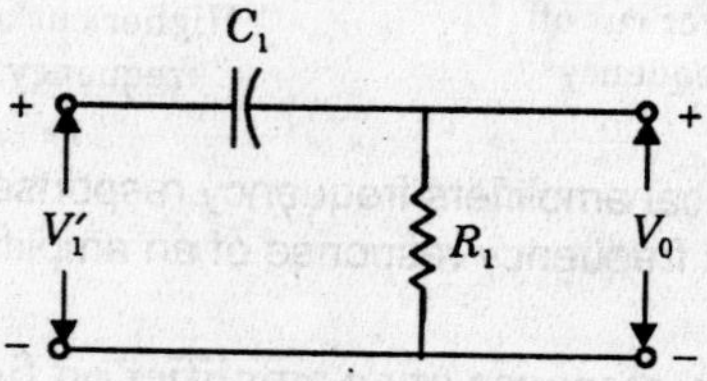


**Fig. 5.7** A high pass RC circuit used to calculate the Low-frequency response of an amplifier.

Thus the voltage transfer function at low frequencies is

$AL(s) = \dfrac{V_0(s)}{V_i(s)}$, has one zero at $s = 0$ and one pole at $s = -1/R_1C_1$

For real frequencies i.e, $s = jw = j\,2\,\pi f$,

$$\text{Eq (1) becomes } Av_L = \frac{1}{1 - j\left(\dfrac{f_1}{f}\right)} \qquad \ldots(2)$$

In the presence of amplifier the expression can be modified as

$$Av_L = \frac{Av_m}{1 - j\left(\dfrac{f_1}{f}\right)}$$

Where $$f_1 = \frac{1}{2\pi R_1C_1} \qquad \ldots(3)$$

The magnitude $|A_L|$ and the phase lead of the gain are given by

$$|Av_L| = \frac{Av_m}{\sqrt{1 + \left(\dfrac{f_1}{f}\right)^2}} \qquad \ldots(4)$$

$$\theta_L = \tan^{-1}(f_1/f) \qquad \ldots(5)$$

at $f = f_1$, $A_L = \frac{1}{\sqrt{2}} = 0.707$, where as in the mid band region ($f >> f_1$) i.e. $A_L \rightarrow 1$. Hence $f_2$ is that frequency at which the gain has fallen to 0.707 times its mid band value $A_0$. This drop in signal level corresponds to a decibel reduction of $20 \log \left(\frac{1}{\sqrt{2}}\right)$, or 3 *dB*. Therefore $f_1$ is referred to as the lower 3 *dB* frequency. From eq (3) $f_1$ is that frequency for which the resistance $R_1$ equals the capacitive reactance $\frac{1}{2\pi f_1 C_1}$.

## *High frequency Response*

In the high-frequency region above the mid-band the simple low-pass circuit of fig 5.8 (b) can approximate the amplifier stage. In terms of complex variable s, we find

$$V_0(s) = \frac{\frac{1}{sC_2}}{R_2 + \frac{1}{sC_2}} V_i(s) = \frac{1}{1 + sR_2C_2} V_{i(s)} \quad \ldots(5)$$

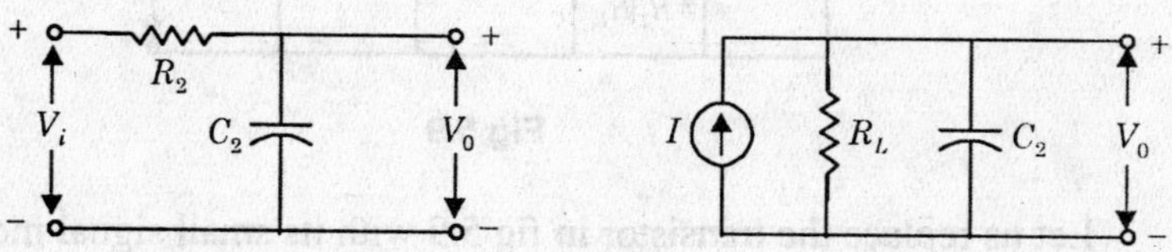


**Fig. 5.8** (a) Alow-pass RC circuit used to calculate the high frequency response of an amplifier. (b) Norton's equivalent of the circuit in (a) where $I = vi/R_2$

Hence the transfer function in this region has a single pole of $s = -1/R_2C_2$. For real frequencies i.,.e. $s = jw = j2\pi$ magnitude is given by

$$|Av_H| = \left|\frac{V_0(s)}{V_i(s)}\right|_{s = j2\pi f}$$

and for the phase lead angle '$\theta_H$' of the gain in the high-frequency region,

$$|Av_H| = \frac{1}{\sqrt{1 + \left(\frac{f}{f_2}\right)^2}} \text{ and } \theta_H = 180 - \tan^{-1}(f/f_H) \quad \ldots(6)$$

In the presence of the amplifier the expression can be modified as $Av_H = \frac{Av_m}{1 + j\frac{f}{f_2}}$

where $$f_2 = \frac{1}{2\pi R_2 C_2} \quad ...(7)$$

Since at $f = f_2$ the gain is reduced to $\frac{1}{\sqrt{2}}$ times its mid band value, then $f_H$ called the upper 3 – *dB* frequency this also represents that frequency at which the resistance $R_2$ equals the capacitive reactance $1/2\pi f_2 C_2$.

In the above expressions $\theta_L$ and $\theta_H$ represent the angle by which the output leads the input , neglecting the initial 180° phase shift through the amplifier. Bandwidth is the frequency range from $f_L$ to $f_H$ of the amplifier stage.

As $Av_L$ and $Av_H$ depends on $Av_m$ .let us go for mf analysis

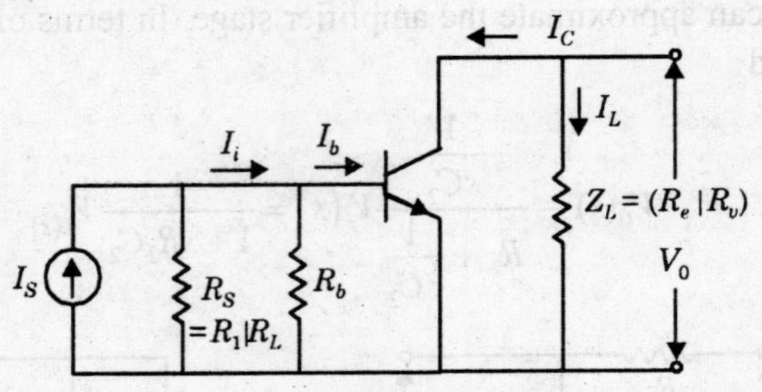


Fig 5.9

Let us replace the transistor in fig 5.9 with its small signal model.

## 5.6 SMALL SIGNAL MODELS

When the collector-emitter voltage and current swings are very small, the transistor is considered to be linear and can be replaced, for purposes of analysis, by a small signal equivalent circuit model.

### *Transistor Models (Small Signal Amplifiers)*

In Design of small signal current or voltage amplifiers we consider the following parameters

1. Hybrid Parameters (h-parameters)
2. *r*-parameters
3. $\pi$-Parameters

### 1. Hybrid Parameters Model

Before this, it is better to know a transistor can be treated as two port network. The representation of two port network is shown 5.10 below.

From figure 5.10 current *i* enter at point $i_1$ and $i_2$ entering at port 2. Terminal voltage is across port 1 and voltage $v_2$ across port 2. If the two port is linear device then we can write

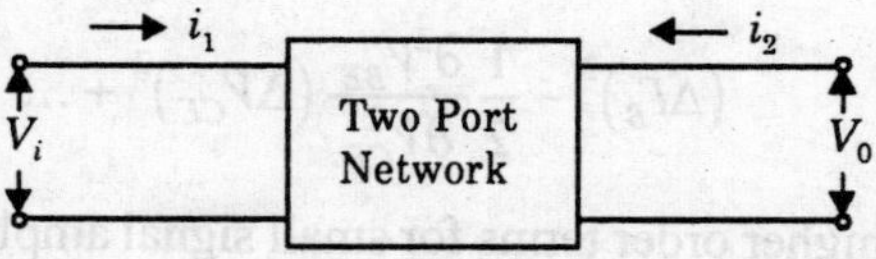


**Fig. 5.10** Two port network

$$v_1 = h_{11}\, i_1 + h_{12}\, v_2 \text{ and}$$

$$i_2 = h_{21}\, i_1 + h_{22}\, v_2$$

where $h_{11}$, $h_{12}$, $h_{21}$ and $h_{22}$ are called the $h$-parameters

$v_1$ is input voltage

$v_2$ is output voltage

$i_1$ is input current and $i_2$ is output current

Above expressions can write only $i_1$ (input current ) and $v_2$ (out put voltage) are taken as independent variables. The basic assumption of a transistor linear model or equivalent circuit is that the variation about the quiescent point is assumed small, so that the transistor parameters can be considered constant over the signal emission. The operating (quiescent) values of current and voltages are determined by the method employed to bias the transistor.

The transistor model is given in terms of the *h-parameters* which all real numbers of audio frequencies are easy to measure, can also be obtained from the transistor static characteristic curves and are particularly convenient to use in circuit analysis and design.

To derive a hybrid model for a transistor let us consider the common emitter connection shown in figure 5.11.

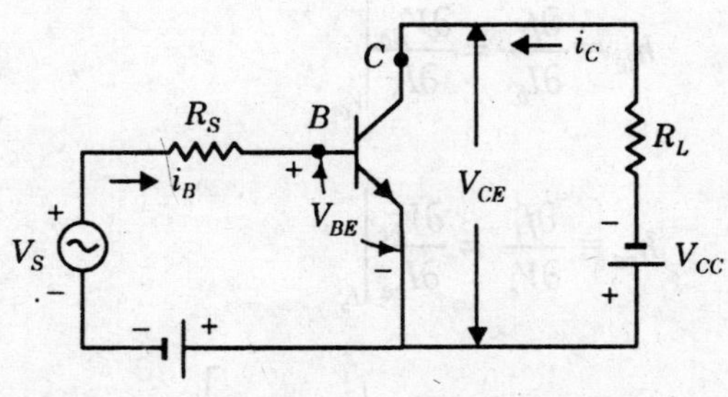


**Fig. 5.11** CE transistor configuration

## *Input Characteristic Equation*

$$V_{BE} = f_1\,(I_B, V_{CE}) \qquad \ldots(1) \text{ (for both } AC \text{ and } DC)$$

Making Taylor series expansion of equation around the quiescent point $I_B$, $V_{CE}$ we obtain

$$\Delta V_{BE} = \left( \frac{\partial V_{BE}}{\partial I_B}\, \Delta I_B + \frac{\partial V_{BE}}{\partial V_{CE}}\, \Delta V_{CE} \right) - \frac{1}{2}\, \frac{\partial^2 V_{BE}}{\partial_B^2}$$

$$(\Delta I_B)^2 - \frac{1}{2}\frac{\partial^2 V_{BE}}{\partial V_{CE}^2}(\Delta V_{CE})^2 + \ldots \quad \ldots(2)$$

Neglecting the higher order terms for small signal amplifier. Where as for large signal amplifiers we can't neglect higher order terms. Therefore for large signal amplifiers the model becomes very complicated

$\Delta I_B$ is small and therefore $(\Delta I_B)^2$ is very very small

We obtain

$$\Delta V_{BE} = \left.\frac{\partial f_1}{\partial I_B}\right|_{V_{CE}} \Delta I_B + \left.\frac{\partial f_1}{\partial V_{CE}}\right|_{I_B} \Delta V_{CE} \quad \ldots(3)$$

The partial derivatives are taken keeping the collector voltage or the base current constant.

$$\therefore \quad v_{be} = h_{ie}\, i_b + h_{re}\, v_{ce} \text{ (For } AC)$$

Where $V_{be}$ is the terminal voltage and

$h_{ie}\, i_b$ is the voltage drop

$h_{re}\, V_{ce}$ is the voltage controlled voltage source

$h_{ie}$ is input impedance

$h_{re}$ is reverse voltage gain

$$Avf \text{ (forward voltage gain)} = \frac{1}{h_{re}}$$

Where $$h_{ie} = \frac{\partial f_1}{\partial I_b} = \left.\frac{\partial V_{Be}}{\partial I_b}\right|_{V_{ce}}$$

$$h_{re} = \frac{\partial f_1}{\partial V_c} = \left.\frac{\partial V_{bc}}{\partial I_{ce}}\right|_{I_b}$$

Where $$h_{fe} = \frac{\partial f_2}{\partial I_b} = \left.\frac{\partial I_c}{\partial I_b}\right|_{V_{ce}} \text{ and}$$

$$h_{oe} = \frac{\partial f_2}{\partial V_{ce}} = \left.\frac{\partial I_c}{\partial V_{ce}}\right|_{I_b} \quad \ldots(4)$$

The partial derivations of equation (2) and (4) define the h-parameters for the common emitter connection .The common emitter (*CE*) *h-parameter* model is shown in fig. 5.12.

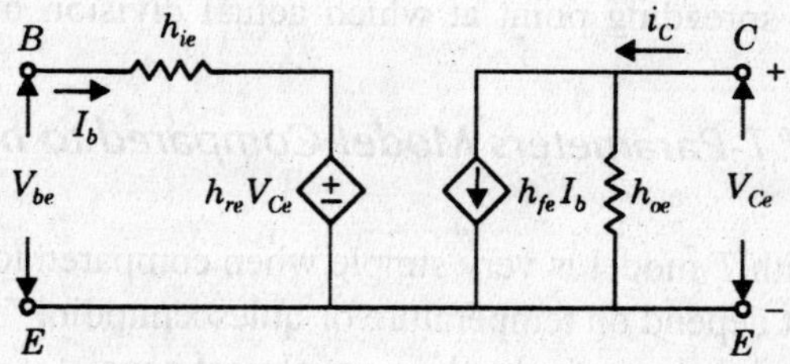


**Fig. 5.12** The hybrid small-signal nodes for the common emitter.

### *Output Characteristic Equation*

$$I_c = f_2\,(I_B, V_{CE})$$

Making Taylor series expansion and neglecting higher order terms we get

$$\Delta Ic = \frac{\partial I_C}{\partial I_B}\,\Delta I_B + \frac{\partial I_C}{\partial V_{CE}}\,\Delta V_{CE}$$

The partial derivatives are taken, keeping the collector voltage or the base current constant.

$$i_c = h_{fe}.\, i_b + h_{oe}.\, V_{ce} \text{ (for } AC\text{)}$$

where $i_c$ is the terminal current

$h_{fe}$ is forward current gain

$h_{oe}$ is output admittance

$h_{fe}\, i_b$ is the current controlled current source

$h_{oe}\, V_{ce}$ is the current flow

The variables $i_b$, $V_{be}$ and $V_{ce}$ represent total instantaneous currents and voltages. We can select current $i_b$ and voltage $V_{ce}$ as independent variables.

Since $V_{be}$ is same function $f_1$ of $I_B$ and $V_{CE}$ and since $I_c$ is another function $f_2$ of $I_B$ and $V_{CE}$.

*Disadvantages of h-parameters:*

1. h-parameters vary with respect to $Q$-point and temperature .
2. Very complicated expressions for analysis.

## 2. r-Parameter or T-Parameter Model

*r*-parameter model is developed for common base and it is also called *T*-model.

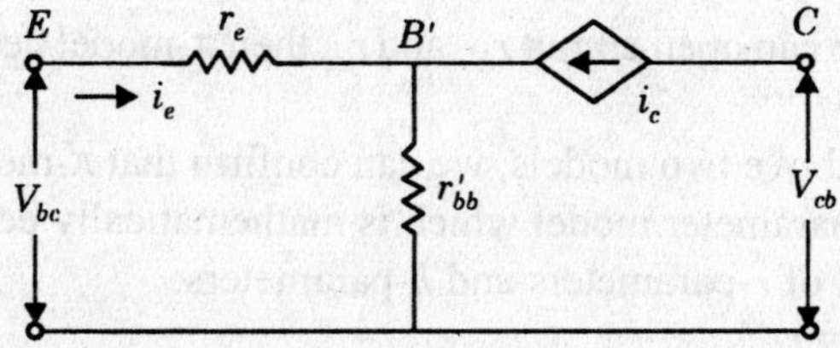


**Fig. 5.13** T-model of a *CB* transistor

$B'$ is called base spreading point at which actual division of current takes place.

### Advantages of T-Parameters Model Compared to h-Parameters Model.

1. The result with $T$-model is very simple when compared to $h$-parameters.
2. Result do not depend on temperature or quiescent point
3. The theoretical and practical values are almost equal.

## 3. π-parameter Model

π-model is also developed for common emmiter. Its validity is compared with $h$-parameter model.

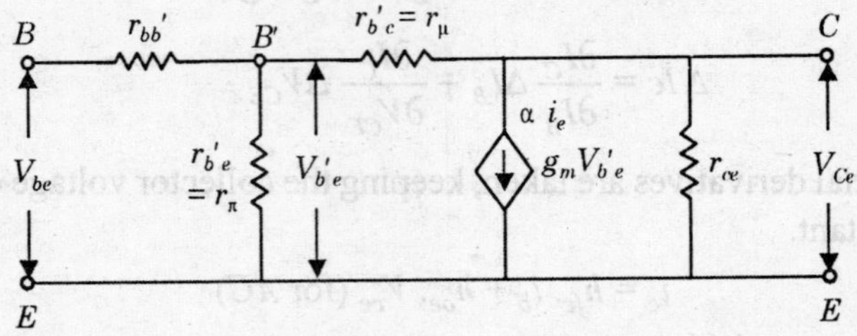


**Fig. 5.14** The hybrid-π model at low frequencies

Conversion of π-parameter model into $h$-parameter model (derived in 6th chapter):

$$h_{fe} = \beta$$

1. $g_m = \dfrac{I_c}{V_T}$
2. $g_{b'e} = \dfrac{g_m}{h_{fe}}$
3. $g_{b'c} = g_{b'e}\, h_{re}$
4. $r_{bb'} = h_{ie} - r_{b'e}$
5. $g_{ce} = h_{oe} - (1 + h_{fe})\, g_{b'c}$

Typical values for a given transistor

$r_{bb'} = 100\ \Omega$, $r_{b'e} = 1\ \text{k}\Omega$, $r_{b'c} = 4\ \text{M}\Omega$, $r_{ce} = 80\ \Omega$, $g_m = 50$ ma\V

Therefore we can open circuit $r_{b'c}$ and $r_{ce}$ then π-model becomes as shown in the fig. 5.15.

Comparing above two models, we can confirm that π-model is also valid as it becomes $h$-parameter model which is mathematically developed.

Comparision of $r$-parameters and $h$-parameters:

1. $r_e = h_{re} = r_\pi = r_e$
2. $\beta = h_{fe}$
3. $i_c = h_{fe}\, i_b$.

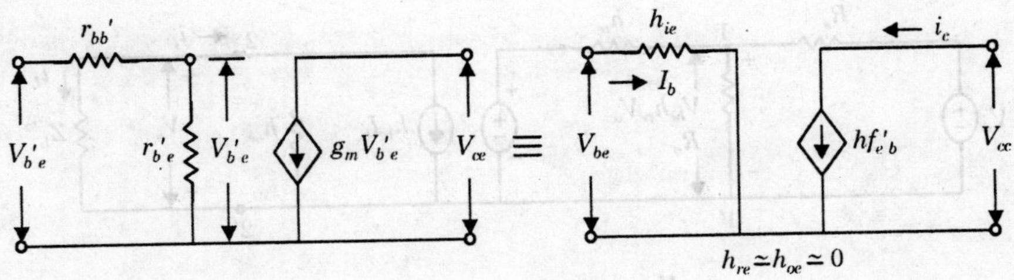


**Fig. 5.15**

Since we have converted $r$-parameter models into $h$-paremeters. Let us analyse amplifier using $h$-parameters.

## 5.7 EXACT ANALYSIS AT MID FREQUENCY

1. *Current gain without base resistor (Rb):*

$$A_I' = \frac{\text{output current}}{\text{input current}} = \frac{i_L}{i_b} = \frac{-i_c}{i_b} \qquad \ldots(1)$$

from the circuit

$$i_c = h_{fe}\, i_b + h_{oe}\, V_o \qquad \ldots(2)$$

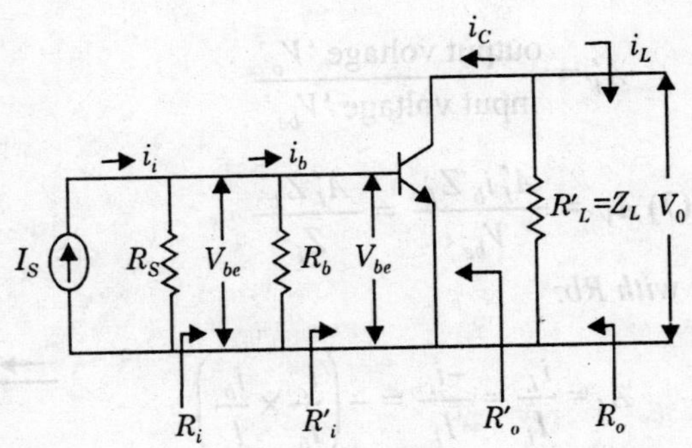


Substituting $V_o = -I_c Z_L$ in the equation (2)

$$i_c = h_{fe}\, i_b - h_{oe}\, i_c\, Z_L$$

$$[i_c + h_{oe}\, i_c\, Z_L] = h_{fe}\, i_b$$

$$i_c\,[1 + h_{oe}\, Z_L] = h_{fe}\, i_b$$

$$\frac{i_c}{i_b} = \frac{h_{fe}}{1 + h_{oe}\, Z_L} \Rightarrow -\frac{i_c}{i_b} = \frac{-h_{fe}}{1 + h_{oe} \cdot Z_L} = A_I' \qquad \ldots(3)$$

2. *Input impedance without Rb:*
   The impedance which is looking into the amplifier input terminals 1 & 1′ is the amplifier input impedance.

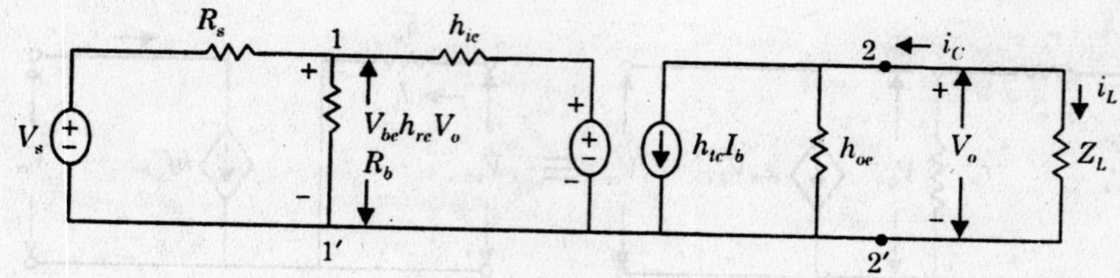

$$R_i' = \frac{V_{be}}{i_b} \qquad \text{...(4)}$$

from the input circuit, $V_{be} = h_{ic}\, i_b + h_{re}\, V_o$ ...(5)

$$\therefore \qquad R_i' = \frac{h_{ie}\, i_b + h_{re}\, V_o}{i_b} = h_{ie} + h_{re}\frac{V_o}{i_b} \qquad \text{...(6)}$$

Substituting $\quad V_0 = -i_c \cdot Z_L = \frac{-i_c'}{i_b} \cdot i_b \cdot Z_L = A_I'\, i_b \,.\, Z_L$ ...(7)

in Equation (6).

$$R_i' = h_{ie} + h_{re}\; A_I' Z_L$$

It is important to note that input impedance is a function of the load impedance.

3. *Voltage gain without Rb:*

$$A_V' = \frac{\text{output voltage '}V_o\text{'}}{\text{input voltage '}V_{be}\text{'}}$$

from the eq. (7) $A_{V'} = \dfrac{A_I'\, i_b\, Z_L}{V_{be}} = \dfrac{A_I' Z_L}{Z_i}$ ...(8)

4. *Current gain with Rb:*

$$A_I = \frac{i_L}{I_i} = \frac{-i_c}{I_i} = -\left(\frac{i_c}{i_b} \times \frac{i_b}{I_i}\right)$$

$$A_I = A_I' \times \frac{i_b}{I_i} = A_I' \frac{R_b \times I_i}{R_b + I_i} \times \frac{1}{I_i}$$

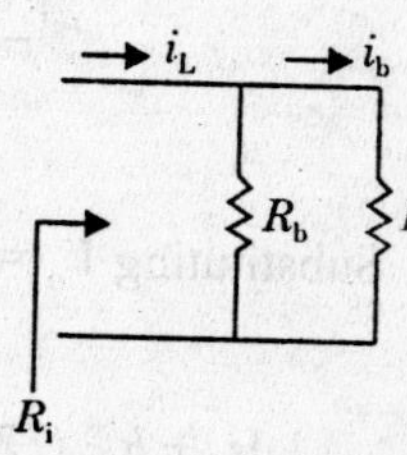

$$A_I = A_I' \cdot \frac{R_b}{R_b + I_i} \qquad \text{...(9)}$$

5. *Input impedance with Rb:*

$$R_i = \frac{V_{be}}{-I_i}$$

from fig. 3 $R_i = R_b \,//\, R_i$ ...(10)

6. *Voltage gain with Rb:*

$$A_V = \frac{V_o}{V_{be}} = \frac{i_L \cdot Z_L}{R_i \cdot I_i} = A_I \cdot \frac{Z_L}{R_i}$$

7. *Current gain with $R_S$ ($A_{IS}$):*

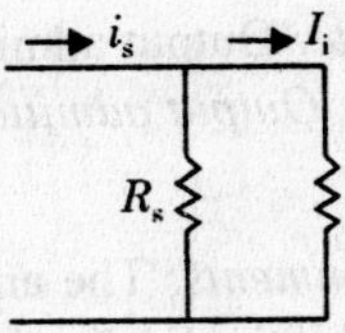


$$A_{IS} = \frac{i_L}{i_S} = \frac{-i_C}{I_i} \times \frac{I_i}{i_S} = A_i \left( \frac{R_S \cdot i_S}{R_S + R_i} \right) \cdot \frac{1}{i_S}$$

$$A_{IS} = A_I \cdot \frac{R_S}{R_S + R_i} \quad \text{...(11)}$$

8. Voltage gain with $R_S$:

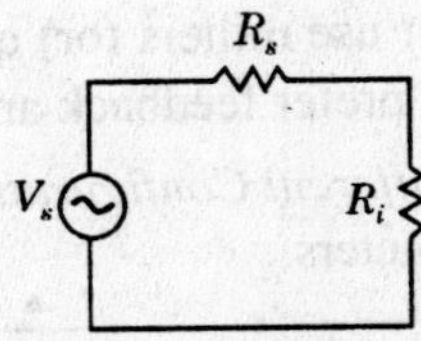


$$A_{VS} = \frac{V_o}{V_S} = \frac{V_o}{V_{be}} \cdot \frac{V_{be}}{V_S}$$

$$= A_V \left\{ \frac{R_i \cdot V_S}{R_S + R_i} \right\} \frac{1}{V_S}$$

$$= A_V \left\{ \frac{R_i}{R_S + R_i} \right\} \quad \text{...(12)}$$

output impedance without $Z_L$:

$$Y_o' = \frac{1}{Z_o'} \bigg/ \begin{matrix} V_S = 0 \\ Z_L = \infty \end{matrix} \quad \text{...(12)}$$

$$Y_o' = \frac{i_c}{V_o} \text{ from eq. (2)}$$

$$Y_o' = \frac{h_{fe} \cdot i_o - h_{oe} V_o}{V_o} = h_{fe} \frac{i_b}{V_o} + h_{oe} \quad \text{...(13)}$$

from fig. 2 with $V_S = 0$

$$R_S' ib + h_{ie} i_b + h_{re} V_o = 0$$

$$i_b (R_S' + h_{ie}) = -h_{re} V_o$$

$$\frac{i_b}{V_o} = \frac{-h_{re}}{(R_S' + h_{ie})} \quad \text{...(14)}$$

where $R_S' = R_S // R_b$

substitute (14) in Eq. (13)

$$Y_o' = h_{oe} - \frac{h_{fe}\, h_{re}}{(R_S' + h_{ie})} \quad \ldots(15)$$

*Note:* Output admittance is a function of the source resistance.

10. *Output admittance with $Z_L$:*

$$R_o = R_o \,//\, Z_L \quad \ldots(16)$$

*Comments:* The analysis is for the circuit without feedback and if the feedback exists we should go by millers (or) duality of millers or applying the feed back concepts.

*Example:* If there is $C_e$ it by passes, if $C_e$ is not there go by two appraoches.

Approaches → Duality (of) millers (Approximate)
Approaches → Negative feed back analysis (better)

Never use millers (or) quality of millers unless and otherwise asked for. Always prefer feedback analysis.

(a) *Different Configurations:* Other configurations we can analysis using their parameters.

| *Parameter* | *CE* | *CB* | *CC* |
|---|---|---|---|
| $A_I'$ | $\frac{-h_{fe}}{1+h_{oe}\, R_L'}$ | $\frac{-h_{fb}}{1+h_{ob}\cdot R_L'}$ | $\frac{-h_{fe}}{1+h_{oc}\, R_L'}$ |
| $R_I'$ | $h_{ie} + h_{re}\, A_I'\, R_L'$ | $h_{ib} + h_{rb}\, A_I'\, R_L'$ | $h_{ic} + h_{rc}\, A_I'\, R_L'$ |
| $Y_o'$ | $h_{oe} - \frac{h_{re}\, h_{fe}}{h_{ie} + R_S'}$ | $h_{ob} - \frac{h_{rb}\cdot h_{fb}}{h_{ib} + R_S'}$ | $h_{oc} - \frac{h_{rc}\, h_{fc}}{h_{ic} + R_S'}$ |

*Conversion of h-parameters:*

| *Parameter* | *CE* | *CC* | *CB* |
|---|---|---|---|
| $h_f$ | $\beta = h_{fe}$ | $h_{fc} = (-1 + h_{fe})$ | $h_{fb} = \frac{-h_{fe}}{1+h_{fe}} \simeq 1$ |
| $h_i$ | $h_{ie}$ | $h_{ic} \simeq h_{ie}$ | $h_{ib} = \frac{h_{ie}}{1+h_{fe}}$ |
| $h_r$ | $h_{re}$ | $h_{rc} \simeq 1$ | $h_{rb} = \frac{h_{oe}\cdot h_{ie}}{1+h_{fe}} - h_{re}$ |
| $h_o$ | $h_{oe}$ | $h_{oc} \simeq h_{oe}$ | $h_{ob} = \frac{h_{oe}}{1+h_{fe}}$ |

1. Unity current gain in CB and Unity vol. gain in cc configuration.
2. a.c gain generally follows d.c gain.
3. $R_i$ of CB is very low.
4. $R_o$ of CB is very high.

(b) Only (1), (2) & (9) varies from exact to approximate because only $h$-parameter model changes from exact to approximate.

*Approximate Analysis:*

*CE without* $R_e$: $h_{oe} \cdot R'_L \le 0.1$

$$(1)\quad A'_I = \frac{-h_{fe}}{1 + h_{oe} \cdot R'_L} = -\,h_{fe}$$

$\because \quad h_{oe} \simeq h_{re} \simeq 0.$

$$(2)\quad R'_i = h_{ie} + h_{re} A_I R'_L = h_{ie}$$

$$R'_i = h_{ie}$$

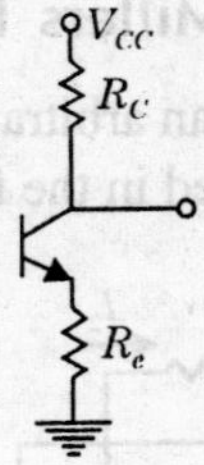


$$(9)\quad Y'_o = h_{oe} - \frac{h_{re} \cdot h_{fe}}{h_{ie} + R'_S} = 0$$

$$R'_o = \frac{1}{0} = \infty$$

*CE with* $R_e$: $h_{oe} \simeq h_{re} \simeq 0$

$$h_{oe}\left\{R_e + R'_L\right\} \le 0.1$$

$$(1)\quad A'_I = -\,h_{fe}$$

$$(2)\quad R'_i = h_{ie} + h_{re} A'_I R_L + R_e (1 - A'_I)$$

$$= h_{ie} + h_{re} A'_I R_L + R_e \left(1 - (-h_{fe})\right)$$

$$R'_i = h_{ie} + (1 + h_{fe}) R_e$$

$$(3)\quad Y'_o = 0$$

$$R'_o = \infty$$

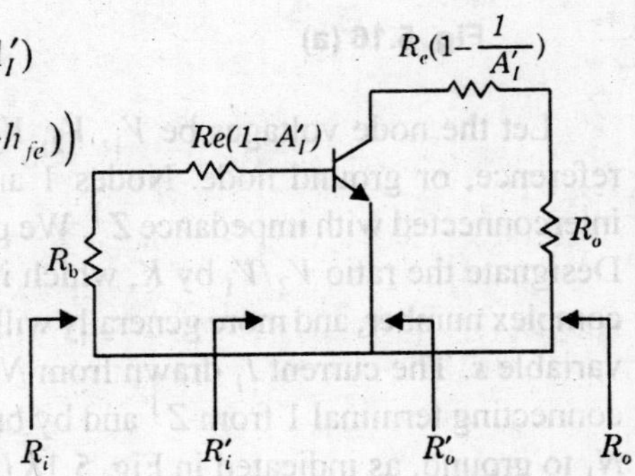


CB: $h_{rb} \simeq h_{ob} \simeq 0$

$$1.\quad A'_I = \frac{-h_{fb}}{1 + h_{ob} R_2^1} = \frac{-(-h_{fe})}{1 + h_{fe}}$$

$$2.\quad R'_i = h_{ib} + h_{rb} A'_I R'_L = \frac{h_{ie}}{1 + h_{fe}}$$

$$Y'_o = h_{ob} - \frac{h_{rb}\, h_{fb}}{h_{ib} + R'_S} = 0$$

$\Rightarrow \quad R_o' = \infty.$

$CC: n_{oc} \simeq 0 \;\; h_{rc} \simeq 1$

1. $A_I' = \dfrac{-h_{fc}}{1 + h_{oc} R_L'} = (1 + h_{fe})$

2. $R_i' = h_{ic} + h_{rc} A_I' R_L' = h_{ie} + 1(1 + h_{fe}) R_L$

$\quad = h_{ie} + 1(1 + h_{fe}) R_L$

3. $Y_o' = h_{oc} - \dfrac{h_{rc} h_{fc}}{h_{ic} + R_S'}$

$\Rightarrow \quad R_o' = \dfrac{h_{ie} + R_S'}{1 + h_{fe}}$

### 5.7.1 Millers Theorem

Consider an arbitrary circuit configuration with $N$ distinct nodes 1, 2, 3, ... $N$ as indicated in the fig. 5.18 (a) below.

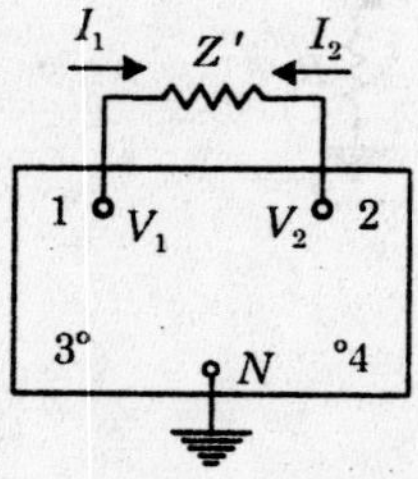


**Fig. 5.16 (a)**

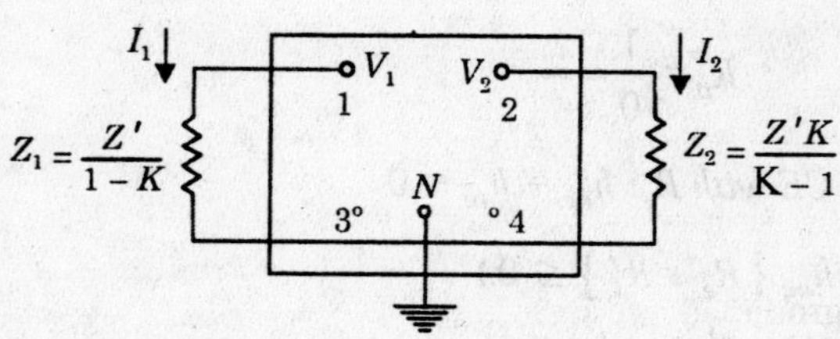


**Fig. 5.16 (b)**

Let the node voltages be $V_1$, $V_2$, $V_3$, ... $V_N$ where $V_N = 0$ since $N$ is the reference, or ground node. Nodes 1 and 2 (referred to as $N_1$ and $N_2$ ) are interconnected with impedance $Z^1$. We postulate that we know the ratio $V_2/V_1$. Designate the ratio $V_2/V_1$ by $K$, which in the sinusoidal steady state will be a complex number, and more generally will be a function of the Laplace transform variable $s$. The current $I_1$ drawn from $N_1$, through $Z^1$ can be obtained by disconnecting terminal 1 from $Z^1$ and by bridging or impedance $Z^1/(1-K)$ from $N_1$ to ground, as indicated in Fig. 5.18 (b).

The current $I_1$ is given by $I_1 = \dfrac{V_1 - V_2}{Z^1} = \dfrac{V_1(1-K)}{Z^1} = \dfrac{V_1}{Z^1/(1-k)} = \dfrac{V_1}{Z_1}$

Therefore if $Z_1 = Z^1/(1-K)$ where shunted across terminals $(N_1 - N)$, the current $I_1$ drawn from $N_1$ would be the same as that from the original circuit

Hence the same expression is obtained for $I_1$ in terms of the node voltages for the two configurations. The current $I_2$ drawn from $N_2$ may be calculated by removing $Z^1$ and by connecting between $N_2$ and ground an impedance $Z_2$ given by $Z_2 = \dfrac{Z^1}{1 - 1/k} = \dfrac{Z^1 k}{K - 1}$

Since identical nodal equations (*KCL*) are obtained from the configuration of Fig. 5.16 (a) and 5.16 (b), these two networks are equivalent. If must be emphasized that this theorem will be useful in making calculations only if it is possible to find the value of *k* by same independent means.

### Dual of Millers Theorem

Consider the network of fig 5.17 (a) with arbitrary active or passive linear elements betweens nodes 1, 2, and 3 and with as impedance $Z^1$ between node 3 and ground *N*, the two loops indicated are coupled by means of the common element $Z_1$. We postulate that we know the current ratio $A_I = -I_2/I_1$.

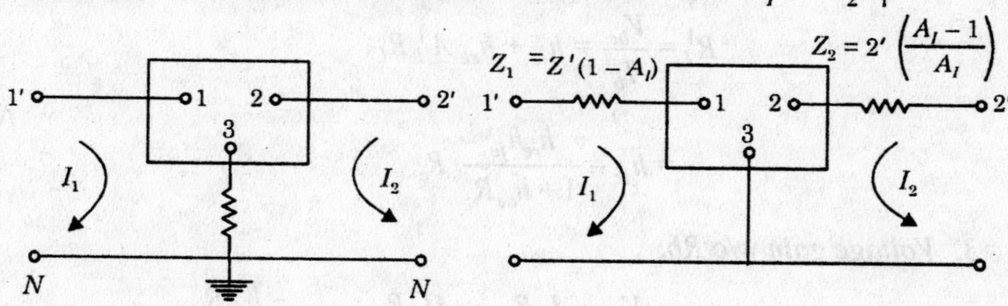


**Fig. 5.17 (a)** **Fig. 5.17 (b)**

The dual of Millers theorem is indicated in Fig. 5.17 (b) where node 3 is grounded, an impedna *ce* $Z_1$ , is placed in mesh 1 and $Z_L$ is added to mesh 2.

It is verified that the voltage $I_1\ Z_1$ equals the drop $(I_1 + I_2)\ Z^1$ across $Z^1$ if $Z_1 = Z^1\ (1 - A_I)$. Hence $V_{IN}$ is the same in the two circuits in Fig. 5.19 (a) and (b). In a similar manner $V_2N$ has the same value in the two circuits if $Z_2 = [(A_I - 1)/A_I]\ Z^1$. The two networks are therefore identical in the reverse that if the same voltages $V_I N$ and $V_2N$ are impressed on both, the same current $I_1$ will flow in mesh 1, and $I_2$ in mesh 2.

## 5.8 EXACT ANALYSIS OF DIFFERENT AMPLIFIER CIRCUITS

**Note:** All these circuits are made up of previous biasing circuits.

*Circuit: 1*

*1. Current gain w/o Rb:*

$$A_I^1 = \frac{-I_C}{I_b} = \frac{-h_{fe}}{1 + h_{oe} R_c}$$

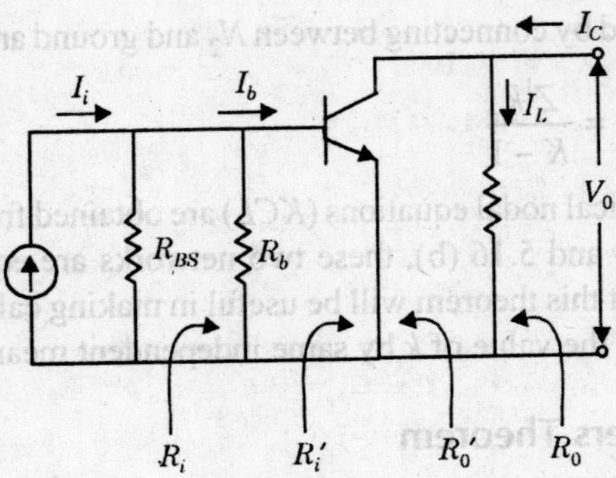


**Fig. 5.18**

2. *I/P Impedance w/o Rb:*

$$R_I^1 = \frac{V_{bc}}{I_b} = h_{ie} + h_{re} A_I^1 R_C.$$

$$= h_{ie} - \frac{h_{re} h_{fe}}{1 + h_{oe} R_c} \cdot R_c$$

3. *Voltage gain w/o Rb:*

$$A_v^1 = \frac{V_{ce}}{V_{be}} = \frac{I_L R_C}{I_b R_i^1} = \frac{A I^1 R_C}{R_i^1} = \frac{-h_{fe} R_c}{(1 + h_{oe} R_c) R_i^1}$$

4. *Current gain with Rb:*

$$A_I = \frac{I_L}{I_i} = \left(\frac{I_L}{I_b}\right)\left(\frac{I_b}{I_i}\right)$$

$$A_I = A_I^1 \cdot \frac{R_b}{R_b + R_i^1} = \frac{-h_{fe}}{(1 + h_{oe} R_c)} \frac{R_b}{(R_b + R_i^1)}$$

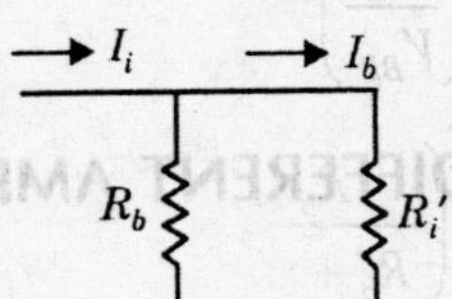


$$I_b = \left[\frac{I_i}{R_b + R_i'}\right] R_b$$

**Fig. 5.19 (a)** current gain with $R_B$

5. *I/P impedance with $R_b$:*

$$R_i = \frac{V_{be}}{I_i} R_i$$

$$= R_b \| R_i^1 = \frac{R_b R_i^1}{R_b + R_i^1}$$

6. *Voltage gain with $R_b$:*

$$A_V = \frac{V_{ce}}{V_{be}} = \frac{I_L R_C}{I_i R_i} = \frac{A_I \cdot R_C}{R_i}$$

$$A_v = \left(\frac{-h_{fe}}{1 + h_{oe} R_C}\right)\left(\frac{R_b}{R_b + R_i^1}\right)\left(\frac{R_C}{R_i}\right)$$

7. *Current gain with $R_{BB}$:*

$$A_{IS} = \frac{I_L}{I_{BB}} = \frac{I_L}{I_i} \cdot \frac{I_i}{I_b}$$

$$= A_I \left\{\frac{R_b}{R_b + R_i}\right\}$$

$$= \frac{-h_{fe}}{(1 + h_{oc} R_C)} \cdot \frac{R_b}{(R_b + R_i)}$$

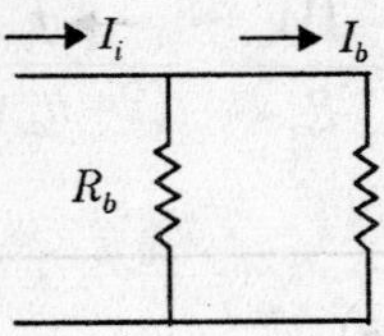


$$I_i = \left[\frac{R_b}{R_i + R_b}\right]$$

**Fig. 5.19 (b)** Current gain with $R_{BB}$

8. *Voltage gain with $R_b$:*

$$A_{VS} = \frac{V_0}{V_{BB}} = \left(\frac{V_0}{V_i}\right)\left(\frac{V_i}{V_{BB}}\right) = A_V \left\{\frac{R_i}{R_i + R_b}\right\}$$

$$= \left(\frac{-h_{fe}}{1 + h_{oe} R_C}\right)\left(\frac{R_b}{R_b + R_i^1}\right)\left(\frac{R_C}{R_i}\right)\left\{\frac{R_i}{R_i + R_b}\right\}$$

$$A_{VS} = \frac{-h_{fe} R_b R_C}{(1 + h_{oc} R_C)(R_b + R_i^1)(R_b + R_i)}$$

9. *Output admittance without $R_C$:*

$$Y_0^1 = \frac{I_C}{V_{Ce}}\bigg|_{V_{BB} = 0}$$

$$= h_{oe} - \frac{h_{re}h_{fe}}{h_{ie} + R_S^1}$$

Where $R_S^1 = (R_S \| R_b)$

$$Z_{oc} = Z_{th} = \left.\frac{V_{oc}}{I_{sc}}\right|_{V_b=0}, R_0^1 = \frac{1}{Y_0^1}$$

*10. O/P impedance with $R_c$:*

$$R_0 = R_0^1 \| R_C = \frac{1}{Y_0^1} \| R_C = h_{oe} - \frac{h_{re}h_{fe}}{h_{ie} + R_{BB}\|R_b} \| R_c$$

$$R_0 = h_{oe} - \frac{h_{re}h_{fe}}{h_{ie} + R_{BB}\|R_b} \| R_c$$

*Circuit 2:*

Same as circuit 1.

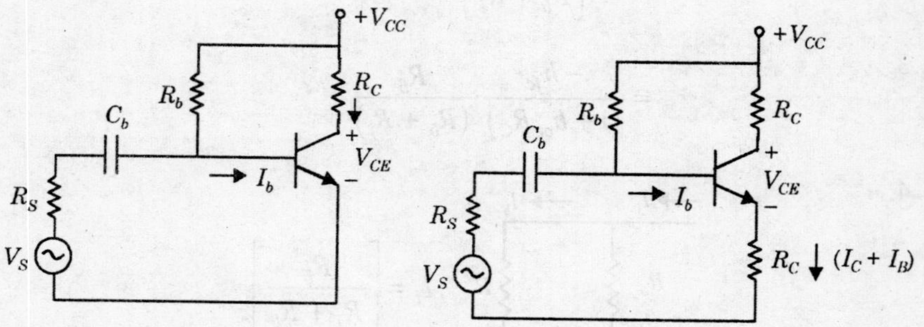


**Fig. 5.20**

*Circuit 3:*

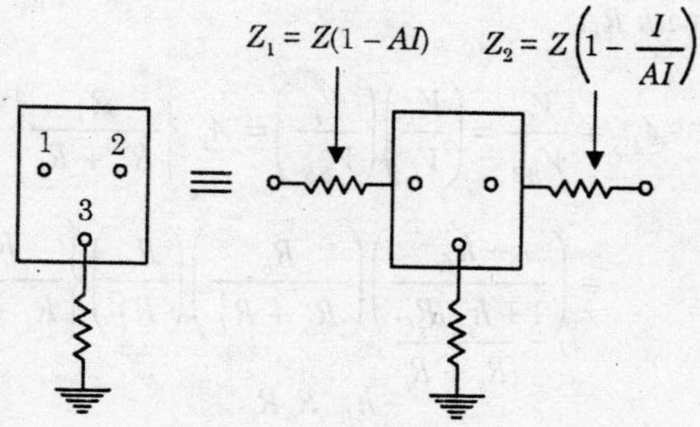


**Fig. 5.21 (a)**

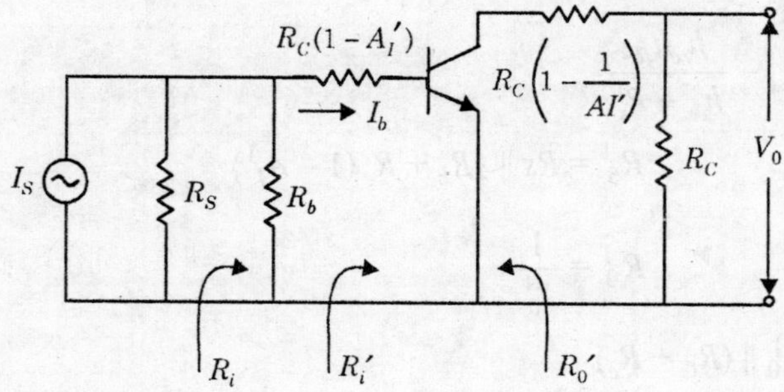


**Fig. 5.21 (b)** The ac equivalent at midband using duality of millers Current gain with out $R_b : h_{oe} < 1$

1. $A_I{}^1 = \dfrac{-h_{fe}}{1 + h_{oe}\,(R_e + R_C)}$

2. $R_i{}^1 = h_{ie} + h_{re}\,A_I^1\,R_C + R_e\,(1 - A_I^1)$

3. $A_V^1 = \dfrac{A_I^1\,(R_e + R_C)}{R_i^1}$

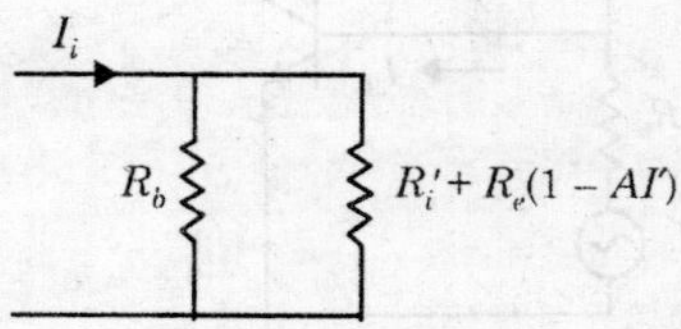


**Fig. 5.21 (c)**

4. $A_I = A_I^1 \left\{\dfrac{I_b}{I_i}\right\}$

From fig (c)

$$I_b = \frac{I_i\,(R_b)}{R_b + R_i^1 + R_e\left(1 - A_I^1\right)}$$

5. $R_i = R_b \| \{R_i^1 + R_e\,(1 - A_i^1)$

6. $A_V = \dfrac{A_i \cdot (R_c + R_e)}{R_i}$

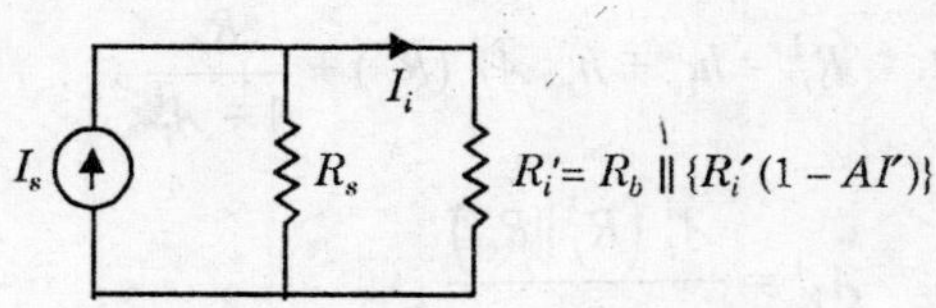


**Fig. 5.21 (d)**

7. $A_{IS} = A_I \left\{\dfrac{I_i}{I_s}\right\}$

From fig (d) $\quad I_I = \dfrac{I_s \cdot R_s}{R_s + R_i}$

$$A_{IS} = A_I \cdot \frac{R_s}{R_s + R_i}$$

8. $A_{VS} = A_V \left\{\dfrac{R_i}{R_i + R_s}\right\}$

9. $Y_0^1 = h_{oe} - \dfrac{h_{re}h_{fe}}{h_{ie} + R_s^1}$

where $R_5^1 = Rs \parallel \{R_b + R_e(1 - A_I^1\}$

$$R_0^1 = \frac{1}{Y_0^1}$$

10. $R_0 = R_0^1 \parallel (R_C + R_e)$

*Circuit 4:*

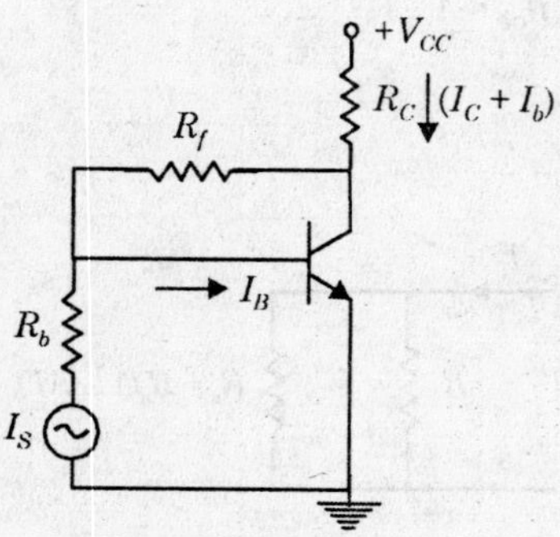


**Fig. 5.22 (a)**

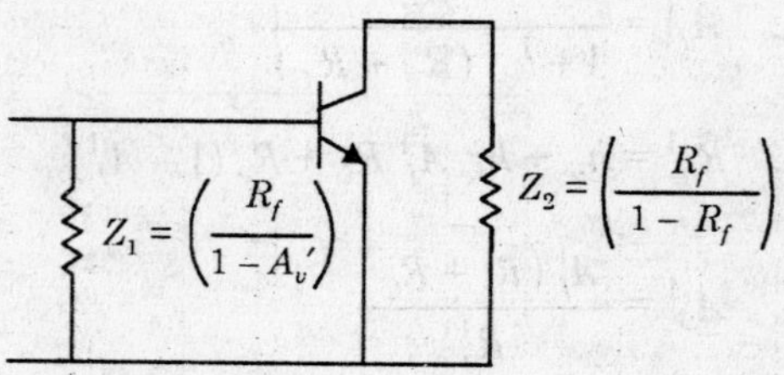


**Fig. 5.22 (b)** A.C. equivalent using millers theorem

1. $A_I^1 = \dfrac{-h_{fe}}{1 + h_{oe}\left(R_f \| R_c\right)}$

2. $R_i^1 = h_{ie} + h_{re} A_I^1 (R_C) + \dfrac{R_f}{1 - A_V^1}$

3. $A_V^1 = \dfrac{A_I^1 \left(R_f \| R_C\right)}{R_i^1}$

4. $A_I = A_I^1 \left(\dfrac{I_b}{I_1}\right)$

from fig (c)

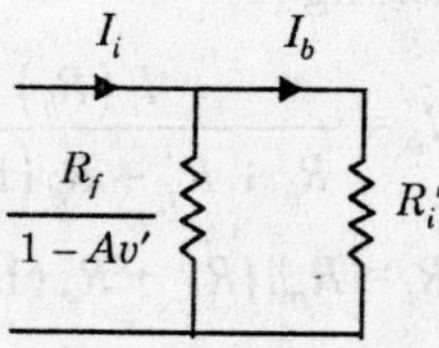


**Fig. 5.22 (c)**

$$I_b = \frac{I_i \dfrac{R_f}{\left(1 - A_V^1\right)}}{\dfrac{R_f}{\left(1 - A_V^1\right)} + R_i^1}$$

$$A_I = \frac{A_I^1 \dfrac{R_f}{\left(1 - A_V^1\right)}}{\dfrac{R_f}{\left(1 - A_V^1\right)} + R_i^1}$$

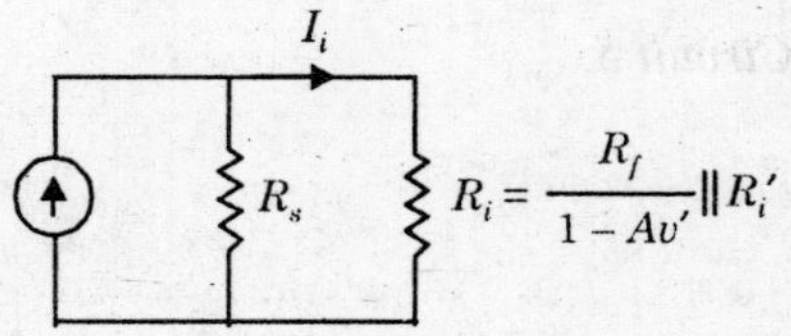


Fig. 5.22 (d)

$$A_I = \frac{A_I^1 R_f}{R_f + R_i^1\left(1 - A_V^1\right)}$$

5. $R_i = \dfrac{R_f}{1 - A_V^1} \| R_i^1$

6. $A_V = \dfrac{A_I\left(R_f \| R_C\right)}{R_i} = \dfrac{A_I R_f R_c}{R_i\left(R_f + R_C\right)}$

7. $A_{IS} = A_I\left\{\dfrac{I_i}{I_S}\right\}$

from fig (d)

$$I_i = \frac{I_s R_s}{R_s + R_i}$$

$$A_{IS} = A_I\left\{\frac{R_s}{R_s + R_i}\right\}$$

8. $A_{VS} = A_V\left\{\dfrac{R_i}{R_i + R_s}\right\}$

9. $Y_0^1 = h_{oe} - \dfrac{h_{re} h_{fe}}{h_{ie} + R_s^1}$

$$R_s^1 = R_S \| \left(\frac{R_f}{1 - A_V^1}\right), R_0^1 = \frac{1}{Y_0^1}$$

10. $R_0 = R_0^1 \ (R_f \| R_C) = R_0^1 \| \dfrac{R_f R_C}{R_f + R_C}$

*Circuit 5:*

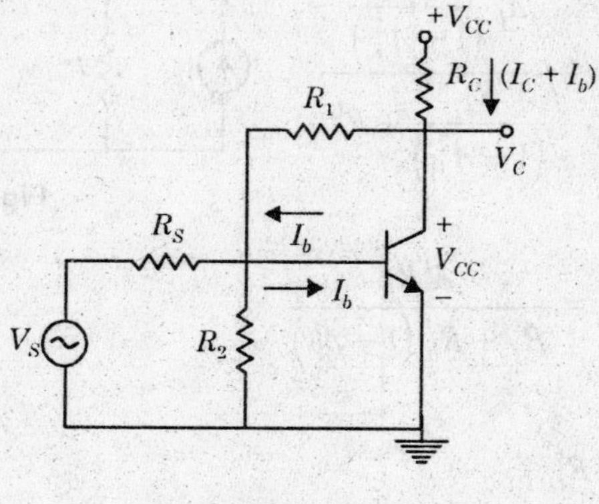


**Fig. 5.23**

Apply millers for $R_1$ and analysis is same as circuit 4.

*Circuit 6:*

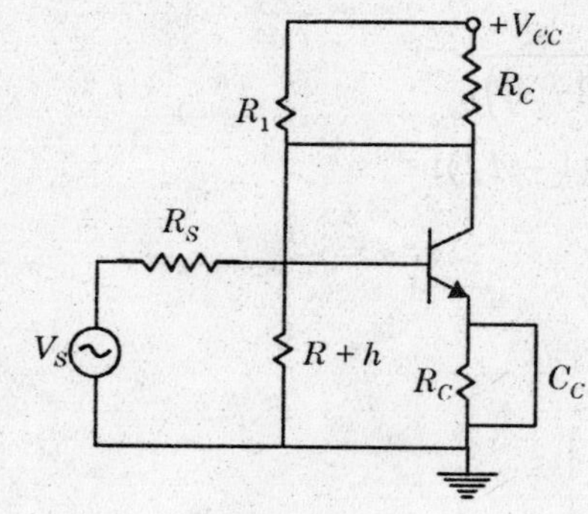


**Fig. 5.24 (a)**

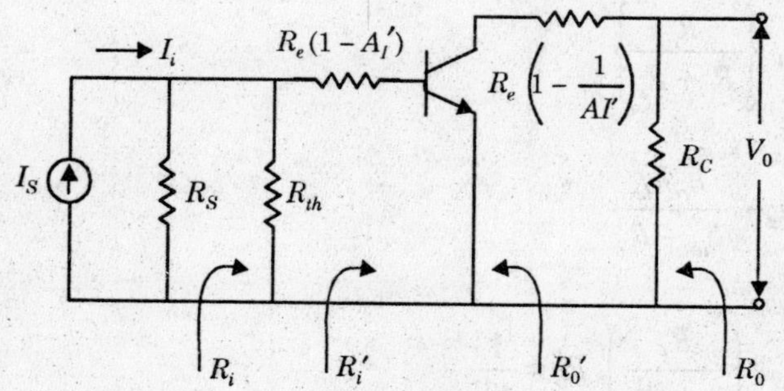


**Fig. 5.24 (b)** The ac equivalent midband using duality of millers

1. $A_I^1 = \dfrac{-h_{fe}}{1 + h_{oe}\{R_e + R_C\}}$
2. $R_i^1 = h_{ie} + h_{re} A_I^1 (R_C) + R_e (1 - A_I^1)$

3. $A_V^1 = \dfrac{A_I^1 (R_e + R_C)}{R_i^1}$

4. $A_I = A_I^1 \dfrac{I_b}{I_i}$

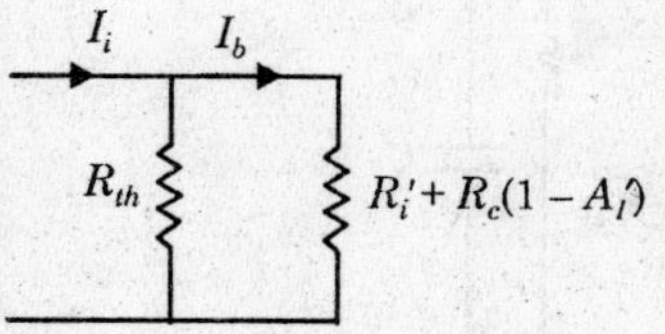


**Fig. 5.24 (c)**

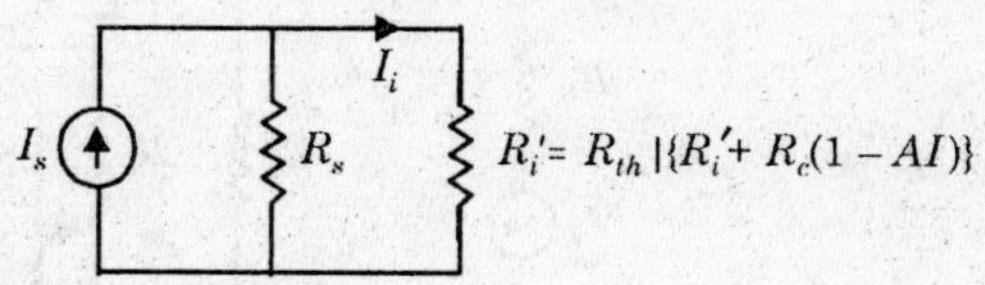


**Fig. 5.24 (d)**

$$A_I = A_I^1 \frac{R_{th}}{R_{th} + R_i^1 + R_e\left(1 - A_I^1\right)}$$

$$I_b = \frac{I_i R_{th}}{R_{th} + R_i^1 + R_e\left(1 - A_I^1\right)}$$

5. $R_i = R_{th} \| \{R_i^1 + R_e (1 - A_I^1)\}$

6. $A_V = \dfrac{A_I (R_C + R_e)}{R_i}$

7. $A_{IS} = A_I \left(\dfrac{I_i}{I_s}\right)$

From the Fig (d)

$$I_I = \frac{I_s R_s}{R_s + R_i}, A_{IS} = \frac{A_I R_s}{R_s + R_i}$$

8. $A_{VS} = A_V \left\{\dfrac{R_i}{R_i + R_s}\right\}$

9. $Y_0^1 = h_{oe} - \dfrac{h_{re} h_{fe}}{h_{ie} + R_S^1}$

Where $R_S^1 = R_S \| \{R_{th} + R_e (1 - A_I^1)\}$

$$R_0^1 = \frac{1}{Y_0^1}$$

10. $R_0 = R_0^1 \| (R_C + R_e)$

## 5.9 LOW FREQUENCY ANALYSIS

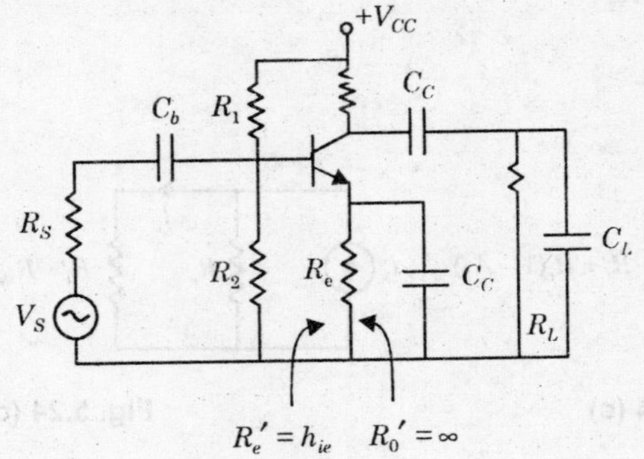


**Fig. 5.25 (a)** Common emitter amplifier

$$A_{VL} = \frac{A_{VM}}{1 - j\left(\frac{f_1}{f}\right)}$$

$f_1$ is calculated in this low frequency analysis, $R_i^1$ and $R_0^1$ are same both for mid frequency and low frequency because the model is same for mid frequency and low frequency analysis. Cutoff frequency due to each capacitor is calculated by short circuiting other capacitance or multiplying the effect of other capacitance. *The overall lower cut off has the highest value and the overall upper cutoff has the lowest value.*

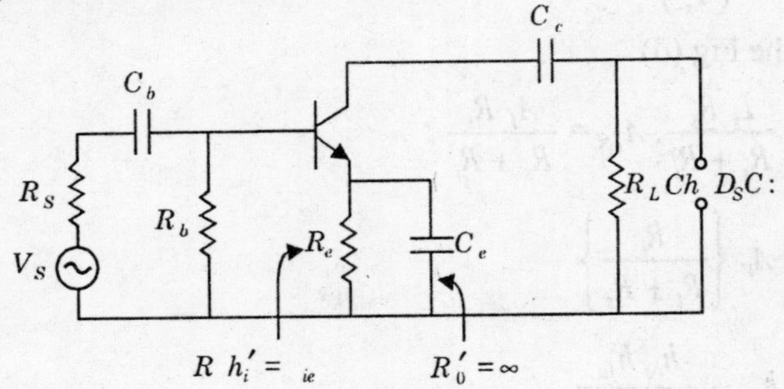


**Fig. 5.25 (b)** AC equivalent of low frequency analysis

$f_1$ is calculated due to different capacitance's that is due to $C_b$, $C_c$ and $C_e$.

The cutoff frequency can be obtained in two ways by Inspection at $C_b$, $C_c$, $C_e$, and by transfer function

### *By Inspection:*

$S_1$: Obtain the circuit connected to that capacitor

$S_2$: The voltage source is short circuited and current source is open circuited

$S_3$: Req across the capacitor terminals is calculated

$S_4$: Cut off frequency is obtained by $f_c = \dfrac{1}{2\pi R_{eq}\, c}$

***Calculation of $f_1$ from $C_b$:***

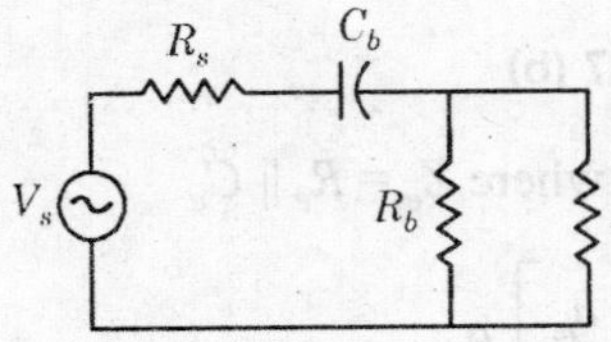


$S_1$: Fig. 5.26 (a)

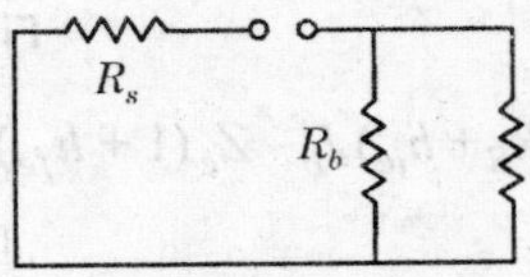


$S_2$: Fig. 5.26 (b)

$S_3$:
$$R_{eq} = R_s + \frac{R_b R_i^1}{R_b + R_i^1}$$

$S_4$:
$$f_1 C_c = \frac{1}{2\pi R_{eq} C_b} = \frac{1}{2\pi \left\{ R_s + \dfrac{R_b R_i^1}{R_b + R_i^1} \right\} C_b}$$

***Calculation of $f_1$ from $C_c$:***

$S_2$:

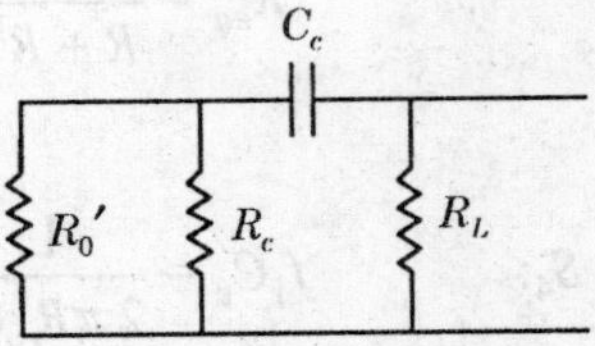


$S_1$: Fig. 5.27

$S_3$:
$$R_{eq} = \frac{R_0^1 R_c}{R_0^1 + R_c} + R_L$$

$S_4$:
$$f_1\, C_c = \frac{1}{2\pi R_{eq} C_c} = \frac{1}{2\pi \left\{ \dfrac{R_0^1 R_c}{R_0^1 + R_c} + R_L \right\} C_c}$$

***Calculation of $f_1$ from $C_e$:***

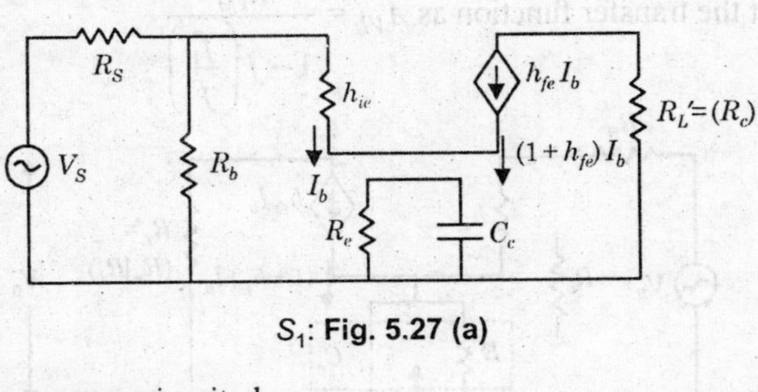


$S_1$: Fig. 5.27 (a)

$S_2$: $R_b \rightarrow \infty$ so open circuited.

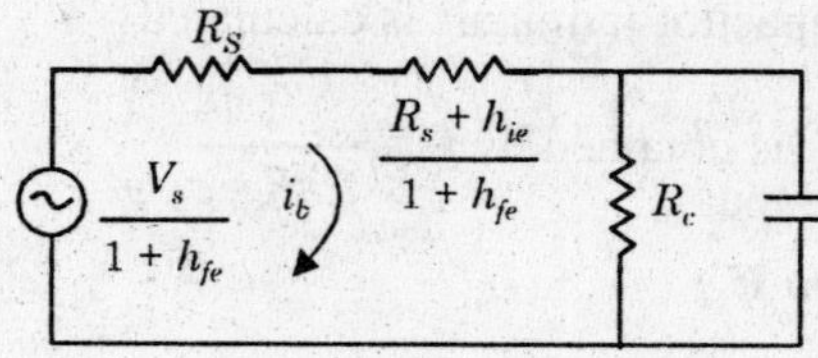


Fig. 5.27 (b)

$S_3$: $V_S - (R_S + h_{ie})\, I_b - Z_e(1 + h_{fe})_b = 0$ where $Z_e = R_e \parallel C_e$

$$R_{eq} = \frac{R_s + h_{ie}}{1 + h_{fe}} \parallel R_e = \frac{\left[\dfrac{R_s + h_{ie}}{1 + h_{fe}}\right] R_e}{\dfrac{R_s + h_{ie}}{1 + h_{fe}} R_e}$$

$$= \frac{(R_s + h_{ie})\, R_e}{R_s + h_{ie} + R_c\left(1 + h_{fe}\right)} = \frac{RR_e}{R + R^1}$$

Where $R_1 = (1 + h_{fe})\, R_e$, $R = R_s + h_{ie}$

$$\therefore \quad R_{eq} = \frac{RR_e}{R + R^1}$$

$S_4$:

$$f_1 C_e = \frac{1}{2\pi R_{eq} c_e} = \frac{1}{2\pi \left\{\dfrac{RR_e}{R + R^1}\right\} C_e} = \frac{1 + \dfrac{R^1}{R}}{2\pi R_c C_e}$$

***By transfer function:***

$S_1$: obtain the transfer function preferably $\frac{V_0}{V_1}$

$S_2$: Adjust the transfer function as $A_{VL} = \dfrac{A_{VM}}{1 - j\left(\dfrac{f_1}{f}\right)}$

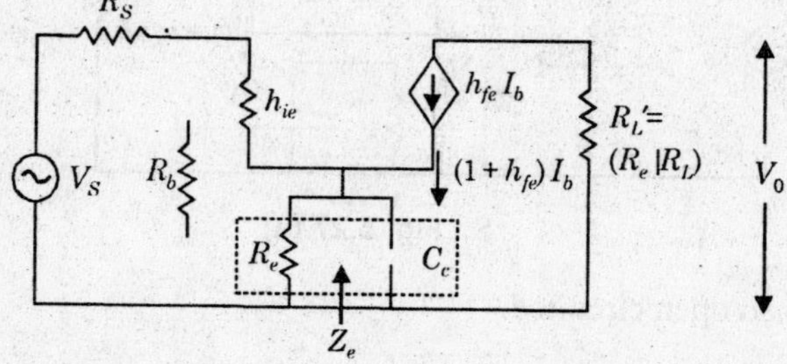


Fig. 5.28 (a)

$S_3$: Identify the cut-off frequency.

$S_1$: $$V_0 = \{-h_{fe} I_b\} R_L^1 \quad \text{...(1)}$$

Applying *KVL* to input

$$V_s - I_b(R_s + h_{ie}) - Z_c(1 + h_{fe}) I_b = 0$$

$$V_s = I_b \left\{ R + \frac{R_e(1 + h_{fe})}{1 + jwR_eC_c} \right\}$$

$$V_s = I_b \left( R + \frac{R^1}{1 + jwR_eC_c} \right)$$

$$V_s = I_b \left\{ \frac{R(1 + jwR_eC_c) + R^1}{1 + jwR_eC_c} \right\}$$

$$\therefore \quad I_b = \frac{V_s(1 + jwR_eC_c)}{R(1 + jwR_eC_c) + R^1}$$

$$I_b = \frac{V_s(1 + jwR_eC_c)}{R + R^1(1 + jwR_eC_c)} \quad \text{...(2)}$$

On substituting (2) in equation (1) we obtain

$$V_0 = \frac{-h_{fe} R_L^1 V_s(1 + jwR_eC_c)}{R + R^1(1 + jwRR_eC_c)}$$

$$\frac{V_0}{V_s} = \frac{-h_{fe}(1 + jwR_eC_c) R_L^1}{R + R^1 + jwRR_eC_c}$$

$S_2$: $$\frac{V_0}{V_s} = \frac{-h_{fe} R_L^1 \left(1 + i\frac{f}{f_2}\right)}{(R + R^1)\left\{1 + \frac{2\pi f RR_eC_e}{R + R^1}\right\}}$$

$$H(w) = \frac{H_o\left(1 + j\frac{f}{f_2}\right)}{1 + j\frac{f}{f_p}} \text{ where } f_p = \frac{R + R^1}{2\pi RR_eC_c} = \frac{1 + \frac{R^1}{R}}{2\pi RR_eC_c}$$

$$A_{VL} = \frac{A_{VM}}{1 - j\left(\frac{f_1}{f}\right)}$$

$$A_{vh} = \frac{A_{VM}}{1 - j\left(\frac{f}{f_2}\right)}$$

From the above discussion the cut-off frequencies resembles the high frequency response

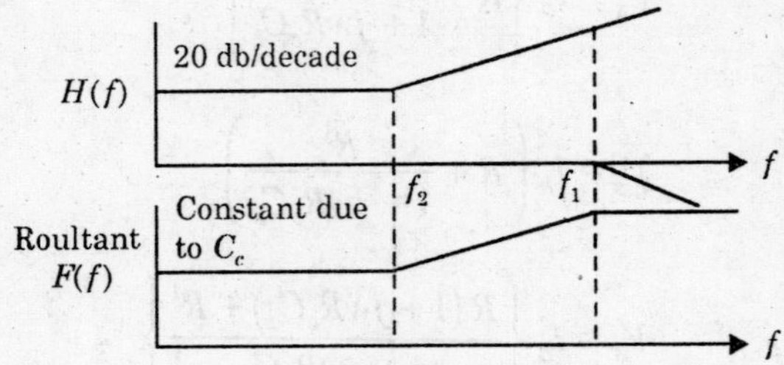


Fig. 5.28 (b)

From the above discussion $f_2$ is behaving like low frequency response and hence due to $C_e$, $f_2$ will dominate

$$f_2 = f_z \text{ when } f_z = \frac{1}{2\pi R_e C_c},$$

Where $R^1 = (\pm h_{fe})\, R_e$, $R = (R_s \,\|\, R_b) + h_{ie}$, $R^1 << R$ under these conditions which is normally not possible

***Conclusion:***

$$f_{1cb} = \frac{1}{2\pi\left\{R_s + R_b // R_f\right\} C_c}, f_{1ce} = \frac{1}{2\pi\left\{R_0^1 // R_c\right\} R_L\right\} C_c}$$

$$f_{1ce} = \frac{1}{2\pi R_e C_e} \text{ at } L_F \text{ the highest frequency dominates that is } f_{1cb}$$

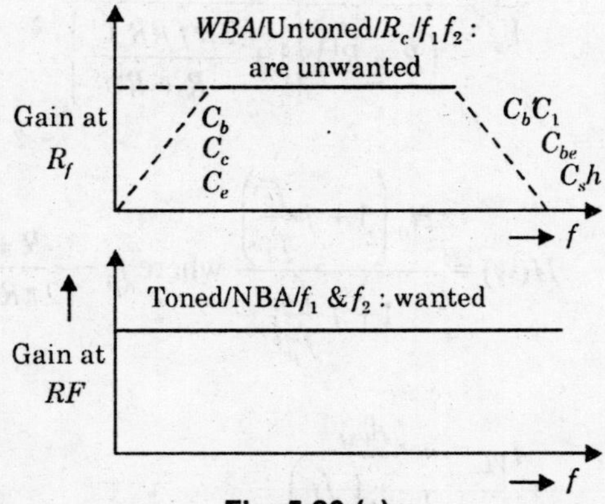


Fig. 5.28 (c)

## 5.10 COMPARISON OF DIFFERENT CONFIGURATION

The different configurations are nothing but *CE*, *CB* and *CC* configurations. *Comparison of amplifier characteristics calculated using the exact equations obtained from small signal analysis of a transistor amplifier using h-parameters.*

| *Quantity* | *CE* | *CB* | *CC* |
|---|---|---|---|
| $A_V$ | High | High | Low |
| $A_1$ | High | Low | High |
| $R_{in}$ | Medium | Low | High |
| $R_{out}$ | *Medium* | *High* | *High* |

### Comparison of (*h*-parameters) Different Configurations

**Table 5.1**

| *S.No.* | *Parameter* | *CE* | *CC* | *CB* |
|---|---|---|---|---|
| 1 | $h_{fe}$ | $h_{fe}$ | $h_{fc} = -(1+h_{fe})$ | $h_{fb} = \dfrac{h_{fe}}{1+h_{fe}} \approx 1$ |
| 2 | $h_{ie}$ | $h_{ie}$ | $h_{ic} \approx \text{h}_{\text{ie}}$ | $h_{ib} = \dfrac{h_{ie}}{1+h_{fe}}$ |
| 3 | $h_r$ | hre | $h_{rc} = 1$ | $h_{rb} = -\dfrac{h_{oe}\,h_{ie}}{1+h_{fe}} - h_{re} \approx 1$ |
| 4 | $h_o$ | $h_{oe}$ | $h_{oc} \approx h_{oe}$ | $h_{ob} = \dfrac{h_{oe}}{1+h_{fe}} \approx 1$ |

### *Comparison of different amplifiers*

**Table 5.2**

| *S.No.* | *Parameter* | *CE w/o Re* | *CE with Re* | *CC* | *CB* |
|---|---|---|---|---|---|
| 1 | *Condition* | $h_{oe} R_c < 0.1$ | $h_{oe}(R_c + R_e) < 0.1$ | $h_{oe} R_L \leq 0.1$ | $\left(\dfrac{h_{oe}}{1+h_{fe}}\right) R_L$ |
| 2 | $A_I^1$ | $-h_{fe}$ | $-h_{fe}$ | $1+h_{fe}$ | $\dfrac{h_{fe}}{1+h_{fe}} \approx 1$ unity current |
| 3 | $R_i^1$ | $h_{ie}$ | $h_{ie} + (1+h_{fe}) R_e$ | $hie + (1+h_{fe}) R_L$ | $\dfrac{h_{ie}}{1+h_{fe}}$ |

## 5.11 SOLVED PROBLEMS

**1. The transistor in the circuit shown in figure is so biased (*dc* biasing network is not shown) that the dc collector current $I_C = 1$ mA. Supply is $V_{CC} = 5$ V.**

**The network components have following values: $R_C = 2$ kΩ; $R_S = 1.4$ KΩ and $R_E = 100$ Ω. The transistor has specifications: β = 100 and base spreading resistance $r_{bb}' = 100$ Ω.**

**Assume $\frac{KT}{q} = 25$ mV.**

**Evaluate small signal voltage gain $A_{vs}$ at a frequency of 10 KHz, and input resistance $R_i$ for two cases (a) $C_E$, the bypass capacitor across $R_E$ is 25 μF.**

**(b) the bypass capacitor $C_E$ is removed leaving $R_E$ unbypassed.**

**Solution:**

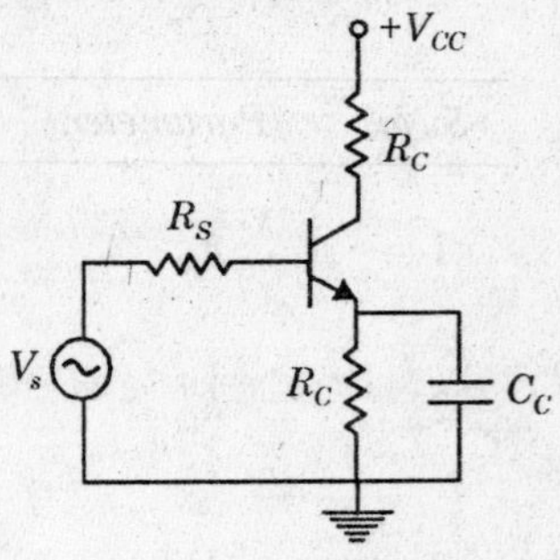


Fig. 5p1

Given $I_c = 1$ mA and $V_{CC} = 5$ V

$$g_m = \frac{I_c}{V_T} = \frac{1}{25} = 40 \times 10^{-3}$$

$$\beta = 100, \gamma\pi = 2.5 \text{ K}$$

With bypass capacitor across $R_E$,

$C_E = 2.5$ μF. Equivalent model is given as

At $f = 10$ KHz,

$$X_C = \frac{1}{2\pi fC} = \frac{1}{2\pi \times 10^4 \times 25 \times 10^{-6}} = \frac{100}{50\pi} = \frac{2}{\pi} = 0.6\ \Omega$$

So it is effectively equivalent to short

$$\therefore \quad V_0 = -\beta\, i_b\, R_C$$

$$i_b = \frac{V_s}{1.4 + 0.1 + 2.5} = \frac{V_s}{4}$$

$$V_0 = -(100)\left(\frac{V_s}{4}\right)(2\text{K}) = \text{small signal voltage gain}$$

$$A_I = \frac{V_0}{V_s} = -50$$

Input Resistance,

$$R_i = (0.1 + 2.5)\, k + (-j\,0.6)\,(1 + \beta)$$
$$= 2.6 \text{ K} + (-j\,0.6)\,(101) = 2.6 \text{ K}\Omega - j\,60\ \Omega$$

$$R_i = 2.6 \text{ K}\Omega - j\,60\ \Omega$$

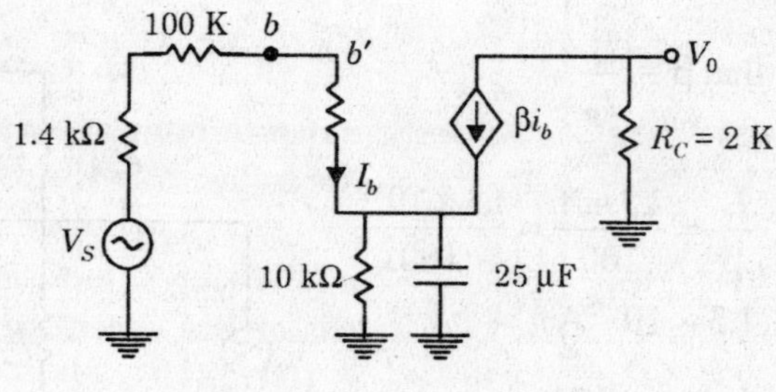


**Fig. 5p2**

(b) If $C_E$ is removed

$$i_b = \frac{V_s}{1.4 + 0.1 + 2.5 + \frac{101}{1000} \times 100} = \frac{V_s}{14K}$$

$$V_0 = -\beta R_C i_b = \frac{-100 \times V_s \times 2}{14} V_s$$

Small signal Voltage gain, $\frac{V_0}{V_s} = -200/14 = -14.2$

Input resistance, $Ri = (0.1 + 2.5) + \frac{100 \times 101}{1000} = 0.1 + 2.5 + 10.1 = 12.7 K\Omega$

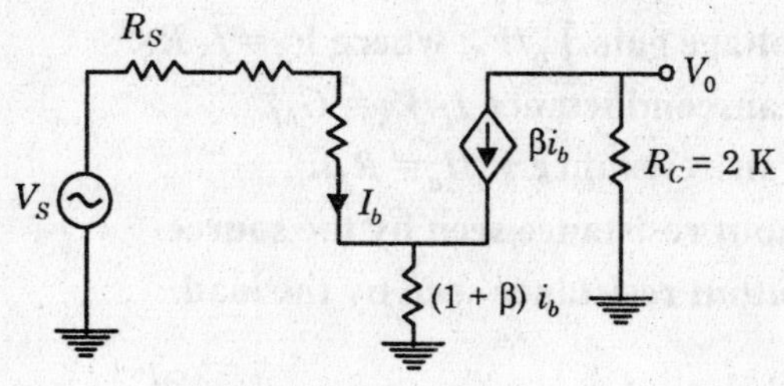


**Fig. 5p3**

**2. For the amplifier of fig., $I_C$ = 1.3 mA, $R_C$ = 2 KΩ, $R_E$ = 500Ω, $V_T$ = $KT/q$ = 26 mV, β = 100, $V_{CC}$ = 15 V, $V_S$ = 0.01 Sin (ωt) V and $C_b = C_e$ = 10 μF.**

**(a) What is the Small signal Voltage gain $A_V = V_o/V_S$?**

**(b) What is the approximate $A_V$ if $C_e$ is removed?**

**(c) What will $V_0$ be if $C_b$ is short circuited?**

**Solution:**

(a) Small signal Voltage gain, $A_V = \frac{\beta_{ac} R_{ac}}{r_{in}} \angle 180°$

We know that $\beta = \dfrac{I_C}{I_B}$

$$\therefore \quad I_B = \frac{I_C}{\beta} = \frac{1.3\,mA}{100} = \frac{1.3\times10^{-3}}{100}$$

$$= 1.3\times10^{-5}\text{A}$$

$$R_{in} = \frac{V_B}{I_B} = \frac{0.01}{1.3\times10^{-5}}$$

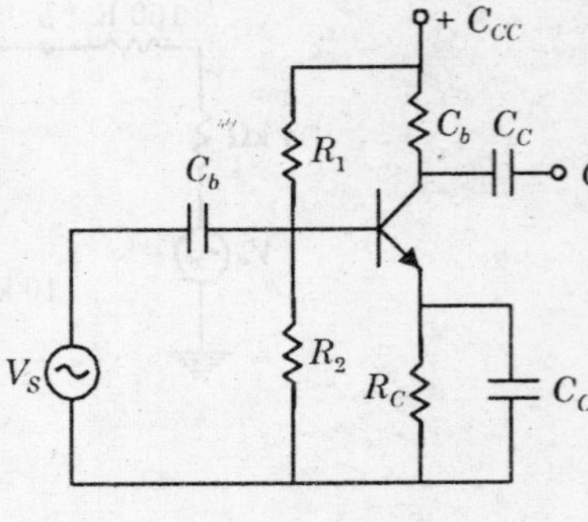

Fig. 5p4

$$\therefore \quad A_V = \frac{100\times 2\text{K}\Omega\times1.3\times10^{-5}}{0.01}\angle 180°$$

(b) We Know that $C_e$ is the bypass capacitor. If we remove $C_e$ then the signal will not be bypassed and feedback will occur, which will reduce the output signal and hence the voltage gain. Therefore, $A_V$ will be reduced in this case.

(c) If $C_b$ will be short circuited then DC signal will also be transmitted because blocking capacitor will not be present. Hence $A_C$ signal as well as DC signal will be present and hence $A_V$ will be increased in this case.

**3. For the circuit shown, with $R_e = 4$ K, $R_L = 4$ K, $R_b$, find**

**(a) The current gain $I_L/I_a = A_I$**

**(b) The voltage gain $V_o/V_S$, where $V_S = I_S R_S$.**

**(c) The transconductance $I_L/V_S = G_M$.**

**(d) The transresistance $V_a/I_a = R_M$.**

**(e) The input resistance seen by the source.**

**(f) The output resistance seen by the load.**

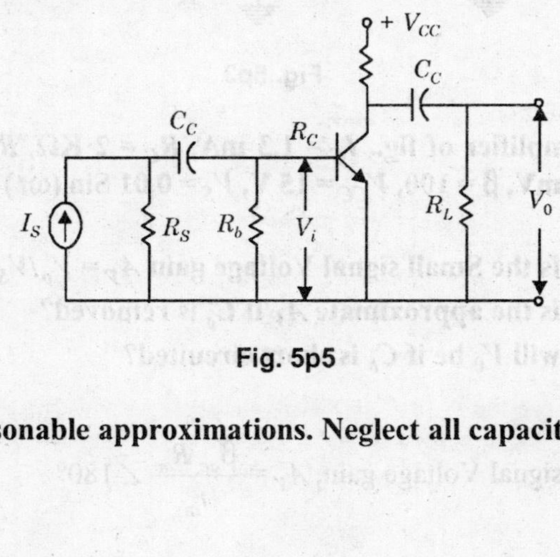

Fig. 5p5

**Make reasonable approximations. Neglect all capacitive effects.**

**Solution:**

(a) From the circuit we have:

$$\frac{I_L}{I_s} = \frac{I_i}{I_s} \cdot \frac{I_b}{I_i} \cdot \frac{I_L}{I_b}$$

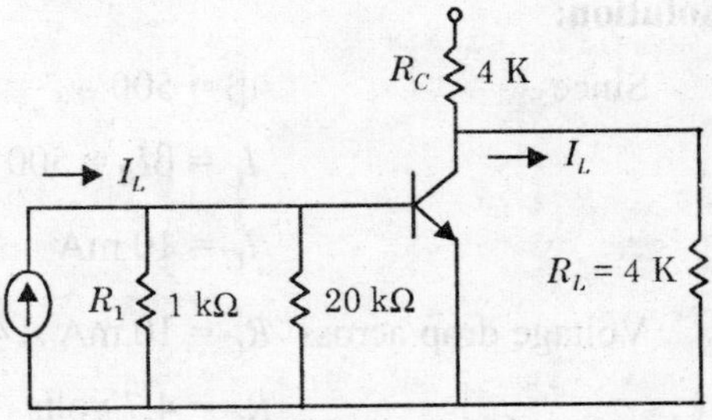



**Fig. 5p6**

where $\frac{I_i}{I_s} = \frac{R_s}{R_s + R_i}$;

$R_i \approx R_b \backslash\backslash h_{ie} = 20\text{ K}\backslash\backslash 1.1\text{ K}$

$$= \frac{(20\times10^3)(1.1\times10^3)}{20\times10^{-3}+1.1\times10^3} = 1.04\ K$$

Or $\frac{I_i}{I_s} = \frac{1}{1+1.04}\ \frac{I_b}{I_i} = \frac{R_b}{R_b + h_{ie}} = \frac{20K}{20K + 1.1K} = 0.95$

$$\frac{I_L}{I_b} = -h_{fe}\frac{R_c}{R_c + R_L} = -50\frac{4}{4+4}\ -50\ (4/8) = -25$$

$$\frac{I_L}{I_S} = \left(\frac{1}{2.04}\right)(0.95)(-25) = -11.65$$

(b) $\frac{V_0}{V_S} = \frac{I_L}{I_S}\frac{R_L}{R_S} = (-11.65)\frac{4K}{1K} = -46.6$

(c) $\frac{I_L}{V_s} = \frac{V_0}{R_L}\frac{1}{V_S} = \left(\frac{V_0}{V_S}\right)\left(\frac{1}{R_L}\right) = \frac{-46.6}{4\times10^3} = -11.65\ \text{mA/V}$

(d) $\frac{V_0}{I_S} = R_S\frac{V_0}{V_S} = 10^3\ (-46.6) = -46.6\ \text{K}$

(e) $R_i = R_b\backslash\backslash h_{ie} = 20\text{ K}\backslash\backslash\ 1.1\text{ K} = \frac{(20\times10^3)(1.1\times10^3)}{20\times10^{-3}+1.1\times10^3} = 1.04\text{ K}$

(f) $R_o = \frac{1}{h_{oe}}\ \backslash\backslash R_C = 40\text{ K}\backslash\backslash\ 4\text{ K} = \frac{(40\times10^3)(4\times10^3)}{40\times10^3+4\times10^3} = 3.64\text{ K}$

**4. The given figure is the circuit of amplifier with voltage feedback biasing. The base current is 20 μA and β is 500. Calculate $R_B$. Also calculate $R_B$ if there is an $R_E$ of 100 Ω.**

**Solution:**

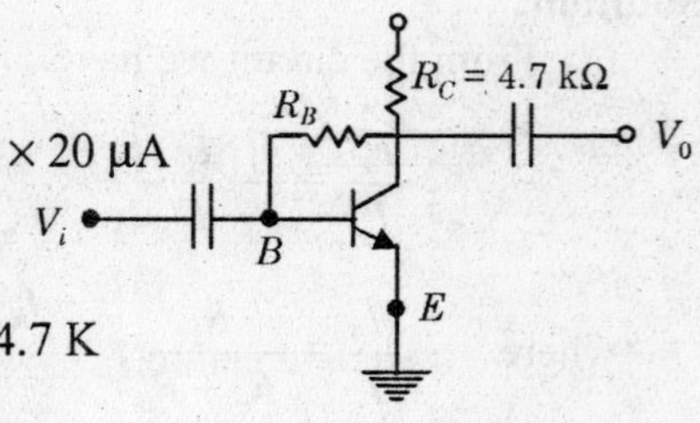

Fig. 5p7

Since $\beta = 500$

$I_C = \beta I_B = 500 \times 20\ \mu A$

$\therefore\quad I_C = 10\ mA$

Voltage drop across $R_C = 10\ mA \times 4.7\ K$

$R_C = 4.7$ volts

The collector voltage $= (10 - 4.7)\ V = 5.3\ V$

Voltage drop across $R_B$ = Voltage at collector – voltage at base

$= 5.3 - 0.6 = 4.7\ V = I_B R_B$

$$\therefore\quad R_B = \frac{4.7}{20\mu A} = 235\ K\Omega$$

Also since $I_C = \beta I_B = 10\ mA$

Voltage at emitter $= 100 \times 10\ mA = 0.1V$

Low end voltage of $R_B$ i.e. Voltage at point $B = (0.6 + 0.1)\ V = 0.7$ volts.

As voltage at collector = 5.3 V

So, $I_B R_B = 5.3 - 0.7 = 4.6\ V$

$$R_B = \frac{4.6}{20\mu A} = 230\ K\Omega$$

5. **An amplifier has an open loop (without feedback) midband voltage gain of magnitude ($A_V$) = 12480 with feedback of 8 *db*, Calculate magnitude of mid band voltage gain of the amplifier with feedback and value of β for α + θ = 0 for mid band frequencies.**

**Solution:**

Voltage gain without feedback = 20 log 12480 = 82 *db*

With feedback, voltage gain = 82 – 8 = 74 *db*

$$20 \log |A^1_v| = 5000 = \frac{A \angle \alpha}{1 - A\beta \angle \alpha + \theta} = \frac{12480}{1 + 12480\beta}$$

$$\beta = 1.2 \times 10^{-4}$$

6. **Calculate the three currents $I_C$, $I_B$ and $I_E$ for transistor circuit shown. β of this silicon transistor is 100.**

**Solution:**

Voltage at base,

$$V_B = \frac{10}{100K + 10K} \times 10K = 0.9\text{ V}$$

$I_e = V_E/R_E = 0.3/100 = 3$ mA

$I_C$ is approximately equal to $I_E$.

$$I_B = \frac{I_c}{\beta} = \frac{3mA}{100} = 30\ \mu\text{A}$$

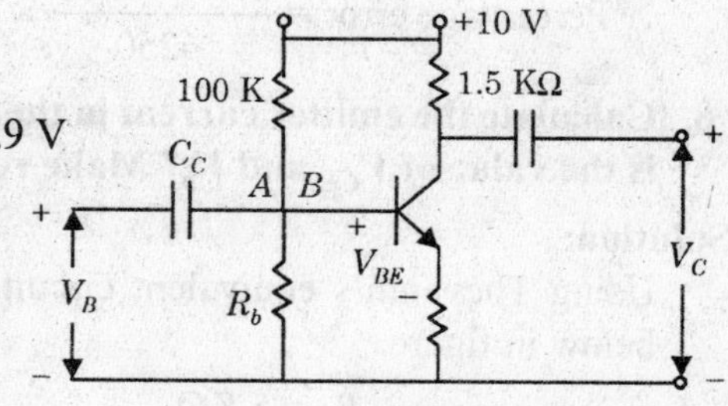


Fig. 5p8

**7. A transistor used in the amplifier circuit shown in figure has the following *h*-parameters: $h_{ie} = 800\ \Omega$, $h_{oe} = 50 \times 10^{-6}\ \Omega^{-1}$ and $h_{ie} = 55$. Calculate the voltage and power gains of the circuit. Find also the percentage error in the values obtained if hoe is neglected.**

**Solution:**

Voltage gain, $A_V = A_I \dfrac{Z_L}{Z_i}$

$$A_I = \frac{h_{fe}}{1 + h_{oe} Z_L} = \frac{-55}{1 + 50 \times 10^{-6} \times 2 \times 10^3} = \frac{-55}{1 + 0.1} = \frac{-55}{1.1}$$

$$Z_i = h_{ie} = 800\ \Omega,\ A_V = \frac{-55}{11} \times \frac{2 \times 10^3}{800} = -125$$

$$\text{Power gain } A_p = A_V, A_I = -125 \times \left(\frac{-55}{1.1}\right) = 6250$$

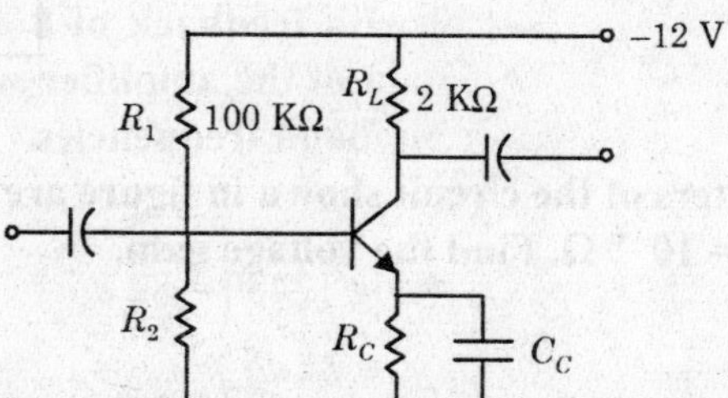


Fig. 5p9

Now if hoe is neglected, then $A_I = h_{fe} = -55$ and $A_V = -137.5$

$$\text{Percentage error} = \frac{137.5 - 12.5}{125} \times 100 = 10\%$$

$$A_P = (-55)(-137.5) = 7562.5$$

$$\therefore \text{ Percentage error} = \frac{7562 - 6250}{6250} \times 100 = 21\%$$

**8. Calculate the emitter current in the voltage bias circuit shown. What is the value of $V_{CE}$ and $V_o$? Make reasonable assumptions.**

**Solution:**

Using Thevenin's equivalent circuit, the circuit is redrawn as shown below in figure.

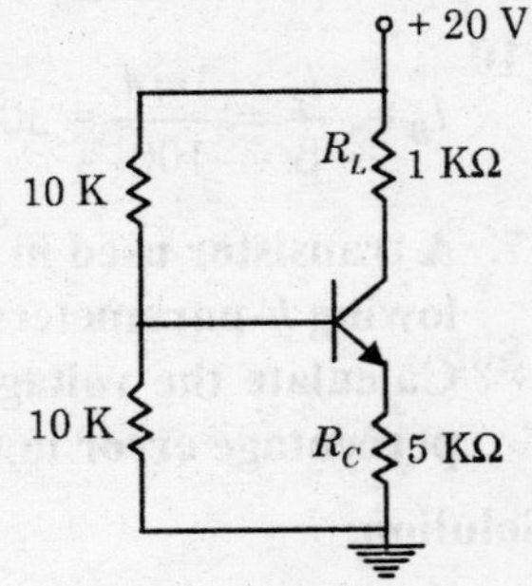


Fig. 5p10

$$R_b = 5\ \text{K}\Omega,$$

$$V_b = \frac{10 \times 20}{10 + 20} = 10\text{V}$$

Assuming $\beta = 50$ and $V_{BE} = 0.6$ V

$$I_C = \beta I_B = 50\ I_B$$

$$V_B = 10\ I_B + 5\ I_C + V_{BE}$$

$$= 10\ I_B + (5 \times 50)\ I_B + 0.6 = 260\ I_B + 0.6$$

Hence $I_B = \dfrac{V_b - 0.6}{260}\text{mA} = \dfrac{10 - 0.6}{260}\text{ mA} = 36.1\ \mu\text{A}$

$$I_C = 50 \times 36.1\ \mu\text{A} = 1.805\text{ mA}$$

$$V_C = 20 - 1.805\text{ mA } 1\text{ K}\Omega = 18.19\text{ V}$$

$$V_{CE} = 18.195 - 5\ (Ic + I_B) = 18.195 - 5\ (1.805 + 0.0361)$$

$VCE = 8.99$ V.

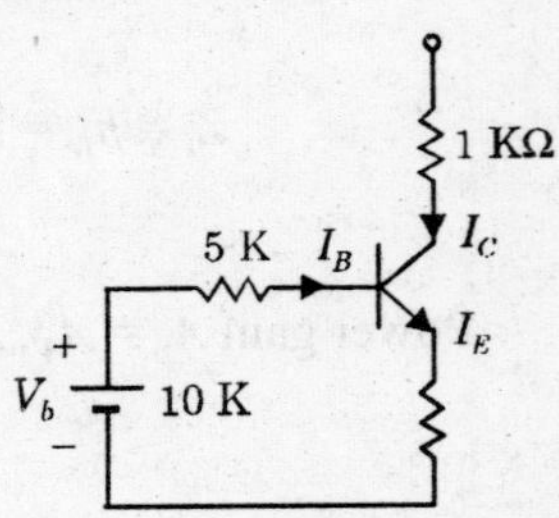


Fig. 5p11

**9. The $h$-parameters of the circuit shown in figure are $h_{ib} = 25\ \Omega$, $h_{fb} = 0.999$ and $h_{ob} = 10^{-6}\ \Omega$. Find the voltage gain.**

**Solution:**

$$\text{Current gain } A_I = \frac{h_{fb}}{1 + h_{ob}\ R_C} = \frac{0.999}{1 + 10^{-6} \times 10 \times 10^3} = \frac{0.999}{1 + 0.01} = 0.999$$

$$Z_i = h_{ib} + h_{ob}\ R_C\ A_I = 25 + 10^{-6} \times 0.999 \times 10^4 = 25$$

$$\text{Voltage gain, } A_V = \frac{A_i\ Z_L}{Z_i} = \frac{0.999 \times 10 \times 10^3}{25}$$

$$\therefore \quad A_V = 400$$

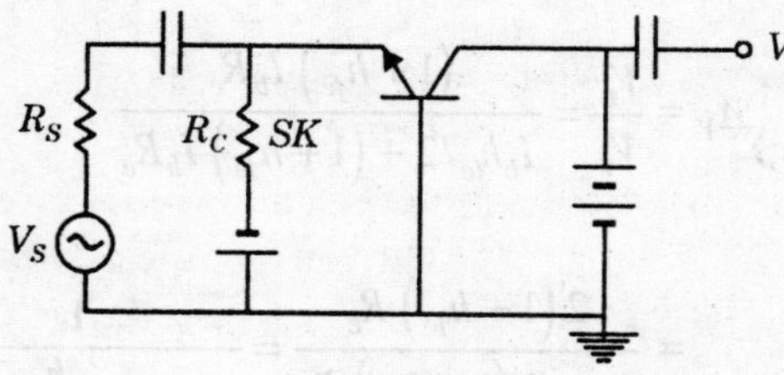


**Fig. 5p12**

**10. Derive the expressions for the voltage gain $A_V$ and the input resistance $R_{in}$ of the amplifier shown. Find the values of $A_V$ and $R_{in}$ for the following values of $h$-parameters for the transistors.**

$$h_{ie} = 100\ \Omega,\ h_{fe} = 100,\ h_{re} = h_{oe} = 0$$

**Solution:**

Equivalent circuit:

for $h_{ie1} = h_{ie2} = h_{ie}, h_{fe1} = h_{fe2} = h_{fe}$

and $h_{re1} = h_{re2} = 0, h_{oe1} = h_{oe2} - 0$

the equivalent circuit reduces to

Which is equivalent to

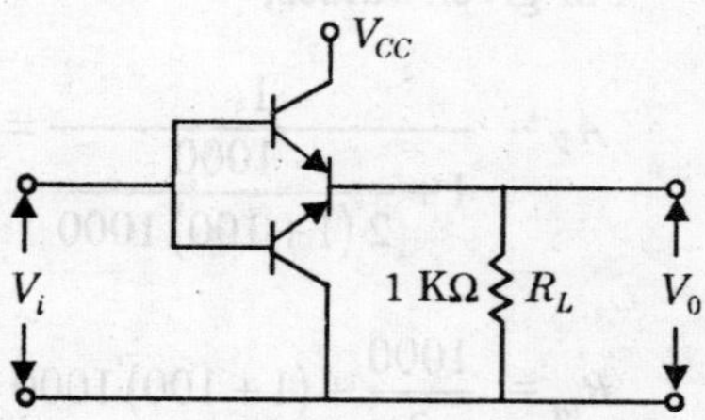


**Fig. 5p13**

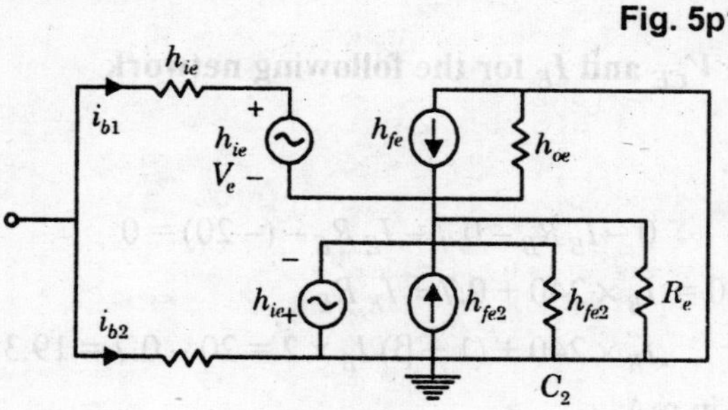


**Fig. 5p14**

$$h_{fe}(i_{b1} + i_b) = h_{fe} I_b$$

By applying *KCL* at *E*,

$$I = I_b + h_{fe} I_b = (1 + h_{fe}) I_b$$

$$V_0 = IR_e = (1 + h_{fe}) I_b R_e$$

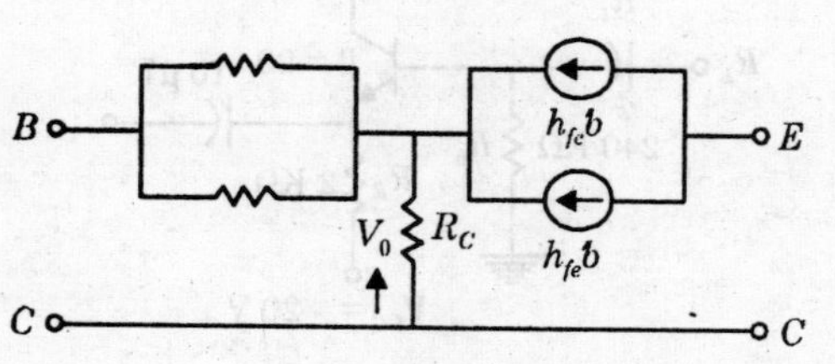


**Fig. 5p15**

Voltage gain $$A_V = \frac{V_0}{V_i} = \frac{(1+h_{fe})\, I_b R_e}{I_b h_{ie}/2 + (1+h_{fe})\, I_b R_e}$$

$$= \frac{2(1+h_{fe}) R_e}{h_{ie} + 2(1+h_{fe}) R_e} = \frac{1}{1 + \dfrac{h_{ie}}{2(1+h_{fe}) R_e}}$$

$$R_{in} = \frac{V_i}{I_b} = \frac{I_b h_{ie}/2 + (1+h_{fe})\, I_b R_e}{I_b} = \frac{h_{ie}}{2} + (1+h_{fe}) R_e$$

For given values,

$$A_V = \frac{1}{1 + \dfrac{1000}{2\,(1+100)\,1000}} = 0.995$$

$$R_{in} = \frac{1000}{2} + (1+100)\,1000 = 101.5\ \text{K}\Omega$$

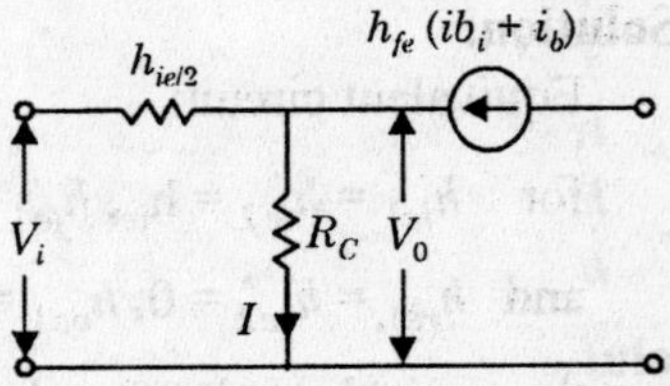

Fig. 5p16

**11. Determine $V_{CE}$ and $I_E$ for the following network**

**Solution:**

In the loop:

$$0 - I_B R_B - 0.7 - I_E R_E - (-20) = 0$$

Or $\quad 20 = I_B \times 240 + 0.7 + I_E R_E$

Or $\quad I_B \times 240 + (1+\beta)\, I_B \times 2 = 20 - 0.7 = 19.3$ V.

where $I_B$ is in mA

Hence $$I_B = \frac{19.3}{240 + (1+90)\times 2} = 0.046\, mA$$

As $\quad I_C = \beta\, I_B = 90 \times 0.046 \times 10^{-3}$

$I_C = 4.11$ mA

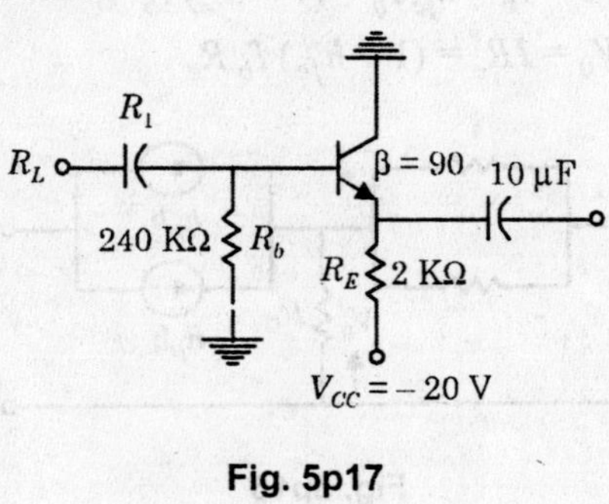

Fig. 5p17

In the collector loop

$$0 - V_{CE} - I_E R_E - (-20) = 0$$

$$V_{CE} = 20 - I_E R_E = 20 - (I_C + I_B) R_E = 20 - (4.11 + 0.046) \times 2$$

$$V_{CE} = 11.67 \text{ V.}$$

**12. For the network shown, determine the following parameters using the complete hybrid equivalent model and compare with the results obtained using the approximate model in which the effects of hre and $h_{oe}$ are neglected.**

**(i) $Z_i$ and $Z_i^1$**

**(ii) $A_V$**

**(iii) $A_i = I_o / I_i$ and $A_i = I_0 / I_i$**

**(iv) $Z_0$**

**The $h$-parameters of the transistors are $h_{fe} = 110$. $h_{ie} = 1.6$ KΩ, $h_{re} = 2 \times 10^{-4}$, $h_{oe} = 20$ μΩ**

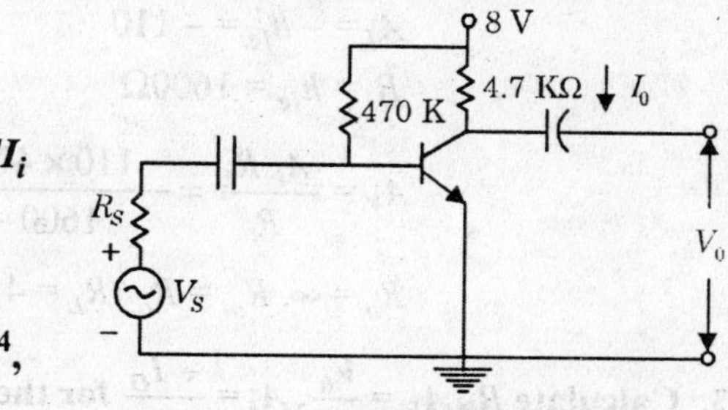


Fig. 5p18

**Solution:**

Hybrid-parameters equivalent circuit is shown in figure

Exact Analysis: We use the exact model shown in figure above neglected $R_B$ (470 KΩ) being much greater than $R_s$ in its parallel.

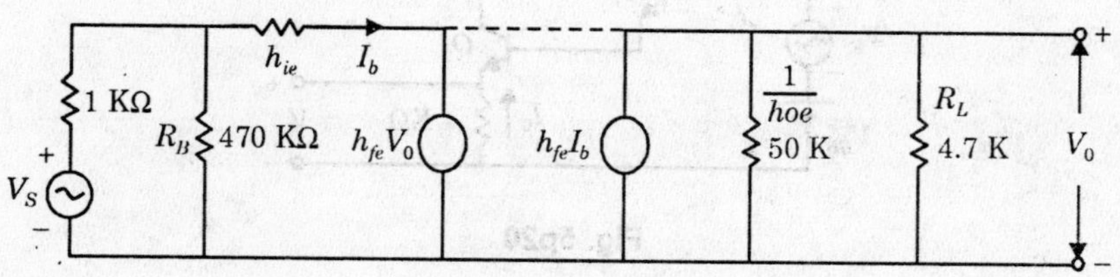


Fig. 5p19

Then current gain is:

$$A_I = \frac{-h_{fe}}{1 + h_{oe}.R_L} = \frac{-110}{\left(1 + 20 \times 10^{-6} \times 4.7 \times 10^3\right)} = -100.5$$

$$R_i = h_{ie} + h_{re} \cdot A_I R_L \cdot = 1600 + (2 \times 10^{-4})(-100.5) \times 4700$$

$$= 1505.5\Omega$$

$$A_V = \frac{A_i \ R_L}{R_i} = \frac{(-100.5) \times 4700}{1505.5} = -313.7$$

$$Y_o = h_{oe} - \frac{h_{fe} h_{re}}{h_{ie} + R_s} = 20 \times 10^{-6} - \frac{110 \times 2 \times 10^{-4}}{1600 + 1000}$$

$$= 20 \times 10^{-6} - = 8.5 \times 10^{-6} = 11.5\ 10^{-6}\,\text{S}$$

Hence $\quad Z_0 = \dfrac{1}{Y_0} = \dfrac{10^6}{11.5}\,\Omega = 87\ \text{K}\Omega$

Output terminal impedance $R_{ot} = Z_0 // R_L = \dfrac{87 \times 4.7}{87 + 4.7}\ \text{K}\Omega = 4.46\ \text{K}\Omega$

Analysis using approximate model (neglecting hre and $h_{oe}$).

$$A_I = -h_{fe} = -110$$

$$R_i = h_{ie} = 1600\Omega$$

$$A_V = \frac{A_I R_L}{R_i} = \frac{-110 \times 4700}{1600} = -32.3$$

$$R_o = \infty,\ R_{ot} = R_o // R_L = 4.7\ \text{K}\Omega$$

**13. Calculate $R_i$, $A_V = \dfrac{V_0}{V_s}$, $A_I = \dfrac{-I_O}{I_i}$ for the circuit shown. Use $h_{ie} = 1000$ $\Omega$, $h_{fe} = 99$, $h_{re} = h_{oe} = 0$**

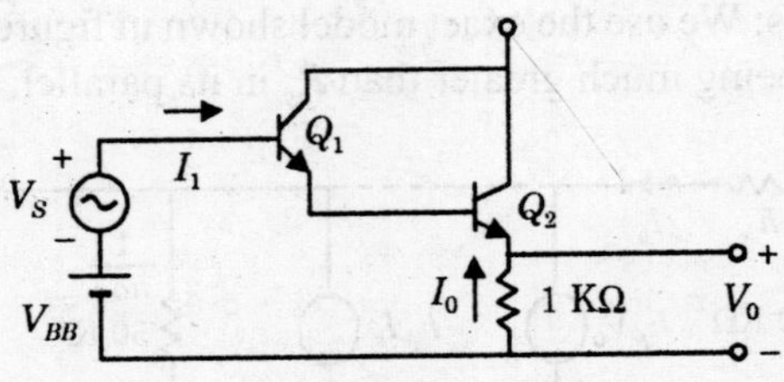


Fig. 5p20

**Solution:**

Small signal *h*-parameter equivalent circuit for the given circuit is considered as shown

$$R_i = h_{ie1} + (1 + h_{fe1})\,[h_{ie2} + 1 + h_{fe2})\,R_E]$$

$$= 1000 + (1 + 99)\,[99 + (1 + 99)\,1 \times 10^3] = 10.0109\ \mu\Omega$$

$$A_V = \frac{V_0}{V_S}$$

$$= \frac{V_S}{R_i} \times \frac{(1 + h_{fe1})(1 + h_{fe2})}{V_S}$$

$$= \frac{(1 + 99)(1 + 99)(1 \times 10^3)}{10.0109 \times 10^6} = 0.999$$

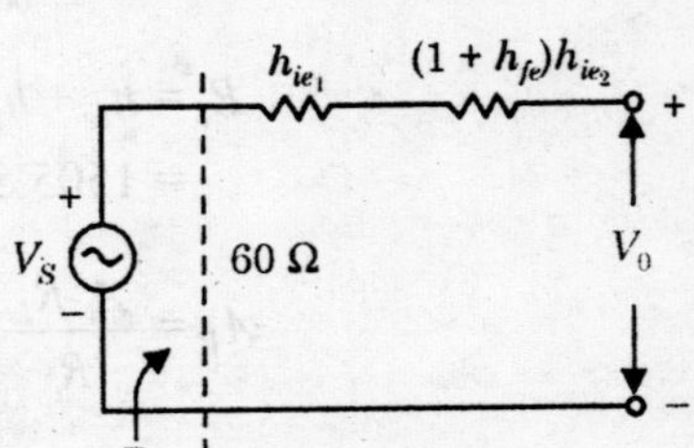


Fig. 5p21

$$A_I = \frac{-(1+h_{fe1})(1+h_{fe2})\,i_{b1}}{i_{b1}} = -(1+99)\,(1+99) = -10^4$$

**14. Figure 1 shows a common emitter amplifier using fixed bias. Draw its ac equivalent circuit. Calculate (a) input impedance (b) voltage gain and (c) current gain assume $h_{ie} = r_i = 2$ KΩ and $h_{ie} = \beta = 100$.**

**Solution:**

ac equivalent circuit of the figure 1 is given below voltage gain $A_V$

$$= \frac{\beta R_{ac}}{r_{in}} \angle 180°$$

There β is 100, $r_{in}$ is 2 kΩ and $R_{ac}$ is 5 kΩ

Substituting these values we get

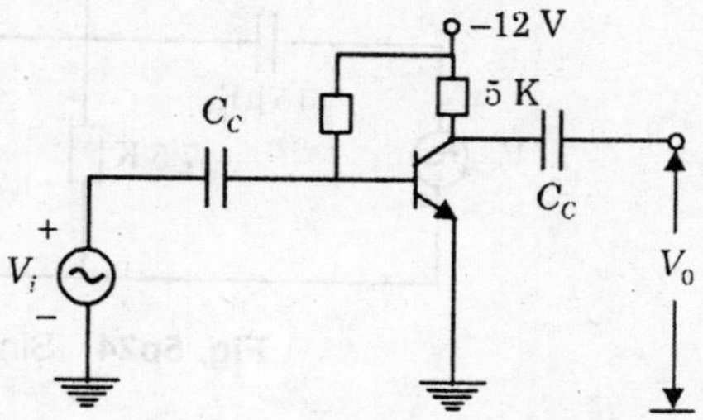


Fig. 5p22

$$A_V = \frac{100 \times 5 \times 10^3}{2 \times 10^3} \angle 180° = 250 \angle 180°$$

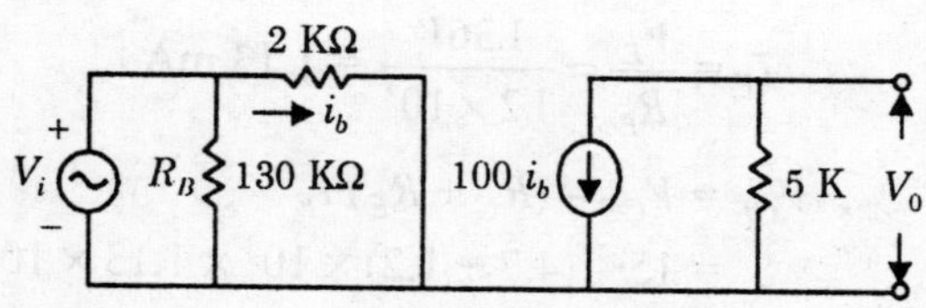


Fig. 5p23

Output current is equal to $i_b$ where as input current is $i_b$

∴ current gain is 100.

**15. In the single stage amplifier circuit shown in figure 2 an *NPN* transistor is used. The parameters of this transistors are $\beta_{ac} = 150$ and $r_{in} = 2$ KΩ Calculate (a) Voltage gain (b) input impedance and (c) *Q* point (neglect $V_{BE}$)**

**Solution:**

In the amplifier circuit, the ac load resistance is $R_{ac} = 4.7$ KΩ//12 KΩ = 3.38 KΩ

(a) The voltage gain $A_V = \dfrac{\beta_{ac}\, R_{ac}}{r_{in}} \angle 180°$

$$\beta_{ac} = 150,\ r_{in} = 2\text{ k}\Omega \text{ and } R_{ac} = 3.38\text{ K}\Omega$$

$$A_V = \frac{150 \times 3.38 \times 10^3}{2 \times 10^3} = 253.5$$

(b) The resistors 7.5 KΩ and 75 KΩ are both connected between the base and ground. Hence the input impedance of amplifier

$$Z_{in} = 75\ \text{K}\Omega \parallel 7.5\ \text{K}\Omega \parallel r_{in} = 1.5\ \text{k}\Omega$$

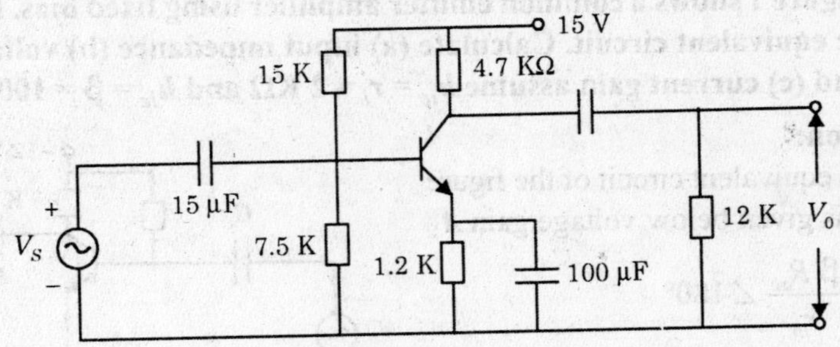


**Fig. 5p24** Single stage amplifier.

(c) $V_B = V_{CC} \dfrac{R_2}{R_1 R_2} = 15 \times \dfrac{7.5\times10^3}{75\times10^3 + 7.5\times10^3} = \dfrac{15}{11} = 1.36\ \text{V}$

Since $\quad V_{BE} = 0,\ V_E = V_B = 1.36\ \text{V}$

$$I_E = \frac{V_E}{R_E} = \frac{1.36V}{1.2\times10^3} = 1.13\ \text{mA}$$

$$V_{CE} = V_{CC} - (R_C + R_E)\, I_E$$
$$= 15 - (4.7 + 1.2)\times 10^3 \times 1.13 \times 10^{-3} = 8.33\ \text{V}$$

**16. A voltage source of internal resistance $R_s = 900\ \Omega$ drive a *CC* amplifier using load resistance $R_L = 2000\ \Omega$. The *CE* h-parameters are hie = 1200 Ω $h_{re} = 2\times10^{-4}$, $h_{fe} = 60$ and $h_{oe} = 25\ \mu\text{A/V}$. Compute the current gain $A_I$, the input impedance $R_i$, voltage gain $A_V$ and output resistance $R_o$ using approximate analysis.**

**Solution:**

Current gain $\quad A_I = \dfrac{-h_{fe}}{1 + h_{oc} R_L}$

$$A_I = \left[\frac{-(61)}{1 + 25\times10^6\left(2\times10^3\right)}\right] = 58.095$$

Input impedance, $R_i = h_{ic} + h_{rc} A_I R_L = 1200 + (1)(58.095)(2000)$

$$= 117.39\ \text{K}\Omega$$

Voltage gain, $\quad A_V = \dfrac{A_I\ R_L}{R_i} = \dfrac{(58.095)\left(2\times10^3\right)}{117.39\times10^3}$

$$Y_0 = \frac{1}{R_0} = 0.9897$$

$$Y_0 = h_{oc} - \frac{h_{fc}\, h_{rc}}{h_{ic} + R_s} = 25 \times 10^{-6} - \frac{(-61)(1)}{(1200) + 900}$$

$$R_0 = 34.396\ \Omega$$

**17. Determine the input impedance, output impedance voltage gain and current gain for the *CE* amplifier of figure. The *h*-parameters of the transistor of $h_{fe} = 60$, $h_{ie} = 500\ \Omega$ at $I_C = 3$ mA**

**Solution:**

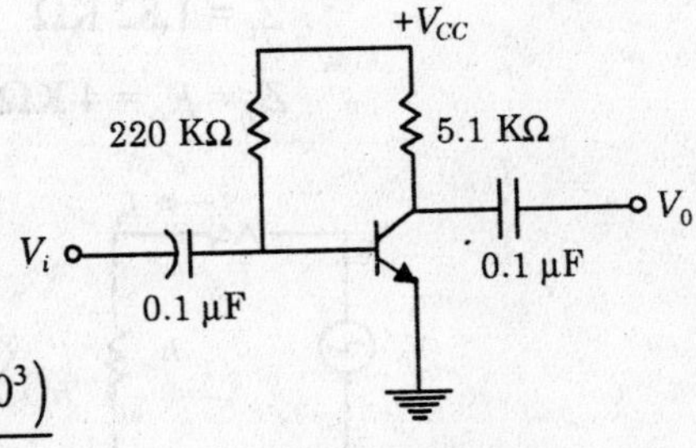

Fig. 5p25

$$R_B = 220\ \text{K}\Omega >> h_{ie} = 500\ \Omega$$

From *h*-parameter model

$$Z_i = h_{ie} = 500\ \Omega$$

$$Z_0 = R_c = 5.1\ \text{K}\Omega$$

$$A_V = \frac{-h_{fe} R_C}{h_{ie}} = \frac{-60\left(5.1 \times 10^3\right)}{500}$$

$$A_V = -612$$

$$A_I = -h_{fe} = -60$$

From $r_e$ model

$$Z_i = \beta r_e \text{ where } r_e = \frac{26\, mV}{I_e}$$

From the circuit $I_b = \dfrac{V_{CC} - V_{BE}}{R_B} = \dfrac{12 - 0.6}{220 \times 10^3} = 51.8\ \mu\text{A}$

$$I_e \approx I_C = \beta I_b = 60 \times 51.8 \times 10^{-6} = 3.108 \text{ mA}$$

$$r_e = \frac{26 \times 10^{-3}}{3.108 \times 10^{-3}} = 8.37\ \Omega$$

$$Z_i = \beta r_e = 60 \times 8.37 = 502.2\ \Omega$$

$$Z_0 = R_C = 5.1\ \text{K}\Omega$$

$$A_V = \frac{-R_c}{r_e} = \frac{-\left(5.1 \times 10^3\right)}{8.37} = -609$$

$$A_I = -\beta = -60$$

*Note:* Small difference in the calculation of amplifier parameters between the *h*-parameters and re models might arise due to the approximations made in the circuits design.

**18. Determine the input impedance, output impedance, voltage gain and current gain of the *CE* amplifier using *h*-parameters and $r_e$ model equivalents for the transistor with $h_{fe}$ = 3.2 kΩ and $h_{fe}$ = 100 at the operating conditions**

**Solution:**

*h*-parameter analysis

$$Z_L = R_B \,\|\, h_{ie}$$

$$R_B = R_1 \,\|\, R_2 = 40\ \text{K}\Omega \,\|\, 4.7\ \text{K}\Omega = 4.2\ \text{K}\Omega$$

$$Z_i = 4.2\ \text{K}\Omega \,\|\, 3.2\ \text{K}\Omega$$

$$Z_i = 1.82\ \text{K}\Omega$$

$$Z_0 = R_c = 4\ \text{K}\Omega$$

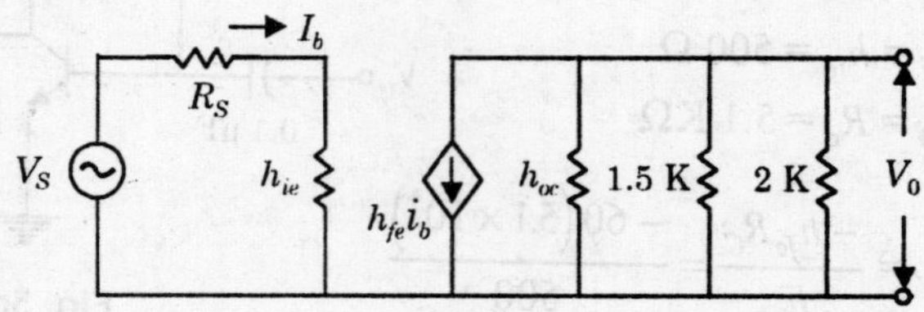


Fig. 5p26

$$A_V = \frac{-h_{fe}R_C}{R_B + h_{ie}} = \frac{-100 \times 4 \times 10^3}{3.2 \times 10^3}$$

$$A_V = -125$$

$$A_I = \frac{-h_{fe}R_B}{R_B + h_{ie}} = \frac{-100 \times 4.2 \times 10^3}{(4.2 + 3.2) \times 10^3}$$

$$A_I = -56.76$$

$r_e$ model

To find $I_B$

$$V_B = \frac{R_2 V_{ce}}{R_1 + R_2}$$

$$h_{ie} = \frac{0.02}{0.024} \times 10^3 = 833\ \Omega$$

The *h*-parameter circuit equivalent is

**Case (a)** Load switch open

$$h_{oe} = 0,\ R_s = 0$$

$$V_i = 1\text{V (assumed)}$$

$$I_b = \frac{V_i}{h_{ie}} = \frac{1}{0.833} = 1.2 \text{ mA}$$

$$h_{fe} I_b = 120 \times 1.2 = 144 \text{ mA}$$

$$A_{vo} = -144 \times 1.5 = -216$$

**Case (b)** Load switch on

$$h_{oe} = 50 \,\mu S \,; R_s = 2 \text{ k}\Omega$$

$$\frac{1}{h_{oe}} = \frac{1}{50} \times 1000 = 20 \text{ K}\Omega$$

Effective resistance at load terminal

$$20 \parallel 1.5 \parallel 2 = 0.822 \text{ k}\Omega$$

$$I_B = \frac{V_i}{R_s + h_{ie}} = \frac{1}{2 + 0.833} = 0.353 \text{ mA}$$

$$= \frac{4.7 \times 16 \times 10^3}{44.7 \times 10^3} = 1.682 \text{ V}$$

Using Thevenin equivalent for input part

$$I_B = \frac{V_B - V_{BE}}{R_B + (1+\beta)\, R_E}$$

$$= \frac{1.682 - 0.6}{4.2 \times 10^3 + (1+100)(1.2 \times 10^{-3})} = \frac{1.082}{125.4 \times 10^3}$$

$$= 8.628 \,\mu\text{A}$$

$$I_C = I_E = 0.86 \text{ mA}$$

$$r_e = \frac{26mV}{I_E} = \frac{26 \times 10^{-3}}{0.86 \times 10^{-3}} = 30.23 \,\Omega$$

$$Z_i = R_B \parallel \beta r_e = (4.2 \times 10^3) \parallel (100 \times 30.23)$$

$$= 4200 \parallel 3023 = 1.76 \text{ K}\Omega$$

$$Z_o = RC = 4 \text{ K}\Omega$$

$$A_V = \frac{-R_C}{r_e} = \frac{-4000}{30.23}$$

$$A_V = -132.3$$

$$A_I = \frac{-\beta R_B}{R_B + \beta r_e} = \frac{-100(4.2 \times 10^3)}{4.2 \times 10^3 + (100 \times 30.23)} = -58.147$$

**19. The transistor of $C_E$ amplifier circuit of figure 1 has the following parameters $h_{fe} = 120$, $h_{ie} = 0.02/I_B$ $h_{re} = h_{oe} = 0$**
**(a) Find $h_{ie}$ and use the $h$-parameters circuit model to find the gain $A_{vo} = V_0/V_i$; $V_0$ = signal component of the voltage at collector (b) Find $A_{vL}$ when the output switch as on. If $h_{oe}$ = 50 μs and the source has an internal resistance of 2 kΩ, Recalculate $A_{vL}$**

**Solution:**

Finding Thevenin's equivalent of the potential divider in the circuit

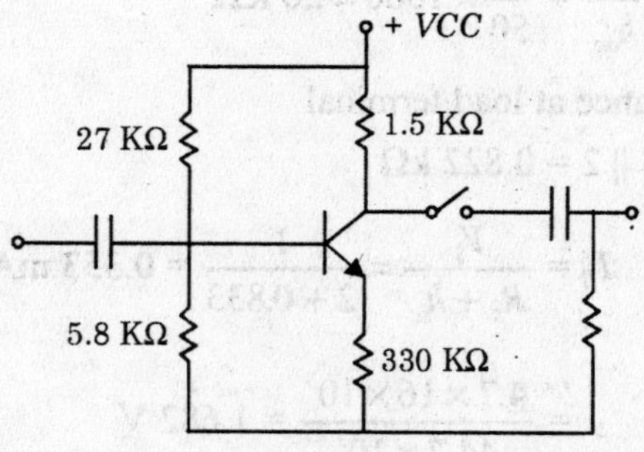


**Fig. 5p27**

$$V_{BB} = 10 \times \left(\frac{5.8}{2.7 + 5.8}\right) = 1.77$$

$$R_B = 27 \parallel 5.8 = 4.77 \text{ K}\Omega$$

$$V_{BB} - V_{BE} = R_B I_B + (1 + \beta) I_B R_E$$

$$1.77 - 0.7 = 4.77 \times 10^3 \times I_B + (121) I_B (0.33)$$

$$I_B = 0.024 \text{ mA.}$$

$$h_{fe} I_b = 120 \times 0.353 = 42.36$$

$$A_{VL} = - h_{fe} I_b \times R_{eff} = -34.8$$

**20. A transistor amplifier in $CE$ configuration operating at high freque ncies has the following parameters. $f_T$ = 6 MHz $h_{fe}$ = 50, $R_s$ = 800 Ω, gm = 0.04 S, $r_{bb}$ = 100 Ω, $CC$ = 10 pF. The load connected is of 1000 Ω. Find the voltage gain, current gain, voltage gain Upper cutoff frequency voltage gain bandwidth product & current gain bandwidth product.**

**Solution:**

$$r_{b1_e} = \frac{h_{fe}}{gm} = \frac{50}{0.04} = 1250\ \Omega$$

$$C_e = \frac{g_m}{2\pi \times f_T} = \frac{0.04}{2\pi \times 6 \times 10^6}$$

$$C_e = 1060 \text{ pF}$$

$$C = C_e + C_c (1 + g_m R_L)$$

$$= 1060 + 10 (1 + 0.04 \times 1000)$$

$$C = 1460 \text{ pF}$$

$$h_{ie} = r_{bb} + r_{b'e} = 100 + 1250 = 1350\ \Omega$$

$$R = (R_S + r_{bb}) \parallel r_{b'e} = (500 + 100) \parallel 1250$$

$$= \frac{600 \times 1250}{600 + 1250} = 405.4\Omega$$

$$f_2 = \frac{1}{2\pi\ RC} = \frac{1}{2\pi \times 405.4 \times 1460 \times 10^{-12}}$$

$$f_2 = 0.27 \text{ MHz}$$

Which gives the voltage gain upper cutoff frequency.

$$A_{IS} = \frac{-h_{fe}\ R_S}{R_S + h_{ie}}$$

$$= \frac{-50 \times 1000}{500 + 1350} = -270$$

Voltage gain bandwidth product is

$$|A_{VS} f_2| = (270.28)\ (0.27 \times 10^6) = 72.98 \text{ MHz}$$

Current gain bandwidth product is

$$|A_{IS} f_2| = (135.14)\ (0.27 \times 10^6) = 36.49 \text{ MHz}$$

**21. A *CE* amplifier is drawn by a voltage source of internal resistance $r_s = 800\Omega$ and the load impedance is a resistance $R_L = 1000\ \Omega$. The *h*-parameter are $h_{ie} = 1\ \text{k}\Omega$ $h_{re} = 2 \times 10^{-4}$ $h_{fe} = 50$ and $h_{oe} = 25\ \mu\text{A/V}$. Compute the current gain *A*, input resistance $R_i$, voltage gain $A_v$, and output resistance $R_o$.**

**Solution:**

Current gain, $$A_I = \frac{-h_{fe}}{1 + h_{oe} R_L} = \frac{-50}{1 + 25 \times 10^{-6} \times 10^3}$$

$$A_I = -48.78$$

Input resistance, $$R_I = h_{ie} - \frac{h_{fe}\ h_{re}}{h_{oe} + \frac{1}{R_L}} = 1000 - \frac{50 \times 2 \times 10^{-4}}{25 \times 10^{-6} + \frac{1}{1000}}$$

$$R_i = 990.24\ \Omega$$

Voltage gain, $A_V = \dfrac{A_I R_L}{R_i} (-48.78) \times \dfrac{100}{990.24} = -49.26$

Output resistance $R_0$, $Y_0 = h_{oe} - \dfrac{h_{fe}\, h_{re}}{h_{ie} + R_S} = 25 \times 10^{-6} - \dfrac{50 \times 2 \times 10^{-4}}{1000 + 800}$

$$= 1.94 \times 10^{-5}\ \text{mho}$$

$$R_0 = \frac{1}{Y_0} = 51.42\ \text{K}\Omega$$

Approximate analysis

$$A_I = -h_{fe} = -50$$

$$R_i = h_{ie} = 1\ \text{K}\Omega$$

$$A_V = \frac{-h_{fe} R_L}{h_{ie}} = \frac{-50 \times 1000}{1000} = -50$$

$$R_0 = \alpha$$

**22. Determine the overall voltage gain of the cascade amplifier shown in figure with $R_{B1} = 7.5\ \text{K}\Omega$ $R_{B2} = 6.8\ \text{K}\Omega$ $R_{B3} = 3.3\ \text{K}\Omega$ $R_E = 1.3\ \text{K}\Omega$ and $R_C = 2.2\ \text{K}\Omega$ for the two transistor $\beta_1 = \beta_2 = 120$ and supply voltage $V_{CC} = 18$ V.**

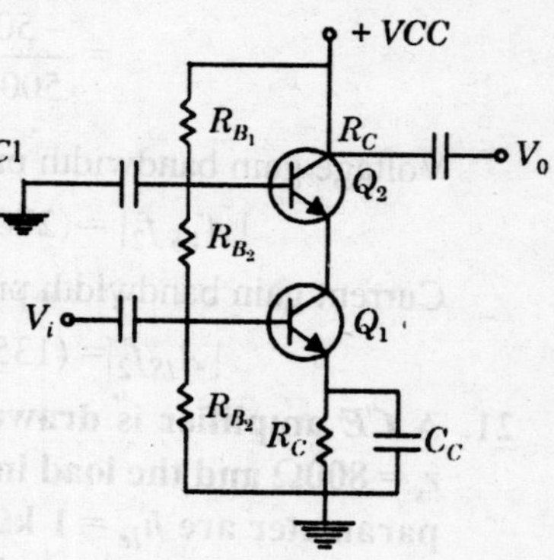


Fig. 5p28

**Solution:**

$$I_{E2} = I_{E1} \text{ and hence } I_{c2} \approx I_{C1}$$

$$\beta_1 = \beta_2$$

$$I_{B1} = \frac{I_{C1}}{\beta_1};\ \frac{I_{C2}}{\beta_2} = I_{B2}$$

By voltage division

$$V_{B1} = \frac{R_{B3}\, V_{CC}}{R_{B3} + R_{B2} + R_{B1}}$$

$$= \frac{3.3 \times 18 \times 10^3}{(3.3 + 6.8 + 7.5) \times 10^3} = 3.375\ \text{V}$$

$$I_{E1} = \frac{V_{E1}}{R_E} = \frac{V_{B1} - V_{BE1}}{R_E} = \frac{3.375 - 0.7}{1.3\text{K}\Omega} = 2.06\text{mA}$$

$$R_{e1} = \frac{26mV}{I_{E1}} = \frac{26}{2.06} = 12.62\ \Omega$$

$$R_{e2} = 12.62\ \Omega \text{ (since } I_{E2} = I_{E2})$$

Voltage gain of first stage

$$A_{V1} = -\frac{R_{e1}}{R_{c1}} = -1$$

Voltage gain of second stage $A_{v2} = -\frac{R_c}{R_{e2}} = \frac{2.2\times10^3}{12.62} = 174$

**23. The BJT switch of Fig. shown has the following device and circuit parameters: $V_{CC} = 5\text{V}$, $R_L = 250\ \Omega$, $V_1 = +5\text{ V}$, $R_B = 25\text{ K}$, $V_{CS} = 0.2\text{ V}$, $\beta_F = 200$, $V_{BS} = 0.8\text{ V}$. Find the forced values of $\beta_F$ for which the BJT will be in saturation state. Assume $V_{CON} = 0.3\text{ V}$.**

**Solution:**

From the circuit fig., the current for a saturated BJT will be:

$$I_{CON} = \frac{V_{CC}-V_{CON}}{R_L} = \frac{5-0.3}{250} = 18.8\times10^{-3}A$$

$$I_{BON} = \frac{I_{CON}}{\beta_F} = \frac{18.8\times10^{-3}}{200} = 94\times10^{-6}A$$

$$I_{BS} = \frac{V_1 - V_{BS}}{R_B} = \frac{5-0.8}{25K} = 168\times10^{-6}A$$

Thus, $I_{BS} \geq I_{BON}$ and hence BJT is saturated,

Now $$I_{CS} = \frac{V_{CC}-V_{CS}}{R_L} = \frac{5-0.3}{250} = 192\text{ mA}$$

$$\therefore \quad \beta_{\text{forced}} = \frac{I_{CS}}{I_{BS}} = \frac{19.2\ mA}{168\mu\ A} = 114 < \beta_F$$

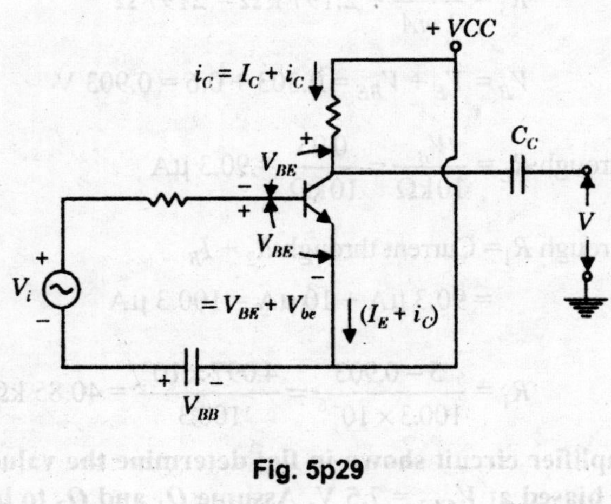


Fig. 5p29

**24. In the common emitter amplifier shown in the fig. the transistor hasa forward current gain of 100, and a base-emitter voltage, $V_{BE} = 0.6$ V. Assume $I_{CO}$ to be negligible. Choose values of $R_1$ and $R_3$ such that the transistor has collector current of 1 mA and a collector to emitter voltage of 2.5 V.**

**Solution:**

Given $\quad I_C = 1$ mA, $\beta = 100$

As $\quad I_C = \beta I_B$

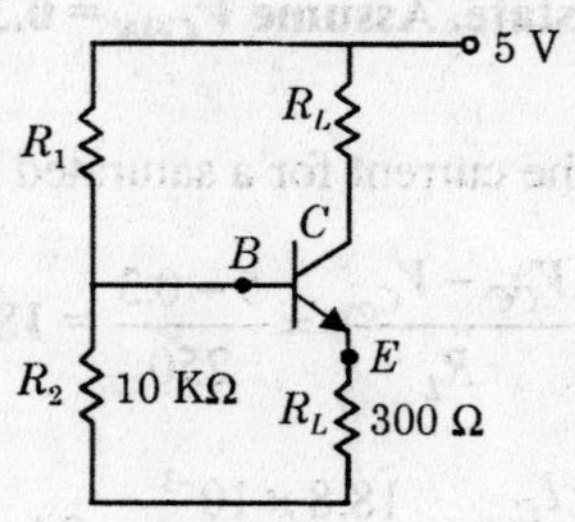


**Fig. 5p30**

$\therefore \quad I_B = 0.01$ mA = 10 μA

$$I_E = (I_C + I_B) = 1.01 \text{ mA}$$

As we have $\quad V_E = I_E R_E = (1.01) \cdot 10^{-5} (300) = 0.303$ V

$$V_{CE} = 0.303 + 2.5 = 2.803 \text{ V}$$

Drop across $\quad R_3 = 5 - 2.803 = 2.197$ V

$$R_3 = \frac{2.197}{1\,mA} = 2.197\text{ k}\Omega = 2197\ \Omega$$

$$V_B = V_E + V_{BE} = 0.303 + 0.6 = 0.903 \text{ V}$$

Current through $R_L = \dfrac{V_B}{10\text{k}\Omega} = \dfrac{0.93}{10\text{k}\Omega} = 90.3$ μA

Current through $R_1$= Current through $R_2 + I_B$

$$= 90.3\ \mu\text{A} + 10\ \mu\text{A} = 100.3\ \mu\text{A}$$

$$R_1 = \frac{5 - 0.903}{100.3 \times 10^{-6}} = \frac{4.097 \times 10^6}{100.3} = 40.85\text{ k}\Omega$$

**25. In the amplifier circuit shown in fig; determine the value of $R$ such that $Q_2$ is biased at $V_{CE2} = 7.5$ V. Assume $Q_1$ and $Q_2$ to be identical,**

**$V_{BE}$ = 0.7 V and neglect base current. Also determine the small signal input impedance of $Q_1$ and $Q_2$, if both of them have β = 200. Use $V_T$ = 26 mV.**

**Solution:**

Given $V_{CE2} = 7.5$ V, $V_{BE} = 0.7$ V, $\beta = 200$, $V_T = 26$ mV.

$$I_1 = \frac{V_{CC} - V_{BE}}{R} = \frac{15 - 0.7}{10} = 1.43 \text{ mA}$$

This $I_1$ is reflected to $I_2 = I_1$ ($\because V_{BE1} = V_{BE2}$)

$$R = \frac{V_{CC} - V_{CE\,sat}}{I_2} = \frac{15 - 7.5}{1.43} k = 5 \text{ k}$$

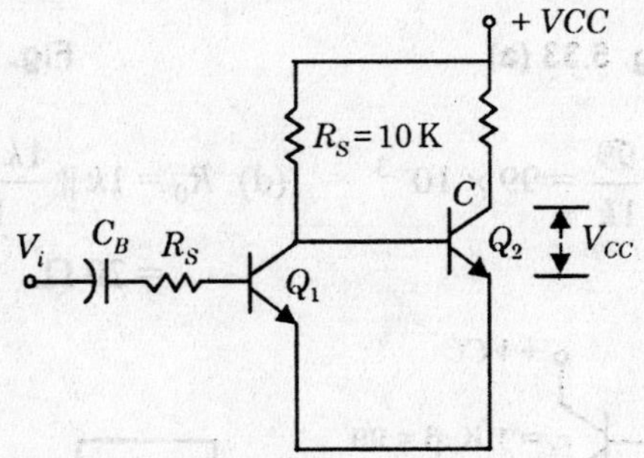


**Fig. 5p31**

For small signal impedance $Z_2 = r\pi_2$

$$= \frac{\beta}{g_{m_2}} = \frac{\beta V_T}{I_{C2}} = \frac{200 \times 25}{1.43} 3.5k$$

$$Z_1 = R_1 \parallel r_{c1} \parallel Z_2$$

$$= r_{e1} \neq \frac{1}{g_{m1}} = \frac{V_1}{I_{C1}} = \frac{25}{1.43} \Omega = 16\,\Omega$$

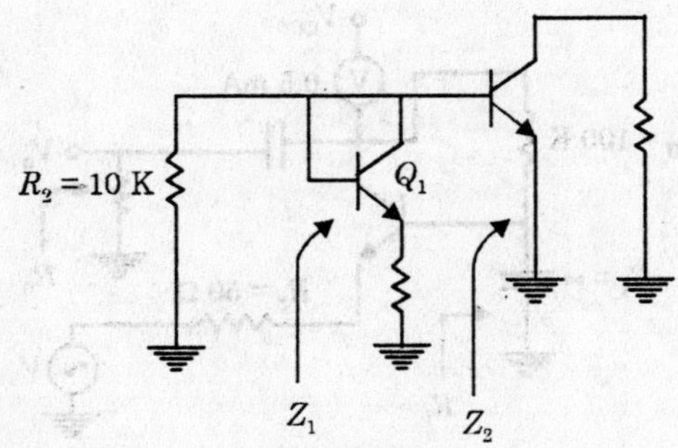


**Fig. 5p32**

**26. In the circuit of fig. determine the resistance $R_0$ seen by the output terminals.**

**Solution:**

(a) Make $V_S = 0$

(b) Ground all D.C supply point.

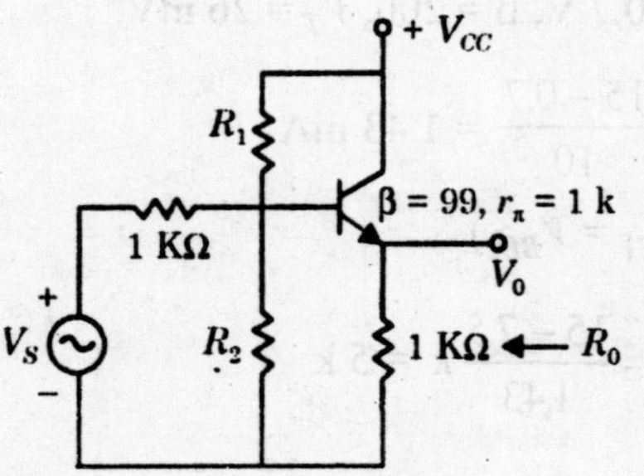


Fig. 5.33 (a)

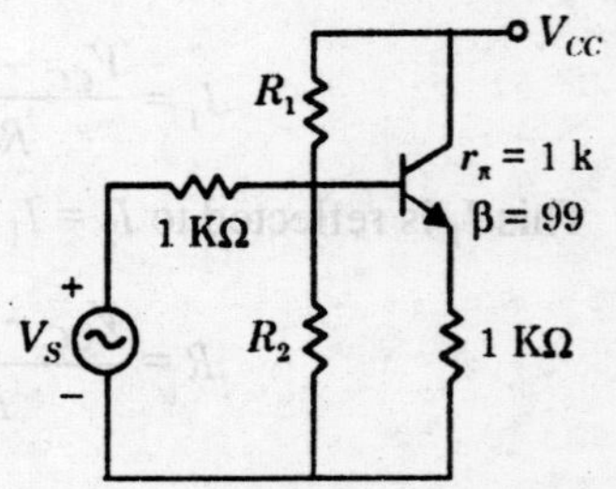


Fig. 5.33 (b)

(c) $g_m' = \dfrac{\beta}{r_\pi} = \dfrac{99}{1k} = 99 \times 10^{-3}$

(d) $R_0 = 1k \,\|\, \dfrac{1k + 1k}{100} = 1\text{ k} \,\|\, 20\ \Omega$

$= 20\ \Omega.$

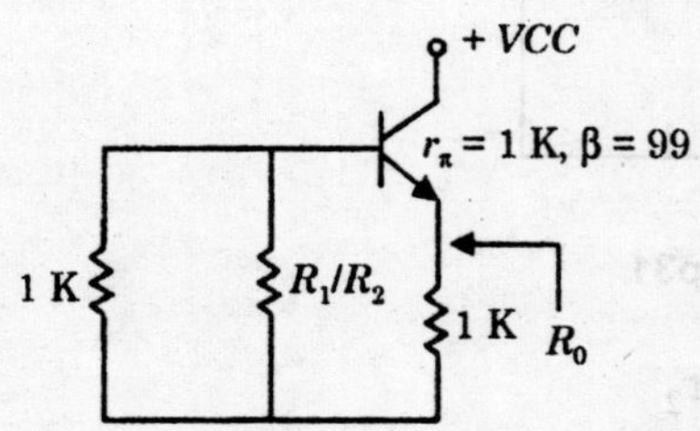


Fig. 5.33 (c)

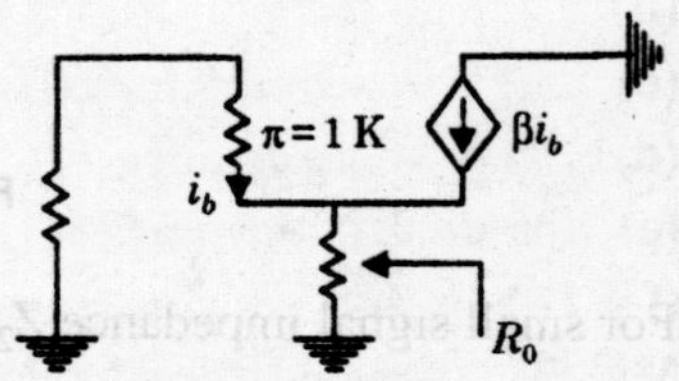


Fig. 5.33 (d)

**27. A bipolar junction transistor amplifier circuit is shown in fig. Assume that the current source $I_{bias}$ is ideal, and the transistor has very large $\beta$, $r_b = 0$ and $r_o \to \infty$. Determine the a.c. small signal midband voltage gain ($Vo/Vs$), input resistance ($R_i$), and output resistance ($R_0$) of the circuit. Assume $V_T = 26$ mV.**

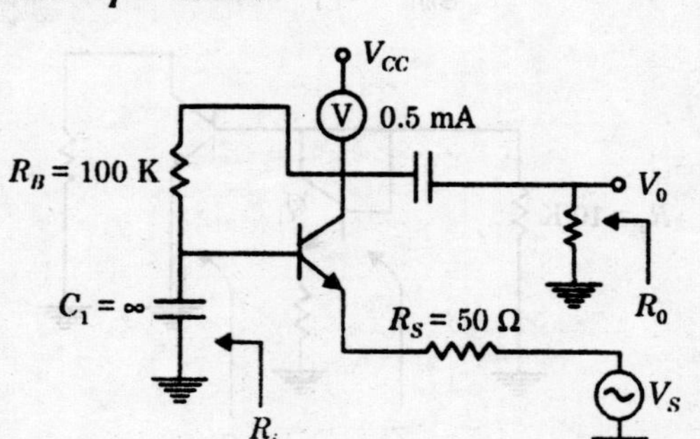


Fig. 5p34

**Solution:**

The given circuit is working in common base configuration with input at emitter and output taken from collector. Neglecting $r_o$, $r_\mu$ and charge storage elements, *T* model reduces to as shown.

Assuming output resistance $r_o \to \infty$ (large). And $r_b = 0$ small signal equivalent circuit for *CB* stage is as below:

$$R_{in} = \frac{\alpha_0}{g_m} = \frac{\frac{\beta_0}{1+\beta_0}}{g_m}$$

$$g_m = \frac{I_C}{V_T} = \frac{0.5mA}{26mA},\ R_{\text{out}} = R_C = 1\ \text{k}\Omega$$

$$A_v = g_m R_c = \frac{0.5mA}{26mA}\ 1\ \text{k}\Omega$$

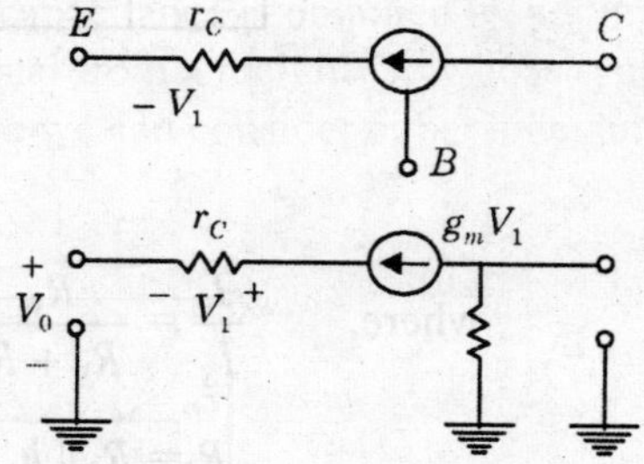


Fig. 5p35

Hence the input impedance is very low and output impedance high. Therefore, it is used as a current source.

**28. For the circuit shown, with $R_e = 4$ k, $R_L = 4$ k, $R_b$, find:**

**(a) The current gain $I_L/I_a = A_I$.**

**(b) The voltage gain $V_o/V_C$, where $V_S = I_S R_S$.**

**(c) The transconductance $I_L/V_S = G_M$.**

**(d) The transresistance $V_a/I_a = R_M$.**

**(e) The input resistance seen by the source**

**(f ) The output resistance seen by the load.**

**Make reasonable approximations. Neglect all capacitive effects.**

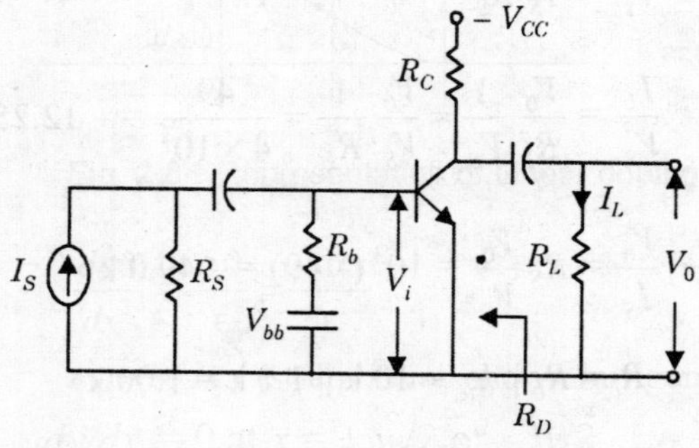


Fig. 5p36

**Solution:**

From the circuit we have $\dfrac{I_L}{I_S} = \dfrac{I_i}{I_S} \cdot \dfrac{I_b}{I_i} \cdot \dfrac{I_L}{I_b}$

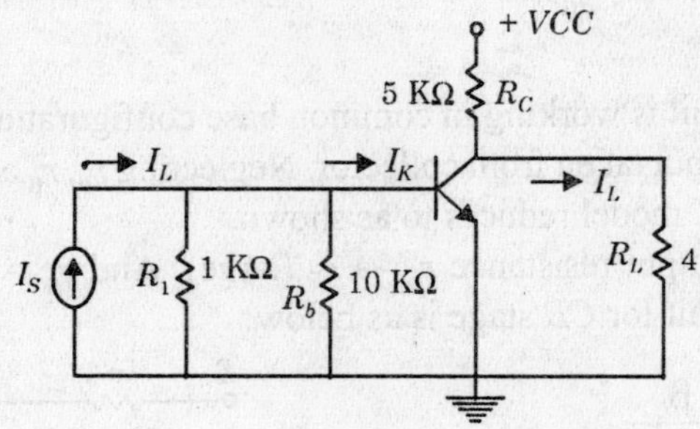


where, $$\frac{I_i}{I_S} = \frac{R_S}{R_S + R_i}$$

$$R_i = R_b \| h_{ie} = 10 \text{ k} \| 1.1 \text{ k}$$
$$= 1.00\text{k}$$

or $$\frac{I_i}{I_S} = \frac{1}{2.04} = \frac{I_b}{I_i} = \frac{R_b}{R_b + h_{ie}} + \frac{10k}{10k + 1.1k} = 0.90$$

$$\frac{I_L}{I_b} = -h_{fe}\frac{R_C}{R_C + R_L} = -50\,\frac{5}{9} = -27.77$$

$$\therefore \quad \frac{I_L}{I_S} = \left(\frac{1}{2.04}\right)(0.90)(-27.7) = -12.25$$

(b) $$\frac{V_0}{V_s} = \frac{I_L R_L}{I_S R_S} = (-12.25)\frac{4k}{1k} = -49$$

(c) $$\frac{I_L}{V_S} = \frac{V_0}{R_L}\frac{1}{V_S} = \frac{V_0}{V_S}\frac{1}{R_L} = \frac{49}{4 \times 10^3} = -12.25 \text{ mA/V.}$$

(d) $$\frac{V_0}{I_S} = R_S\frac{V_0}{V_S} = 10^3(-49) = -49.0 \text{ k}$$

(e) $$R_i = R_b \| h_{ie} = 10 \text{ k} \| 1.1 \text{ k} = 1.00 \text{ k}$$

(f) $$R_o = \frac{1}{h_{oe}} \| R_C = 40 \text{ k} \| 5 \text{ k} = 4.44 \text{ k}$$

**29. The given figure is the circuit of amplifier with voltage feedback biasing. The base current is 20 μA and β is 500. Calculate $R_B$. Also calculate $R_B$ if there is an $R_E$ of 100 Ω.**

**Solution:**

Since $\beta = 500$

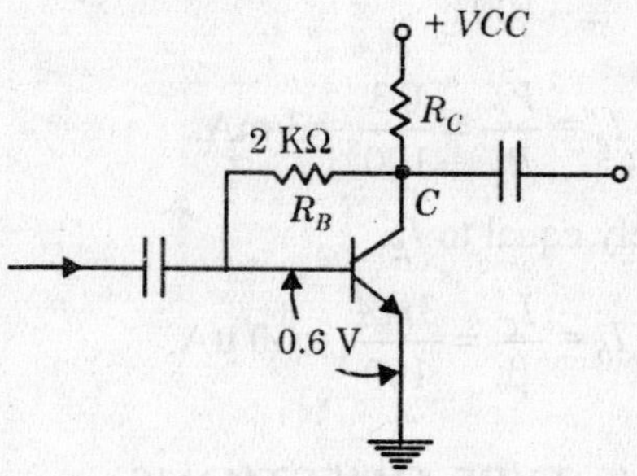


**Fig. 5p37**

$$I_C = \beta I_B = 500\ 20\mu A = 10 \text{ mA.}$$

Voltage drop across $R_C = 10 \text{ mA} \times 4.7 \text{ k} = 4.7$ V

The collector voltage $= (10 - 4.7)$ V $= 5.3$ V.

Voltage drop across $R_B$ = voltage at collector – voltage at base

$= 5.3 - 0.6$

$= 4.7 \text{ V} = I_B R_B$

$\therefore \qquad R_B = \dfrac{4.7}{20\mu A} = 235 \text{ k}\Omega$

Also as $\qquad I_C = \beta I_B = 10$ mA as above

Voltage emitter = 100 10 mA. = 0.1 V

Low end voltage of $R_B$ i.e.

Voltage at point $\quad B = (0.6 + 0.1)$ V $= 0.7$ V

Voltage at collector = 5.3 V and voltage at point $B = 0.7$ V

$$I_B R_B = 5.3 - 0.7 = 4.6 \text{ V}$$

$\Rightarrow \qquad R_B = \dfrac{4.6}{20\mu A} = 230 \text{ k}\Omega.$

**30. Calculate the three currents $I_C$, $I_B$ and $I_E$ for transistor circuit shown. β of this silicon transistor is 100.**

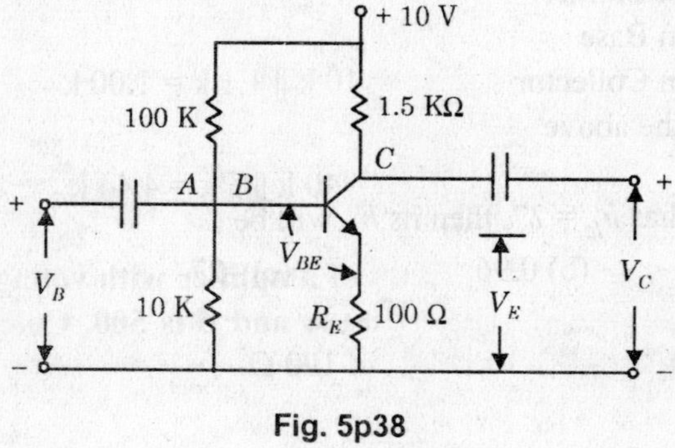


**Fig. 5p38**

**Solution:**

$$\text{Voltage at base, } V_B = \frac{10V}{100k} + 10k = 0.9 \text{ V}$$

$$I_e = \frac{V_E}{R_E} = \frac{0.3}{100} = 3 \text{ mA.}$$

$I_C$ is approximately equal to $I_E$.

$$I_b = \frac{I_C}{\beta} = \frac{3mA}{100} = 30 \ \mu\text{A.}$$

## 5.12 OBJECTIVE TYPE QUESTIONS

1. For good stabilized biasing of the transistor of the CE amplifier of figure. We should have

   (a) $\frac{R_E}{R_B} << 1$ (b) $\frac{R_E}{R_B} >> 1$ (c) $\frac{R_E}{R_B} << h_{rb}$ (d) $\frac{R_E}{R_B} >> h_{rb}$

   **Ans:** (b)
2. Current stability of a *CC* amplifuier can be increased by
   (a) Reducing both Emitter and Base resistance
   (b) Increasing both Emitter and Base resistance
   (c) Reducing Emitter resistance and increasing Base resistance
   (d) Increasing Emitter resistance and decreasing Base resistance

   **Ans:** (d)
3. Which of the following statements are correct for basic transistor amplifier configurations?
   (a) *CB* amplifier has low input impedance and a low current gain
   (b) *CC* amplifier has low output impedance and a low current gain
   (c) *CE* amplifier has very poor voltage gain but very high i/p impedance
   (d) The current gain of *CB* amplifier is higher than the current gain of *CC* amplifier

   **Ans:** (a), (b)
4. Which of the following configuration ifs nomally used in cascading
   (a) Common Emitter
   (b) Common Base
   (c) Common Collector
   (d) Non of the above

   **Ans:** (a)
5. A transistor has $h_{fe} = 27$, then its $h_{fc}$ will be

   (a) –0.96 (b) 0.96 (c) –27 (d) –28

   **Ans:** (d)

**6.** In the BJT amplifier, the transistor is biased in the forward active region. Putting a capacitor across $R_E$ will .

(a) decrease the voltage gain and decrease the input impedance
(b) increase the voltage gain and decrease the input impedance
(c) Decrease the voltage gain and increase the input impedance
(d) Increase the voltage gain and increase the input impedance

**Ans:**

**7.** In a common emitter BJT amplifier, the maximum usable supply voltage is limited by

(a) avalanche breakdown of Base-emitter junction
(b) collector-Base breakdown voltage with emitter open (BVCBO)
(c) Collector-emitter breakdown voltage with base open (BVCEO)
(d) Zener breakdown voltage of the emitter-base junction.

**Ans:** (c)

**8.** The transconductance $g_m$ is defined as $g_m = \frac{\partial i_c}{\partial V_{BE}}$ its value in terms of *h*-parameters is

(a) $\frac{h_{ie}}{h_{fe}}$ (b) $\frac{h_{fe}}{25}$ (c) $\frac{h_{fe}}{h_{ie}}$ (d) $h_{fe}\,h_{ie}$

**Ans:** (c)

**9.** Introducing a resistor in the emitter of a common emitter amplifier stabilizes the DC operating point against variations in

(a) only the temperature (b) only the β of the transistor
(c) both temperature and β (d) none of the above

**Ans:** (c)

**10.** In a *CE* transistor a mplifier, if collector emitter voltage increases, the instantaneous operating point

(a) move up the load line
(b) move down the load line
(c) move at right angle to the load line
(d) remains stationary

**Ans:** (a)

**11.** The '*h*' parameter equivalent circuit of a junction transistor is valid for

(a) high frequency, large signal operation
(b) high frequency, small signal operation
(c) low frequency, small signal operation
(d) low frequency, large signal operation

**Ans:** (c)

**12.** In a transistor $h_{fe} = 50$ $h_{ie} = 830$ ohms $h_{oe} = 10^{-4}$ mho when used *CB* then its output resistance

(a) 2 M Ohms (b) 500 K (c) 2.5 M ohms (d) 780 K

**Ans:** (b)

**13.** The small signal input impedance of a transistor when the output is shorted for the measuring signal, is (where the symbols have then usual measuring)

(a) $h_{11} = \left.\frac{V_1}{i_1}\right|_{v_2=0}$ (b) $h_{12} = \left.\frac{V_1}{i_1}\right|_{v_1=0}$

(c) $h_{21} = \left.\frac{i_2}{i_1}\right|_{v_2=0}$ (d) $h_{22} = \left.\frac{i_2}{i_1}\right|_{v_1=0}$

**Ans:** (a)

**14.** For obtaining hybrid parameters of a transistor

(a) variable $V_{be}$ and $i_e$ are taken as independent variables

(b) the two independent variables are the ones that are most easily measurable for a *CE* configuration

(c) variable $i_b$ and $V_{ce}$ are taken as dependent variables

(d) variable $V_{be}$ and ie are taken as dependent variables

**Ans:** (b)

**15.** Typical values of *h-parameters*, at about collector currant, for small signal audio transistors in the *CE* configuration are

| | $h_{ie}$ | $h_{re}$ | $h_{fe}$ | $h_{oe}$ |
|---|---|---|---|---|
| (a) | 100 Ω | $10^{-1}$ | 50 | 1 m Ω |
| (b) | 5 Ω | $10^{-4}$ | 200 | 20 m Ω |
| (c) | 5 K Ω | 0 | 20 | 3 m Ω |
| (d) | 100 Ω | $10^{-2}$ | 100 | 10 m Ω |

**Ans:** (d)

**16.** The condition necessary to calculate $h_{oe}$ of a transistor

(a) *DC* base current is to be zero

(b) base to emitter voltage is to be constant

(c) collector current is to be constant

(d) base current is to be constant

**Ans:** (d)

**17.** The approximate value of input impedance of a common emitter amplifier with emitter resistance $R_e$ is given by

(a) $h_{ie} + A_I R_e$ (b) $h_{ie} + (1 + h_{fe}) R_e$

(c) $h_{ie}$ (d) $(1 + h_{fe}) R_e$

**Ans:** (b)

## 5.13 CONVENTIONAL QUESTIONS

1. Draw the circuit diagram of a *CE* configuration and give its *h*-parameter model.
2. State and draw the circuit diagram of Miller's and dual of Miller's theorem.
3. Draw the circuit diagram of a *CB* configuration and give its *h*-parameter model.
4. Draw the circuit diagram of a *CC* configuration and give its *h*-parameter model.
5. Prove that (a) $h_{oc} = h_{oe}$ (b) $h_{fc} = -(h_{fe} + 1)$ (c) $h_{ic} = h_{ie}$ (d) $h_{rc} = 1 - h_{re}$
6. Using approximate *h* = parameter model obtain the expressions for (a) $A_I$ (b) $A_V$ (c) $R_i$ (d) $R_o$ for *CE* Configuration
7. Derive the expression for (a) $A_V$ in terms of $A_I$ (b) $A_{Vs}$ in terms of $A_V$ and (c) $A_{Is}$ in terms of $A_I$
8. (a) $h_{oe}$ (b) $h_{fe}$ (c) $h_{ie}$ (d) $h_{re}$ define in words
9. In *CE*, *CB* and *CC* which of the configurations has the (a) lowest $R_i$ (b) highest $R_i$ (c) lowest $R_o$ (d) highest $R_o$ (e) lowest $A_I$ (f) highest $A_I$.
10. compare Class *A*, Class *B*, Class *AB* and Class *C* amplifiers.

## 5.14 EXERCISE PROBLEMS

1. Circuit shown in figure determine (a) $r_e$ (b) $Z_i$ (c) $Z_o$ (d) $A_V$ (e) $A_i$

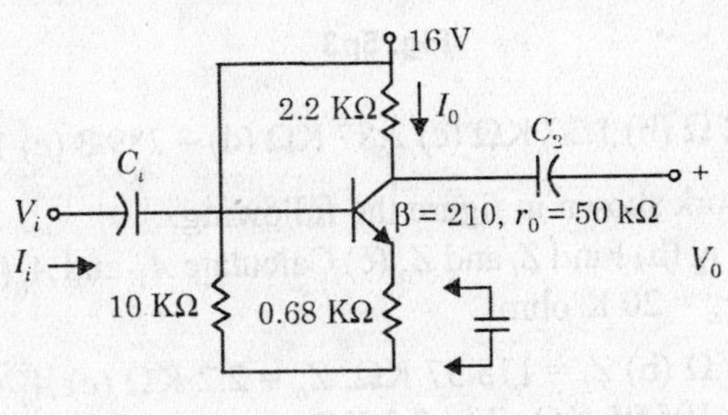


Fig. 5p1

**Ans:** (a) 19.64 Ω (b) 8.47 Ω (c) 2.2 KΩ (d) – 3.24 (e) 12.47

2. For the Emitter follower net work shown in figure determine the following.

   (a) $r_e$ (b) $Z_i$ (c) $Z_o$ (d) $A_V$ (e) $A_i$

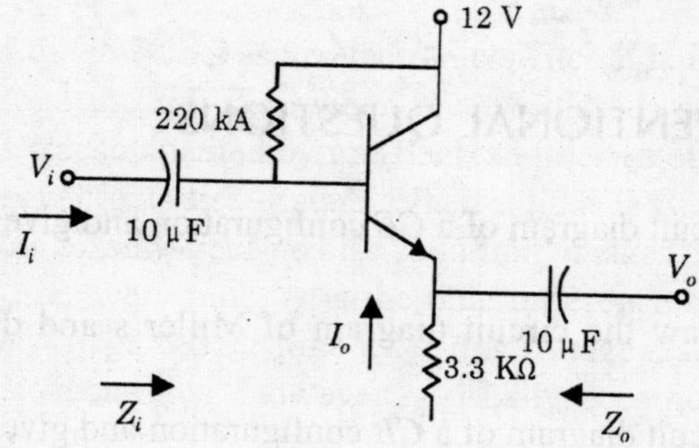


**Fig. 5p2**

**Ans:** (a) 12.61 Ω (b) 132.72 KΩ (c) 12.56 Ω (d) 0.996 (e) – 40.06

3. For the net work shown in figure determine the following.
   (a) $r_e$ (b) $Z_i$ (c) $Z_o$ (d) $A_V$ (e) $A_i$

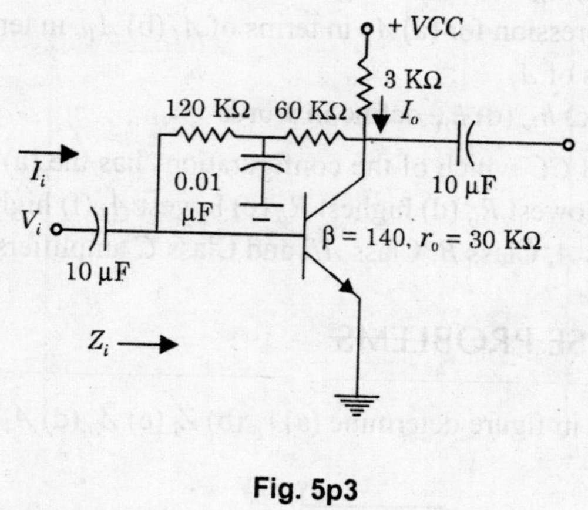


**Fig. 5p3**

**Ans:** (a) 9.92 Ω (b) 1.37 KΩ (c) 2.87 KΩ (d) – 289.3 (e) 122.8

4. For the net work shown in figure the following.
   (a) determine $r_e$ (b) Find $Z_i$ and $Z_o$ (c) Calculate $A_V$ and $A_i$ (d) repeat parts *b* and *c* with $r_o$ = 20 K ohm

   **Ans:** (a) 5.34 Ω (b) $Z_i$ = 118.37 KΩ, $Z_o$ = 2.2 KΩ (c) $A_V$ = – 1.81, $A_i$ = 97.39 (d) $Z_i$ = 105.95 KΩ, $Z_o$ = 2.2 KΩ $A_V$ = – 1.81, $A_i$ = 87.17

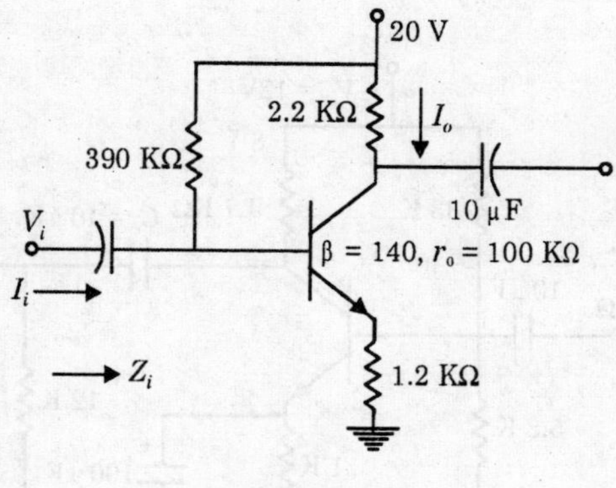


**Fig. 5p4**

5. Circuit shown in figure determine (a) $A_V$ and (b) $A_i$
**Ans:** $A_V = 163.2, A_i = 0.9868$

## 5.15 LAB EXPERIMENTS

### *1. Common Emitter Amplifier*

**AIM:** To plot the frequency response of common emitter amplifier and to calculate the bandwidth

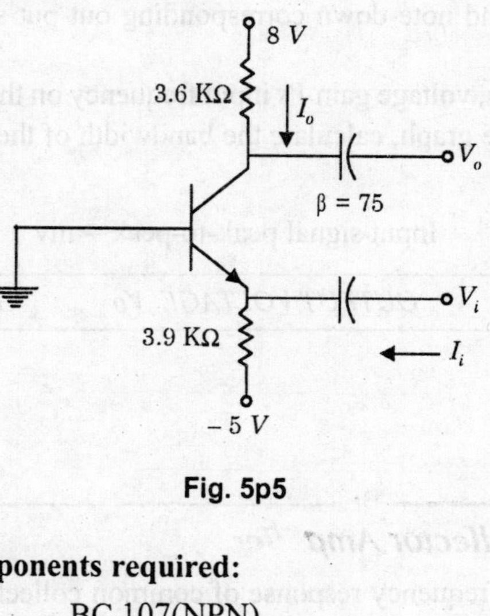


**Fig. 5p5**

**Equipment & components required:**

| | |
|---|---|
| 1. Transistor | BC 107(NPN) |
| 2. Resistor | 4.7 k? |
| 3. Ammeter | 0-25 mA |
| 4. Voltmeter | 0-25 volt |
| 5. function generator | |
| 6. Power supply | 0-30 volt |
| 7. Breadboard and connecting wires. | |

**Circuit Diagram:**

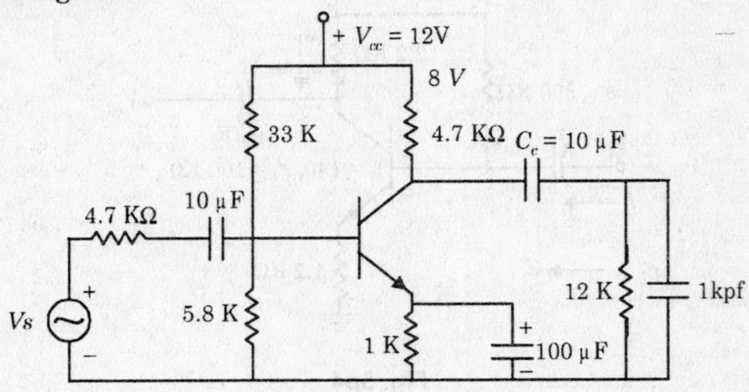


**Fig. 5L1**

**Procedure:**

- Connect The Circuit as shown in the circuit diagram
- Select the input signal as sinusoidal wave form the function generator such that the output is undistorted by using the oscilloscope. Keep this value as constant throughout the experiment.
- Select *Vs* = 40 mv. Such that the out put is not distorted.
- Vary the input signal frequency from 50 Hz to 500 KHz as shown in the tabular form and note down corresponding out put signal peak to peak from *CRO*.
- Draw the graph, voltage gain *Vs* input frequency on the semi graph paper.
- From the above graph, calculate the bandwidth of the amplifier.

**Tabular form:**

Input signal peak-to-peak = mv

| *FREQUENCY* | *OUTPUT VOLTAGE Vo* | *GAIN Vo/Vs* |
|---|---|---|
| | | |

## *2. Common Collector Amp.'ˈfier*

**AIM:** To plot the frequency response of common collector amplifier and to calculate the bandwidth

**Equipment and components required:**

| | |
|---|---|
| 8. Transistor | BC 107 (NPN) |
| 9. Resistors | 4.7 k, 100 k, 10 k, 10 k? |
| 10. capacitors | 10 uf, 10 uf |
| 11. CRO | DUAL |

12. Ammeter 0 – 25 mA
13. Voltmeter 0 – 25 volt
14. Power supply 0 – 30 volt
15. Breadboard and connecting wires.

**Circuit Diagram:**

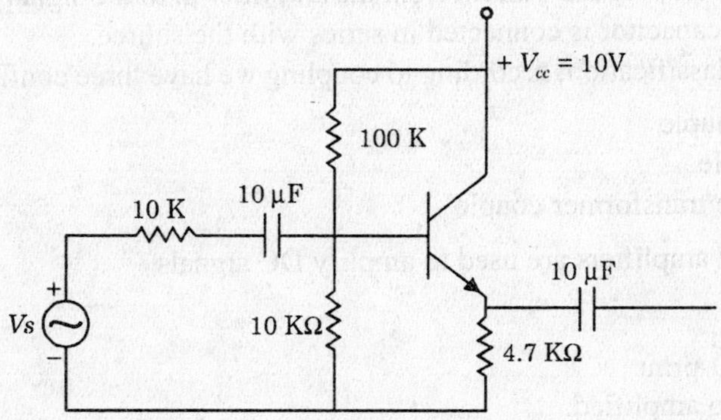


**Fig. 5L2**

**Procedure:**

1. Connect The Circuit as shown in the circuit diagram
2. Select the input signal as sinusoidal wave form the function generator such that the output is undistorted by using the oscilloscope. Keep this value as constant throughout the experiment.
3. Select $Vs$ = 40 mv. Such that the out put is not distorted.
4. Vary the input signal frequency from 50 Hz to 500 KHz as shown in the tabular form and note down corresponding out put signal peak to peak from CRO.
5. Draw the graph, voltage gain $Vs$ input frequency on the semi log graph paper.
6. From the above graph, calculate the bandwidth of the amplifier.

**Tabularform:**

Input signal peak-to-peak = mv

| *FREQUENCY* | *OUTPUT VOLTAGE Vo* | *GAIN Vo/Vs* |
|---|---|---|

According to coupling in many amplifier applications the source or the load, or both cannot be subjected to a DC voltage or be permitted to conduct DC current for example an electromagnetic speaker is designed to respond to ac foundations only and may not operate properly if it conducts a dc current. To prevent the dc component of an amplifiers output voltage from producing DC current in the load, a capacitor is connected in series with load. Similarly, to prevent the flow of DC current from the amplifier in to the signal source or vice versa, a capacitor is connected in series with the source.
Now under classification: according to coupling we have three configurations

1. Direct couple
2. RC couple
3. Inductive/transformer couple

Direct couple amplifiers are used to amplify DC signals

**Limitations:**

1. Drift in Q-print
2. Ico is also amplified.

# ❮6❯

# BJT AT HIGH FREQUENCY

## 6.1 INTRODUCTION

At low frequency it is assumed that the transistor responds instantly to changes of input voltage or current. This is not the reason because the mechanism of the transport of charge carriers from emitter to collector is essentially one of diffusion. Hence, in order to know the transistor behavior at high frequencies, it is necessary to have a clear description on this diffusion mechanism. Such an analysis is complicated, and the resulting equations are suggestive to those which are in connection with a lossy transmission line. The time delay in response is mainly contributed by the process of diffusion. At low frequencies, this time delay is small compared with the periodic time $T$ (= $1/f$) and may, therefore, be neglected. However, at high frequencies, this time delay becomes a significant part of the periodic time and can not be neglected in the analysis of the amplifier. Taking into consideration the diffusion mechanism and the consequent time delay, we arrive a high frequency model for the transistor called the high frequency hybrid-$\pi$ model.First let us consider the high frequency $T$-model and then the high frequency hybrid-$\pi$ model.

## 6.2 THE HIGH-FREQUENCY T-MODEL

As a first reasonable approximation, the diffusion phenomenon is to be taken into account by modifying the basic common-base $T$ model of a complete physical model of a $CB$ transistor as follows; the collector resistor $r_c^1$ is shunted by a capacitor $C_e$, as indicated in figure 6.1 shown. Also the dependent current generator is made proportional to the current $i_1$ in $r$ and not to the emitter current that is the low-frequency alpha is denoted by $\alpha_0$. If an input current step is applied, then initially this current is bypassed by $C_e$ and $i_1$, remains zero. Hence the output current starts at zero and rises slowly with time. Such a response is that because of the diffusion process. A better approximation is to replace $C_e$ and $r_e^1$ by a lumped transmission line consisting of a capacitance.

The physical significance of $C_e$ is not difficult to know. It represents the sum of the diffusion capacitance $C_{De}$ and the transition capacitance $C_{Te}$ across the emitter junction.

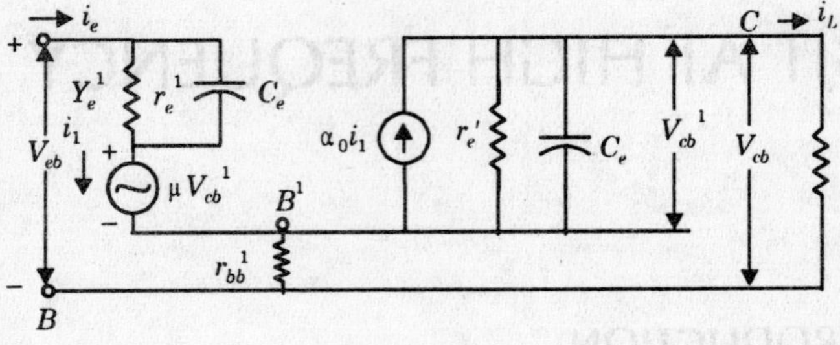

**Fig. 6.1** Transistor *T* model at high frequency

$Ce = C_{De} + C_{Te}$. The diffusion capacitance is directly proportional to the quiescent emitter current. As $C_{De} >> C_T$, except for very small values of emitter current, and hence $C_e$ is approximately equal to the diffusion capacitance $C_{De}$. Since the collector-junction is reverse-biased, the collector diffusion capacitance $C_{Dc}$ *is* negligible, so that $C_C$ is equal to the collector transition capacitance $C_{Tc}$. Also it is that, $C_e$ is at least 30 times as large as $C_C$.

### *The High Frequency Alpha:*

Assume that the input excitation is sinusoidal of frequency $f = \omega/2\pi$.

Therefore phase current, we have from figure;

$$I_1 r^1_e = \frac{I_e}{1/r^1_e + j\omega C_e} \quad \text{...(1)}$$

Or $$I_1 = \frac{I_e}{1 + j(f/f_\alpha)} \text{ where } f_\alpha = \frac{I_e}{2\pi r^1_e C_e} \quad \text{...(2)}$$

It is possible to consider the generator to be proportional to the current rather than the current through $r^1_e$ provided that the proportionality factor $\alpha$ to be a complex function of frequency thus, if

$$\alpha_0 I_1 = \alpha I_e \quad \text{...(3)}$$

Then form equation (1)

$$\alpha = \frac{\alpha_0}{1 + j(f/f_\alpha)} \quad \text{...(4)}$$

The magnitude of the complex or high-frequency alpha $\alpha$ is $\alpha_o$ at zero frequency and falls to 0.707 $\alpha_0$ at $f = f_\alpha$. This frequency $f_\alpha$ is called the *alpha cut off frequency*. The diffusion equation leads to the solutions for $\alpha$ equal to the hyperbolic secant of a complex quantity. If this expression is expanded into a power series in the variable $f/f_\alpha$ and only the first two terms are retained, equation (4) is obtained. Hence equation 4 and the equivalent circuit of figure are valid at frequencies which are appreciably less than $f_\alpha$. General-purpose transistors have values of $f_\alpha$ in the range of hundreds of kilohertz. High frequency transistor can have alpha cut off frequencies in the tens, hundreds, or even thousands of megahertz.

Since $\alpha = -h_{fb}$,

### *The Approximate CB T-model*

If the load resistance $R_L$ is small, the output voltage is $v_{cb}$, and hence $v^1_{cb}$, under these conditions the network of figure, reduces to the circuit of figure 6.2, which is referred to as the approximate *CB* high frequency model.

The order of magnitudes of the parameters in figure 6.2 are $r^1_e = 20\ \Omega$ $r^1_{bb} = 100\ \Omega$ $r^1_C = 1$ M $C_C = 1 - 50$ PF and $C_e = 30 - 10{,}000$ PF.

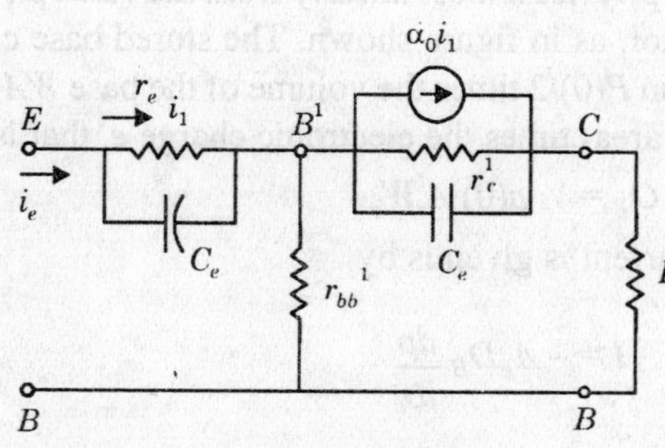


**Fig. 6.2** The approximate high frequency *T*-model

### *The common-Base short-circuit-current frequency response*

Consider a transistor in the common-base configuration excited by a sinusoidal current $I_e$ of frequency *f*. If terminals *C* and *B* are connected together in figure 6.2, then $r^1_{bb}$, $r^1_c$ and $C_c$ are placed in parallel. Since $r^1_c >> r^1_{bb}$, neglect $r^1_c$.

As $r^1_{bb}\ C_c << r^1_e\ C_e$ and under these conditions, the response is determined by the larger time constant $r^1_e C_e$. Now $C_c$ from figure can also be neglected. With these simplifications, $I_L = \alpha_0 I$, or from the previous equations that is 3 and 4, the common-base short-circuit current gain is given by

$$A_{ib} = \frac{I_L}{I_e} = \frac{\alpha_0 I_1}{I_e} = \alpha = \frac{\alpha_0}{1 + j\,(f/f\alpha)} \qquad \ldots(5)$$

The magnitude of a and its phase angles are given by

$$|\alpha| = \frac{\alpha_0}{\sqrt{1+(f/f_\alpha)^2}},\ \theta = -\tan^{-1}(f/f_\alpha) \qquad \ldots(6)$$

If $f = f_\alpha$, $\alpha = \alpha_0/\sqrt{2}$, and $20 \log|\alpha/\alpha_0| = -20 \log\sqrt{2} = -3$dB. Hence the alpha cutoff frequency $f_\alpha$ is called the 3 – dB *dB* frequency of the *CB* short-circuit current gain.

## 6.3 THE ALPHA CUTOFF FREQUENCY

For high-frequency applications fa has to be very large. In order to construct a transistor with a definite value of $f_\alpha$, it is necessary to know all the parameters upon which $f_\alpha$ depends. Expression for the emitter capacitance is obtained from the equation for $f_\alpha$.

### *The Diffusion Capacitance:*

Considering figure 6.3 shown represents the injected hole concentration vs distance in the base region of *p-n-p* transistor. The base width $W$ is assumed to be small compared with the diffusion length $L_B$ of the minority carriers. Since the collector is reverse-biased, the injected charge concentration part in the collector junction is zero.

If $W << L_B$, then $p$ varies almost linearly from the value $p(0)$ at the emitter to zero at the collector, as in figure shown. The stored base charge $Q_B$ is the average concentration $P(0)/2$ times the volume of the base $WA$ (where $A$ is the base cross-sectional area) times the electronic charge $e$, that is,

$$Q_B = ½\, p(0)\, A\, W_e \quad \text{...(7)}$$

The diffusion current is given is by

$$I = -A_e D_B \frac{dp}{dx}$$

$$= A_e D_B \frac{P(0)}{W} \quad \text{...(8)} \quad \left( J_P = -eD_B \frac{dp}{dx} \right)$$

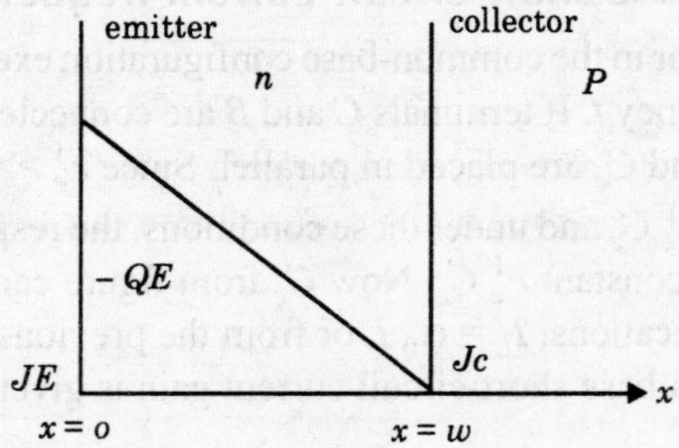


**Fig. 6.3** In the base region Minority carrier charge distribution

Where $D_B$ is the diffusion minority carriers in the base. Combining equations (7) and (8)

$$Q_B = \frac{Iw^2}{2D_B} \quad \text{...(9)}$$

The emitter diffusion capacitance $C_{De}$ is given by the rate of change of $Q_B$ with respect to emitter voltage $V$ or

$$C_{De} = \frac{d_{QB}}{dV} = \frac{W^2}{2D_B}\frac{dI}{dV} = \frac{W^2}{2D_B}\frac{1}{r_e^1} \quad ...(10)$$

Where $r_e^1 = d_v/d_I$ is the emitter-junction incremental resistance considering equation $r = \frac{\eta\, v_T}{I}$ and neglecting junction recombination, $r_e^1 = V_T/I_E$,

where $V_T = \bar{k}_T/e$, $\bar{k}$ = Boltzman's constant in $J/^\circ k$, $\bar{k}$ = k/q

$T$ = absolute temperature

$e$ = electronic charge

Hence
$$C_{De} = \frac{w^2 I_E}{2D_B V_T} = g_m \frac{w^2}{2D_B} \quad ...(11)$$

This indicates that the diffusion capacitance is proportional to the emitter bias current $I_E$. Since $D_B$ varies approximately inversely with $T$, and $V_T$ is proportional to $T$, then $C_{de}$ is almost independent of temperature. Except for very small values of $I_E$, the diffusion capacitance is much greater than the transition capacitance $C_T$, and hence $C_e = C_{De} + C_{Te} \cong C_D$.

### Dependence of $f_\alpha$ Upon Base Width or Transit Time:

From the equations (1) and (10) and also since $c_e \approx C_{de}$, then

$$2\pi f_\alpha = \omega_\alpha = \frac{1}{r_e^1 c_e} = \frac{2D_B}{W^2} \quad ...(12)$$

The above equation indicated that alpha cut off frequency varies inversely as the square of the base thickness $W$.

For a *p-n-p* germanium transistor with $W = 2.54 \times 10^{-3}$cm $= 25^{-4}$ microns

$\therefore$ $f_\alpha$ becomes, $f_\alpha = 2.3$ MHz.

Now $\omega_\alpha$ is obtained by combining equation (9) and (12),

$$I = Q_B\, \omega_\alpha \quad ...(13)$$

If $t_B$ is the base transit time that is the number of seconds it takes a carrier to cross the base, then in time $t_B$ an amount of charge equal to the charge $Q_B$ reaches the collector. Then the resulting current is given as,

$$I = \frac{Q_B}{t_B} \quad ...(14)$$

From equation (13) and (14) we have that $\omega_\alpha = 1/t_B$, or it is that the alpha cutoff (angular) frequency is the reciprocal of the base transit time.

### The Common-Emitter Short Circuit Current Frequency Response:

The $T$-model of figure shown in the previous discussion is applicable in the $C_E$ configuration if $E$ is grounded, the signal is applied to $B$, and the load is placed between $C$ and $E$. The $C_E$ short circuit current gain $A_{ie}$ is obtained by shorting the collector terminal $C$ to $E$ as shown in figure below.

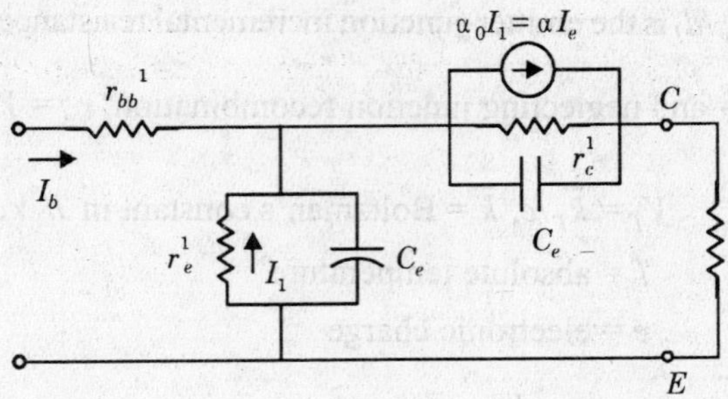


**Fig. 6.4** The circuit in the *CE* configuration under short circuit condition

Since $r_c^1 >> r_e$ and $C_e >> C_c$ the parallel elements $r_c^1$ and $c_c$ can be neglected, and then $I_L = \alpha_0$

$$I_1 = \alpha_0 I_1 = \alpha I_e$$

Now from *KCL*, applying we get

$$I_L = I_b + I_e$$

that is $\quad I_e(1-\alpha) = -I_b$

$$\therefore \quad A_{ie} = \frac{I_L}{I_b} = \frac{\alpha I_e}{I_b} = \frac{-\alpha(\omega)}{1-\alpha(\omega)} \quad \text{...(15)}$$

Using equation (4) $A_{ie}$ is written as

$$A_{ie} = \frac{-\beta_0}{1 + J\left(f/f_\beta\right)} \quad \text{...(16)}$$

Where
$$\beta_0 = \frac{\alpha_0}{1-\alpha_0} \quad \text{...(17)}$$

And
$$f_\beta = f_\alpha(1-\alpha_0) \quad \text{...(18)}$$

At zero frequency the $C_E$ short-circuit current amplification is $\beta_0 \approx h_{fe}$ and the corresponding *CB* parameter is $\alpha_0 = -h_{fb}$.

The *CE* 3dB frequency, or the beta cutoff frequency, is $f_\beta$ which is also denoted as $f_{hfe}$ or $f_{\alpha e}$

From equations (17) and (18)

$$\beta_0 f_\beta = h_{fe} f_\beta = \alpha_0 f_\alpha \quad \text{...(19)}$$

Since $\alpha_0$ is close continuity, the high-frequency response for the *CE* configuration is much worse than that for the *CB* circuit. Where as, the amplification for the *CE* configuration is much greater than that for the *CB* circuit.

An important to note is that the short-circuit-current gain, band-width produce which is the amplification times 3-dB frequency is the same for both the configurations.

## 6.4 THE HIGH FREQUENCY π-MODEL

As it is studied earlier, at low frequencies, as the time delay becomes a significant part of the periodic time and cannot be neglected in the analysis of the amplifier taking into consideration the diffusion mechanism and the consequent time delay. We prefer high frequency model for the transistor called the high frequency hybrid-π model.

### *High Frequency Common Emitter Transistor π-Model*

As the common-emitter circuit is the most important practical configuration let us consider a *CE* model which is valid at high frequencies. The circuit of figure 6.1 which is the transistor *T* model at high frequencies can be used in the *CE* configuration, but it is too complicated to be useful for analysis. Also taking into consideration the model of figure 4 that is the *T* circuit in the *CE* configuration under short-circuit conditions with a load $R_L$ between *C* and *E* instead of the short-circuit is simple but in accurate except for small values of $R_L$ as it neglects the early generator.

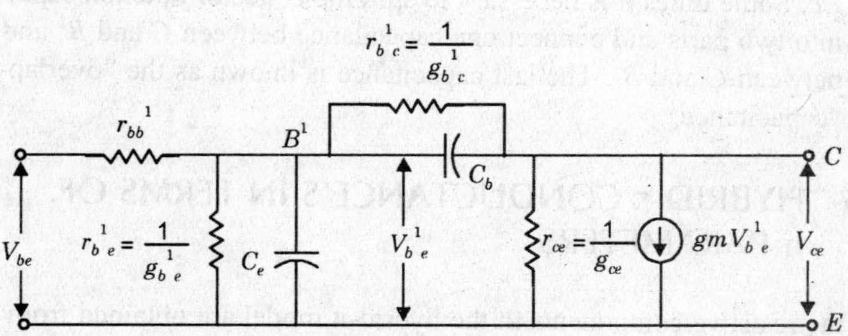


**Fig. 6.5** The hybrid π-model for a transistor in the *CE* configuration.

A circuit, called the hybrid-π or GiaColetto model named after the scientist who presented this model, which does not have the above defects, is indicated in figure 6.5. The resistive components in this circuit are obtained further from the low-frequency *h* parameters. All parameters that, is resistances and capacitances in the model are assumed to be independent of frequency. These are to be varied with quiescent operating point but under given bias conditions that are reasonably constant for small signal.

### *Various Circuit Parameters:*

1. *Resistance* $r^1_{bb}$: In the high frequency hybrid π-model of figure 6.5 node $B^1$ represents the internal base while node *B* represents the external base.

The base spreading resistance $r_{bb^1}$ shown as a lumped parameter connects the external base $B$ to be the internal base $B^1$

2. *Current Generator* $gmV_{b^1e}$: For small changes in the voltage $v_{b^1e}$ across the emitter junction, the excess minority-carrier concentration injected into the base in proportional to $v_{b^1e}$, and therefore the resulting small-signal collector current, with the collector shorted to the emitter, is proportional to $v_{b^1e}$. This effect accounts for the current generator $V_{b^1e}$.
3. *Conductance* $g_{b^1e}$: The increase in minority carriers in the base results in increased recombination base current. This effect is taken into account by inserting a conductance $g_{b^1e}$ between nodes $B^1$ and $E$.
4. *Capacitance Ce*: The excess minority carrier storage in the base is accounted for by the diffusion capacitance $C_e$ connected between $B^1$ and $E$.
5. *Conductance* $g_{b^1c}$: The varying voltage across the collector-to-base junction causes the base width modulation, which referred to as Early effect. This change in base width causes the slope of the minority carrier distribution to changes. This in turn changes the emitter feedback effect between output and input is taken into account by connecting $r_{b^1c}$ between $B^1$ and $C$.
6. *Conductance* $g_{ce}$: the conductance between $C$ and $E$ is $g_{ce}$.
7. *Capacitance* $C_c$: The collector junction barrier capacitance is included in $Cc$. Some times it is necessary to split the collector junction capacitance into two parts and connect one capacitance between $C$ and $B^1$ and other between $C$ and $B$ . The last capacitance is known as the "overlap-diode "capacitance.

## 6.5 HYBRID-π CONDUCTANCE'S IN TERMS OF h-PARAMETERS

All the resistive components in the hybrid-π model are obtained from the *h*-parameters in the $C_E$ configuration. These *h*-parameters are discussed briefly in the following manner.

*1. Transistor Transconducatance*: Figure 6.6 shows a *p-n-p* transistor in the *CE* configuration with the collector shorted to the emitter for time-varying signals. In the active-region the collector current given by equation $I_c = -\alpha I_E + I_{co}$ is applicable here with $\alpha_N = \alpha_0$:

The Transconductance is given by

$$g_m = \frac{\partial I_c}{\partial V_{B^1E}} / Vce = -\alpha_0 \frac{\partial I_E}{\partial V_{B^1E}} = \alpha_0 \frac{\partial I_E}{\partial V_E} \quad \ldots(1)$$

In the above our assumption is that $\alpha_N$ is independent of $V_E$. For a *p-n-p* transistor $V_E = -V_{B^1E}$ as shown in figure 6.6.

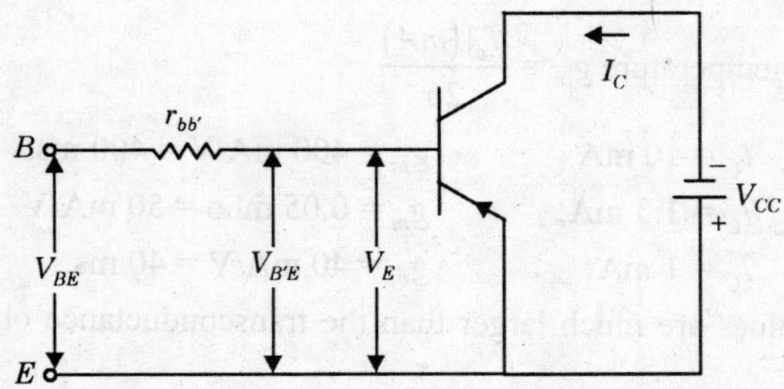


**Fig. 6.6** *p-n-p* transistor in *CE* configuration for the derivation of Transconduction (gm):

If the emitter diode resistance is $r^1_e$, then $r^1_e = \dfrac{\partial V_E}{\partial I_E}$ and hence

$$g_m = \frac{\alpha_0}{r^1_e} \quad \ldots(2)$$

From Ebers-Molleq to evaluated $r^1_e$ with $V_c = -V_{cc}$, we have

$$I_E = \alpha_{11}\,(\varepsilon^{V_E/V_T} - 1) + \alpha_{12}\,(\varepsilon^{V_E/V_T} - 1) \quad \ldots(3)$$

Where $\quad \alpha_{11} = A_q\left(\dfrac{D_p\,P_{no}}{w} + \dfrac{D_n n_{eo}}{L_E}\right)$ and $\alpha_{12} = -\left(\dfrac{A_q D_p P_{no}}{w}\right)$

At cut off, $V_E$ is very much negative and the cutoff current $I_E$ is small. Since the cut off current is very small, we neglected it in equation (3).

Hence $\quad I_E = \alpha_{11}\,\varepsilon^{V_E/V_T}$ and $\dfrac{1}{r^1_e} = \dfrac{\partial V_E}{\partial I_E} = \dfrac{a_{11}\varepsilon^{V_E/V_T}}{V_T} = \dfrac{I_E}{V_T} \quad \ldots(4)$

Substituting equation (4) in (2) equation, we have

$$g_m = \frac{\alpha_0 I_E}{V_T} = \frac{I_{co} - I_c}{V_T} \quad \ldots(5)$$

For a *p-n-p* transistor $I_c$ is negative, for a *n-p-n* transistor $I_c$ is positive, but for the foregoing analysis with $V_E = +V_{B^1E}$ leads to $g_m = \dfrac{(I_c - I_{Co})}{V_T}$

Hence for either type of transistor $g_m$ is positive.

Since $|I_c| >> |I_{co}|$ then $g_m$ is given by $g_m = \dfrac{|I_c|}{V_T} \quad \ldots(6)$

$g_m$ is directly proportional to current and inversely proportional to temperature.

At room temperature $g_m = \dfrac{|I_c|(mA)}{26}$ ...(7)

For $I_C = 10$ mA, $g_m = 400$ mA/V = 400 ms.

For $I_C = 1.3$ mA, $g_m = 0.05$ mho = 50 mA/V

For $I_C = 1$ mA $g_m = 40$ mA/V = 40 ms.

These values are much larger than the transconductance obtained with tubes.

*2. Input conductance* $g_{b^1e}$: Consider the figure 6.7 (a) of the hybrid-pi model valid at low frequencies, where all capacitances are negligible figure 6.7 (b) represents the same transistor, using the *h*-parameter equivalent circuit. In general $r_{b^1e} << r_{b^1c}$. Hence almost the complete base current $I_b$ flows into $r_{b^1e}$ and nothing flows through $r_{b^1c}$.

Hence $V_{b^1e} = I_b\, r_{b^1e}$ ...(8)

The short-circuit collector current is given by

$$I_C = g_m\, v_{b^1e} \approx g_m\, I_b\, r_{b^1e} \quad ...(9)$$

The short circuit current gain $h_{fe}$ is defined by $h_{fe} = \dfrac{I_c}{I_b} |v_{ce} = g_m\, r_{b^1e}$

Or $$r_{b^1e} = \frac{h_{fe}}{g_m} = \frac{h_{fe}\, V_T}{|I_c|}$$

or $$g_{b^1e} = \frac{g_m}{h_{fe}} \quad ...(10)$$

Hence, the over range of currents for which $h_{fe}$ remains constant, $r_{b^1e}$ is directly proportional to temperature and inversely proportional to current.

Since $g_m = \alpha_0/r_e^1$ and $h_{fe} = \alpha_0/(1 - \alpha_0)$, then $r_{b^1e}$ can be expressed in terms of the *T*-model emitter resistor $r_e^1$ as

$$r_{b^1e} = \frac{h_{fe}}{g_m} = \frac{r_e^1}{1 - \alpha_0} \quad ...(11)$$

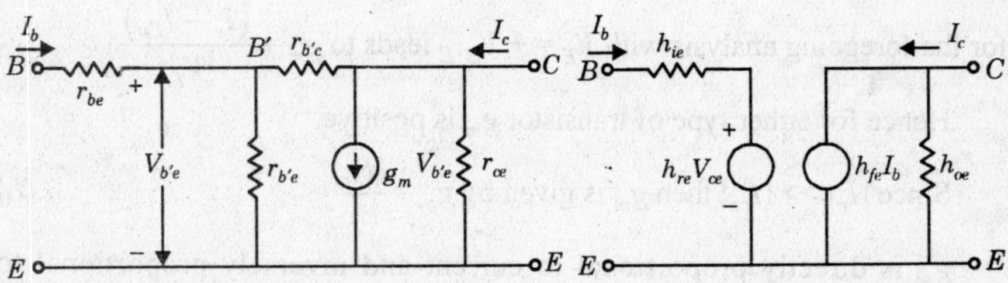


**Fig. 6.7** (a) The hybrid *pi* model at low frequency (b) The *h*-parameter model at low frequency

*3. Feedback conductance $g_{b^1c}$:* Parameter $h_{re}$ gives the reverse voltage gain with input open-circuited that is with $I_b = 0$ in the high frequency hybrid-π *CE* model of figure 6.7 (a).

Thus $$h_{re} = \frac{V_{b'e}}{V_{ce}} = \frac{r_{b'e}}{r_{b'e} + r_{b'c}} \quad \ldots(12)$$

Or $r_{b^1e}(1 - h_{re}) = h_{re} \cdot r_{b^1c}$

Since $h_{re} << 1$, then to a good approximation

$$r_{b^1e} = h_{re} \cdot r_{b^1c} \quad \ldots(13)$$

Or $$g_{b^1c} = h_{re} \cdot g_{b^1e} \quad \ldots(14)$$

But $h_{re} <<1$. Hence $r_{b^1c} >> r_{b^1e}$ or $g_{b^1c} << g_{b^1e}$. (that is since $h_{re} = 10^{-4}$ the above equation verifies that $r_{b^1c} >> r_{b^1e}$)

It is found that $h_{re}$ is quite insensitive to current and temperature. Therefore $r_{b^1e}$ has not the same dependence upon $|I_c|$ and $T$ as does $r_{b^1e}$.

*4.Base-spreading resistance $r_{bb^1}$:* Parameter hie forms the input resistance of the transistor with the output short circuited. With reference to the circuit of figure 6.7 (a), with output short-circuited, $r_{b^1c}$ is in parallel with $r_{b^1e}$.

But $r_{b^1c} >> r_{b^1e}$.

Hence $r_{b^1c} \parallel r_{b^1e} \approx r_{b^1e}$ so that the input resistance approximately equals to $r_{bb^1} + r_{b^1e}$.

Hence $$h_{ie} = r_{bb^1} + r_{b^1e}. \quad \ldots(15)$$

Or $$r_{bb^1} = h_{ie} - r_{b^1e}$$

$$= h_{ie} - \frac{h_{fe}}{g_m} \quad \ldots(16)$$

Equations above give the desired expression for $r_{bb^1}$.

*5. Output conductance $g_{ce}$:* Parameter $h_{oe}$ constitutes the output conductance with input open circuited that is with $I_b = 0$

From the ckt of figure 6.7 (a) with $I_b = 0$ we get

$$I_c = \frac{V_{ce}}{R_{ce}} + \frac{V_{ce}}{r_{b'c} + r_{b'e}} + g_m V_{b'e} \quad \ldots(17)$$

with $I_b = 0$, we have from equation (12), $V_{b^1e} = h_{re} \cdot V_{ce}$.

Substituting this value of $V_{b^1e}$ in the above equation (7) and neglecting $r_{b^1e}$ in comparison with $r_{b^1c}$, we get,

$$h_{oe} = \frac{I_c}{V_{ce}} = \frac{1}{r_{ce}} + g_m h_{re} + \frac{1}{r_{b'e}} \quad \ldots(18)$$

On substituting the values of $g_m$ and $h_{oe}$ from equations (10) and (14) and assuming that $r_{b^1c} >> r_{b^1e}$ we get,

$$h_{oe} = g_{ce} + g_{b'e} + g_{b'e}\, h_{fe} \frac{g_{b'e}}{g_{b'c}} \qquad \text{...(19)}$$

$$= g_{ce} + (1 + h_{fe})\, g_{b'c} \qquad \text{...(20)}$$

but if $h_{fe} >> 1$ , equation (20) is written as,

$$g_{ce} = h_{oe} - g_{b'c} \cdot h_{fe} \qquad \text{...(21)}$$

On using equations (10) and (13) equations (21) is written as

$$g_{ce} \approx h_{oe} - g_m\, h_{re}$$

*6. feedback conductance* $g_{b'c}$: $g_{b'c} = h_{re}\, g_{b'e}$

*7. Transition capacitance* $C_{b'c}$: $C_{b'c} = C_{ob} = 3pf$ *(constant)*

*Conclusion:* If the *CE h*-parameters at low frequencies are known at a given collector $I_c$, the conductances or resistances in the hybrid-π circuit are calculated from the following five equations in the order given.

(i) $g_m = \dfrac{|I_c|}{V_T}$

(ii) $r_{b'e} = \dfrac{h_{fe}}{g_m}$ or $g_{b'c} = \dfrac{g_m}{h_{fe}}$ (21a)

(iii) $r_{bb'} = h_{ie} - r_{b'e}$

(iv) $r_{b'c} = \dfrac{1}{g_{b'e}} = \dfrac{r_{b'e}}{h_{re}}$ or $g_{b'c} = h_{re} \cdot g_{b'e}$

(v) $g_{ce} = h_{oe} - (1 + h_{fe})\, g_{b'c} = 1/r_{ce}$.

(vi) $C_{b'c} = C_{ob}$

## *Hybrid-π Capacitances*

The collector-junction capacitance $C_c = C_{b'e}$ is the measured *CB* output capacitance with the input open that is $I_E = 0$, and is specified by the manufacturers as $C_{ob}$. Since in the active region the collector junction is reverse-biased, then $C_C$ is a transition capacitance; and hence varies as $V_{CB^{-n}}$, where n is ½ or 1/3 for an abrupt or gradual junction, respectively.

Since $C_c = C_{b'e}$ represents, principally the diffusion capacitance across the emitter junction, it is directly proportional to the current and is approximately independent of temperature

That is $C_e$ is sum of emitter junction diffusion capacitance $C_{De}$ and emitter junction transition capacitance $C_{Te}$ for forward biased emitter junction $C_{De} >> C_{Te}$.

Hence $$C_e = C_{De} + C_{Te} = C_{De} \qquad \text{...(22)}$$

Experimentally, $C_e$ is determined from a measurement of the frequency $f_T$ at which the *CE* short-circuit current gain drops to unity.

$$\therefore \qquad C_e = \frac{g_m}{2\pi f_T} \qquad \ldots(23)$$

It is proved in our previous discussion (6.2) that the diffusion capacitance $C_{De}$ is proportional to the emitter bias current $I_E$ and is almost independent of temperature $T$.

Thus from the above discussion we conclude that:

1. $g_m$ is directly proportional to the collector current and inversely proportional to the temperature.
2. Over the range of currents for which hfe remains fairly constant, $r_{b^1e}$ is directly proportional to the temperature and inversely proportional to the current.
3. As $h_{re}$ is quite insensitive to current and temperature, $r_{b^1c}$ has the same dependence upon collector current and temperature as does $r_{b^1e}$.
4. The base-spreading resistance $r_{bb^1}$ varies with current and temperature in the following manner: $r_{bb^1} = h_{ie} \dfrac{h_{fe} V_T}{|I_c|}$
5. For $h_{fe}$ >>1, the resistance $r_{ce}$ varies in the following manner.

   $$r_{ce} = \frac{1}{h_{oe} - g_m h_{re}}$$
6. The transition capacitance $C_c$ varies with the output voltage $V_{CE}$ only.
7. The diffusion capacitance $C_e$ is directly proportional to the current and is approximately independent of temperature.

### *Frequency Limit of Validity of Hybrid-π Model:*

In the derivation of Transconductance $g_m$ and diffusion capacitance $C_e$, it is assumed that $V_{BE}$ changes so slowly with time that in the base region, concentration of minority carrier holes is along straight line from $J_E$ to $J_C$ as shown in figure 3. Thus the slope of minority carrier charge distribution curve at $x = 0$ is the same at $x = W$ (that is at $J_C$) and hence the collector current $I_c$ remains equal to the emitter current $I_E$ and the base current is extremely small compared with $I_C$. Hence under dynamic condition, the hybrid-π model is valid only when the rate of change of $V_{BE}$ with time is so small that the base current increment $I_b$ is small in comparison with the collector current increment current $I_c$. Giacoletto proved that the network elements in the hybrid model of figure 6.5 are frequency invariant provided that

$$2\pi f \frac{W^2}{2D_B} << 1 \qquad \ldots(24)$$

But from previous sections $C_e$ and $C_{De}$

That is $C_e = \dfrac{g_m}{2\pi f_T}$ and $C_{De} = \dfrac{W^2}{2D_m} g_m$ as proved earlier we get,

$$\frac{W^2}{6D_B} = \frac{C_e}{3g_m} = \frac{1}{6\pi f_T} \quad ...(25)$$

Hence the equation (24) reduces to $f << \frac{6\pi f_T}{2\pi}$ or $f << 3 f_T$ ...(26)

Thus we conclude the hybrid-π model is valid for frequency up to about $f_T/3$.

### Variation of Hybrid-p Parameters:

The hybrid-π parameters vary with collector current magnitude $|I_c|$, collector -to-emitter voltage magnitude ($V_{CE}$) and temperature *T*. *Increasing* $|V_{CE}|$ *decreases the effective base width*. The decrease of $r_{bb^1}$ with $|Ic|$ is due to conductivity modulation of the base with increasing collector current. Whereas $r_{bb^1}$ increases with increasing temperature because the mobility of majority and minority carriers decreases, and this results in conductivity. The increase of $h_{fe}$ with temperature has been experimentally, *whereas the increase with* $|V_{CE}|$ *is due to the decrease of the base width and the reduction in recombination which increases the transistor alpha*. Table below gives in brief the dependence of $g_m$, $r_{b^1e}$, $c_e$ $c_c$, $h_{fe}$ and $h_{ie}$ with parameters on $|I_c|$, $|V_{CE}|$ and *T*.

Dependence Hybrid-π parameters on $|Ic|$, $|V_{CE}|$ and *T*.

**Table 6.1** Parameters variation with increasing $|Ic|$, $|V_{CE}|$ and *T*.

| *S.No* | *Parameter* | $|Ic|$ | *VCE\|* | *T* |
|---|---|---|---|---|
| 1 | $G_m$ | As $|I_C|$ | independent | as 1/T |
| 2 | $r_{b^1e}$ | $1/|I_c|$ | increases | increases |
| 3 | $r_{bb^1}$ | decreases | complicated | increases |
| 4 | $c_e$ | as $|I_c|$ | decreases | complicated |
| 5 | $c_c$ | independent | decreases | independen |
| 6 | $h_{fe}$ | complicated | increases | increases |
| 7 | $h_{ie}$ | $1/|I_c|$ | increases | increases |

The word complicated in table implies that the relevant parameter varies with $|I_c|$, $|V_{CE}|$ and *T* in a complicated manner.

## 6.6 SIMPLIFIED MODEL

## Short Circuit Analysis of BJT

In this we mainly deal with the current gain under short circuit and loaded conditions. Also, about the transistor amplifier response taking source resistance into account by considering the hybrid π model of the transistor at high frequencies.

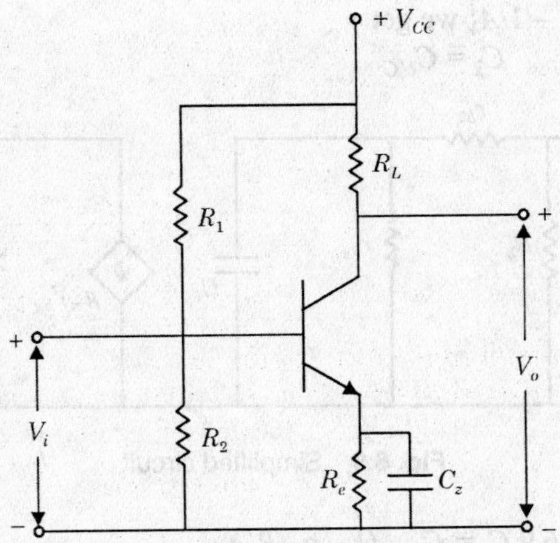


(a) Single stage *CE* amplifier

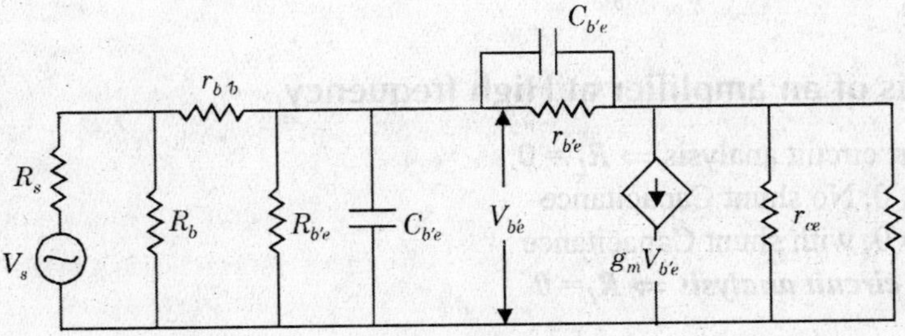


(b) Hybrid-π Equivalent circuit

**Fig. 6.8** Single stage *CE* amplifier and its hybrid-π equivalent circuit

1. $r_{b'c} = 4\text{M}\Omega$ (unconditionally open circuited)
2. $r_{ce} = 80\text{K}\Omega$

$$r_{ce} >> R_L' \qquad \therefore r_{ce} \text{ is conditionally open circuited.}$$

$$A_V = \frac{h_{fe}}{h_{ie}} R_L^1$$

If $R_L$ increases then $A_V$ increases and also bandwidth decreases.
But we want large bandwidth. So $R_L$ should decrease.

3. $C_{b'c}$ is drawn at input and output using Millers theorem.

$$Z_1 = \frac{R}{1 - A_V'}$$

$$\frac{1}{j\omega C_1} = \frac{1/j\omega C_{b'c}}{1 - A_V'}$$

$$C_1 = C_{b'c}(1 - A_V) = C_{b'c}\left\{1 + g_m R_L^1\right\}$$

$$C_2 = C_{b'c}\left(1 - 1/A_V^1\right)$$

Neglecting $1 - 1/A_V^1$ we get

$$C_2 = C_{b'C}.$$

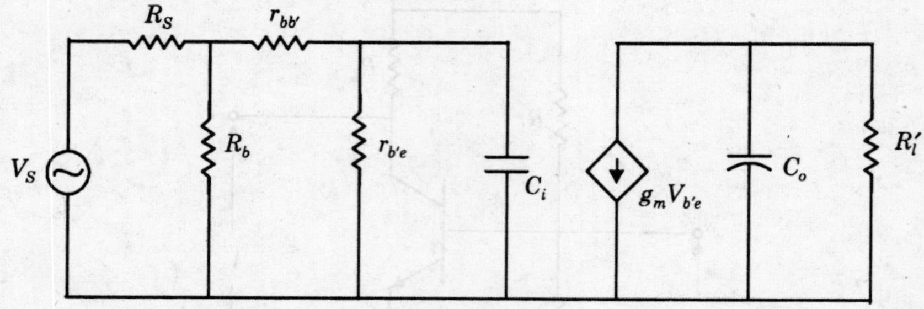


Fig. 6.9 Simplified circuit

In the figure 6.9 $C_i = C_{b^1e}\ (1 - g_m R_L')$

and $C_0 = C_{b^1c}$

## Analysis of an amplifier at High frequency

1. Short circuit analysis $\Rightarrow R_L = 0$
2. $R_L \neq 0$, No shunt Capacitance
3. $R_L \neq 0$, with shunt Capacitance

***1. Short circuit analysis $\Rightarrow R_L = 0$***

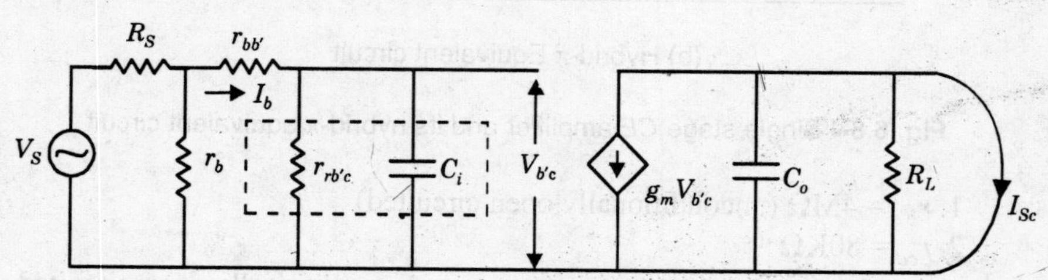


Fig: 6.10(a)

$$I_{sc} = -g_m V_{b^1e}$$

$$V_{b^1e} = \{V\} I_b$$

$$\therefore \quad A_{Isc} = \frac{I_{sc}}{I_b} = -g_m Z$$

$$Z = r_{b^1e} \parallel \frac{1}{jwC_i} = \frac{r_{b^1e}}{1 + jwr_{b^1e} C_i}$$

$$\therefore \quad A_{Isc} = \frac{-g_m r_{b^1e}}{1 + jwr_{b^1e} C_i}$$

$$= \frac{-h_{fe}}{1 + j\left(\frac{f}{f_\beta}\right)}, \text{ where } f_\beta = \frac{1}{2\pi r_{b'e} C_i} = \frac{1}{2\pi r_{b'e}\left(C_{b'e} + r_{b'c}\right)}$$

$$|A_{ISC}| = \frac{h_{fe}}{\sqrt{1 + \left(\frac{f}{f_b}\right)^2}}, f << f_\beta$$

From above figure $f_\beta$ = short circuit upper cut off frequency of *CE* amplifier

$f_\tau$ = gain band width product of short circuit *CE* amplifier.

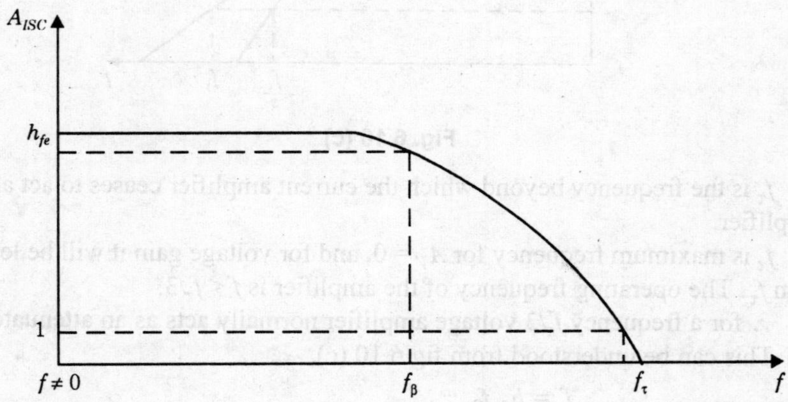


**Fig. 6.10(b)**

At $\quad f = f_\tau, A_{Isc} = 1$

$\therefore$
$$1 = \frac{h_{fe}}{\sqrt{1 + \left(\frac{f}{f_b}\right)^2}}$$

Since $\quad f_\tau >> f_\beta$

$$\frac{f_\tau}{f_\beta} >> 1$$

$\therefore \quad f_\tau = h_{fe} f_\beta$

$f_\beta$ is short circuited for the upper cut off frequency in *CE* configuration.
When short circuited $A_I \neq 0$ and $A_V = 0$
$f_\alpha$ is short circuited for the upper cut off frequency in *CB* configuration.

$$f_\alpha = \frac{f_\beta}{1-\alpha_0}$$

$$\alpha_0 = \frac{h_{fe}}{1+h_{fe}} \cong 1$$

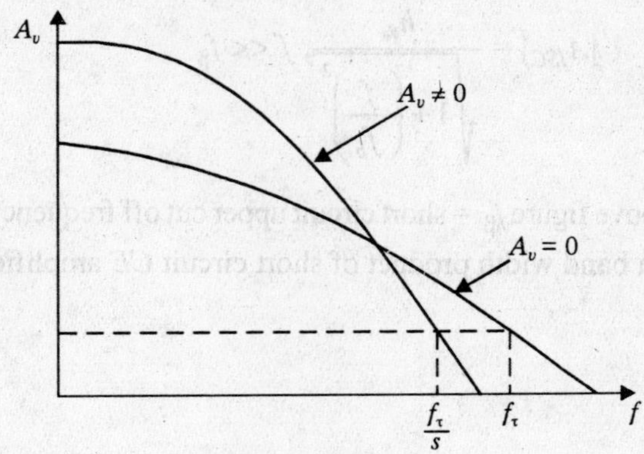


**Fig. 6.10 (c)**

$f_\tau$ is the frequency beyond which the current amplifier ceases to act as an amplifier.

$f_\tau$ is maximum frequency for $A_V = 0$, and for voltage gain it will be lesser than $f_\tau$. The operating frequency of the amplifier is $f < f_\tau/3$.

$\therefore$ for a frequency $f_\tau/3$ voltage amplifier normally acts as an attenuator.

This can be understood from fig 6.10 (c).

$$f_\tau = h_{fe} f_\beta$$

$f_\tau$ is the gain bandwidth product of short circuit amplifier.

At high frequencies $C_c$ and $C_e$ acts as short circuit.

Gain band width product of a short circuit amplifier is always constant as they depend on internal parameters.

***2. $R_L \neq 0$, No shunt capacitor:***

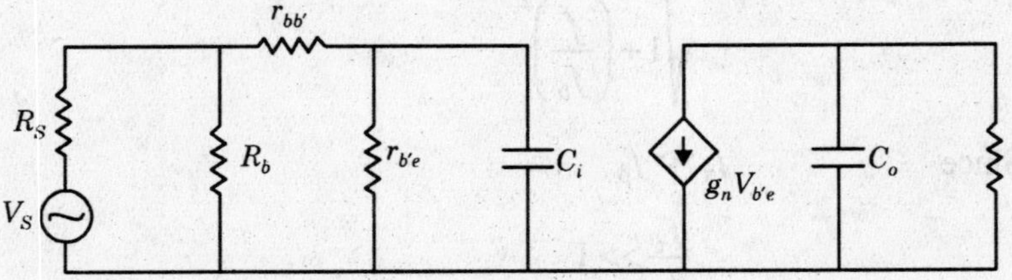


**Fig. 6.11 (c)**

$$f_2 = \frac{1}{2\pi\tau}.$$

$$\tau_{20} = R_L C_0$$

$$= 2 \times 10^3 \times 3 \times 10^{-2} = 6 \text{ ns.}$$

$$\tau_{21} = \{R_s // R_b + R_{bb'}\}$$
$$= 1 \times 10^3 \{100 \times 10^{-12} + 3 \times 10^{-12} (1 + 50 \times 10^{-3} \times 2 \times 10^{-3})$$
$$= 403 \times 10^{-9} = 403 \text{ ns.}$$

at high frequency the lowest cut off frequency dominates *i.e.* the highest time constant dominates.

***3. $R_L \neq 0$, with shunt capacitance:***

$$\tau_{20} = R_L \{C_C + C_{sh}\} = 2 \times 10^3 \times 100 \times 10^{-12}$$
$$= 2 \times 10^{-6} = 200 \text{ ns}$$
$$\tau_{2i} = 403 \text{ ns}$$
$$\tau_{20} >> \tau_{2i}$$
$$f_Q = \frac{1}{2\pi R_L \{C_c + C_{sh}\}}$$
$$C_C << C_{sh} \text{ so } C_c \text{ is neglected.}$$

$\therefore$ By changing $C_{sh}$ without changing $R_L$, we can change bandwidth without varying (effecting) the gain.

## 6.7 GAIN BAND WIDTH PRODUCT OF AN AMPLIFIER

Gain-band width product is given by for the voltage gain as it is the product of the low frequency voltage gain $A_{vs}$ and the 3-dB frequency $f_H$.

Assume $R_b$ is tending to $\propto$

$$C = C_{b'e} + C_{b'c} (1 + g_m R_L)$$

$$A_{VS_o} = A_V \left[\frac{R_i}{R_i + R_s}\right] = \left(\frac{A_I R_L}{R_i}\right)\left(\frac{R_i}{R_i + R_s}\right)$$
$$= \frac{-h_{fe} R_L}{h_{ie} + R_s} (\text{as } R_i = h_{ie})$$

$$f_H = f_{2i} = \frac{1}{2\pi R_i C_i}$$

$f_H = f_{2i}$ when $C_{sh}$ is not considerd.

$$R_i = \{(R_s \backslash\backslash R_b) + r_{bb'}\} // r_{b'e} = \frac{(R_s + r_{bb'})\, r_{b'e}}{R_s + r_{bb'} + r_{b'e}} = \frac{(R_s + r_{bb'})\, r_{b'e}}{R_s + h_{ie}}$$

$$A_{VS0} f_h = \left\{\frac{-h_{fe} R_L}{h_{ie} + R_s}\right\} \left[\frac{1}{2\pi \left(\dfrac{R_s + r_{bb'}}{R_s + h_{ie}}\right) r_{b'e}\, C}\right]$$

$$|A_{VSO} f_h| = \left\{\frac{-h_{fe} R_L}{2\pi (R_s + r_{bb'}) r_{b'e} C}\right\} = \frac{g_m R_L}{2\pi C (R_s + r_{bb'})}\left(\frac{h_{fe}}{r_{b'e}} = g_m\right)$$

$$|A_{VSO} f_h| = \frac{g_m}{2\pi \{C_{b'e} + C_{b'c}(1 + g_m R_L)\}}\left\{\frac{R_L}{R_s + r_{bb'}}\right\}$$

$$\frac{g_m}{2\pi C} = \frac{g_m}{2\pi \{C_{b'e} + C_c(1 + g_m R_L)\}} = \frac{g_m}{2\pi \left\{C_e + C_c\left(1 + \frac{g_m R_L C_c}{C_e + C_c}\right)\right\}}$$

where $f_\tau = \dfrac{g_m}{2\pi (C_e + C_c)}$ and $\dfrac{g_m}{C_e + C_c} = 2\pi f_\tau$

$$\frac{g_m}{2\pi C} = \frac{f_\tau}{1 + 2\pi f_\tau R_L C_c}$$

$$A_{VSO} f_h = \frac{f_\tau}{1 + 2\pi f_\tau C_c R_L}\left(\frac{R_L}{R_s + r_{bb'}}\right)$$

If $(2\pi f_\tau C_c R_L) >>$ then the gain bandwidth product is constant.

Similarly for current gain it is the product of the low frequency current gain $A_{Is}$ and the 3-dB frequency $f_h$. It is given as,

$$|A_{Is} . f_H| = \frac{g_m R_s}{2\pi c (R_s + r_{bb'})} = \frac{f_T R_s}{(1 + 2\pi f_T c_c R_L)(R_s + r_{bb'})}$$

It is seen the low frequency current gain $A_{Is}$ is a function of $R_s$ while the 3-dB frequency $f_H$ is a function of both $R_L$ and $R_s$. The 3-dB frequency $f_H$ for current gain has the same value as for the voltage gain and this $f_H$ reduces with the increase of either $R_L$ or $R_s$. The current gain $A_{Is}$ reduces as $R_s$ increases.

As a result, the current gain band-width product decreases with the increase of $R_L$ and also with the increase of $R_s$.

Let us show that $f_{20} < f_{2i} < f_\beta < f_\alpha < f_\tau$

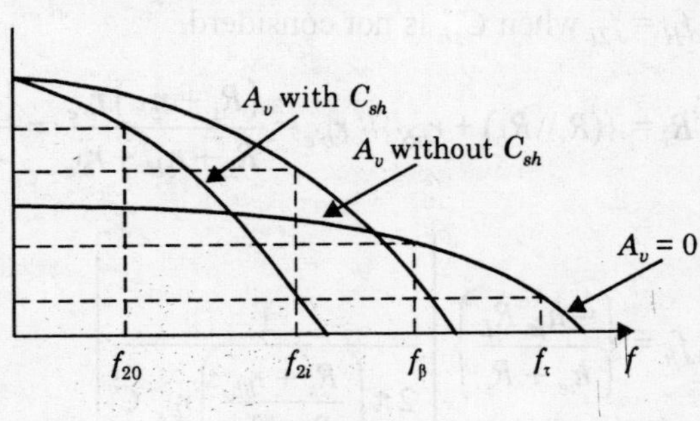


Fig. 6.12

Let us show the value of $C_{sh}$ for output time constant $\tau_{20}$ to dominate.

$$f_{20} \leq \frac{f_{2i}}{4}$$

$$\frac{1}{2\pi\tau_{20}} = \frac{1}{4}\frac{1}{2\pi\tau_i}$$

$$\tau_{20} \leq 4\tau_{2i}$$

$$R_L\,(C + C_{sh}) \geq 4 \times 403 \times 10^{-9}$$

$$C + C_{sh} \geq 806 \text{ pf}$$

$$C_c = 3 \text{ pf}$$

So $\quad C_{sh} \geq 803$ pf.

## 6.8 SOLVED PROBLEMS

**1. The following low frequency parameters are known for a given transistor at $I_c = 10$ mA, $V_{CE} = 10$ V and at room temperature $h_{ie} = 500\ \Omega$, $h_{oe} = 4 \times 10^{-5}$A/V, $h_{fe} = 100$, $h_{re} = 10^{-4}$. At the same operating point $f_T$ = 50 MHz, and $C_0$ = 3 PF, compute the values of all the hybrid-π parameters.**

**Solution:**

Given $I_c = 10$ mA, $V_{CE} = 10$ V, $h_{ie} = 500\ \Omega$, $h_{oe} = 4 \times 10^{-5}$ A/V, $h_{fe} = 100$, $h_{re} = 10^{-4}$, $f_T = 50$ MHz, $C_0$ = 3 PF, at room temparature $V_T = 26$ mV

1. $g_m = \dfrac{I_C}{V_T} = \dfrac{10}{26} = 385$ mA/V = 0.38 A/V

2. $g_{b^1e} = \dfrac{g_m}{h_{fe}} = \dfrac{0.38}{100} = 3.84 \times 10^{-3} \Rightarrow V_{b^1e} = 260\ \Omega$

3. $g_{b^1e} = g_{b^1e}\,h_{re} = (3.84 \times 10^{-3})10^{-4} = 0.384 \times 10^{-6} \Rightarrow r_{b'c} = 26$ MΩ

4. $r_{b^1b} = h_{ie} - V_{b^1e} = 500 - 260 = 240\ \Omega$

5. $g_{ee} = h_{oe} - (1 + h_{fe})\,g_{b^1c} = 1.2 \times 10^{-6}$

6. $C_{b^1e} = \dfrac{g_m}{2\pi f_T} = \dfrac{0.38}{2\pi\left(50 \times 10^6\right)} = 1209.5$ PF; $r_{ce} = 822.3$ KΩ

**2. The following transistor measurements made at $I_C = 5$ mA, $V_{CE} = 10$ V, and at room temperature $h_{fe} = 100$, $h_{ie} = 600\ \Omega$, $|A_{ie}| = 10$ at 10 MHz, $C_c = 3$ PF find, $f_\beta$, $f_T$, $C_e$, $r_{b^1e}$ and $r_{bb^1}$.**

**Solution:**

Given $I_C = 5$ mA, $V_{CE} = 10$ V, $h_{fe} = 100$, $h_{ie} = 600\ \Omega$ $|A_{ie}| = 10$ at 10 MHz, $C_c = 3$ pF.

1. $|A_{ie}| = \dfrac{-h_{fe}}{\left[1+\left(\dfrac{f}{f_B}\right)^2\right]^{1/2}} \Rightarrow 10 = \dfrac{-100}{\sqrt{1+\left(\dfrac{10\times10^6}{f_B}\right)^2}} \Rightarrow f_B = 1.01 \text{ MHz}$

2. $f_T = h_{fe} \cdot f_B = 100\,(1.01 \times 10^6) = 101 \text{ MHz}$

3. $C_e = C_{b^1e} = \dfrac{g_m}{2\pi f_T} = \dfrac{0.19}{2\pi\left(101\times10^6\right)} = 299.4 \text{ PF}, g_m = \dfrac{I_C}{V_T} = \dfrac{5}{26} = 0.19$

4. $r_{b^1e} = \dfrac{h_{fe}}{g_m} = \dfrac{100}{0.19} = 520\ \Omega$

5. $r_{bb^1} = h_{fe} - r_{b^1e} = 600 - 520 = 80\ \Omega$

3. Given Ge *p-n-p* Transistor $W_B = 10^{-4}$ cm, $I_E = 2$ mA at room temperature, $D_B = D_P = 47$ Find $C_{DE}, f_T$.

**Solution.**

(a) $C_{DE} = \dfrac{I_E}{V_T} \cdot \dfrac{W_B^2}{2D_B} = \dfrac{2\times10^{-3}\left(10^{-4}\right)^2}{26\times10^{-3}\,2(47)} = 8.18 \text{ PF}$

(b) $F_T = \dfrac{g_m}{2\pi C_b^1 e} = \dfrac{\dfrac{I_E}{V_T}}{2\pi C_{be}^1} = 1.5 \text{ GHz}$

**4. Given a single stage $C_E$ transistor amplifier with $R_L$ shunted by $C_L$**

**(a) Prove $K = \dfrac{V_{ce}}{V_{be}} = \dfrac{-g_m R_L}{1+JW(C_C+C_L)R_L}$**

**(b) $f_H = \dfrac{1}{2\pi(C_C+C_L)R_L}$ given internal voltage gain $K = \dfrac{V_{ce}}{V_{b^1e}}$**

**Solution**

(a) $A_{vh} = \dfrac{A_{vm}}{1+J\left(\dfrac{f}{f_2}\right)}$ ...(1)

(b) $F_H = \dfrac{1}{2\pi(C_c+C_L)R_L}$ provided the given condition is satisfied $g_{b^1e}$

$g_{b'e} R_L\,(C_c + C_L) >> C_e + C_C\,(g_m R_L)$

$\Rightarrow R_L\,(C_C + C_L) >> r_{b^1e}\,(C_e + C_C\,(1 + g_m R_L)) \Rightarrow \tau_2 >> r_{b^1e}\,(C_e + C_c\,(1 + g_m R_L)) \Rightarrow f_{20}$ is lesser. For upper cut off frequency the lower frequency is dominated.

$$F_{20} = \frac{1}{2\pi\,\tau_{20}} \quad \text{where } \tau_{20} = (R_L\,(C_c + C_L))$$

$$\therefore \qquad f_2 = f_{20} = \frac{1}{2\pi R_L\,(C_C + C_L)}$$

From (1) $$A_{Vh} = \frac{A_{vm}}{1 + J2\pi\,(C_C + C_L)\,R_L} = \frac{A_{vm}}{1 + J\omega\,(C_c + C_L)\,RL}$$

**5. Given a single stage $C_E$ transistor amplifier $g_m = 50$ mA/V, $r_{bb^1} = 100$ Ω, $r_{b^1e} = 1$ kΩ, $r_{b^1c} = 4$ MΩ, $r_{ce} = 80$ K. $C_C = 3$ PF. What value of source resistance $R_S$ will give a 3 *dB* frequency $f_2$ which is (a) half the value for $R_s = 0$ (b) Twice the value for $R_s = \alpha$, $R_s$ depend upon $R_L$.**

**Solution:**

(a) $f_2 = \frac{1}{2} f_{20}$ (b) $f_2 = 2f_{20}$'

for $$R_s = 0 \Rightarrow f_{20} = \frac{1}{2\pi\left(\frac{r_{bb^1}\,r_{b^1e}}{r_{bb^1} + r_{b^1e}}\right)C}$$

$$f_2 = f_{2i} = \frac{1}{2\pi R_i C_i} = \frac{1}{2\pi\left(\frac{(r_{bb^1}\,r_{b^1e})\,r_{b^1e}}{R_s + r_{bb^1} + r_{b^1e}}\right)\{C_e\,(C_C\,(1 + gmR_L))\}}$$

$$\Rightarrow \qquad f_{20} = \frac{1}{2\pi r^1_{bc} C}$$

(b) $$f_2 = \frac{1}{2} f_{20} \Rightarrow \frac{1}{2\pi\left(\frac{(R_s + r_{b^1e})\,r_{b^1e}}{R_s + r_{bb^1} + r_{b^1e}}\right)C} = \frac{1}{2}\,\frac{1}{2\pi\left(\frac{r_{bb^1}\,r_{b^1e}}{r_{bb^1} + r_{b^1e}}\right)C}$$

$$\Rightarrow \qquad R_s = 122\ \Omega$$

(c) $$f_2 = 2f_{2\alpha} \Rightarrow \frac{1}{2\pi\left(\frac{(R_s + r_{b^1e})\,r_{b^1e}}{R_s + r_{bb^1} + r_{b^1e}}\right)c} = 2\,\frac{1}{2\pi r_{b'e} C} \Rightarrow R_s = 900\ \Omega$$

(d) $R_s$ does not depend on $R_L$

**6. Given Ge *p-n-p* transistor whose base width $W_B = 5 \times 10^{-4}$ cm At room temperature $I_E = 2$ mA Find (a) $R_e$ (b) $f_\alpha$ (c) $C_{D^1E}$ (d) Base transistor Time, given $D_p = D_B = 47$**

**Solution:**

(a) $r_e^1 = \frac{V_T}{I_E} = \frac{26}{2} = 13\ \Omega$

(b) $f_\alpha = \frac{g_m}{2\pi\left(C_{D^1E} + C_{b^1c}\right)} \cong \frac{I_E/V_T}{2\pi\left(C_{D^1E}\right)} = \frac{2/26}{2\pi\left(204.6\times10^{-12}\right)} = 59.84$ MHz

$$f_\alpha = \frac{2D_B}{W^2(2\pi)} = \frac{2(47)}{\left(5\times10^{-4}\right)^2 2\pi} = 59.8 \text{ MHz}$$

(c) $C_{DE}^1 = \frac{I_E}{V_T}\left(\frac{W_B^2}{2D_B}\right) = \frac{2\times10^{-3}}{26\times10^{-3}}\frac{\left(5\times10^{-4}\right)^2}{2(47)} = 204.6$ PF

(d) Base transition Time $t_B = \frac{1}{W_\alpha}$, $Q_B = \frac{IW^2}{2D_B}$ and $I = \frac{Q_B}{t_B} = \frac{IW^2}{2D_B t_B}$

$$t_B = \frac{W^2}{2D_B} = \frac{\left(5\times10^{-4}\right)^2}{2(47)} = 2.65 \text{ n sec}$$

**7. Single stage $C_E$ amplifier $f_H = 5$ MHz., $R_L = 500\ \Omega$, $h_{fe} = 100$, $g_m = 100$ mA/V · $r_{bb}^1 = 100\ \Omega$, $C_C = 1$ PF and $f_T = 400$ MHz. Find the value of source resistance $R_S$, midband voltage gain $V_0/V_s$**

**Solution:**

$$f_H = \frac{1}{2\pi RC} \quad C = C_e + C_C(1 + g_m R_L) \quad C_e = \frac{g_m}{2\pi f T} = 0.0405\times10^{-9}$$

$$R = \frac{1}{2\pi f_H C} \quad C = 0.0405\times10^{-9} + 1\text{PF}\{1 + 100\times10^{-3}(500)\} = 91\text{PF}$$

$$R = \frac{1}{2\pi\, 5\times10^6\times91\times10^{-12}} = 350\Omega$$

$$R = \frac{R_s^1\, r_{b'e}}{R_S^1 + r_{be}^1},\ r_{be}^1 = \frac{h_{fe}}{g_m} = \frac{100}{100\times10^{-3}} = 1\text{K where } R_s^1 = R_s + r_{bb1}$$

$0.35\text{ K} = R_s // r_{be}^1 \Rightarrow R_S = 0.539\text{ K}\Omega$,

$R_s = R_s^1 - R_{bb}^1 = 539\ \Omega - 100 = 439\ \Omega$

$A_{VS} = \frac{V_0}{V_s} = \frac{-g_m R_L G_s^1}{G_s^1 + g_b^1 e + Sc}$, $S = j\omega$ For mid band gain $w = 0$ $\therefore S = 0$

$$A_{VS} = \frac{V_0}{V_s} = \frac{-g_m R_L G_s^1}{G_s^1 + g_b^1 e} = -32.5, G_S^1 = \frac{1}{R_s^1},$$

$$g_b^1 e = \frac{1}{V_s^1 e} = 1.85 \times 10^{-3} = 10^{-3}.$$

**8. Given a germanium *p-n-p* transistor whose base width is $10^{-6}$ cm. at room temperature and for a *dc* emitter current of 4 mA, find a) the emitter diffusion capacitance b) $f_T$**

**Solution:**

Given Ge *p-n-p* transistor $W_B = 10^{-6}$ cm

$I_E = 4$ mA at room temperature $D_B - D_P = 47$,

(a) $$C_{DE} = \frac{I_E}{V_T} \frac{W_B^2}{2D_B}$$

$$= \frac{4 \times 10^{-3}}{26 \times 10^{-3}} \frac{10^{-6}}{2(47)} = 0.0016$$

(b) $$f_T = \frac{g_m}{2\pi C_{b'e}} \frac{\frac{I_E}{V_T}}{2\pi\, C_{b'e}}$$

$$= \frac{\frac{4 \times 10^{-3}}{26 \times 10^{-3}}}{2\pi \times 0.0016 \times 10^{-12}} = 1.526 \times 10^3$$

$\therefore$ $f_T = 15298$G Hz

## 6.9 OBJECTIVE TYPE QUESTIONS

1. α-cut off frequency of a bipolar junction transistor
   (a) increases with the increase in base width
   (b) increases with the increases in emitter width
   (c) increases with the increase in the collector width
   (d) increases with the decrease in the base width
   **Ans:** (d)
2. The common-emitter short-circuit current gain β of a transistor
   (a) is a monotonically increasing function of the collector current $I_C$
   (b) is a monotonically decreasing function of $I_C$
   (c) increases width $I_C$ for low $I_C$, reaches a maximum, and then decreases with further increase in $I_C$
   (d) is not a function of $I_C$
   **Ans:** (c)

**3.** An *NPN* transistor has a beta cut-off frequency $f_\beta$ of 1 MHz, and common-emitter short-circuit low- frequency current gain $\beta_0$ of 200. Its unity-gain frequency β and the alpha cut-off frequency $f_\alpha$ respectively are

(a) 200 MHz, 201 MHz (b) 200MHz, 199 MHz
(c) 199MHz, 200MHz (d) 201MHz, 200MHz

**Ans:** (a)

**4.** The $f_T$ of a BJT is related to its gm, $c_\pi$ and $c_\mu$ as follows:

(a) $f_T = (c_\pi + c_\mu)/g_m$ (b) $f_T = 2\pi\,(c_\pi + c_\mu)/g_m$
(c) $f_T = g_m/(c_\pi + c_\mu)$ (d) $f_T = g_m/[2\pi\,(c_\pi + c_\mu)]$

**5.** An *NPN* transistor (with $c_\mu = 0.3$ pF) has a unity-gain cut off frequency $f_T$ of 400 MHz at a *dc* bias current $I_C = 1$ mA. The value of its $c_\pi$ (in pF) is approximately ($V_T = 26$ mv)

(a) 15 (b) 30
(c) 50 (d) 96

**Ans:** (a)

**6.** The current gain of a bipolar junction transistor drops at high frequencies because of

(a) Transistor capacitance (b) high current effects in thebase
(c) Parasitic inductive elements (d) the early effect.

**Ans:** (a)

**7.** The upper 3 dB frequency in a common emitter amplifier is given in terms of the hybrid parameters as

(a) $g_{b'e}/2\,\Pi c$ (b) $g_{b'e}/c$
(c) $h_{fe}/g_{b'e}$ (d) $g_m/h_{fe}$

**Ans:** (a)

**8.** The transfer function of an amplifier is given by:

$$A_V = \frac{V_o}{V_s} = \frac{2810}{\left(1 + j\dfrac{f}{5.85 \times 10^5}\right)\left(1 + j\dfrac{f}{5.85 \times 10^6}\right)}$$ The high 3-dB frequency of the amplifier will be approximately

(a) 5850kHz (b) 585kHz
(c) 5850Hz (d) 585Hz

**Ans:** (a)

**9.** If $R_s$ is the source resistance, the output resistance of an emitter follower using the simplified hybrid model would be

(a) $\dfrac{h_{ie} + R_s}{1 + h_{fe}}$ (b) $\dfrac{h_{ie} + R_s}{h_{fe}}$

(c) $R_s + \dfrac{1}{h_{oe}}$ (d) $\dfrac{1}{h_{oe}}$

**Ans:** (a)

**10.** In the high frequency hybrid-π model of a *CE* transistor, typical value of $C_C$ is

(a) 3 PF (b) 100 PF
(c) 1000 PF (d) 0.01 μF

**Ans:** (a)

**11.** In the high frequency hybrid-π model of a *CE* transistor, capacitor $C_e$ accounts for:

(a) excess minority carrier storage in the base region
(b) collector junction barrier capacitance
(c) emitter junction barrier capacitance
(d) collector junction diffusion capacitance

**Ans:** A

**12.** Parameter $f_T$ of a transistor is the frequency at which the magnitude of *CE* short circuit current gain is

(a) Half the midband gain (b) $1/\sqrt{2}$ of the midband gain
(c) One-tenth of midband gain (d) unity

**Ans:** (b)

**13.** As the temperature of a transistor increases, the base spreading resistance *rbb'* in the hybrid-π model at high frequencies

(a) Increases, because the concentration of the current-carrier in the base region increases.
(b) Increases, because the mobility of the carrier reduces.
(c) Decreases, because the base-width reduces.
(d) Decreases, because the base-width increases.

**Ans:** (b)

**14.** The gain-band width of an amplifier is

(a) Always constant (b) always variable
(c) None of these

**Ans:** (a)

**15.** High frequency response of an amplifier can be determined from

(a) *h*-parameter model of the amplifier
(b) hybrid-*T* model
(c) hybrid-π model
(d) none of these

**Ans:** (c)

**16.** The *CE* short circuit current gain ($h_{fe}$) can be expressed in terms of *CB* short circuit current gain ($h_{fb}$) as

(a) $h_{fe} = -h_{fb}$ (b) $h_{fe} = -\left(\dfrac{1+h_{fb}}{h_{fb}}\right)$

(c) $h_{fe} = -\dfrac{h_{fb}}{1+h_{fb}}$ (d) none

**Ans:** (c)

**17.** The small signal short circuit current gain is defined with reference to

(a) *CE*-configuration (b) *CB*-configuration

(c) *CC*-configuration (d) high frequency response only

**Ans:** (a)

**18.** In the high frequency hybrid-π model of a *CE* transistor, the conductance $g_{b'e}$ equals:

(a) $h_{fe}/g_m$ (b) $g_m/h_{fe}$

(c) $g_m/h_{ie}$ (d) $h_{ie}/g_m$

**Ans:** (b)

**19.** In the high frequency hybrid-π model of a *CE* transistor, the conductance $g_{b'c}$ equals:

(a) $h_{re}\, g_{b'e}$ (b) $h_{fe}\, g_{b'e}$

(c) $g_{b'e} + 1/r_{bb'}$ (d) $g_{b'e}/h_{re}$

**Ans:** (a)

**20.** In the high frequency hybrid-π model of a *CE* transistor, the conductance $g_{ce}$ equal to

(a) $h_{ie} - g_m h_{re}$ (b) $g_{b'e} - g_m h_{re}$

(c) $h_{oe} - g_m h_{re}$ (d) $g_m h_{re}$

**Ans:** (c)

**21.** The frequency $f_\beta$ at which the short circuit current gain of a *CE* amplifier falls to $1/\sqrt{2}$ of its low frequency value, is equal to:

(a) $g_{b'e}/2\pi\,(C_c + C_e)$ (b) $g_{be}1\,/(C_c + C_e)$

(c) $\frac{g_m}{h_{fe}} \cdot \frac{1}{Cc} + Ce$ (d) $(C_c + C_e)/g_{be'}$

**Ans:** (a)

**22.** Parameter $f_T$ of a transistor is approximately given by

(a) $g_m/C_e$ (b) $gm/2\pi\, C_e$

(c) $2\pi C_e/g_m$ (d) $h_{fe}/f_\beta$

**Ans:** (b)

**23.** As the collector current $I_c$ increases, the value of $f_T$:

(a) remains constant

(b) decreases

(c) increases, reaches a maximum and then falls

(d) decreases, reaches a minimum and then rises

**Ans:** (d)

**24.** The upper 3-db frequency of *CE* amplifier equals:

(a) $g_{b'e}/2\pi C$ (b) $g_{be}/C$

(c) $h_{fe}/g_{be'}$ (d) $g_m/h_{fe}$

where *C* is the total effective shunt capacitance of the input circuit

**Ans:** (a)

**25.** The most sought after specifications for the transistor in the high frequency applications are the $f_T$ and junction capacitances.

## 6.10 CONVENTIONAL QUESTIONS

1. Draw hybrid π-model for a transistor in the *CE* configuration. Define various parameters.
2. Write the following hybrid-π conductance's in terms of *h*-parameters.
   (i) Transistor Transconducatance:
   (ii) Input conductance $g_{b^1e}$:
   (iii) Feedback conductance $g_{b^1c}$:
   (iv) Base-spreading resistance $r_{bb^1}$:
   (v) Output conductance $g_{ce}$:
3. Explain about Beta cut of frequency.
4. What is figure of merit $f_t$?
5. Write a short notes on short circuit analysis of BJT.
6. What happens in gain band width product of an amplifier if increase of $R_L$ and also with the increase of $R_s$?
7. Derive the expression for *CE* short circuit emitter gain $A_i$ as a function of frequency.
8. What is the order of magnitude of each resistsnce in the hybrid π-model?
9. Draw the circuit diagram of a Single stage CE amplifier and its hybrid-π equivalent circuit.

## 6.11 EXERCISE PROBLEMS

1. The transistor shown in figure below has α = 0.98 and a base current of 30 μA. Find $I_{CQ}$ and $I_{EQ}$ if leakage current is negligible. **Ans:** 1.50 mA

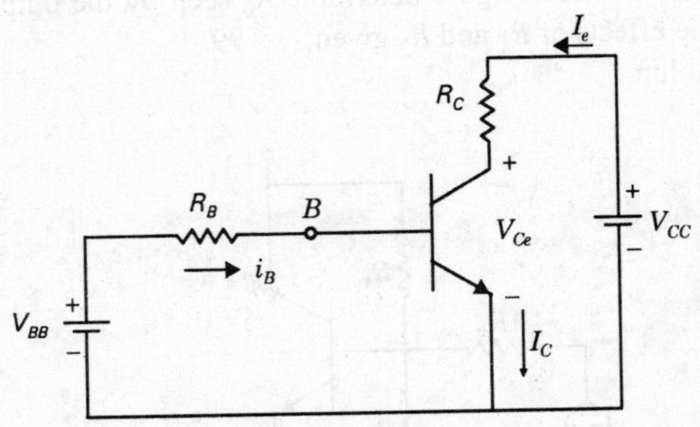


**Fig. 6p1**

2. In the *CE* amplifier shown, has a forward current gain of 100 and $V_{BE}$= 0.6 V. Assume $I_{CO}$ to be negligible. Choose values of $R_1$ and $R_3$ such that the transistor has a collector current of 1 mA and collector to emitter voltage of 2.5 V.

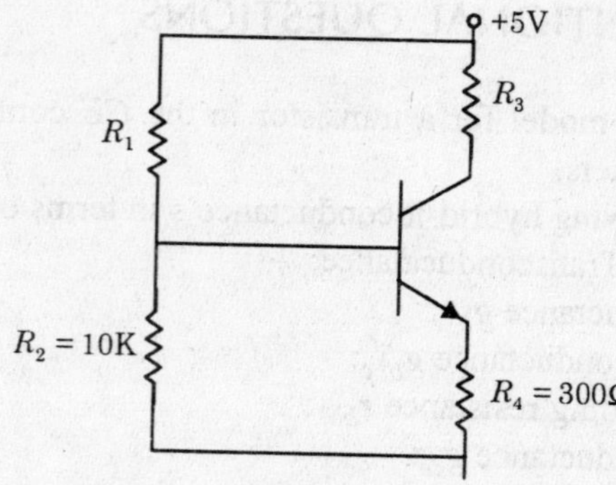


**Fig. 6p2**

**Ans:** $R_1 = 40.85$ K and $R_3 = 2197$ ohm

**3.** A *CE* amplifier with $C_C$ connected across the base and the collector, given $g_m = 5$ mA/V $r_\pi =$ 20 k ohm, $C_\pi = 1.5$ pF and $C_\mu =$ 0.5 pF

(a) determine *AC* small signal mud-band voltage gain $\dfrac{V_0}{V_s}$

(b) Upper cut off frequency $f_H$ of the amplifier.

**Ans:** (a) – 33.33 (b) 459 kH.

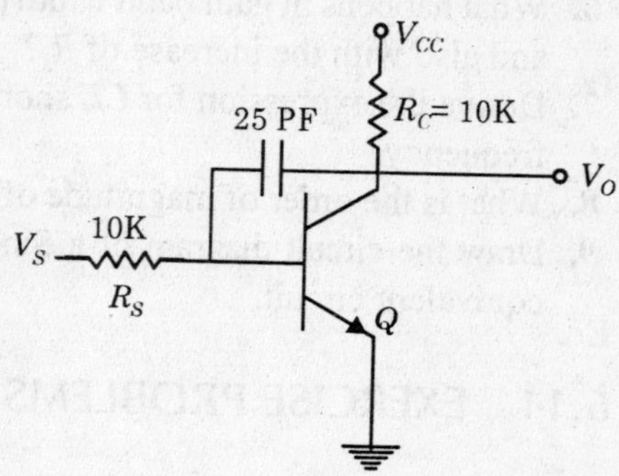


**Fig. 6p3**

**4.** The circuit shown in figure determine $R_0$ seen by the output terminals. Ignore the effects of $R_1$ and $R_2$ given = 99.

**Ans:** 20 ohm

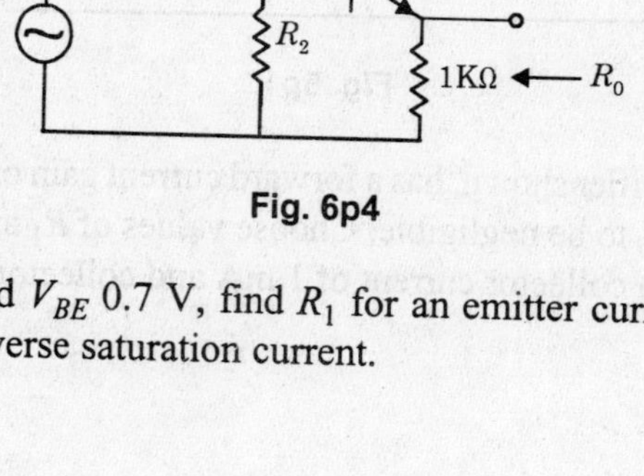


**Fig. 6p4**

**5.** If $\alpha = 0.98$ and $V_{BE}$ 0.7 V, find $R_1$ for an emitter current $I_E = -\,2$ mA. Neglect the reverse saturation current.

**Ans:** $R_1 = 52$ K

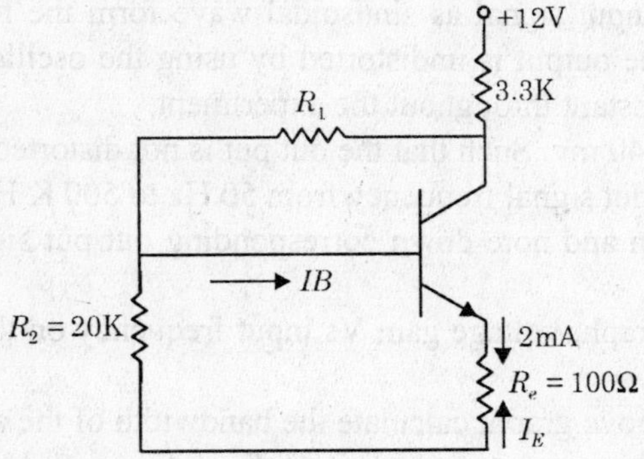


**Fig. 6p5**

## 6.12 LAB EXPERIMENTS

### *1. Millers Theorem*

**AIM:** To verify the miller's theorem.

**Equipments and components required:**

1. FET BF W11
2. Resistors 4.7 k, 100 K, 10 k
3. capacitors 10 µf, 0.001 µf
4. CRO DUAL
5. function generator
6. Ammeter
7. Voltmeter
8. Power supply 0 – 30 volt
9. Breadboard and connecting wires.

**Circuit Diagram:**

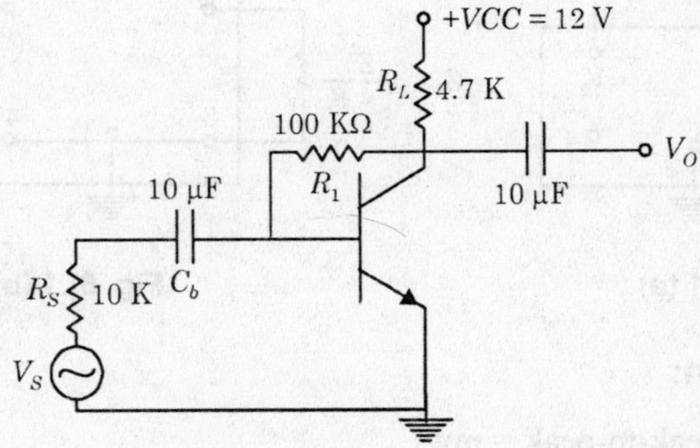


**Fig. 6L1**

**Procedure:**

1. Connect The Circuit as shown in the circuit diagram
2. Select the input signal as sinusoidal wave form the function generator such that the output is undistorted by using the oscilloscope. Keep this value as constant throughout the experiment.
3. Select $V_s = 40$ mv. Such that the out put is not distorted.
4. Vary the input signal frequency from 50 Hz to 500 K Hz as shown in the tabular form and note down corresponding out put signal peak to peak from *CRO.*
5. Draw the graph, voltage gain Vs input frequency on the semi log graph paper.
6. From the above graph, calculate the bandwidth of the amplifier.

**Theory:** Consider an arbitrary circuit configuration with $N$ distant nodes 1, 2, 3, … $N$ as indicated in figure. Let the node voltages be $v_1, v_2, v_3 \ldots V_N$. Where $V_N = 0$ and $N$ is the reference or ground node. Node 1 and 2 are intermediate with an impedance $Z^1$:

Designate the ratio $\frac{V_2}{V_1}$ by $k$, which in the sinusoidal study state will be a complex member and more generally will be a function of the Laplace Transform variables. The current $I_1$ drawn from $N_1$ through $Z^1$ can be obtained by disconnecting terminal 1 from $z^1$ and by bridging an impedance $\left(\frac{Z^1}{1-k}\right)$ from $n_1$ to ground as indicated in figure (b) $I_1 = \frac{V_1 - V_2}{z^1} = \frac{V_1(1-k)}{z^1} = \frac{\frac{V_1}{z_1}}{(1-k)} = \frac{V_1}{z^1}$.

In a similar way. It may be established that the coirrect $I_2$ drawn from $N_2$ may be calculated by removing $z^1$ and by connecting between $N_2$ and ground.

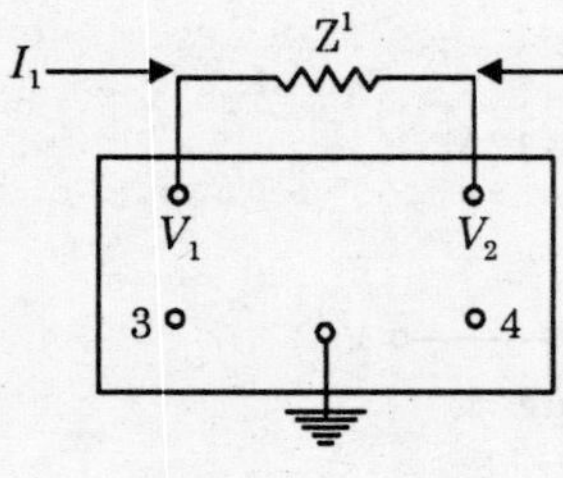


**Fig. 6L1 (a)**

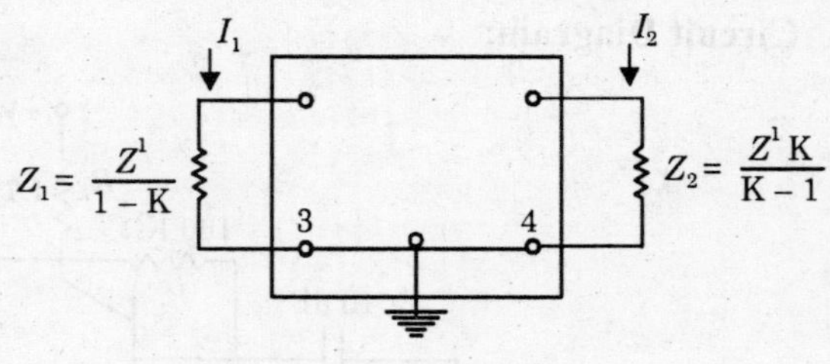


**Fig. 6L1 (b)**

## Tabularform:

Input signal peak-to-peak = mv

| Input voltage $V_i$ | Output voltage $V_o$ | $A_V = V_o/V_s$ |
|---|---|---|
| | | |

## 2. Two Port Parameters

**Objectives:** These experiments are aimed at

1. Measuring *z*, *y* transmission and hybrid parameters for any two-port network.
2. Characterize the network in terms of its parameters and hence draw its equivalent circuit.
3. Measure the small signal hybrid parameters of a transistor, in the common emitter mode: $h_{ie}$, $h_{fe}$, $h_{re}$, $h_{oe}$

**Components:**

1. Resistors: 1 kΩ – 2
   2 kΩ – 3
2. Transistor–12N2222A
3. Other components as calculated in individual experiments.

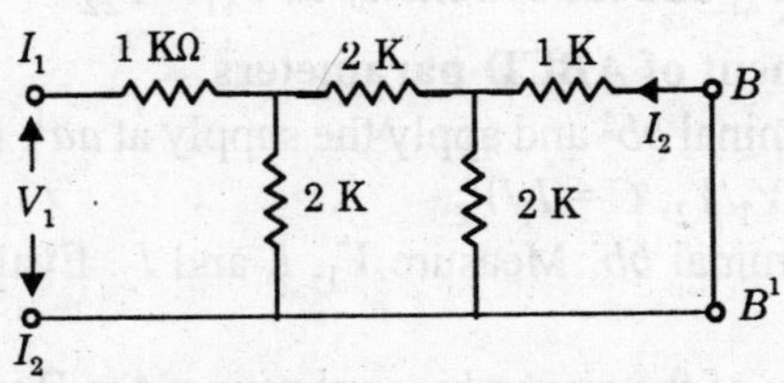


**Fig. 6L2 (a)** A resistive network.

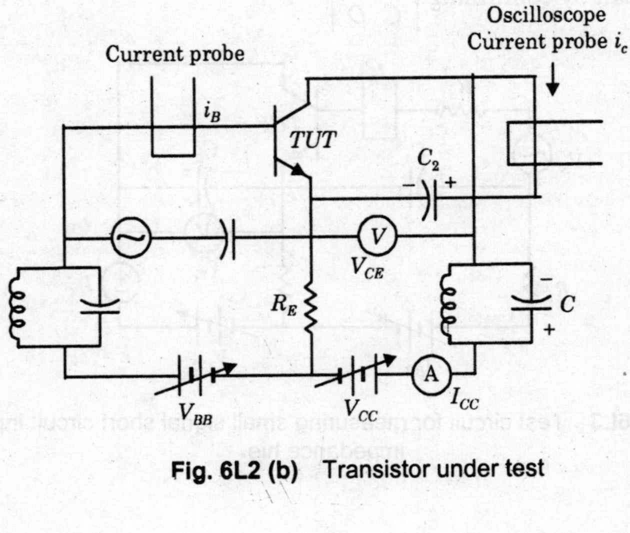


**Fig. 6L2 (b)** Transistor under test

**Equipment:**

1. 10 V power supply
2. CRO-with current probes
3. *rms* voltmeter
4. *rms* ammeter with micro amps and milliamps range
5. dc voltmeter
6. dc ammeter

**Procedure:**

**Phase 1: Measuring Z-parameters of a network**

1. Connect a circuit as shown in figure 1
2. Apply a 1 V dc supply at terminal *aa*', and keep *bb*' open measure $V_{aa}$' – $V_1$, the current $I_1$ and voltage $V_2$. Evaluate $Z_{11} = V1/I_1$, $Z_{21} = V_2/I_1$
3. Apply the 1 V dc supply at terminal *bb*' keep terminal aa' open. Measure $V_2$, $I_2$ and $V_1$ evaluate $Z_{22} = V_2/I_2$ and $Z_{12} = V_1/I_2$ Note that the circuit in both reciprocal and symmetric confirm this by verifying $z_{11} = z_{22}$ and $Z_{12} = Z_{21}$

**Phase 2: Measure of Y-parameters**

1. Short circuit terminal *bb*' and apply 1 *V* to $aa^1$ measure $I_1$, $V_1$ and $I_2$ evaluate $Y_{11} - I_1/V_1$; $Y_{21} = I_2/V_1$
2. Short circuit terminal $aa^1$ and apply a IV voltage source at $bb^1$. Measure $I_1$, $V_2$, $I_2$ evaluate $Y_{12} = I_1/V_2$; $Y_{22} = I_2/V_2$ verify the reciprocity of the circuit as $Y_{12} = Y_{21}$ and the symmetry as $Y_{11} = Y_{22}$

**Phase 3: Measurement of ABCD parameters**

1. Open circuit terminal *bb*' and apply the supply at $aa^1$. Measure $V_1$, $V_2$ and $I_1$ Evaluate $A = V_1/Y_2$; $C = I_1/V_2$.
2. Short circuit terminal *bb*' Measure $V_1$, $I$, and $I_2$. Evaluate $B = V_I/I_2$ and $D = I_1/I_2$
3. Verify symmetry of the circuit by confirming $A = D$ verify reciprocity of the circuit by confirming $\begin{vmatrix} A & B \\ C & D \end{vmatrix} = 1$

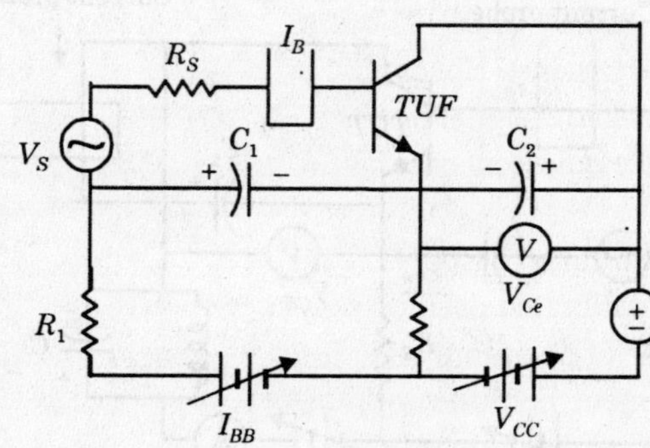


**Fig. 6L3** Test circuit for measuring small signal short circuit input impedance hie

**Phase 4: Measurement of small signal hybrid parameters of the transistor.**

**A. Small signal forward current gain $h_{fe} = \dfrac{\delta I_C}{\delta I_B}$ when $V_{CE}$ is constant.**

1. Connect the circuit as shown in figure 5. the $LC$ circuits have a very large impedance at the operating frequency, 1 KHz. The capacitors $C_1$ and $C_2$ are short circuits at this frequency, thus providing an ac short at the output terminal. Thus $\delta V_{CE} = 0$. The tank circuit of $LC$ combination completely isolates the ac and dc circuits, because of their very high impedance anti resonance. $V_{BB}$, $V_{cc}$ are biasing voltages which can be varied to provide a range of $I_{BB}$ and $I_{cc}$ values. $V_{BB}$ is variable 0–IV dc supply. $V_{CC}$ is a variable 0–20 V dc power supply $RE$ is the emitter resistance providing dc bias stability. It is a 220 W resistor.
   Figure 5: $L = 200$ mH $L = 5$ μH; $C_1$, $C_2 = 10$ μF, $RE = 220\ \Omega$ $V_{BB} = 0$–1 $V_{dc}$ $V_{CE} = 0$–20 V $d_c$ $V_S = 0.6\ V_{PP}$, 1 KHz sine wave TUT Transistor under test
2. Measure $i_c$ and $i_B$ with calibrated current probes of the oscilloscope evaluate $h_{fe} = i_c / i_B$.
3. The test condition to be specified are
   (a) Case temperature
   (b) Collector to emitter voltage $V_{CE}$ measured by the dc voltmeter V.
   (c) Collector dc current $I_C$ measured by the dc Ammeter $A$
   (d) Frequency of operation: 1 KHz.

**B. Small signal short circuit Input impedance $h_{ie}$**

1. Connect the circuit as shown in figure (6L3) Note the following points Figure (6L2b) test circuit for measuring small signal short circuit input impedance hie
   (i) $V_{BB}$ and $V_{CC}$ are biasing voltages of range 0–5 V and 0–20 V. $V_{CC}$ can be varied to test the circuit at different operating points. The base bias voltage can be varied by the potentiometer $R_{BB} = 50$ kΩ.
   (ii) $RE = 220\ \Omega$ Emitter resistance to provide feedback stability.
   (iii) Capacitors $C_1$ and $C_2$ 10 μF: These are short circuits at the operating frequency (1 kHz here). Hence $\Delta V_{CE} = 0$
   (iv) $V_S$: 1 KHz sinusoidal signal frequency with a range of about ± 0.3 V swing around the quiescent base bias voltage and has an internal source resistance $R_s$.
   (v) *TUT*: Transistor under Test 2N2222A
2. Measure $i_B$ with a calibrated oscilloscope current probe and $\delta V_{BE}$ on the scope, for a number of operating conditions. Calculate $h_{ie} = \delta V_{BE} / i_B$
3. For each measurement note the following test conditions collector to emitter voltage: $V_{CE}$ Collector current: $I_{CC}$ frequency $f = 1$ kHz operating or case temperature $T_c$

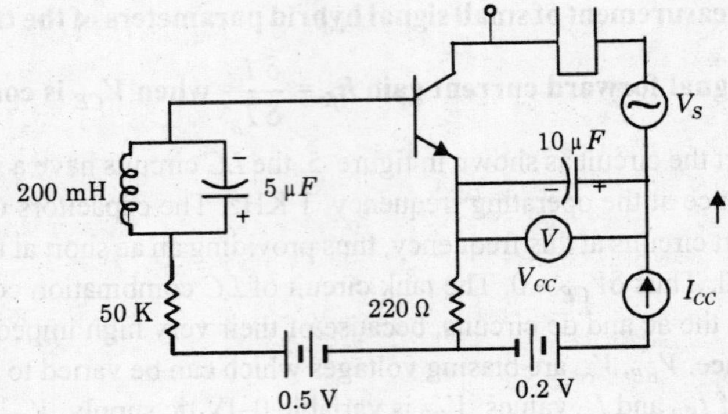


**Fig. 6L4** Test circuit for measuring small signal open circuit output admittance hoe measurement.

**C. Small signal open circuit output admittance ($h_{oe}$)**

Test circuit for small signal open-circuit output admittance hoe, measurement.

Since $hoe = \delta I_C/\delta V_{CE}|_{\delta IB=0}$, the input must be ac open circuit. This is done by the $LC$ circuit which has a very high impedance at the operating frequency.

1. $C$ is a short-circuit at the operating frequency.
2. Measure $\delta V_{CE}$ with a scope and $i_c$ with current probe for different operating conditions.
3. for each such measurement specify the operating conditions $V_{CE}$, $I_{CC}$, $T_C$ and frequency of operation $\delta o$.

**D. Small signal open circuit reverse voltage gain $h_{re}$.**

1. In the same circuit as shown in figure1. Measure $\delta V_{CE}$ and $\delta V_{BE}$ for each operating condition with scope calculate $h_{re} = \left.\dfrac{\delta V_{CE}}{\delta V_{be}}\right| \delta_{I_B=0}$. For each measurement, note the operating conditions $V_{CE}$, $I_{CC}$, $f$ and $T_C$.

# ❮ 7 ❯

# FIELD EFFECT TRANSISTOR (FET)

## 7.1 INTRODUCTION

The field effect transistor is a semiconductor device, which depends, for its operation on the control of current by an electric field. *FET* is a unipolar device, that is current involves only majority carriers where as BJT is a bipolar device. *FET* is a three terminal device in which the current through terminals is controlled by a voltage at the third terminal.

*Comparison of BJT and FET*

| *BJT* | *FET* |
|---|---|
| 1. Bipolar device because there are both majority and minority carriers | 1. Unipolar device because there are only majority carriers |
| 2. There is thermal runaway | 2. There is no thermal runaway. |
| 3. There is offset voltage or cut in voltage existing. | 3. There is no offset voltage. Therefore it is good for signal chopping |
| 4. Ri decreases | 4. $R_i$ increases |
| 5. Ro increases as output junction is reverse biased | 5. $R_o$ decreases as current passes through the channel |
| 6. Current controlled device | 6. Voltage controlled device. |
| 7. Noisy | 7. No noise |
| 8. Bulky | 8. Small |
| 9. Gain voltages are large | 9. Gain voltages are small |
| 10. Cheap | 10. Costly |

There are two types of field effect transistors.

1. The junction field effect transistors (JFET or simply FET) in which the control (gate) voltage varies the depletion width of the reverse biased *p-n* junction and
2. The metal-oxide-semiconductor transistor (MOST Or MOSFET).

The basic structure of an *n*-channel JFET is illustrated in figure 7.1.

It consists of a *n-type* bar which

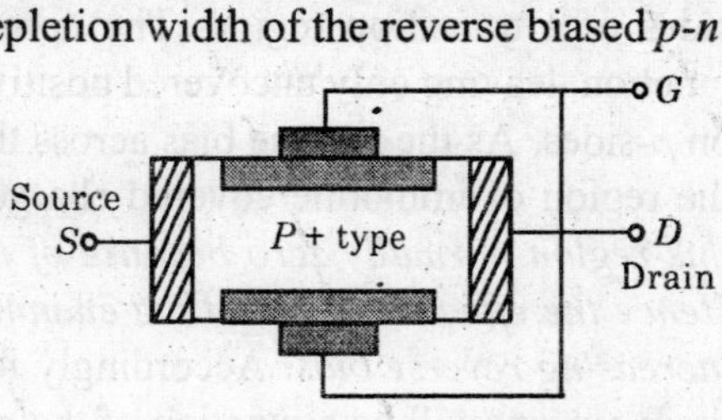


**Fig. 7.1** *n*-channel JFET

is made of silicon Ohmic contacts made at the two ends of the bar, are called source and the drain.

*Source (S):* This terminal is connected to the negative pole of the battery. Electrons, which are majority carriers in the *N*-type bar, enter the bar through this terminal.

*Drain (D):* This terminal is connected to the positive pole of the battery. The majority carriers leave the bar through this terminal.

*Gate (G):* Heavily doped *p*-type *Si* is diffused on both sides of the *N*-type *Si* bar by which PN junction are formed, these layers are joined together and called gate (G).

*Channel:* The region in figure 7.2 of the *n*-type bar between the depletion regions is called the channel.

*Shield or Substrate:* It is to protect the FET from the affect of electromagnetic fields outside the FET. Arrow at the gate is in opposite direction of the conventional current when the gate junction is forward biased.

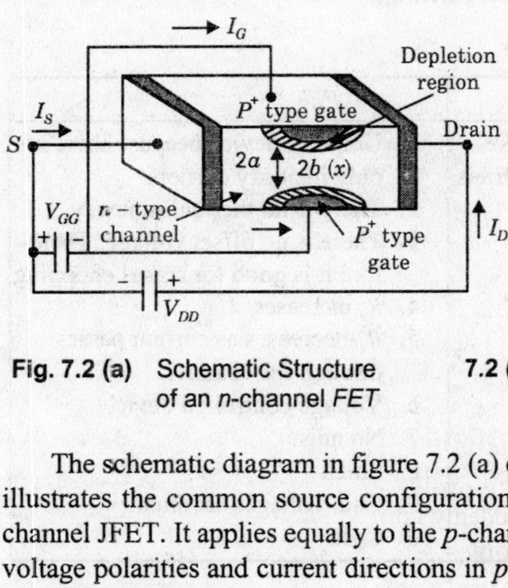


**Fig. 7.2 (a)** Schematic Structure of an *n*-channel *FET*

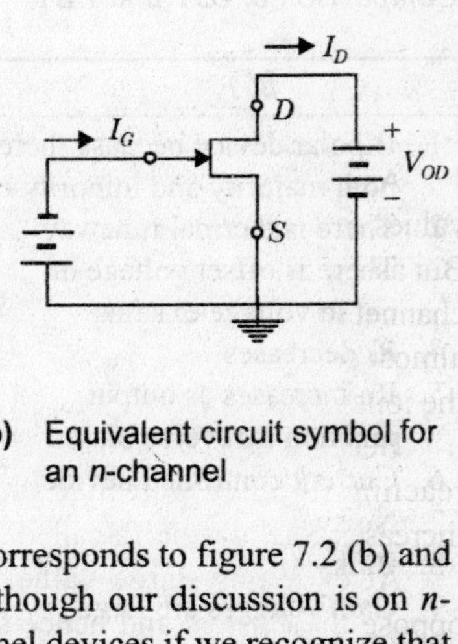


**7.2 (b)** Equivalent circuit symbol for an *n*-channel

The schematic diagram in figure 7.2 (a) corresponds to figure 7.2 (b) and illustrates the common source configuration though our discussion is on *n*-channel JFET. It applies equally to the *p*-channel devices if we recognize that voltage polarities and current directions in *p*-channel devices are opposite to those of *n*-channel .

In a reverse biased *p-n* junction there are space charge regions on the two sides of a transition region. The current carriers have diffused across the junction, leaving only uncovered positive ions on the *n-side* and negative ions on *p*-sides. As the reverse bias across the junction increases, the thickness of the region of immobile covered charges also increases. *The conductivity of this region normally zero because of the unavailability of current carriers. Hence the effective width of the channel in* figure 7.2 (a) *will decrease with increasing reverse bias*. Accordingly for a fixed drain to source voltage, the drain current will be a junction of the reverse biasing voltage across the gate junction. The term *Field Effect* is used to describe this device because the mechanism of current *control is the effect of the extension with increasing reverse bias, of the field association with the depletion region.*

## 7.2 JFET CHARACTERISTICS

$$I_D = f(V_{GS}, V_{DS})$$

Consider the effect of varying $V_{DS}$ and $V_{GS}$ on the drain current $I_D$.

*Output characteristics:* It is simpler to begin by assuming $V_{GS} = 0\ V$ as in figure 7.3

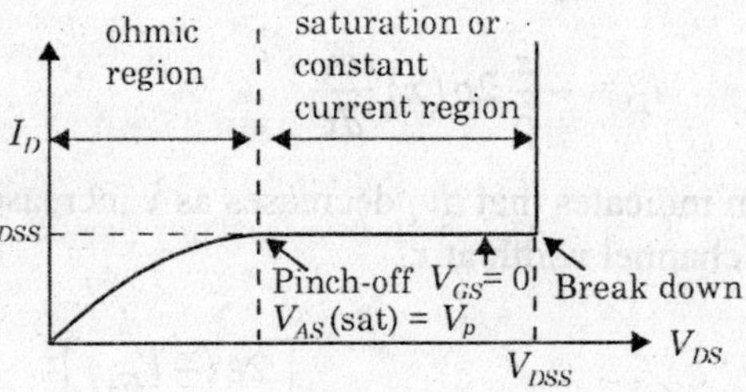


**Fig. 7.3** Pinch off action due to channel current.

As the voltage drop $V_{DS}$ increases then current $I_D$ also increases for small values of $V_{DS}$ and acts as a resistor. So this region is called the *Ohmic region.* But as $V_{DS}$ increases the distributive potential develops along the length of the channel and that oppose the increases in current $I_D$. There fore the current remains almost constant instead of increasing. The distributive potential is affected by the ions in the junction there fore it is called the "*space change region*".

Because of this increase in the space region some electrons are struck up reacting negative potential and that opposes increases in $I_D$ even if $V_{DS}$ increases. Such a region is called "*Pinch off region*" or "*Constant current region*".

At extremely large value of $V_{DS}$, the space charge region could not oppose the carriers and hence suddenly current increases and this region is called "*saturation region*". From output characteristic $V_P$ is a value of $V_{DS}$ from which $I_D$ becomes constant and it is numerically equal to $V_P$ in terms of $V_{GS}$ at which $I_D$ becomes zero.

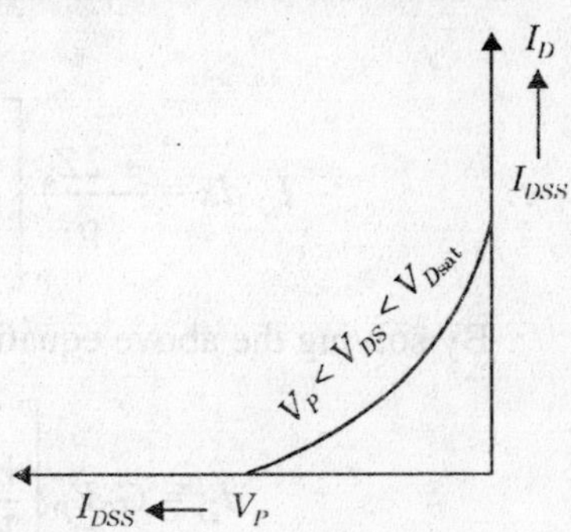


Fig 7.4

*Transfer characteristics:*

From the figure 7.4 as negative $V_{GS}$ increases then junction width increases and channel width increases then $I_D$ decreases. As negative $V_{GS}$

continues further at one value of $V_{GS}$, $I_D$ becomes zero, and that is $V_P$ called pinch off voltage.

### V-I equation of JFET:

The center of the channel at the drain end is taken as origin. The length of the channel in the $x$-direction is $a$. If the depth of the channel is $z$ and the resistivity of the material is ρ, then the differential volume = $2\,b\,(x)\,z \cdot dx$.

$$\therefore \quad \text{The resistance of the volume element} = \frac{\rho dx}{z\,2b(x)}$$

Since the current does not change along the length of the channel, $I_D$ is related to differential voltage drop in the element $-\,dv_x$ is given by

$$I_D = -\frac{z}{\rho}\,2b(x)\frac{dv_x}{dx}$$

Negative sign indicates that $dv_x$ decreases as $x$ increases.
$2\,b\,(x)$ is the channel width at $x$

$$\therefore \quad b(x) = a - w(x) = a - \left[\frac{2\varepsilon(-V_{Gx})}{qN_D}\right]^{\frac{1}{2}}$$

$$b(x) = a\left[1-\left(\frac{V_x - V_G}{V_P}\right)^{\frac{1}{2}}\right]$$

$$V_{Gx} = V_G - V_x$$

$$V_P = \frac{qN_D}{2\varepsilon}a^2$$

$$\therefore \quad I_D = \frac{-2z}{\rho}\frac{dv_x}{dx}a\left[1-\left(\frac{V_x - V_{Gx}}{V_P}\right)^{\frac{1}{2}}\right]$$

$$\therefore \quad -I_D\,dx = \frac{+2Z_a}{\rho}\left[1-\left(\frac{V_X - V_G}{V_P}\right)^{\frac{1}{2}}\right]dv_x$$

∴ By solving the above equation

$$I_D = G_0 V_P\left[\frac{V_D}{V_P} + \frac{2}{3}\left(\frac{-V_G}{V_p}\right)^{\frac{3}{2}} - \frac{2}{3}\left(\frac{V_D - V_G}{V_P}\right)^{\frac{3}{2}}\right]$$

Where $G_O = \frac{2Z_a}{\rho l}$: conductance. $V_G$ is negative.

The above equation is valid upto punch off region.

$$\Rightarrow \qquad V_D - V_G = V_P$$

If we assume that the saturation current remains constant.

$$I_D\,(\text{sat}) = G_0 V_P\left[\frac{V_D}{V_P} + \frac{2}{3}\left(\frac{-V_G}{V_P}\right)^{\frac{3}{2}} - \frac{3}{2}\right] = G_0 V_P\left[\frac{V_D}{V_P} + \frac{2}{3}\left(\frac{-V_G}{V_P}\right)^{\frac{3}{2}} - \frac{1}{3}\right]$$

Where $\frac{V_D}{V_P} = 1 + \frac{V_G}{V_P}$

It is experimentally found that, the drain saturation current following the square law which can be deduced as

$$I_D = I_{DSS}\left(1 + \frac{V_{GS}}{V_P}\right)^2$$

Since $V_G$ is negative

$$I_D = I_{DSS}\left(1 - \frac{V_{GS}}{V_P}\right)^2$$

(a) *Transconductance:* The Trans conductance gm defines how the drain current varies in relation to the gate source voltage. Units of $g_m$ are microamperes per volt ($\mu A/v$) or micro siemens ($\mu s$). It can be measured as the slope of the transfer characteristic. Since slope varies, the $I_D$ or $V_{GS}$ level at which $g_m$ is measured.

Transconductance is defined as.

$$g_m = \frac{\text{Variation in drain current}}{\text{Variation in gate source voltage}}$$

$$g_m = \left.\frac{\Delta I_{DS}}{\Delta V_{GS}}\right|_{V_{DS}}$$

$$g_m = \frac{2I_{DSS}}{-V_P}\left[1 - \frac{V_{GS}}{V_P}\right]$$

$$g_m = g_{mo}\left[1 - \frac{V_{GS}}{V_P}\right]$$

$$g_{mo} = g_m \,|\, V_{GS} = 0.$$

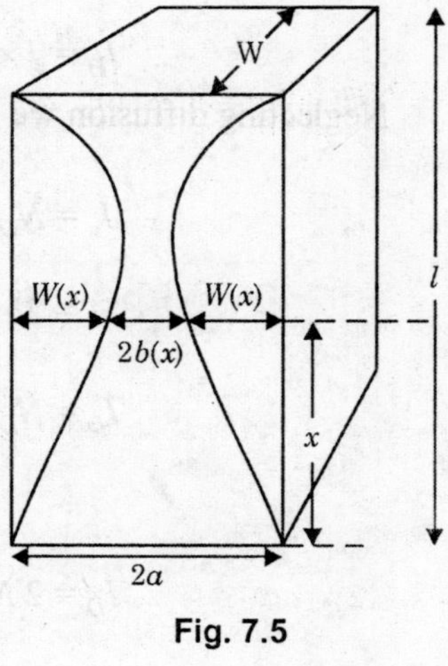


Fig. 7.5

For any device to act as an amplifier $g_m$ should be always positive.

$$\frac{I_{DS}}{g_m} = \frac{-V_P}{2}\left[1 - \frac{V_{GS}}{V_P}\right]$$

$$\left|\frac{I_{DS}}{g_m}\right| = \frac{1}{2}\{|V_P| - |V_{GS}|\}$$

The space charge width, $W_n(x) = W(x)$ at a distance $x$ along the channel.

$$W(x) = a - b(x) = \left\{\frac{2\varepsilon}{qN_D}[|V_0| - |V_{GS}|]\right\}^{\frac{1}{2}}$$

When $b(x) = b = 0$ then $|Vo| << |V_{GS}|$ we obtain the pinch off voltage

$$V_p = \frac{qN_D}{2\varepsilon} a^2$$

$$V_{GS} = V_p\left\{1 - \frac{b}{a}\right\}^2$$

(b) *Drain resistance:* The drain resistance $r_d$ is the static resistance between drain and source terminals when the *FET* is operating in the pinch off region. It is also the slope of the drain characteristics in pinch off region. Drain resistance $r_d$ is defined as

$$r_d = \frac{\text{drain voltage}}{\text{drain current}}$$

$$r_d = \left|\frac{V_{DS}}{I_D}\right|_{V_{DS}}$$

$$I_D = J \times A$$

Neglecting diffusion we get

$$J_n = N_D \mu_n q \left\{\frac{V_{DS}}{L}\right\}$$

$$A = 2b(x) \times W$$

$$I_D = N_D \mu_n q \left\{\frac{V_{DS}}{L}\right\} 2b(x) \times W$$

$$I_D = 2 N_D \mu_n q \left\{\frac{V_{DS}}{L}\right\}\left\{a\left\{1 - \left(\frac{V_{GS}}{V_P}\right)^{\frac{1}{2}}\right\}\right\}$$

$$V_{GS} = V_P \left\{1 - \frac{b}{a}\right\}^2$$

$$\left\{\left(\frac{V_{GS}}{V_P}\right)^{\frac{1}{2}}\right\} = \left\{1 - \frac{b}{a}\right\}$$

$$b = \left[1 - \left\{\frac{V_{GS}}{V_P}\right\}^{\frac{1}{2}}\right] \cdot a$$

$$r_d = \frac{V_{DS}}{I_D} = \frac{L}{2a\,\mu_n\, w\, N_D\, q \left\{1 - \frac{V_{GS}}{V_P}\right\}^{\frac{1}{2}}}$$

(c) *Zero-drift drain current:* Figure 7.6 shows the dependence of the transfer characteristics on temperature. Observe from this figure that there exits a value of $V_{GS}$ for which $I_D = I_Q$ does not change with temperature $T$. It is therefore possible to bias a field effect transistor for zero-drift drain current. An explanation of this effect is possible if we note that two factor affect the variation of drain current.

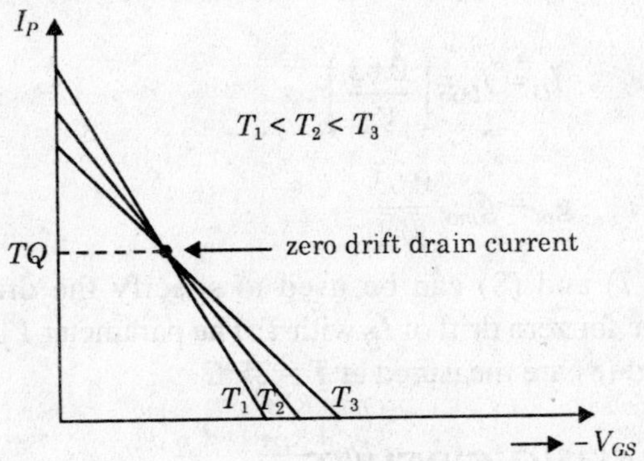


**Fig. 7.6** Transfer characteristics

The first factor is the decreases of majority carrier mobility with temperature. As $T$ increases the lattice ions vibrate more rigorously and hence the carriers cannot move as freely in crystalline structure. Thus, for a given field strength, their velocity is decreased and this reduces the current. It has been found that the reduction in $I_D$ is 0.7% per °C.

The second factor is the decreases of the width of the gate to channel barrier width increasing temperature. This follows $I_D$ to increases and it has been found that the increases in $I_D$ are equivalent to change of 2.2 mv/°C in $|V_{GS}|$. This is a similar phenomenon to that which gives a bipolar transistor a change of $|V_{BE}|$ of 2.5 mv/°C.

Since a change in gate voltage $\Delta V_{GS}$ causes in drain current of $gm\ \Delta V_{GS}$, then the condition for zero drift.

$$0.007\,|I_D| = 0.0022\text{ gm} \qquad \text{...(1)}$$

or

$$\frac{|I_D|}{g_m} = 0.314\text{ V} \qquad \text{...(2)}$$

If we substitute equation

$$I_{DS} = I_{DSS}\left(1 - \frac{V_{GS}}{V_P}\right)^2 \qquad \text{...(3)}$$

$$g_m = g_{mo}\left(1 - \frac{V_{GS}}{V_P}\right) \qquad \text{...(4)}$$

$$g_{mo} = \frac{-2\,I_{DSS}}{V_P} \qquad \text{...(5)}$$

(3) (4) (5) in (1) we obtain

$$|V_p| - |V_{GS}| = 0.63\text{ V} \qquad \text{...(6)}$$

Equation (6) gives the value of $V_{GS}$ for zero drift if $V_P$ is known. If $V_P$ = 0.63 V, $V_{GS}$= 0 and $I_D = D_{SS}$ from equation (3) (4) and (6)

$$I_D = I_{DSS}\left(\frac{0.63}{V_P}\right)^2 \qquad \text{...(7)}$$

And

$$g_m = g_{mo}\frac{0.63}{|V_P|} \qquad \text{...(8)}$$

Equations (7) and (8) can be used to specify the drain current and transconductance for zero drift of $I_D$ with $T$. The parameter $V_P$, $I_{DSS}$ and $g_{mo}$ in equations (6) and (8) are measured at $T$ = 25°C.

## 7.3 JFET BIASING CIRCUITS

### *1. Two battery bias circuit:*

Consider the circuit in figure 7.7. The gate of the FET is connected via resistor $R_G$ to a bias voltage – $V_G$. The gate voltage controls the level of drain current in this circuit. Biasing method is called fixed bias because the gate to source voltage is fixed by the voltage applied across the terminals.

Writing Kirchhoffs voltage law around the output loops we find

$$V_{DS} = V_{DD} - I_D R_D \qquad \text{...(1)}$$

Writing Kirchhoff's voltage law around the input loops we find

$$V_{GS} = -V_{GG} \quad \ldots(2)$$

There is no loss of gain since there is no feedback.

A FET has a much input resistance. To take advantage of it, $R_G$ should be as large as possible so that circuit input resistance remains high. If $R_G$ is extremely large a charge accumulated on the gate may take a long time to leak off. *A* reasonable upper limit is 1MΩ. Normally $R_G$ should not exceed this value. $I_{GSS} R_G \leq 10$ mv. To act as short circuit $R_{GSS} \leq \frac{10 \times 10^{-3}}{10 \times 10^{-3}} \leq 1$ MΩ

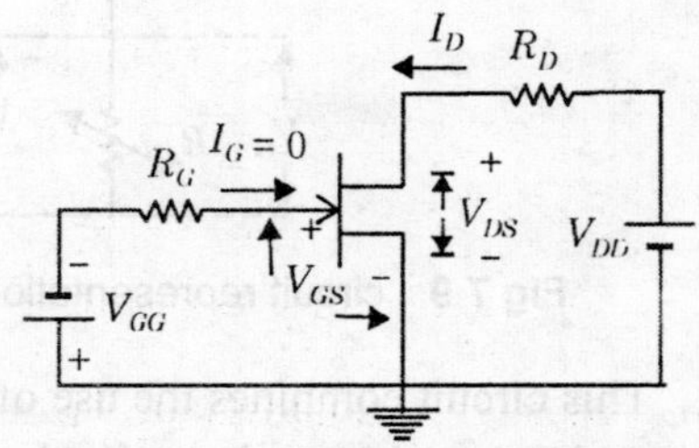


**Fig. 7.7** Two battery bias circuit:

## 2. Self bias

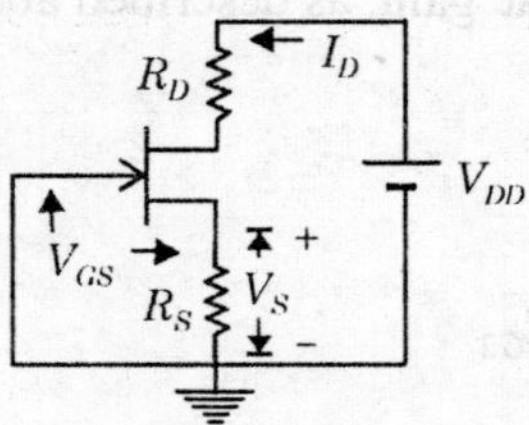


**Fig. 7.8 (a)** Self bias circuit

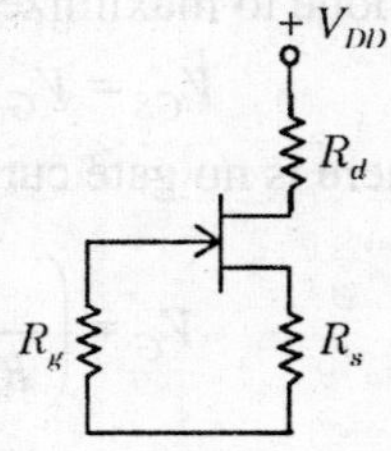


**Fig. 7.8 (b)** Self bias with $R_G$

Figure 7.8 shows a bias circuit that provides improved stability and requires only a single supply voltage. This bias method is called self bias, because the voltage drop across $R_S$ due to flow of quiescent current determines the quiescent value of $V_{GS}$. the current $I_D$ in resistor $R_S$ creates the voltage $V_D = I_D R_S$ at source terminal with respect to ground. This means gate is negative with respect to source, since gate is grounded.

$$V_{GS} = -I_D R_S \quad \ldots(1)$$

The above equation describes straight when plotted on $V_{GS} - I_D$ axes. Each line is called bias line for its respective type. The quiescent value of $I_D$ in self bias circuit can be determined graphically by plotting the bias line on the same net of axis with transfer characteristics. The $Q$-value of $V_{DS}$ can be found by writing Kirchoff's voltage law around the output loop. That is

$$V_{DS} = V_{DD} - I_D R_D - I_D R_S \quad \ldots(2)$$

## 3. Self bias with potential divider:

Potential divider bias allows the use of reasonably large $R_s$ values without making $I_D$ very small. The potential divider bias circuit using FET is shown in figure 7.9.

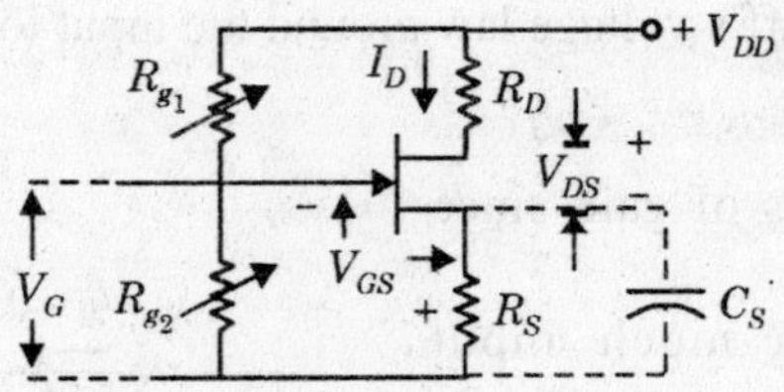


**Fig 7.9** circuit representation of self bias with Potential divider

This circuit combines the use of a source resistor, as in the self- bias circuit with a gate bias voltage $V_G$ derived from supply voltage by means of a potential divides. From figure 7.9 it is seen that $V_G$ makes gate positive with respect to ground. The voltage drop across RS namely $V_S = I_D R_S$ makes the source terminal positive with respect to ground. $V_s$ is larger than $V_G$ so the source terminal is at a higher potential than the gate. Thus, the gate is negative with respect to source. The circuit employs a by pass capacitors $C_S$ across source resistors $R_S$.

This is done to maximize the circuit ac gain, as described above

$$V_{GS} = V_G - I_D R_S \quad \ldots(1)$$

Since there is no gate current

$$V_G = \left(\frac{V_{DD}}{R_{G1} + R_{G2}}\right) R_{G2} \quad \ldots(2)$$

By substituting (2) in (1) we get

$$V_{GS} = \frac{V_{DD}\, R_{G2}}{R_{G1} + R_{G2}} - I_D\, R_S \quad \ldots(3)$$

Maximum gain is achieved by making $R_D$ as large as possible and for a given level of $I_D$ this requires maximum voltage drop across $R_D$. However, greatest bias stability is achieved by making $R_S$ as large as possible and this dictates maximum $V_S$. Applying Kirchoff's law to outer loop we get

$$V_{DD} = I_D R_S + V_{DS} + I_D R_D \quad \ldots(4)$$

## 7.4 BIASING AGAINST DEVICE VARIATION

The maximum and minimum valves of $I_{DSS}$ and $V_P$ (pinch off voltage) at room temperature are usually given by FET manufactures. They also supply data to correct these quantities for temperature variations. The transfer characteristics for a given type of $n$-channel FET may be seen in figure 7.10 (a) where the top and bottom curves are for extreme values of temperature and device variation.

It is necessary to bias the device at a current which does not drift outside of $I_D = I_A$ and $I_D = I_B$. Then the bias line $V_{GS} = -\, I_D\, R_S$ must intersect the transfer characteristics between $A$ and $B$ as indicated in figure 7.10 (a). The slope of the bias line is determined by source resistance $R_S$. For any transfer characteristic between the two extremes indicated, the current $I_Q$ is such that $I_A < I_Q < I_B$, as desired.

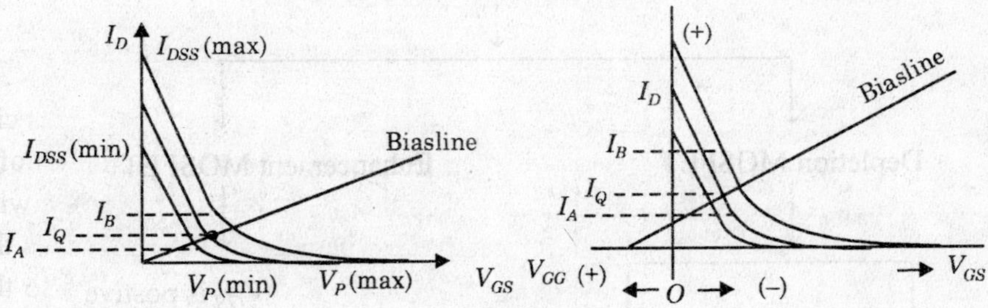


**Fig. 7.10 (a)** transfer characteristics for the n-channel FET **7.10 (b)** The bias line does not pass through origin.

Consider the situation in figure 7.10 (b) where a line drawn to pass between points $A$ and $B$ does not pass through the origin. This bias line satisfies the equation.

$$V_{GS} = V_{GG} - I_D R_S \qquad \ldots(1)$$

Such a bias relationship may be obtained by adding a fixed that bias to the gate in addition to the source self bias as indicated in figure 7.11.

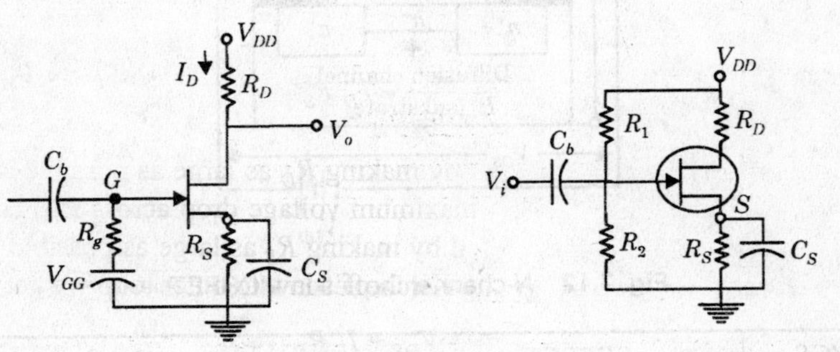


**Fig. 7.11 (a)** **7.11 (b)**

A circuit requiring only one power supply and which can satisfy equation (1) is shown in figure 7.11(b). For this circuit.

$$V_{GG} = \frac{R_2 V_{DD}}{R_1 + R_2},\ R_g = \frac{R_1 R_2}{R_1 + R_2}$$

We have assumed that gate current is negligible. It is also possible for $V_{GG}$ to fall in reverse biased region so that the line in figure 7.11 (b) intersects the axis of abscissa to the origin. Under such circumstances two separate supplies must be used.

## 7.5 MOSFET—CHARACTERISTICS

MOSFET is Metal Oxide Semi conductor Field Effect Transistor and is the common term for Insulated Gate Field Effect Transistor (IGFET).

MOSFET

- Depletion MOSFET
  - Depletion mode: $I_D$ decreases, $V_{GS}$ is negative
  - Enhancement mode: $I_D$ increases, $V_{GS}$ is positive
- Enhancement MOSFET
  - $V_{GS}$ is postive
  - No permanent channel exists (induced channel developed)
  - $V_{GS} = 0, I_D = 0$

### *Depletion MOSFET:*

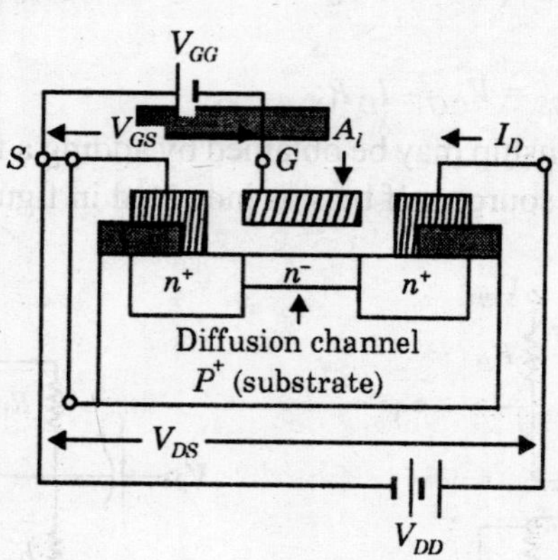


**Fig. 7.12** *N*-channel Depletion MOSFET

| *VGS* | *EFFECT* | *ID* |
|---|---|---|
| Negative | Produces positive carriers at *n*_channel. So recombination takes place. | Decreases |
| Zero | Here neither holes nor electrons are generated | It exists and neither increases nor decreases but it flows. |
| Positive | Produces negative carriers at *n*-channel. ∴ Electron concentration increases | Increases. |

The channel is lightly doped to avoid the mesh formation when $V_{GS}$ is positive. Substrate supplies the required type of carriers according to the supply at gate.

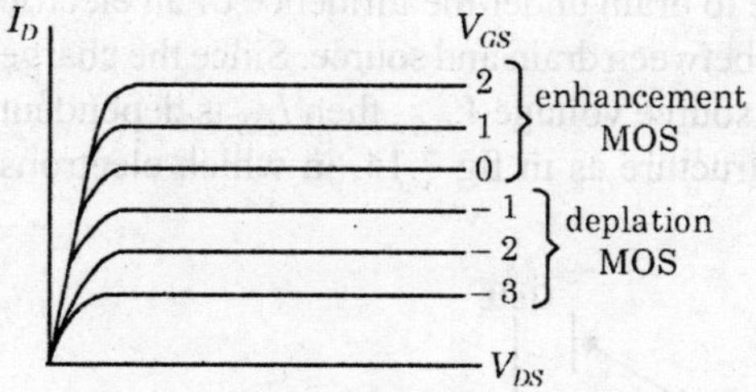


**Fig7.12 (a)** Drain Characteristics

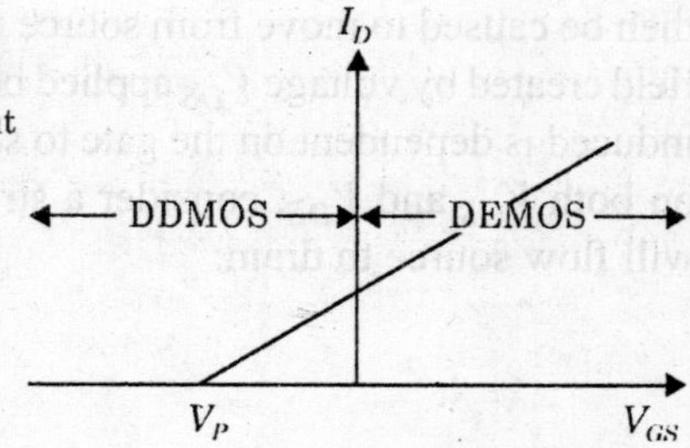


**7.12.(b)** Transfer Characteristics

## *Enhancement MOSFET:*

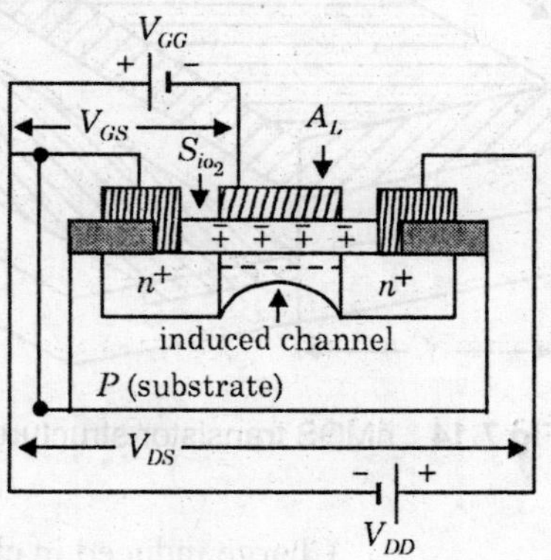


**Fig. 7.13** Enhancement MOSFET

| $V_{GS}$ | EFFECT | ID |
|---|---|---|
| Negative | It produces positive carrier. ∴ No channel exists. | Zero |
| Zero | No carriers are produced. | Zero |
| Positive | It produces negative carrier. So channel is developed. | Flows |

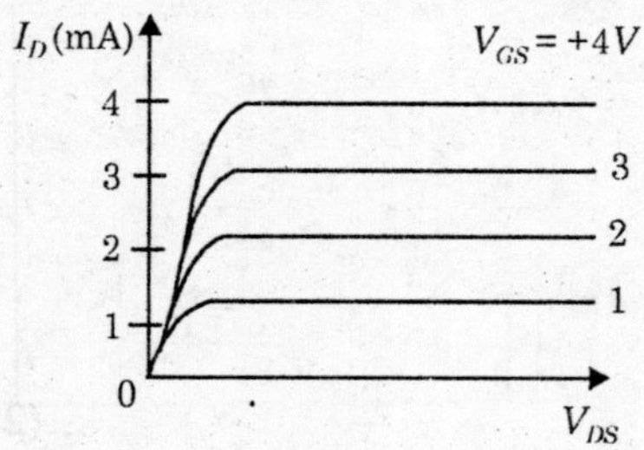


**Fig. 7.13 (a)** Drain Characteristics

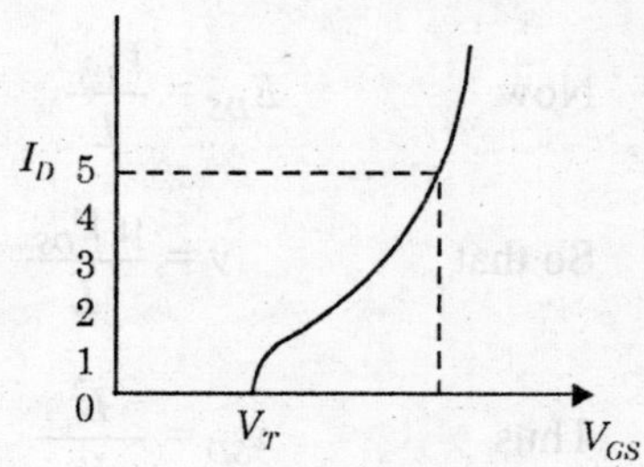


**7.13 (b)** Transfer Characteristics

### *V-I equation of MOSFET:*

The concept of the MOS transistor evolves from the use of a voltage on the gate to induce a charge in the channel between source and drain, which may then be caused to move from source to drain under the influence of an electric field created by voltage $V_{DS}$ applied between drain and source. Since the charge induced is dependent on the gate to source voltage $V_{GS}$, then $I_{DS}$ is dependent on both $V_{GS}$ and $V_{DS}$. consider a structure as in fig 7.14, in which electrons will flow source to drain:

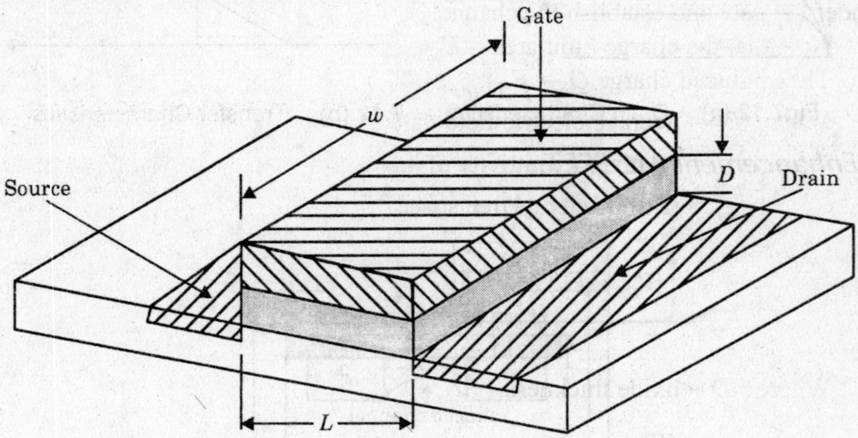


**Fig 7.14** nMOS transistor structure

$$I_{DS} = -I_{SD} = \frac{\text{Charge induced in channel } (Q_C)}{\text{Electron transit time } (\tau)} \qquad \ldots(1)$$

First, transit time:

$$\tau_{SD} = \frac{\text{length of channel } (L)}{\text{velocity } (v)}$$

but velocity $\quad v = \mu E_{DS}$

where $\quad \mu$ = electron or hole mobility (surface )

$\quad E_{DS}$ = electric field (drain to source)

Now $$E_{DS} = \frac{V_{DS}}{L}$$

So that $$v = \frac{\mu V_{DS}}{L}$$

Thus $$\tau_{SD} = \frac{L^2}{\mu V_{DS}} \qquad \ldots(2)$$

Typical values of μ at room temperature are:

$$\mu_n = 650 \text{ cm}^2/\text{V sec (surface)}$$

$$\mu_p = 240 \text{ cm}^2/\text{V sec (surface)}$$

***Non saturated region:***

The charge that is induced in the channel due to the gate voltage is due to the voltage difference between the gate and the channel, $V_{GS}$. the effective voltage $V_G = V_{GS} - V_T$ where $V_T$ is the threshold voltage needed to invert the charge under the gate and establish the channel.

Note that the charge /unit area = $E_G \varepsilon_{ins} \varepsilon_0$.

Thus induced charge $Q_c = E_G \varepsilon_{ins} \varepsilon_0 W_L$.

Where $E_G$ = average electric field gate to channel.

$\varepsilon_{ins}$ = relative permittivity of insulation between gate and channel

$\varepsilon_0$ = permittivity of free space

$$E_G = \frac{\left[(V_{GS} - V_T) - \frac{V_{DS}}{2}\right]}{D}$$

Where $D$ = oxide thickness.

$$\text{Thus} \quad Q_c = \frac{WL\varepsilon_{ins}\varepsilon_0}{D}\left[(V_{GS} - V_T) - \frac{V_{DS}}{2}\right] \quad \text{...(3)}$$

Now combining equations (2) and (3) in equation (1), we have

$$I_{DS} = \frac{\varepsilon_{ins}\, \varepsilon_0\, \mu}{D} \frac{W}{L}\left[(V_{GS} - V_T) - \frac{V_{DS}}{2}\right] V_{DS}$$

$$\text{Or} \quad I_{DS} = K\frac{W}{L}\left[(V_{GS} - V_T)V_{DS} - \frac{V_{DS^2}}{2}\right] \quad \text{...(4)}$$

in the non saturated or resistive region where $V_{DS} < V_{GS} - V_T$ and

$$K = \frac{\varepsilon_{ins}\, \varepsilon_0 \mu}{D}$$

The factor $W/L$ is written as $\beta = K\dfrac{W}{L}$

$$\text{So that } I_{DS} = \beta\left[(V_{GS} - V_T)V_{DS} - \frac{V_{DS^2}}{2}\right] \quad \text{...(4a)}$$

Which is an alternative form of equation (4)

Noting that gate/channel capacitance

$$C_G = \frac{\varepsilon_{ins}\,\varepsilon_0\,WL}{D}\ \text{(parallel plate)}$$

We also have $\quad K = \dfrac{C_G\mu}{WL}$

So that $$I_{DS} = \frac{C_G\,\mu}{WL}\left[(V_{GS}-V_T)V_{DS}-\frac{V_{DS}^2}{2}\right] \qquad \text{...(4b)}$$

Which is a further alternative form of equation (4).sometimes it is convenient to use gate capacitance per unit area $C_0$ rather than $C_G$ in this and other expressions.

Where $\quad C_G = C_0 WL$

We may also write

$$I_{DS} = \frac{C_0\,\mu W}{L}\left[(V_{GS}-V_T)V_{DS}-\frac{V_{DS}^2}{2}\right] \qquad \text{...(4c)}$$

### *Saturated region*

Saturation begins when $V_{DS} = V_{GS} - V_T$ since at this point the $I_R$ drop in the channel equals the effective gate to channel voltage at the drain and we mat assume that the current remains fairly constant as $V_{DS}$ increases further. Thus

$$I_{DS} = K\frac{W}{L}\frac{(V_{GS}-V_T)^2}{2}$$

Or, we may write

$$I_{DS} = \frac{\beta}{2}(V_{GS}-V_T)^2$$

$$I_{DS} = \frac{C_G\,\mu}{2L^2}(V_{GS}-V_T)^2$$

We may also write

$$I_{DS} = C_0\,\mu\,\frac{W}{2L}(V_{GS}-V_T)^2$$

The expressions derived for $I_{DS}$ hold for both enhancement and depletion mode devices, but it should be noted that the threshold voltage for the nMOS depletion mode device (denoted as $V_{TD}$) is negative.

Typical charecteristics for nMOS transistors are given in fig. 7.15. pMOS transistor charecteristics are similar, with suitable reversal of polarity.

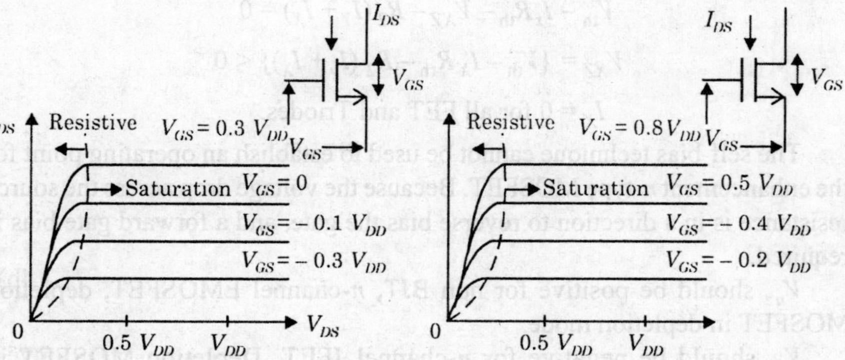


**Fig. 7.15 (a)** Depletion mode device **7.15 (b)** Enhancement mode device

## 7.6 BIASING ACTION OF MOSFETS

### *Universal biasing circuit: (self-bias):*

Consider the bias circuit in figure 7.16. The circuit employs a depletion enhancement FET, so $V_{GS}$ may be positive, negative or zero. In figure 7.16 the gate terminal is connected to source via resistor $R_G$. The figure shown below can be used to bias junction FET devices or depletion-mode MOS transistors. For specified drain current $I_D$, the corresponding $V_{GS}$ can be obtained by using $I_{DS} = I_{DSS}(1 - V_{GS}/V_p)^2$, it gives an excellent fit, with the experimentally determined transfer characteristics for FETs made by the diffusion process.

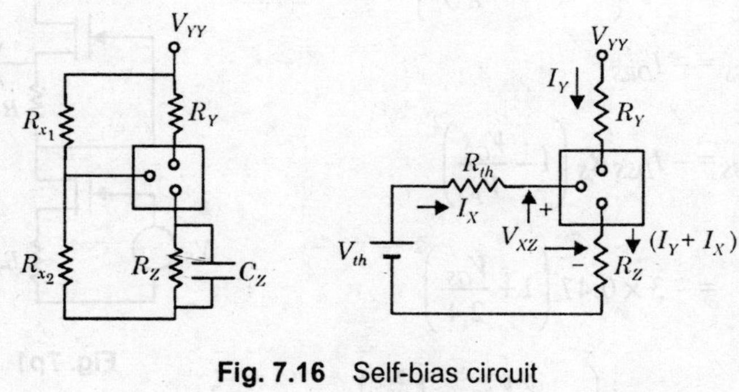


**Fig. 7.16** Self-bias circuit

$$V_{\text{th}} = \left(\frac{V_{YY}}{R_{x_1} + R_{x_2}}\right) R_{X2}$$

$$R_{\text{th}} = R_{X_1} \parallel R_{X_2} = \left(\frac{R_{x_1}\ R_{x_2}}{R_{x_1} + R_{x_2}}\right)$$

By applying Kirchoff's law we get

$$V_{th} - I_x R_{th} - V_{XZ} - R_2 (I_Y + I_X) = 0$$

$$V_{XZ} = \{V_{th} - I_X R_{th} - R_2 (I_y + I_X)\} < 0$$

$$I_X = 0 \text{ for all FET and Triodes.}$$

The self-bias technique cannot be used to establish an operating point for the enhancement *n*-type MOSFET. Because the voltage drop across the source resistance is in a direction to reverse bias the gate, and a forward gate bias is required.

$V_{nz}$ should be positive for npn BJT, *n*-channel EMOSFET, depletion MOSFET in depletion mode.

$V_{xz}$ should be negative for *n*-channel JFET. Depletion MOSFET in depletion mode and triode.

## 7.7 SOLVED PROBLEMS

**1. The *CS* amplifier stage shown in figure 7p1 has the following parameters. $R_d = 12$ k, $R_g = 1$ M, $R_s = 470\ \Omega$, $V_{DD} = 30$ *v*, Cs is arbitrarily large $I_{DSS} = 3$ mA, $V_D = -2.4$ V and $r_d >> R_d$. Determine (a) the gate to-source bias voltage $V_{GS}$, (b) the drain current $I_D$, (c) the quiescent voltage $V_{DS}$, (d) the small signal voltage gain $A_V$.**

**Solution:**

(a) $$I_D = I_{DSS}\left\{1 - \left(1 - \frac{V_{GS}}{V_P}\right)^2\right\}$$

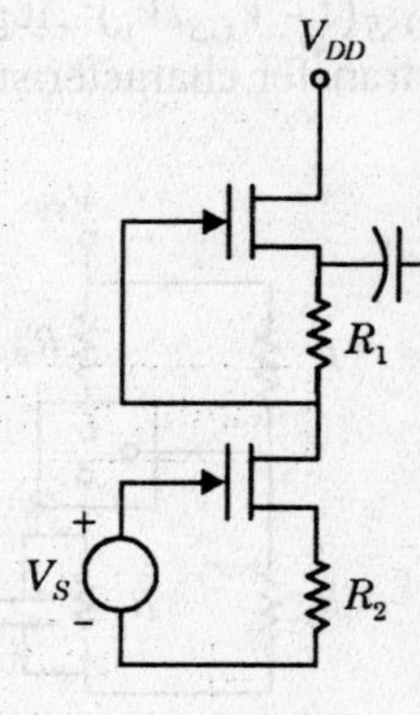

Fig. 7p1

$$V_{GS} = -I_{DRS}$$

$$V_{GS} = -I_{DSS} R_S \left(1 - \frac{V_{GS}}{V_P}\right)^2$$

$$= -3 \times 0.47 \left(1 + \frac{V_{GS}}{2.4}\right)^2$$

$$= -1.41 \left(1 + \frac{2V_{GS}}{2.4} + \frac{V_{GS}^2}{2.4^2}\right)$$

$$V_{GS} = -1.4 - 1.175\, V_{GS} - 0.24\, V_{GS}$$

$$0.24\, V_{GS}^2 + 2.175\, V_{GS} + 1.41 = 0$$

$$V_{GS} = \frac{-2 \pm \sqrt{(2.175^2) - 4\,(1.41)\,0.24}}{2 \times 0.24} = \frac{-2.754 \pm 1.837}{0.48}$$

$$= -0.7 \text{ V}$$

(b) $$I_D = 3\left(1-\frac{0.7}{2.4}\right)^2 = 3\left(1-\frac{1.7}{0.48}\right)^2 = 1.5\text{mA}$$

(c) $$V_{DS} = V_{DD} - I_D\,(R_d + R_s)$$
$$= 30 - 1.5 \times 12.47$$
$$= 11.29 \text{ V}$$

(d) Since $r_d >> R_d$ then $A_V = -\,g_m\,R_d$

$$g_m = \frac{2I_{DSS}}{V_P}\left(1-\frac{VGS}{V_P}\right)$$

$$= \frac{2\times 3\times 10^{-13}}{2.4}\left(1-\frac{0.7}{2.4}\right)$$

$$= 1170\ \mu\text{ mho}$$
$$= 1.77 \text{ mA/V}$$

Hence $$A_V = -\,1.77 \times 12$$
$$= -\,21.2$$

**2. The amplifier stage shown uses an *n*-channel *FET* having $I_{DSS}$ = 1 mA, $v_p$ = 1 V. if the quiescent drain-to-ground voltage is 10 v, find $R_1$.**

**Solution:**

$$I_D = \frac{V_{DD} - V_{ON}}{R_d} = \frac{24-10}{56} = 0.25 \text{ mA}$$

$$I_{DSS}\left(1-\frac{VGS}{V_P}\right)^2 = (V_{GS})^2$$

$$1 + V_{GS} = \left(\frac{1}{4}\right)^{\frac{1}{3}} = \frac{1}{2}$$

Therefore $$V_{GS} = -\,0.5 \text{ V}$$

But $$V_{GS} = -\,I_D R_1$$

$$\frac{-V_{GS}}{I_D} = \frac{-0.5}{0.25\times 10^{-3}} = 2\ K$$

**3. The FET shown has the following parameters: $R_1 = I_{DSS}$ = 4 mA and $V_P$ = – 4v**

**(a) If $V_i$ = 0 find $V_o$**

**(b) If $V_i$ = 10 v, find $V_o$**

**(c) If $v_o$ = 0 find $V_i$**

**Note: $V_i$ and $V_o$ are constant voltages. Fig. 7p2**

**Solution:**

(a) $$V_i = 0$$

$$V_i - V_{GS} - 2\,I_D + 12 = 12 = 0$$

$\Rightarrow$ $$V_{GS} = -(2\,I_D - 12) \quad \left[\text{Since } I_D = I_{DSS}\left[1 - \frac{V_{GS}}{V_P}\right]^2\right]$$

$$I_D = 4\left[1 + \frac{2\,I_D + 12}{+4}\right]^2 = 1/4\,[-2\,I_D + 16]^2 = [-I_D + 4]^2$$

$$I_D = (I_D - 4)^2$$

$$I_D^2 - 9\,I_D + 16 = 0$$

$$I_D = \frac{9 \pm \sqrt{81 - 64}}{2}$$

$$I_D = 6.56,\ 2.44$$

$\therefore$ $$V_O = V_{GS} = 2\,I_D - 12$$

$$V_O = -7.12\text{ V},\ 1.12\text{ V}.$$

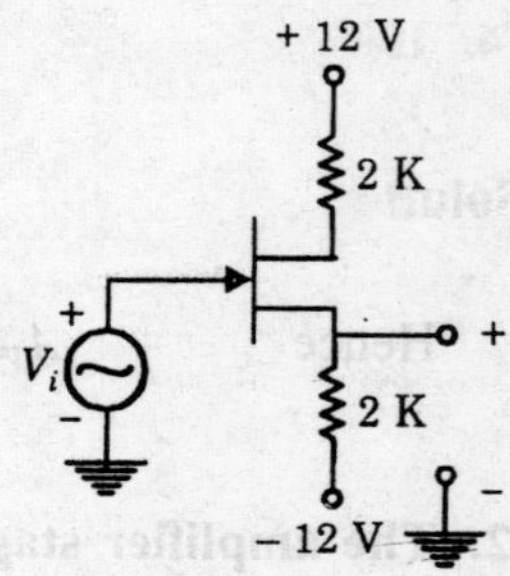


**Fig. 7p2**

(b) if $$V_I = 10\text{ V}$$

$$V_{GS} = -2\,I_D + 22$$

$$I_D = 4\left[1 + \frac{-2\,I_D + 22}{+4}\right]^2 = 4\left[\frac{-2\,I_D + 26}{+4}\right]^2$$

$$I_D = (-I_D + 13)^2$$

$$I_D = (I_D - 13)^2$$

$$I_D^2 - 27\,I_D + 169 = 0$$

$$I_D = \frac{27 \pm \sqrt{729 - 676}}{2}$$

$$= \frac{27 \pm 7.28}{2} = 17.14,\ 9.86$$

$$V_o = V_{GS} = 2.28\text{ V},\ -12.28\text{ V}$$

Or $$V_{GS} \cong 1.4\text{ V}$$

$$I_D = 2.34\text{ ma}$$

(c) if $$V_o = 0$$

$$I_d = \frac{12V}{2K} = 6 \text{ mA}$$

Therefore $\quad 6 \text{ mA} = 4 \text{ mA}\left(1+\frac{V_{GS}}{4}\right)^2$

$$1+\frac{V_{GS}}{4} = \pm 1.225$$

$$V_{GS} = 0.9 \text{ V}, -8.9 \text{ V}$$

Therefore $\quad V_O = V_{GS} = -8.9 \text{ V}$

$$V_{GS} = -ve,\ V_O = +ve$$

**4. If $|I_{DSS}| = 4$ mA, $V_P = 4$ V, calculate the quiescent value of $I_D$, $V_{GS}$ and $V_{DS}$.**

**Solution:**

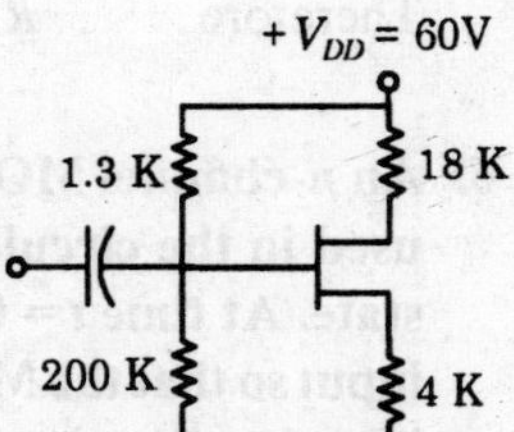

**Fig. 7p3**

$$R_{TH} = 200 \text{ K} \,||\, 1.3 \text{ M}$$
$$= 173.5 \text{ K}$$

$$-V_{\text{TH}} = \frac{200K}{1500K}(1-60) = -8 \text{ V}$$

$$V_{GS} = -4\,I_D - 8$$

Or $\quad I_D = -\frac{8+V_{GS}}{4};\ I_D = I_{DSS}\left(1-\frac{VGS}{V_P}\right)^2$

$$\Rightarrow \quad \left(\frac{-8-V_{GS}}{4}\right) = 4\left(1-\frac{V_{GS}}{V_P}\right)^2$$

$$V_{GS} = I_V \Rightarrow I_D = \left(\frac{-8-V_{GS}}{4}\right) = -2.25 \text{ mA.}$$

Solving we get $V_{GS} = I_V$

$$I_D = -2.25 \text{ mA}$$

Hence, $\quad V_{DS} = -60-(18+4)\,(2.25)$

$$= -60 + 49.5$$
$$= -10.5 \text{ V}$$

**5. The *JFET* in the circuit shown has an $I_{dss} = 10$ mA, and $V_P = -5$ V, find the value of resistance $R_S$ for a drain current $I_{DS} = 6.4$ mA.**

**Solution:**

Given $\quad I_{DSS} = 10 \text{ mA},\ V_p = -5 \text{ v}$

$I_{ds} = 6.4$ mA, $R_s = ?$

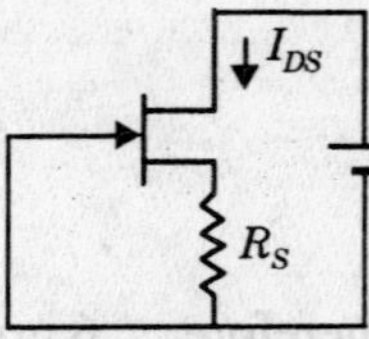

Fig. 7p5(a)

$$As = I_{DS} = I_{DSS}\left(1 - \frac{V_{GS}}{V_P}\right)^2$$

$$6.4 = 10\left(1 - \frac{V_{GS}}{V_P}\right)^2$$

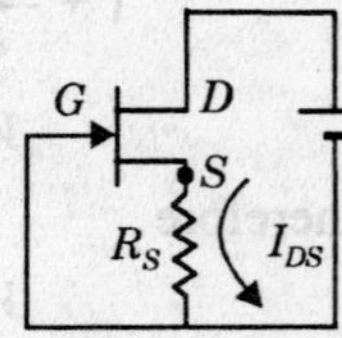

Fig. 7p5(b)

$$0.8 = \left(1 - \frac{V_{GS}}{V_P}\right)$$

$$V_{GS} = 0.2\ V_P = -1\ \text{V}$$

$$\Rightarrow \quad I_{DS}\, R_S = 1$$

Therefore $\quad R_s = \dfrac{1}{I_{DS}} = \dfrac{1}{6.4 \times 10^{-3}}\ 156\ \Omega$

**6. An *n*-channel MOSFET (*T*) having a $V_T$ of 2 V(Threshold voltage) is used in the circuit shown in figure. Initially *T* is OFF and in steady state. At time $t = 0$, a step voltage of magnitude 4 V is applied to the input so that the MOSFET turns on instantaneously. Draw the equivalent circuit and calculate the time taken for the output $V_o$ to fall to 5 V. The device constant of the MOSFET, $K = 5$ mA/V$^2$, $R_{DS} = \infty$, $C_{DS} = 0$; $C_{DG} = 0$.**

**Solution:**

Given *n*-channel MOSFET

$V_T = 2$ $\qquad$ *T* OFF and steady state so, MOS turns ON.

$K = 5$ mA/V$^2$, $R_{DS} = \infty$, $C_{DS} = 0$; $C_{DG} = 0$

Assuming initially capacitor is charged to 10 V as MOSFET is OFF

Now $\qquad V_{GS} = 4$ v

$$I_D = K\,(V_{GS} - V_T)^2$$

$$= 5\,(4 - 2)^2 = 20\ \text{mA.}$$

In saturation region

$$V_{GS} > V_T \text{ satisfied}$$

$$V_{GD} > V_T$$

$$\alpha_1 - V_0 \geq 2 \Rightarrow -V_0 \geq -2$$

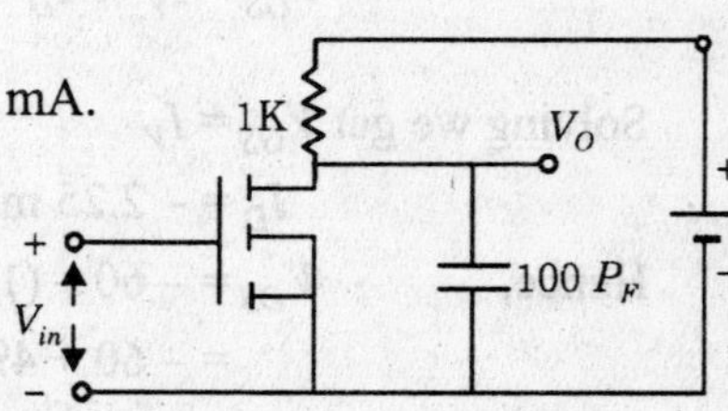

Fig. 7p6(a)

Therefore $\qquad V_0 \leq 2$ V

Since $V_0$ falls only upto 5 v

So MOSFET is in pinch off region

Discharging model:

Application of $KCL$ to the model gives:

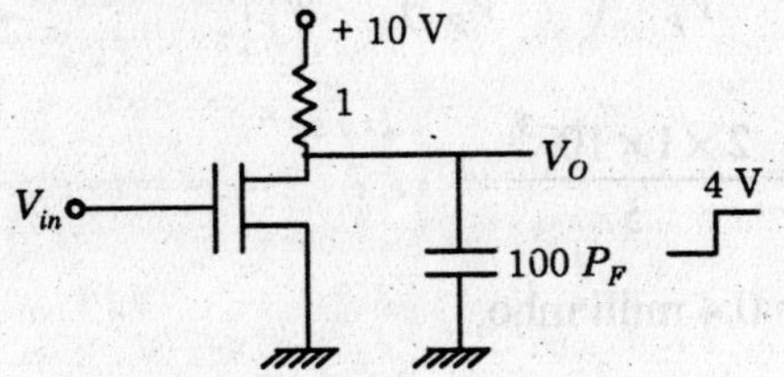


Fig. 7p6 (b)

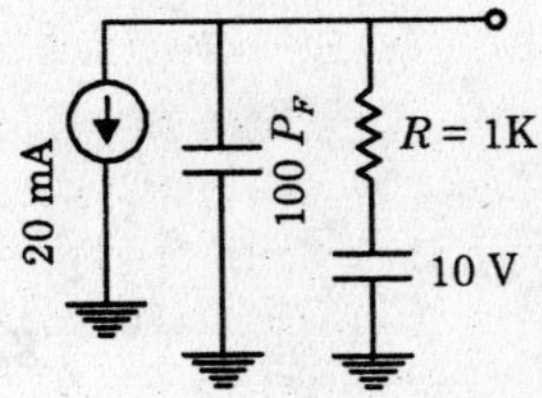


Fig. 7p6 (c)

$$2.\times 10^{-3} = -\frac{CdV_O}{dt} + \frac{10 - V_O}{R}$$

Taking Laplace transform;

$$\frac{20\times 10^{-3}}{5} = 10\times 10^{-12}\,[SV_o(s) - V_c(0)]$$

$$+\frac{10\times 10^{-3} V_O(S)\times 10^{-3}}{5} + \frac{10\times 10^{-3}}{5}$$

$$= -V_O(S)\,[10\times 10^{-12} S + 10^{-3}] + 100\times 10^{-12}$$

$$(S + 10^7)\,V_o(s) = -\frac{10^8}{5} - 10$$

$$V_O(S) = \frac{10^8}{S\left(S+10^7\right)} = \frac{10^8}{S\left(S+10^7\right)}$$

$$V_O(S) = \frac{10}{5}\;\frac{10}{S+10^7} - \frac{10}{S\left(S+10^7\right)}$$

Inverse Laplace gives:

$$V_O(t) = 10^2\, e^{-t}\,(10^7)$$

$$V_O = 5\text{ V}$$

$\Rightarrow$ $5 = 20\,(1^{-t}\times 10^7)$

$\Rightarrow$ $t = 10^{-7}\log^4_e = 13.8\times 10^{-8} = 138$ ns

Therefore $t = 138$ ns

**7. An $n$-channel has $I_{DSS} = 1$ mA and $V_P = -5$ v. Find the maximum transconductance.**

**Solution:**

$I_{DSS} = 1$ mA (given) $n$-channel JFET $V_P = -5$ V

Transconductance, $$g_m = \frac{2\, I_{DSS}}{V_P}\left(1-\frac{V_{GS}}{V_P}\right) = \frac{2\, I_{DSS}}{|V_P|}$$

$$= \frac{2 \times 1 \times 10^{-3}}{5}$$

$$g_m = 0.4 \text{ milli mho}$$

**8. Given an NMOS circuit as shown in figure. The specifications of the circuit are:**
**$V_{DD} = 10$ V; $\beta = K = \mu n\, C_{ox}\, (W/L) = 10^{-4}$ A/V$_2$**
**$V_T = I_1$ and $I^{DS} = 0.5$ mA. Evaluate $V_{DS}$ and $R_D$ for the circuit. Neglect body-effect for $V_T$.**

**Solution:**

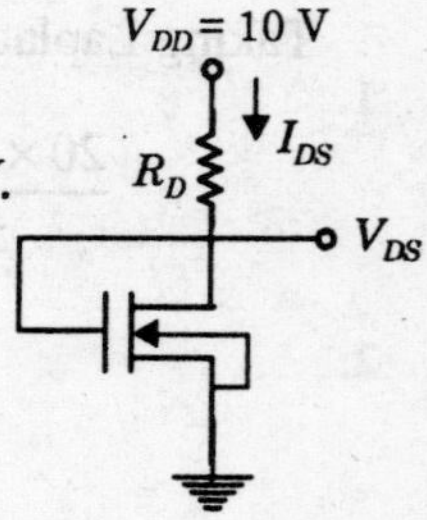


Fig. 7p10

Given an NMOS circuit;

$$\beta = 10^{-4} \text{ A/V}^2,\ V_{DD} = 10\text{V};\ V_T = IV.$$

$$I_{DS} = 0.5 \text{ mA.}$$

We know, $I_D = K\,(V_{GS} - V_T)^2$ in saturation

$$5 \times 10^{-14} = 10^{-4} = (V_{GS} - 1)^2$$

$$V_{DS} = V_{gs} = 3.23 \text{ V} = 3.24 \text{ V}$$

and $$R_D = \frac{V_{DD} - V_{DS}}{I_{DS}} = \frac{10 - 3.24}{0.5} = 13.5\text{K}$$

Therefore $R_D = 13.5$ K.

**9. A JFET amplifier with a voltage divider biasing circuit shown in figure below has the following parameter: $V_P = -2$ V, $I_{DSS} = 4$ mA $R_D = 910\ \Omega$, $R_S = 3$ K$\Omega$, $R_1 = 12$ M$\Omega$, $R_2 = 8.57$ M$\Omega$ and $V_{DD} = 24$ V. Find the value of the drain current $I_D$ at the operating point. Verify whether the FET will operate in the pinch-off region.**

**Solution:**

$$V_{GG} = V_D \cdot \frac{R_2}{R_1 + R_2} = 24 \times \frac{8.57 \times 10^6}{(12 + 8.57)\, 10^6} = 10 \text{ V}$$

Where $V_{GS} = V_{GG} - I_D\, R_S$ we have $I_D = 4\left(1 - \frac{10 - I_D \times 3}{2}\right)^3$.

$$9I_D^2 - 73\, I_D + 144 = 0$$

$$I_D = 3.39 \text{ mA or } 4.72 \text{ mA}$$

As $I_D = 4.72 \text{ mA} > 4 \text{ mA} = I_{DSS}$

This value is inappropriate so, $I_{DQ} = 3.39$ mA is selected

$$V_{GSQ} = V_{GG} - I_{DQ} R_S$$
$$= 10 - (3.39 \times 10^{-3} \times 10^3) = -0.17 \text{ V}$$
$$V_{DSQ} = V_{DD} - I_{DQ}(R_D + R_S)$$
$$= 24 - 3.39 \times 10^{-3}(0.91 + 3) \times 10^3 = 10.74$$
$$V_{DGQ} = V_{DSQ} - V_{GSQ} = 10745 + 0.17 = 10.915 \text{ V}$$

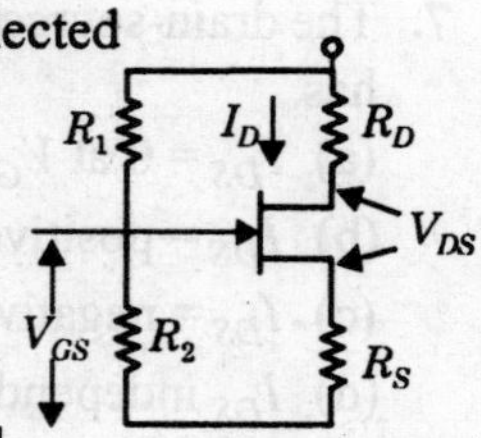


**Fig. 7P11**

Which is greater than $|V_D| = 2$ V.

Hence the *FET* is in pinch off region.

## 7.8 OBJECTIVE QUESTIONS

1. The "Pinch off" voltage of a JFET is 5.0 volts. Its "cut off" voltage is
   (a) (5.0) ½ V (b) 2.5 V
   (c) 5.0 V (d) $(5.0)^{3/2}$ V
   **Ans:** (c)
2. An *n*-channel JFET has a pinch-off voltage of $V_P = -5$ V, $V_{DS\,(max)} = 20$ V, and $g_m = 2$ mA/V. The minimum 'ON' resistance is achieved in the JFET for
   (a) $V_{GS} = -7$ V and $V_{DS} = 0$ V (b) $V_{GS} = 0$ V and $V_{DS} = 0$ V
   (c) $V_{GS} = 0$ V and $V_{DS} = 20$ V (d) $V_{GS} = -7$ V and $V_{DS} = 20$ V
   **Ans:** (b)
3. The threshold voltage of an *n*-channel MOSFET can be increased by
   (a) increasing the channel dopant concentration
   (b) reducing the channel dopant concentration.
   (c) reducing the gate oxide thickness
   (d) reducing the channel length.
   **Ans:** (b)
4. Two identical FET's each characterized by the parameters $g_m$ and $r_d$ are connected in parallel. The composite FET is then characterized by the parameters.
   (a) $g_m/2$ and $2\, r_d$ (b) $g_m/2$ and $r_d/2$
   (c) $2\, g_m$ and $r_d/2$ (d) $2\, g_m$ and $2\, r_d$
   **Ans:** (c)
5. An *n*-channel JFET has $I_{DSS} = 2$ mA and $V_p = -4$ v. Its transconductance gm (in milli mho) for an applied gate-to-source voltage $V_{GS}$ of $-2$ V is
   (a) 0.25 (b) 0.5
   (c) 0.75 (d) 1.0
   **Ans:** (b)
6. For quiet reception the front end of FM tuner contains
   (a) BJT (b) FET
   (c) UJT (d) SCR
   **Ans:** (b)

7. The drain-source output V-I characteristics of an n-channel depletion FET has
   (a) $I_{DS} = 0$ at $V_{GS} = 0$
   (b) $I_{DS}$ = positive maximum at $V_{GS} = 0$
   (c) $I_{DS}$ = negative maximum at $V_{GS} = 0$
   (d) $I_{DS}$ independent of $V_{GS}$
   **Ans:** (b)
8. The output V-I characteristics of an enhancement type MOSFET has
   (a) only an ohmic region
   (b) only a saturation region
   (c) an ohmic region at low voltage value followed by a saturation region at higher voltages.
   (d) an ohmic region at large voltage values preceded by a saturation region lower voltages.
   **Ans:** (c)
9. For an *n*-channel JFET, having drain-source voltage constant if the gate-source voltage is increased (more negative) pinch-off would occur for
   (a) high values of drain current.
   (b) saturation value of drain current
   (c) zero drain current
   (d) gate current equal to the drain current
   **Ans:** (c)
10. For a junction FET in the pinch off region, as the drain voltage is increased, the drain current
    (a) becomes zero
    (b) abruptly decreases
    (c) abruptly increases
    (d) remains constant
    **Ans:** (d)
11. In modern MOSFET's the material used for the gate is
    (a) high purity silicon
    (b) high purity silica
    (c) heavily doped polycrystalline silicon
    (d) epitaxial grown silicon
    **Ans:** (c)
12. An *n*-channel JFET has *IDS* whose value is
    (a) maximum for $V_{GS} = 0$, and minimum for $V_{GS}$ = negative and large
    (b) minimum for $V_{GS} = 0$, and maximum for $V_{GS}$ = negative and large
    (c) maximum for $V_{GS} = 0$, and minimum for $V_{GS}$ = positive and larged
    (d) minimum for $V_{GS} = 0$, and maximum for $V_{GS}$ = positive and large
    **Ans:** (a)
13. The threshold voltage of an *n*-channel enhancement mode MOSFET is 0.5v. When the device is biased at a gate voltage of 3v. Pinch-off would occur at a drain voltage of

(a) 1.5 V (b) 2.5 V
(c) 3.5 V (d) 4.5 V
**Ans:** (b)

**14.** Compared to field-effect photo transistor, bipolar photo transistor are:
(a) more sensitive and faster (b) less sensitive and slower
(c) more sensitive and slower (d) less sensitive and faster
**Ans:** (a)

**15.** Which of the following is ideally suited for choppers?
(a) JFET (b) BJT
(c) UJT (d) SCR
**Ans:** (a)

**16.** The main factor, which differentiates a D-MOSFET from an E-MOSFET, is the absence of
(a) PN junction (b) insulated gate
(c) electrons (d) channel
**Ans:** (d)

**17.** In order to protect a MOSFET against damage from any stray voltage at the gate.
(a) grounding rings are provided
(b) terminals are shorted
(c) source terminal is earthen during transit
(d) none
**Ans:** (c)

**18.** *N*-Channel FET's are superior to *P*-channel FET's because
(a) mobility of electrons is smaller than that of holes
(b) mobility of electrons is greater than that of holes
(c) they consume less power
(d) they have high switching time
**Ans:** (b)

**19.** The amplification factor of FET is 40 and drain resistance is equal to 10 kΩ and load resistance is 10 kΩ, the voltage gain is
(a) – 40 (b) 40
(c) – 20 (d) – 4
**Ans:** (c)

**20.** Which of the following transistor are symmetrical in the sense that emitter and collector, or source and drain terminals can be interchanged
(a) JFET (b) NPN transistor
(c) MOSFET (d) PNP transistor
**Ans:** (c)

**21.** In JFET, the primary control on drain current is exerted by
(a) channel resistance (b) size of depletion regions
(c) voltage drop across channel (d) gate reverse bias
**Ans:** (d)

**22.** The parameters of JFET are related as

(a) $g_m = r_d/\mu$ (b) $g_m = \mu/r_d$

(c) $g_m = r_d * \mu$

**Ans: (c)**

**23.** Pinch off voltage $V_p$ for an FET is the drain voltage at which

(a) significant drain current starts flowing

(b) drain current becomes zero

(c) all free charges get removed from the channel

(d) avlanche breakdown takes place

**Ans: (c)**

**24.** The saturation drain current $I_{DS}$ in an FET equals:

(a) $I_{DSS}\left(1-\frac{V_{GS}}{V_P}\right)$ (b) $I_{DSS}\left(1-\frac{V_{GS}}{V_P}\right)^2$

(c) $I_{DSS}\sqrt{V_{GS}/V_p}$. (d) $I_{DSS}^2\left(\frac{V_{GS}}{V_P}\right)$

**25.** The transconductance $g_m$ of a FET in the saturation region equals:

(a) $\frac{-2\,I_{DSS}}{V_P}\left(1-\frac{V_{GS}}{V_P}\right)$ (b) $\frac{-2\,I_{DSS}}{V_P}\left(1-\frac{V_{GS}}{V_P}\right)^2$

(c) $2\,I_{DSS}\left(1-\frac{V_{GS}}{V_P}\right)^{\frac{1}{2}}$ (d) $1/V_P\,(I_{DSS}-I_{DS})^{½}$

**Ans: (a)**

**26.** The transconductance $g_m$ of a diffused JFET is of the order of:

(a) 1 mS (b) 1 S

(c) 100 S (d) 1000 S

**Ans: (a)**

**27.** The gate to source resistance of an FET is of the order of:

(a) 0.1 MΩ (b) 1 MΩ

(c) 10 MΩ (d) 100 MΩ

**Ans: (d)**

**28.** Inter electrode capacitances in an FET are of the order of:

(a) 1 pF (b) 100 pF

(c) 0.1 μF (d) 1 μF

**Ans: (a)**

**29.** FET has offset voltage of about:

(a) 0.2 V (b) 0.6 V

(c) 1.5 V (d) Zero

**Ans: (d)**

**30.** The ON resistance rd, ON of an FET is the ratio:

(a) $V_{DS}/I_D$ at the origin

(b) $V_{DS}/I_D$ in the saturation region
(c) $\Delta V_{DS}/\Delta I_D$ in the saturation region
(d) $V_{GS}/I_D$ at the origin
**Ans:** (a)

**31.** A JFET has a potential divider bias arrangement if the resistor between the gate and power supply terminal is removed. The JFET will
(a) continue to work as an amplifier
(b) have a forward bias gate w.r.t source
(c) not work as an amplifier but will work as a switch.
(d) immediately burn out.
**Ans:** (a)

**32.** The output V-I characteristics of a FET is given in the figure, in which region is the device biased for small signal amplification?
(a) *AB* (b) *BC*
(c) *CD* (d) *BD*
**Ans:** (b)

**33.** The following symbol in figure represents
(a) *N*-channel depletion MOSFET
(b) *P*-channel depletion MOSFET
(c) *P*-channel enhancement MOSFET
(d) *N*-channel enhancement MOSFET
**Ans:** (d)

**33.** In the MOSFET amplifier of figure, the signal outputs $V_1$ and $V_2$ obey the relationship
(a) $V_1 = V_2/2$ (b) $V_1 = -V_2/2$
(c) $V_1 = 2V_2$ (d) $V_1 = -2V_2$
**Ans:** (a)

**34.** The JFET in the circuit shown in figure has an $I_{DSS} = 10$ mA and $V_P = -5$ v. The value of the resistance $R_S$ for a drain current $I_{DS} = 6.4$ mA is (select the nearest value)
(a) 150 ohms (b) 470 ohms
(c) 560 ohms (d) 1kilo ohms
**Ans:** (a)

**35.** Channel current is reduced on application of a more positive voltage to the gate of a depletion mode *n*-channel MOSFET (True/False)
**Ans:** False

## 7.9 CONVENTIONAL QUESTIONS

1. Define the pinch off voltage.
2. In the saturation region, how does the drain current vary with gate voltage?
3. Sketch the basic structure of an n-channel JFET transistor.

4. Explain switching action of JFET.
5. Discuss about different types of JFET biasing circuits.
6. Sketch the circuits of Enhancement MOSFET and Depletion MOSFET and explain there operations.
7. Define transconductance $g_m$, and drain resistance $r_d$ of an FET.
8. Draw the circuit symbol of JFET.

## 7.10 EXERCISE PROBLEMS

**1.** Determine the following for the circuit shown in figure

(a) $V_{gs}$ and $I_D$ (b) $V_D$

(c) $V_S$ (d) $V_{DS}$

(e) $V_{DG}$

**Ans:** (a) – 1.8 V, 2.4 mA (b) 10.24 V

(c) 3.6 V (d) 6.64 V

(e) 8.42 V

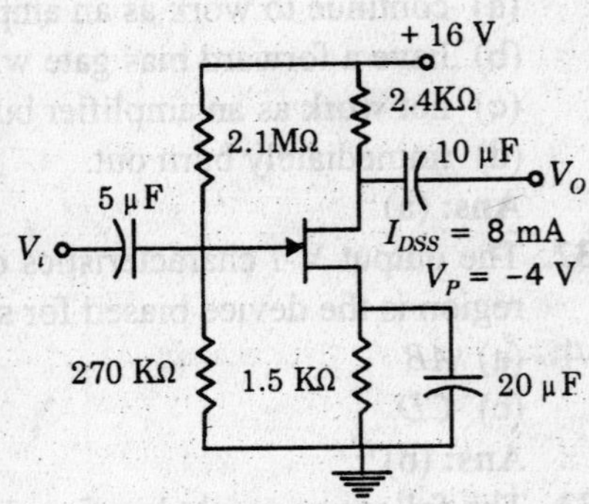


Fig. 7p15

**2.** Figure shows n-channel depletion type MOSFET, determine

(a) $I_D$ and $V_{GS}$ (b) $V_{DS}$

**Ans.** (a) 10.67mA, 1.5 V (b) 10.1 V

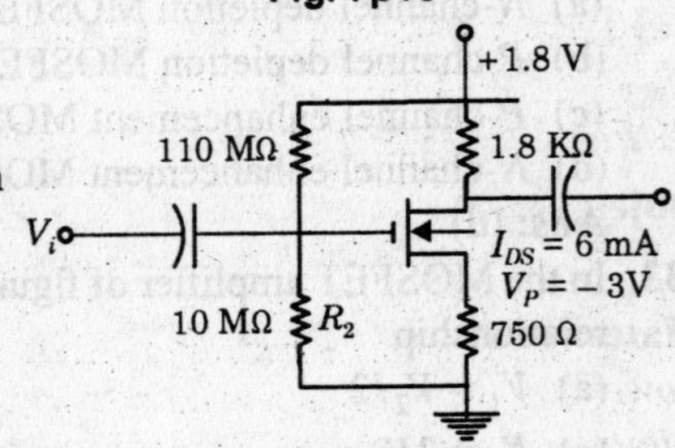


Fig. 7p16

**3.** Determine $R_S$ if $V_D$ = 12 V and $V_{GS}$ = – 2 V for voltage divider bias circuit shown below.

**Ans:** 3.35 k ohm

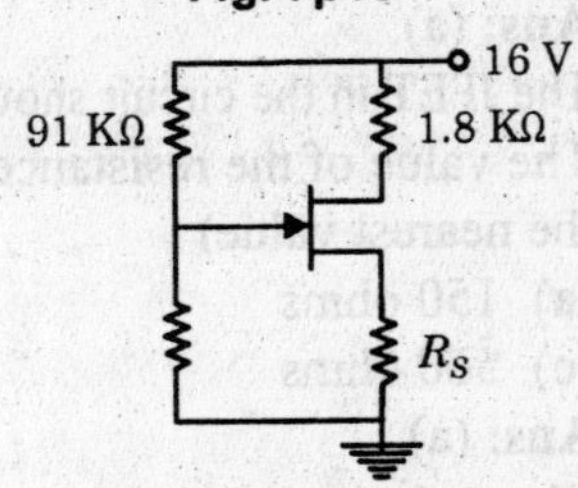


Fig. 7p17

**4.** Given $V_D$ = 9 determine

(a) $I_D$ (b) $V_{DS}$

(c) $V_{GG}$

**Ans:** 3.125 mA, 9 V, 1.5 V

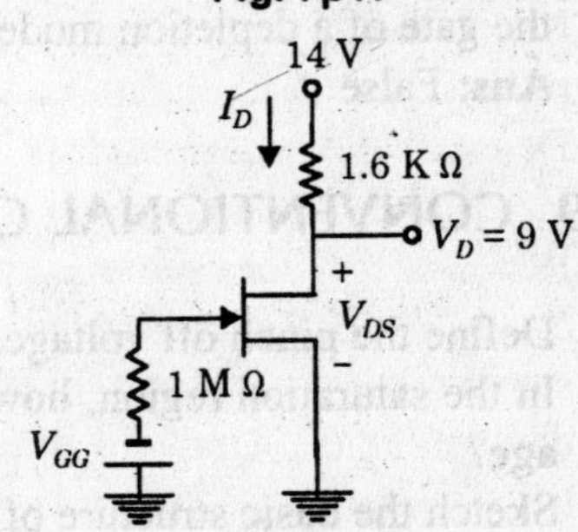


Fig. 7p18

**5.** Dermine $V_D$ for fixed bias configuration shown in figure.

**Ans:** 18 V

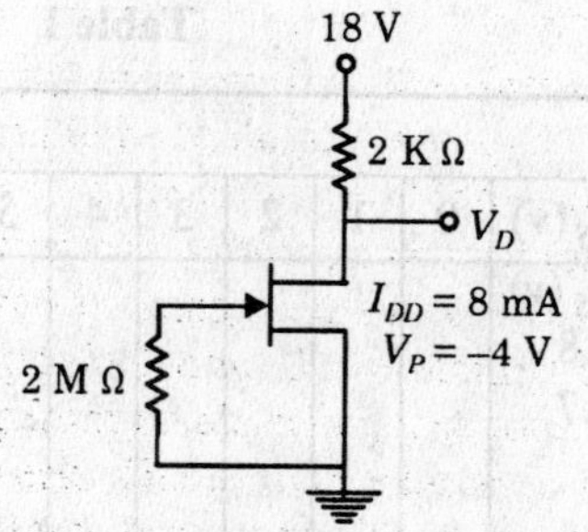


**Fig. 7P19**

**6.** Dermine $V_S$ for the configuration shown in figure.

**Ans:** 1.4 V

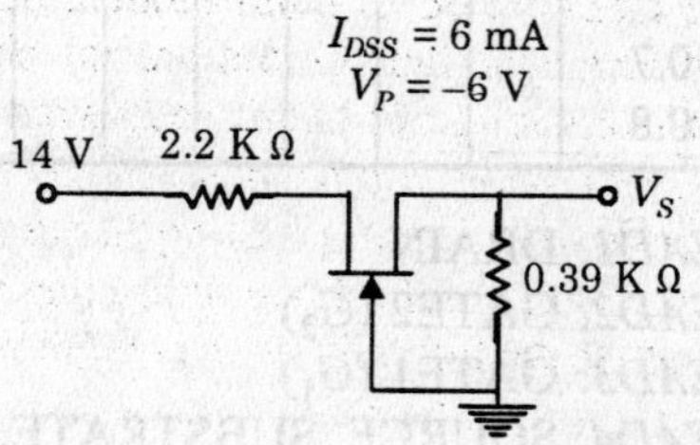


## 7.11 LAB EXPERIMENTS

### *1. Field Effect Transistors*

**Objective:** (1) To obtain Drain characteristics

(2) To calculate the gain of common-source amplifier.

**Material Required:**

*Power supply:* Two independent variable regulated low-voltage dc sources,

*Digital multimeter:* 0 – 10mA dc milliammeter or equivalent range on VOM.

*Resistors:* 1 kΩ, 10 kΩ, 2.2 MΩ ½ w

*Capacitors*: Two 0.047 µF, 100 µF 50 V

*Semiconductors:* 3N187 (MOSFET) or equivalent.

**Drain Characteristics:**

1. Figure 1 is a bottom view of the terminals of the 3N187. Connect the circuit of figure 2. $S_1$ and $S_2$ are off. Set $V_{DD}$ at 0 V, $V_{GG}$ at – 0.8 V.
2. Close $S_1$ and $S_2$ measure $I_D$ for $V_{GS}$ = – 0.8 V, $V_{DS}$ = 0, and record in Table1.
3. Maintain $V_{GS}$ at – 0.8 V. Increase $V_{GS}$ to + 1 V, + 3 V etc as in Table 1 and record the measured values of $I_D$
4. Decrease the negative bias $V_{GS}$ to – 0.7 V. Measure and record $I_D$ for each value of $V_{DS}$ listed in Table 1.
5. Repeat step 4 for each negative value of $V_{GS}$ and record $I_D$ in Table1.
6. $S_1$ and $S_2$ off. Reverse the polarity of $V_{GG}$, the gate bias supply, and repeat step 4 for $V_{GS}$ = 0 V and for each positive value of $V_{GS}$ and $V_{DD}$. From the date in Table 1. Draw the drain characteristics curves of the 3N187. Identify each curve.

**Table 1** Drain Characteristics

| | *ID (mA)* | | | | | | | | | | | | | | |
|---|---|---|---|---|---|---|---|---|---|---|---|---|---|---|---|
| $V_{DS}$(v) | 0 | 1 | 2 | 3 | 4 | 5 | 6 | 7 | 8 | 9 | 10 | 11 | 12 | 13 | 14 |
| $V_{GS}$ (v) | | | | | | | | | | | | | | | |
| – 0.8 | | | | | | | | | | | | | | | |
| – 0.7 | | | | | | | | | | | | | | | |
| . | | | | | | | | | | | | | | | |
| . | | | | | | | | | | | | | | | |
| . | | | | | | | | | | | | | | | |
| . | | | | | | | | | | | | | | | |
| + 0.7 | | | | | | | | | | | | | | | |
| + 0.8 | | | | | | | | | | | | | | | |

*LEAD1:* DRAIN
*LEAD2:* GATE2 ($G_2$)
*LEAD3:* GATE1 ($G_1$)
*LEAD4:* SOURCE, SUBSTRATE, AND CASE

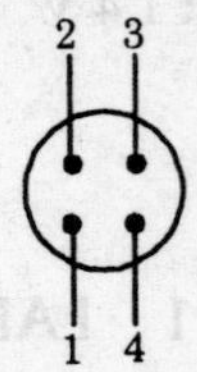


**Fig. 7L1**

Figure 1 Bottom view of 3N187 showing terminal arrangement

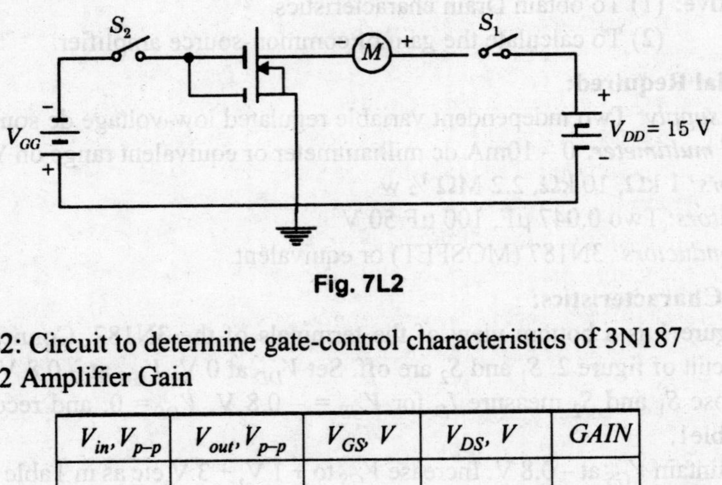


**Fig. 7L2**

Figure2: Circuit to determine gate-control characteristics of 3N187

Table 2 Amplifier Gain

| $V_{in}$, $V_{p\text{–}p}$ | $V_{out}$, $V_{p\text{–}p}$ | $V_{GS}$, $V$ | $V_{DS}$, $V$ | *GAIN* |
|---|---|---|---|---|
| | | | | |

**Common-source Amplifier:**

7. Open $S_1$. Connect the circuit of figure 2. Set $V_{DD}$ at + 15 V. Set the output of the sine-wave generator at 1000 Hz, minimum output.
8. Close $S_1$: with an oscilloscope, monitor the output signal $V_{out}$. Draw $I_D$ versus $V_{DS}$ characteristic curves for the voltage values Gradually increase the input signal for the maximum undistorted signal, $V_{out}$.

9. Experimentally determine the effect of increasing and decreasing the drain load resistor (a) on input signal level $V_{in}$ (b) on amplifier output and gain.

## 2. FET Characteristics

**Aim:** To plot the static characteristics of field effect transistor in common source configuration and to find $g_m$ and $r_d$ from the characteristics.

**Equipment and components required:**

| | |
|---|---|
| 1. N-Channel FET | BFW 10 |
| 2. Resistor | 1M-Ohm |
| 3. Ammeter | 0 – 25mA |
| 4. Voltmeter | 0 – 25volt |
| 5. Dual power supply | 0 – 30volt |
| 6. Breadboard and connecting wires. | |

**Circuit Diagram:**

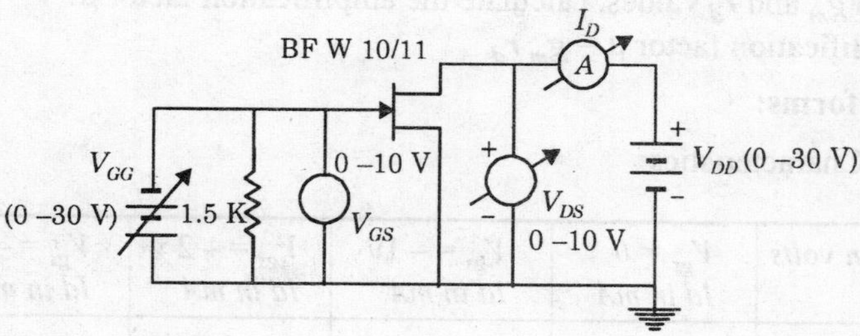


**Fig. 7L3**

**Theory:** The acronym FET stands for field effect transistor. It is three terminal uni- polar solid-state devices in which current is controlled by an electric field. It can be fabricated with either an *N*-channel or *P*-channel through *N*-channel is generally preferred. For fabricated an *N*-channel FET. First a narrow bar of *N*-type semiconductor material is taken and then two *P*-type junctions are diffused on opposite sides of its middle part. These junctions from two *PN* diodes or gates and the area between these gates is called the gate channel. The two *P* regions are internally connected and a single lead is brought out which is called the gate terminal. Ohmic contacts (direct electrical connections) are made at the two ends of the bar. One lead is called source(s) and the other is called the drain terminal (D). When potential difference is applied between drain and source, current flows through the channel. The current consists of only majority carriers. Therefore FET is a uni-Polar device.

### *Procedure:*

**Drain characteristics: Output characteristics:**

Connect the circuit as shown in the circuit diagram. Keep $V_{gs}$ constant at 0,– 1, – 2, – 3 volt etc. for each fixed value of $V_{gs}$, very $V_{ds}$ in steps of 1 V from 0 to 10 volts and note down the corresponding drain current $I_d$. Plot the graph

$I_d$ versus $V_{ds}$ for each value of $V_{gs}$. the set of curves obtained is called drain or output characteristics of common source FET configuration. From the above readings, for $V_{gs}$ = 0 note down the pinch off voltage $V_{ds}$ (sat).This is the voltage at which the drain current is maximum and remains constant at The value $I_{dss}$. From the graph calculate rd in the constant current region.

$$R_d = \text{drain resistance} = V_{ds}/I_d \text{ for constant } V_{gs}.$$

### *Transfer Characteristics:*

Keep $V_{ds}$ constant at a Value $V_{ds} > V_{ds}$ (SAT). For each value of $V_{ds}$ that should be greater than the pinch off voltage, vary $V_{gs}$ in steps of 0.5 volts. Proceed until to get a zero drain current and note down the corresponding drain current $I_d$ for each step. Take readings for different values of $V_{ds}$. Draw the plot $I_d$ versus $V_{gs}$. This is called transfer characteristics of FET. From the graph calculate the trans-conductance $g_m$.

Trans – conductance $g_m = I_d/V_{gs}$ at constant $V_{ds}$.

From $g_m$ and $r_d$ values, calculate the amplification factor μ.

Amplification factor $\mu = g_m\, r_d$.

**Tabular forms:**

1. Drain Characteristics:

| *$V_{ds}$ in volts* | *$V_{gs} = 0$ Id in mA* | *$V_{gs} = -1v$ Id in mA* | *$V_{gs} = -2v$ Id in mA* | *$V_{gs} = -3v$ Id in mA* |
|---|---|---|---|---|
| | | | | |

2. Trnasfer Characteristics:

| *$V_{gs}$ in volts* | *$V_{ds} > V_{ds}$(Sat) Id in mA* | *$V_{ds} > V_{ds}$(sat) Id in mA* | *$V_{ds} > V_{ds}$(sat) Id in mA* |
|---|---|---|---|
| | | | |

# ‹8›

# FET AMPLIFIER

## 8.1 INTRODUCTION

FET amplifiers provide an excellent voltage gain with the added feature of a high input impedance, they are also considered low power consumption configurations with minimal size and weight. While a BJT device controls a large output current by means of a relatively small input current. FET device controls an output current by means of a small input voltage therefore, in general we say the BJT is a current controlled device and FET is a voltage controlled device. FETs are used in high frequency applications and buffering applications. The amplifier analysis for JFET and MOSFET is same and they only differ in biasing.

## 8.2 LOW FREQUENCY SMALL SIGNAL MODEL OF FET AMPLIFIER

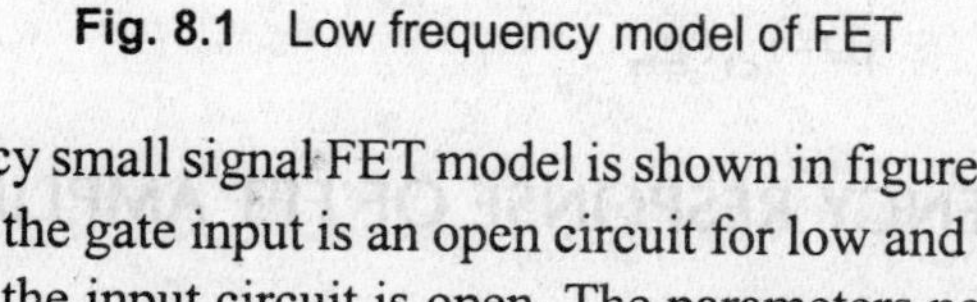


**Fig. 8.1** Low frequency model of FET

The low frequency small signal FET model is shown in figure 8.1. As the input is reverse biased the gate input is an open circuit for low and mid frequencies, so $R_i$ is $\infty$.Thus, the input circuit is open. The parameters needed to describe the FET are transconductance $g_m$ and drain-source output resistance $r_{ds}$.

The V-I equation of FET $I_D = f(V_{GS}, V_{DS})$. If both gate and drain voltages are varied, the change in drain current is given approximately by the first two terms in Taylors series expansion and higher order terms are neglected as variation of signal is small.

$$\Delta I_D = \frac{\partial I_D}{\partial V_{GS}} \Delta V_{GS} + \frac{\partial I_D}{\partial V_{DS}} \Delta V_{DS} \qquad \ldots(1)$$

In small signal notation

$\Delta I_D = i_d$, $\Delta V_{GS} = v_{gs}$ and $\Delta V_{DS} = v_{ds}$ so that equation (1) becomes

$$i_d = g_m v_{gs} + \frac{1}{r_d} v_{ds} \qquad \ldots(2)$$

Transconductance $g_m$:

$$g_m = \frac{\partial I_D}{\partial V_{GS}} = \frac{i_D}{V_{gs}} \qquad \ldots(3)$$

is mutual conductance or transconductance. It is also called forward transadmittance.

While the voltage gain of a FET is neglecting $r_{ds}$.

$$Av = \frac{v_{ds}}{v_{gs}} = -g_m R_L. \qquad \ldots(4)$$

*Drain source resistance:*

Drain source resistance is defined as

$$r_{ds} = \frac{\partial V_{DS}}{\partial i_{DS}} \approx \frac{\Delta V_{DS}}{\Delta i_D} |V_{GS} = \frac{v_{ds}}{i_d} |V_{GS} \qquad \ldots(5)$$

Reciprocal of $r_d$ is drain conductance $g_d$.

*Amplification factor:*

An amplification factor μ is defined as the product of $g_m r_{ds}$.

$$\mu = \frac{\partial V_{DS}}{\partial V_{GS}} |I_D = \frac{-\Delta V_{DS}}{\Delta V_{GS}} I_D = \frac{v_{ds}}{v_{gs}} \qquad \ldots(6)$$

We can verify that μ, $r_d$, $g_m$ are related by

$$\mu = r_{ds} \cdot g_m \qquad \ldots(7)$$

## 8.3 FREQUENCY RESPONSE OF FET AMPLIFIER

In the low frequency region, below the midband, an amplifier stage behaves like the simple high- pass circuit of figure 8.2 of time constant $T_1 = R_1 C_1$, from this circuit we find that

$$V_0 = \frac{V_i R_1}{R_1 - J/wC_1} = \frac{V_i}{R_1 - J/wR_1 C_1}$$

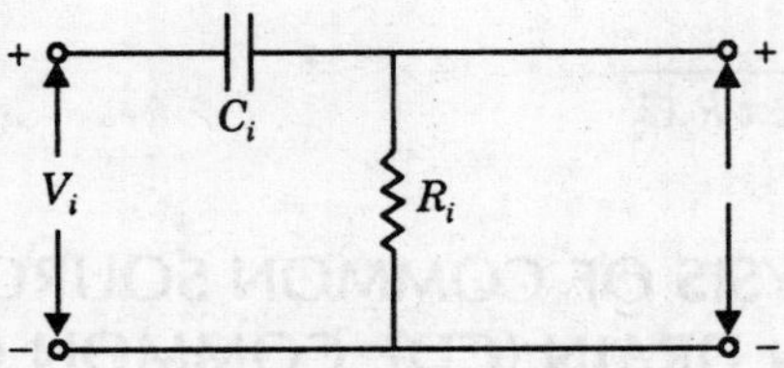

**Fig. 8.2** A high-pass *RC* circuit to calculate low frequency response of amplifier.

The voltage gain at low frequencies $A_{vL}$ is defined as the ratio of the output voltage $V_o$ to the input voltage $V_i$, or

$$Av_L = \frac{V_o}{V_i} = \frac{A_{vm}}{1 - j(f_1/f)} \quad \text{where } f_1 = \frac{1}{2\pi R_1 C_1}$$

The magnitude $|Av_L|$ and phase lag $\theta_1$, of the gain are given by

$$|A_{VL}| = \frac{A_{vm}}{\sqrt{1 + (f_1/f)^2}} \quad \theta = \text{Tan}^{-1}\,(f_1/f).$$

at the frequency $f = f_1$, $A_{vL} = \frac{A_{vm}}{\sqrt{2}} = 0.707$ whereas in midband region

$(f >> f_1)$, $A_{vL} \rightarrow A_{Vm}$. Hence $f_1$ is that frequencies at which gain has fallen to 0.707 times its midland value $A_{vh}$, $f_1$ is referred to as lower $3dB$ frequency.

*Mid frequency response:* Mid band frequencies is a range over the amplification is reasonably constant and equal to $A_{Vm}$ and over which the delay is also quite constant. we assume that midband gain is normalized to unity, $A_{Vm} = 1$

$$A_{vm} = \frac{V_o}{V_s} = g_m\,(r_d \| R_L)$$

*High frequency response:* In the high frequency response, above the midband, amplifier stage behaves like the simple for low pass circuit with time constant $R_2\,C_2$. Procedure is as above, we obtain for the magnitude $|A_{Vm}|$ and the phase lag $\theta_2$ of the gain

$$|A_{V\mu}| = \frac{A_{Vm}}{\sqrt{1 + \left(\frac{f}{f_2}\right)^2}} \quad \theta_2 = \tan^{-1}\,(f/f_2)$$

Since $f = f_2$ the gain is reduced to $\frac{1}{\sqrt{2}}$ times its midland value, then $f_2$ is called the upper 3-db frequency

Where $\quad f_2 = \dfrac{1}{2\pi R_2 C_2}$

## 8.4 MF ANALYSIS OF COMMON SOURCE (CS), COMMON DRAIN (CD), COMMON GATE (CG)

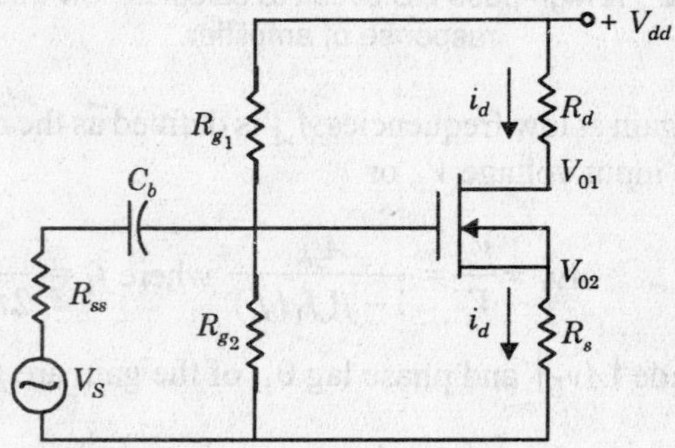


Fig. 8.3(a) Common source FET

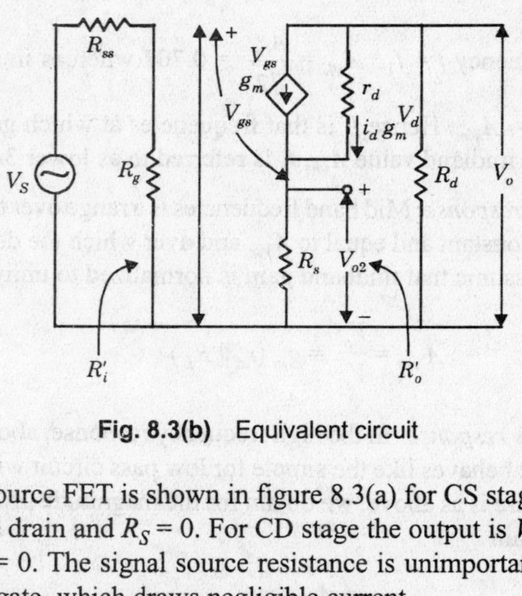


Fig. 8.3(b) Equivalent circuit

The common source FET is shown in figure 8.3(a) for CS stage the output is $V_{01}$ taken at the drain and $R_S = 0$. For CD stage the output is $V_{02}$ taken at the source and $R_d = 0$. The signal source resistance is unimportant since it is in series with the gate, which draws negligible current.

Replacing FET by its small signal model the equivalent circuit of figure 8.3(b) is obtained. Applying KVL to the output we get

$$i_d R_s + i_d R_d + (i_d - g_m V_{gs})\, r_d = 0$$

$$i_d \times \{R_s + R_d + r_d\} = g_m r_d V_{gs}$$

Since $\mu = r_d g_m$.

$$i_d \{R_s + R_d + r_d\} = \mu V_{gs} \quad \cdots(1)$$

From figure 8.3(b) the voltage from $G$ to $S$ is

$$V_{gs} = V_i - i_d R \quad \cdots(2)$$

Substitute equation (2) In (1) we get

$$i_d \{R_s + R_d + r_d\} = \mu \{V_i - i_d R_s\}$$

$$i_d \{R_s + R_d + r_d\} = \mu V_i - \mu i_d R_s$$

$$i_d \{R_s (1 + \mu) + R_d + r_d\} = \mu V_i$$

$$i_d = \frac{-\mu V_i}{R_d + R_d + (\mu + 1) R_s} \quad \ldots(3)$$

*CS Amplifier*: Across $R_d$

*Voltage gain $A_v$*: since $V_{01} = -i_d R_d$ ...(4)

Substitute (3) in (4)

$$V_{01} = \frac{-\mu V_i R_d}{r_d + R_d + (\mu + 1) R_s} \quad \ldots(5)$$

$$A_v = \frac{V_{01}}{V_i}, \qquad A_v = \frac{-\mu_i R_d}{r_d + R_d + (\mu + 1) R_s} \quad \ldots(6)$$

If $R_s$ is by passed with a large capacitance or if the source is grounded, then $R_s = 0$. Under these circumtances

$$A_v = \frac{\mu R_d}{r_d + R_d} \quad \ldots(7)$$

$$= -g_m (r_d \| R_d)$$

*Input Resistance:*

$$R_i = \infty$$

$$R_i^1 = R_i \| R_g = \infty \| R_g = R_g \quad \ldots(8)$$

*Output resistance:*

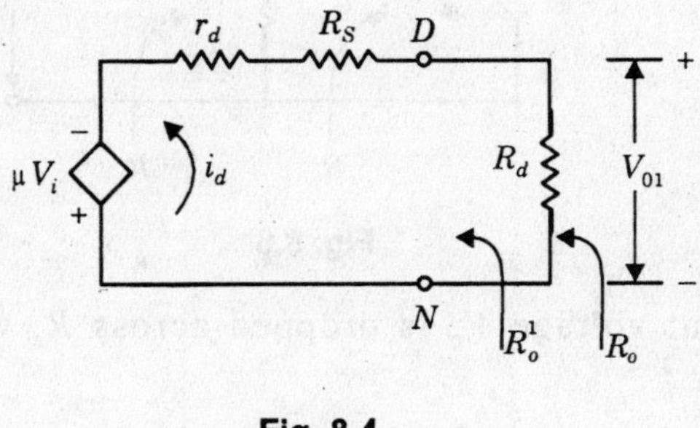


**Fig. 8.4**

The open circuit voltage is $-\mu V_i$, and output resistance $R_o$ is $R_0^1 = r_d + (\mu + 1) R_s$. When $R_s = 0$

$$R'_0 = r_d$$

The output resistance $R_o = (R_0^1 \| R_d)$ ...(9)

*CD Amplifier:*

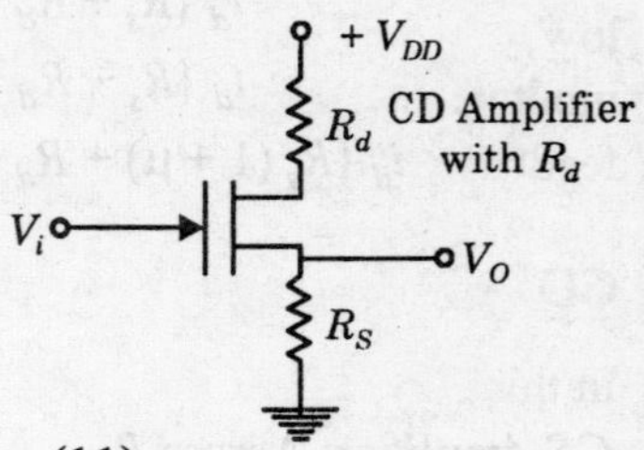

Fig. 8.5

*Voltage gain $A_v$:* The output is taken from the source and the output voltage is $V_o$ given by

$$V_o = i_d R_s \quad \text{...(10)}$$

From equation (3) $i_d$ can be written as

$$I_d = \frac{\mu V_i}{r_d + R_d + (\mu + 1) R_s} \quad \text{...(11)}$$

$$V_o = \frac{\mu V_i}{r_d + R_d + (\mu + 1) R_s} Rs \quad \text{...(12)}$$

$$\frac{V_o}{V_i} = \frac{\mu R_s}{r_d + R_d + (\mu + 1) R_s} \text{ with } R_d$$

$$\frac{V_o}{V_i} = \frac{\mu R_s}{r_d + R_d + (\mu + 1) R_s} \text{ without } R_d$$

Dividing the numerator and denominator by $(\mu + 1)$

$$i_d = \frac{\left(\frac{\mu}{\mu + 1}\right) V_i}{\frac{r_d + R_d}{(\mu + 1)} + R_s} \quad \text{...(13)}$$

*Output resistance:*

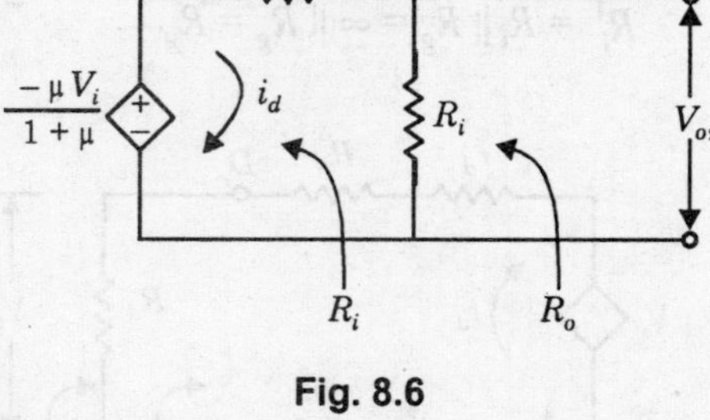

Fig. 8.6

The output voltage $V_o$ is dropped across $R_s$ where the source voltage $\left(\frac{\mu}{\mu + 1}\right) V_i$ is supplied to two resistors in series as shown in the figure

$\therefore$ The output resistance $R'_O = \dfrac{r_d + R_d}{1+\mu}$ ...(15)

$$R_O = R'_O \parallel R_s \qquad ...(16)$$

In the CD amplifier normally we don't take $R_d$ because gain should not betoo low, output impedance is very small. In CC & CD total output is feedback to input instead of part of output. This gain can become far less than 1, if another feedback is also allowed due to $R_d$ or $R_s$.

## CD Amplifier Without $R_d$:

In this confriguation $R_d = 0$. The voltage gain reduces to

$$A_v = \frac{\left(\dfrac{\mu}{\mu+1}\right)R_s}{\dfrac{r_d}{\mu+1} + R_s} \qquad ...(17)$$

Multiplying numerator and denominator by $(\mu + 1)$

$$A_v = \frac{\mu R_s}{r_d + (\mu+1)R_s} \qquad ...(18)$$

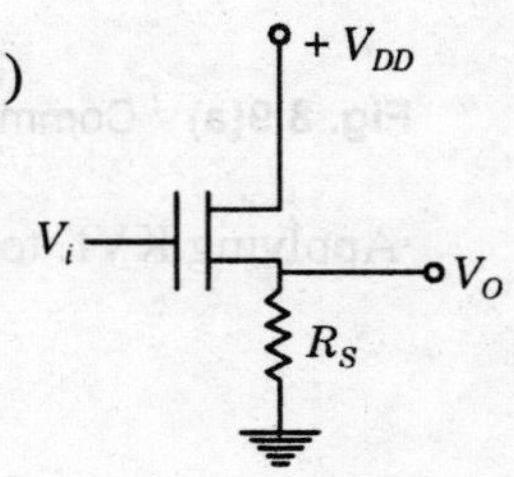

Fig. 8.7

If $(\mu + 1)R_s >> r_d$ then $r_d$ can be ignored

$$\therefore \quad A_v = \frac{\mu R_s}{(\mu+1)R_s} = \frac{\mu}{\mu+1} \qquad ...(19)$$

$\because$ $\mu >> 1;\quad A_v \approx 1$

Since $A_V \approx 1$, the source voltage is almost equal to input voltage, this circuit is known as *"source follower"* similar to follower for BJT.

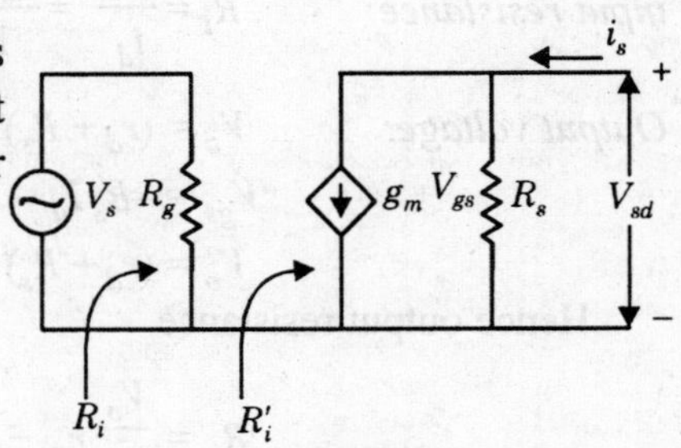

Fig. 8.8

*Input resistance:*

The input resistance is

$$R'_i = \infty$$

$$R_i = \infty \parallel R_g = R_g \qquad ...(20)$$

*Output resistance:*

Since $R_d = 0$ equation (15) reduces to

$$R'_o = \frac{r_d}{\mu+1}$$

Since μ >>1 hence ( μ + 1) = μ

$$\therefore \qquad R_0' = \frac{r_d}{\mu} = \frac{r_d}{g_m r_d} = \frac{1}{g_m}$$

$$R_0 = R_0' \parallel R_s.$$

## Common Gate Amplifier

1. The common gate FET is shown in figure 8.9(*a*).

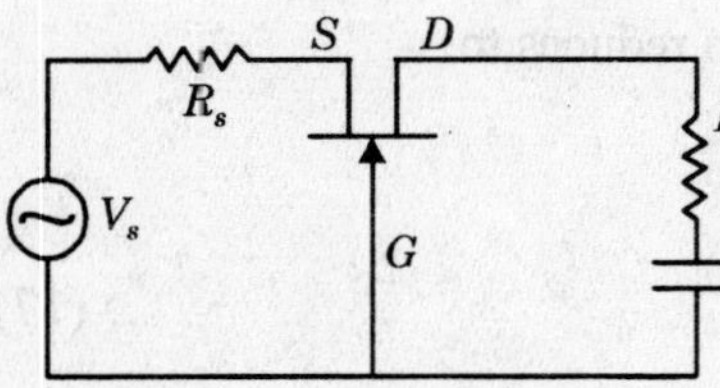


**Fig. 8.9(a)** Common gate FET

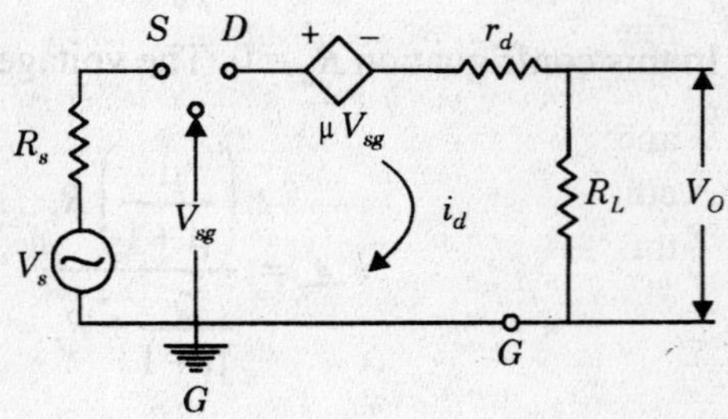


**Fig. 8.9(b)** Equivalent circuit

Applying KVL to the output we get

$$V_{sg} = \mu V_{gs} + (r_d + R_L)\, i_d$$

$$= \mu(-V_{sg}) + (r_d + R_L)\, i_d$$

$$(1+\mu)\, V_{sg} = (r_d + R_L)\, i_d$$

*input resistance:* $$R_i = \frac{V_{sg}}{i_d} = \frac{r_d + R_L}{1+\mu}$$

*Output voltage:* $$V_o = (r_d + R_s)\, i_d - \mu V_{gs}$$

$$V_{gs} = -R_s I_d$$

$$V_o = (r_d + R_s)\, i_d + R_s i_d = \{r_d + (1+\mu)\, R_s\} i_d$$

Hence output resistance

$$R_o = \frac{V_o}{i_o} r_d + (1+\mu)\, r_s$$

$$V_i = (r_s + r_d + R_L)\, i_d + \mu\, V_{gs} = 0$$

$$V_{sg} = -V_{gs} = V_i - R_i i_d$$

Combining above two equations

Hence $$i_d = \frac{(1+\mu)V_i}{r_d + R_2 + (1+\mu)r_s}$$

$$V_o = R_L i_d = \frac{(1+\mu)R_L V_i}{r_d + R_L + (1+\mu)r_s}$$

Voltage gain $$A_v = \frac{(1+\mu)R_L}{r_d + R_L + (1+\mu)R_i}$$

## 8.5 LOW FREQUENCY ANALYSIS OF CS

In the low frequency range let us assume that the bypass capacitor Cs is infinitely large and the coupling capacitors have finite reactance.

At low frequency, all inter electrode capacitance behave as open circuit and do not play any role in its analysis. Thus the small signal equivalent circuit of figure 8.10(a) is reduced to figure 8.10 (b). The inter electrode capacitors behave as open circuit at low frequency.

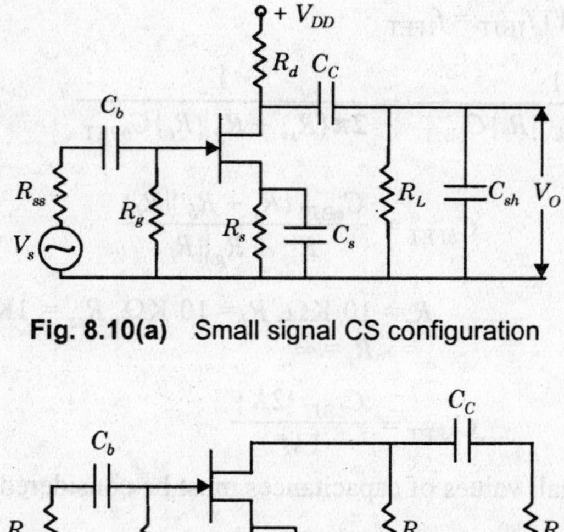


**Fig. 8.10(a)** Small signal CS configuration

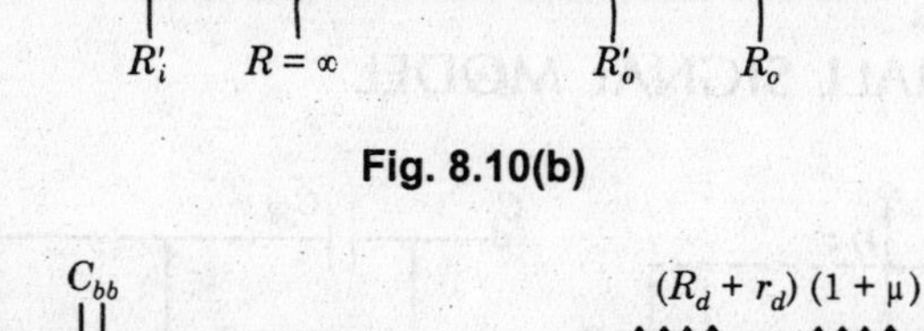


**Fig. 8.10(b)**

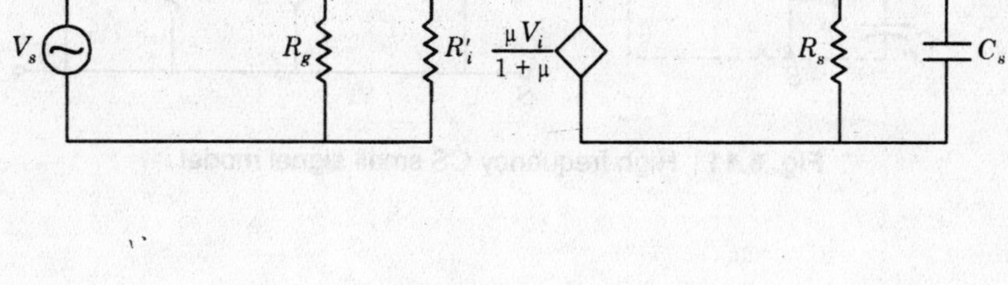

Low frequency range when $Xs \neq 0$

$$f_{1Cb} = \frac{1}{2\pi R_{eq} C_b}$$

$$= \frac{1}{2\pi\{R_{ss} + (R_g \| R_i^1)\}\, C_b}$$

$$f_{1_{cc}} = \frac{1}{2\pi\{R_o^1 \| R_d + R_l\}\, C_C}$$

$$f_{1_{cs}} = \frac{1}{2\pi\left\{\left(\frac{R_d + r_d}{1+\mu}\right) \| R_s\right\} C_s}$$

In order to have equal $f_1$ using BJT and FET, the value of $C_b$ (FET) in terms of $C_b$(BJT) $f_{1\text{BJT}} = f_{1\text{FET}}$

$$\frac{1}{2\pi\{R_s + R_b \| R_i\} C_{b\text{BJT}}} = \frac{1}{2\pi\{R_{ss} + R_g \| R_i\} C_{b\text{FET}}}$$

$$C_{b\text{FET}} = \frac{C_{b\text{BJT}}\{R_s + R_b \| R_i\}}{R_{ss} + R_g \| R_i}$$

where $R_s = 10\ \text{K}\Omega$, $R_b = 10\ \text{K}\Omega$, $R_{ss} = 1\text{K}\Omega$, $R_g = 1\text{M}\Omega$, $R_i = \infty$

$$C_{b\text{FET}} = \frac{C_{b\text{BJT}}\{2K\}}{1M}$$

for FET small values of capacitances must be considered

$$C_{b\text{FET}} = \frac{1}{500} C_{b\text{BJT}}$$

## 8.6 HF SMALL SIGNAL MODEL

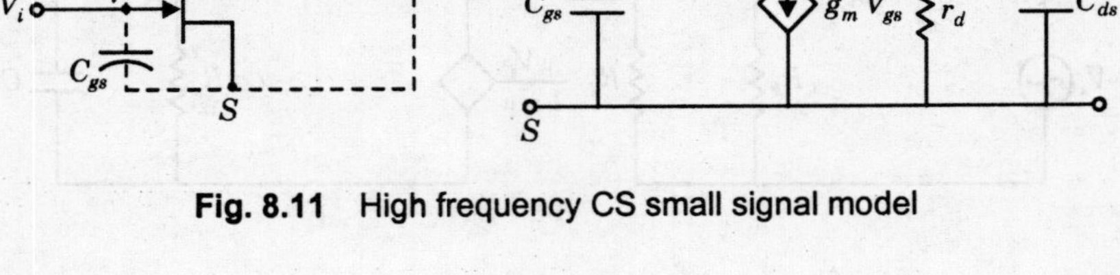


**Fig. 8.11** High frequency CS small signal model

The FET also exhibits inter electrodes capacitances due to *Pn* junction and the channel which limits the frequency response of the FET amplifiers at high frequency. The capacitor $C_{gd}$ works as the feedback element. This capacitor can be replaced by its equivalent values across its input and output terminals using Miller's theorem.

According to Miller's theorem

$$Z_i = \frac{Z_f}{1-A_v} = \frac{1}{(1-A_v)j\,\omega\,C_{gd}}$$

Hence the portion of $C_{gd}$ reflected across the input terminals is $(1-A_v)C_{gd}$.

Similarly the impedance reflected across the output terminals due to the presence of $C_{gd}$ is

$$Zo = \frac{A_v Z_f}{(1-A_v)} \equiv Z_f = \frac{1}{j\,\omega C_{gd}}$$

The total input capacitances

$$C_i = C_{gs} + (1-A_v)\,C_{gd}.$$

Hence $C_{gd}$ split in to two portions works as two time constants. Since the total input capacitance is much larger than the output capacitance, the effect of $C_{gd}$ on the output side is neglected.

**Case(1):** *$f_2$ with out shunt capacitor $c_{sh}$:*

$$T_{2i} = (R_s \,\|\, R_g)\,(C_i)$$

$$T_{2o} = (r_d \,\|\, R_L)\,(C_o)$$

At high frequency lowest cut off frequency or largest constant dominates $T_{2i}$ is far greater than $T_{20}$.

$$\therefore \qquad f_2 = \frac{1}{2\pi\tau_{2i}}$$

**Case (2):** *$RL \neq 0$ with shunt capacitor*

$T_{2i}$ remains same.

$$T_{20} = (r_d \,\|\, R_L)\{C_{ds} + C_{gd} + C_{sh}\}$$

$$T_{20} \approx R_L\,C_{sh}.$$

$$f_2 = f_{20} = \frac{1}{2\pi\,R_L C_{sh}}$$

Input admittance at High frequency: $Y_i = \dfrac{1}{R_g} + j\omega\,C_i$

Output impedance $Y_0 = \dfrac{1}{r_d} + \dfrac{1}{R_L}\,j\omega\,C_o$

$$\text{Voltage gain } A_v\,(\text{H.F}) = \frac{V_o}{V_1} = \frac{-g_m R_{eq}}{1 + j\omega C_{r_{eq}}} = \frac{A_v\,(M.F)}{1 + j\left(\dfrac{\omega}{\omega_2}\right)}$$

Where $\omega_2 = \dfrac{1}{C_{\text{Req}}}$

## HF analysis of CD amplifier

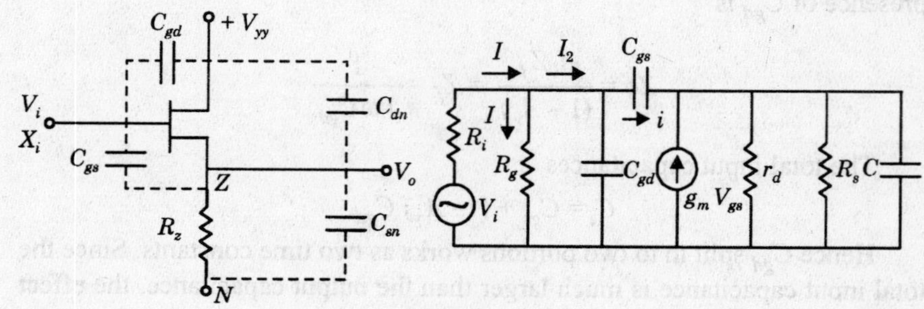

**Fig. 8.12(a)** CD at high frequency **Fig. 8.12(b)** Simplified equiva lent circuit of CD at high frequency

The coupling and bypass capacitors behaves as short circuit as depicted in figure 8.12

*Input Admittance:*

$$I_1 = V_i\,(j\omega\, C_{gd})$$

$$I_2 = (V_i - V_o)\, j\omega\, C_{gs}$$

$$= V_i\,(1 - A_v)\,(\omega\, j\, C_{gs})$$

$$Y_i = \frac{I}{V_i} = \frac{I_1 + I_2}{v_i}$$

$$Y_i = j\omega\, C_{gd} + j\omega\, C_{gs}\,(1 - A_v)$$

Input resistance is given by

$$C_i = C_{gd} + C_{gs}\,(1 - A_v)$$

*Output Admittance:*

The output admittance $Y_o$ with considered external to the amplifier, is given by

$$Y_o = g_m + g_d + j\omega C$$

$$A_v \equiv \frac{(g_m + j\omega C_{gs})\, R_s}{1 + (g_m + g_d + j\omega\, C)\, R_s}$$

## 8.7 GAIN BANDWIDTH PRODUCT

Gain-Bandwidth product is the product of mid frequency gain and upper cut off frequency. This can be studied in two cases.

Let us consider common source amplifier

**Case (1):** $R_L \neq 0$ without shunt capacitor of

$$|Av_m f_2| = |Av_m f_{2i}|.$$

$$= \frac{g_m\, R_L}{2\pi\,(R_{ss} \| R_g)(C_{gs} + C_{gd}\,(1 + g_m R_L)}$$

$$g_m R_L >> 1 \text{ and } C_{gs} << C_{gd}\, g_m\, R_L$$

$$\therefore \quad Av_m f_2 = \frac{1}{2\pi\,(R_{ss} \| R_g)}$$

Therefore gain bandwidth product of loaded amplifier without shunt capacitot is almost constant.

**Case (2):** $R_L \neq 0$ with shunt capacitor of

$$|Av_m f_2| = |Av_m f_{20}|.$$

$$= \frac{g_m R_L}{2\pi R_L C_{sh}}$$

$$= \frac{g_m}{2\pi C_{sh}}$$

Therefore by changing shunt capacitor we can change gain bandwidth product. Hence it is not constant if shunt capacitor is connected.

## 8.8 SOLVED PROBLEMS

1. **Calculate the voltage gain $A_V = V_o/V_i$ at 5 KHz for the circuit shown. (a) The FET parameters are $g_m = 2mA/V$ and $r_d = 10K$. Neglect capacitances. (b) Repeat part (a) if the capacitance 0.025μF is taken under consideration.**

**Solution:**

$$g_m = 2mA/V;\ r_d = 10K$$

**(a)** $R_L^I = 30\text{K} \parallel 30\text{K} = \dfrac{30\times 30}{30+30} = 15\text{K}\Omega$

$$A_V = \frac{V_o}{V_i} = \frac{-\mu R_L^I}{R_L^I + r_d + R_S(1+\mu)} = -\frac{g_m r_d R_L^I}{R_L^I + r_d}$$

$$= \frac{-(2\times 10^{-3})(10\times 10^{3})(15\times 10^{3})}{(15\times 10^{-3})+(10\times 10^{3})}$$

$A_V = -29.99 \approx -30$

**(b)** $C = 0.025\mu F$

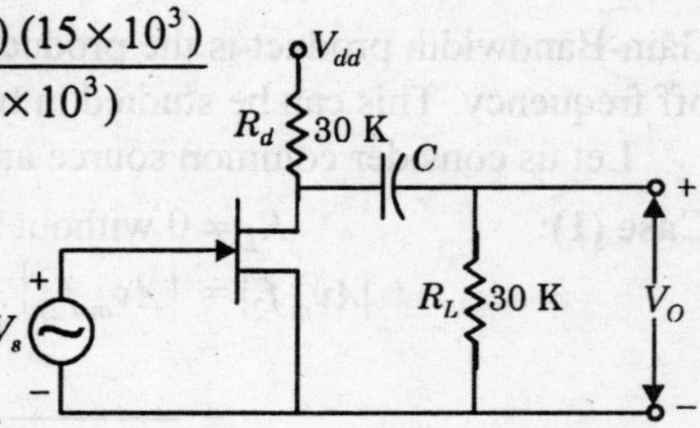


Fig. 8P1

$$f_1 = \frac{1}{2\pi(r_d \parallel R_d + R_L)C_C}$$

$$f_1 = \frac{1}{2\pi((10\text{K} \parallel 30\text{K}) + 30\text{K})0.025\times 10^{-6}} = 169.7\text{Hz}$$

$$\therefore \quad A_{VL} = \frac{A_v}{\sqrt{1+\left(\frac{f_1}{f}\right)^2}} = \frac{-30}{\sqrt{1+\left(\frac{169.7}{5k}\right)^2}}$$

**2. If an input signal $V_i$ is impressed between gate and ground, find the amplification, $A_V = V_O/V_i$. Apply Miller's theorem to the 80k resistor. The FET parameters are $\mu = 30$, $r_d = 5$k. Neglect capacitances.**

**Solution:**

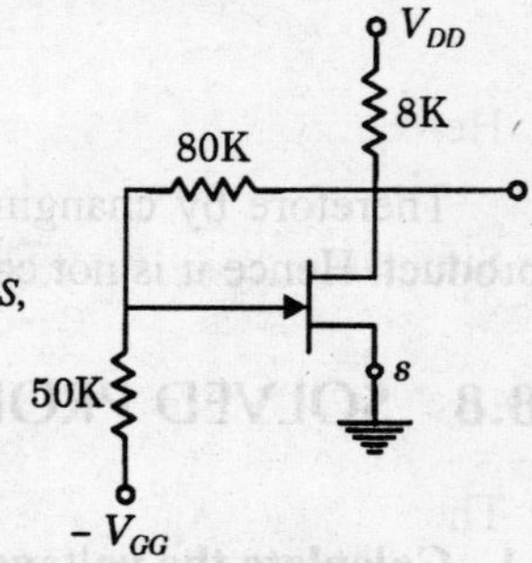


Fig. 8P2

$\mu = 30, \quad r_d = 5\text{k}$

$$A_V = \frac{V_o}{V_i} = \frac{-\mu R_D^1}{R_D^1 + r_d + R_S(1+1)} \text{ with } R_S,$$

$$A_V = \frac{-\mu R_D^1}{R_D^1 + r_d} \text{ and without } R_S,$$

$$R_D^1 = R_D \parallel \frac{50}{\left(1-\frac{1}{A_V}\right)}$$

$$\text{Therefore } R_D^1 = \frac{80\text{K} \times 8\text{K}}{80\text{K} + 8\text{K}\left(1 - \frac{1}{A_V}\right)}$$

$$A_V = \frac{V_o}{V_i} = \frac{-\mu R_D^1}{R_D^I + r_d} = \frac{\dfrac{-(30)\,640\text{M}}{80\text{K}+8\text{K}\left(1-\frac{1}{A_V}\right)}}{\dfrac{640\text{M}+5\text{K}\{80\text{K}+8\text{K}(1-1/A_V)\}}{80K+8\text{K}\left(1-\frac{1}{A_V}\right)}} = -19200\text{M}$$

$$A_V(640\text{M} + 400 + 40\text{M}) = 19200\text{M} + 40\text{M}$$

$$A_V = \frac{-18800}{1080} = -17.4$$

Therefore $\quad A_V = -17.4$

**3. In the above problem 2, the signal $V_i$ is impressed in series with the 60k resistor (instead of from gate to ground). Find $A_V = \frac{V_o}{V_i}$**

**Solution:**

As we got $\quad A_V = \frac{V_o}{V_i} = -17.4$, from above problem 2

Here $\quad A_V = \frac{V_o}{V_i} = \frac{V_o}{V_i^1}\frac{V_i^1}{V_i}$

Substitute $\quad A_V = -17.4,\ R_G = 80\text{K}$

$$\text{Therefore } A_V = \frac{(-17.4)\left(\frac{R_{G1}}{1-A_V}\right)}{\left(\frac{R_{G1}}{1-A_V}\right) + 60\text{K}} = \frac{(-17.4)\left(\frac{80}{1+17.4}\right)}{\left(\frac{80}{1+17.4}\right)+60} = -1.175.$$

**4. (a) A MOSFET connected in CS configuration works into a 10k resistive load. Calculate the complex voltage gain and the input admittance of the system for frequencies of 500Hz and 500KHz. Take the**

**inter electrode capacitances into consideration. The MOSFET parameters are $\mu = 100$, $r_d = 40K$, $g_m = 2.5mA/V$, $C_{gs} = 4.0PF$, $C_{ds} = 0.6PF$, and $C_{gd} = 2.4PF$. Compare these results with those obtained when the inter electrode capacitances are neglected.**

**(b) Calculate the input resistance and capacitance.**

**Solution:**

Given $\mu = 100$, $r_d = 40K$, $g_m = 2.5mA/V$, $C_{gs} = 4pF$, $C_{ds} = 0.6pF$,

$C_{gd} = 2.4pF$, $R_D = R_L = 10K$

(a)
$$A_{Vm} = \frac{-\mu R_D^1}{R_D^1 + r_d} = \frac{-100\,(10K)}{10K + \alpha_1 0K} = -20$$

$$f_{20} = \frac{1}{2\pi\, R_O C_O}$$

$$R_o = R_D \,\|\, r_D = \frac{(40K)\,(100K)}{40K + 100K} = 28.57k\Omega$$

$$= \frac{(40K)\,(10K)}{40K + 10K} = 8k\Omega$$

$$C_O = C_{ds} + C_{gd} = 0.6pF + 2.4pF = 3pF$$

$$f_{20} = \frac{1}{2\pi(8\times 10^3)\,(3\times 10^{-12})}$$

$\therefore$
$$f_{20} = 6.6MHz$$

$\therefore$
$$A_{Vh} = \frac{1}{1 + j(f/f_{2\alpha})}$$

At $f = 500Hz$,

$$A_{Vh} = \frac{-20}{1 + j\left(\dfrac{500}{1.856M}\right)} = -20$$

At $f = 100Hz$,

$$A_{Vh} = -20.1$$

(b)
$$C_1 = C_{gs} + C_{gd}\,(1 - A_{Vm})$$
$$= 4\times 10^{-12} + 2.4\times 10^{-12}\,(1-(-20))$$
$$= 4\times 10^{-12} + 2.4\times 10^{-12}\,(1 + 20)$$

$$C_i = 54.4\text{pF}$$

$$R_i^1 = \alpha, R_i = R_i^1 \parallel R_G$$

$$\therefore \quad R_i = R_G$$

**5. Consider the JFET circuit of figure (a) Determine the resistance seen from terminal 2 and ground at low frequencies (b) Evaluate the resistance in part (a) for $R_D$= 4KΩ, $R_S$= 2.5KΩ, $R_1$= 200KΩ, $R_2$= 100KΩ, $g_m$ = 2.5ms and $r_d$= 60 kΩ (c) Repeat part (b) if $R_D$ = 0**

**Solution:**

The small signal model of the circuit is below

Use of Thevenin's equivalent, converts the circuit to that given below:

If an input signal of 1V is applied

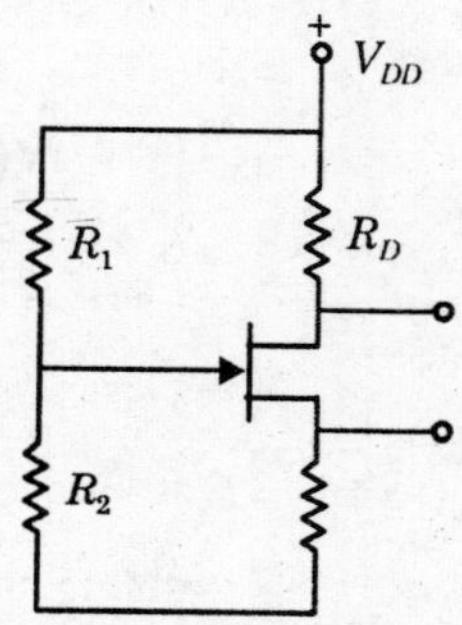


Fig. 8P3(a)

$$V_{gs} = 1 - \mathrm{R_s}\left(\frac{\mu V_{gs}}{r_d + R_S + R_D}\right)$$

$$V_{gs} = \left(\frac{r_d + R_S + R_D}{r_d(1+\mu)R_S + R_D}\right)$$

O.C voltage $V_{2G}\,(\text{O.C.}) = \left(\dfrac{\mu V_{gs}}{r_d + R_S + R_D}\right) \times R_S$

$$= \left(\frac{\mu R_S}{r_d + (1+\mu)R_S + R_D}\right)$$

Short circuit current (terminal 2 shorted to $G$)

$$V_{gs} = V_i = 1\text{V as } R_S \text{ is shorted}$$

$$I_{2G}(S.C.) = \frac{\mu V_{gs}}{r_d + R_D} = \frac{\mu V_{gs}}{r_d + R_D}$$

Resistance as seen from terminal 2 and $G$

$$R_0 = V_{2G}(O.C)/I_{2g}(S.C)$$

$$= \frac{\mu R_s}{r_d + (1+\mu R_S) + R_D} \times \frac{(r_d + R_d)}{\mu}$$

$$= \frac{1}{1 + \dfrac{(1+\mu)R_S}{r_d + R_D}}$$

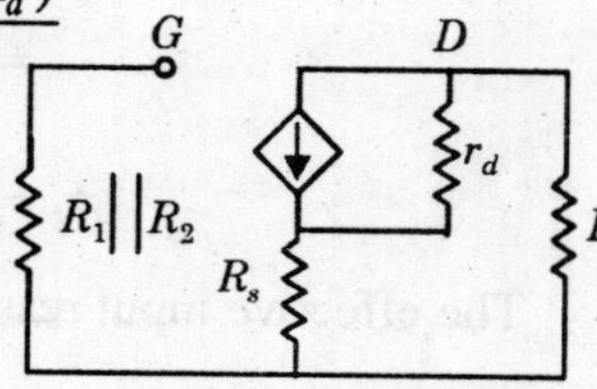


Fig. 8P3(b)

(b) $$R_0 = \frac{2.5}{1+\frac{(1+2.5+60)2.5}{60+4}} = 362\Omega$$

(c) $R_D = 0$

$$R_o = \frac{2.5}{1+\frac{(1+2.5+60)2.5}{60+4}} = 343\Omega.$$

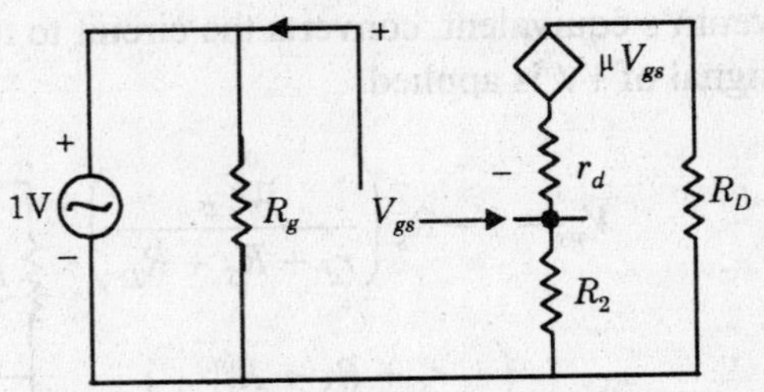


Fig. 8P3(c)

**6. Design a source follower circuit at *Q*-point $V_{DS}$ = 14V, $I_{DQ}$ = 3mA, $V_{DD}$ = 20V, $g_m$ = 2ms, $r_d$ = 50k, $V_{GS}$ = –1.5V**

**Solution:**

The circuit of bootstrapped source follower may be considered for this Hence 20V= 14V + 3mA $(R_1 + R_2)$

$$R_1 + R_2 = 2K$$

$$-1.5 = -3\text{mA } R_1 \quad \Rightarrow \quad R_1 = 0.5K$$

$$R_2 = 2 - 0.5 = 1.5K$$

Output resistance $R_o = 1/g_m = 1/2\text{ms} = 0.5\text{k}\Omega$

$$V_s = A_v^1 V_g \frac{(R_1 + R_2)}{R_1 + R_2 - \frac{1}{g_m}}$$

$$= A_v^1 V_g \frac{2k}{2\text{ k} + 0.5\text{ k}}$$

$$A_V = V_s/V_g = 0.8\, A_v^1$$

The effective input resistance is expressed as

$$R_1 = \frac{R_3}{1+\frac{V_s}{V_g}\left(\frac{R_2}{R_1+R_2}\right)}$$

$$= \frac{R_3}{1-0.8A_V \times \frac{0.5\text{ K}}{2\text{ K}}}$$

$$= \frac{R_3}{1-0.8\times 0.25} = \frac{R_3}{0.8} = 1.25R_3$$

**7. Calculate voltage if the input voltage is connected in series with the $R_G$ (40k) as indicated in figure.**

**Solution:**

The small signal equivalent circuit is shown below

$$\frac{V_iV_o}{R_F} g_m V_{gs} + \frac{V_o}{r_d \parallel R_L}$$

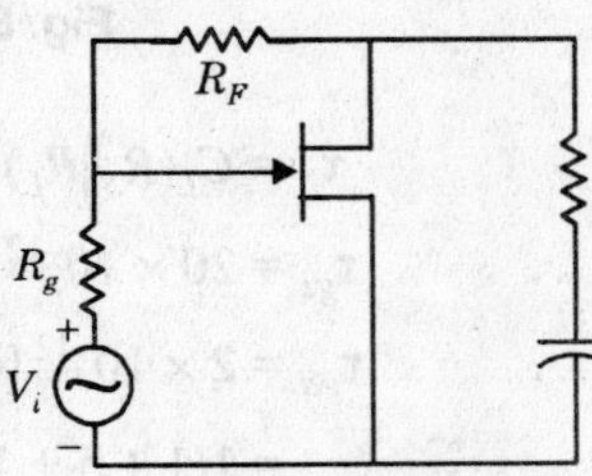


Fig. 8P4(a)

$$V_L = R_F g_m V_{gs} + R_F \frac{V_o}{r_d \parallel R_L} + V_o$$

$$V_{gs} = V_g - V_s = V_g - 0 = V_g$$

$$V_i(1 - R_F g_m) = R_F \frac{V_o}{r_d \parallel R_L} + V_o = \frac{R_F + r_d \parallel R_L}{r_d \parallel R_L} V_o$$

$$\frac{V_o}{V_i} = \frac{(1-R_F g_m) r_d \parallel R_L}{R_F + r_d \parallel R_L}$$

$$\frac{V_o}{V_i} = \frac{(1-6\times 50)3.3\text{ K}}{5.3\text{ m}}$$

$$V_o = -18.7\text{ V}$$

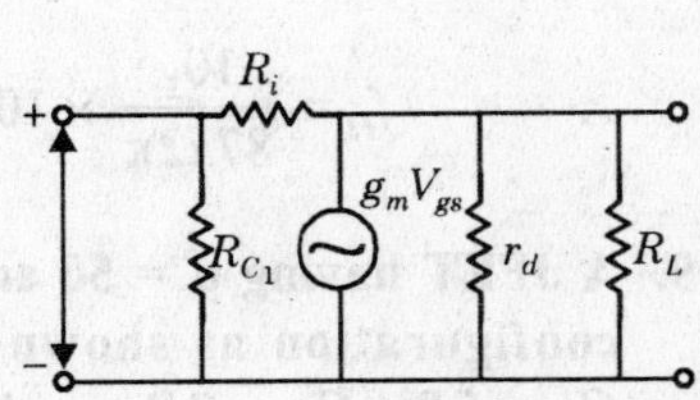


Fig. 8P4(b)

**8. In the JFET circuit shown in figure assume that $R_1/R_2$= 1MW and the total stray capacitance at the output to be $2p_F$. The JFET used has $g_m$= 2mA/V, $C_{gs}$ = $20p_F$ and $C_{gd}$ = $2p_F$. Determine the upper cut-off frequency of the amplifier.**

**Solution:**

$$\tau_{gs} = C_{gs}(R_{in} \| R) \qquad R_i = R_{in} \| R = 1\text{K}$$

$$\tau_{gd} = C_{gd}[(1 + g_m R_L^1) R_1 + R_L^1] \qquad R_L^1 = 2.5\text{k}$$

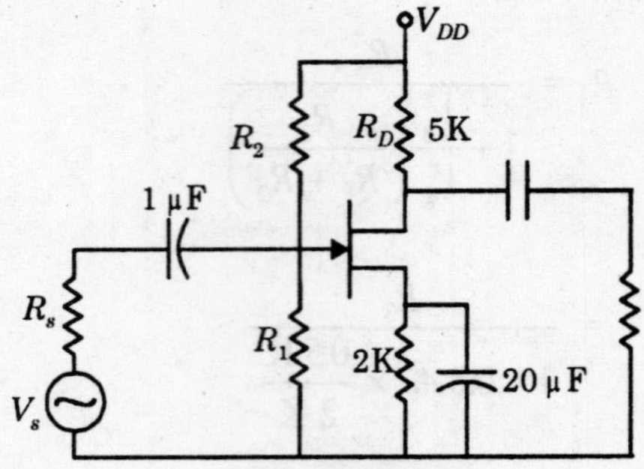


Fig. 8P5(a)

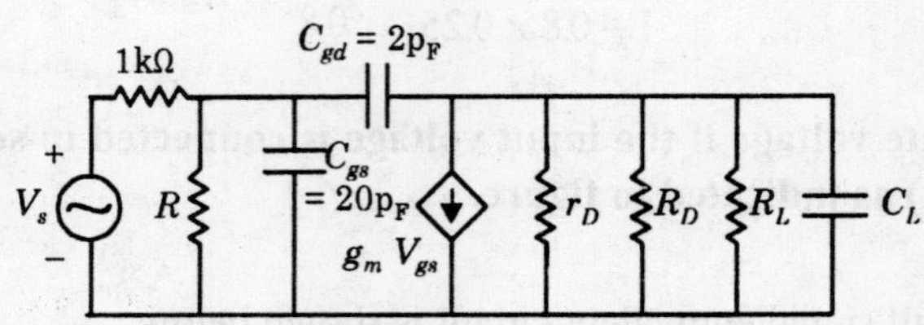


Fig. 8P5(b) Equivalent circuit

$$\tau_L = C_L(R_S \| R_L) = C_L R_L^1$$

$\therefore$ $$\tau_{gs} = 20 \times 10^{-12} (1 \times 10^3) = 20 \times 10^{-9}$$

$\therefore$ $$\tau_{gd} = 2 \times 10^{-12} [(1 + 2 \times 10^{-3} + 2.5 \times 10^3) + 2.5] \times 10^3$$

$$= 1(1 + 5 + 2.5) \times 10^{-9} = 17 \times 10^{-9}\ pF$$

and $$\tau_L = 20 \times 10^{-12} \times (2.5 \times 10^3) = 50 \times 10^{-9}\ pF$$

$$\tau_{eq} = (20 + 17 + 50) \times 10^{-9} = 87 \times 10^{-9}$$

$\therefore$ $$f_H = \frac{10_3}{87x2\pi} \times 106 = 1.8\text{MHz}$$

**9. A JFET having μ = 50 and $r_d$ = 10kΩ is used in a common-source configuration as shown in figure. The JFET capacitances are $C_{gs}$ = 5$P_F$, $C_{gd}$ = 2$P_F$, and $C_{ds}$ = 2$P_F$. Determine the *ac* small-signal midband voltage gain ($V_o/V_s$) and the upper-3*dB* frequency of the circuit.**

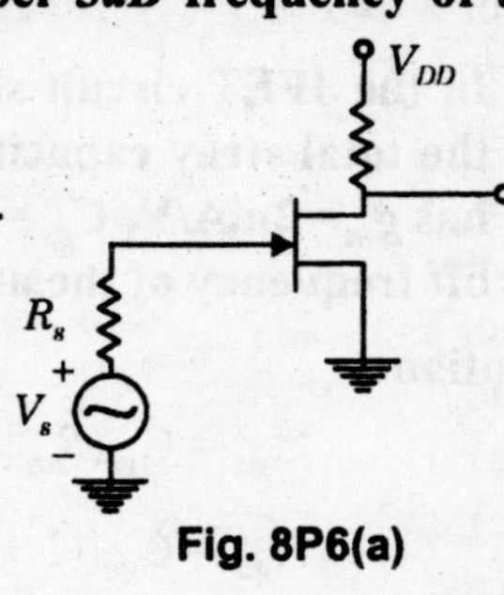


Fig. 8P6(a)

**Solution:**

Given *JFET* in common source configuration.

$$\mu = 50,\ r_d = 10\text{kW}$$

$$C_{gs} = 5\ pF \text{ and } \mu = g_m\, r_d$$

$$C_{gd} = 2\ pF \text{ and}$$

$$G_m = \frac{\mu}{r_d} = \frac{50}{10 \times 10^3} = 5 \times 10 - 3\ C_{ds} = 2P_F$$

Voltage gain $\frac{V_o}{V_s} = -g_m \frac{r_d R_D}{r_d + R_D} = \frac{\mu R_D}{r_d + R_D}$

$$= \frac{50 \times 10 \times 10^3}{10 \times 10^3 + 10 \times 10^3} = -25.$$

In mid frequency range, all inter-electrode capacitors $C_{gs}$, $C_{gd}$ and $C_{ds}$ behave as open circuits and only resistive compounds are present.

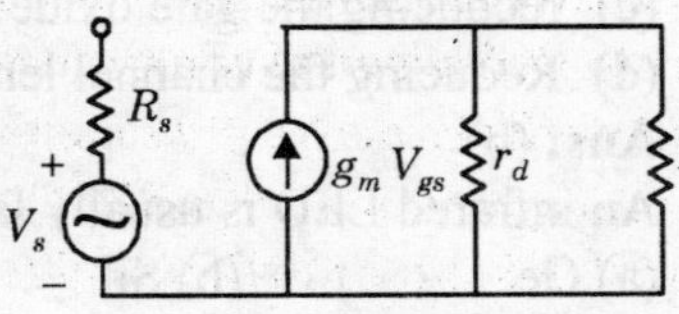

**Fig. 8P6(b)**

Upper 3dB frequency,

$$f_2 = \frac{1}{2\pi c_o R_{eq}} = \frac{1}{2\pi \times 2 \times 10^{-12} \times 5 \times 10^5} = 15.9\text{MHz}$$

Where, $C_o = C_{gd}(1 + g_m) = 2\ pF$

$R_e = C_{gd}(1 + g_m) = 2\ pF$

$$R_{eq} = r_d \| R_D = \frac{r_d R_D}{r_d + R_D} = \frac{10 \times 10}{10 + 10} = \frac{100}{20}$$

Therefore $R_{eq} = 5\text{k}.$

## 8.9 OBJECTIVE QUESTIONS

**1.** For an n-channel *JFET* having drain-source voltage constant if the gatesource voltage is increased (more negative) Pinch-off would occur for:

(a) High values of drain current (b) saturation value of drain current
(c) Zero drain current
(d) gate current equal to drain current

**Ans:** (a)

**2.** For a *UJT*, if $R_1$ = resistance from emitter to the base 1, $R_2$ = resistance from emitter to the base 2 and $R_{BB} = (R_1 + R_2)$, then the intrinsic stand-off ratio (η) is :

(a) $R_1/R_2$ (b) $R_1/R_{BB}$ (c) $R_2/R_1$ (d) $R_2/R_{BB}$

**Ans:** (a)

**3.** For a junction Fet in the pinch off region as the drain voltage is increased, the drain current:

(a) Becomes zero (b) abruptly decreases
(c) abruptly increases (d) remains constant

**Ans:** (a)

**4.** In modern MOSFETs, the material used for the gate is:
(a) high purity silicon
(b) high purity silica
(c) Heavily doped polycrystalline silicon
(d) epitaxially grown silicon
**Ans:** (c)

**5.** The threshold voltage of an n-channel MOSFET can be increased by:
(a) increasing the channel dopant concentration
(b) reducing the channel dopant concentration
(c) recducing the gate oxide thickness
(d) Reducing the channel length
**Ans:** (b)

**6.** An infrared LED is usually fabricated from:
(a) Ge (b) Si (c) Ga As (d) Ga As P
**Ans:** (c)

**7.** An *n*-channel JFET has a pinch-off voltage of $V_P = -5V$, $V_{DS}$ (max) = 20V and $g_m$ = 2mA/V. The minimum 'ON' resistance is achieved in *n*th JFET for,
(a) $V_{GS} = -7V$ and $VDS = 0V$ (b) $V_{GS} = 0V$ and $V_{DS} = 0V$
(c) $V_{GS} = 0V$ and $V_{DS} = 20V$ (d) $V_{FGS} = -7V$ and $V_{DS} = 20V$
**Ans:** (b)

**8.** The JFET in the given current has an $I_{DSS}$ = 10mA and $V_p$ = 5V. The value of the resistance $R_s$ for a drain current $I_D$ = 6.4 mA is:
(a) 150 ohms (b) 470 ohms
(c) 560 ohms (d) 1 kilo-ohms
**Ans:** (a)

**9.**

| List I | List II |
|---|---|
| (a) Voltage controlled device | 1. Bipolar Junction transistro |
| (b) Current controlled device | 2. Unijunction transistor |
| (c) Conductivity modulation device | 3. Field effect transistor |
| (d) Negative conductance device | 4. IMPATT diode |

| | A | B | C | D |
|---|---|---|---|---|
| (a) | 2 | 3 | 1 | 4 |
| (b) | 2 | 3 | 4 | 1 |
| (c) | 3 | 1 | 2 | 4 |
| (d) | 3 | 1 | 4 | 2 |

**Ans:** (d)

**10.** In an FET, tranconductance $g_m$ is proportional to:
(a) $I_{DS}$ (b) $I^2$ *DS* (c) $\sqrt{I_{DC}}$ (d) $1/I_{DC}$
**Ans:** (c)

**11.** In an FET, $g_{mo}$ is proportional to:
(a) $I_{DSS}$ (b) $\sqrt{I_{DSS}}$ (c) $I^2$ *DSS* (d) $1/I_{DSS}$
**Ans:** (a)

**12.** In a JFET, transconductance $g_m$ is of the order of:

(a) 1 mS (b) 100 mS (c) 1S (d) 100S

**Ans:** (a)

**13.** In a FET, dynamic drain resistance $r_d$ is of the order of:

(a) 1KΩ (b) 10kΩ (c) 100Ω (d) 100kΩ

**Ans:** (c)

**14.** In a MOSFET, dynamic drain resistance $r_d$ is of the order of:

(a) 10KΩ (b) 1kΩ (c) 10Ω (d) 100kΩ

**Ans:** (a)

**15.** The input resistance $r_{gs}$ in small signal model of MOSFET is of the order of:

(a) 100kΩ (b) 1MΩ (c) 100MΩ (d) $10^4$MΩ

**Ans:** (d)

**16.** The feedback resistance $r_{gd}$ in small signal model of MOSFET is of the order of:

(a) 1MΩ (b) 100MΩ (c) $10^4$MΩ (d) $10^6$MΩ

**Ans:** (d)

**17.** The feedback capcitance $C_{gd}$ in small signal high frequency model of a JFET is of the order of:

(a) 5pF (b) 5–pF (c) 500pF (d) 1pF

**Ans:** (a)

**18.** The drain-to-source resistance $C_{ds}$ in high frequency model of a JFET is of the order of:

(a) 1pF (b) 10pF (c) 100pF (d) 1000PF

**Ans:** (a)

**19.** The gate -to-source capacitance $C_{gs}$ in small signal high frequency model of a JFET of the order of:

(a) 5pF (b) 50pF (c) 500pF (d) 5000pF

**Ans:** (a)

## 8.10 CONVENTIONAL QUESTIONS

1. Sketch the circuit of MF analysis of CS amplifier and derive the expression for $A_v$.
2. Derive the expression of $A_v$ *for CD amplifier.*
3. Explain the MF analysis of CG amplifier with neat diagram.
4. Draw the circuit diagram of small signal CS configuration and derive the expression for $A_v$.
5. Explain about High frequency analysis of Common Source Amplifier.
6. Show that $Av = \dfrac{\mu}{\mu + 1}$ = for CD amplifier without $R_d$.

## 8.11 EXERCISE PROBLEMS

**1. If $V_{GS}=-2.2$v and $I_D=2.03$ mA calculate (a) $g_m$ (b) $r_d$ (c) determine $V_0$ with and with out $r_d$**

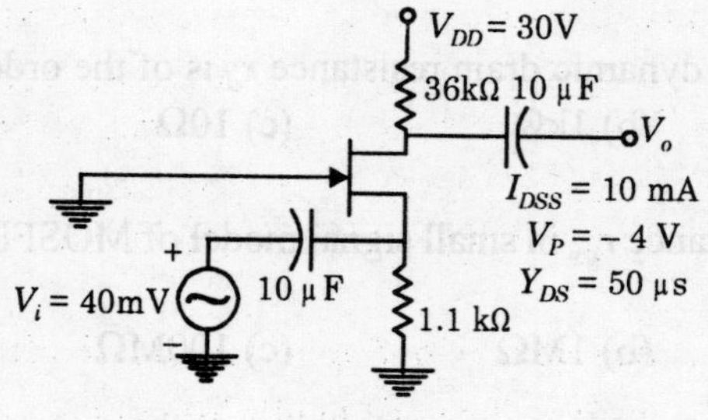


**Fig. 8P1**

**Ans: (a) 2.25mS (b) 20 k ohm (c) 280.8 mV, 324 mV**

**2. Shown in figure bellow. If $V_{GSQ}$ = 1.5V $I_D$ = 7.6mA determine (a) $g_m$ (b) $r_d$ (c) $A_v$**

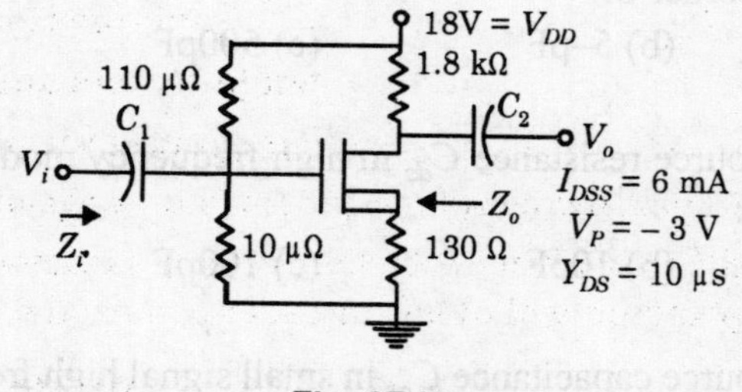


**Fig. 8P13**

**Ans: (a) 6mS (b)100k ohm (c) 10.8**

**3. Design the fixed bias network of figure to have an AC gain of 10. That is determine the value of $R_D$.**

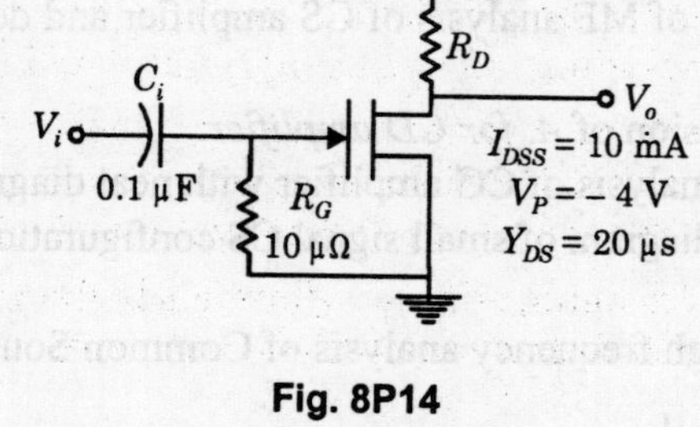


**Fig. 8P14**

**Ans. $R_D$ = 2k ohm**

**4. In the MOSFET amplifier shown in figure below, the transistor has $\mu = 50$, $r_d = 10K\Omega$, $C_{gs} = 5pf$, $C_{gd} = 1pf$ and $C_{ds} = 2pf$. Draw a small signal equivalent circuit for the amplifier for midband frequencies and calculate its midband voltage gain.**

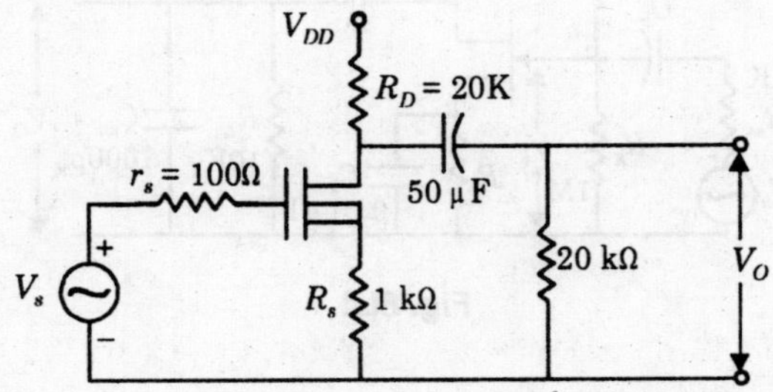


**Fig. 8P15**

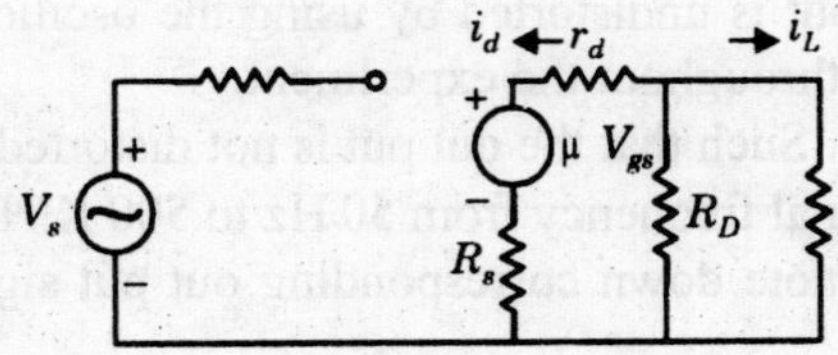


**Ans.** $A_V = 7.04$

## 8.12 LAB EXPERIMENTS

### *1. FET Amplifier*

**Aim:** To plot the frequency response of FET amplifier and to calculate the bandwidth

**Equipments & components required:**

| | | |
|---|---|---|
| 1. | FET | BF W11 |
| 2. | Resistors | 1M,1K, 10k? |
| 3. | capacitors | 10uf, 0.001uf |
| 4. | CRO | DUAL |
| 5. | function generator | |
| 6. | Ammeter | 0-25mA |
| 7. | Voltmeter | 0-25volt |
| 8. | Power supply | 0-30volt |
| 9. | Breadboard and connecting wires. | |

**Circuit Diagram:**

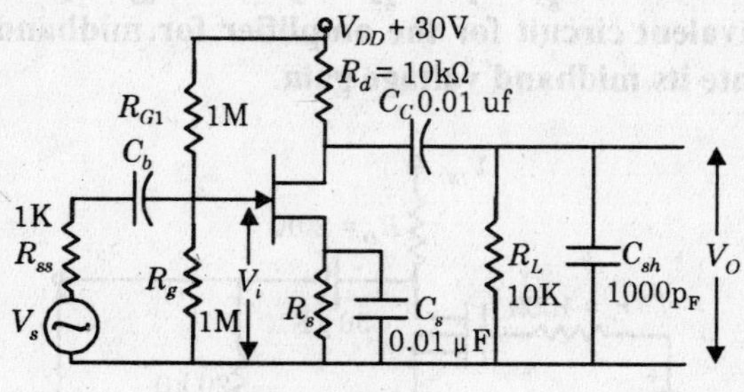


**Fig. 8L1**

## Procedure:

1. Connect The Circuit as shown in the circuit diagram.
2. Select the input signal as sinusoidal wave form the function generator such that the output is undistorted by using the oscilloscope. Keep this value as constant throughout the experiment.
3. Select Vs = 40mv. Such that the out put is not distorted.
4. Vary the input signal frequency from 50 Hz to 500 K Hz as shown in the tabular form and note down corresponding out put signal peak to peak from CRO.
5. Draw the graph, voltage gain Vs input frequency on the semi log graph paper.
6. From the above graph, calculate the bandwidth of the amplifier.

# ❮ 9 ❯

# MULTI STAGE AMPLIFIER

## 9.1 INTRODUCTION

The purpose of multistage amplifiers or cascaded amplifiers is to increase voltage gain, increase input impedance and even sometimes making amplifier unilateral. Whenever voltage gain is increased bandwidth will decrease. Each cascaded amplifier has its own applications which will be discussed in the next sections of this chapter.

## 9.2 DIFFERENT POSSIBLE CASCADINGS OF AMPLIFIERS

*CE-CE* : Audio frequency voltage amplifiers with large gain.
*CE-CC* : Audio frequency voltage amplifiers with impedance matching.
*CE-CB* : Cascode amplifiers used as unilateral amplifier.
*CC-CC* : High input impedance circuits called Darlington and Bootstrap circuits.

Overall gain of cascaded common base amplifiers is approximately equal to first stage gain. Therefore cascading of common base stages is not used.

## 9.3 TYPES OF CASCADED AMPLIFIERS

There are two types of cascaded amplifiers, classified according to loading as the previous stages. The comparison of these are as given below.

| Non-interacting stages (identical) | Interacting stages(non-interacting and non-identical) |
|---|---|
| 1. $R_L << R_{in+1}$ <br> $\therefore R_L n' = R_{Ln} \parallel R_{in+1} = R_{Ln}$ | 1. $R_{Ln} \not<\not< R_{in+1}$ <br> $\therefore R_L n' = R_{Ln} \parallel R_{in+1}$ |
| 2. $Av^{(n)} = (A_{v1})^n$ | 2. $Av^{(n)} = A_{v1} A_{v2} \ldots$ |
| 3. $f_1^{(n)} \; \dfrac{f_1}{\sqrt{2^{\frac{1}{n}} - 1}}$ | 3. $f_1^{(n)} \; \sqrt{f_{11}^2 + f_{12}^2 + \ldots\ldots\ldots}$ |

| | |
|---|---|
| 4. $f_2^{(n)} = f_2 \times \sqrt{2^{\frac{1}{n}} - 1}$ | 4. $f_2^{(n)} = \dfrac{1}{\sqrt{\dfrac{1}{f_{21}^2} + \dfrac{1}{f_{22}^2} + \ldots\ldots\ldots}}$ |
| 5. Generally cascaded FET and operational amplifiers. | 5. Generally cascaded BJT amplifiers except *CC* amplifiers. |

Let us prove overall $f_1$ and $f_2$ for both non-interacting and interacting stages.

**Case (i):** *Non-interacting (identical) stages:*

$$A_{VL}^{(n)} = (A_{VL1})^n = \left\{\frac{A_{Vm1}}{\sqrt{1+\left(\dfrac{f_1}{f}\right)^2}}\right\}^n$$

At $\quad f = f_1^{(n)}, A_{VL}^{(n)} = \dfrac{(A_{V1})^n}{\sqrt{2}}$

$$\frac{(A_{Vm1})^n}{\left\{\sqrt{1+\left(\dfrac{f_1}{f_1^{(n)}}\right)^2}\right\}^n} = \frac{\left(A_{V_{m1}}\right)^n}{\sqrt{2}}$$

$$f_1^{(n)} = \frac{f_1}{\sqrt{2^{\frac{1}{n}} - 1}}$$

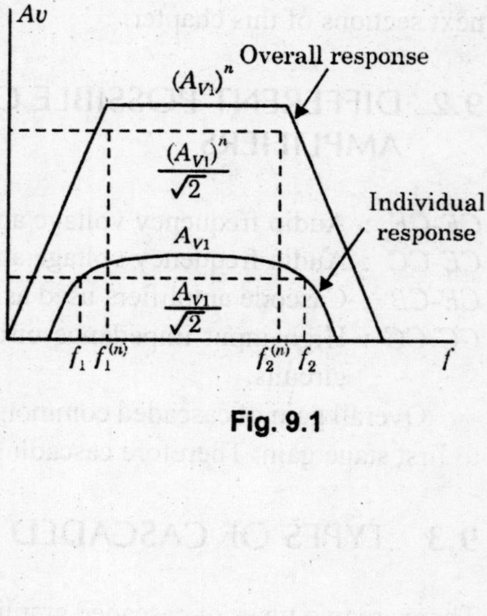


**Fig. 9.1**

$$\frac{(A_{Vm1})^n}{\left\{\sqrt{1+\left(\dfrac{f_2^{(n)}}{f_2}\right)^2}\right\}^n} = \frac{(A_{Vm1})^n}{\sqrt{2}}$$

$$1 + \left(\frac{f_2^{(n)}}{f_2}\right)^2 = (2)^{\frac{1}{n}}$$

$$f_2^{(n)} = f_2\left[\sqrt{2^{\frac{1}{n}} - 1}\right]$$

The overall response will never cross the individual responses as shown in the fig. 9.1

**Case (ii):** interacting (non-interacting and non-identical) stages

$$f_{11} f_{12} < f^2$$

$$A_{VL}^{(n)} = A_{VL1} A_{VL2} \,.........\, A_{VLn}$$

$$\frac{A_{Vm1} A_{Vm2}}{\sqrt{1+\left(\frac{f_1^{(n)}}{f}\right)^2}} = \left\{\frac{A_{Vm1}}{\sqrt{1+\left(\frac{f_{11}}{f}\right)^2}}\right\}\left\{\frac{A_{Vm2}}{\sqrt{1+\left(\frac{f_{12}}{f}\right)^2}}\right\}..............$$

$$1+\left(\frac{f_1^{(n)}}{f}\right)^2 = 1+\left(\frac{f_{12}}{f}\right)^2+\left(\frac{f_{11}}{f}\right)^2+\left(\frac{f_{11} f_{12}}{f^2}\right)^2+.....$$

$$f_1^{(n)} = \sqrt{f_{11}^2 + f_{12}^2 + .............}$$

$$\frac{A_{Vm1} A_{Vm2}}{\sqrt{1+\left(\frac{f_2}{f_2^{(n)}}\right)^2}} = \left\{\frac{A_{Vm1}}{\sqrt{1+\left(\frac{f}{f_{11}}\right)^2}}\right\}\left\{\frac{A_{Vm2}}{\sqrt{1+\left(\frac{f}{f_{12}}\right)^2}}\right\}.............$$

$$f_2^{(n)} = \frac{1}{\sqrt{\frac{1}{f_{21}^2}+\frac{1}{f_{22}^2}+.......}}$$

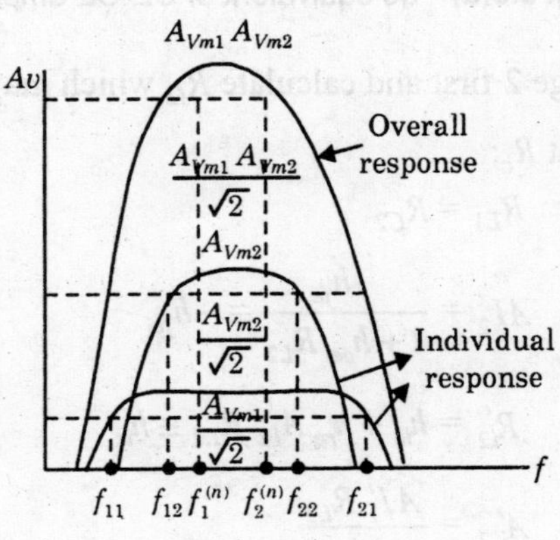


**Fig. 9.2**

The overall frequency response at low frequency range is greater than both the individual stages as shown in fig. 9.2 .

## 9.4 ANALYSIS OF CASCADED AMPLIFIERS

### 9.4.1 *CE-CE* cascaded amplifier

Let us demonstrate the analysis of *CE-CE* amplifier as a basis for understanding all other cascaded amplifiers.

The a.c equivalent of the circuit in fig 9.3 is shown in fig 9.3(a).

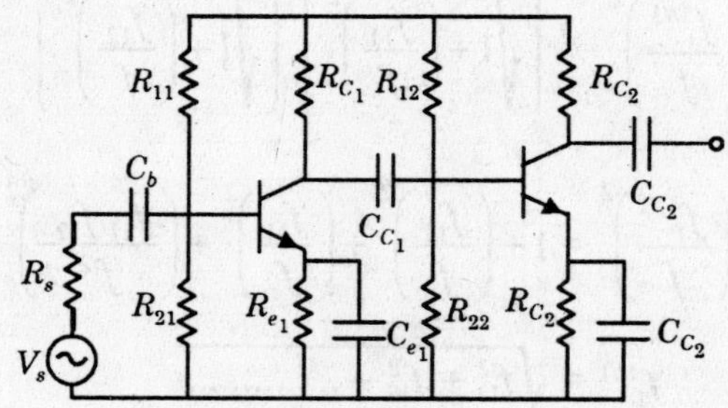


**Fig. 9.3** CE-CE amplifier

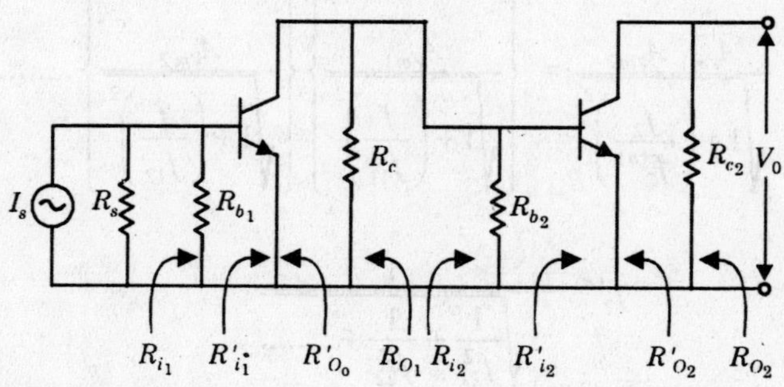


**Fig. 9.3(a)** ac equivalent of CE-CE amplifier

We analyse stage 2 first and calculate $R_{i2}$ which may load $R_{C1}$

**Stage 2:** CE without $R_c$:

$$R_{L1} = R_{C2}$$

1. $$AI_2' = \frac{-h_{fe}}{1 + h_{oe} R_{L2}} \cong -h_{fe}$$

2. $$R_{i2}' = h_{ie} + h_{re} A_{I2}' R_{L2} \cong h_{ie}$$

3. $$A_{V2}' = \frac{AI_1' R_{L2}}{R_{i2}'}$$

4. $$AI_1 = AI_1'\left(\frac{R_{b1}}{R_{b1} + R_{i1}'}\right)$$

5. $$R_{i2} = R_{b2} \parallel R_{i2}'$$

6. $$A_{V2} = \frac{AI_2 R_{L2}}{R_{i2}}$$

**Stage 1:** CE without $R_e$:

$$R_{L1} = R_{C1} \parallel R_{i2}$$

$$h_{oe} R_{L1} \leq 0.1 \begin{cases} \text{if yes approximate analysis} \\ \text{if no exact analysis} \end{cases}$$

1. $$AI_2' = \frac{-h_{fe}}{1 + h_{oe} R_{L1}} \cong -h_{fe}$$

2. $$R_{i2}' = h_{ie} + h_{re} A_1' R_{L1} \cong h_{ie}$$

3. $$A_{V1}' = \frac{AI_1' R_{L1}}{R_i'}$$

4. $$AI_1 = AI_1'\left(\frac{R_{b1}}{R_{b1} + R_{i1}'}\right)$$

5. $$R_{i1} = R_{b1} \parallel R_{i1}'$$

6. $$AV_1 = \frac{AI_1 R_{L1}}{R_{i1}}$$

*Output impedance's:*

**Stage 1:**

1. $$Y_{01}' = h_{oe} - \frac{h_{re} h_{fe}}{h_{ie} + R_{s1}'} \cong 0$$

$$R_s' = R_s \parallel R_{b1}$$

$$R_{01}' = \frac{1}{Y_{01}'} \cong \infty$$

2. $$R_{01}' = R_{01}' \parallel R_{c1} \cong R_{c1}$$

**Stage 2:**

1. $$Y_{02}' = h_{oe} - \frac{h_{re} h_{fe}}{h_{ie} + R_{s2}'} \cong 0$$

$$R'_{s2} = R_{01} \parallel R_{b2}$$

$$R'_{02} = \frac{1}{Y'_{02}} \cong \infty$$

2. $$R'_{02} = R'_{02} \parallel R_{c2} \cong R_{c2}$$

*Overall analysis:*

1. $$A_V = A_{V1} A'_{V2} = \frac{AI_1 R_{L2}}{R_{i1}}$$

2. $$A_I = \frac{A_V R_{i1}}{R_{L2}}$$

3. $$R_i = R_{i1}$$

4. $$R_0 = R_{02} \cong R_{c2}$$

## 9.4.2 *CE-CC* cascaded amplifier

As we studied CE-CE with biasing resistors, the analysis becomes complicated. So sometimes we can ignore biasing resistors in the analysis as $R_b > R'_i$. Therefore let us analyse CE-CC without biasing resistors. We must use the respective *h*-parameters.

The ac equivalent of CE-CC amplifier shown in fig 9.4 is shown in fig 9.4(a)

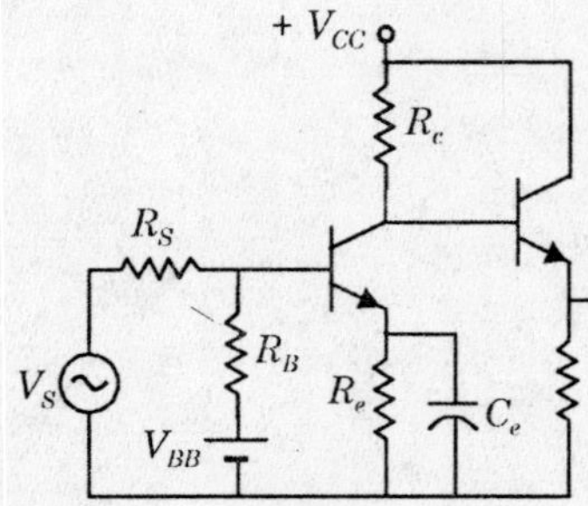


**Fig 9.4** CE-CC amplifier

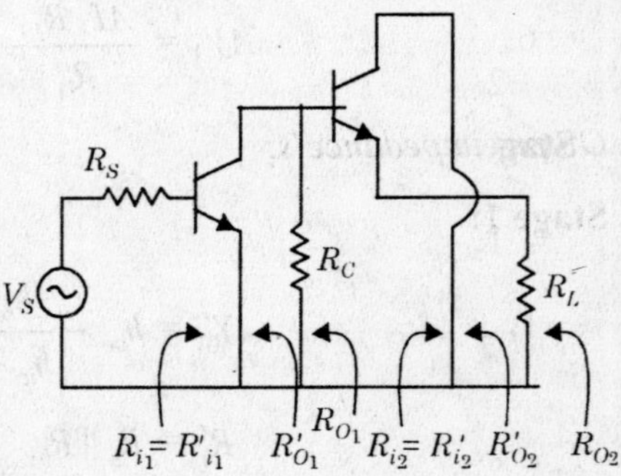


**Fig 9.4(a)** ac equivalent of CE-CC amplifier

**Stage 2:** CC amplifier:

$$h_{oc} R_{L1} \leq 0.1$$

$$R_{L2} \cong R_L$$

1. $$AI_2 = AI_2' = \frac{-h_{fc}}{1+h_{oc}R_{L2}} \cong 1+h_{fe}$$

2. $$Ri_2 = R_{i2}' = h_{ic} + h_{rc}A_{I2}'R_{L2} \cong h_{ie} + (1+h_{fe})R_{L2}$$

3. $$A_{V2} = A_{V2}' = \frac{AI_2 R_{L2}}{R_{i2}} = \frac{(1+h_{fe})R_{L2}}{h_{ie}+(1+h_{fe})R_{L2}} \cong 1 - \frac{h_{ie}}{R_{i2}} < 1$$

**Stage 1:** CE without $R_e$:

$$h_{oe}R_{L1} \le 0.1$$

1. $$AI_1 = AI_1' = \frac{-h_{fe}}{1+h_{oe}R_{L1}} \cong -h_{fe}$$

2. $$R_{i1} = R_{i1}' = h_{ie} + h_{re}A_1'R_{L1} \cong h_{ie}$$

3. $$A_{V1} = A_{V1}' = \frac{AI_1 R_{L1}}{R_i}$$

Output impedances:

**Stage 1:**

1. $$Y_{01}' = h_{oe} - \frac{h_{re}h_{fe}}{h_{ie}+R_{s1}'} \cong 0$$

$$R_{01}' = \frac{1}{Y_{01}'}$$

2. $$R_{01} = R_{01}' \parallel R_{L1}$$

**Stage 2:**

1. $$Y_{02}' = h_{oc} - \frac{h_{rc}h_{fc}}{h_{ic}+R_{s2}'} \cong 0$$

$$R_{02}' = \frac{1}{Y_{02}'}$$

2. $$R_{02} = R_{02}' \parallel R_{L2}$$

Overall analysis:

1. $$A_V = A_{V1}A_{V2}'$$

2. $$Ri = R_{i1}$$

3. $$R_0 = R_{02}$$

4. $$A_I = \frac{A_V R_{i1}}{R_{L2}}$$

### 9.4.3 *CE-CB* cascaded amplifier ( Cascode amplifier )

CE-CB is used for unilateral amplification as $h_{rb} << h_{re}$. It is called cascode amplifier. We must use the respective $h$-parameter. It is used to avoid the direct feed through or reverse transmission of signal through antenna in radio receivers. Here also we ignore the biasing resistors to ease the analysis.

The ac equivalent of CE-CB amplifier shown in fig. 9.5 is shown in fig. 9.5(a)

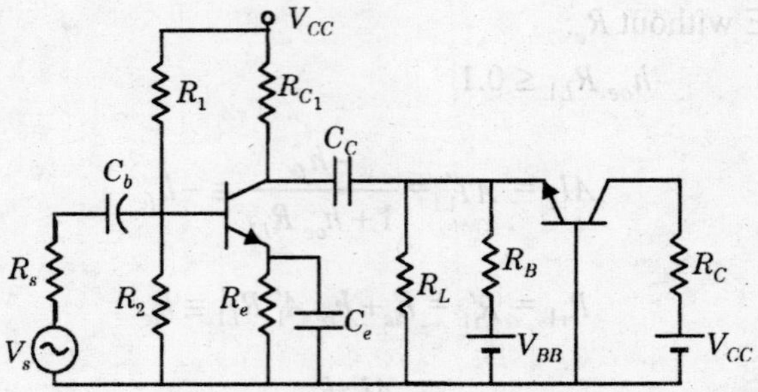


**Fig. 9.5** CE-CB amplifier

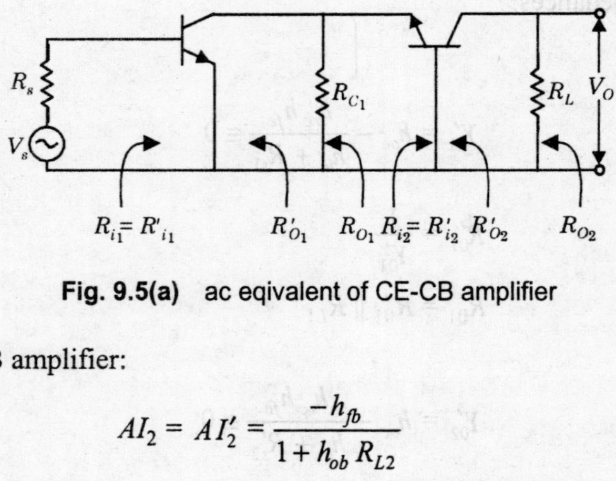


**Fig. 9.5(a)** ac eqivalent of CE-CB amplifier

**Stage 2:** CB amplifier:

1. $$AI_2 = AI_2' = \frac{-h_{fb}}{1 + h_{ob} R_{L2}}$$

2. $$R_{i2} = R_{i2}' = h_{ib} + h_{rb} A_{I2}' R_{L2}$$

3. $$A_{V2} = A_{V2}' = \frac{AI_2 R_{L2}}{R_{i2}'}$$

**Stage 1:**

$$R_L = R_{C_1} \parallel R_{i_2}$$

1. $$AI_1 = AI_1' = \frac{-h_{fc}}{1 + h_{oc} R_L}$$

$$R_{i_1} = R_{i1}' = h_{ic} + h_{rc} A_I' R_{L1}$$

3. $$A_{V_1} = A'_{V1} = \frac{AI_1 R_{L1}}{R_i}$$

Output impedances:

**Stage 1:**

1. $$Y'_{01} = h_{oe} - \frac{h_{re} h_{fe}}{h_{ie} + R'_{s1}} \cong 0$$

$$R'_{01} = \frac{1}{Y'_{01}}$$

2. $$R_{01} = R'_{01}$$

**Stage 2:**

1. $$Y'_{02} = h_{ob} - \frac{h_{rb} h_{fb}}{h_{ib} + R'_{s2}} \cong 0$$

$$R'_{02} = \frac{1}{Y'_{02}}$$

2. $$R_{02} = R'_{02} \parallel R_{L2}$$

Overall analysis:

1. $A_V = A_{V_1} A_{V_2}$
2. $R_i = R_{i1}$
3. $R_0 = R_{02}$
4. $$A_I = \frac{A_V R_{i1}}{R_{L2}}$$

### 9.4.4 CC–CC Cascaded Amplifier (Darlington and Bootstrap Amplifier)

CC-CC cascaded amplifiers is also called as darlington pair. It is a three terminal device and direct-coupled amplifier is readily available for use. These circuits provide large input impedance. So let us analyse the amplifier for input impedance and rest of the analysis is same as any other cascaded amplifiers along with their respective *h*-parameters.

**Circuit 1:**

Darlington circuit

$$R'_{i2} = R_{i2} = h_{ie} + (1 + h_{fe}) R_{L2} = h_{fe} R_L$$

where $R_{L2} = R_L$

$$R_{L1} = h_{fe} R_L$$

$$R'_{i1} = R_{i1} = h_{ie} + (1 + h_{fe})\,R_{L1} = (h_{fe})^2\,R_L$$

In general for n stages $R_1 = (h_{fe})^n\,R_L$

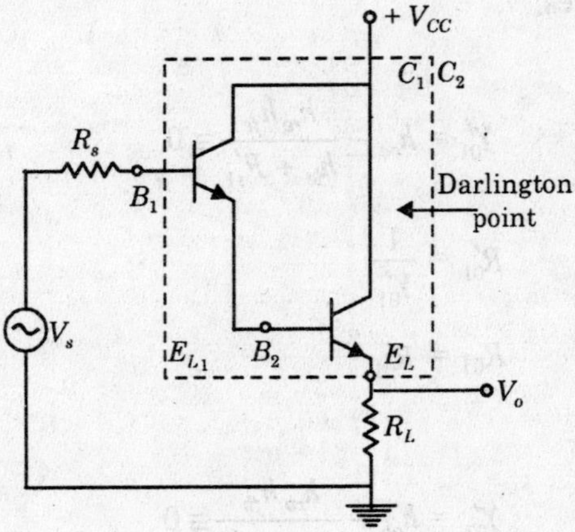


**Fig. 9.6** Darlington circuit

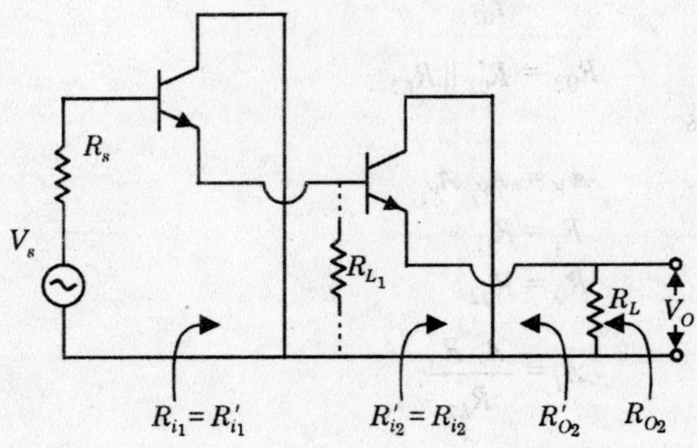


**Fig. 9.6 (a)** ac equivalent of Darlington circuit

**Circuit 2:**

Direct coupled amplifier:

$$R_{i1} = R_{b1} \parallel R'_{i1} = R_b \parallel (h_{fe})^2\,R_L$$

Advantage is that the input bias is given.

Disadvantage is that all the impedance that is obtained is lost.

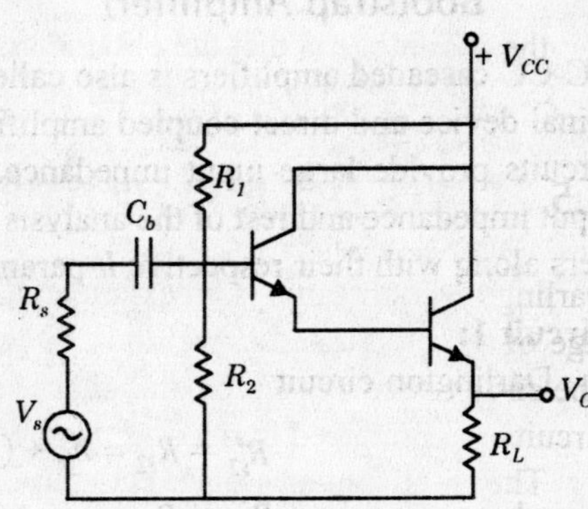


**Fig. 9.7** Direct coupled amplifier

**Circuit 3:**

Bootstrap circuit

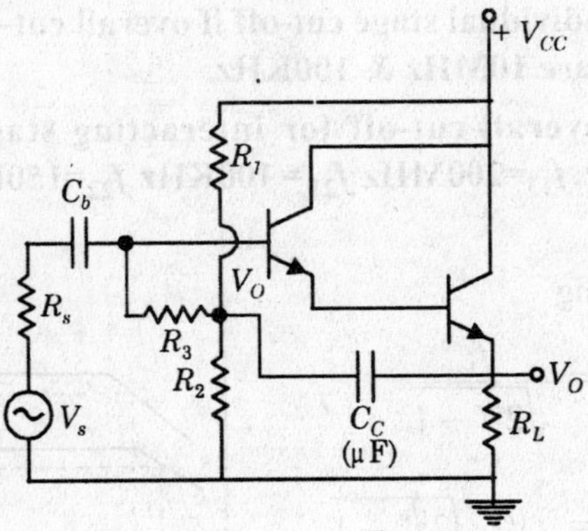


**Fig. 9.8** Bootstrap circuit

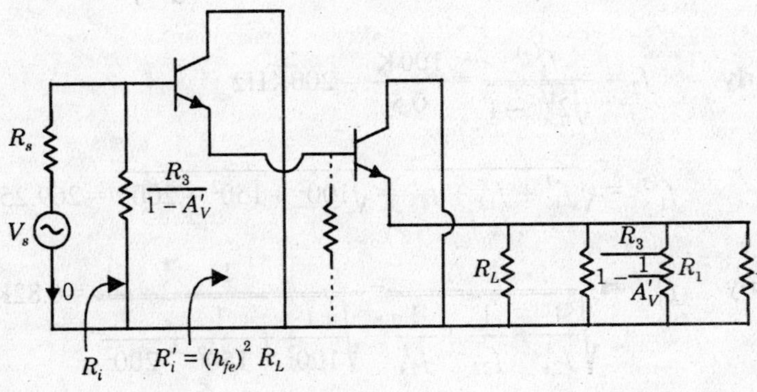


**Fig. 9.8(a)** ac equivalent of the bootstrap circuit

$$R_i = \left(\frac{R_3}{1 - A'_V}\right) \| (h_{fe})^2 R_L = (h_{fe})^2 R_L$$

the advantage is that the obtained impedance is retained.

∴ Boot strap is the practical version of Darlington.

## 9.5 DIRECT-COUPLED AMPLIFIERS

Darlington connection is an example of direct-coupled amplifier. The advantage of direct coupled is we don't need biasing resistors for the next stages. The circuit becomes simple and takes less space and therefore direct coupled circuits are preferred in making integrated circuits.

The disadvantages of direct-coupled amplifiers are drift in $Q$-point and amplification of $I_{co}$ by cascaded amplifiers and hence number of cascaded direct coupled amplifiers will be restricted.

## 9.6 SOLVED PROBLEMS

**1. (a) Calculate individual stage cut-off if overall cut-off of a stage non interacting are 10MHz & 100KHz.**

**(b) Calculate overall cut-off for interacting stages $f_{11}$=100MHz $f_{12}$=150MHz, $f_{13}$=200MHz $f_{21}$ = 100KHz $f_{22}$=150KHz $f_{23}$=200KHz**

**Solution:**

For non interacting

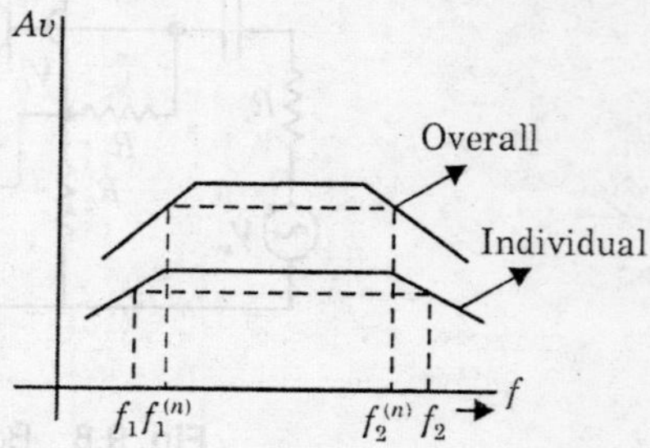


Fig: 9p1

(a) $$f_1^{(n)} = \frac{f_1}{\sqrt{2^{1/n}-1}}$$

Therefore $$f_1 = f_1^{(n)}\sqrt{2^{1/n}-1}$$

$$= 100\sqrt{2^{1/3}-1} = 50\text{KHz}$$

similarly $$f_2 = \frac{f_1^{(n)}}{\sqrt{2^{1/n}-1}} = \frac{100\text{K}}{0.5} = 200\text{KHz}$$

(b) $$f_1^{(3)} = \sqrt{f_{11}^2 + f_{12}^2 + f_{13}^2} = \sqrt{100^2 + 150^2 + 200^2} = 269.25\text{Hz}$$

similarly $$f_3^{(3)} = \frac{1}{\sqrt{\frac{1}{f_{21}^2}+\frac{1}{f_{22}^2}+\frac{1}{f_{23}^2}}} = \frac{1}{\sqrt{\frac{1}{100^2}+\frac{1}{150^2}+\frac{1}{200^2}}} = 6.82\text{KHz}$$

**2. It is desired that the voltage gain of an *RC*-coupled amplifier at 60Hz should not decrease by more than 105 from its mid band value. Show that the coupling capacitance *C* μ*F* must be at least equal to 5.5/$R^1$, where $R^1 = R_0^1 + R_1^1$ is expressed in kΩ.**

**Solution:**

$$\frac{A_V\text{ (low frequency)}}{A_V\text{ (mid frequency)}} = \frac{1}{\sqrt{1+\left(\frac{f_L}{f}\right)^2}}$$

at 60Hz the gain is 10% less than midband value

Therefore $$\frac{A_V\text{ (60 Hz)}}{A_V\text{ (mid frequency)}} = 0.9 = \frac{1}{\sqrt{1+\left(\frac{f_L}{f}\right)^2}}$$

Taking squares on both sides

$$0.81 = \frac{1}{1+\left(\frac{f_L}{f}\right)^2}$$

$$1+\left(\frac{f_L}{f}\right)^2 = 1/0.81 = 1.2346$$

$$\left(\frac{f_L}{f}\right)^2 = 0.2346$$

$$\frac{f_L}{f} = \sqrt{0.2346} = 0.484$$

$$f_L = f \times 0.484$$

$$= 60\text{Hz} \times 0.483 = 29.06\text{Hz}$$

Now $f_L$, the lower 3db frequency is also given by $f_L = \dfrac{1}{2\pi\,(R_0^1 + R_1^1)\,C_b}$

$$C_b = \frac{1}{f_L\, 2\pi\,(R_0^1 + R_1^1)} \quad \text{since } R_1 = R_0^1 + R_1^1 \text{ in k}\Omega$$

Therefore $\quad C_b = \dfrac{1}{f_L\, 2\pi\left(R_1^1 + 10^3\right)}$

Since $R_1$ is in kilo-ohms

$$C_b = \frac{1}{29.06 \times 2\pi R^1 + 10^3} = \frac{5.477}{R^1} \times 10^{-6}$$

$$C_b \approx \frac{5.5}{R^1}\ \mu\text{F}$$

**3. A two-stage FET *RC*-coupled amplifier has the following parameters: $g_m$ = 10mA/V, $r_d$ = 5.5k $R_d$ = 8k and $R_g$=1M for each stage. Assume C in figure to be arbitrarily large.**

**(a) what must be the value of $C_b$ in order that the frequency characteristics of each stage be flat within 1db down to 10Hz?**

**(b) Repeat part a if the overall gain of both stages is to be down 1db at 10Hz**

**(c) what is the overall mid-band voltage gain?**

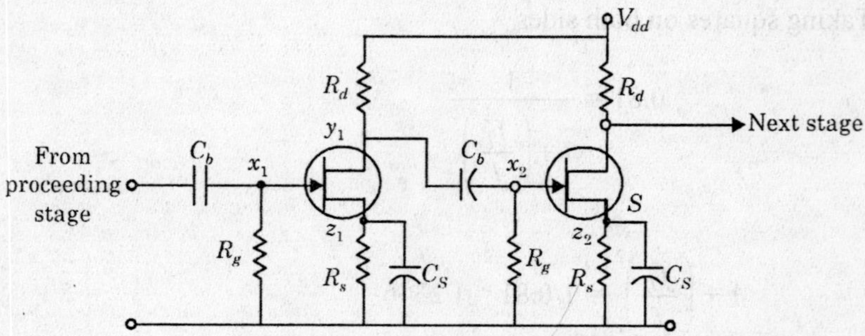


Fig. 9p3.

From Equation $\quad f_L = \dfrac{1}{2\pi\,(R_o^1 + R_i^1)\,C_b}$

Where $\quad R_o^1 = r_d \,||\, R_d = 5.5\text{k} \,||\, 8\text{k}$

$R_i^1 = R_g = 1\text{M}$ hence

$$f_L = \frac{1}{2\pi\,(1003) \times 10^3\, C_b}$$

$$\left|\frac{A}{A_{V_o}}\right| = \frac{1}{\sqrt{1+\left(\dfrac{f_L}{f}\right)^2}} = -\,10 \log\left(1+\left(\frac{f_L}{f}\right)^2\right)$$

(a) Where $A_o$ is the midband gain. This equation is valid here since each stage has a single capacitor that introduces one porl and one zero we want for $f = 10\text{Hz}$

$$-\,10 \log\left(1+\left(\frac{f_L}{f}\right)^2\right) = -1\text{db}$$

or $\quad \left(1+\dfrac{f_L^2}{f^2}\right) = 1.26$ or

$$f_L = \sqrt{0.26} \times y = 0.509 \times 10 = 5.09\text{Hz}$$

solving for $C_b$, we obtain $\quad C_b = \dfrac{10^{-6}}{\pi \times 5.09} \quad C_b = 0.0621\mu\text{F} = 62\text{nF}$

(b) for the two stage, $20 \log_{10}\left|\dfrac{A}{A_o}\right|^2 = -\,20 \log_{10}\left(1+\left(\dfrac{f_L}{f}\right)^2\right) = -\,1\text{db}$

or $$1+\left(\frac{f_L}{f}\right)^2 = 1.125\ f_L/f = 0.352$$

Therefore $$f_L = 0.352 \times 10 = 3.52\text{Hz}.$$

Hence $$C_b = (0.0621)\frac{5.0}{3.52} = 0.9\ \mu\text{F} = 90\ \mu\text{F}$$

(c) at the midband the gain of each stage equals the gain of the other stages and it is given by

$$A_O = A_{O1}\,A_{O2} = (A_{01})^2 = g_m^2\ (R_d \parallel r_d)^2$$
$$= (10 \times 10^{-3})^2\ (3.26)^2$$
$$= 1062.76$$

**4. Three identical cascaded stages have an overall upper 3-db frequency of 10KHz and a lower 3-db frequency of 40 kHz. What are $f_L$ and $f_H$ of each stage? Assume non-interacting stages.**

**Solution:**

$$\frac{f_H^*}{f_H} = \sqrt{2^{1/3}-1}$$

$$f_H^* = 0.509 f_H\,,\ f_H^* = 40\text{kHz}$$

$$f_H = \frac{40\,\text{KHz}}{0.509} = 78.58\text{kHz}$$

$$\frac{f_L^*}{f_L} = \frac{1}{\sqrt{1^{1/3}-1}}$$

$$f_L^* = 1.96 f_L\,,\ f_L^* = 40\text{Hz}$$

$$f_L = \frac{40\,\text{KHz}}{1.96}$$
$$= 20.4\text{Hz}$$

**5. A three-stage *RC*-coupled amplifier uses FET with the following parameters: $g_m$ = 2.6mA/V $r_d$= 7.7k $R_d$= 12k, $R_g$ = 1m, $C_b$= 0.005 μf and $C_s = \infty$.**

**Evaluate (a) the overall mid-band voltage gain in decibels**

**(b) $f_L$ of each individual stage.**

**(c) the overall lower 3-db frequency.**

(a) $$|A_o| = g_m R \text{ where } 1/R = \left(\frac{1}{7.7} + \frac{1}{12} + \frac{1}{1000}\right) \times 10^{-3}$$

$$1/R = 0.214 \times 10^{-3}$$

$$g_m/R = |A_o| = \frac{2.6 \times 10^{-3}}{0.214 \times 10^{-3}} \text{ or } |A_o| = 12.14$$

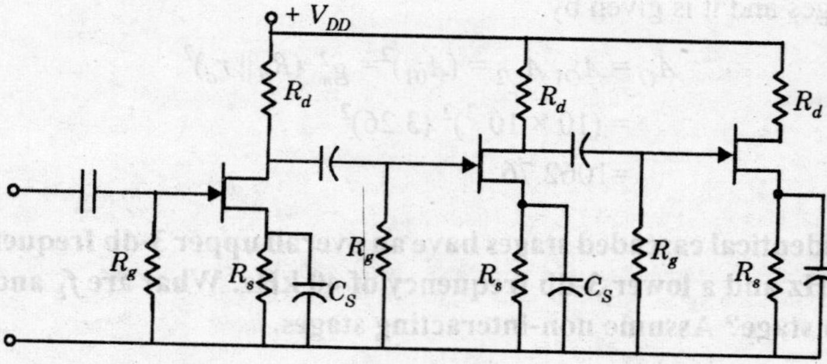


**Fig. 9p4**

Therefore $N = 20 \log_{10} (10.8) = 21.68\text{db}$
Hence the overall mid-band gain of three stages is 3 × 2168 = 65db

(b) From equation $$f_L = \frac{1}{2\pi\,(R_o^1 + R_i^1)\,C_b}$$

where $$R_o^1 = r_d \,\|\, R_d = \frac{7.7 \times 12}{7.7 + 12}\ \text{k} = 4.69\text{k}$$

and $$R_i^1 = R_g = 1\text{M}$$

Thus $$f_L = \frac{1}{2\pi\,(5 \times 10^{-9})\,(1004.7 \times 10^3)}$$

$$f_L = 31.68\text{Hz}$$

(c) From equation $$\frac{f_L^*}{f_L} = \frac{1}{\sqrt{2^{1/3} - 1}}$$

$$\frac{f_L^*}{f_L} = 1.96 f_L$$

$$f_L^* = 1.96 \times 31.68$$
$$= 62.1\text{Hz}$$

**6. The parameters of the transistors in the circuit shown are $h_{fe} = 50$ $h_{ie} = 1.1k$ $h_{re} = h_{oe} = 0$. Find**

**(a) the mid-band gain**

**(b) the value of $C_b$ necessary to give a lower 3-db frequency of 20Hz. Assume that $C_z$ represents a short-circuit at this frequency.**

**(c) find the value of $C_b$ necessary to ensure less than 10% tilt for a 100Hz square wave input:**

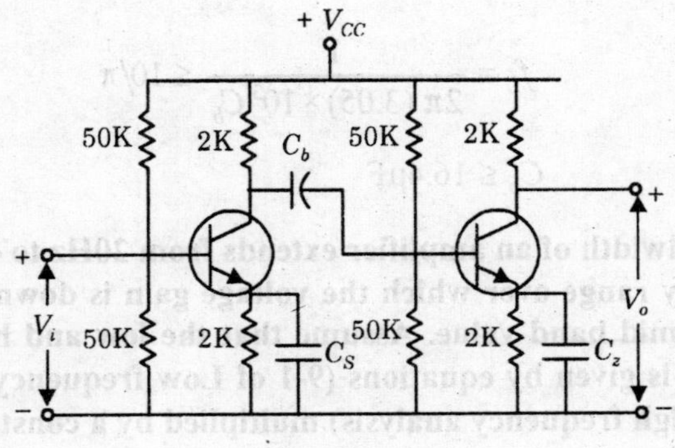


**Fig. 9p5**

**Solution:**

(a) Assuming that for small signal operation, $C_z$ is a short circuit and starting from second stage we have.

$$R_{L_2} = 2K \; R_{iL} = h_{ie} = 1.1k \; A_{I_2} = -50$$

$$A_{V_2} = \frac{A_{I2}\, R_{L2}}{R_{i2}} = \frac{-50 \times 2}{1.1} = 91$$

For the first stage $\quad R_{L_2} = 2 \,||\, 25 \,||\, R_{i_2} = 1/1.45 = 0.69K$

$$R_{i_1} = h_{ie} = 1.1k$$

$$A_{I_1} = -50$$

$$A_{V_1} = \frac{A_{I1}\, R_{LI}}{R_{i1}} = \frac{-50 \times 0.6}{1.1} = 31.4$$

Hence $\quad A_{VO} = A_{V_1} A_{V_2} = 31.4 \times 91 = 2857$

(b) at low frequencies we cannot consider $C_b$ as short circuit. Then $C_b$ will introduce a pole and a zero as it can be seen easily by drawing the equivalent circuit for small signal operation at low frequencies. Hence using equation

$$f_L = \frac{1}{2\pi(R_o^1 + R_i^1)\, C_b}$$

but $\qquad R_o^1 = 2\text{k and } R_i^1 = 25 \,||\, 1.1 = 1.05\text{k}$

then $\qquad f_L = \dfrac{1}{2\pi\,(2 + 1.05) \times 10^3\, C_b} = 20\text{Hz}$

$$C_b = 2.61\mu\text{F}$$

(c) from equation $P = \dfrac{\pi\, f_L}{f} \times 100\%$

but $\qquad f_L = \dfrac{1}{2\pi\,(3.05) \times 10^3\, C_b} \leq 10/\pi$

$$C_b \leq 16.4\mu\text{F}$$

**7. The bandwidth of an amplifier extends from 20Hz to 40Hz. Find the frequency range over which the voltage gain is down less than 1db from its mid band value. Assume that the low and high frequency response is given by equations (9-1 of Low frequency analysis) and (9-5 of High frequency analysis) multiplied by a constant A.**

**Solution:**

$$V_0(s) = \frac{V_i(s)\, R_1}{R_1 + 1/sC_1} = V_1(s)\, \frac{s}{s + 1/R_1C_1} \quad \text{\_\_\_\_\_\_(9-1)}$$

$$L_F\, V_O(S) = V_i(S)\, \frac{S}{S + 1/R_1C_1}$$

$$V_0(s) = \frac{1/sC_2}{R_2 + 1/sC_2} V_i(s) = \frac{1}{1 + sR_2C_2} V_i(s) \quad \text{\_\_\_\_\_\_ (5)}$$

$$H_{FR}\, V_o(s) = V_i(s)\, \frac{S}{1 + SR_2C_2}$$

It is given that $f_L = 20\text{Hz}$ and $f_H$ 20KHz. At low frequencies, using equation (9-1) and the given assumption, we have

$$A_V = \frac{V_o(S)}{V_i(S)} = A_{VO}\, \frac{S}{S + 1/R_1C_1}$$

Or $\qquad \dfrac{A_V}{A_{VO}} = \dfrac{S}{S + 1/R_1C_1}$

And from equation (10-2)

$$\frac{A_V}{A_{VO}} = \frac{1}{1 - j\left(\frac{f_1}{f}\right)} \text{ hence}$$

$$\frac{A_V}{A_{VO}} \text{ is } -1 \text{ db or } 20 \log\left(1 + \frac{f_L^1}{f^2}\right)^{1/2} = 1$$

$$|A_1(jf)| = \frac{1}{\sqrt{1 + \left(\frac{f_L}{f}\right)^2}} \quad \theta_L = \text{are tan } f_L/f$$

$$\log\left(1 + \frac{f_L^2}{f^2}\right)^{1/2} = 0.1 \text{ hence } \left(1 + \frac{f_L^2}{f^2}\right) = 1.26$$

$$t_L = 20.35\text{Hz}$$

Similarly at high frequencies using equation (9-1) and equation (9-2) we obtain

$$\log\left(1 + \frac{f_L^2}{f_H^2}\right)^{1/2} = 1 \text{ or } 1 + f_2/f_H^2 = 1.26$$

$$f_H = 78\text{KHz}$$

at low frequencies $\dfrac{A_L}{A_{VO}} = \dfrac{1}{\left[1 + \left(\frac{f_L}{f}\right)^2\right]^{1/2}}$

$$= \frac{1}{\left[1 + (0.1)^2\right]^{1/2}} = \frac{1}{(0.1)^{1/2}}$$

$$= \frac{1}{1.005} = 0995$$

1. the gain is constant within 0.5/ in the frequency $10f_L \leq f \leq 0.1\, f_H$

$$\text{Tan}^{-1}\left(\frac{f_L}{f}\right) = -\tan^{-1}(0.1) = -0.1 \text{ rad}$$

Since for small $\theta$ $\tan\theta \approx \theta$.

Similarly $\theta = \tan^{-1}\left(\frac{f}{f_H}\right) = \tan^{-1}(0.1) \approx 5.73$

For $10f_L \le f \le 0.1f_H$

**8. Prove that over the range of frequencies from $10f_L$ to 0.1gH the voltage amplification is constant to within 0.5 percent and the phase shift to within ± 0.1 rad. Make the same assumption as in above problem.**

**Solution:**

The gain is constant within 0.5% in the frequency $10f_L \le f \le 0.1f_H$

$$\text{Tan}^{-1}\left(\frac{f_L}{f}\right) = -\tan^{-1}(0.1) = -0.1 \text{ rad}$$

Since for small angle $\tan\theta \approx \theta$

Similarly $\qquad \theta = \tan^{-1}\left(\frac{f}{f_H}\right) = \tan^{-1}(0.1) \approx \theta$

Hence the phase shift is constant to 5.730 for $10f_L \le f \le 0.1f_H$

## 9.7 OBJECTIVE TYPE QUESTIONS

1. In a multistage *R-C* coupled amplifier the coupling capacitor
   (a) limits the low frequency response
   (b) limits the high frequency response
   (c) does not affect the frequency response
   (d) blocks the d.c. component without affecting the frequency response
   **Ans:** (a)
2. A cascade amplifier stage is equivalent to
   (a) a common emitter stage followed by a common base stage
   (b) a common base stage followed by an emitter follower
   (c) an emitter follower stage followed by a common base stage
   (d) a common base stage followed by a common emitter stage
   **Ans:** (a)
3. A multistage amplifier has a low-pass response with three real poles at $s = -\omega_1, -\omega_2$ and $-\omega_3$. The approximate bandwidth $B$ of the amplifier will be given by
   (a) $B = \omega_1 + \omega_2 + \omega_3$ (b) $1/B = 1/\omega_1 + 1/\omega_2 + 1/\omega_3$
   (c) $B = (\omega_1\omega_2\omega_3)^{1/3}$ (d) $B = \sqrt{\omega_1^2 + \omega_2^2 + \omega_3^2}$
   **Ans:** (d)
4. In the cascode amplifier shown in figure if the common-emitter stage (Q1) has a transconductance gm1, and the common-base stage (Q2) has a transconductance $g_{m1}$, and the common-base stage (*q*20 has a

transconductance $g_{m2}$, then the overall transconductance $g_{mc} = (i_o/v_i)$ of the cascode amplifier is

(a) $g_{m1}$ (b) $g_{m2}$

(c) $g_{m1/2}$ (d) $g_{m2/2}$

**Ans:** (a)

**5.** Which of the following amplifier has higher voltage gain and impedance matching?

(a) *RC* coupling (b) inductive coupling

(c) transformer coupling (d) direct coupling

**6.** Which fo the following amplifier is having minimum possible non-linear distortion

(a) *RC* coupling (b) inductive coupling

(c) transformer coupling (d) direct coupling

**Ans:** (a)

**7.** Effect of cascading several amplifier stages is to:

(a) reduce the overall gain

(b) reduce the overall frequency response

(c) overall gain and reduce the frequency response

(d) decrease the overall gain and increase the frequency response

**Ans:** (c)

**8.** An advantage of *RC* coupled amplifier is its:

(a) high efficiency (b) economy

(c) excellent frequency response (d) good impedance matching

**Ans:** (d)

**9.** When a multistage transistor amplifier is required to amplify dc signals also, we must use:

(a) *RC* coupling (b) direct coupling

(c) transformer coupling (d) double tuned circuits

**Ans:** (b)

**10.** Transformer coupling provides high efficiency because the:

(a) collector voltage is stepped up

(b) dc resistance in the collector circuit is low

(c) collector voltage is stepped down

(d) flux linkages are incomplete

**Ans:** (b)

**11.** In a cascade amplifier, the coupling method which is capable of providing highest gain is :

(a) *RC* coupling (b) direct coupling

(c) transformer coupling (d) impedance coupling

**Ans:** (c)

**12.** In *RC* coupled amplifier, the dc component is blocked by:

(a) load resistor $R_L$ (b) coupling capacitance $C_b$

(c) the transistor

(d) the bypass capacitor $C_z$ in the self bias circuit.
**Ans:** (b)

**13.** In the $R_C$ coupled amplifier, the coupling capacitor $C_b$ must be large enough:
(a) to dissipate high power
(b) to pass *dc* current to the next stage
(c) not to attenuate the low frequencies
(d) to give good bias stability
**Ans:** (c)

**14.** Presence of emitter circuit by pass capacitor adversely effects the
(a) low frequency response (b) midband response
(c) high frequency response
(d) response over the compute frequency range.
**Ans:** (a)

**15.** The dissipation at the collector is zero in the queiscent state and increases with excitation in case of
(a) class *A* series-fed amplifier
(b) class *A* transistor coupled amplifier
(c) class *AB* amplifier
(d) class *B* amplifier
**Ans:** (b)

**16.** *RC* coupling is popular in low-level audio amplifiers because it
(a) has better low frequency response
(b) is inexpensive and needs no adjustments
(c) provides an output signal in phase with the input signal
(d) needs low voltage battery for collector supply.
**Ans:** (b)

**17.** The decibel gain of a cascaded amplifier equals the
(a) product of individual gains (b) sum of individual gains
(c) ration of stage gains
(d) product of voltage and current gains
**Ans:** (-)

**18.** Two cascaded stages have gains of 15 and 30. The overall gain will be
(a) 15 (b) 45
(c) 450 (d) none
**Ans:** (-)

**19.** The biggest disadvantage of direct coupled d.c. amplifiers is that
(a) they cannot amplify a.c. voltage
(b) in cascading, each stage $v_c$ gets larger which leads to cut-off after a few stages when $v_c$ becomes equal to $v_{cc}$
(c) they provide low amplification per stage
(d) they down use capacitors between different stages.
**Ans:** (b)

**20.** If two stages of a cascaded amplifier have decibel gains of 40 and 20, then overall gain is –dB

(a) 60 (b) 800

(c) 2 (d) 20

**Ans:** (a)

**21.** Direct coupling is especially suited for amplifying

(a) high frequency a.c. signals (b) changes in d.c. voltages

(c) high-level voltages (d) sinusoidal signals

**Ans:** (b)

**22.** Multistage amplifiers one used to achieve greater

(a) voltage amplification (b) frequency response

(c) power gain (d) all of the above

**Ans:** (d)

**23.** In single stage *RC* coupled amplifier stages, the phase shift at high 3-dB frequency is

(a) 0° (b) 180°

(c) 135° (d) 225°

**Ans:** (c)

**24.** The thermal noise voltage in a conductor is proportional to

(a) $B$ (b) $B2$

(c) $\sqrt{B}$ (d) $1/B$ where $B$ is the Bandwidth

**Ans:** (c)

**25.** The shot noise current in an electron device is proportional to

(a) B3 (b) $B2$

(c) $\sqrt{B}$ (d) $\sqrt{B}$, where $B$ is the band width

**Ans:** (-)

**26.** The lower 3-dB frequency of an $n$-stage amplifier with non interacting stages equals

(a) $\frac{f_2}{\sqrt{2^{1/n} - 1}}$ (b) $f_2\sqrt{2^{1/n} - 1}$

(c) $f_2/n$ (d) $nf_2$

**Ans:** (a)

**27.** The higher 3-dB frequency of an $n$-stage amplifier with non-interacting stages equals

(a) $f_H\sqrt{2^{1/n} - 1}$ (b) $\frac{f_H}{\sqrt{2^{1/n} - 1}}$

(c) $nf_H$ (d) $f_H/n$

**Ans:** (a)

**28.** The rise time $t_r$ of an amplifier in reproducing a square wave is related to the higher 3-dB frequency $f_H$ by the relation.

(a) $t_r = \frac{0.35}{\sqrt{f_H}}$ (b) $t_r = \frac{0.35}{f_H}$

(c) $t_r = 0.35 f_H$ (d) $t_r = 0.35\sqrt{f_H}$

**Ans:** (b)

**29.** In an *RC* coupled transistor amplifier, typical value of coupling capacitor is

(a) 1000pF (b) 0.1μF

(c) 0.01μ0 (d) 10μF

**Ans:** (d)

**30.** One advantages of transformer coupling in transistor amplifiers is that

(a) it is simple and less expensive than the coupling methods

(b) it provides excellent response

(c) low power supply may be used

(d) high efficiency and high power output is obtained

**Ans:** (d)

**31.** In a cascade amplifier, the coupling method capable of providing highest gain is

(a) *RC* coupling (b) *dc* coupling

(c) transformer coupling (d) inductor coupling

**Ans:** (d)

**32.** In an *R.C* coupled amplifier stage, as the value of coupling capacitor *cb* is increased, the low 3-dB frequency $f_L$:

(a) remains unaltered (b) increases

(c) decreases (d) may increase or decrease

**Ans:** (c)

**33.** In an *CE RC*-coupled amplifier stage, as the value of effective shunt capacitance increases, the high 3-dB frequency $f_H$:

(a) remains unaltered (b) increases

(c) decreases (d) may increase or decrease

**Ans:** (c)

**34.** In transformer-coupled amplifiers

(a) *dc* load line is nearly vertical

(b) *ac* load line is nearly vertical

(c) both dc as well as ac load line is nearly vertical

(d) both load lines are nearly horizontal

**Ans:** (a)

**35.** The disadvantage of the complementary Darlington amplifier is that

(a) its *i/p* impedance is very low

(b) its current gain is nearly same as that of Darlington amplifier

(c) matched *NPN-PNP* transistors is required

(d) it is highly temperature-sensitive

**Ans:** (c)

**36.** The 3-dB frequency of an amplifier is one at which gain reduces to

(a) unity (b) zero

(c) $1/\sqrt{2}$ of its midband value (d) half of its medband value

**Ans:** (-)

**37.** Low frequency response of an *RC* coupled amplifier can be improved by:
(a) increasing the coupling capacitors only
(b) increasing both the bypass capacitors only
(c) increasing both the coupling and bypass capacitors
(d) decreasing the bypass capacitor
**Ans:** (c)

**38.** Frequency distortion in an amplifier is caused by
(a) none linear dynamic characteristic of the active device
(b) reactive elements in the circuit
(c) ripple components in the circuit
(d) high temperature of operation
**Ans:** (b)

**39.** Non linear distortion in an amplifier is caused by
(a) non linear dynamic characteristic of the active device
(b) reactive elements in the circuit
(c) ripple components in the circuit
(d) high temperature of operation
**Ans:** (a)

## 9.8 CONVENTIONAL QUESTIONS

**1.** (a) Define the frequency magnitude characteristic of an amplifier
(b) Sketch a typical response curve
(d) Indicate the high and low 3-dB frequencies
(e) Define bandwidth.

**2.** Draw the circuit diagram of Transformer Coupled amplifiers. Determine current gain and voltage gain.

**3.** Draw the circuit diagram of Direct coupled amplifier stages using conventional bias methods. Derive the expressions for voltage gain of first and second stages.

**4.** Sketch the Darlington amplifier circuit diagram what are the advantages of this when compare with single stage amplifier, what is main drawback off this amplifier?

**5.** What is Boostrapping? Draw the circuit diagram of Bootstrapped Darlington circuit and explain Bootstrap effect in FET circuit.

**6.** Sketch the circuit diagram of Cascade amplifier.

## 9.9 EXERCISE PROBLEMS

**1. A cascade amplifier is shown , find the value of $R_C$, which will set the *dc* component of the output voltage to 0 V. Assume $h_{fe}$ = 50 for all transitors.**

**Ans: 3.3k ohms**

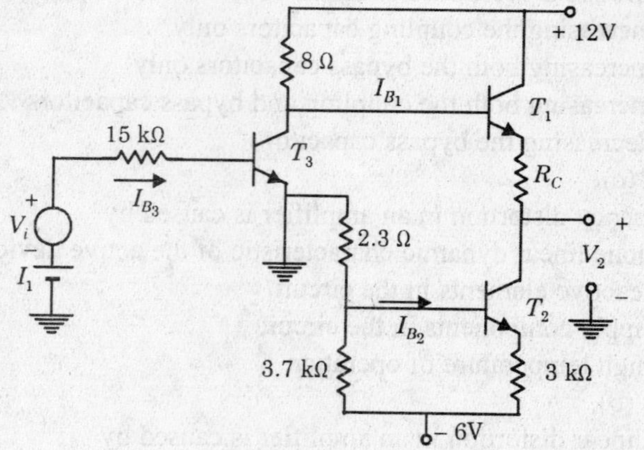


Fig. 9p6

2. **The cascaded amplifier of given figure is *CC* stage at first and then *CE* second stage. Given $R_S$ = 0, $R_{11}$ = 100kΩ, $R_{12}$ = 90kΩ, $R_{21}$=10kΩ, $R_{22}$ = 90kΩ, $R_L = R_C$ = 5kΩ and $R_E$ = 9kΩ. For transistor $Q_1$ $hoc \approx 0$, $h_{ic}$ = 1kΩ , $h_{rc} \approx 1$ and $h_{fc} = -100$. For transistor $Q_2$ $h_{re} \approx 0$, $h_{oe} \approx 0$, $h_{fe}$ = 100 and $h_{ie}$ = 1kΩ. Find**

**(a) overall voltage gain ratio $A_V = \frac{v_L}{v_s}$ (b) overall current gain ratio $A_i = \frac{i_L}{i_s}$**

**Ans: (a) 98 (b) –595.2**

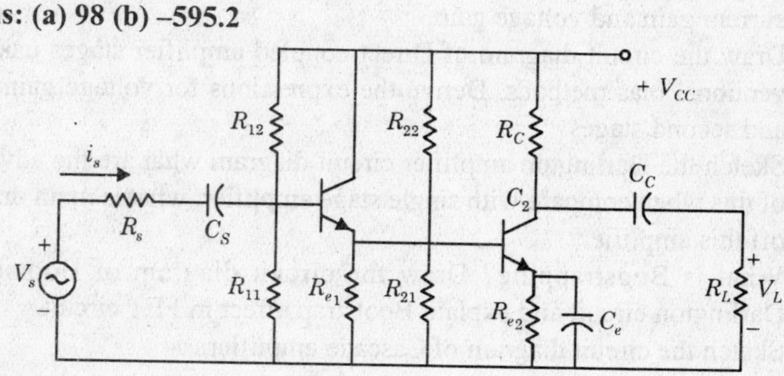


Fig. 9p7

3. **The cascaded amplifier of given figure built of two identical transistors for which $h_{re} = h_{oe} \approx 0$, $h_{fe} \approx 100$ and $h_{ie}$ = 1kΩ. Let $R_{E1}$ = 1kΩ, $R_{C1}$ = 10kΩ, $R_{E2}$ = 100Ω, $R_{C2} = R_L$ = 3kΩ and $C_C = C_E \rightarrow \infty$. Determine**

**(a) overall voltage gain ratio $A_V = \dfrac{v_L}{v_s}$ (b) overall current gain ratio $A_i = \dfrac{i_L}{i_s}$**

**Ans: (a) 133.6 (b) 4545.4**

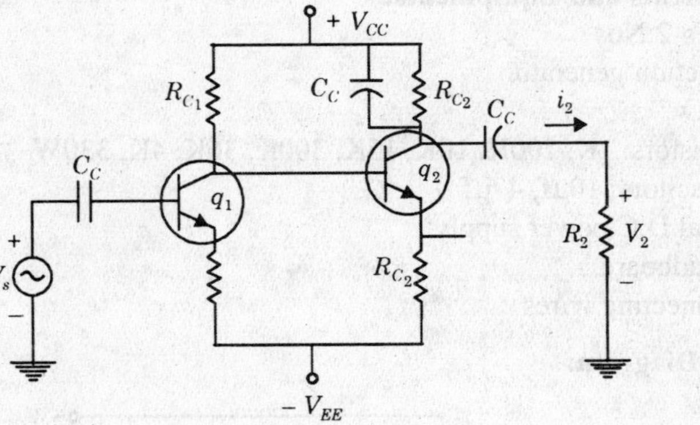


**Fig. 9p8**

**4. For the JFET-BJT Darlington amplifier of figure 9p9**

**(a) voltage gain ratio $A_V = \dfrac{v_o}{v_i}$ and (b) output impedance $R_o$. Assume $h_{re} = h_{oe} = 0$ and that $RG >> R_1, R_2$.**

**Ans: (a) $\dfrac{\mu(h_{fe}+1)(R_1+R_2)}{r_{ds}+(\mu+1)\{h_{ie}+(h_{fe}+1)(R_1+R_2)\}}$ (b) $\dfrac{r_{ds}(\mu+1)h_{ie}}{(\mu+1)(h_{fe}+1)}$**

**5. Calculate $A_v$, $A_I$ for the circuit shown in the figure below.**

**Ans: $A_v = 0.98$, $A_I = 1120$**

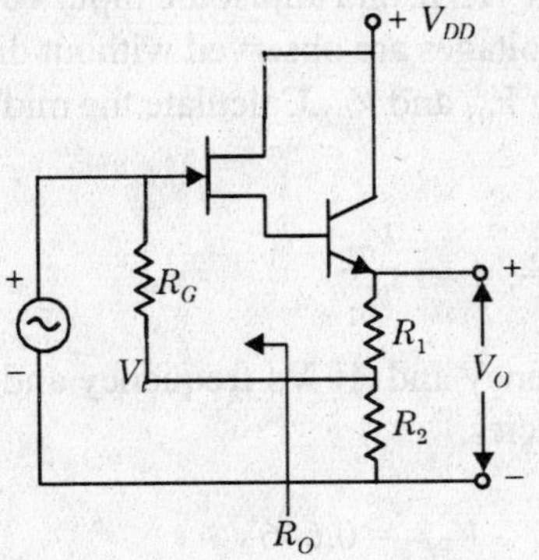


**Fig. 9p9**

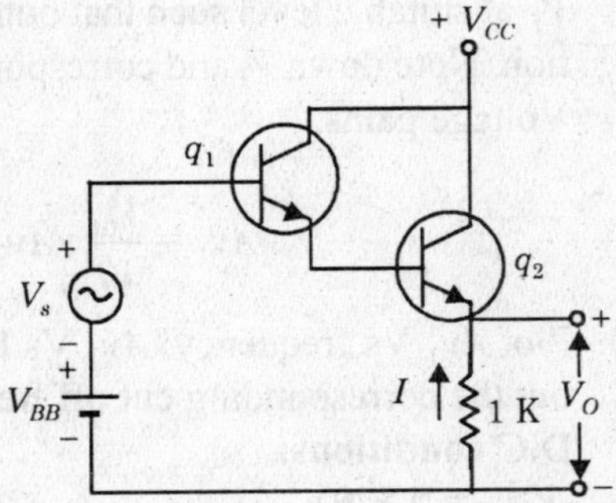


**Fig. 9p10**

## 9.10 LAB EXPERIMENTS

### *1. RC Coupled Amplifier(Two Stage)*

**Aim:** To study the frequency response of a *RC* coupled BJT amplifier i.e., gain *Vs* frequency response.

**Components and Equipments:**

1. BJTs-2 Nos
2. Function generator
3. CRO
4. Resistors: 1K, 200K, 10K, 15K, 300K, 36K, 4K, 330W
5. capacitors: 10µf, 47µf
6. Dual D.C power supply
7. Breadboard
8. Connecting wires

**Circuit Diagram:**

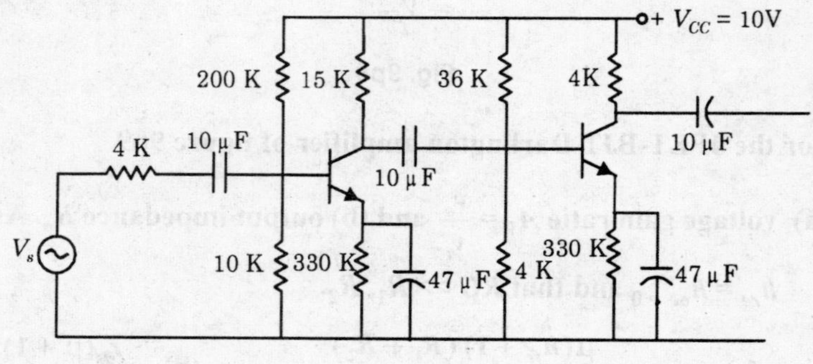


Fig. 9L1

**Procedure:**

1. Connect the circuit as shown in the circuit diagram.
2. keep the signal generator frequency at 1KHz and adjust the input voltage $V_i$ at suitable level such that output voltages are observed without distortion. Note down $V_i$ and corresponding $V_{01}$ and $V_{02}$.Calculate the midband Voltage gains.

$$Av_1 = \frac{V_{01}}{Vi};\ Av_2 = \frac{V_{02}}{Vi};\ Av = \frac{V_{02}}{V_{01}}$$

3. Plot $Av_1$ Vs frequency; $Av_2$ Vs frequency and $Av$ Vs frequency and find out the corresponding cut off frequencies.

**D.C conditions:**

$V_{BE1} = 0.579V$ ; $V_{BE2} = 0.646V$

$I_{B1} = 0.3\mu A$ ; $I_{B2} = 5.8\mu A$

$I_{C1} = 0.144\text{mA}$ ; $I_{C2} = 1.94\text{mA}$

$V_{CE1} = 10.61\text{V}$ ; $V_{CE2} = 4.35\text{V}$

**Theoretical calculations:**

2[nd] stage: $R_{L2} = R_{C2} = 4\text{K}$

1. $A_{I2}^{1} = -h_{fe} = -70$

2. $R_{i2}^{1} = h_{ie} = 2.2\text{K}\Omega$

3. $A_{V2}^{1} = A_{I2}^{1} \dfrac{R_{L2}}{R_{i2}^{1}} = -127.27 = A_v$

4. $R_{i2} = R_{b2} \,||\, R_{i2}^{1} = 1.37\text{K}\Omega$

# ❮ 10 ❯

# NEGATIVE FEEDBACK AMPLIFIER

## 10.1 INTRODUCTION

The amplifiers without negative feedback are called basic amplifiers, their a.c gain is not stable, their impedances are not according to expected values, and they have lot of distortion and effected noise. All these limitations can be eliminated by using negative feedback in the basic amplifiers. Therefore the purpose of negative feed back amplifier is to improve the characteristic of basic amplifier.

## 10.2 LIMITATIONS OF BASIC AMPLIFIER

1. The instability of a.c gain is due to the following
   - (i) Change in supply.
   - (ii) Change in $h$-parameters.
   - (iii) Age of the device
2. The input and output impedances are not according to the requirements of the basic amplifier.
3. Distortion is large.
4. Noise is more
5. Bandwidth is not sufficiently large.

## 10.3 DIFFERENT TYPES OF BASIC AMPLIFIERS

For understanding the concepts of feedback, amplifiers have been classified into four broad categories:

- (i) Voltage amplifiers.
- (ii) Current amplifiers
- (iii) Transconductance amplifiers
- (iv) Transresistance amplifiers.

The relative magnitudes of the input impedance as compared to the source impedance and that of output impedance as compared to load impedance are the factors, which determine the category of the amplifier.

### *Voltage Amplifiers:*

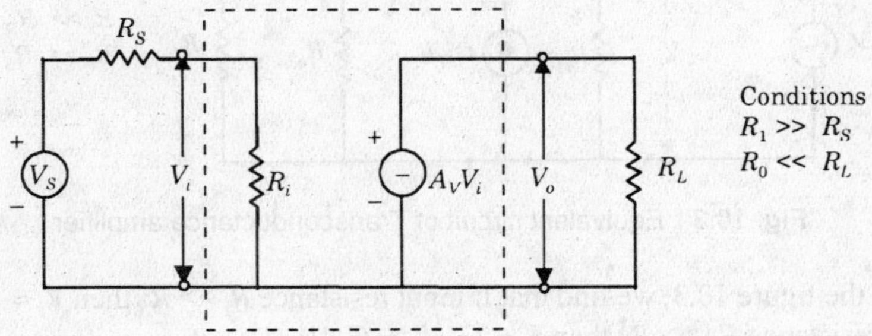


**Fig. 10.1** Equivalent circuit of voltage amplifier

From the figure 10.1 we find that if input resistance $R_i >> R_s$ then $V_i \approx V_s$. Also, if load resistance $R_L >> R_o$

Then $\quad V_o \approx A_V.$

$$V_i \approx A_V V_S \qquad \therefore \qquad A_V = \frac{V_0}{V_S}$$

An ideal voltage amplifier should have infinite input resistance ($R_i = \alpha$) and zero output resistance ($R_o = 0$).

### *Current Amplifier:*

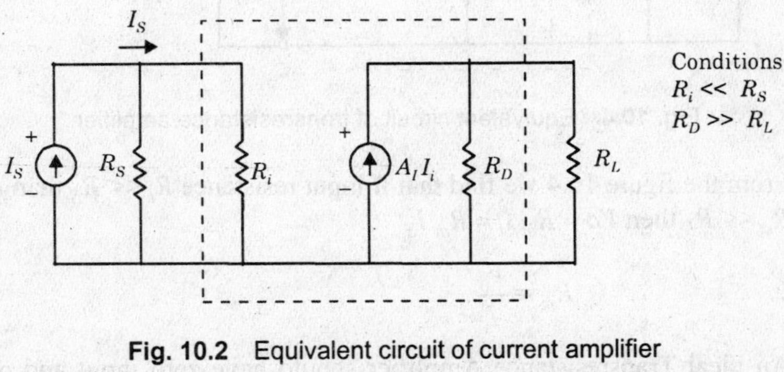


**Fig. 10.2** Equivalent circuit of current amplifier

From the figure 10.2 we find that if the input resistance $R_i << R_S$ then $I_i \approx I_S$

and if $R_0 >> R_L$ then $I_L \approx A_i I_i \approx A_i I_s \therefore A_I = \dfrac{I_L}{I_S}$

*An ideal current amplifier should have zero input resistance (i.e. $R_i = 0$) and infinite output resistance ($R_o = \alpha$)*

### *Transconductance Amplifier:*

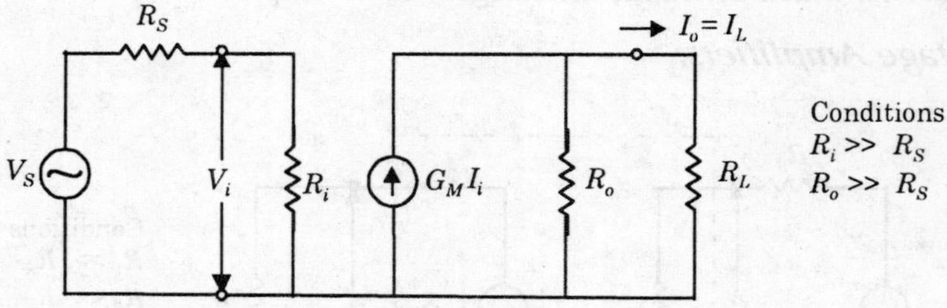


**Fig. 10.3** Equivalent circuit of Transconductance amplifier

From the figure 10.3, we find that if input resistance $R_i >> R_S$ then $V_i \approx V_S$ and load resistance $R_o >> R_L$ then $I_L \approx G_m V_i \approx G_m V_S$

$$\therefore \qquad G_m \equiv \frac{I_L}{V_i}$$

An ideal transconductance amplifier should have infinite input and output resistances (i.e. $R_i = \alpha$, $R_o = \infty$)

### *Transresistance Amplifier:*

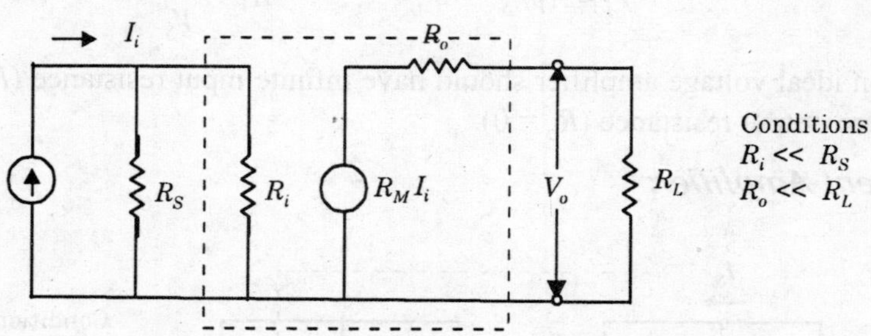


**Fig. 10.4** Equivalent circuit of transresistance amplifier

From the figure 10.4 we find that if input resistance $R_i << R_S$ than $I_i \approx I_S$ and $R_o << R_L$ then $Vo \approx R_m I_i \approx R_m I_S$

$$\therefore \qquad R_m = \frac{V_0}{I_i}.$$

An ideal Transresistance Amplifier should have zero input and output resistance (i.e. $R_i = 0$; $R_o = 0$)

Ideal amplifier classification

| | *Voltage amplifier* | *Current amplifier* | *Transresistance amplifier* | *Transconductance amplifier* |
|---|---|---|---|---|
| Input Resistance ($R_I$) | ∞ | 0 | ∞ | 0 |
| Output resistance ($R_o$) | 0 | ∞ | ∞ | 0 |
| Input quantity | $V_S$ | $I_S$ | $V_S$ | $I_S$ |
| Output quantity | $V_o$ | $I_L$ | $I_L$ | $V_o$ |
| *Transfer characteristics* | $A_V = \frac{V_S}{V_O}$ | $A_V = \frac{I_L}{I_S}$ | $G_M = \frac{I_L}{V_S}$ | $R_M = \frac{V_O}{I_S}$ |

## 10.4 DISTORTION IN BASIC AMPLIFIERS

| *Name of the distortion* | *Effect* | *Cause* | *Remedy* |
|---|---|---|---|
| 1. Amplifier/ non-linear. | Some new harmonics which are not given at the input are seen at the output because of non-linearity. | *Q*-point is in non-linear or *Q*-point is in linear but the signal has gone to non-linear. | $V_0 = A_V V_I$ (a) as negative feed-back amplifier is applied voltage gain decreases and the signal is decreased and operated in linear region. (b) as DC negative feedback amplifier is applied the *Q*-point is decreased to linear region. |
| 2. Frequency | Different harmonics are multiplied, amplified to different strength. | µF capacitors at low frequency range and *pF* capacitors at high frequency range. | (a) frequency equali-zers (or) compen-sating circuit. (b) Negative feed-back amplifiers is applied then the vol-tage gain decrea-ses which causes an increase in the band-width. |
| 3. Phase distortion or delay distortion | Different frequencies are shifted to different phases. | µF capacitors at low frequency range and *pF* capacitors at high frequency range | (a) Phase equalizers. (b) Negative feedback amplifiers |

## 10.5 BLOCK DIAGRAM OF NEGATIVE FEEDBACK AMPLIFIER

### *Block Diagram of* NFBA

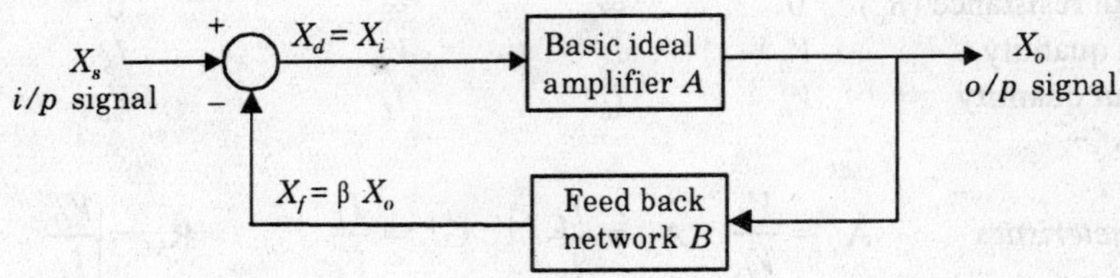


**Fig. 10.5** Block diagram of negative feed back amplifier

The basic amplifier of figure 10.5 may be an ideal voltage, transconductance, current, or transresistance amplifier connected in a feedback configuration. The input signal $X_S$, the output signal $X_o$, the feedback signal $X_f$ and difference signal $X_d$ each represent either a voltage or a current.

$X_d = X_s - X_f$, $X_d$ = difference signal or error signal $X_d$ represents different between the applied signal and the fedback to the input, $X_f$.

The feedback signal $X_f$ is defined by $X_f \equiv \beta X_o$, β network is generally a resistive network. The symbol $X_o$ is output voltage given by $X_o = AX_i$ For an ideal amplifier, the output is proportional to the input and that this proportionality factor A is independent of the magnitude of the source and load impedance. The gain with feedback $A_f$ is given by

$$A_f = \frac{X_0}{X_s} = \frac{A}{1+\beta A}$$

If $|A_f| > |A|$, the feedback is termed negative, or degenerative.

If $|A_f| < |A|$, the feedback is termed as positive, or regenerative.

## 10.6 STABILITY OF GAIN WITH FEEDBACK

**Case (i)** Approximate analysis:

$$A\beta >> 1$$

$$A_f = \frac{A}{1 + A\beta} \cong \frac{1}{\beta}$$

β should not contain active device and frequency dependent components.

∴ β network is resistive network.

**Case (ii)** Exact analysis:

$$A_f = \frac{A}{1+A\beta}$$

On differentiating with respect to $A$ we get

$$\frac{dA_f}{dA} = \frac{1}{(1+A\beta)^2}$$

$$\frac{dA_f}{dA} = \frac{1}{(1+A\beta)} \frac{A}{1+A\beta} \frac{1}{A}$$

$$\frac{dA_f}{A_f} = \left\{\frac{1}{1+A\beta}\right\} \frac{dA}{A}$$

$$\left|\frac{dA_f}{A_f}\right| << \left|\frac{dA}{A}\right|$$

$$D = 1 + A\beta$$

Where $D$ is the desensitive factor.

## 10.7 ADVANTAGES OF NEGATIVE FEEDBACK AMPLIFIER

1. Gain is stabilized as discussed in previous section.
2. Frequency phase distortion is decreased as bandwidth is increased, their bandwidth is called "Distortion free zone ".
3. Non linear distortion is decreased as gain decreases.
4. Effect of noise decreases, as gain is decreased.
5. $R_{if}$ and $R_{0f}$ are increased or decreased in order to meet the requirements of amplifiers according to feedback arrangement.

## Disadvantages:

All the above advantages are at the cost of only one drawback of reduction in gain.

### 10.7.1 Topologies of Feedback

Voltage series Feedback: In voltage series feedback, the output voltage is sampled and feedback quantity is mixed in series with input.

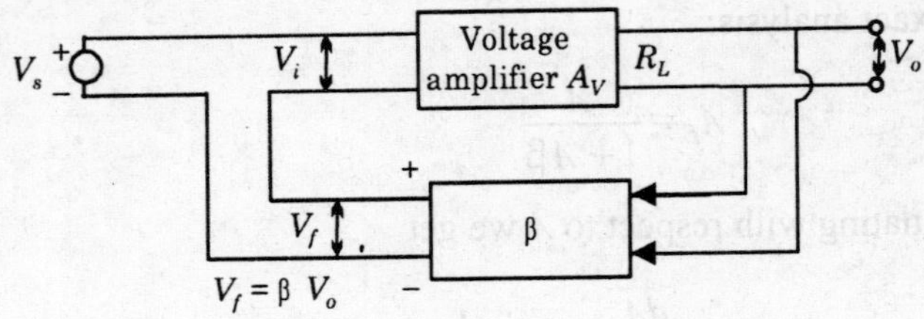


**Fig. 10.6** Voltage amplifier with voltage series feedback

The feedback quantity $V_f = \beta_{Vo}$. Therefore the net input to the main amplifier, which is voltage amplifier is $V_i = V_S - V_f = V_S - \beta_{Vo}$

$$V_S = V_i + \beta_{\text{Vo}}$$

$$= I_i R_i + \beta_{Vo}$$

1. Voltage gain $A_V = \dfrac{V_0}{V_i}$
2. Feedback factor $\beta = \dfrac{V_S}{V_0}$
3. Desensitivity $D = 1 + A_V\beta$
4. Voltage gain with feedback $A_{Vf} = \dfrac{A_V}{D}$
5. Input resistance with feedback $R_{if} = R_i D$
6. Output resistance with feedback $R_{of} = \dfrac{R_0}{D}$

$A_{Vf}$ (Voltage gain with feedback):

$$A_{Vf} = \frac{V_0}{V_S} = (\because \text{ output voltage is assured unchanged}).$$

Thus $$A_{Vf} = \frac{A_V V_i}{V_S} = \frac{A_V}{1 - \beta A_V}$$

$A_{Vf}$ closed loop gain input resistance with feedback $= R_{if}$

$$R_{if} = \frac{V_S}{I_i} = \frac{V_S}{I_i}\frac{V_i}{V_i} = \frac{V_S}{I_i}\left(\frac{V_S}{V_i}\right) = R_i\,(1 - \beta A_V) = R_i D$$

Output resistance with feedback( $R_{of}$)

$$R_{of} = \frac{V_\infty}{I_0} = \frac{A_V V_i}{I_0}$$

$$R_{of} = A_V \frac{V_i}{I_0} = \left(\frac{V_i}{V_S}\right)\left(\frac{V_0}{I_0}\right) = \frac{R_0}{D}$$

### *Current series Feedback:*

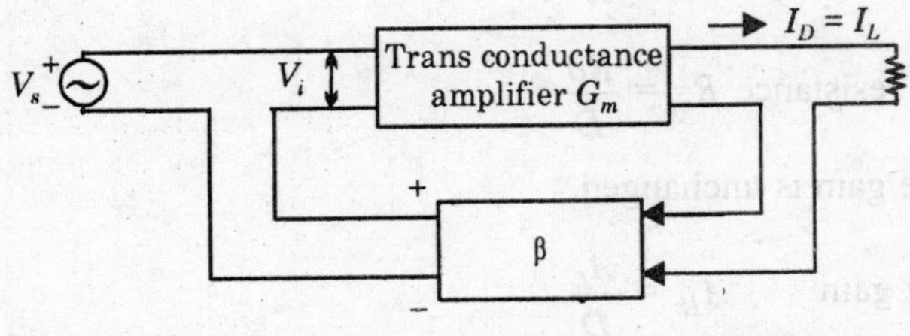


**Fig. 10.7** Current amplifier with current shunt feedback

The feedback quantity is proportional to the output current and is fed in series with input in this transconductance amplifier, as its output quantity is current $I_o$ with input quantity is voltage $V_I$

$$V_f = \beta I_o \; R_{if} = R_i(1 + \beta G_M)$$

$$V_i = V_S - \beta I_o \; D = 1 + \beta G_M \; G_M = I_o/V_I$$

$$G_M = I_L/V_S$$

Input resistance $\quad R_{if} = R_i(D)$

Output resistance $R_{of} = R_o(D)$

Current gain $A_{IF}$ = is unchanged

Voltage gai $A_{Vf}$ is $A_V/D$

### *Voltage Shunt Feedback:*

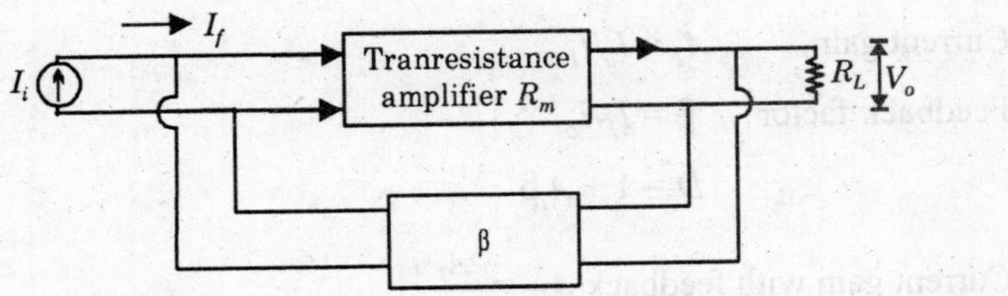


**Fig. 10.8** Transresistance amplifier with voltage-shunt feedback

In this feedback amplifier the feedback quantity is proportional to output voltage $V_o$ and is fed in parallel to the input signal. This is a transresistance amplifier, because its output quantity is voltage ($V_o$) and input quantity is current ($I_i$).

$$I_F = \beta V_o$$
$$I_I = I_S - \beta V_o$$
$$R_M = V_o/I_i$$

Input resistance $R_{if} = \frac{R_i}{D}$

Output resistance $R_{of} = \frac{Ro}{D}$

Voltage gain is unchanged

Current gain $A_{IF} = \frac{A_I}{D}$

### *Current-shunt Feedback:*

In this, the feedback quantity is proportional to output voltage $I_o$ is fed in parallel with input. This main amplifier is a current amplifier.

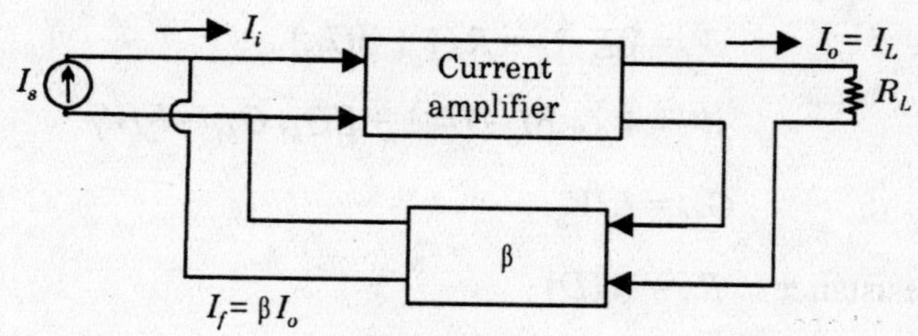


**Fig. 10.9** Current amplifier with current-shunt feedback

$$I_F = \beta Io \qquad D = (1 + \beta A_i)$$

∴ $I_I = I_S - \beta I_o$

Current gain $A_I = I_o/I_I$

Feedback factor $\beta = I_F/I_o$

$$D = 1 + A_i\beta$$

Current gain with feedback $A_{IF} = \frac{A_I}{D}$

Voltage gain with feedback $A_V$ is unchanged

Input resistance with feedback $R_{if} = \frac{R_i}{D}$

Out resistance with feedback $R_{OF} = R_{OD}$

### 10.8.2 Comparision of Negative Feedback Amplifier:

| Parameter | Voltage series | Current shunt | Voltage shunt | Current series |
|---|---|---|---|---|
| 1. $X_0$ | Voltage $V_0$ | Current $I_O$ | Voltage $V_0$ | Current $I_O$ |
| 2. $X_s$, $X_i$, $X_f$ | Voltage $V_s$, $V_i$, $V_f$ | Current $I_s$, $I_i$, $I_f$ | Current $I_s$, $I_i$, $I_f$ | Voltage $V_s$, $V_i$, $V_f$ |
| 3. Basic amplifier | Voltage amplifier | Current amplifier | Trans resistance | Trans conductanc |
| 4. basic amplifier gain $\frac{X_0}{X_f}$ | $A_v = \frac{V_0}{V_i}$ | $A_v = \frac{I_0}{I_i}$ | $R_H = \frac{V_0}{I_i}$ | $G_M = \frac{I_0}{V_i}$ |
| 5. $\beta = \frac{X_f}{X_0}$ | $\beta = \frac{V_f}{V_0}$ | $\beta = \frac{I_f}{I_0}$ | $\beta = \frac{I_f}{V_0}$ | $\beta = \frac{V_f}{I_0}$ |
| 6. $A_f = \frac{A}{D}$ | $Av_f = \frac{A_I}{D}$ | $AI_f = \frac{A_I}{D}$ | $R_{Mf} = \frac{R_M}{\beta}$ | $G_{Mf} = \frac{G_M}{\beta}$ |
| 7. $R_{if}$ | $R_{if} = R_i$ D | $R_{if} = R_i/D$ | $R_{if} = R_i/D$ | $R_{if} = R_0 D$ |
| 8. $R_{0f}$ | $R_{0f} = R_0/D$ | $R_{0f} = R_0 D$ | $R_{0f} = R_0/D$ | $R_{0f} = R_0 D$ |
| 9. $BW_f \cong BW \times D = BW(1 + A_v \beta)$ | $BW \times D$ $(1 + A_I \beta)$ | $BW = BW$ | $BW = BW(1 + R_M \beta)$ | $BW = BW(1 + G_M)$ |
| 10. $f_{1f} = f_1/D$ | $f_{1f} = f_1/(1 + A_V\beta)$ | $f_{1f} \cong f_1/D$ | $f_{1f} = f_1/D$ <br> $f_{1f} = f_1/(1+R_M\beta)$ | $f_{1f} \cong f_1/D$ |
| 11. $f_{2f} = f_2 \times D$ | $f_{2f} = f_2 \times D$ | $f_{2f} = f_2 \times D$ | $f_{2f} = f_2 \times D$ | $f_{2f} = f_2 \times D$ |
| 12. $D_{2f} = D_2/D$ | $D_{2f} = D_2/D$ | $D_{2f} = D_2/D$ | $D_{2f} = D_2/D$ | $D_{2f} = D_2/D$ |
| 13. Noise | Reduces | Reduces | Reduces | Reduces |
| 14. $D = 1 + A\beta$ | $1 + A_V\beta$ | $1 + A_I\beta$ | $1 + R_M\beta$ | $1 + G_M\beta$ |
| 15 Other names | Parallely driven serially return. Voltage controlled voltage source. | Serially driven parallely return. Current controlled current source. | Parallely driven parallely return. Current controlled voltage source. | Serially driven serially return. Voltage controlled current source. |

## 10.8 EFFECT OF NEGATIVE FEEDBACK AMPLIFIER UPON INPUT AND OUTPUT RESISTANCES

### *Input Resistance for Feedback:*

Let us consider the voltage amplifier and its equivalent circuit can be drawn as shown in fig 10.10

Input *kvl*:

$$V_s = I_i R_i + V_f \;\; = I_i R_i + \beta A_v \qquad \text{...(1)}$$

$$V_0 = \left( \frac{A_V V_i}{R_0 + R_L} \right) R_L = A_V R_i I_i \qquad \text{...(2)}$$

$$\therefore \qquad A_v = \frac{V_0}{V_i} = \left( \frac{R_V R_L}{R_0 + R_L} \right) \qquad \text{...(3)}$$

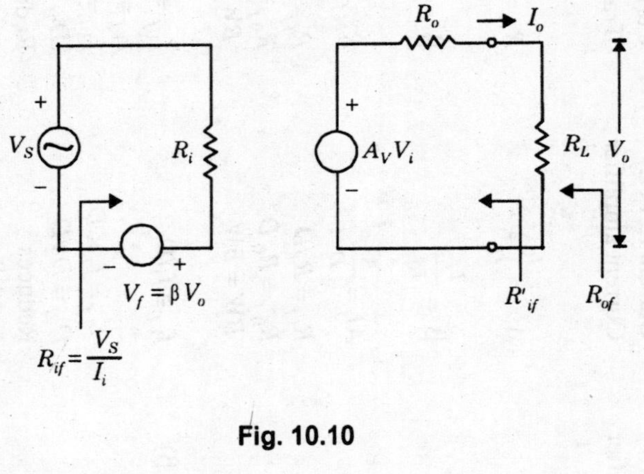


**Fig. 10.10**

From equation (1) and (2) we get

$$V_S = I_i R_i + \beta V_0$$

$$= I_i R_i + \beta A_V R_i I_i$$

$$= I_i R_i (1 + \beta A_V)$$

$$R_f = \frac{V_i}{I_i} = R_i (1 + \beta A_v) \;\; = R_i D$$

where $\qquad D = 1 + \beta A_v$

### *Output Resistance for Voltage Sample:*

From output side:

$$I = \frac{V - A_V V_i}{R_0}$$

$$V_i = -V_f = -\beta A_v$$

$$I = \frac{V + \beta A_V V_i}{R_0} = \frac{V(1 + A\beta)}{R_0}$$

$$R'_{0f} = \frac{V}{1} = \frac{R_0}{1 + \beta A_V} = \frac{R_0}{D}$$

Similarly when $R_L$ is connected

$$R_0 = R'_0 \parallel R_L$$

$$R_{0f} = \frac{R'_0}{1 + \beta A_V} = \frac{R'_0}{D}$$

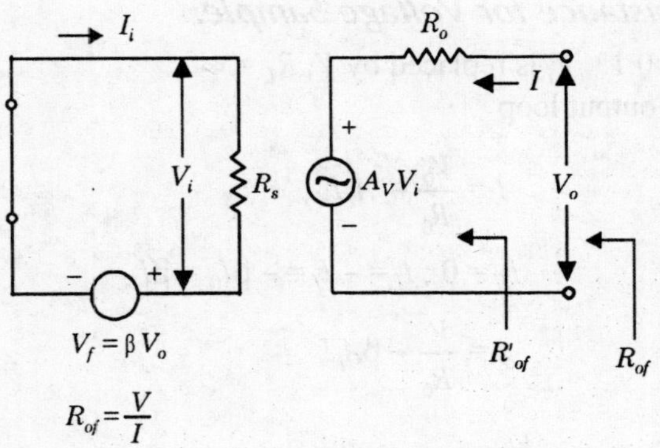


**Fig. 10.11**

## *Input Resistance for Shunt Feedback:*

Let us consider the current amplifier and its equivalent circuit can be drawn as shown in Fig 10.12

Input *kcl*

$$I_S = I_i + I_f = I_S + \beta I_0 \quad \ldots(1)$$

$$I_0 = \left(\frac{A_I I_i}{R_0 + R_L}\right) R_0 = A_I I_i \quad \ldots(2)$$

$$\frac{I_0}{I_i} = A_I = \frac{A_I R_0}{R_0 + R_L} \quad \ldots(3)$$

From equation (1) and (3)

$$I_s = I_i + \beta I_0 = I_i + \beta A_I I_i = I_i(1 + \beta A_I)$$

$$R_i = \frac{V_i}{I_i}$$

$$R_{if} = \frac{V_i}{I_s} = \frac{V_i}{I_i(1 + \beta A_I)} = \frac{R_i}{(1 + \beta A_I)} = \frac{R_i}{D}$$

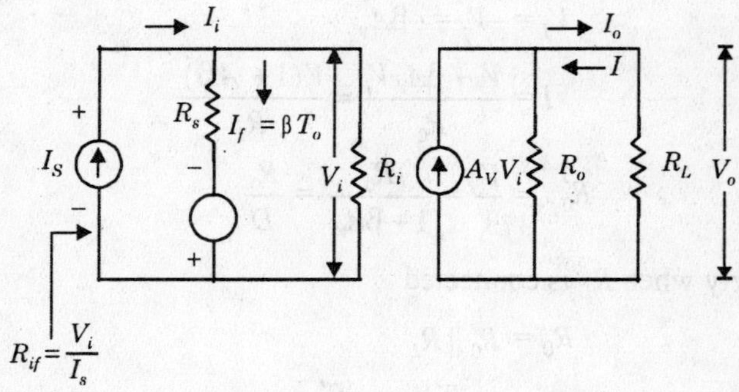


Fig. 10.12

## *Output Resistance for Voltage Sample:*

In the figure 10.13, $V_i$ is replaced by $V$, $R_L = \infty$

From the output loop

$$I = \frac{V_0}{R_0} - A_I I_i$$

With $$I_S = 0\,;\, I_i = -I_f = -\beta I_0 = \beta I$$

$\therefore$ $$I = \frac{V}{R_0} - \beta A_i I$$

$$\frac{V}{R_0} = I + \beta A_i I$$

$$\frac{V}{R_0} = I(1 + \beta A_i)$$

$\therefore$ $$R'_{0f} = \frac{V}{I} = R_0(1+\beta A_i) = R_0 D.$$

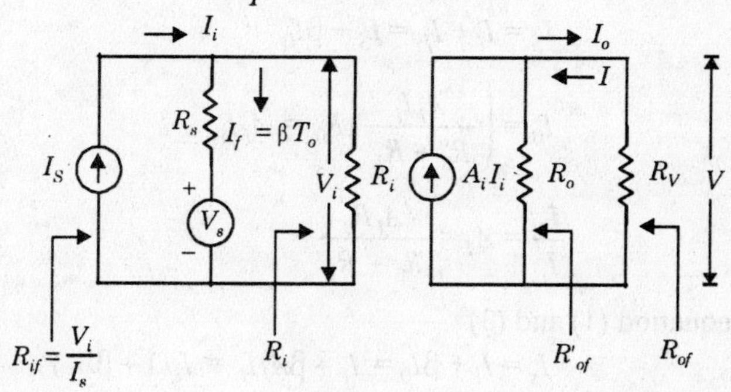


Fig. 10.13

when $$R_{0f} = R'_{0f} \parallel R_L$$

$$R_{0f} = R_0(1 + \beta A_i) = R_0 D$$

## 10.9 PROCEDURE FOR ANALYSIS OF NEGATIVE FEEDBACK AMPLIFIER

### $S_1$ : Identify the topology

(a) If β network is directly taken from $V_0$ which is voltage sample or otherwise current sample.

(b) If β network is directly connected to base or gate or opamp signal point then shunt mixing otherwise series mixing.

$S_2$ : Calculate β accordingly.

$S_3$ : Draw basic amplifier.

Assumption of feedback amplifiers:

1. When the signal is going through a forward path it can go through β network also.
   ∴ It will load on the input of basic amplifier even if the signal through the β network is nullified.
2. When the signal is going through the reverse path it loads $A$ at output.
   ∴ Drawing the basic amplifier is nothing but basic amplifier with loading of β network.
   (a) to draw input circuit go to output and put $X_0 = 0$
   if $V_0 = 0$ then output is short circuited.
   if $I_0 = 0$ then output is open circuited.
   (b) to draw output circuit go to input and see that if it is in series then cut it and if it is in shunt then ground it.
   (c) From the above discussion the basic amplifier is with the loading of β network but not signal through β.

$S_4$ : Calculate $A$, $R_i$, $R_0$ using (i) ten steps (ii) $h$-parameter model using kirchoffs laws.

$S_5$ : Calculate $A_{if}$, $R_{if}$, $R_{0f}$ using comparison table.

## 10.10 ANALYSIS OF DIFFERENT TOPOLOGIES

Let us analyse each topology in terms of circuits by using the above procedure for analysis and comparision of topologies table.

### 10.10.1 Voltage Shunt Feedback Amplifier

**Case (i)** $R_e = 0$

$S_1$ : $R_f$ is acting as β network.

(a) β network is directly taken from $V_0$. ∴ It is voltage sampled.

(b) β network is directly connected to base to form a node. ∴ shunt mixing.

Therefore it is a voltage shunt feedback amplifier.

$X_0$ is voltage. $X_S$, $X_f$, $X_i$ are currents.

$S_2$:
$$\beta = \frac{X_f}{X_0} = \frac{I_f}{V_0}$$

$$I_f = \frac{V_i - V_0}{R_f}$$

∴ $V_i << V_0$, because $V_0$ is amplified.

$$\frac{V_i - V_0}{R_f}$$

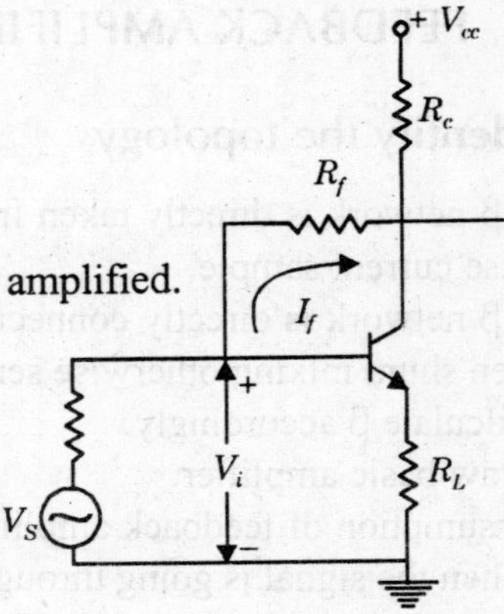


Fig. 10.14

∴
$$\beta = \frac{R_f}{V_0} = -\frac{1}{R_f}$$

$S_3$ : Drawing basic amplifier

(a) For the input circuit go to output and put $X_0 = 0$ i.e. $V_0 = 0$.

(b) For output circuit go to input and put $V_i = 0$.

$S_4$: Analysis of basic amplifier using ten standard steps and if that is not possible we go by replacing the transistor with its equivalent model. In this problem we do using ten standard steps.

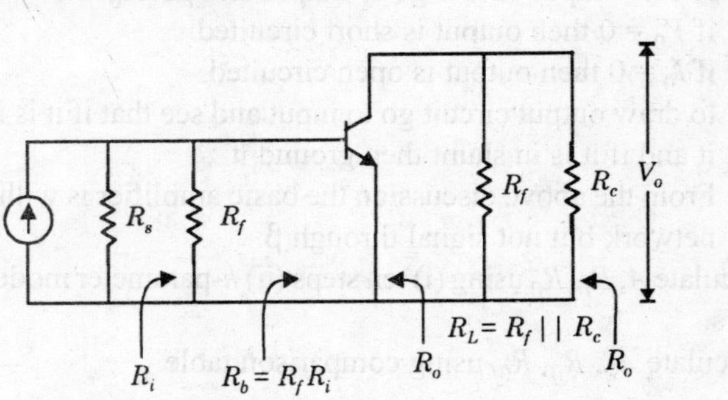


Fig. 10.14(b)

1. $$A_I' = \frac{h_{fe}}{1 + h_{oe} R_L} = \frac{I_0}{I_b}$$

2. $$R_i' = h_{ie} + h_{re} A_I' R_L = \frac{V_{be}}{I_b}$$

3. $$A_V' = \frac{A_I' R_L}{R_i'} = \frac{V_0}{V_{be}}$$

4. $$A_I = \frac{I_0}{I_i} = A_I' \left( \frac{R_b}{R_b + R_i} \right)$$

5. $$R_i = R_b \| R_i$$

6. $$R_M = \frac{V_0}{I_i} = \frac{I_0 R_L}{I_i} = A_I R_L$$

7. $$Y_0' = h_{oe} - \frac{h_{re} h_{fe}}{h_{ie} + R_S'} \text{ where } R_S' = R_S \| R_f$$

$$R_0' = \frac{1}{Y_0'}$$

8. $$R_0 = R_0' \| R_L$$

$S_5$ : Analysis with feedback amplifier

1. $$D = 1 + R_M \beta$$

2. $$R_{Mf} = \frac{R_M}{D}$$

3. $$R_{if} = \frac{R_i}{D}$$

4. $$R_{Of} = \frac{R_0}{D}$$

**Case (ii) $R_e \neq 0$**

$S_1$: We treat $R_e$ as local feedback and hence it does not change topology. ∴ It is voltage shunt.

$S_2$: $\beta = -\frac{1}{R_f}$

$S_3$:

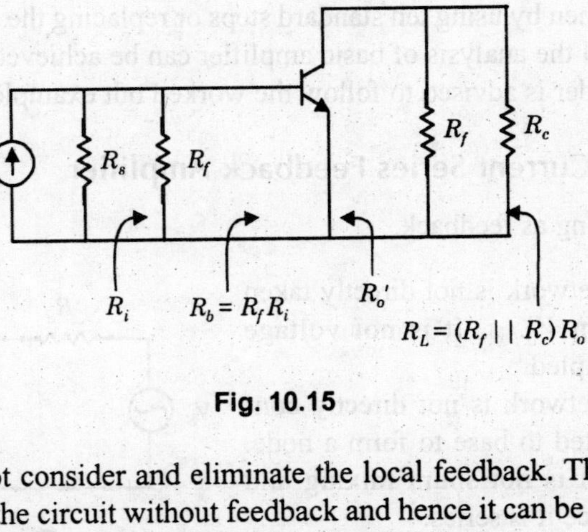


**Fig. 10.15**

We need not consider and eliminate the local feedback. Therefore $R_e$ is present even in the circuit without feedback and hence it can be treated as $CE$ without $R_e$ and approximate analysis by assuming $h_{oe} R_c \leq 0.1$

$S_4$: 1. $$A_I' = -h_{fe}$$

2. $$R_i' = h_{ie} + (1 + h_{fe})R_e$$

3. $$A_I = A_I'\left(\frac{R_b}{R_b + R_i}\right)$$

4. $$R_i = R_i' \,||\, R_b$$

5. $$R_M = A_I R_L$$

6. $$Y_0' = 0$$

$$R_0' = \frac{1}{Y_0'} = \infty$$

7. $$R_0 = R_0' \,||\, R_L = R_L$$

$S_5$ : Analysis with feedback amplifier

1. $$D = 1 + R_M \beta$$

2. $$R_{Mf} = \frac{R_M}{D}$$

3. $$R_{if} = \frac{R_i}{D}$$

4. $$R_{Of} = \frac{R_0}{D}$$

For the remaining topologies we will do identification and draw basic amplifier. Then by using ten standard steps or replacing the device with small signal model the analysis of basic amplifier can be achieved.

The reader is advised to follow the worked out examples for other steps.

## 10.10.2 Current Series Feedback Amplifier

$S_1$: $R_e$ is acting as feedback.

(a) $\beta$ network is not directly taken from $V_0$. $\therefore$ It is not voltage sampled.

(c) $\beta$ network is not directly connected to base to form a node. $\therefore$ it is not shunt mixing and hence it is series.

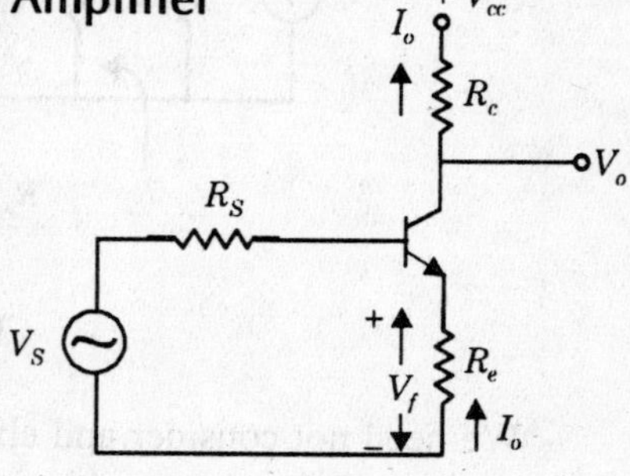


Fig. 10.16

Therefore it is a current series shunt feedback amplifier.

$S_2$: $$\beta = \frac{V_f}{I_0} = -\frac{I_0 R_e}{I_0} = -R_e$$

$S_3$: Drawing basic amplifier

(a) For the input circuit go to output and put $I_0 = 0$ i.e. output is open circuited.

(b) For output circuit go to input and open circuit input.

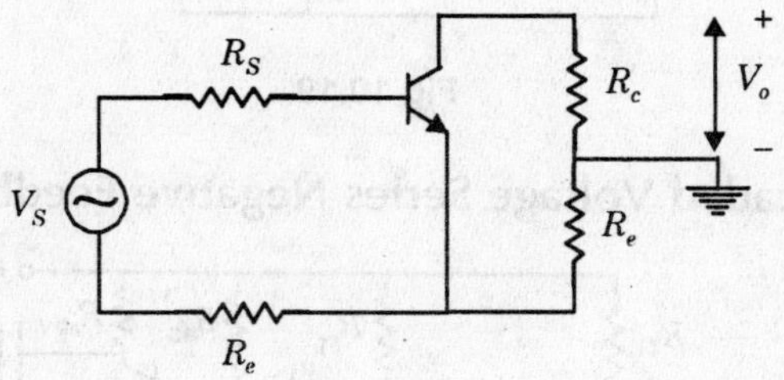


**Fig 10.17**

### 10.10.3 Voltage Series Feedback Amplifier

$S_1$: $R_e$ is acting as feedback.

(a) β network is not directly taken from $V_0$. ∴ So it is not voltage sampled.

(b) β network is not directly connected to base ∴ So it is not shunt mixing and therefore it is series mixing.

Hence the topology is voltage series. $X_0$, $X_s$, $X_i$, $X_f$ are voltages. Basic amplifier is voltage amplifier.

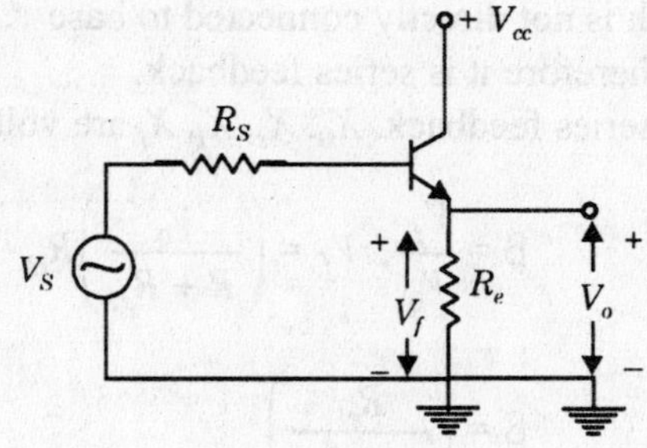


**Fig. 10.18**

$S_2$: $$\beta = \frac{X_f}{X_0} = \frac{V_f}{V_0} = 1$$

$S_3$ : Drawing basic amplifier

(c) For the input circuit go to output and put $X_0 = 0$ i.e. $V_0 = 0$.

(d) For output circuit go to input and input is open circuited.

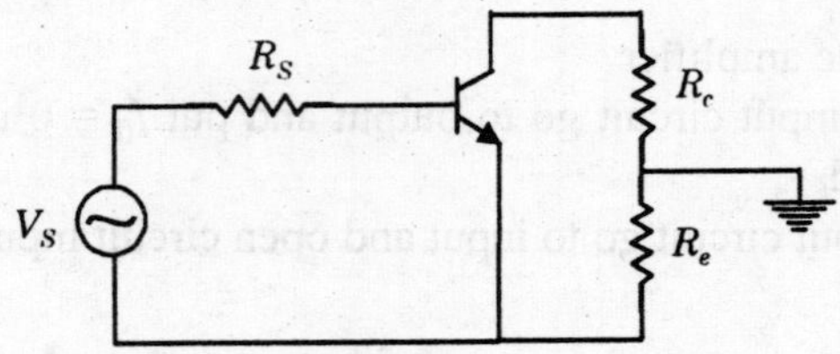


Fig 10.19

### 10.10.4 Cascaded Voltage Series Negative Feedback Amplifier

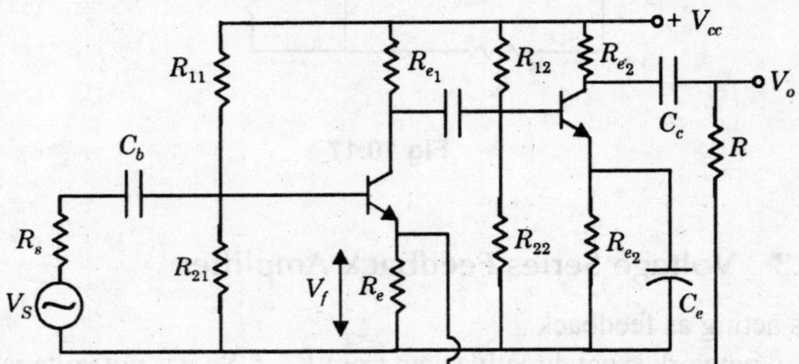


Fig. 10.20

$S_1$: $R$ and $R_{e1}$ are acting as feedback.

(a) β network is directly taken from $V_0$. ∴ So it is voltage sampled.

(b) β network is not directly connected to base ∴ So it is not shunt mixing and therefore it is series feedback.

∴ Voltage series feedback. $X_0$, $X_s$, $X_i$, $X_f$ are voltages.

$S_2$:

$$\beta = \frac{V_f}{V_0}, \quad V_f = \left(\frac{V_0}{R + R_{e1}}\right) R_{e1}$$

$$\beta = \left(\frac{R_{e1}}{R + R_{e1}}\right)$$

$S_3$ : Drawing basic amplifier

(e) For the input circuit go to output and put $X_0 = 0$ i.e. $V_0 = 0$.

(f) For output circuit go to input and put $I_i = 0$.

Let
$$R_e = R_{e1} \parallel R$$

$$R_{L2} = R_{C2} \parallel (R + R_{e1})$$

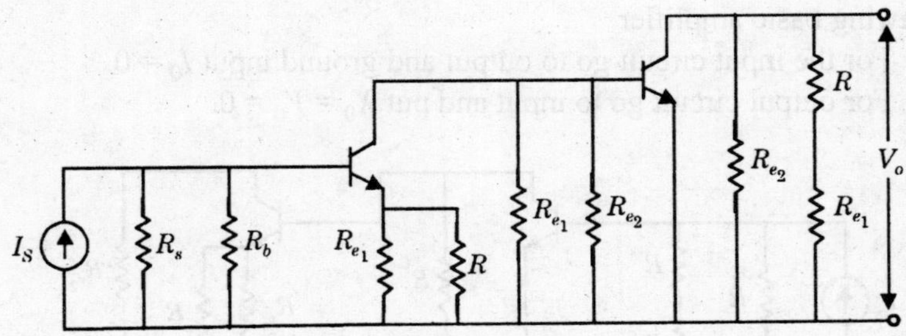


**Fig. 10.21**

First stage is *CE* with $R_e$ acting as local feedback and $R$ and $R_{e1}$ acting as global feedback.

$S_4$ : Analysis is same as multistage amplifier as discussed in the 9th chapter.

$S_5$ :
$$D = 1 + A_v\beta.$$

$$A_{vf} = \frac{A_v}{D}$$

$$R_{if} = R_i \times D.$$

$$R_{of} = R_o / D.$$

## 10.10.5 Cascaded Current Shunt-Negative Feedback Amplifier

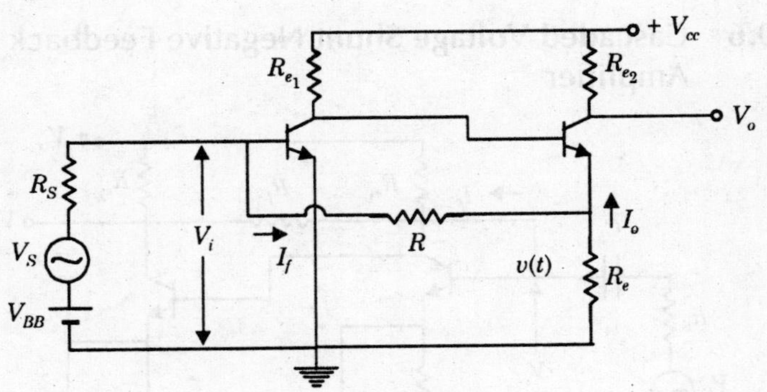


**Fig 10.22**

$S_1$: $R$ and $R_e$ are acting as feedback.

(a) $\beta$ network is not directly taken from $V_0$. ∴ So it is not voltage sampled and hence it is current sampled.

(b) $\beta$ network is directly connected to base ∴ So it is shunt mixing. ∴ current shunt feedback. $X_0, X_s, X_i, X_f$ are current.

$S_2$:
$$\beta = \frac{I_f}{I_0} = \left(\frac{R_{e1}}{R + R_{e1}}\right)$$

$S_3$ : Drawing basic amplifier

(g) For the input circuit go to output and ground input $I_0 = 0$.

(h) For output circuit go to input and put $X_0 = V_0 = 0$.

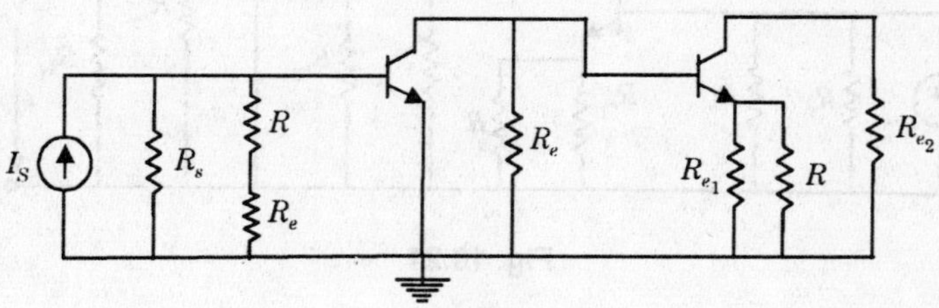


**Fig. 10.23**

$S_4$ : Analysis is same as multistage amplifier as discussed in the 9th chapter.

$S_5$ :

$$D = 1 + A_I\beta.$$

$$A_{If} = \frac{A_I}{D}$$

$$R_{if} = R_i/D.$$

$$A_{vf} = \frac{A_v}{1 + A_v\beta}$$

$$R_{of} = R_o \times D.$$

## 10.10.6 Cascaded Voltage Shunt Negative Feedback Amplifier

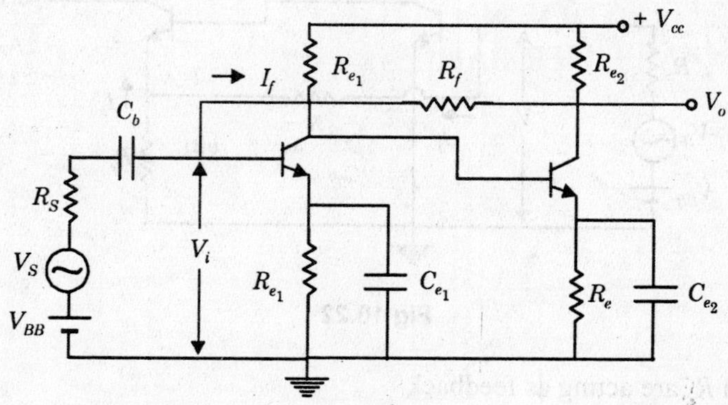


**Fig. 10.24**

$S_1$ : $R_f$ is acting as feedback.

(a) β network is directly taken from $V_0$. β voltage sampled.

(b) β network is directly connected to base ∴ shunt mixing.

$\therefore$ Voltage shunt feedback. $X_0$ is voltage and $X_s$, $X_i$, $X_f$ are currents.

$S_2$ :
$$\beta = \frac{I_f}{V_0} = \frac{\dfrac{V_i - V_0}{R_f}}{V_0} = \frac{-1}{R_f}$$

$S_3$ : Drawing basic amplifier

(i) For the input circuit go to output and put $X_0 = 0$ i.e. $V_0 = 0$.

(j) For output circuit go to input and put $I_0 = 0$.

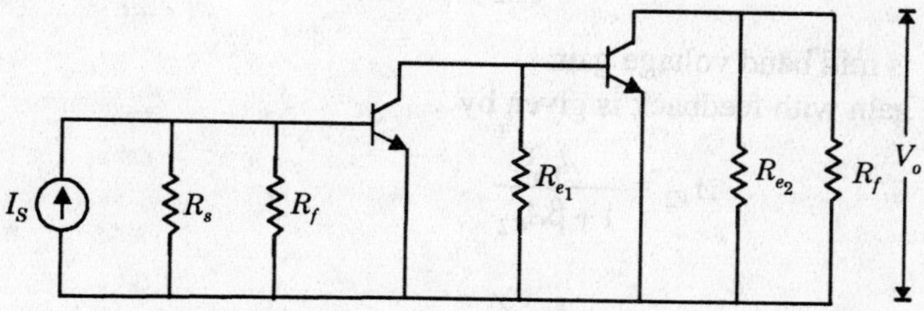


**Fig. 10.25**

$S_4$ : Analysis is same as cascaded amplifier for $R_M$, $R_i$, $R_0$.

$S_5$ :
$$D = 1 + R_M\beta.$$
$$R_{Mf} = \frac{R_M}{D}$$
$$R_{if} = R_i/D.$$
$$R_{of} = R_o/D.$$

## 10.11 EFFECT OF NEGATIVE FEEDBACK ON AMPLIFIER BANDWIDTH

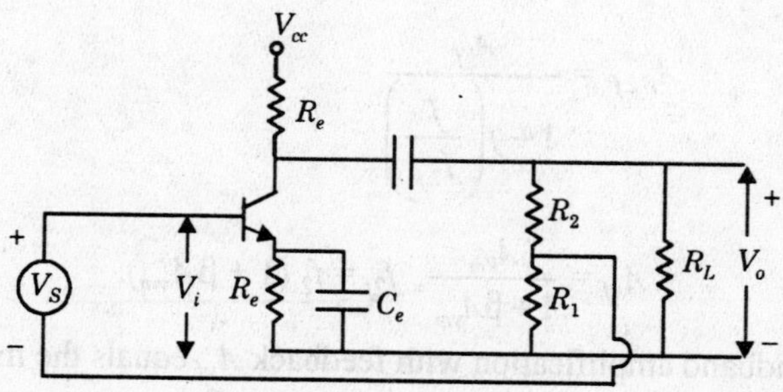


**Fig. 10.26**

We know that $\quad A_{vf} = \dfrac{A_V}{1 + \beta A_v}$

If $\qquad \beta A_V >> 1$

$$\Rightarrow \qquad A_{vf} = \frac{A_V}{\beta A_V} = \frac{1}{\beta}$$

The high frequency voltage gain $A_{V2}$ without feedback is given by

$$A_{V2} = \frac{A_{Vm}}{1 + j\left(\frac{f}{f_2}\right)}$$

$A_{Vm}$ is mid band voltage gain

The gain with feedback is given by

$$A_{V2} = \frac{A_{Vm}}{1 + \beta A_{V2}}$$

$$= \frac{\dfrac{A_{Vm}}{1 + j\left(\frac{f}{f_2}\right)}}{1 + \beta\left(\dfrac{A_{Vm}}{1 + j\left(\frac{f}{f_2}\right)}\right)}$$

$$= \frac{A_{Vm}}{1 + \beta A_{Vm} + j\left(\frac{f}{f_2}\right)}$$

By dividing numerator and denominator by $(1 + \beta A_{Vm})$ we will get

$$A_{V2f} = \frac{A_{Vf}}{1 + j\left(\frac{f}{f_{2f}}\right)}$$

where $\qquad A_{vf} = \dfrac{A_{Vm}}{1 + \beta A_{vm}}, \; f_{2f} = f_2\,(1 + \beta A_{vm}).$

∴ The midband amplification with feedback $A_{vf}$ equals the midband amplification without feedback $A_{vm}$ is divided by $1 + \beta A_{vm}$.

∴ The upper 3dB frequency with feedback $f_{2f}$ equals the corresponding 3dB frequency without feedback($f_2$) multiplied by the factor $D = 1 + \beta A_{vm}$.

Similarly

$$A_{VL} = \frac{A_{Vm}}{1 - j\left(\frac{f_1}{f}\right)}$$

where $$f_1 = \frac{1}{2\pi R_1 C_1}$$

$$A_{Vf} = \frac{A_{Vm}}{1 + \beta A_{Vm}}$$

$$= \frac{\dfrac{A_{Vm}}{1 - j\left(\frac{f_1}{f}\right)}}{\left(1 + \beta \dfrac{A_{Vm}}{1 - j\left(\frac{f_1}{f}\right)}\right)}$$

$$= \frac{A_{Vm}}{1 + \beta A_{Vm} - j\left(\frac{f_1}{f}\right)}$$

By dividing numerator and denominator by $\left(1 - j\left(\frac{f_1}{f}\right)\right)$ we will get

$$A_{V2f} = \frac{A_{Vf}}{1 - j\left(\frac{f}{f_{1f}}\right)}$$

where

$$f_{1f} = f_2/(1 + \beta A_{Vm})$$

## 10.12 STABILITY CONSIDERATIONS

The condition for stability: If an amplifier is designed to have negative feedback in a particular frequency range but breaks out into oscillation at some high or low frequency, it is useless as an amplifier. Hence, in the design of a feedback amplifier, it must be ascertained that the circuit is stable at all frequencies, and not merely over the frequency range of interest. A system is unstable if a transient disturbance persists indefinitely or increases until it is limited only by some non-linearity in the circuit. Thus the question of stability may be considered to involve a study of transient response of the system. If L.T. notation is used, the transfer function $V_o/V_s = A_f$ is a function of complex frequency $S = (\sigma + jw)$. The poles of the transfer function determine the transient behavior of the network. If the pole exists with a positive value of $\sigma$, this will result in a disturbance increasing exponentially with time. Hence the condition which must be satisfied, if a system is to be stable, is that the poles of the transfer function must all lie on the left-hand half of the complex-frequency plane. If the system w/o feedback is stable, the poles of $A$ do be in the left-hand half plane. Therefore, the stability condition requires that the zeros of $1 + A\beta$ all lie in the left half of the complex-frequency plane.

*Nyquist criterion:* The criterion of Nyquist is that the amplifier is unstable if the curve encloses the point $(-1 + j0)$, and the amplifier is stable if the curve does not enclose this point.

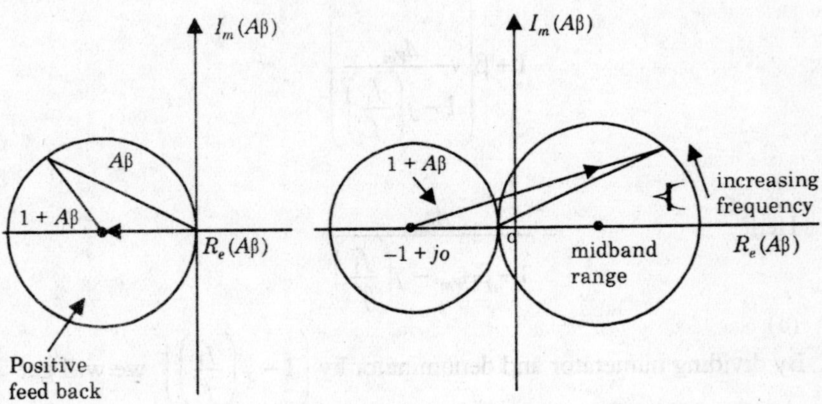


**Fig. 10.27** Representation of Nyquist criterion

From figure 10.27 we see that $|1 + A\beta| = 1$ represents a circle of unit radius, with its center at the point-1 + $j0$. If, for any frequency, $AB$ extends outside circle, the feedback is negative, since then $|1 + AB| > 1$. If, however, $A\beta$ lies within this circle, then

$|1 + AB| < 1$, and the feedback is positive. In latter case the system will not oscillate unless Nyquist criterion is satisfied.

The locus of $A\beta$ for all frequencies is plotted in complex plane. This curve shows a polar plot of the gain $A$ of the circuit. Furthermore, since this curve does not enclosed the point $-1 + j0$, the amplifier is stable and the feedback is negative for all frequencies, if $|1 + AB| > 1$ for all frequencies which is condition for negative feedback. The feedback is negative for this amplifier in the frequency range from 0 to $f_1$. Positive feedback exists in the frequency range from $f_1$ to $\infty$. Note: however, that the locus of $A\beta$ does not enclose the point $(-1 + j0)$. Hence, according to the Nyquist criterion, oscillations will not occur.

## 10.13 SOLVED PROBLEMS

**1. An amplifier with open-loop voltage gain $AV = 1000 \pm 100$ is available. It is necessary to have an amplifier whose voltage gain varies by no more than ± 0.1%**

**(a) Find the reverse transmission factor β of the feedback network used.**

**(b) Find the gain with feedback.**

**Solution:**

From the equation $\left|\dfrac{dA_f}{A_f}\right| = \dfrac{1}{|1+\beta A|}\left|\dfrac{dA}{A}\right|$

$$\frac{0.1}{100} = \frac{A}{1+\beta A}\frac{100}{1000}$$

$$1 + A\beta = 100$$

or $$\beta A = 99$$

Hence $$\beta = \frac{99}{1000} = 0.099$$

(c) $$A_f = \frac{A}{1+\beta A} = \frac{1000}{1+99} = 10$$

**2. An amplifier without feedback gives a fundamentals output of 36 V with 7% second-harmonic distortion when the input is 0.028 V.**

**(a) If 1.5% of the output is feedback into the input in a negative voltage-series feedback circuit, what is the output voltage?**

**(b) For an output of 36 V with 1% second-harmonic distortion, what is the input voltage?**

**Solution:**

$$A = \frac{36}{0.028} = 1285$$

$$\beta = 0.012$$

From equation $A_f = \dfrac{A}{1+\beta A}$

$$= \frac{1285}{1+(0.015)(1285)} = 63.38$$

Therefore $V_o = A_f V_s = 63.38 \times 0.028 = 1.77\text{V}$

(b) If the output remains constant at 36v, then the distortion produced within the active devices of the amplifier is unchanged. However since the distortion at the output is less than in part a by a factor of 7, it follows that the feedback now increased by 9 and hence, the voltage gain decreases by 9. Thus the input signal required to produce the same output (as in part a without *F.B*) must be $V_s = 9\ (0.028\text{v}) = 0.252\text{v}$

**3. An amplifier with an open-loop voltage gain of 2000 delivers 20w of output power at 10% second-harmonic distortion within the input signal is 10mV. If 40db negative voltage –series feedback is applied and the output power is to remain at 10w, determine (a) the required input signal (b) the percent harmonic distortion.**

**Solution:**

(a)
$$-40\text{db} = 20\log 10 \frac{1}{|1+\beta A|}$$

$$= -20\log_{10} |i + \beta A|$$

Therefore $|1 + \beta A| = 100$

$$\text{But } |A_f| = \frac{|A|}{|1+\beta A|} = \frac{2000}{100} = 20$$

When the amplifier delivers 20W, its output voltage is $V_0 = A_{Vs} = 2000\ (10 \times 10 - 3) = 20\text{V}$

If the output power is to remain at 10w, then the output voltage also must remain at 10v. hence the input signal required when $I_B$ is applied will be $V_s = \frac{V_o}{A_f} = \frac{20\text{v}}{20}$

(b) The distortion of the amplifier with *FB* will be reduced by *FB* factor i.e by

$$|1+\beta A| = 100$$

Hence $$D_4 = \frac{10\%}{100} = 0.1\%$$

**4. An amplifier consists of three identical stages connected in cascade. The output voltage is sampled and returned to the input in series opposing. If it is specified that the relative change $dA_f/A_f$ in the closed-loop voltage gain $A_f$ must not exceed y/f, show that the minimum value of the open-loop gain $A$ of the amplifier is given by**

$$A = 3A_f\left|\frac{\psi_1}{\psi_f}\right|$$

Where $\psi \equiv dA_1/A_1$ is the relative change in the voltage gain of each stage of the amplifier.

**Solution:**

From $$\left|\frac{dA_f}{A_f}\right| = \frac{1}{|1+\beta A|}\left|\frac{dA}{A}\right|$$

We obtain $$\left|\frac{dA_f}{A_f}\right| \equiv |\psi_f| = \frac{1}{|1+\beta A|} = \left|\frac{dA}{A}\right| \text{ where } A = A_1^3$$

Or $$dA = 3A_1^2 dA_1$$

Then $$\left|\frac{dA}{A}\right| = 3\frac{dA_1}{A_1} = 3\psi_1$$

Since $$A_f = \frac{A}{1+\beta A}$$

$$\frac{A_f}{A} = \frac{1}{1+\beta A}$$

$$|\psi_f| = \frac{A_f}{A}3|\psi_1|$$

or $$A = 3A_f\frac{|\psi_1|}{|\psi_f|}$$

**5. We have an amplifier of 60db gain. It has an output impedance $Z_o$ = 10kΩ. It is required to modify its output impedance to 500Ω by applying negative feedback. Calculate the value of the feedback factor. Also find the percentage change in the overall gain, for 10% change in the gain of the internal amplifiers.**

**Solution:**

We know that

$$Z_{of} = \frac{Z_o}{1+A\beta}$$

Given

$$A = 60\text{db} = 1000$$

$$Z_0 = 10{,}000\Omega$$

$$Z_{of} = 500\Omega$$

$$500 = \frac{10{,}000}{1 + 1000\beta}$$

$$1 + 1000\beta = \frac{10{,}000}{500} = 20$$

$$1000\beta = 19$$

$$\beta = 19/1000 = 0.019 = 1.9\%$$

Again $\dfrac{dA_f}{A_f} = 1/1 + A\beta \dfrac{dA}{A}$

$$= \frac{1}{1 + 1000 \times 0.019} \times 0.1$$

$$= \frac{0.1}{1 + 19} = \frac{0.1}{20}$$

$$\frac{dA_f}{A_f} = 0.005 = 0.5\%$$

**6. For the circuit shown in the fig 10p1, with $R_c = 4$ K, $R_L = 4$ K, $R_b = 20$ K, $R_s = 1$ K, find**

**(a) the current gain $I_L/I_s = A_I$.**

**(b) the voltage gain $V_0/V_s$, where $V_s = I_s R_s$.**

**(c) the transconductance $I_L/V_s = G_M$.**

**(d) the transresistance $V_0/I_s = R_M$.**

**(e) the input resistance seen by the source.**

**(f) The output resistance seen by the load.**

**Make reasonable approximations. Neglect all capacitive effects.**

**Solution:**

$$\frac{I_l}{I_s} = \frac{I_i}{I_s}\frac{I_b}{I_i}\frac{I_L}{I_b}$$

here

$$\frac{I_i}{I_s} = \frac{R_s}{R_s + R_i}$$

$$R_i = R_b \parallel h_{ie} = 20\text{ K} \parallel 1.1\text{ K} = 1.04\text{ K or}$$

$$R_i = 1/2.04.$$

$$\frac{I_b}{I_s} = \frac{R_b}{R_b + h_{ie}} = \frac{20\text{K}}{20\text{K} + 1.1\text{K}} = 0.05.$$

(a) $$\frac{I_L}{I_b} = -h_{fe}\frac{R_C}{R_C + R_L} = -50.\frac{1}{8} = -25.$$

$$\therefore \quad \frac{I_L}{I_s} = \left(\frac{1}{2.04}\right)(0.95)\,(-25) = -11.65.$$

(b) $$\frac{V_0}{V_s} = \frac{I_L R_L}{I_s R_s} = -11.65\frac{4\text{K}}{1\text{K}} = -46.6.$$

(c) $$\frac{I_l}{V_s} = \frac{V_0}{R_L}\frac{1}{V_s} = \frac{V_0}{V_s}\frac{1}{R_L} = \frac{46.6}{4\times10^3} = -11.65 \text{ mA/V}$$

(d) $$\frac{V_0}{I_s} = R_s\frac{V_0}{V_s} = 10^3\,(-46.6) = -46.6\text{K}.$$

(e) $$R_i = R_b \,||\, h_{fe} = 20\text{K} \,||\, 1.1\text{K} = 1.04\text{K}.$$

(g) $$R_0 = 1/h_{oe} \,||\, R_c = 40\text{K} \,||\, 4\text{K} = 3.64\text{K}.$$

**7. For the transistor feedback-amplifier stage shown in fig 10p2, $h_{fe}$ = 100, $h_{ie}$ = 1K, while $h_{re}$ and $h_{oe}$ are negligible. Determine with $R_e$ = 0.**

(a) $R_{Mf} = \dfrac{V_0}{I_0}$ where $I_s = \dfrac{V_s}{R_s}$

(b) $A_{Vf} = \dfrac{V_0}{V_s}$

(c) $R_{if}$

(d) $R'_{of}$

(e) Repeat the four preceeding calculations if $R_e$ = 1K.

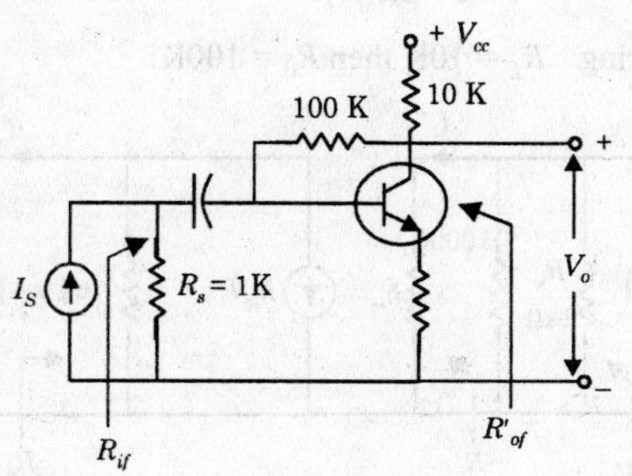


Fig 10p2

**Solution:**

(a) This is a voltage –shunt configuration, so we have Norton's equivalent of the source. Notice that $I_f = \frac{V_f - V_0}{100K}$ or $-\frac{V_0}{100K}$ or $\beta = -\frac{1}{100K}$ $= -10^{-4}$

We find the amplifier without feedback by setting $V_1 = 0$ to find the output circuit. The amplifier without feedback is as shown figure 10*p*3. Since this a voltage shunt feedback amplifier. It stabilizes $R_M$. Thus we should calculate $R_M$ for the amplifier without feedback.

$$R_M = \frac{V_0}{I_s} = \frac{R_L I_0}{I_s} = R_L \frac{I_0}{I_1}\frac{I_1}{I_s} \text{ but } \frac{I_0}{I_1} = -h_{fe}\frac{100}{110} = -91.$$

$$\frac{I_1}{I_s} = \frac{R_2 \| 100\text{K}}{h_{ie} + (R_s \| 100\text{K})} = \frac{1}{2} = 0.5.$$

Thus $\quad R_M = 10 \times (-91) \times 0.5 \times 10^3 = -455\text{K}.$

$$D = 1 + \beta R_M = 1 + 4.55 = 5.55$$

And $\quad R_{Mf} = R_M / D = -\frac{4.55 \times 10^3}{5.55} = 8.20 \times 10^3 \Omega.$

(b) $\quad A_{vf} = \frac{V_0}{V_s} = \frac{V_0}{I_s R_s} = \frac{R_{Mf}}{R_s} = -82$

(c) $\quad R_1 = R_S \| h_{fe} \| 100 = 0.5$ K.

Thus $\quad R_{if} = \frac{R_f}{D} = \frac{0.5\text{K}}{5.5} = 90\Omega.$

(d) $\quad R_{0f} = \frac{R_0}{1 + \beta R_M}$ but $R_M = \lim_{R_L \to \infty} R_M$

Considering $R_L = 10$K then $R_0 = 100$K.

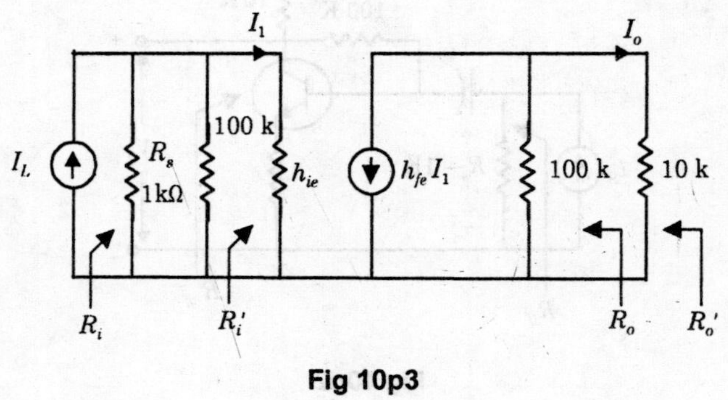


**Fig 10p3**

Then $V_0 = -h_{fe}\, I_1\ 100\text{K}$ thus $R_M = \dfrac{V_0}{I_s} = -h_{fe} \times 100\text{K} \times \dfrac{I_1}{I_s}$

$$= -100 \times 10^3 \times 0.5 = -5 \times 10^4$$

And $R_{of} = \dfrac{100\text{K}}{1+50} = 1.96\text{K}.$

Thus $R'_{of} = 10\text{K} \,||\, 1.96\text{K} = 1.64\text{K}.$

(e) With $R_e = 1\text{K}$ the equivalent circuit of the amplifier without feedback is as indicated.

Then $\dfrac{I_0}{I_1} = -h_{fe}\dfrac{100\text{K}}{110\text{K}}\ -91$ and $\dfrac{I_1}{I_s} = \dfrac{R_s \,||\, 100}{R_i + (R_s \,||\, 100)}$

Where $R_i = h_{fe} + (1 + h_{fe})\, R_e = 102\text{K}$

Thus $\dfrac{I_1}{I_s} = \dfrac{1}{103} = 0.0097 = 9.7 \times 10^{-3}$

Hence $R_M = R_L \times (-91) \times (9.7 \times 10^{-3}) = -8.82 \times 10^3\ \Omega$

Again $\beta = -10^{-3}$

Thus $D = 1 + \beta R_M = 1 + 0.088 = 1.088$

So $R_{Mf} = \dfrac{R_M}{D} = \dfrac{8.82 \times 10^3}{1.088} = -8.10\text{K}$

$$A_{vf} = \frac{R_{Mf}}{R_s} = -8.10$$

$$R_1 = 1\text{K} \,||\, 100\text{K} \,||\, R_I = 980\Omega.$$

Then $R_{if} = \dfrac{R_f}{D} = \dfrac{980}{1.088} = 910\Omega$

Finally $R_{of} = \dfrac{R_0}{1+\beta R_M}.$

To find $R_M$

$$V_0 = -h_{fe}\, I_1 \times 10^5$$

Thus $R_M = -100 \times 9.7 \times 10^{-3} \times 10^5 = -9.7 \times 10^4$

and $1 + \beta R_M = 1.97$

$$R_0 = 100\text{K},\ R_{of} = \frac{100\text{K}}{1.97} = 50.7\text{K}$$

Thus $\qquad R_{of} = R_{of} \,\|\, 10\text{K} = 8.35\text{ K}.$

**8. For the circuit shown in the figure 10*p*4, find**

**(a)** $A_{If} = \dfrac{I_0}{I_s}$

**(b)** $R_{if}$

**(c)** $A_{Vf} = \dfrac{V_0}{V_s}$ **where** $I_s = \dfrac{V_s}{R_s}$

**(d)** $A'_{Vf} = \dfrac{V_0}{V_s}$

**(e)** $R'_{of}$

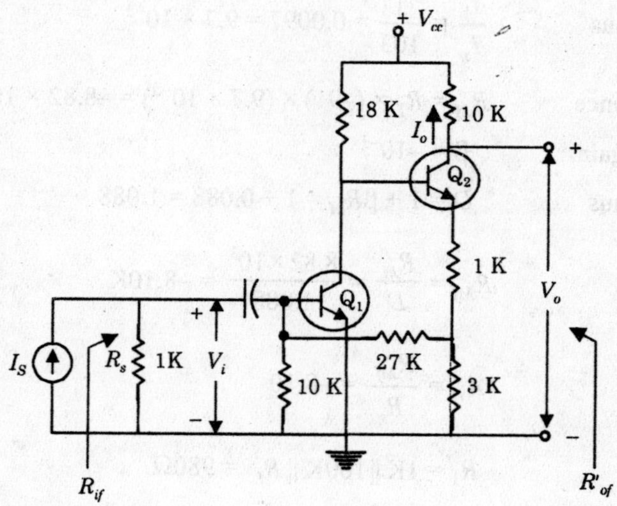


**Solution:**

(a) 1. Type of feedback: the mixing is of shunt type and $I_f = \dfrac{V_1 - V}{27\text{K}}$ where $V$ is the voltage drop across the 3K resistor. Since $V >> V_1$ then $I_1 = -\dfrac{V}{27\text{K}} = \dfrac{3}{27}(I_0 - I_1)$ or $I_f = \dfrac{3}{30} I_0 - 0.1 I_0 = 8 I_0$. Hence this is again a current shunt feedback.

2. To obtain the basic amplifier without feedback we open the output loop $I_0 = 0$, and we thus have at the input a resistor $27 + 3 = 30\text{K}$ in parallel with $R_s$. Then we let $V_1 = 0$ and we have at the output loop a resistor $27 \,\|\, 3\text{K} = 2.7\text{K}$. Hence the equivalent circuit is as shown in fig 10p5.

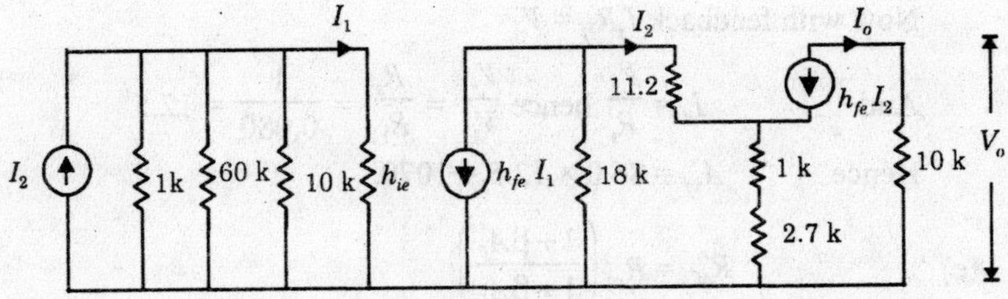


**Fig 10p5**

3. Since the circuit is a current-shunt feedback amplifier the current gain will be stabilized. We now find $A_I$ for the basic amplifier without feedback.

$$A_I = \frac{I_O}{I_2}\frac{I_2}{I_1}\frac{I_1}{I_s}, \frac{I_O}{I_s} = -h_{fe} = -50, \frac{I_2}{I_1} = -h_{fe}\frac{18}{18+R_{if}}$$

where $R_{if} = h_{fe} + (1 + h_{fe})\ 3.7$ or $R_{if} = 2 + 51 \times 3.7 = 190\text{K}$.

or $$\frac{I_1}{I_s} = -50 \times \frac{18}{208} = -4.32$$

finally $$\frac{I_1}{I_s} = \frac{1\|10\|30}{2+(1\|10\|30)}$$

but $$1\|10\|30 = \frac{1}{1+0.1+0.39} = \frac{1}{1.133} = 0.0884\text{K}$$

or $$\frac{I_1}{I_s} = \frac{0.884}{2.884} = 0.308$$

hence $$A_I = \frac{A_I}{D} \text{ but } D = 1 + \beta A_I = 7.66 \text{ or } A_{If} = \frac{66.6}{7.66} = 8.69$$

(b) $$R_I = 1\|10\|30\|h_{fe} = 0.884\|2 = \frac{1.768}{2.884} = 0.615$$

And $$R_{if} = \frac{6.15}{7.66} = 80.2\text{W}$$

(c) $$A_{Vf} = \frac{V_O}{V_1} = \frac{I_O R_C}{I_s R_s} = A_{If} = \frac{10}{1} = 86.9$$

(d) $$A_{Vf} = \frac{V_O}{V_1} = \frac{V_O}{V_s}\frac{V_s}{V_1}$$

Now with feedback $I_s R_{If} = V_1$

And $I_s = \dfrac{V_s}{R_s}$ hence $\dfrac{V_s}{V_1} = \dfrac{R_s}{R_{11}} = \dfrac{1}{0.080} = 12.5$

Hence $A_{vf} = 86.0 \times 12.5 = 1070.$

(e) $R'_{of} = R_{of} \cdot \left(\dfrac{1+\beta A_I}{1+\beta A_I}\right)$

Since $A_I = \lim\limits_{R_L \to 0}$ and $A_I$ is independent of $R_L$ then $A_I - A_I$

and $R'_{of} - R'_0 = 10\text{K}$

9. The transistors in the feedback amplifier shown are identical. Make reasonable approximations whenever appropriate, and neglect the reactance of the capacitors. Calculate $R_{if} = V_s/I_I$, $A_{if} = -I/I_I$, $A'_{Vf} = V_0/V_I$, $A_{Vf} = V_0/V_s$ and $R'_{of}$.

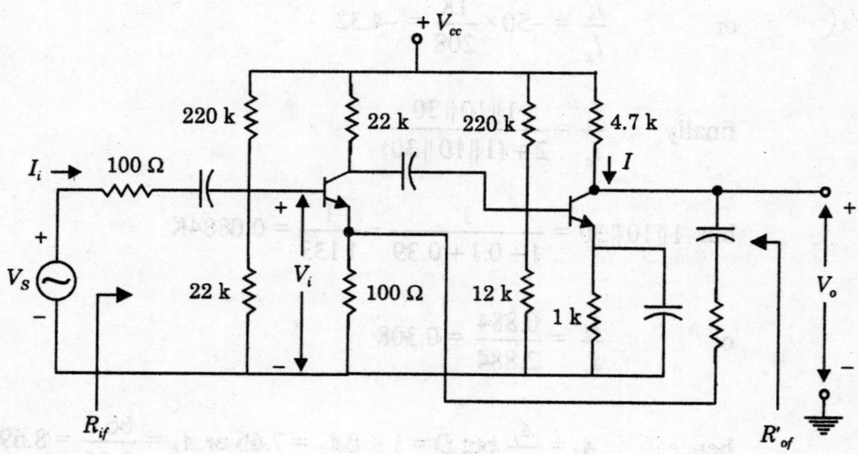


Fig 10p6

**Solution:**

1. Type of feedback. We sample output voltage and $V_f = V_0 \dfrac{0.1}{10.1} = \text{b}V_0$ hence it is a voltage series feedback with b = 0.0099 – 0.01
2. We obtain the basic amplifier without feedback to fine the input circuit we short circuit the output and to fine the output circuit we open the input loop. Thus we have fig.10p7

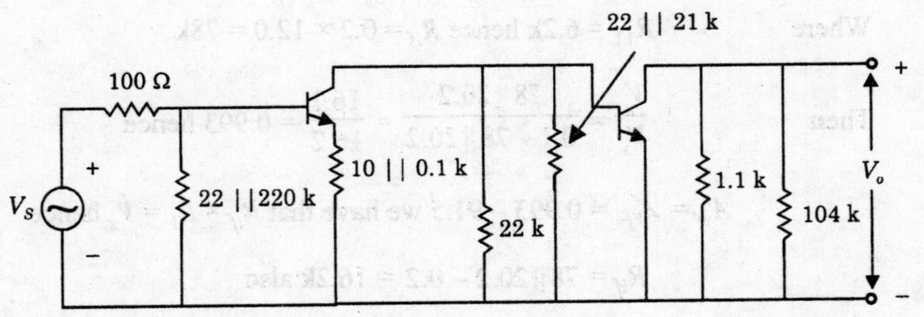


**Fig 10p7 (a)**

3. Replacing transistors with the appropriate hybrid equivalent small signal model we have fig 10p7 (b)

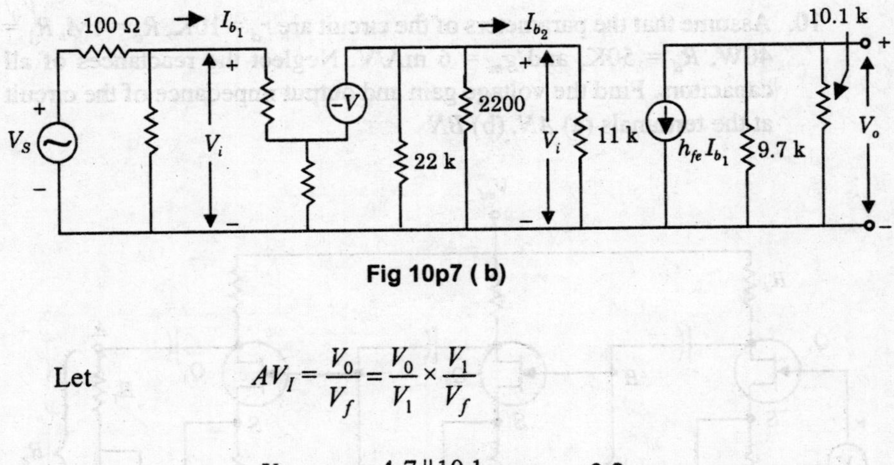


**Fig 10p7 ( b)**

Let $$AV_I = \frac{V_0}{V_f} = \frac{V_0}{V_1} \times \frac{V_1}{V_f}$$

$$\frac{V_0}{V_f} = -h_{ie}\frac{4.7 \| 10.1}{h_{ie}} = -50 \times \frac{3.2}{1.1} = -145.5$$

$$\frac{V_1}{V_f} = -h_{fe}\frac{R_{L1}}{R_{f1}} \text{ but } R_{f1} = h_{ie} + (I + h_{fo})\,R_e = 1.1 + 51 \times 0.1 = 6.2\text{k}$$

and $$R_{L1} = 22 \| 20.2 \| h_{ie} = 990\ \Omega \text{ hence}$$

$$\frac{V_1}{V_f} = -50 \times \frac{0.99}{6.2} = -8.0 \text{ now that}$$

$A_{VI}\, n = (-8) \times (-145.5) = 1100$. Since $D = 1 + \beta A_{VI} = 1 + 11.60 - 12.6$

$$A'_{Vf} = \frac{A_{VI}}{D} = \frac{1160}{12.6} = 92.1 \text{ where } \beta = 0.01 \text{ and } R'_{if} = R_{f1}D$$

Where $R_{11} = 6.2\text{k}$ hence $R_{if} = 0.2 \times 12.0 = 78\text{k}$

Then $$\frac{V_i}{V_s} = \frac{78 \,||\, 20.2}{0.1 + 78 \,||\, 20.2} = \frac{16.1}{16.2} = 0.993 \text{ hence}$$

$$A_{vf} = A'_{Vf} = 0.993 - 91.5 \text{ we have that } R_{if} \times L_1 = V_s \text{ hence}$$

$$R_{if} = 78 \,||\, 20.2 - 0.2 = 16.2\text{k also}$$

$$A_{vf} = -\frac{V_0}{V_s} = -\frac{IR_L}{I_1 R_{if}} = A_{if} = 91.5 \times \frac{10.2}{4.7} = 314$$

Finally $R'_0 = 4.7 \,||\, 10.1 - 3.2\text{k}$ and $R'_{of} = \frac{R'_Q}{D} = \frac{3.2}{12.6} = 253\,\Omega$

10. Assume that the parameters of the circuit are $r_d = 10\text{K}$, $R_e = 1\text{M}$, $R_1 = 40\text{W}$, $R_d = 50\text{K}$, and $g_m = 6$ mA/V. Neglect the reactances of all capacitors. Find the voltage gain and output impedance of the circuit at the terminals (a) *AN*, (b) *BN*

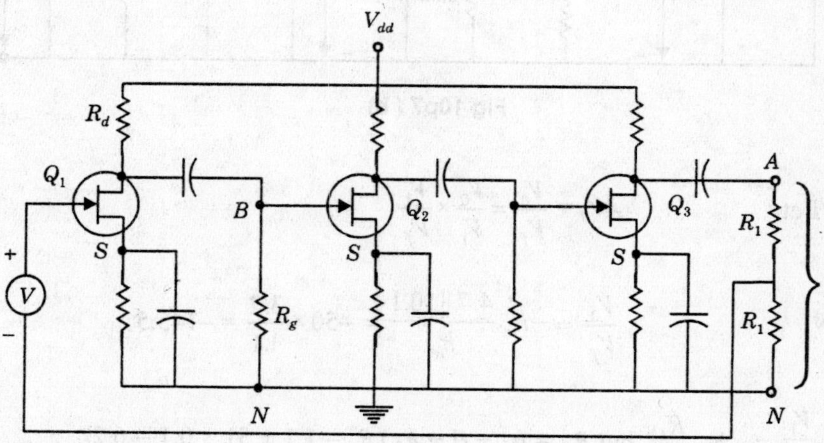


Fig. 10p8

**Solution:**

1. we observe $X_f = V_f$
2. $\beta = \frac{V_f}{V_0} = -\frac{R_1}{R_g}$ hence we have voltage series feedback
3. To find the input circuit short-circuit the output node to ground. Then we obtain resistance $R' = 0 \,||\, (Rg - R_f)$ or $R' = 40\text{W}$ in series with the input source as shown
4. To find output circuit open the input 100 p, then we have have $R_C$ loading the output

5. We replace each FET with his small signal equivalent circuit and thus we obtain the equivalent circuit shown in the figure 10p9

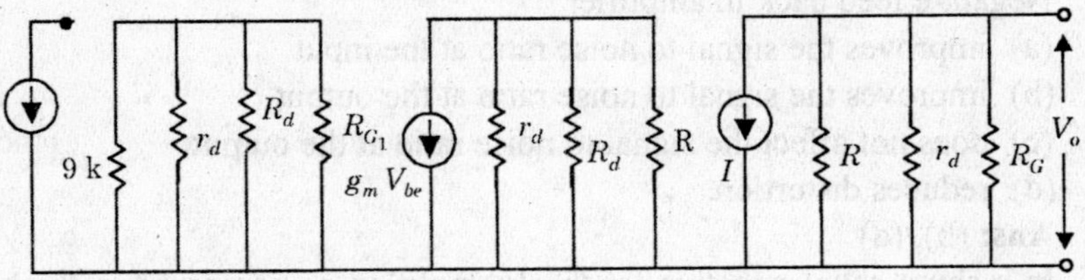


**Fig. 10p9**

For this circuit $A_{VI} = \dfrac{V_{BS}}{V} = \dfrac{V_{BS}}{V_{GS}} = -g_m\,(r_d \,\|\, R_d \,\|\, R_C) = A_{V2} = A_{V3}$

Hence $A_V = A_{v1}^{1} = \left(-6\times 10^{-B}\dfrac{1}{0.1\times 10^{-3} + 1\times 10^{-2} + 0.02\times 10^{3}}\right)^{3}$

$= (-50)2 = -1.25 \times 10^3$ But $s = -\dfrac{10}{10^4} = -4 \times 10^{-6}$

hence $D = 1 + \beta A_V = 1 + 5 = 6$ we include that $A_{vf} = \dfrac{A_V}{D} = -2.08 \times 10^4$.

Considering $R_g$ port of the stage then it follows that $R_{of} = \dfrac{R_o}{1+\beta A_V}$

$$= \frac{R_0}{1+\beta A_V} = \frac{0.22}{6} = 1.39\text{k}$$

(c) Taking the output at terminals *BN* makes the last two stages part of the network. The forward gain without feedback is the gain of since *I*

thus $A_V = -50$ . Now $B = \dfrac{V_f}{V_{BN}} - \dfrac{V_f}{V_{AN}} - \dfrac{V_{AN}}{V_{BN}} - \dfrac{R_1}{R_g}\,A_{V2}A_{V3}$

$$= \frac{40}{10^6} \times 25 \times 10^2 = 0.1$$

Hence $D = 1 + \beta A_V = 6$. Note that the densitivity and the loop gain is as in part (1). This is as it should be since in taking the output at a different point we do not change the loop in any way. Now $A_{vf} = \dfrac{A_V}{D} = \dfrac{-50}{6} = -$ 8.33 and $R_0 = 8.32$k hence $R_{of} = 1.39$k as in part (a).

## 10.14 OBJECTIVE TYPE QUESTIONS

1. Negative feed back in amplifier
   (a) improves the signal to noise ratio at the input
   (b) improves the signal to noise ratio at the output
   (c) does not affect the signal to noise ratio at the output
   (d) reduces distortion.
   **Ans:** (b), (d)
2. In a shunt-shunt negative feedback amplifier, as compared to the basic amplifier,
   (a) both, input and output impedance, decrease
   (b) input impedance decreases but output impedance increases
   (c) input impedance increases but output impedance decreases
   (d) both input and output impedance increase.
   **Ans:** (b)
3. Negative feedback in an amplifier
   (a) reduces gain (b) increases frequency and phase distortions
   (c) reduces band width (d) increases noise
   **Ans:** (a)
4. An amplifier has an open-loop gain of 100, an input impedance of 1KΩ and output impedance of 100Ω. A feedback network with a feedback factor of 0.99 is connected to the amplifier in a voltage-series feedback mode. The new input and output impedance respectively are
   (a) 10Ω and 1Ω (b) 10Ω and 10kΩ
   (c) 100kΩ and 1Ω (d) 100kΩ and 10 kΩ
   **Ans:** (c)
5. An amplifier with resistive negative feedback has two left half plane poles in its open-loop transfer function. The amplifier
   (a) will always be unstable at high frequencies
   (b) will be stable for all frequencies
   (c) may be unstable, depending on the feedback factor
   (d) will oscillate at low frequencies
   **Ans:** (b)
6. Negative feedback
   (a) decreases higher and lower cutoff frequencies
   (b) increases higher and lower cut off frequencies
   (c) decreases lower cut off and increases higher cut off frequencies
   (d) none
   **Ans:** (c)
7. Transmission gain in negative feedback amplifier
   (a) $A\beta$ (b) $1/A\beta$
   (c) $A/(1 + A\beta)$ (d) $A/(1 - A\beta)$
   **Ans:** (a)

**8.** It is desired to reduce total harmonic distortion of an amplifier from 85 to 20% by use of 5% feedback. What is the gain of the amplifier with original distortion and with reduced distortion?

(a) 60, 15 (b) 15, 90
(c) 6, 1.5 (d) 1.5, 6

**Ans:** (a)

**9.** In a feedback amplifier, sensitivity *D* equals:

(a) $A\beta$ (b) $1 - A\beta$
(c) $1 + A\beta$ (d) $1/(A\beta + 1)$

**Ans:** (c)

**10.** In a feed back amplifier, loop gain is:

(a) $A\beta$ (b) $-A\beta$
(c) $1/A\beta$ (d) $-1/A\beta$

**Ans:** (b)

**11.** In a negative feedback amplifier, voltage sampling

(a) tends to decrease the output resistance
(b) tends to increase the out resistance
(c) does not alter the output resistance
(d) produces the same effect on output resistance as current sampling:

**Ans:** (a)

**12.** In a negative feedback amplifier, current sampling:

(a) tends to decrease the output resistance
(b) tends to increase to output resistance
(c) does not alter the output resistance
(d) produces the same effect on output resistance as voltage sampling

**Ans:** (b)

**13.** In a negative feedback amplifier, series mixing

(a) tends to increase the input resistance
(b) tends to decrease the input resistance
(c) does not alter the input resistance
(d) produces the same effect on input resistance as the shunt mixing

**Ans:** (a)

**14.** In a negative feedback amplifier, shunt-mixing

(a) tends to increase the input resistance
(b) tends to decrease the input resistance
(c) does not alter the input resistance
(d) produces the same effect on input resistance as the series mixing

**Ans:** (b)

**15.** FET source follower is a negative feedback amplifier using :

(a) voltage series feedback
(b) current series feedback
(c) current shunt feedback
(d) voltage shunt feedback

**Ans:** (a)

**16.** *CE* amplifier with unbypassed resistor in emitter-to-ground circuit forms a case of negative feedback amplifier with
(a) voltage series feedback
(b) current series feedback
(c) current shunt feedback
(d) voltage shunt feedback
**Ans:** (b)

**17.** FET common source amplifier with unbypassed resistor in source-to-ground circuit forms a case of 4negative feedback amplifier using:
(a) voltage series feedback
(b) current series feedback
(c) current shunt feedback
(d) voltage shunt feedback
**Ans:** (c)

**18.** *CE* amplifier with a resistor connected between collector and base forms a case of negative feedback amplifier using:
(a) voltage series feedback
(b) current series feedback
(c) current shunt feedback
(d) voltage shunt feedback
**Ans:** (d)

**19.** Emitter follower is a negative feedback amplifier using:
(a) voltage series feedback
(b) current series feedback
(c) current shunt feedback
(d) voltage shunt feedback
**Ans:** (a)

**20.** Feedback is said to be positive if :
(a) the feedback signal gets subtracted from the input signal
(b) the feedback signal gets added to the input signal
(c) any increase in the output signal results in a feedback signal which on being mixed with the input signal causes further increase in the magnitude of the output signal
(d) none of these
**Ans:** (c)

**21.** Emitter follower is used in electronic instruments because
(a) its voltage gain is very high
(b) its voltage gain is less than unity
(c) its output impedance is high and input impedance is low
(d) its output impedance is low and input impedance is high
**Ans:** (d)

**22.** The voltage of an amplifier is 100. On applying negative feedback with $\beta = 0.03$, its gain will reduce to

(a) 25 (b) 70

(c) 95 (d) 3

**Ans:** (a)

**23.** The negative feedback is more effective if the loop gain is

(a) small (b) large

(c) unity (d) zero

**Ans:** (b)

**24.** An amplifier has a gain of 20 without feedback. if 10% of the output voltage is fed back by means of a resistance negative feedback circuit, the overall gain would be

(a) 16.55 (b) 19.80

(c) 10.85 (d) 6.67

**Ans:** (d)

**25.** The circuit of figure is an example of feedback of following type:

(a) current (b) current shunt

(c) voltage series (d) voltage shunt

**Ans:** (d)

## 10.15 CONVENTIONAL QUESTIONS

1. Draw the block diagram of feed back amplifier, and state its each function.
2. What is the concept of feedback, explain characteristics of negative feedback amplifier?
3. How can you say that, the feed back effects on bandwidth of an amplifier?
4. Draw the equivalent circuit for a voltage amplifier, what are the values of $R_i$ and $R_o$. What are the dimensions of the transfer gain?
5. Draw the equivalent circuit for a current amplifier, what are the values of $R_i$ and $R_o$ what are the dimensions of the transfer gain?
6. Draw the equivalent circuit for a transconductance voltage amplifier, what are the values of $R_i$ and $R_o$. What are the dimensions of the transfer gain?
7. Draw the equivalent circuit for a transresistance amplifier, what are the values of $R_i$ and $R_o$. What are the dimensions of the transfer gain?
8. What are the four possible topologies of feed back amlpifier? Identify the output signal $X_o$ and feedback signal $X_f$.
9. How the negative feedback effect on input and output resistance's?
10. What is the relationship between the transfer gain with feedback $A_f$ and what with out feedback $A$?

## 10.16 EXERCISE PROBLEMS

1. **Determine the voltage gain, input and output impedance with feedback for voltage series feedback having $A = -100$, $R_i = 10$ k ohms Ro=20 k ohms for feed back of (a) $\beta = -0.1$ (b) $\beta = -0.5$.**

**Ans:** (a) –9.09,110 k ohms, 182 k ohms (b) –1.96,510 k ohms, 392.16 k ohms.

2. **Calculate the voltage gain of the circuit shown in figure.**

   **Ans:** $A_{vf} = -4.2$.

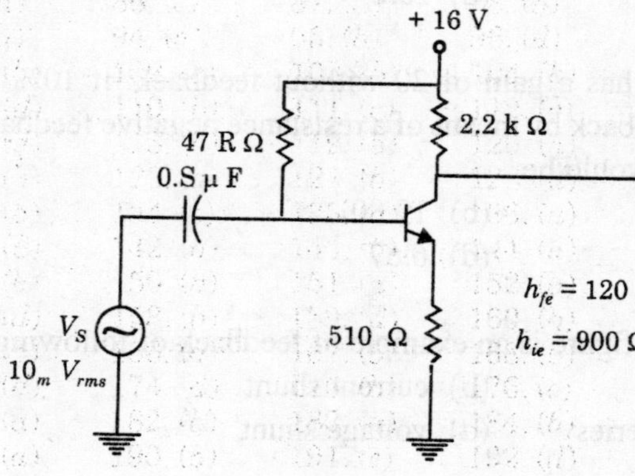


Fig. 10p10

3. **Calculate the voltage gain with and with out feedback for the circuit of figure, with values of $g_m = 5$mS, $R_D = 5.1$ k ohms $R_S = 1$ k ohms and $R_F = 20$ k ohms.**

   **Ans:** with out feedback ($A_v$) = – 25.5, with feedback ($A_{vf}$) = – 11.2.

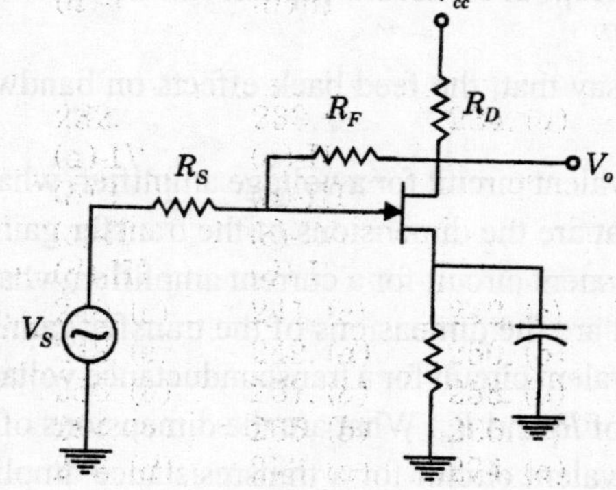


Fig. 10p11

4. **Calculate the gain of a negative feedback amplifier having $A = -2000$, $\beta = -1/10$.**

$A_f = -9.95$

**5.** Calculate the gain, input and output impedances of a voltage series feedback amplifier having $A = -3000$, $R_I = 1.5$ k ohms, $R_o = 50$ k ohms and $\beta = -1/15$.

**Ans:** $A_f = -14.3$, $R_{if} = 31.5$ k ohms, $R_{of} = 2.4$ k ohms.

**6.** A modified second-collector to first-emitter feedback pair is shown with dc biasing omitted for simplicity. All transistors are identical. Neglecting $h_{re}$, $h_{rb}$, $h_{oe}$, $h_{ob}$ and assuming that $h_{fe} >> 1$, $h_{fe}R_1 >> R_s + h_{ie}$ and $R_2 >> h_{ie}b_3$.

Show that (a) the voltage gain $A_V = \dfrac{V_o}{V_i} \approx R_2/R_1$

(b) the output resistance $R_o \gg R_c \parallel (R_2/h_{fe})$

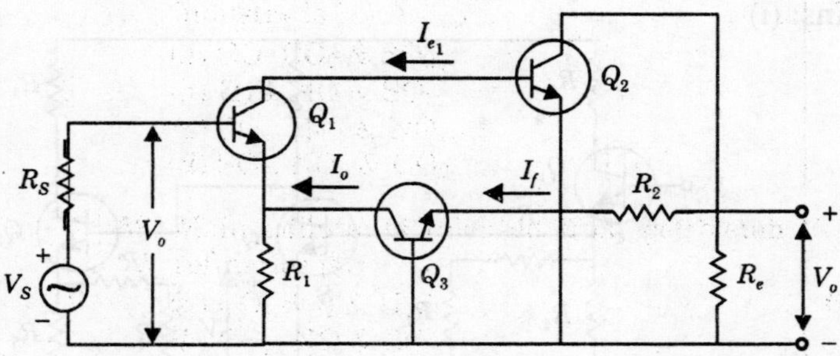


**Fig. 10p12**

**7.** For the transistor feedback-amplifier stage shown, $h_{fe} = 100$, $h_{ie} = 1$k. while hre and hoe are negligible. Determine with $R_e = 0$ the following

(a) $A_V = V_O/V_i$ (b) $A_{VS} = V_O/V_s$ (c) $R_{if}$ (d) $R_{of}$

**Ans:** (a) –910 (b) –82.6 (c) 100Ω (d) 1960Ω.

**8.** An amplifier has $A = 60000$ and $A_f = 10000$. Calculate the amount of negative feedback and the value of feedback factor $B$.

**Ans:** $\beta = 8.33 \times 10^{-5}$

**9.** An amplifier without feedback has an output voltage $V_o = 50$V with second harmonic distortion of 10% for $V_i$ 0.5v. Calculate (i) the amount of feedback necessary to reduce $D$ to 1%, (ii) the resulting gain $A_f$ and (iii) the new input voltage required to restore $V_o$ to 50V with 1% distortion.

**Ans:** (i) 0.09 (ii) 10 (iii) 5v

**10.** For the feedback amplifier shown in the figure

(i) draw the circuit without feedback but taking the loading of feedback network into account

(ii) find the feedback factor β

(iii) assuming loop gain to be much larger than unity find the voltage gain with feedback

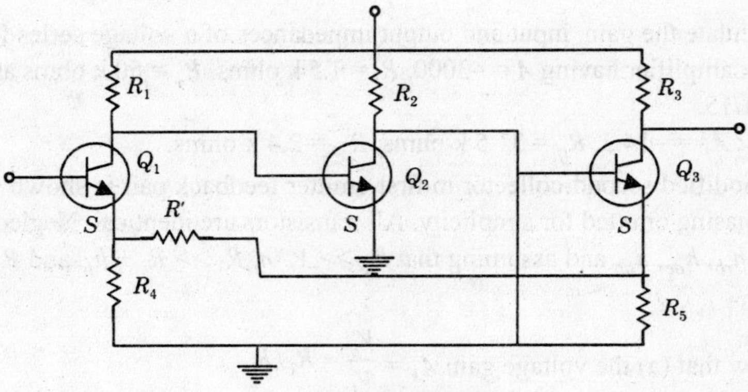


Fig. 10p13(a)

**Ans:** (i)

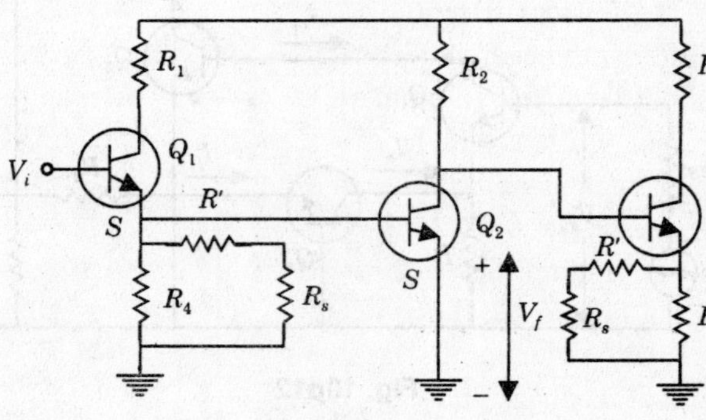


Fig. 10p13(b)

(ii) $b = -\dfrac{R_5 R_4}{R_4 + R^1 + R_5}$

(iii) $A_{VF} = \dfrac{R_3}{\beta} = -\dfrac{R_3(R_5 + R^1 + R_4)}{R_4 R_5}$

**11.** **An amplifier with open loop voltage gain $A_V = 1000 \pm 100$ is available. It is required to have an amplifier whose gain varies by no more than ± 0.2%. find (i) reverse transmission factor β of the feedback network (ii) gain with feedback. Derive the formula you used.**

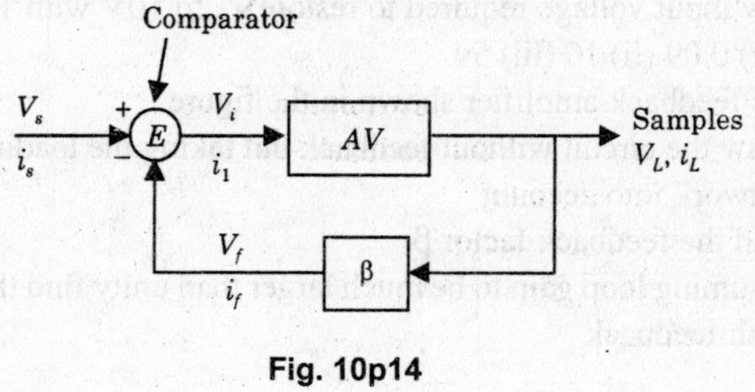


Fig. 10p14

**Ans:** (i) b = 5% (ii) $A_{Vf}$ = 19.60

**12.** An amplifier with an open-loop voltage gain of 1000 delivers 10W of output power at 10 percent second-harmonic distortion when the input signal is 10mV. If 40db negative voltage-series feedback is applied and the output power is to remain at 10W, determine

(a) The required input signal

(b) The % harmonic distortion.

**Ans:** (a) To retain the same power at the output, the input voltage should be increased to 10mV to 1V (ii) 0.1%.

**13.** The overall gain of multi stage amplifier is 160. When negative feedback is applied, the gain is reduced to 19.5.

(a) Find the fraction of the output that feedback to the input.

(b) Find the gain with internal gain $A = 100 + \beta = 1/20$ $A = 160, A_f = 19.5$

**Ans:** (a) $\beta = 0.045$ (b)16.66

**14.** An amplifier with negative feedback has a voltage gain of 100. it is found that without feedback an input signal of 40mV is required to produce a given output, whereas with feedback, the input signal must be 0.5v for the same output calculate the value of $A$ and $\beta$.

**Ans:** $A = 1250, \beta = 0.92$ %

**15.** The gain of an amplifier without feedback is 40 whereas with negative feedback, it falls to 20. If due to aging, the amplifier gain falls to 3. Find the percentage reduction in stage gain

(i) Without feedback and

(ii) with negative feedback.

**Ans:** (i) 25% (ii) 45.3%

**16.** To an amplifier of 50db gain of feedback negative of $\beta = 0.005$ is applied. What would be the change in overall gain of the feedback amplifier? If the internal amplifier is subjected to a gain reduction of 10%.

**Ans:** 1.6%

## 10.17 LAB EXPERIMENTS

### EXPERIMENT No: 1

### FREQUENCY RESPONSE OF AMPLIFIER WITH AND WITHOUT FEEDBACK

**AIM:** To find the response of the amplifier with and without feedback

COMPONENTS AND EQUIPMENT REQUIRED:

1. BJT Transistor: BC 548
2. Resistors: 5.6kΩ, 33kΩ, 10kΩ, 4.7kΩ, 1kΩ, 22kΩ
3. Capacitors: 10mF, 1kpF, 47mF.

CIRCUIT DIAGRAM:

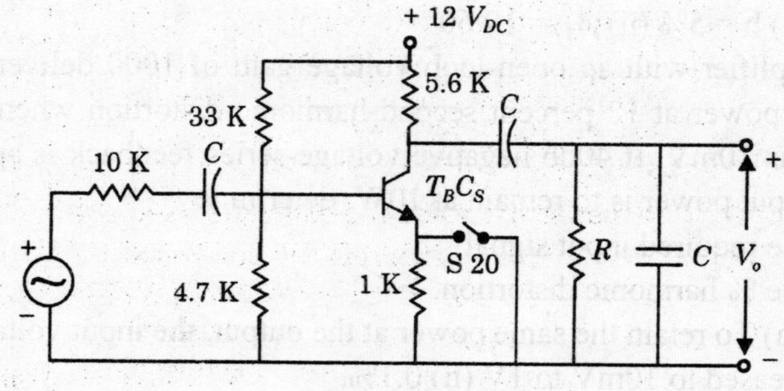


**Fig. 10L1**

**PROCEDURE:**

**Response without feedback**

**(1)** **Connect the circuit as shown with the switch being closed such that any AC signal appearing at the emitter of the transistor must be grounded through the shunting capacitor.**

**(2)** **Set the $V_s$ at 40mV peak to peak and $V_{CC}$ = 12V and vary the frequency of the input signal from 50Hz to 250Hz shown in the tabular column and note down the corresponding output. $A_{vs} = V_0/V_s$, $A_{vsf} = V_{0f} / V_s$.**

**(3)** **Plot the frequency *vs* output voltage and locate $f_H$ and $f_L$ and $B_W = f_H - f_L$ from the graph.**

**Response with feedback**

**(1)** **Connect the circuit as shown in the figure with the switch open such that there is no AC path provided.**

**(2)** **Plot frequency *vs* output voltage and locate $f_{LF}$ and $f_{HF}$ from the graph.**

OBSERVATIONS

*Without feedback*

| *Frequency (Hz)* | $V_i(mV)$ | $V_O\ (V)$ | $A_V = V_o/V_i$ |
|---|---|---|---|
| 50 | | | |
| 70 | | | |
| 100 | | | |
| 150 | | | |
| 200 | | | |
| 500 | | | |
| 700 | | | |
| 1k | | | |
| 5k | | | |
| 7k | | | |
| 10k | | | |

| Frequency (Hz) | $V_i(mV)$ | $V_o(mV)$ | $A_v = V_0/V_i$ |
|---|---|---|---|
| 50k | | | |
| 70k | | | |
| 100k | | | |
| 200k | | | |

*With Feedback*

| *Frequency (Hz)* | $V_i(mV)$ | $V_o(mV)$ | $A_v = V_0/V_i$ |
|---|---|---|---|
| 20 | | | |
| 30 | | | |
| 40 | | | |
| 50 | | | |
| 70 | | | |
| 100 | | | |
| 150 | | | |
| 200 | | | |
| 300 | | | |
| 500 | | | |
| 700 | | | |
| 1k | | | |
| 2k | | | |
| 5k | | | |
| 7k | | | |
| 10k | | | |
| 30k | | | |
| 50k | | | |
| 70k | | | |
| 100k | | | |

*RESULT:*

With feedback the gain is ____________________

Without feedback the gain is ____________________

# ‹ 11 ›

# SINUSOIDAL OSCILLATORS

## 11.1 INTRODUCTION

Oscillator is an amplifier with positive feedback which produces an output without any input of course with biasing voltages. They are used for experimental work, as carrier frequency for radios and for TVs and as a clock for computers and switching circuits.

There are so many types of oscillators like sinusoidal oscillators, square wave oscillator and triangular wave oscillators but we consider only sinusoidal oscillators in this chapter.

## 11.2 GENERATION AND SUSTAINING OF SINUSOIDAL OSCILLATORS

In this section we study how oscillations are generated and how they are sustained.

### 11.2.1 Block Diagram

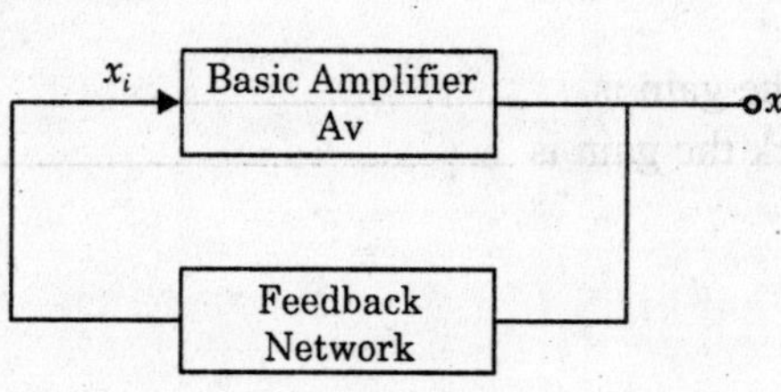


**Fig. 11.1** Block diagram of a feed back system

Basic amplifier contains active device, power supply, resistors and capacitors. Feedback network also contains passive elements. The drift in power supply, changes in active device, changes in passive elements will produce small signal at the input of basic amplifier, and a part of output is feedback to the input through feedback network and added to the previous input as it is positive feedback amplifier. This process repeats and sinusoidal oscillations are produced.

Among the oscillations generated, frequency is selected according to the feedback network and that signal is sustained when condition for generation and sustaining of oscillations is by Bharkhausen criteria as follows

### *Bharkhausen Criteria*

1. The total phase shift around the loop gain $\angle A\beta$ must be $2\pi$ or integer multiple of $2\pi$.
2. The magnitude of the product of the transfer gain of the amplifier and the gain of feedback network should not be less than unity.
   Note: if $|A\beta|$ is less than unity then the oscillator will produce nonsinusoidal oscillations.

## 11.3 CLASSIFICATION OF SINUSOIDAL OSCILLATORS

Sinusoidal oscillators are classified according to feedback network and frequency of oscillations.

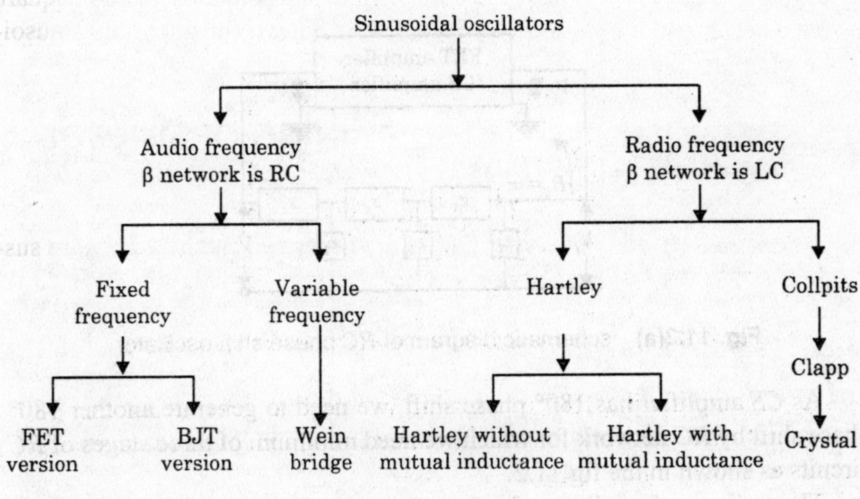


## 11.4 REQUIREMENTS OF OSCILLATORS

1. The frequency of oscillations should be independent of internal parameters of active device
   So that the frequency of oscillations may be stable.
2. $f_o$ should be independent of external parameters of an amplifier so that $f_0$ and gain may be independently varied.
3. Conditions for sustaining oscillations should be independent of parameters of active device.

4. Easy way of varying $f_o$ i.e. variable frequency without disturbing sustaining condition.
5. $f_o$ should be independent of discrete components.

## 11.5 PROCEDURE FOR ANALYSIS OF OSCILLATORS

Step 1: Calculate $A = \frac{X_0}{X_i}$

Step 2: Calculate $\beta = \frac{X_f}{X_0} = \frac{X_i}{X_0}$

Step 3: Calculate $A\beta$

Step 4: put $j$ term zero of $A\beta$ and get $f_o$.

Step 5: $|A\beta|_{f=fo} \geq 1$ and get condition for sustaining oscillations.

## 11.6 RC PHASE SHIFT OSCILLATOR

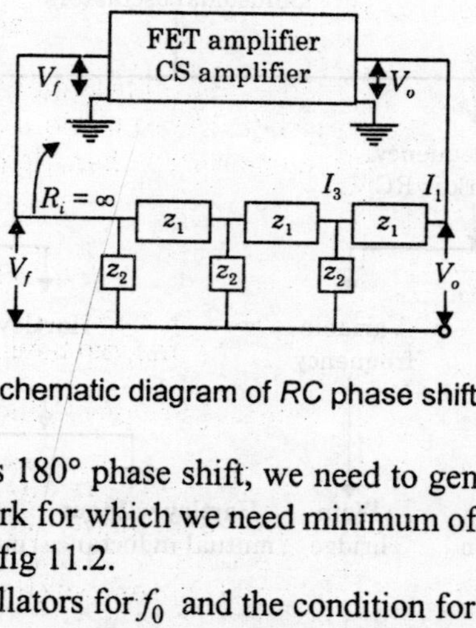


**Fig. 11.2(a)** schematic diagram of *RC* phase shift oscillator

As *CS* amplifier has 180° phase shift, we need to generate another 180° phase shift by *RC* network for which we need minimum of three stages of *RC* circuits as shown in the fig 11.2.

The analysis of oscillators for $f_0$ and the condition for sustaining oscillator i.e. according to the procedure given below as follows.

$S_1$: $$A = \frac{X_0}{X_i}$$

$$A_V = \left(\frac{-\mu R_d}{R_d + r_d}\right) \rightarrow \text{Exact}$$

$$= -g_m r_d \,||\, R_d \quad \text{if } r_d << R_d$$

$$A_V = -g_m r_d = -\mu \rightarrow \text{approx.}$$

$S_2$: $$\beta = \frac{V_f}{V_0}$$

$$V_f = I_6 Z_2 = I_5 Z_2 \qquad \text{...(1)}$$

$$KVL = I_4 Z_2 = I_5 Z_1 + I_6 Z_2$$

$$I_4 = I_5(Z_1 + Z_2)$$

$$I_4 = I_3(k+1) \qquad \text{...(2)}$$

$$\left(k = \frac{Z_1}{Z_2}\right) \; KVL\ I_3 = I_4 + I_5$$

$$\beta = \frac{V_f}{V_0} = \frac{1}{K^3 + 5K^2 + 6K + 1}$$

$S_3$: $$A\beta = \frac{A}{K^3 + 5K^2 + 6K + 1}$$

Case ( I ) $$Z_1 = R : Z_2 = \frac{1}{j\omega c}$$

$\therefore k = jx,\ x = \omega RC$

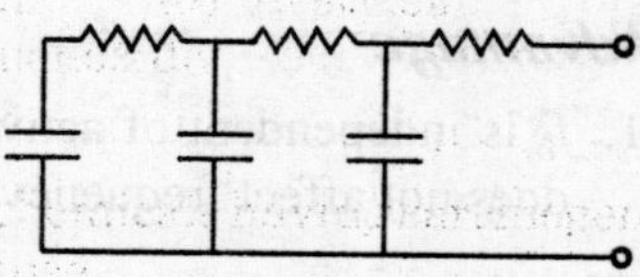

Fig. 11.2(b)

$$A\beta = \frac{A}{(jx)^3 + 5(jx)^2 + 6(jx) + 1}$$

$$= \frac{A}{1 - 5x^2 + j(6x - x^3)}$$

$S_4$: Put $j = 0,\ (6x - x^3) = 0$

$$X = 0,\ (\omega RC) = 0.$$

$$X = \pm\sqrt{6} \quad (\omega_o RC = \pm\sqrt{6}\ )$$

$\therefore$ only possibility is $x = \sqrt{6}$, as cant be zero or negative.

$$\omega_o RC = \sqrt{6}$$

$$f_o = \frac{\sqrt{6}}{2\pi\ RC}$$

$S_5$: $$|A\beta|_f = f_0 \geq 1 \left|\frac{A}{1 - 5\left(\sqrt{6}\right)^2}\right| \geq 1 \qquad \therefore |A| \geq 29$$

For FET $\left(\dfrac{\mu\ R_d}{R_S + r_d}\right) \geq 29$ is highly impossible

Case (ii) $Z_1 = \frac{1}{j\omega c}$ $Z_2 = R$

$$f_o = \frac{1}{2\pi\sqrt{6}RC} \quad |A| \geq 29$$

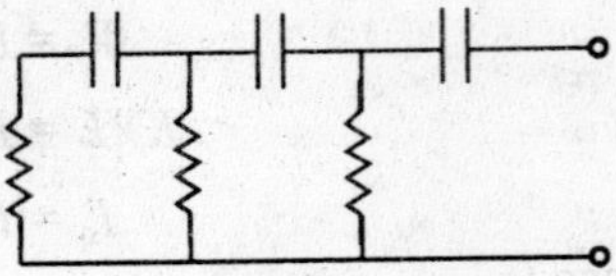

Fig. 11.2(c)

$S_6$: $|AB|_{f=fo} \geq 1$

$$\left|\frac{A}{1-5\left(\sqrt{6}\right)^2}\right| \geq 1 \qquad \therefore |A| \geq 29$$

For FET $\left(\frac{\mu R_d}{R_S + r_d}\right) \geq 29$ is highly impossible

## Advantage

1. $f_o$ is independent of active device parameters and elements of amplifier does not affect frequency stability.

## Disadvantages

1. Condition for sustaining oscillation is dependent of parameters of active device.
2. *fo* is very difficult to vary.
3. *fo* depends on discrete components.
4. $|A| \geq 29$ is not possible by single stage FET.

To get $|A| \geq 29$ we need to take two stages of FET amplifier, but with two stages the phase angle of basic amplifier itself will become 360°. There we need β network to select frequency. The analysis of such an oscillator is as follows:

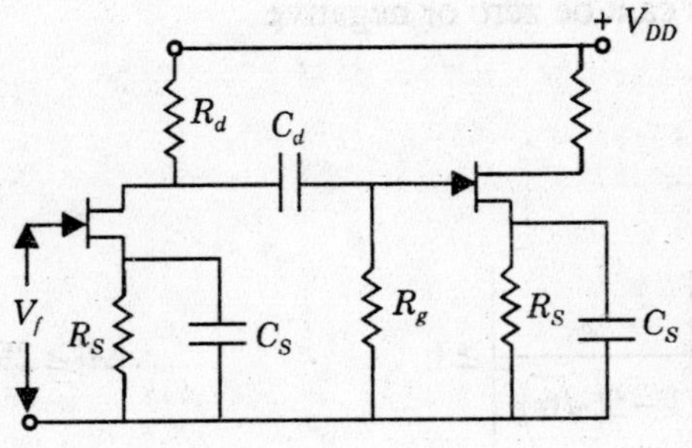


Fig. 11.3 (a) basic amplifier

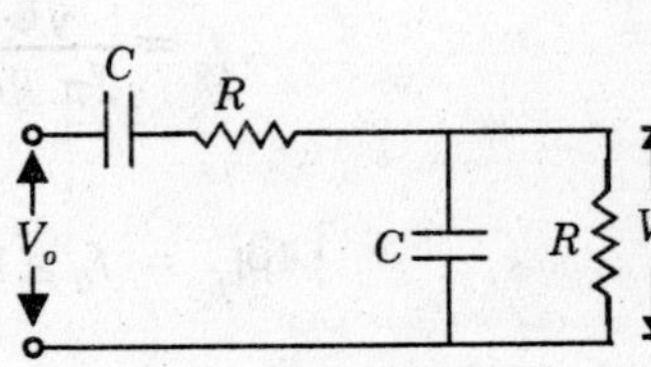


Fig. 11.3 (b) β network

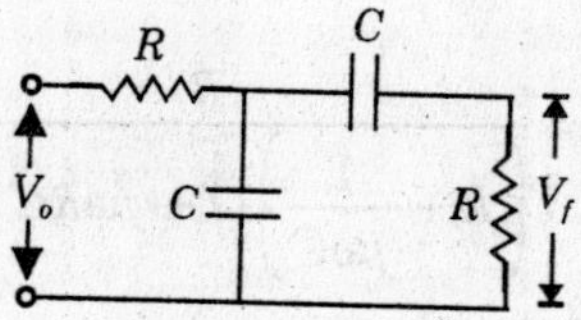


**Fig. 11.3(c)** β network

Case (ii) $\quad Z_1 = \dfrac{1}{j\omega c}\; Z_2 = R$

$S_1$: $\quad A_v = \left|\dfrac{-\mu R_d}{R_d + r_d}\right|^2$

$S_2$: Case (i):

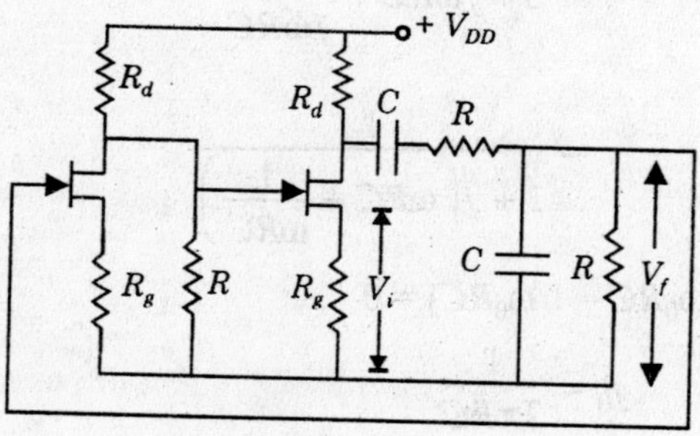


**Fig. 11.4(a)**

$$\frac{V_f}{V_0} = \left(\frac{Z_1}{Z_1 + Z_2}\right)$$

$$Z_1 = R + \frac{1}{j\omega C}$$

$$Z_2 = \frac{R\dfrac{1}{j\omega C}}{R + \dfrac{1}{j\omega C}} = \frac{R}{1 + j\omega RC}$$

$$\frac{V_f}{V_0} = \left(\frac{\dfrac{R}{1+\ j\omega RC}}{R + \dfrac{1}{j\omega C} + \dfrac{R}{1 + j\omega RC}}\right)$$

$$= \frac{R}{\left(R + \frac{1}{j\omega C}\right)(1 + j\omega RC) + R}$$

$$= \frac{R}{R + j\omega R^2 C + \frac{1}{j\omega C} + R + R}$$

$$= \frac{R}{3R + j\omega R^2 C + \frac{1}{j\omega C}}$$

$$= \frac{1}{3 + j\omega RC + \frac{1}{j\omega RC}}$$

$$= \frac{1}{3 + j\left(\omega RC + \frac{1}{\omega RC}\right)}$$

Put $j$ term = 0 i.e. $(\omega_0 RC - 1/\omega_0 RC) = 0$

$$f_0 = \frac{1}{2\pi RC}$$

$$|A\beta| \geq 1$$

$$\left|\frac{-\mu R_d}{R_d + r_d}\right|^2 \geq 3$$

Gain condition is also satisfied but we feel that we can manage with single stage.

Case (ii):

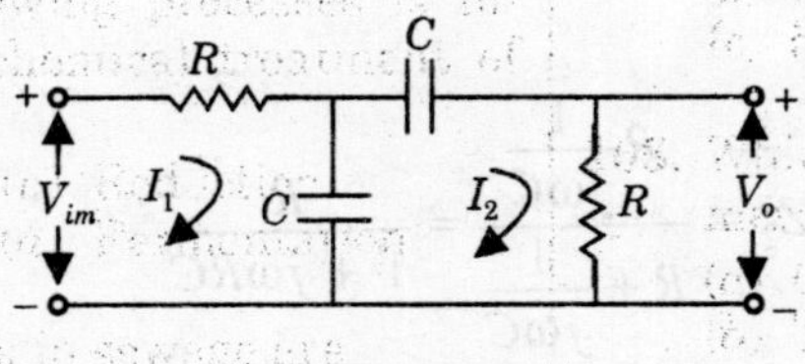


**Fig. 11.4(b)**

Let $X = \frac{1}{\omega C}$ then $V_i = I_1(R - jX) - I_2(-jX)$

$$0 = -I_1(-jX) + I_2(R - j_2 X)$$

$$I_1 = \left(\frac{R - j2X}{jX}\right)I_2 = \left(2 + j\frac{R}{X}\right)I_2$$

So $V_i = I_2\left\{(R - jX)\left(2 + \frac{jR}{X}\right) + jX\right\} = I_2\left[3R + j\left(\frac{R^3}{X} - X\right)\right]$

$$\frac{V_O}{V_i} = \frac{I_2R}{V_i} = \frac{R}{3R + j\left(\frac{R^3}{X} - X\right)} = \frac{1}{3 + j\left(\frac{R}{X} - \frac{X}{R}\right)}$$

$$= \frac{1}{3 + j\left(\omega RC - \frac{1}{\omega RC}\right)}$$

For zero phases shift $\left(\omega_0 RC - \frac{1}{\omega_0 RC}\right) = 0$ or $\omega_0 RC = 1$

and $$f_0 = \frac{1}{2\pi RC}$$

Since $\beta = \frac{V_O}{V_i} = \frac{1}{3}$ and $|A\beta|_{f=f_0} > 1$ then A > 3

We can take three stages of basic amplifier and three stages of β network. As three stages gives 180° we need three stages of $RC$.

$S_1$: $$|A| = \left|\frac{-\mu R_d}{R_d + r_d}\right|^3$$

Analysis of β network is sane as procedures.

$$A\beta = \frac{A}{k^3 + 5k^2 + 6k + 1}$$

$$|A| \geq 29.$$

$$f_0 = \frac{1}{2\pi\sqrt{6}RC}$$

$|A| \geq 29$ is very much possible for three stages.

## 11.7 RC PHASE SHIFT WITH BJT VERSION

### BJT *RC* phase shift

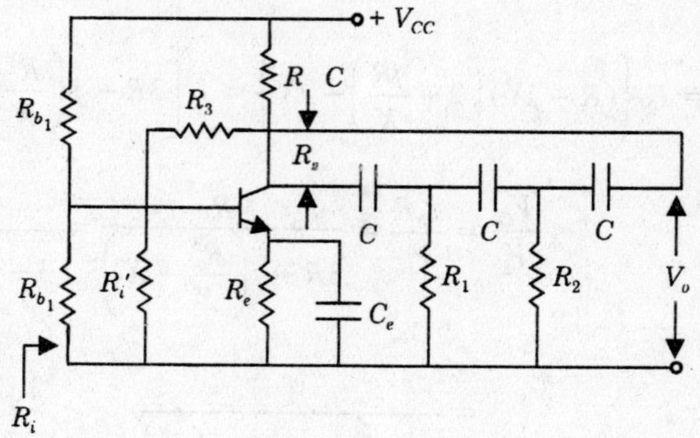


**Fig. 11.5 (a)** Representation of BJT *RC* Phase shift oscillator

$$R_1 = R_2 = (R_3 + R_i) = R$$

$$R_b \parallel h_{ie} = h_{ie}$$

$$\therefore \quad R_3 = R - h_{ie}$$

$$\frac{I_3}{I_0} = \left(\frac{I_3}{I_0}\right)\left(\frac{I_0}{I_b}\right)$$

$$= \{\beta\}\ \{A_I\}$$

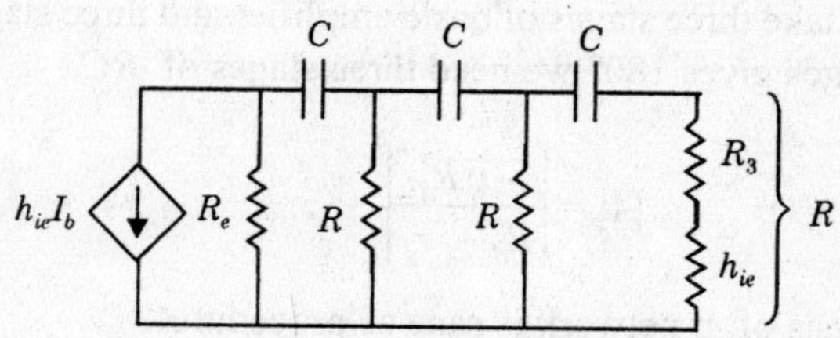


**Fig. 11.5(b)** equivalent circuit

Current to Voltage Converter:

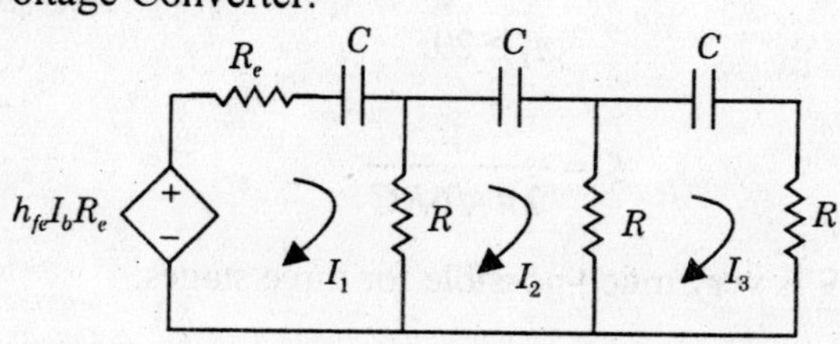


**Fig. 11.5(c)**

$S_3$: Using mesh analysis obtain

$$\left(\frac{I_3}{I_b}\right) = A\beta$$

$S_4$: and put $j$ term = 0

Case (i)

$$f_o = \frac{1}{2\pi\, RC\sqrt{6+4K}} \quad \text{where } K = \frac{R_C}{R}$$

$$f_o = \frac{1}{2\pi\, RC\sqrt{6+4K}}$$

$S_5$: $$|A\beta|_{at\ f = fo} \geq 1 \qquad h_{fe} \geq 4K + 23 + \frac{29}{K}$$

***Advantages:*** $f_o$ *is independent of* $C_i$ & $C_o$

***Disadvantages:***

1. $f_o$ is independent of active parameters but depends on external elements of amplifier.
2. Condition for sustaining oscillations depends on internal parameter $h_{fe}$.
3. Variation of $f_o$ is difficult.
4. $f_o$ depends on discrete components.
   Application: Fixed audio frequency oscillations.

Case (ii) $$f_o = \frac{\sqrt{6+4k}}{2\pi\, RC} \qquad h_{fe} \geq 4K + 23 + \frac{29}{K}$$

In BJT $RC$-phase shift oscillator $f_{oRC} = (6 + 4k)\, f_{oCR}$

In FET phase shift oscillator $f_{oRC} = 6f_{oCR}$

To show that for the BJT $RC$ phase shift oscillator, the frequency of oscillation is given by $\omega_O = \dfrac{1}{RC}\dfrac{1}{\sqrt{6+4K}}$

Where $K = R_C/R$, $R_C$ being the collector load and value of the $h_{fe}$ has to be $h_{fe} > 4K + 23 + 29/K$. Show that the value of K = 2.7 for minimum $h_{fe}$ and the corresponding value of $h_{fe} = 44.5$

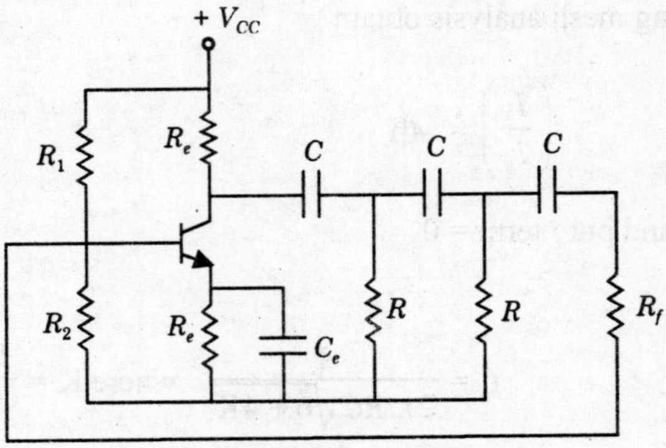


**Fig. 11.6(a)**

Analysis:

The equivalent circuit can be drawn by omitting $R_1$ and $R_2$ and neglecting $h_{re}$ and $h_{oe}$

Let $$R = R_f + h_{ie}$$

$$0 = [(R + R_C) - jX_C]\, I_1 - RI_2 - h_{fc}\, R_C I_3$$

$$0 = (2R - jX_C)\, I_2 - RI_1 - RI_3$$

$$0 = (2R - jX_C)\, I_3 - RI_2$$

$$\therefore \quad \begin{vmatrix} R + R_C - jX_C & -R & -h_{fc}\, R_C \\ -R & 2R - jX_C & -R \\ 0 & -R & 2R - jX_C \end{vmatrix}$$

$$(R_C + R - jX_C)\, [(2R - jX_C)^2 - R^2] + R[-R\,(2R - jX_C) - Rh_{fc}\, R_C]$$

$$R_C + R - jX_C\, [(3R^2 - X_C^2 - 4jRX_C) + R\,\{-R\,(2R^2 + jRX_C - RR_C h_{fc})\} = 0$$

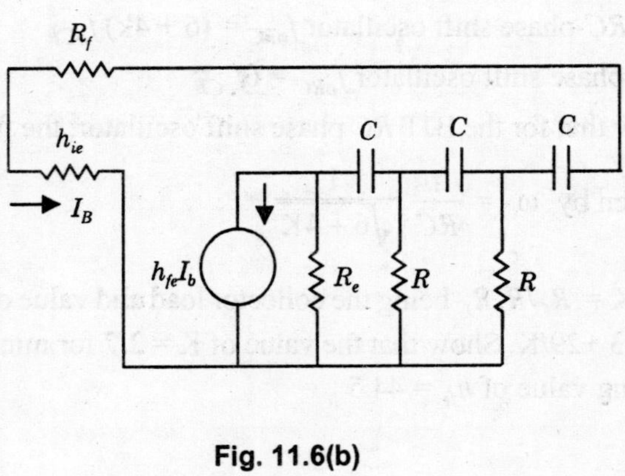


**Fig. 11.6(b)**

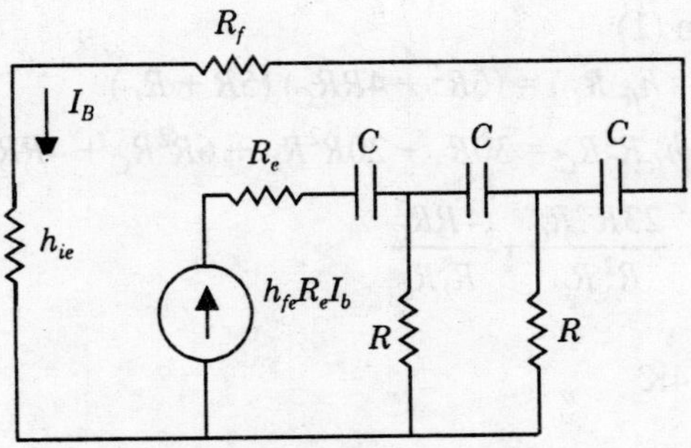


**Fig. 11.6(c)**

$3R^2R_C - R_CX_C^2 - 4jRR_CX_C + 3R^3 - RX_C^2 - 4jR^2X_C - j3R^2X_C + jX_C^2 -$
$4RX_C^2 - 2R^3 + jR_2X_C - R^2R_Ch_{fc} = 0$

$(R^3 + 3R^2R_C - h_{fe}\, R_C\, R_2 - 5RX_C^2 - R_C\, X_C^2) + j(X_C^2 - 6R^2X_C - 4RR_CX_C) = 0$

Equating the imaginary part to zero

$X_C^2 - 6R^2\, X_C - 4RR_CX_C = 0$

$$X_C^2 = 6R^2 + 4RR_C$$

$$\frac{1}{\omega_0\, C^2} = 6R^2 + 4RR_C$$

$$\omega_0^2 = \frac{1}{C^2\left(6R^2 + 4RR_C\right)} = \frac{1}{C^2R^2\left(6 + 4\dfrac{R_C}{R}\right)}$$

$$\omega_0 = \frac{1}{RC\sqrt{6+4\text{K}}}$$

Where K = $R_C/R$ is the frequency of oscillation.

Equating the real part to zero.

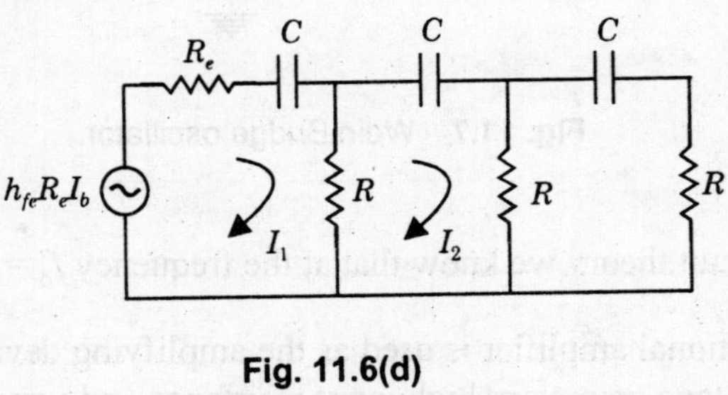


**Fig. 11.6(d)**

$R^3 + R^2\,(3R_C - h_{fc}\, R_C) - 5R\; X_C^2\; - R_CX_C^2\; = 0$

$R^3 + R^2\,(3R_C - h_{fc}\, R_C) = X_C^2\;\; (5R + R_C)$

From equation (1)

$$R^3 + R^2 (3R_C - h_{fc} R_C) = (6R^2 + 4RR_C)(5R + R_C)$$

$$R_3 + 3R^2R_C - h_{fc}R^2R_C = 30R_3 + 20R^2R_C + 6R^2R_C + 4RR^2C$$

$$-h_{fc} = \frac{29R^3}{R^2R_C} + \frac{23R^3R_C}{R^2R_C} + \frac{4RR_C^2}{R_2R_C}$$

$$> \frac{29}{K} + 23 + 4K$$

If $K = 2.7$, $h_{fe} = 44.5$

### *Applications of RC, BJT, FET Versions:*

As variation of frequency is very difficult, they are used for fixed frequency oscillations.

## 11.8 *RC* WEIN BRIDGE OSCILLATOR

Figure 11.7 shows a Wein bridge oscillator, which is one type of *RC* oscillator, makes use of Wein Bridge as the feedback network.

$Z_1$, $Z_2$, $R_3$ and $R_4$ are the four arms of the Wein Bridge. $Z_1$ is a $R - C$ series-circuit and $Z_2$ is a $R$ - $C$ parallel circuit.

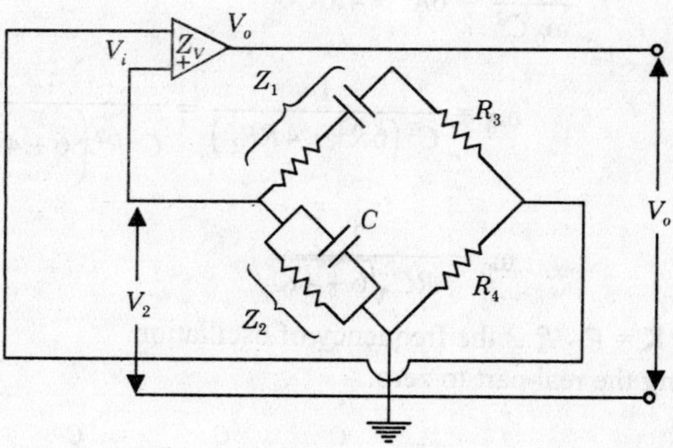


**Fig. 11.7** Wein Bridge oscillator.

From circuit theory we know that at the frequency $f_o = \dfrac{1}{2\pi RC}$

An operational amplifier is used as the amplifying device, Op-amp.have very large voltage gain, very high input resistance and very low output resistance.

Thus, a Wein bridge oscillator will oscillate at the frequency determined by

$$f_o = \frac{1}{2\pi RC}$$

and necessary condition is

$$\frac{R_3}{R_3 + R_4} \leq \frac{1}{3}$$

**Calculation of $f_0$:**

$S_1$: The voltage gain $A = \dfrac{V_0}{V_i}$

$$A_V = \left(1 + \frac{R_2}{R_1}\right)$$, **Non-inverting amplifier.**

$S_2$: $$\beta = \frac{V_f}{V_0}$$

$$V_f = \frac{V_0}{Z_1 + Z_2} Z_2$$

$$Z_1 = R + \frac{1}{j\omega c} \quad Z_2 = R \,||\, \frac{1}{j\omega c}$$

$$\beta = \frac{1}{3 + j\left(\omega Rc - \dfrac{1}{\omega RC}\right)}$$

$S_3$: $$A\beta = \frac{A}{3 + j\left(\omega Rc - \dfrac{1}{\omega RC}\right)}$$

$S_4$: put $j$ term = 0 get $f_o$ = ?

$$\left(\omega_0 RC - \frac{1}{\omega_0 RC}\right) = 0$$

frequency of oscillation $f_o = \dfrac{1}{2\pi\, RC} \quad \omega_o = \dfrac{1}{RC}$

$S_5$: $$|A\beta|_{at\ f = f_0} = \left|\frac{A}{3 + j}\right| \geq 1$$ ($\because$ **$j$ term is ignored**)

$$\left|\frac{A}{3}\right| \geq 1 \qquad \therefore\ A \geq 3$$

$$\left(1+\frac{R_2}{R_1}\right) \geq 3$$

$$\left(\frac{R_2}{R_1}\right) = 2 \Rightarrow R_2 = 2R_1$$

This is the condition for sustaining frequency.

### *Advantages*

1. $f_o$ is independent of active device parameters and elements of Amplifier do not affect frequency stability.
2. Conditions for sustaining oscillations should be independent of parameters of active device.
3. $f_o$ is variable with $\beta$ network.
4. $f_o$ is independent of internal capacitance ($C_i$ & $C_o$) of active device.
   Disadvantages: fo depends on discrete components.

## 11.9 LC OSCILLATORS

*LC* oscillators make use of *LC* resonant circuit as the frequency determining circuit. In the following analysis, we assume an active device with infinite input resistance such as an FET. There are several circuits available under this category, they are:

(a) Tuned *LC* oscillator
(b) Hartley oscillator
(c) Colpitts oscillator
(d) Clapp oscillator.
(e) Crystal oscillator

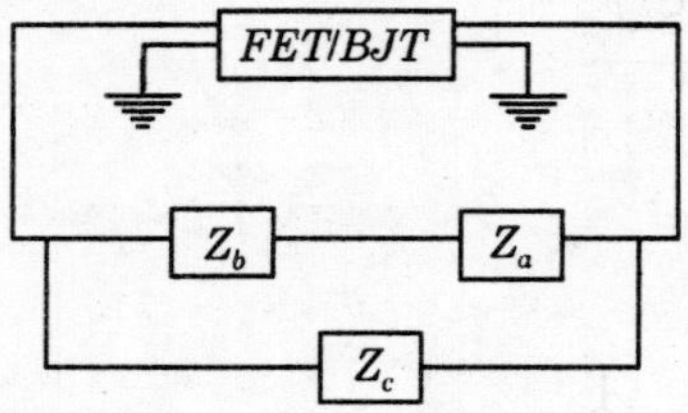


**Fig. 11.8(a)** *LC* oscillator

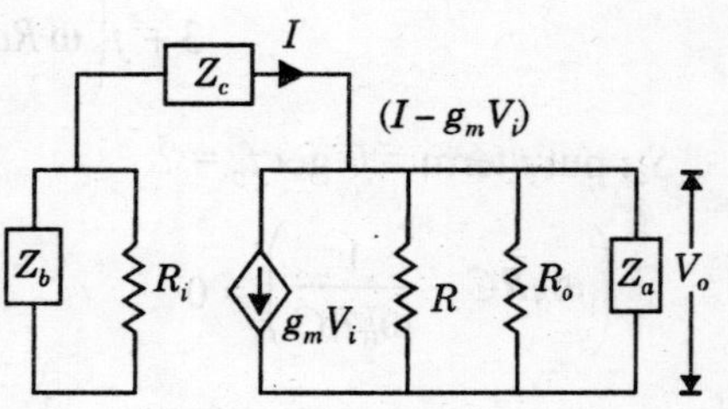


**11.8(b)** Equivalent circuit of *LC* oscillator.

*LC* tuned oscillators are used to generate sine waves in the range of a few KHz to a few MHz. They use reactive elements *L* and *C* which determine the frequency of oscillations.

General analysis:

$$A = \frac{V_0}{V_i}$$

$$V_o = \{I - g_m V_i\} (R_o \parallel Z_a)$$

$$\{(Z_b \parallel R_i) + Z_c\} I - V_o = 0$$

$$\therefore \quad I = \frac{-V_0}{(Z_b \parallel R_i) + Z_C}$$

$$\therefore \quad V_o = \left\{ \frac{-V_0}{(Z_b \parallel R_i) + Z_C} - g_m V_i \right\} (R_o \parallel Z_a)$$

$$\therefore \quad V_o \left\{ \frac{1 + Z_a \parallel R_0}{(Z_b \parallel R_i) + Z_C} \right\} = g_m V_i (R_o \parallel Z_a)$$

$$A = \frac{V_0}{V_i} = \frac{-g_m (Z_a \parallel R_o)(Z_c + Z_b \parallel R_i)}{Z_c + (Z_b \parallel R_i) + Z_a \parallel R_o}$$

$S_2$: $$\beta = \frac{V_f}{V_0} = \frac{V_i}{V_0}$$

$$V_i = \left\{ \frac{V_0}{(Z_b \parallel R_i) + Z_C} \right\} Z_b \parallel R_i$$

$$\frac{V_i}{V_0} = \beta = \left\{ \frac{Z_b \parallel Z_i}{(Z_b \parallel R_i) + Z_C} \right\} \quad \text{...(2)}$$

$S_3$: $$A\beta = \left\{ \frac{-g_m (Z_b \parallel R_0)(Z_b \parallel R_i)}{Z_c + (Z_b \parallel R_i) + (Z_a + R_a)} \right\}$$

$$Za = jX_a \quad Z_b = jX_b \quad Z_c = jX_c$$

$$A\beta = \frac{g_m X_a X_b X_i R_0}{-X_a X_b R_i - X_a X_b R_0 - X_a X_c R_i - X_b X_c R_0 + jR_i R_0 (X_a + X_b + X_c) - jX_a X_b X_c)}$$

–At high frequency $-j X_a X_b X_c$ is zero.

Step 4: Put $Z$ term = 0 $\therefore (X_a + X_b + X_c) = 0$

S5: $|A\beta|_{f=fo} \geq 1 \quad \left|\dfrac{g_m X_a X_b R_i R_0}{-R_i X_a (X_b + X_c) - R_0 X_b (X_a + X_c)}\right| \geq 1$

Case (i): for FET:

$$\text{Divide with } X_a X_b R_i, \quad \left\{\frac{g_m R_0}{\left(\dfrac{R_i X_a^2}{R_i X_a X_b}\right) + \left(\dfrac{R_a X_b^2}{R_i X_a X_b}\right)}\right\} \geq 1$$

$$|A\beta| = \frac{A_v X_b}{X_a} \geq 1$$

$$A_v \geq \frac{X_a}{X_b}$$

$$\left|-\frac{\mu R_d}{r_d + R_d}\right| \geq \frac{X_a}{X_b} \text{ if FET}$$

(a) if $\quad r_d << R_d$

$$g_m r_d = \mu$$

(b) $\quad R_i \to \infty$

$$\mu \geq \frac{X_a}{X_b}$$

as $\mu$ is positive $X_a$ and $X_b$ should be of same type reactance.

$\therefore \quad X_c = -(X_a + X_b)$

for BJT divide with $X_a$, $X_b$ and $R_0$

$$\left\{\frac{g_m R_i}{\left(\dfrac{R_i X_a^2}{R_0 X_a X_b}\right)\left(\dfrac{X_b^2}{X_a X_b}\right)}\right\} \geq 1$$

$$h_{fe} \geq \frac{X_b}{X_a} + \frac{h_{ie}}{R_c}\frac{X_a}{X_b}$$

## HARTLEY OSCILLATOR

In figure 11.9 (a) shows a Hartley oscillator using an inverting amplifier, where $X_1$ and $X_L$ are inductors and $X_C$ is the capacitance.

In Hartley oscillator, the *CE* stage provides 180° phase shift between collector and base voltage. Additional 180° phase shift is by β network.

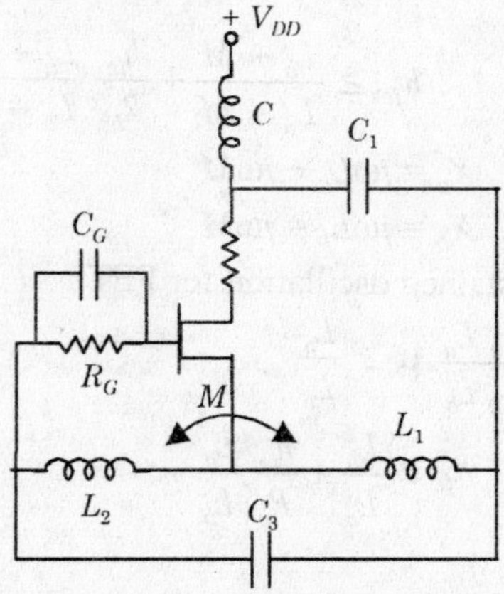


**Fig. 11.9(a)** Hartley oscillator with inverting amplifier

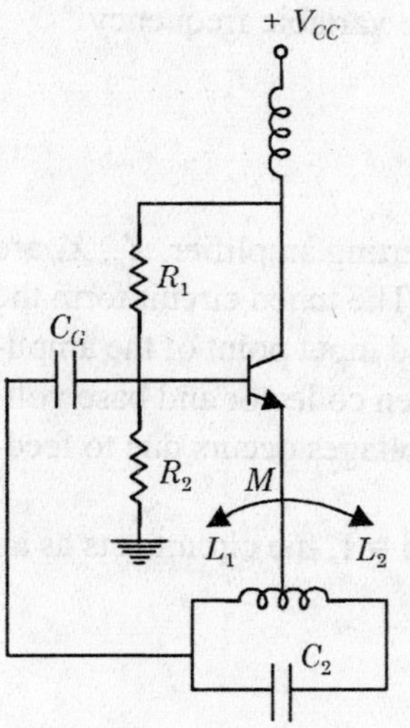


**Fig. 11.9(b)** non-inverting amplifier

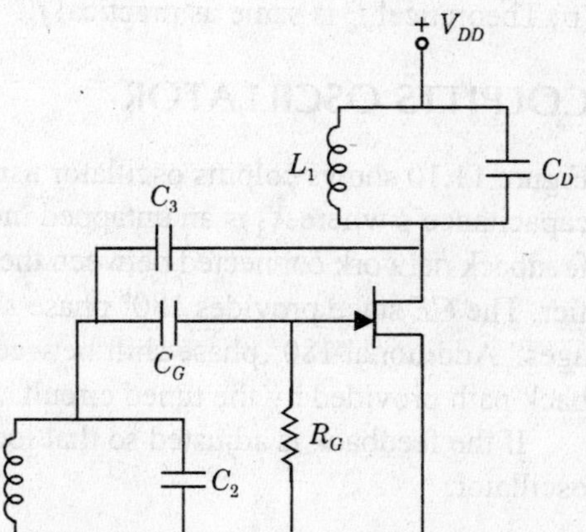


**11.9(c)** Tuned input – Tuned output version.

Case (i): $A\beta = 1$ with $X_a = \omega L_a$, $X_b = \omega L_b$ and $X_c = -\dfrac{1}{\omega Cc}$

$$X_a + X_b + X_c = 0 \qquad \omega L_a + \omega L_b - \frac{1}{\omega_0 c_c} = 0$$

$$f_o = \frac{1}{2\pi\left(\sqrt{L_a + L_b}\right)C_c} \qquad L = L_a + L_b + 2M$$

Where $M$ is the coefficient of mutual inductance between coils $L_a$ and $L_b$. The condition for sustained oscillation is

$$\mu \geq \frac{L_a + M}{L_b + M},$$

BJT,

$$h_{fe} \geq \frac{L_b + M}{L_a + M} + \frac{h_{ie}}{R_{bc}} \frac{L_a + M}{L_b + M}$$

$$X_a = j\omega L_a + j\omega M$$

$$X_b = j\omega L_b = j\omega M$$

Condition for sustained oscillation for FET

$$\mu \geq \frac{\omega_0 L_a}{\omega_0 L_b} \quad \mu \geq \frac{L_a}{L_b} \qquad \text{for FET}$$

$$h_{fe} \geq \frac{L_b}{L_a} + \frac{h_{ie}}{R_e} \frac{L_a}{L_b} \qquad \text{for BJT}$$

### *Advantage*

(a) $C_i$ and $C_o$ are not directly affecting $L_a$ and $L_b$
Note: as gain condition is independent of $X_c$. It can be varied to get variable frequency. Therefore all $LC$ oscillators are variable frequency

(b) Theoretical $f_o$ is same as practical $f_o$.

## COLPITTS OSCILLATOR

Figure 11.10 shows colpitts oscillator using an inverting amplifier, $X_a$, $X_b$ are capacitance's where $X_3$ is an untapped inductance. The tuned circuit form the feedback network connected between the output and input point of the amplifier. The *CE* stage provides 180° phase shift between collector and base voltages. Additional 180° phase shift between these voltages occurs due to feedback path provided by the tuned circuit.

If the feedback is adjusted so that loop gain $A\beta = 1$, the circuit acts as an oscillator.

The frequency of oscillation is $f_o = \dfrac{1}{2\pi\sqrt{LC_{eq}}}$

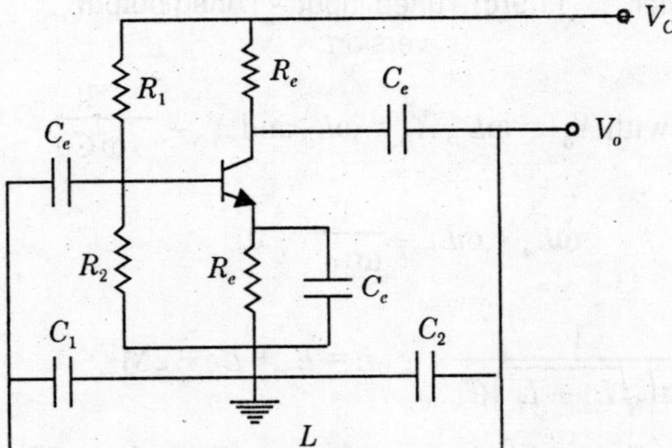


**Fig. 11.10(a)** Colpitts oscillator

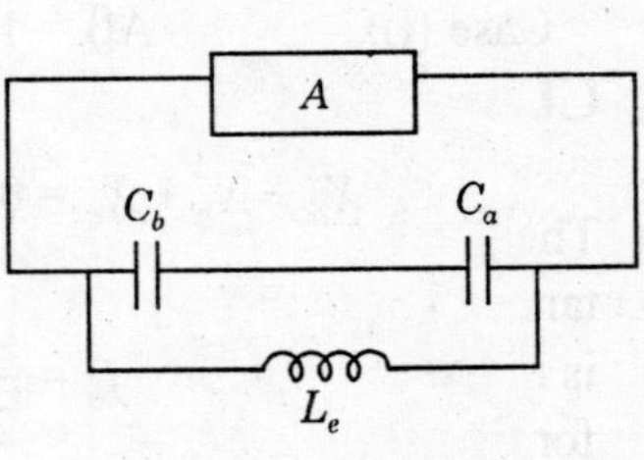


**11.10(b)** equivalent circuit

$$X_a + X_b + X_c = 0$$

$$-\frac{1}{\omega_0 C_a} - \frac{1}{\omega_0 C_b} + \omega_o L_c = 0$$

$$\frac{1}{C_{eq}} = \frac{1}{C_a} + \frac{1}{C_b} \qquad C_{eq} = \frac{C_a C_b}{C_a + C_b}$$

$$f_o = \frac{1}{2\pi}\sqrt{\frac{C_a + C_b}{L\, C_a C_b}}$$

$$\mu \geq \frac{X_a}{X_b} = \frac{\dfrac{-1}{\varpi_0 C_a}}{\dfrac{-1}{\varpi_0 C_b}}$$

$$\mu \geq \frac{C_a}{C_b}$$

$$h_{fe} \geq \frac{C_a}{C_b} + \frac{h_{ie}}{R_e}\frac{C_b}{C_a}$$

### *Advantages*

1. $f_o$ is variable by varying inductance
2. It occupies small space
3. No mutual inductance $M$.

### *Disadvantages:*

1. Internal capacitances loads as b network.

   $C_a^1 = C_a + C_o, \quad C_b^1 = C_b + C_i$

   ∴ Practical $f_o$ is not same as theoretical $f_o$. Therefore $f_o$ is unstable as $C_i$ & $C_o$ depends on active device.
2. $f_0$ depends on discrete components.

## CLAPP OSCILLATOR

The clapp oscillator is a variation of the colpitts oscillator, in which a capacitance $C_S$ is in series with $L_3$ as shown in figure below. The series combination is inductive in nature $C_1$ and $C_2$ are usually made large enough to compensate for transistors inherent junction capacitances, thereby negating transistor variations and junction capacitances changes with temperature.

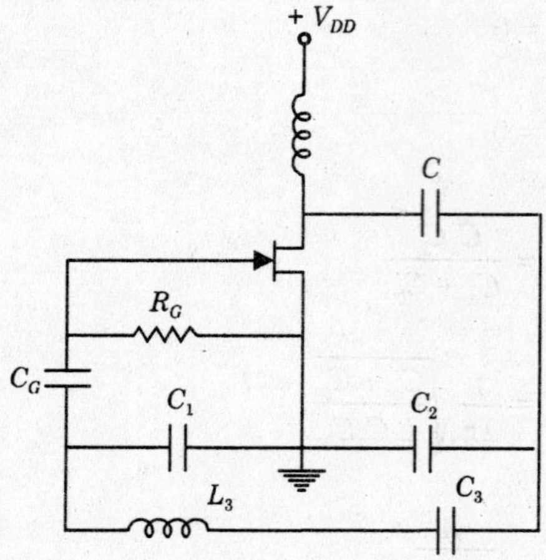


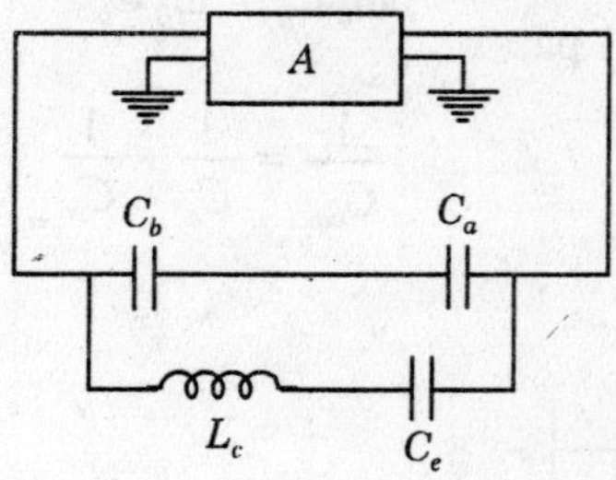


**Fig. 11.11 (a)** Clapp Oscillator **11.11(b)** equivalent circuit

The resonant frequency is $f_o = \dfrac{1}{2\pi\sqrt{LC_{eq}}}$

$$\frac{1}{C_{eq}} = \frac{1}{C_a} + \frac{1}{C_b} + \frac{1}{C_c}$$

$$X_a + X_b + X_c = 0$$

$$-\frac{1}{\omega_0 C_a} - \frac{1}{\omega_0 C_b} - \frac{1}{\omega_0 C_c} + \omega_0 L_c = 0$$

Condition for sustaining oscillations is same as Calpitts Oscillator.

$$C_c >> C_a, C_b \quad f_o = \frac{1}{2\pi\sqrt{LC\left(\frac{1}{C_a} + \frac{1}{C_b} + \frac{1}{C_c}\right)}}$$

Since it is independent of $C_i$ & $C_o$, it is stable.
Disadvantages: $f_0$ depends on discrete components

## CRYSTAL OSCILLATOR

Crystal oscillator is used when exceptional frequency stability is desired. It uses a piezo-electric crystal, usually quartz, as the inductive element of an *LC* tank circuit. It is a colpitts oscillator in which the inductor is replaced by the crystal. The crystal is a thin slice of piezo electric material, such as quartz, tourmaline and Rochelle salts, which exhibits a property called piezo electric effect. The piezo electric effect means the crystal reacts to any mechanical stress by producing electric charge, in the converse effect, an electric field results in mechanical strain. However, since the resonant frequencies of the crystals are temperature dependent, it is necessary to enclose the crystal in a temperature controlled oven to achieve the frequency stability of the order of 1 part in $10^{10}$.

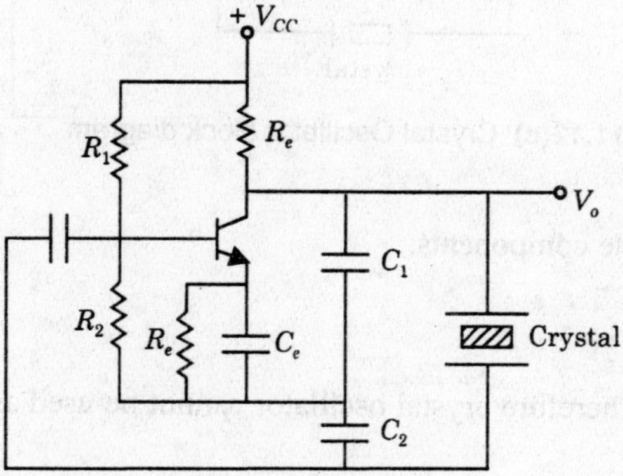


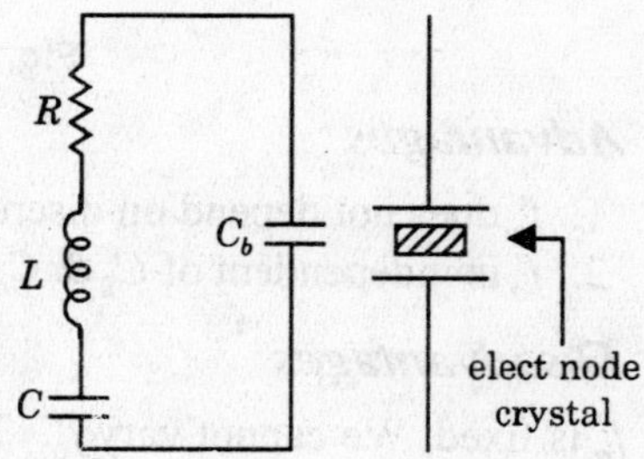


**Fig. 11.12(a)** Crystal Oscillator **11.12(b)** equivalent circuit

The equivalent circuit has a parallel resonant frequency $\omega_p$ and a series resonance frequency $\omega_s$ given by

$$\omega_p = \frac{1}{\left(\dfrac{LC_1C_2}{C_1 + C_2}\right)} \qquad (1)$$

$$\omega_s = \frac{1}{\sqrt{LC_2}} \qquad (2)$$

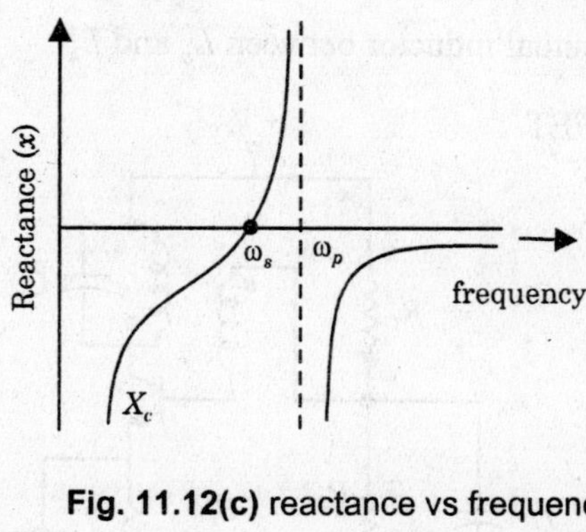


**Fig. 11.12(c)** reactance vs frequency graph

Since $C_i \geq C_2$, $\omega_p$ and ws are very close. The capacitance $C_1$ is the header or inter-holding plate capacitance. The quality factor $Q$ of the crystal is given by

$$Q = \frac{\sqrt{\frac{L}{C_2}}}{R} \quad ...(3)$$

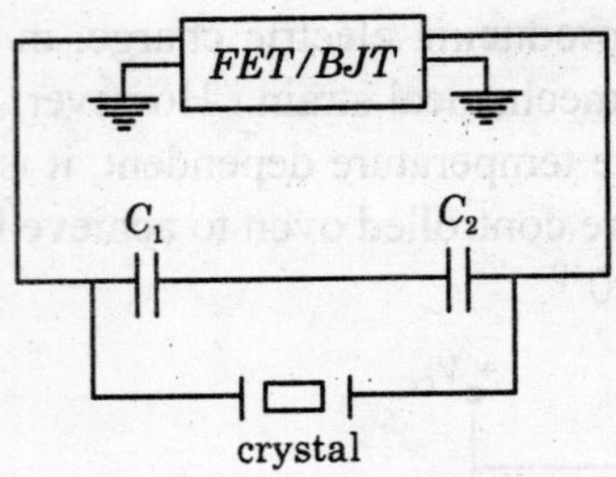


**Fig. 11.12(c)** Crystal Oscillator block diagram

### *Advantages*

1. $f_o$ does not depend on discrete components.
2. $f_o$ is independent of $C_i$ & $C_o$

### *Disadvantages*

$f_o$ is fixed. We cannot vary $f_o$. Therefore crystal oscillator cannot be used as carrier in direct *Fm*.

## 11.10 TUNED COLLECTOR OSCILLATORS

Tuned *LC* oscillator use tuned circuits in the input as well as output side of the amplifier as shown in fig. 11.13. The feedback is helped by the center electrode input-output feedback capacitance $C_3$.

The resonant frequency of the oscillator is given by $f_o = \dfrac{1}{2\pi\sqrt{L_p C}}$.

The inductor $L_p$ has some small resistance. Also the reflected load from the secondary winding $L_s$ presents some resistance. The effect of these two resistances is to slightly change the resonant frequency. The gain required of the amplifier to maintain oscillation is given by: $|A_V| \geq \dfrac{L_p}{M}$ for BJT

Where M = mutual inductor between $L_p$ and $L_s$

$\mu \geq \dfrac{L_p}{M}$ for FET.

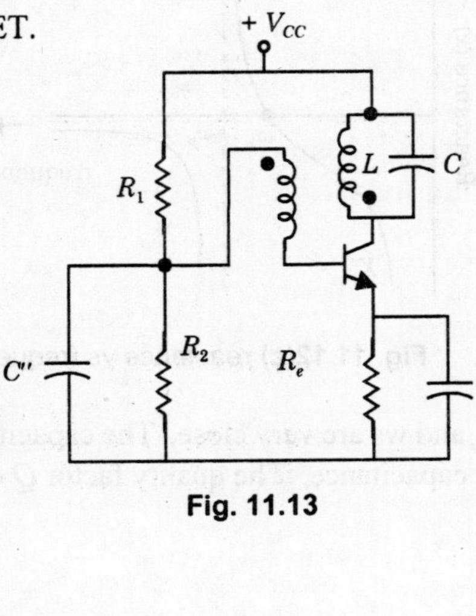


**Fig. 11.13**

## 11.11 AMPLITUDE AND FREQUENCY STABILITY OF OSCILLATORS

*Amplitude stability:* The amplitude of oscillations is determined by factors, which reduces amplifier gain to the point where the loop gain is unity. These factors include non-linearity of amplifying device, such as the onset of saturation or self-bias, and externally provided amplitude clipper. In any case, the amplitude is subject to variation with load, operating conditions, and supply variations. Very good amplitude stability can be obtained by this means, even under varying load conditions.

*Frequency Stability:* Practically all the components in an oscillator will have some effect in determining the frequency of oscillation. The frequency of the *LC* oscillator for example, is dependent on series impedance of $Z_a + Z_b + Z_c$. Amplifier input and output resistance and circuit resistance, parasitic capacitance can vary over wide range, depending on the amplifier supply voltage, temperature and loading and will thus change the resonant frequency.

The calpp circuit provides a greater degree of stability, because the oscillating frequency is almost entirely due to series reactance of $Z_c$. More gain is required from the amplifier to maintain oscillations.

The tuned circuit itself may experience changes of parameters which will cause a change of oscillator frequency. Temperature changes can cause significant changes of parameters. Each component in the tank circuit must be a rigid entity and must be protected from mechanical vibrations. Even very small distortions of a coil will cause a shift of the oscillating frequency.

A low frequency in the tank circuit (because of coil resistance or loading) results in a broadening of the notch. Which shifts the frequency of oscillation. The higher frequency becomes, the less this shift is allowed to become circuit frequency from 10 to 1000 yield frequency stabilities to about 1 part in $10^4$. For stabilities greater than this, crystals must be used. A quartz crystal run at ambient temperature can give stabilities of about 1 to $10^5$. While a temperature –controlled oscillator can give about 1 in $10^6$.

## 11.12 SOLVED PROBLEMS

**1. Find the value of *R′* in the circuit of the figure for generally sinusoidal oscillations. Find the frequency of oscillations.**

**Solution:**

At node a: $\dfrac{V_a}{R} + \dfrac{V_a - V_C}{R'} = 0$

$$V_C = V_a\left[1 + \frac{R'}{R}\right] \qquad ...(1)$$

At node b: $V_a = V_b$

$$V_C = V_b\left[1+\frac{R'}{R}\right] \quad \text{...(2)}$$

$$0 + (V_b)\,SC + \frac{V_b - V_d}{R} = 0$$

$$V_b\,(1 + SCR) = V_d \quad \text{...(3)}$$

At node d: $(V_d - V_c)\,SC + \dfrac{V_d}{R} + \dfrac{(V_d - V_b)}{R} = 0$

$$V_d\,(2 + SCR) = V_C\,(SCR) + V_b \quad \text{...(4)}$$

From (2), (3), (4)

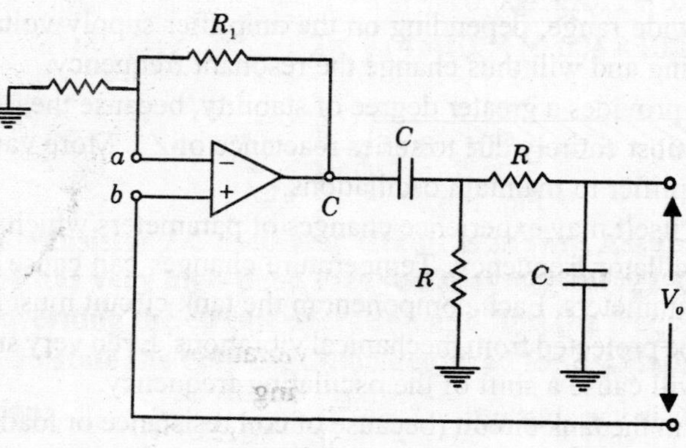


Fig: 11p1

$$V_b\,(1 + SCR)\,(2 + SCR) = V_b\left(1+\frac{R'}{R}\right)(SCR) + V_b$$

$$2 + 3SCR + S^2C^2R^2 - \left(1+\frac{R'}{R}\right)(SCR) - 1 = 0$$

$$1 + S^2C^2R^2 + \left(2-\frac{R'}{R}\right)(SCR) = 0$$

For oscillation $R^1 = 2R$ and $\omega = \dfrac{1}{CR}$

**2. In a Wien bridge oscillator, the capacitors are variable type. The maximum and minimum values of capacitance are 900PF and 90PF respectively. The value of $R = 100\text{K}\Omega$.**

**(a) Determine the range of the operating frequency of the oscillator.**

**(b) Determine the value of $R_3$ if $R_4 = 10K\Omega$, so that oscillation can be maintained.**

**Solution:**

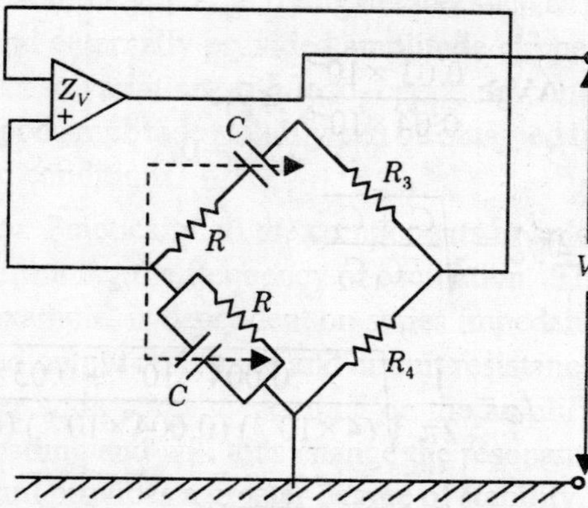


**Fig. 11p2**

(a) The frequency of oscillation is given by

$$f_O = \frac{1}{2\pi RC}$$

The capacitor $C$ is variable and

$C_{\text{maximum}} = 900\text{PF}$

and $C_{\text{minimum}} = 90\text{PF}$

When the $C$ is the minimum, we get the minimum frequency and

$$f_{O\,\text{minimum}} = \frac{1}{2\pi RC_{\text{maximum}}} = \frac{1}{2\pi \times 100\text{K} \times 900\text{PF}} = 1.768 \text{ KHz}$$

When the $C$ is maximum, we get the maximum frequency as

$$f_{O\,\text{maximum}} = \frac{1}{2\pi RC_{\text{minimum}}} = \frac{1}{2\pi\, 100\text{k} \times 90\text{PF}} = 17.68 \text{ KHz}$$

∴ The range of oscillation frequency is from 1.768 KHz to 17.68 KHz

(b) From equation $\dfrac{R_3}{R_3 + R_4} \leq \dfrac{1}{3}$

$R_3 = 2R_4$

$R_3 = 2 \times 10K\Omega = 20K\Omega.$

**3. Find the minimum voltage gain and the frequency of oscillation for a colpitts oscillator with $C_1 = 0.004\mu F$, $C_2 = 0.03\mu F$, and L= 4.0mH.**

**Solution:**

$$A_V \geq \frac{C_2}{C_1}$$

$$AV \geq \frac{0.03 \times 10^{-6}}{0.04 \times 10^{-6}} \geq 7.5$$

So
$$2\pi f_O = \sqrt{\frac{C_1 + C_2}{LC_1C_2}}$$

$$f_O = \frac{1}{2\pi}\sqrt{\frac{0.004 \times 10^{-6} + 0.03 \times 10^{-6}}{(4 \times 10^{-3})(0.004 \times 10^{-6})(0.03 \times 10^{-6})}}$$

$$= \frac{1}{2\pi}\sqrt{7.08 \times 10^{10}} = 42.4 \times 10^3 \text{ Hz} = 42.4 \text{ KHz}$$

**4. A transistor *LC* oscillator circuit is shown. Assume that the transistor has very high β (so that you may neglect $r_\pi$). Derive an equation governing the circuit operation and find the frequency of oscillation. Also state the gain condition required for oscillations to start.**

**Solution:**

$$Z_1 = \frac{1}{j\omega C_1} = \frac{-j}{\omega C_1}$$

$$Z_2 = \frac{1}{j\omega C_2} = \frac{-j}{\omega C_2}$$

$$Z_3 = j\omega L_1$$

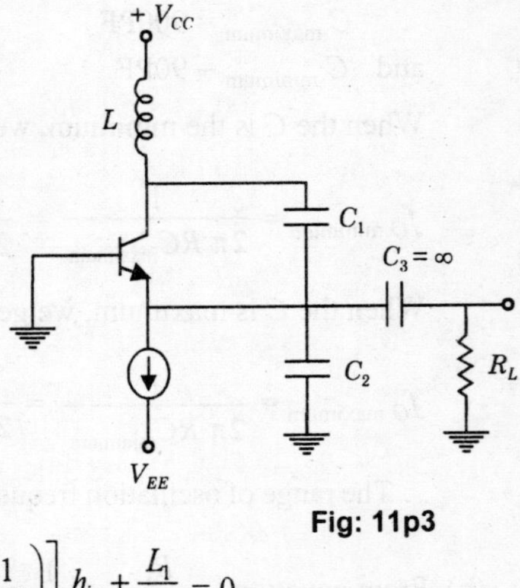


Fig: 11p3

$$\frac{-1 + h_{fe}}{\omega^2 C_1C_2} + j\omega\left[L_1 - \frac{1}{\omega^2}\left(\frac{1}{C_1} + \frac{1}{C_2}\right)\right]h_{ie} + \frac{L_1}{C_2} = 0$$

$$\omega^2 L_1 = \frac{1}{C_1} + \frac{1}{C_2} = \frac{C_1 + C_2}{C_1C_2}$$

$$X_C^2 = \frac{C_1 + C_2}{L_1 C_1 C_2}$$

Equating real part to zero

$$1 + h_{fe} - \frac{1}{\omega_0^2 C_1 C_2} + \frac{L_1}{C_2} = 0$$

$$(1 + h_{fe}) = \omega^2 C_1 L_1 = \frac{C_1 + C}{C_1 C_2} C_1$$

$$h_{fe} = \frac{C_1}{C_2} \text{ Condition of oscillation}$$

**5. A Hartley oscillator as shown in the figure the circuit parameters are as follows:**

**$L_1 = 500\mu H$, $L_2 = 5000\mu M$, M = 300μH and C = 150PF**

**(a) Determine the frequency of oscillation.**

**(b) If the transistor has the following parameters, determine whether the circuit will oscillate or not**

**$R_L$ = 10KΩ  $g_m$ = 8mA/V  $r_o$ = 50KΩ**

**Solution:**

(a) Frequency of oscillation $f_O = \dfrac{1}{2\pi\sqrt{L_T C}}$

$$L_T = L_1 + L_2 + 2M$$

$$= 500\mu H + 5000\mu H + 2 \times 300\mu H = 6.1MH$$

and $C$ = 150 PF

$$f_O = \frac{1}{2\pi\sqrt{6.1mH \times 150PF}} = 166.4 \text{ KHz}$$

The voltage gain using the approximate formula is $A_V = -g_m R_L^1$

The effective $R_L^l = R_L \parallel r_O$ = 10KΩ || 50kΩ = 8.33kΩ

$$A_V = -8mA/V \times 8.33K\Omega = -66.64$$

$$|A_V| = 66.64$$

From equation $\dfrac{N_2}{N_1} = \dfrac{L_2 + M}{L_1 + M} = \dfrac{500\mu H + 300\mu H}{500\mu H + 300\mu H} = 6.625$

There fore using condition for maintaninig sustained oscillation is given by

$$A_V \frac{N_2}{N_1} \geq 1$$

$$|A_V| \frac{N_2}{N_1} = 66.64 \times 6.625 = 441.5$$

Which is much larger than 1.
Hence the circuit will oscillate.

**6. A piezo oscillator has the following circuit and the device parameters $C_{gs} = 5PF$ $C_{ds} = 1PF$ $g_m = 10mA/V$ $r_d = 50k$ and $R_G = 10M$. The crystal parameters are $L = 0.5H$, $C_2 = 0.05PF$, $R_{se} = 1K$ and $C_1 = 1PF$ Find (i) the equivalent series-resonating capacitance $C_r$ (ii) The frequency of oscillations $f_O$ (iii) The series and the parallel resonant frequencies $f_S$ and $f_P$ respectively and $Q$ of the crystal (iv) the loop gain $AB$ at zero bias and (V) the bias time constant.**

**Solution:**

(i) From the figure, we obtain the total capacitance $C_T$ in series with $L$ as:

$C_T = C_2$ in series with $[C_1 \| \{C_{ds}$ in series with $C_{gs}\}]$

$$= \frac{1}{\dfrac{1}{0.05} + \dfrac{1}{1 + \left(\dfrac{1 \times 5}{1+5}\right)}} = 0.049PF$$

(ii) The series resonant frequency of the clapps like piezo oscillator is

$$f_O = \frac{\sqrt{2}}{2\pi\sqrt{LC_T}} = \frac{\sqrt{2}}{2\pi\sqrt{0.5 \times 0.049 \times 10^{-12}}} = 1.017 \text{ MHz}$$

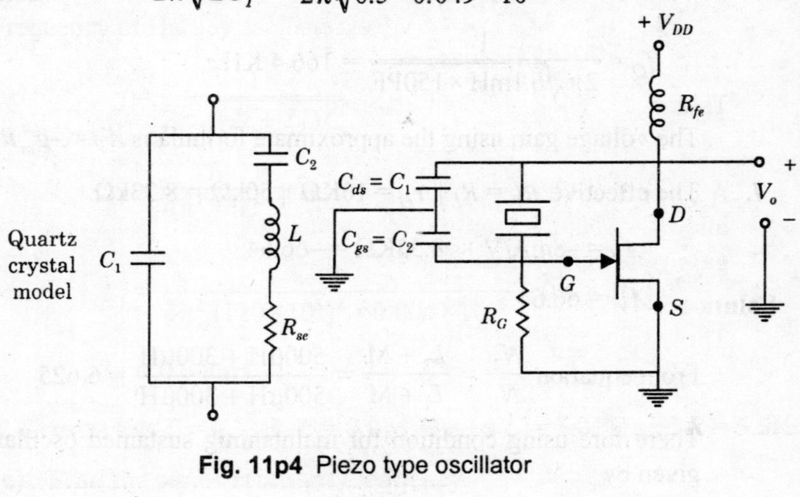


**Fig. 11p4** Piezo type oscillator

(iii) Parallel resonant frequency $\omega_p = \dfrac{1}{\left(\dfrac{LC_1C_2}{C_1+C_2}\right)^{1/2}}$

$$f_P = \frac{1}{2\pi\left(\dfrac{0.5\times10^{-12}\times0.05\times10^{-12}}{1\times10^{-12}+0.05\times10^{-12}}\right)^{1/2}} = 1.3\text{MHz}$$

Series resonant frequency $\omega_S = \dfrac{1}{(LC_2)^{1/2}}$

$$f_S = \frac{1}{2\pi(0.5\times0.05\times10^{-12})^{1/2}} = 1.0065\text{MHz}$$

Quality factor $Q$ of the crystal $Q = \dfrac{(L/C_2)^{1/2}}{R_{Se}}$

$$\text{Q} = \frac{1}{10^3}\left(\frac{0.5}{0.05\times10^{-12}}\right)^{1/2} = 316$$

(iv) the loop gain $A\beta = g_m\, r_d \dfrac{C_{ds}}{C_{gs}} = 10\times10^{-3}\times50\times10^3\times\dfrac{1\text{PF}}{5\text{PF}} = 100$

(v) $\text{T}_{\text{bias}} = R_GC_G = R_G\,(C_{gs}\parallel C_{ds}) = 10\times10^6(5+1)\times10^{-12} = 60\mu\text{s}$

$$\frac{1}{\omega_O} = \frac{1}{2\pi\times1.017\times10^6} = 0.45\mu\text{s}$$

Thus $\text{T}_{\text{bias}} >> \dfrac{1}{\omega_O}$ as required for proper operation.

**7. A colpitts oscillator figure has a coil with inductance of $C_1 = 100\mu\text{PF}$ and $C_2 = 1000\text{PF}$. Find (a) frequency of oscillation (b) The minimum gain required of the amplifier to maintain oscillation.**

**Solution:**

The frequency of oscillation is

$$f_O = \frac{1}{2\pi\sqrt{L_1C_{eq}}}$$

$$L_1 = 100\mu\text{H} = 100\times10^{-6}$$

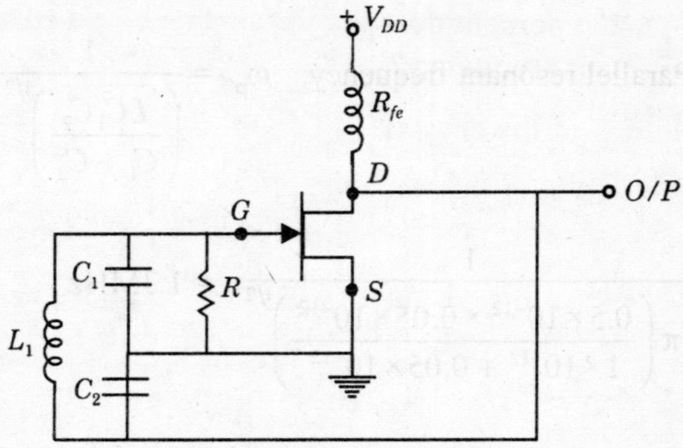


**Fig. 11p5**

$$\text{Ceq} = \frac{C_1 \times C_2}{C_1 + C_2} = \frac{200 \times 10^{-12} \times 1000 \times 10^{-12}}{200 \times 10^{-12} + 1000 \times 10^{-12}} = 166.67 \times 10^{-12}\text{F}$$

$$fo = \frac{1}{2\pi\sqrt{100 \times 10^{-6} \times 166.67 \times 10^{-12}}}$$

$$fo = 123.3 \text{ KHz}$$

The minimum gain required is $|A_V| \geq \frac{C_2}{C_1} = \frac{1000\text{PF}}{200\text{PF}} = 5$

**8. In the Hartley oscillator, $L_2$ = 0.4mH and $C$ = 0.004mF. If the frequency of the oscillation is 120 KHz. Find the value of $L_1$. Neglect the mutual inductance.**

**Solution:**

Frequency of Hartley oscillator is

$$f = \frac{1}{2\pi\sqrt{(L_1 + L_2)C}}$$

$$L_1 = \frac{1}{4\pi^2 f^2 C} - L_2$$

$$L_1 = \frac{1}{4\pi^2 (120 \times 10^3)^2 \times 0.004 \times 10^{-6}} - 0.4 \times 10^{-3}$$

$$L_1 = 0.04\text{mH.}$$

**9. A Crystal has $L$ = 0.33H, $C$ = 0.065PF and $C^1$= 1.0PF and $R$ = 5.5K**

**(a) Find the series resonant frequency.**

**(b) By what percent does the parallel resonant frequency exceed the resonant frequency?**

**(c) Find $Q$ of the crystal.**

**Solution:**

(a) $$f_S = \frac{1}{2\pi}\left(\frac{1}{LC}\right)^{\frac{1}{2}} = \frac{1}{2\pi}\left(\frac{10^{12}}{0.33\times 0.065}\right)^{\frac{1}{2}} = 1.09 \text{ MHz}$$

(b) $$\frac{f_P}{f_S} \doteq \left(1+\frac{C}{C}\right)^{\frac{1}{2}} = \left(1+\frac{0.065}{1.0}\right)^{\frac{1}{2}} \approx 1.033 \text{ MHz}$$

$\therefore$ $f_P$ exceeds $f_S$ by 3.3%

(c) $$Q = \frac{\omega_s L}{R} = \frac{1}{R}\sqrt{\frac{L}{C}} = \frac{1}{5.5\times 10^3}\left(\frac{0.33}{0.065\times 10^{-12}}\right)^{\frac{1}{2}} = 410$$

## 11.13 OBJECTIVE TYPE QUESTIONS

1. A distorted sinusoid has the amplitudes $A_1, A_2, A_3$—— of the fundamental, second harmonic, third harmonic, — respectively. The total harmonic distortion is:

   (a) $(A_2 + A_3 + —)/A_1$ (b) $\sqrt{A_2^2 + A_3^2 + --}/A_1$

   (c) $\sqrt{A_2^2 + A_3^2 + --}/\sqrt{A_1^2 + A_2^2 + A_3^2 + --}$

   (d) $1 - \left(\sqrt{A_2^2 + A_3^2 + --}/A_1\right)$

   **Ans:** (b)

2. An amplifier is assumed to have a single-pole high-frequency transfer function. The rise time of its output response to a step function input is 35 nsec. The upper 3-dB frequency (in MHz) for the amplifier to a sinusoidal input is approximately at

   (a) 4.55 (b) 10

   (c) 20 (d) 28.6

   **Ans:** (d)

3. Frequency of oscillation of a Wein bridge oscillator is given by

   (a) $1/6\pi RC$ (b) $1/2\pi RC$

   (c) $2\pi RC$ (d) $1/RC$

   **Ans:** (b)

4. Which of the following is not true
   (a) An oscillator is circuit that converts DC to AC
   (b) An oscillator is a n amplifier that supplies its own input signal
   (c) All oscillators generate sine wave
   (d) In-phase feedback is called positive feedback

   **Ans:** (c)
5. What do phase-shift oscillators, twin-*T* oscillator and Wein bridge oscillators have in common
   (a) they use *RC* frequency control
   (b) they have a sinusoidal output
   (c) they use amplifier gain to overcome feedback loss
   (d) all the above

   **Ans:** (d)
6. The stability of frequency of oscillation is high if

   (a) $\frac{d\phi}{dt} = 0$ (b) $\frac{d\phi}{dt} = \infty$

   (c) $\frac{d\phi}{d} = 0$ (d) $\frac{d\phi}{dw} = \infty$

   **Ans:** (b)
7. Match List I with List II and select the correct answer using the codes given below the lists:

| *List I* (Oscillator) | *List II* (Characteristics/Features) |
|---|---|
| (a) Wein Bridge | 1. *RF* oscillator; two inductance's and one capacitance on the reactance network |
| (b) Colpitts | 2. *LC* oscillator for *RF* frequency; three capacitances and one inductance *n* the reactance network |
| (c) Hartley | 3. *RC* oscillator for Audio frequency applications |
| (d) Clapp | 4. *RF* oscillator; two capacitances and one inductance the reactance network. |

Codes:

(a) *a b c d*
2 1 4 3

(b) *a b c d*
2 4 1 3

(c) *a b c d*
3 4 1 2

(d) *a b c d*
3 1 4 2

**Ans:** (c)

8. The primary advantage of a crystal oscillator is that
   (a) it can oscillate at any frequency
   (b) it gives a high output voltage
   (c) its frequency of oscillation remains almost constant
   (d) it operates on a very low dc supply voltage

   **Ans:** (c)

**9.** A Hartley oscillator circuits uses
(a) a tapped inductor
(b) a tapped capacitor
(c) both the above
(d) a tapped inductor for inductive feedback
**Ans:** (d)

**10.** A Colpitt's oscillator uses
(a) a tapped inductor
(b) a tapped capacitor
(c) both the above (d) none of the above
**Ans:** (b)

**11.** An oscillator circuit using a quartz crystal has
(a) high frequency stability
(b) low frequency stability
(c) medium frequency stability
(d) none of these
**Ans:** (a)

**12.** An oscillator is basically an amplifier with
(a) zero gain (b) very large gain
(c) infinite gain (d) very low gain
**Ans:** (c)

**13.** In a feed back oscillator, constant amplitude oscillation are obtained when loop gain $-A\beta$ equals
(a) 0 (b) $-1$
(c) 1 (d) $\infty$
**Ans:** (c)

**14.** Crystal oscillator uses
(a) silicon crystal (b) germanium crystal
(c) crystal diode (d) piezo-electric quartz crystal
**Ans:** (d)

**15.** Effective $Q$ of the equivalent electrical circuit of a quartz crystal is of the order of:
(a) 200 (b) 2000
(c) 20,000 (d) $10^5$

**16.** Barkhausen criterion for sustained oscillation gives
(a) $-A\beta = 1$ (b) $A\beta = 0$
(c) $A = \beta$ (d) $A = 1/\beta$
**Ans:** (a)

**17.** Quartz crystal oscillators are popularly used because of
(a) high $Q$ and high frequency stability
(b) low $Q$ and high frequency stability
(c) low $Q$ and large output power
(d) high $Q$ and large output power
**Ans:** (a)

**18.** The crystal oscillator frequency is highly stable due to
(a) crystal structure
(b) high $Q$ of the crystal
(c) vibration of the crystal
(d) rigidity of the crystal
**Ans:** (b)

**19.** The most likely application of a crystal oscillator is
(a) as an *RF* test oscillator
(b) as an electronic organ for home
(c) as a *Hi-Fi* test audio frequency sweep generator
(d) in commercial radio transmitter
**Ans:** (d)

**20.** In *RC* phase shift oscillator using FET and 3-section *RC* phase shift network, the condition for sustained oscillation is
(a) $\beta > 6$ (b) $\beta > 29$
(c) $\beta > 4n + 23 + 29/n$, $n = R_d/R$ (d) $\beta > 23 + 29/n$
**Ans:** (b)

**21.** FET *RC* phase-shift oscillator has angular frequency of oscillation w equal to
(a) $1/3RC$ (b) $1/6\ RC$
(c) $1/\sqrt{6}$ RC (d) $\sqrt{6}/RC$
Where $R$ and $C$ refer to each section of three section *RC* phase shift network.
**Ans:** (c)

**22.** In FET Hartley oscillator, frequency of oscillation w
(a) $\approx \omega_o$ (b) $<< \omega_o$
(c) $>> \omega_o$ (d) $= \omega_o\ (L_1/L_2)$
Where ω is frequency of series resonance $L_1$, $L_2$ and $C$
**Ans:** (a)

**23.** In tuned collector oscillator, frequency ω of oscillation is
(a) $= \omega_o$ (b) $<\omega_o$
(c) $>\omega_o$ (d) $\omega/h_{fe}$
Where $\omega_o$ is frequency of resonance
**Ans:** (c)

**24.** The feedback factor β at frequency of oscillation of Wein bridge oscillator is
(a) 1/3 (b) 3
(c) 1/29 (d) −1/29
**Ans:** (a)

**25.** The minimum number of *RC* sections required in phase shift oscillator are
(a) two (b) three
(c) four (d) none
**Ans:** (b)

**26.** The current amplification factor in radian square of Collpitt's oscillator is
(a) $C_1/C_2$ (b) $C_1\ C_2$
(c) $C_1 + C_2$ (d) $C_1 - C_2$
**Ans:** (a)

**27.** Electronic oscillator is better than mechanical one because
(a) it has better frequency stability
(b) it has higher efficiency
(c) it can produce 20Hz to 200Hz
(d) none
**Ans:** (a)

**28.** Wein bridge oscillator is most often used whenever
(a) wide range of high purity sine waves is to be generated
(b) high feedback ratio is needed
(c) square output waves are required
(d) extremely high resonant frequencies are required
**Ans:** (a)

**29.** If Barkhausen criterion is not fulfilled by an oscillator circuit, it will
(a) stop oscillating (b) produce damped waves continuously
(c) become an amplifier (d) produce high frequency whistles
**Ans:** (c)

**30.** To generate a 1MHz signal, the most suitable circuit is
(a) Phase shift oscillator (b) Wein bridge oscillator
(c) Colpitts oscillator (d) none of the above
**Ans:** (c)

**31.** In oscillator circuit, the energy feedback to its input terminal from the output is
(a) 180° out of phase with input signal
(b) in phase with the input signal
(c) 90° out of phase with the input signal
(d) none
**Ans:** (b)

**32.** For sustaining oscillations in an oscillator
(a) feed back factor should be unity
(b) phase shift should be 0°
(c) feed back should be negative
(d) both (a) and (b)
**Ans:** (d)

## 11.14 CONVENTIONAL QUESTIONS

**1.** What is Barkhausen criterion for oscillation? What are conditions for oscillators?

**2.** Why *R-C* Phase shift oscillators are needed?
**3.** Draw the circuit diagram of BJT *R-C* Phase Shift oscillator, what are the advantages of it?
**4.** Draw the circuit diagram of a Wein bridge oscillator, at what frequency it will oscillate? Derive the expression for $f_o$.
**5.** Draw the circuit diagram of *LC* oscillators, give the expression for $A\beta$.
**6.** What are the important factors in choosing a certain type of oscillator?
**7.** Distinguish between Hartley and Colpitts oscillators and derive the expression for oscillating frequency.
**8.** What are the advantages of Crystal oscillator? What is piezo electric effect? Explain with neat schematic diagram.
**9.** Derive the expression for quality factor in Crystal oscillator.
**10.** Give the expression for sustaining oscillations in Calpits Oscillator.

## 11.15 EXERCISE PROBLEMS

1. Find the minimum voltage gain and the frequency of oscillation for a colpitts oscilator with $C_1 = 0.004\ \mu F$, $C_2 = 0.03\ \mu F$ and $L = 4.0$ mH.
   **Ans:** $A_v \geq 75, f_o = 42.3 \times 10^3$ Hz.
2. A crystal has $L = 0.33$ H, $C = 0.065$ pF and $C^1 = 1.0$ pF, $R = 5.5$ k. Find
   (a) the series resonance frequency
   (b) by what percent does the parellel resonant frequency exceed the series resonance frequency
   (c) $Q$ of the crystal.
   **Ans:** (a) 1.087 MHz (b)1.032 (c) 410

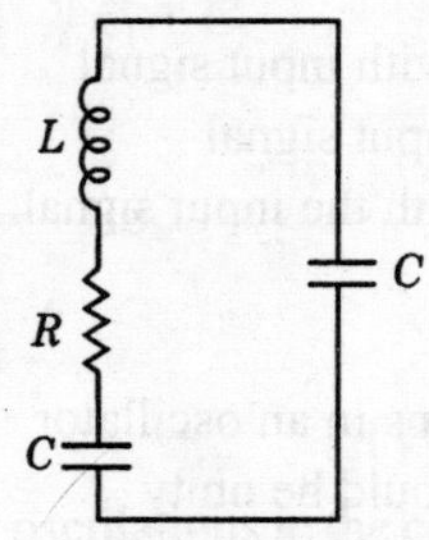


Fig. 11p7

3. Calculate the operating frequency of a BJT phase shift oscillator for $R$ = 6 k ohms, $C$ = 1500 pF and $R_C$ = 18 k ohms.
   **Ans:** $f_o$ = 4.2 kH.

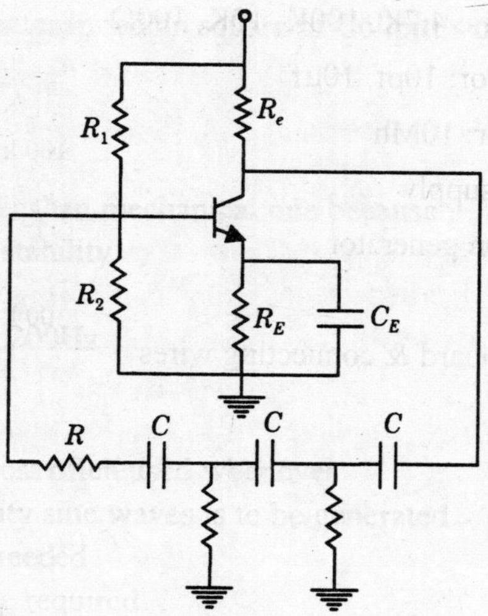


$$f = \frac{1}{2\pi R_c} = \frac{1}{\sqrt{6 + 4\,(R_c/R)}}$$

**Fig. 11p8**

4. Calculate the frequency at which zero transmission is obtained from Wien bridge shown in the figure below.
   **Ans:** $1/2\pi RC$.

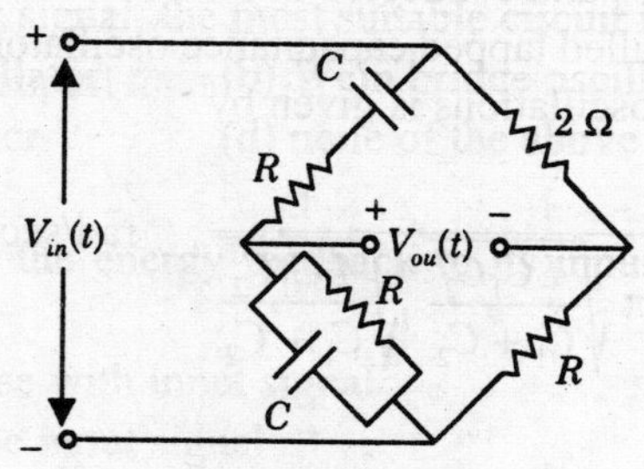


**Fig. 11p9**

## 11.16 LAB EXPERIMENTS

### EXPERIMENT No. 1

### *COLPITT'S OSCILLATOR*

***AIM:*** To measure the frequency of oscillation using CRO.

**APPARATUS and EQUIPMENT REQUIRED:**

1. BJT

2. Resistors: 4.7K, 100K, 10K, 100Ω
3. Capacitor: 10pf, 10μf
4. Inductor: 10Mh
5. Power supply
6. Function generator
7. CRO
8. Bread board & connecting wires

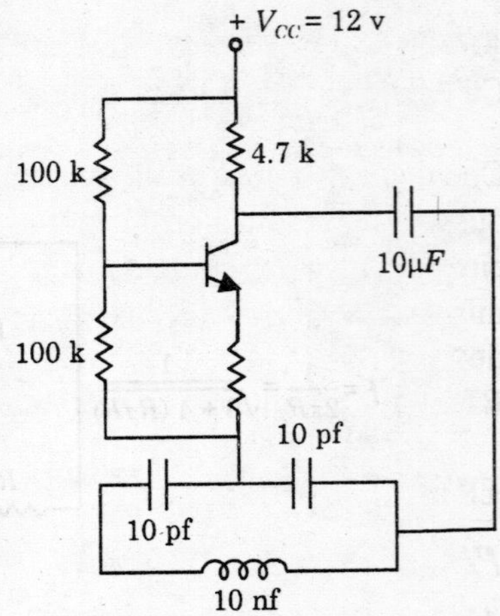


**Fig. 11L1** Circuit diagram

## THEORY

Colpitts oscillator is a variable frequency *R.F.* oscillator. It works on the principle of parallel resonance. The total capacitance of the tank circuit is divided into two parts $C_1$ & $C_2$ and connected in series.

Colpitts is also called tapped capacitance oscillator circuit. The condition for the frequency of oscillations is given by

$$\omega_0 = \frac{1}{2\pi\sqrt{\dfrac{LC_1C_2}{C_1+C_2}}} \frac{1}{\sqrt{\dfrac{LC_1C_2}{C_1+C_2}}} \text{ rad/sec}$$

$$f_0 = \frac{1}{2\pi\sqrt{\dfrac{LC_1C_2}{C_1+C_2}}} \text{ Hz}$$

The condition for sustaining oscillations in the circuit is given by $h_{fe} \geq \dfrac{C_1}{C_2}$.

The frequency of oscillations can be altered by varying the variable inductor.

## PROCEDURE

1. Connect the circuit as shown in figure.
2. Switch on the power supply.
3. Measure dc collector to emitter voltage $V_{CE}$ and emitter-to-ground voltage $V_E$.

Calculate the zero signal collector current using the relation $I_E = \frac{V_E}{R_E}$

4. Connect the output of the oscillator to *y*-plates of the CRO and feed the output of standard signal generator to *x*-plates and vary its frequency till a circle, ellipse (or) straight line is obtained on the screen of the CRO. Note this frequency of the signal generator is same as the frequency of oscillation.

**RESULT:** frequency of oscillation = ____ KHz

## EXPERIMENT No. 2

## RC *PHASE SHIFT OSCILLATOR*

***AIM:*** To study the performance of *RC* phase shift oscillator and to verify the frequency
f oscillation.

**APPARATUS:** 1. Transistor BC548

2. Resistor 4.7K(2), 33K, 5.6 K, 6.8K(2)

3. Capacitor 1kpf (3), 47mf

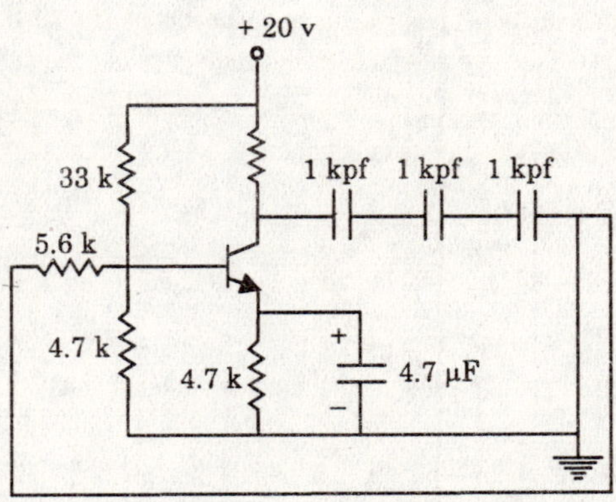


**Fig:11L2** Circuit diagram

**PROCEDURE:**

1. Make the connections as per the circuit diagram.
2. Observe the output signal and note down the output signal amplitude and time period.
3. Calculate the frequency of oscillation theoretically and verify practically.

**OBSERVATIONS**

DC Conditions $V_{cc} =$

$V_{ce} =$

$V_{be} =$

$I_c =$

**Calculation of Frequency:**

Theoretical $f = \dfrac{1}{6 \times \sqrt{2\Pi RC}}$

Practical $f = \dfrac{1}{T}$

# ‹ 12 ›

# POWER ELECTRONIC DEVICES

## 12.1 INTRODUCTION

Study of electronic devices and circuits will be incomplete without study of power devices. Power electronics deals with electronic devices that are operated at power level instead at signal level. They are used in aerospace, commercial, industry, residential, telecommunications and high voltage dc transmission (HVDC).

Starting will the conventional thyristor-type devices in the early days to the recent availability of high frequency high power MOS-gated self controlled device, and high power semiconductor transistors used in radio high power transmitter (HPT) has taken a new direction in technology high power devices with semiconductors has many advantages over the vacuum devices interms of speed, cost and space.

## 12.2 THYRISTOR

Thyristor is a general name given to a family of power semiconductor switching devices, all of, which are characterized, by a bistable switching action depending upon the PNPN regenerative feedback. A thyristor has characteristics similar to a thyratron gas tube. But from the construction point of view, the thyristor (PNPN structure) can be best visualized as consisting of two transistors (a PNP and NPN interconnected to form a regenerative feedback pair). The name thyristor is derived by a combination of THYRatron and transISTOR. Thus, a thyristor is a solid state device like a transistor and has characteristics similar to that of a thyratron tube. Since a thyristor is basically a silicon-made controlled device, it is also known as silicon-controlled rectifier (SCR).

## 12.3 PRINCIPLE OF OPERATION OF SCR

Thyristor (SCR) is a four layer, three junction, P-N-P-N semiconductor switching device. It has three terminals: anode, cathode and gate. The structure and symbol of the SCR is shown in Fig. 12.1

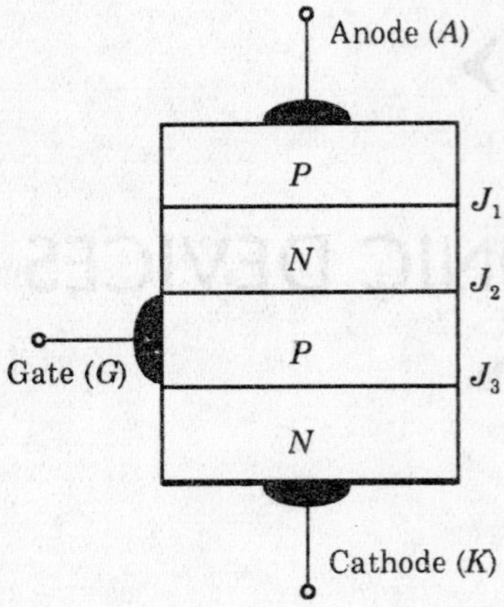


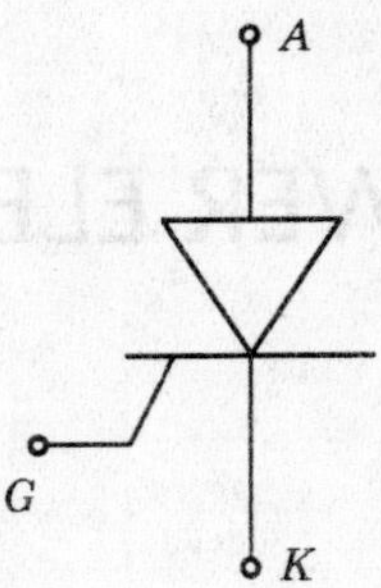


**Fig. 12.1 (a)** Structure **Fig. 12.1 (b)** Symbol

The terminal connected to outer p region is called anode (A), the terminal connected to outer n region is called cathode (K) and that connected to inner p region is called gate (G). the anode and cathode are connected to main power circuit. The gate terminal carries a low level gate current in the direction of gate to cathode. For large current applications thyristors need better cooling and this can be achieved by mountaining them onto heat sinks. Now SCRs of voltage rating 10 KV and an RMS current rating of 3000A with corresponding power handling capacity of 30 Mw are available. As SCRs are solid state devices, they are compact and posses high reliability and have low loss.

### 12.3.1 Static V-I Characteristics of a Thyristor

An element circuit diagram for obtaining static V-I characteristics of a thyristor is shown in Fig 12.2. The anode and cathode are connected to main source through the load. The gate and cathode are fed from another source.

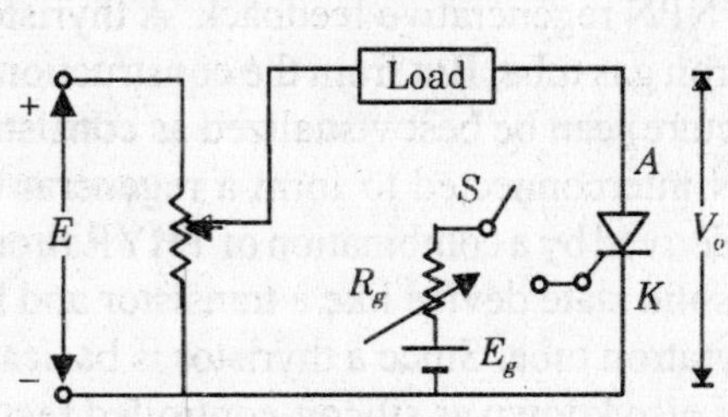


**Fig. 12.2** Elementary circuit

The static V-I characteristics of an SCR is shown in fig 12.3. here $V_a$ is the anode-cathode voltage and $I_a$ is the anode current. The thyristor V-I characteristics is divided into three regions of operation. They are described below.

### *Reverse Blocking Region*

When the cathode is made positive with respect to anode with respect to anode when the switch $S$ is open, the thyristor becomes reverse biased. In the reverse biased condition, the outer junction $J_1$ and $J_3$ are reverse biased and the middle junction $J_2$ is forward biased. The device behaves as if two diodes are connected in series with reverse voltage applied across them. Therefore, only a small leakage current (in mA) flows. If the reverse voltage is increased, then at a critical voltage called reverse breakdown voltage $V_{BR}$, an avalanche will occur at $J_1$ and $J_3$ and the reverse current increases rapidly. A large current associated with $V_{BR}$ gives rise to more losses in the SCR. This may lead to thyristor damage as the junction temperature may exceed its permissible temperature rise. The SCR in reverse blocking may treated as a open switch because it offers very high impedance.

The inner two regions of the SCR are lightly doped compared to the outer two layers. Hence, the thickness of $J_2$ depletion layer during the forward biased condition will be greater than the total thickness of the two depletion layers at $J_1$ and $J_3$ when the device is reverse biased. Therefore, the forward break-over voltage $V_{B0}$ is generally higher than the reverse break-over voltage $V_{BR}$.

### *Forward Blocking Region*

In this region, the anode is made positive with respect to the cathode, with gate circuit open junctions $J_1$ and $J_3$ are forward biased while the junction $J_2$ remains reverse biased. In this mode, a small current called forward leakage current flows as shown in fig 12.3. in this case the forward voltage is increased, then the reverse biased junction $J_2$ will have an avalanche breakdown at a voltage called forward breakover voltage $V_{B0}$, SCR offers a high impedance. Therefore, a thyristor can be treated as an open switch even in the forward blocking mode.

### *Forward Conduction Mode*

A thyristor is brought from forward blocking mode to forward conduction mode by turning it on by exceeding the forward break-over voltage or by applying a gate pulse between gate and cathode. In this mode, thyristor is in on-state and behaves like a closed switch. Voltage drop across thyristor in the on state is of the order of 1 to 2 V depending on the rating of SCR. In conduction mode, anode current is limited by load impedance alone as voltage drop across SCR is quite small. This small voltage drop $V_T$ across the device is due to ohmic drop in the four layers.

### *Latching Current*

It is defined as the minimum value of anode current, which it must attain during turn-on process to maintain conduction when gate signal is removed.

### *Holding Current*

It is defined as the minimum value of anode current below which it must fall for turning off the thyristor.

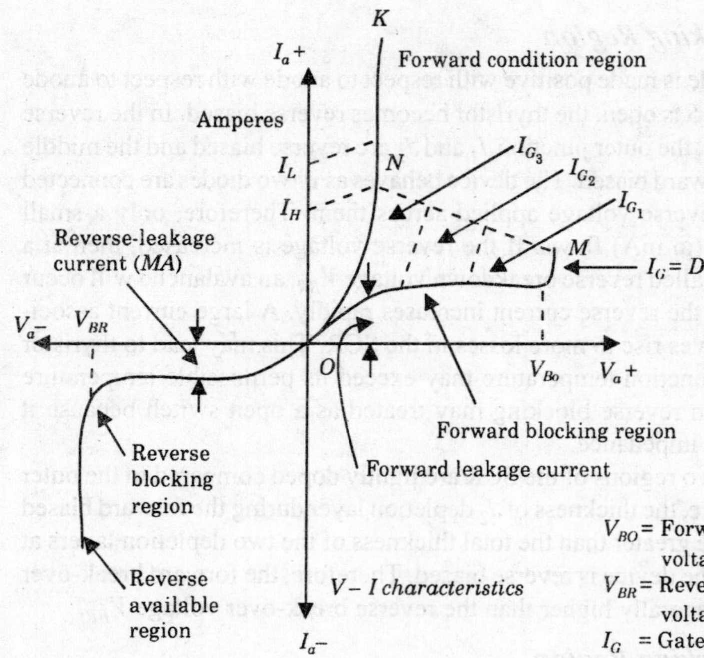


$V_{BO}$ = Forward breakover voltage
$V_{BR}$ = Reverse breakover voltage
$I_G$ = Gate current
$I_L$ = Latching current
$I_H$ = Holding current

**Fig. 12.3**

Generally, the latching current is higher than the holding current. Note that, latching current is associated with turn-on process and holding current with turn-off process. Latching current is two to three times the holding current.

## 12.3.2 Switching Characteristics of Thyristors

Switching characteristics are also known as dynamic or transient characteristics. The static characteristics give no indication as to the speed at which the SCR is capable of being switched from the line forward blocking voltage to the conducting state and vice versa. However, the transition from one state to another state does not take place instantaneously, and it occupies a finite period of time, and this is shown in Fig. 12.4.

During turn-on and turn-off process, a thyristor is subjected to different voltages across it and different currents through it. The time variations of the voltage across a thyristor and the current through it during turn-on and turn-off process give the dynamic or switching characteristics of a thyristor.

### *12.3.2.1 Switching Characteristics During Turn-on*

A forward-biased thyristor is usually turned on by applying a positive gate voltage between gate and cathode. Turn-on time can be divided into three intervals.

(i) delay time $t_d$ (ii) rise time $t_r$ (iii) spread time $t_p$.

*(i) Delay time ($t_d$):* The delay time td is measured from the instant at which gate current reaches 0.9 $I_g$ to the instant at which anode current reaches 0.1 $I_a$. here $I_g$ and $I_a$ are respectively the final values of gate current and anode currents. It can also be defined as the time during which anode voltage falls from $V_a$ to $0.9V_a$ where $V_a$ is initial value of anode voltage, or the another definition is the time during which anode current rises from forward leakage current to 0.1 $I_a$ where $I_a$ is final value of anode current. The delay time can be decreased by applying high gate current and more forward voltage.

*(ii) Rise time ($t_r$):* The rise time $t_r$ is the time taken by the anode current to rise $0.1I_a$ to 0.9 $I_a$. It can also be defined as the time required for the forward blocking off-state voltage to fall from 0.9 to 0.1 of its initial value of 0A. The rise time is inversely proportional to the magnitude of gate current and its build up rate, thus $t_r$ can be reduced if high and steep current pulses are applied to the gate.

During the rise time, turn-on losses in the thyristor are the highest due to high anode voltage ($V_a$) and large anode current ($I_a$) occurring together in the thyristor as shown in fig. 12.4.

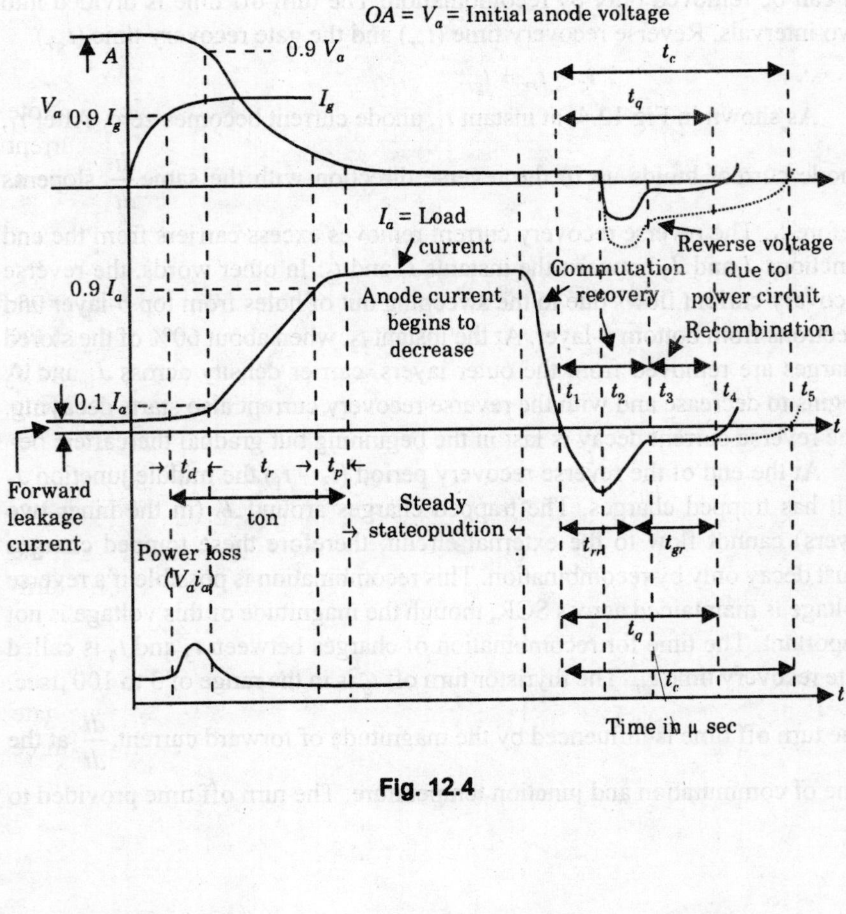


Fig. 12.4

*(iii) Spread time $t_p$:* The spread time is the time taken by anode current to rise from $0.9I_a$ to $I_a$. it is also defined as the time for the forward blocking voltage to fall from 0.1 of its value to the on-state voltage drop. During this time, conduction spreads over the entire cross-section of the cathode of SCR.

#### 12.3.2.2 Switching Characteristics During Turn-off

Thyristor turn-off means that it has changed from on to off state and is capable of blocking the forward voltage. Once, the thyristor is on, gate losses control. The SCR can be turned off by reducing the anode current below latching current. If the forward voltage is applied to the SCR at the moment its anode current falls to zero, the device will not be able to block this forward voltage as the carriers in the four layers are still favourable for conduction. The device will therefore go into conduction immediately even though gate signal is not applied. In order to safe turn off, it is essential that the thyristor is reverse biased for a finite period after the anode current has reached zero.

The turn off time $t_2$ of a thyristor is defined as the time between the instant anode current becomes zero and the instant SCR regains forward blocking capability. During $t_2$, all the excess carriers from the four layers of SCR must be removed. This removal of excess carriers consists of sweeping out of holes from outer *p*-layer and electrons from outer n-layer. The carriers around junction $J_2$ can be removed only by recombination. The turn-off time is divided into two intervals. Reverse recovery time ($t_{rr}$) and the gate recovery time ($t_{gr}$)

$$\therefore \qquad t_q = t_{rr} + t_{gr}.$$

As shown in Fig 12.4, at instant $t_1$, anode current becomes zero. After $t_1$, anode current builds up in the reverse direction with the same $\frac{di}{dt}$ slope as before $t_1$. The reverse recovery current removes excess carriers from the end junctions $J_1$ and $J_3$ between the instants $t_1$ and $t_3$. In other words, the reverse recovery current flows due to the sweeping out of holes from top *p*-layer and electrons from bottom *n*-layer. At the instant $t_2$, when about 60% of the stored charges are removed from the outer layers, carrier density across $J_1$ and $J_3$ begins to decrease and with the reverse recovery current also starts decaying. The reverse current decay is fast in the beginning but gradual thereafter.

At the end of the reverse recovery period ($t_3 - t_1$) the middle junction $J_2$ still has trapped charges. The trapped charges around $J_2$ (in the inner two layers) cannot flow to the external circuit, therefore these trapped charges must decay only by recombination. This recombination is possible if a reverse voltage is maintained across SCR, though the magnitude of this voltage is not important. The time for recombination of charges between $t_3$ and $t_4$ is called gate recovery time $t_{gr}$. The thyristor turn off $t_q$ is in the range of 3 to 100 μsec. The turn off time is influenced by the magnitude of forward current, $\frac{di}{dt}$ at the time of commutation and junction temperature. The turn off time provided to the thyristor by the practical circuit is called circuit turn off time $t_c$. time $t_c$ must be greater than $t_q$ for reliable turn off.

### 12.3.3 Two-Transistor Model of a Thyristor

The operation of an SCR can be explained in a very simple way by considering it in terms of two transistors. This is known as the two transistor analogy of SCR.

The SCR can be considered as an '*npn*' and a '*pnp*' transistor, where the collector of one transistor is attached to the base of the other and vice versa as shown in Fig 12.5. this model is obtained by splitting the two middle layers of the SCR into two separate parts.

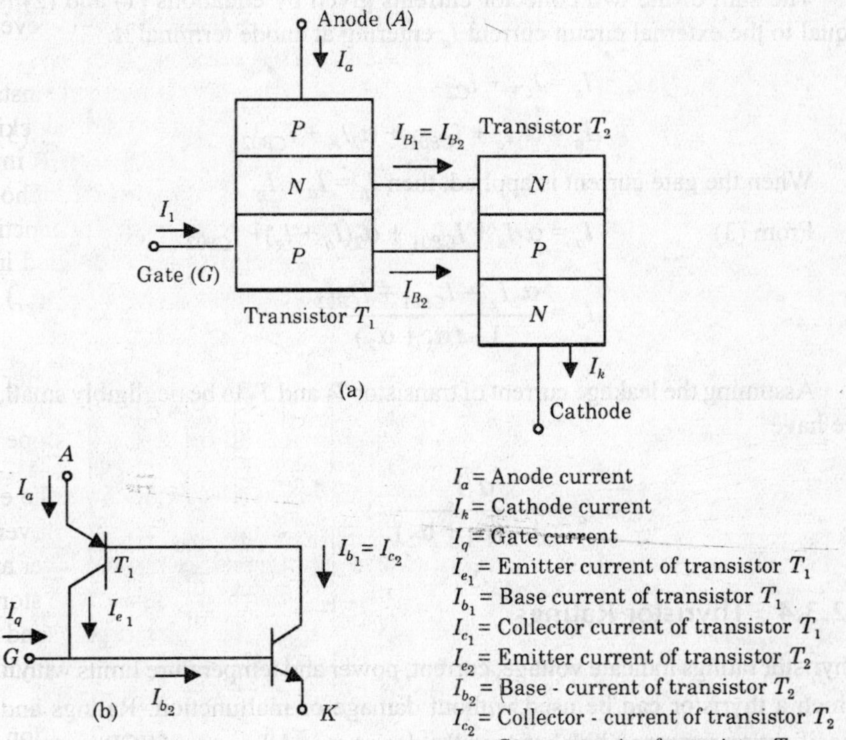


**Fig. 12.5**

In the off-state of a transistor collector current $I_c$ is related to emmitter current $I_E$ as $I_C = \alpha I_E + I_{CB0}$. Where $\alpha$ is the common-base current gain and $I_{CB0}$ is the common-base leakage current of collector-base junction of a transistor. For transistor $T$, in the Fig 12.5, emitter current $I_E$ is anode current $I_a$ and $I_C$ is collector current $I_{CI}$.

$\therefore \quad I_{C1} = \alpha_1 I_a + I_{CB01}$ ...(1)

where $\alpha_1$ = common-base current gain of $T_1$.

$I_{CB01}$ = common-base leakage current of $T_1$.

Similarly for transistor $T_2$, the collector current $I_{C2}$ is given by

$$I_{C2} = \alpha_2 I_K + I_{CB02} \quad ...(2)$$

where $\alpha_2$ = common-base current gain of $T_2$.

$I_{CB01}$ = common-base leakage current of $T_2$.

$I_K$ = emmiter-current of $T_2$.

The sum of the two collector currents given by equations (1) and (2) is equal to the external circuit current $I_a$ entering at anode terminal $A$.

$$\therefore \quad I_a = I_{C1} + I_{C2}$$

$$I_a = \alpha_1 I_a + I_{CB01} + \alpha_2 I_K + I_{CB02} \quad ...(3)$$

When the gate current is applied, then $I_K = I_a + I_g$.

From (3) $\quad I_a = \alpha_1 I_a + I_{CB01} + \alpha_2 (I_a + I_g) + I_{CB02}$

$$\therefore \quad I_a = \frac{\alpha_2 I_g + I_{CB01} + I_{CB02}}{1 - (\alpha_1 + \alpha_2)}$$

Assuming the leakage current of transistor $T_1$ and $T_2$ to be negligibly small, we have

$$\therefore \quad I_a = \frac{\alpha_2 I_g}{1 - (\alpha_1 + \alpha_2)}$$

### 12.3.4 Thyristor Ratings

Thyristor ratings indicate voltage, current, power and temperature limits within which a thyristor can be used without damage or malfunction. Ratings and specification serve as a link between the designer and the user of SCR systems.

A thyristor has several ratings such as voltage, current, power, *dv/dt*, *di/dt*, turn-on time, turn- off time etc. For correct application of the device in thyristor circuits, knowledge of these ratings is desirable,

#### *12.3.4.1 Anode Voltage Ratings*

The anode voltage rating indicate the values of maximum voltages that a thyristor can with stand a breakdown of the junction area with gate circuit open. The different anode voltage ratings are as under:

*(i) $V_{DWM}$ – peak working forward-blocking voltage:* It specifies the maximum forward-blocking voltage that a thyristor can withstand during its working.

*(ii) $V_{DRM}$ – Peak repetitive forward blocking voltage:* It refers to the peak transient voltage that a thyristor can withstand repeatedly or periodically in its forward blocking mode. This rating is specified at a maximum allowable junction temperature with gate circuit open.

*(iii) $V_{DSM}$ – peak surge (non-repetitive) forward-blocking voltage:* It refers to the peak value of the forward voltage that does not repeat. Its value is about 130% of $V_{DRM}$, but $V_{DSM}$ is less than forward breakover voltage $V_{BO}$.

*(iv) $V_{RWM}$ – peak working reverse voltage:* It is the maximum reverse voltage that a thyristor can withstand repeatedly. It is equal to the peak negative value of a sine voltage wave.

*(v) $V_{RRM}$ – peak repetitive reverse voltage:* It specifies the peak reverse transient voltage that may occur repeatedly in the reverse direction at the allowable maximum junction temperature.

*(vi) $V_{RSM}$ – peak non repitive reverse voltage:* It represents the peak value of the reverse surge voltage that does not repeat. Its value is about 130% of $V_{RMM}$. But $V_{RSM}$ is less than reverse breakover voltage $V_{BR}$.

*(vii) forward dv/dt rating:* The *dv/dt* rating of a thyristor indictaes the maximum rate of rise of anode voltage that will not trigger the device without any gate signal. If the rate of rise of forward voltage is higher than the specified maximum value it may cause switching from the OFF-state to the ON-state. When the voltage across the device is increased charges flow through it in a manner analogous to the charging current of a capacitor (I = C *dv/dt*). The greater the rate of rise of applied voltage the greater will be this flow of charges.

The *dv/dt* rating also depends on the junction temperature higher the junction temperature lower the *dv/dt* of the device. Since the *dv/dt* triggering causes random turn-on of a thyristor, it is never employed practically.

### 12.3.4.2 Current Ratings

The current carrying ability of the thyristor is determined by the temperature at this junction. Even for short over currents, the junction temperature may exceed the rated value and the device may be damaged. As the junction temperature is dependent on the current handled by a thyristor, a correct choice of current ratings is essential for a long working life of device.

*(i) Average on the state current ($I_{TAV}$):* As the forward voltage drop across conducting SCR is very low, the power loss in an SCR depends mainly on forward average on state current $I_{TAV}$. The average current rating of a phase controlled thyristor results in different conduction angles. If the same average current is permitted for different conduction angles the instantaneous current increases with the decrease in conduction angle.

The current rating is of repetitive type and is specified at the maximum junction temperature. This rating varies with the case temperature.

*(ii) RMS on state current ($I_{RMS}$):* The RMS current rating can be of importance when applying thyristors to high peak current, low duty cycle waveforms. Although, the average value of the waveform may be well within ratings, it may be that the allowable RMS rating is being exceeded. In order to prevent excessive heating in resistive elements of a thyristor, such as mettalic joints, leads and interfaces, the RMS value is given by manufacturers. This current rating is also of repitive type and is specified at the maximum junction temperature.

*(iii) Surge current rating ($I_{TSM}$):* When an SCR is working within its repetitive voltages and current ratings, its permissible junction temperature is never exceeded. However, a thyristor may be subjected to abnormal operating conditions due to faults or short circuits. The surge current rating indicates the maximum possible non repetitive or surge current, the device can withstand and this may occur due to non-repetitive faults or short-circuits during the life-span of a thyristor.

The subcycle surge current rating $I_{sub}$ can be determined by equating the energies involved in one cycle surge and one subcycle surge as follows.

$$I_{sub}^2 \, t = I^2 \, T.$$

$$I_{sub} = I\sqrt{\frac{T}{t}}$$

Where $T$ = time for one half-cycle of supply frequency (sec).

$I$ = one cycle surge rating (A).

$I_{sub}$ = sub cycle surge current rating(A).

$t$ = duration of sub cycle surge (sec).

*$I^2t$ rating:* $I^2t$ is the maximum allowable non-recurring value of the square of the instantaneous current integrated with respect to time. This rating is required to coordinate with the fast acting fuse for protecting the device during an overload or fault conditions. This rating is the measure of the thermal energy that the device can absorb for a short time before the fault is cleared by the fuse.

*di/dt rating:* The *di/dt* rating of a thyristor indicates the maximum rate of rise in anode current to cathode current. The maximum rate of change of current that the device can with stand during its ON state is called its critical rate of rise of current. The value of a critical rate of rise in current for a particular device is always specified at its highest value of junction temperature that it can safely bear. If the rate of rise in anode current is very rapid compared to the spreading velocity of carriers across the junctions during the turn-on period, the local hot spot heating occurs due to high current density in the junction regions. This increases the junction temperature beyond the safe limit and the device may be damaged.

## Applications

1. In phase controlled rectifiers.
2. In subway cars, trolley buses, battery-operated vehicles, battery-chargings etc.
3. In adjustable-speed ac drivers, induction heating, stand by air craft power supplies, ups for computers, HVDC, transmission lines etc.
4. As AC voltage controllers for domestic and industrial heating, transformer tap changing, lighting control, speed control of 1ϕ and 3ϕ AC drivers and starting of induction motors.
5. As cyclo converters in speed control of high power AC drivers, induction heating, static VAR generation, for converting variable speed alternator voltage to constant frequency output voltage for use as power supply in aircrafts or shipboards.

## 12.4 DIAC

The term Diac is obtained from capital leters, Diode that can work on AC. Diac is a two terminal, bi directional avalanche diode which can be switched from the off state to the on state for either polarity of applied voltage. The Schematic construction, voltage-current characteristics and circuit symbol of the Diac are shown in Fig. 12.6. It can be observed that the two leads are labelled as Terminals $T_1$ and $T_2$ instead of the conventional anode-cathode notation.

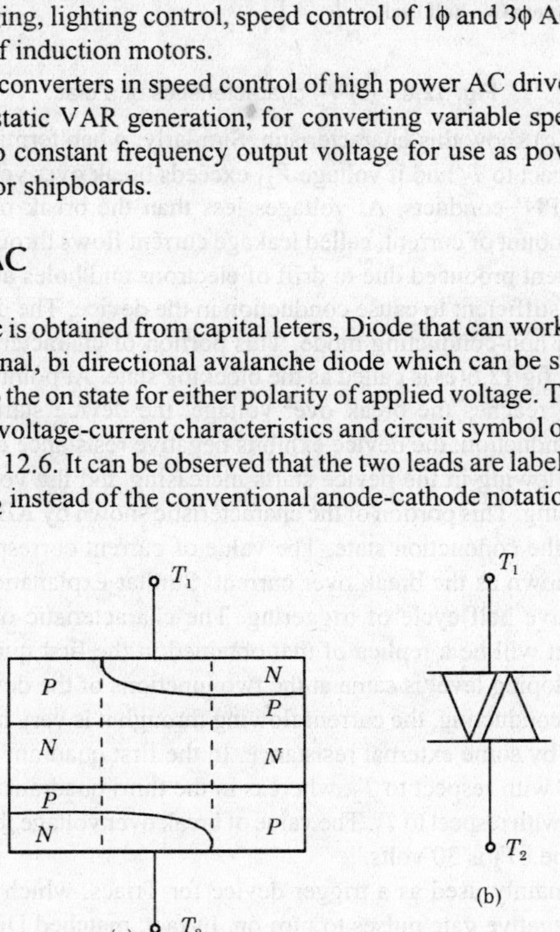


**Fig. 12.6** (a) schematic construction (b) circuit symbol

Conduction occurs in the diac when the break over voltage is reached in either polarity across the two terminals. When $T_1$ is positive with respect to $T_2$ and if voltage $V_{12}$ exceeds $V_{B01}$, then the structure PNPN conducts. The curve

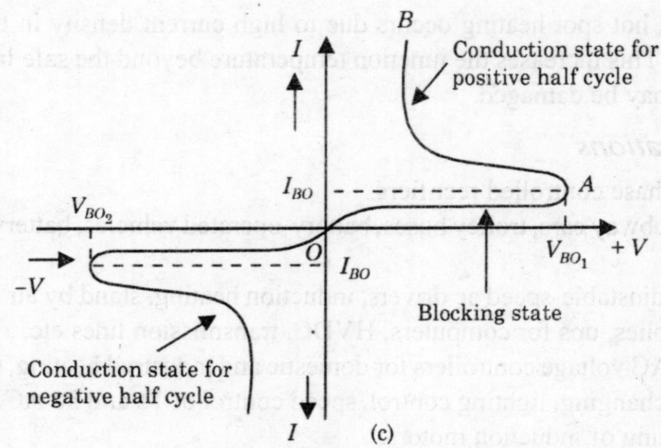


**Fig. 12.6** (c) V-I characteristics of a diac.

in Fig. 12.6 (c) show this characteristic. Similarly, when terminal $T_2$ is positive with respect to $T_1$ and if voltage $V_{21}$ exceeds break over voltage $V_{B02}$, the structure PNPN' conducts. At voltages less than the break over voltage, a very small amount of current, called leakage current flows through the device. Leakage current produced due to drift of electrons and holes at the depletion region is not sufficient to cause conduction in the device. The device remains practically in non-conducting mode. This portion of characteristic shown in region OA in fig 12.6(c) is called as the blocking state. At point 'A', when the voltage level reaches the break over voltage, the device starts conducting. During its conduction, the device exhibits negative resistance characteristics. The current flowing in the device starts increasing and the voltage across it starts decreasing. This portion of the characteristic shown by AB in Fig 12.6(c) is known as the conduction state. The value of current corresponding to the point A is known as the break over current. Similar explanation holds good for the negative half cycle of triggering. The characteristic obtained in the third quadrant will be a replica of that obtained in the first quadrant. This is because the doping level is same at the two junctions of the device. Once the device starts conducting, the current flowing through it is very high which has to be limited by some external resistance. In the first quadrant characteristic, $T_1$ is positive with respect to $T_2$, whereas in the third quadrant characteristic, $T_2$ is positive with respect to $T_1$. The value of break over voltage for a commonly used Diac type $\delta T_2$ is 30 volts.

Diac is mainly used as a trigger device for Triacs, which require either positive or negative gate pulses to turn on. In fact, matched Diac-Triac pairs are available in the market for various types of control circuits.

## 12.5 TRIAC

An SCR is a unidirectional device as it can conduct from anode to cathode only and not from cathode to anode. A triac can conduct in both the directions.

A triac is thus a bi directional thyristor with three terminals. It is used extensively for the control of power in ac circuits. Triac is the word derived by combining the capital letters from the words TRIode and AC. When in operation, a triac is equivalent to two SCRs connected in anti parallel. The circuit symbol and its characteristics are shown in Fig. 12.7.

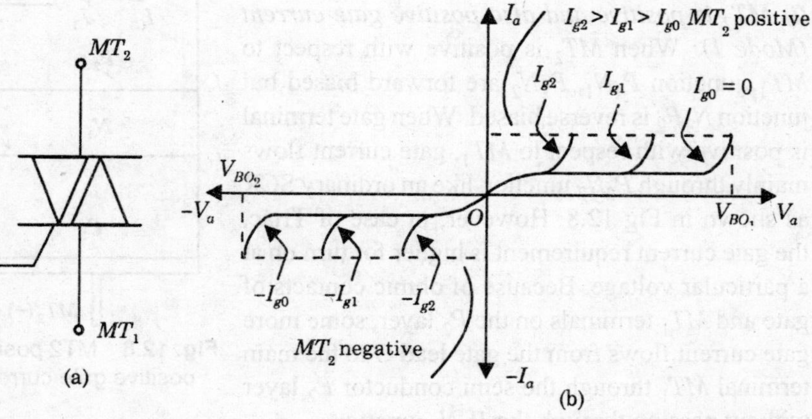


**Fig. 12.7** (a) Circuit symbol (b) static V-I characteristics of a triac

As the triac can conduct in both the directions, the term anode and cathode are not applicable to triac. Its three terminals are usually designated as $MT_1$ (Main Terminal 1), $MT_2$ (Main Terminal 2) and the gate $G$. The gate is near terminal $MT_1$. The first quadrant is the region wherein $MT_2$ is positive with respect to $MT_1$ and vice versa for the third quadrant.

Depending upon the polarity of gate pulse and biasing conditions, the main four layer structure that turns on by a regenerative process could be one of $P_1N_1$, $P_2N_2$, $P_1N_1N_2N_3$ or $P_2N_1P_1N_4$ as shown in Fig 12.8.

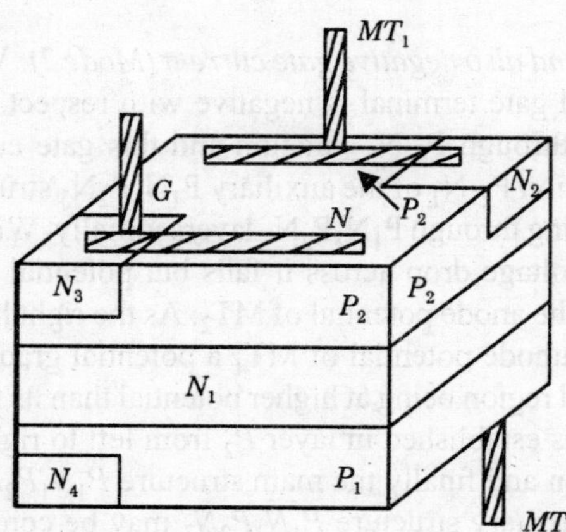


**Fig. 12.8** Cross-sectional view of a triac

### 12.5.1 Triggering Modes of Triac

The Triac can be turned on with positive or negative gate current keeping the $MT_2$ terminal at positive or negative potential. The turn on process of a triac can be explained as below:

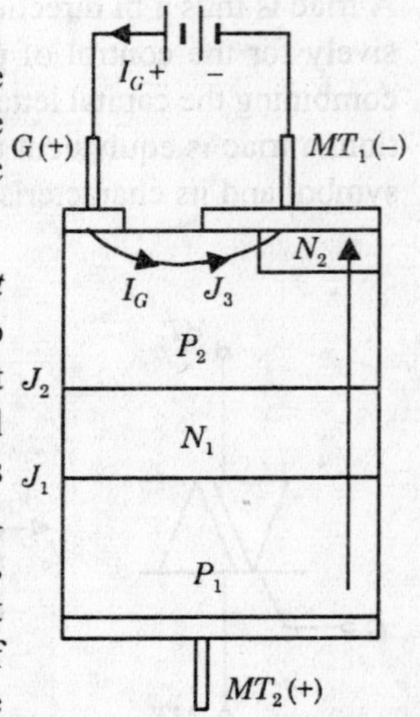


**Fig. 12.8** MT2 positive, positive gate current

*(i) $MT_2$ is positive and also positive gate current (Mode 1):* When $MT_2$ is positive with respect to $MT_1$, junction $P_1N_1$, $P_2N_2$ are forward biased but junction $N_1P_2$ is reverse biased. When gate terminal is positive with respect to $MT_1$, gate current flows mainly through $P_2N_2$ junction like an ordinary SCR as shown in Fig 12.8. However, in case of Triac, the gate current requirement is higher for turn on at a particular voltage. Because of ohmic contacts of gate and $MT_1$ terminals on the $P_2$ layer, some more gate current flows from the gate lead $G$ to the main terminal $MT_1$ through the semi conductor $P_2$ layer without passing through the $P_2N_2$ junction.

When gate current has injected sufficient charge into $P_2$ layer, the $P_2$ layer is flooded with Electrons when the gate current flows across the $P_2$-$N_2$ junction. These electrons diffuse to the edge of the Junction $J_2$, and are collected by the $N_1$ layer. Therefore, the electrons build a space charge in the $N_1$ region and more holes from $P_1$ diffuse into $N_1$ to neutralize the negative space charge. These holes arrive at the junction $J_2$. They produce a positive space charge in the $P_2$ region which results in more Electrons being injected from $N_2$ into $P_2$. This results in positive regeneration and ultimately the structure $P_1N_1$ $P_2N_2$ conducts the external current. The device is more sensitive in this mode. It is recommended method of triggering of the conduction is desired in the first quadrant.

*(ii) $MT_2$ is positive and also negative gate current (Mode 2):* When the terminal $MT_2$ is positive and gate terminal is negative with respect to terminal $MT_1$, gate current flows through $P_2$-$N_3$ junction and this gate current $I_G$ forward biases the gate junction $P_2$-$N_1$ of the auxiliary $P_1N_1P_2N_3$ structure. As a result, Triac starts conducting through $P_1N_1P_2N_3$ layers initially. With the conduction of $P_1N_1P_2N_3$, the voltage drop across it falls but potential of layer between $P_2N_3$ rises towards the anode potential of $MT_2$. As the right hand portion of $P_2$ is clamped at the cathode potential of $MT_1$ a potential gradient exists across layer $P_2$, its left hand region being at higher potential than its right hand region.

A current is thus established in layer $P_2$ from left to right which forward biased $P_2N_2$ junction and finally the main structure $P_1N_1P_2N_2$ beings to conduct. The device auxiliary structure $P_1N_1P_2N_3$ may be considered as a pilot SCR while the structure $P_1N_1P_2N_2$ may be regarded as the main SCR, both being built in one common structure. The anode current of the pilot SCR serves

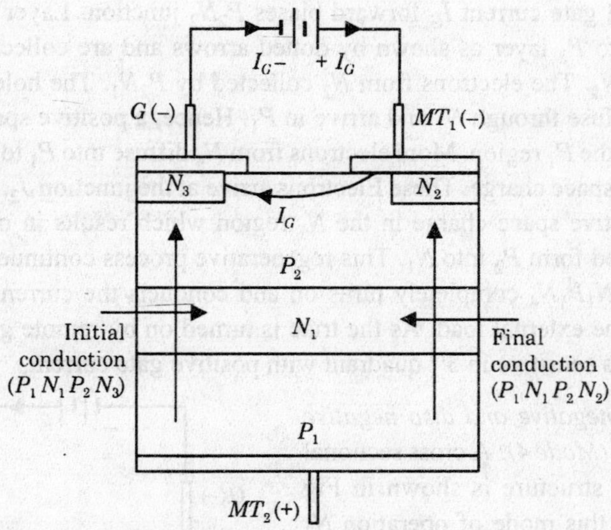


**Fig. 12.9** $MT_2$ positive, negative gate current

as the gate current for the main SCR. As compared with turn on process discussed in (1), the device with $MT_2$ positive but gate current negative is less sensitive and therefore, more gate current is required.

*(iii) $MT_2$ is negative and also positive gate current (Mode 3):* When terminal $MT_2$ is negative and terminal $MT_1$ is positive, the device can be turned on by applying a positive voltage between the gate and terminal $MT_1$. In this mode, the device operates in the third quadrant when it is triggered into conduction. The turnon is initiated by remote gate control. The main structure that leads to turn on is $P_2N_1 P_1N_4$ with $N_2$ acting as a remote gate as shown in Fig. 12.10.

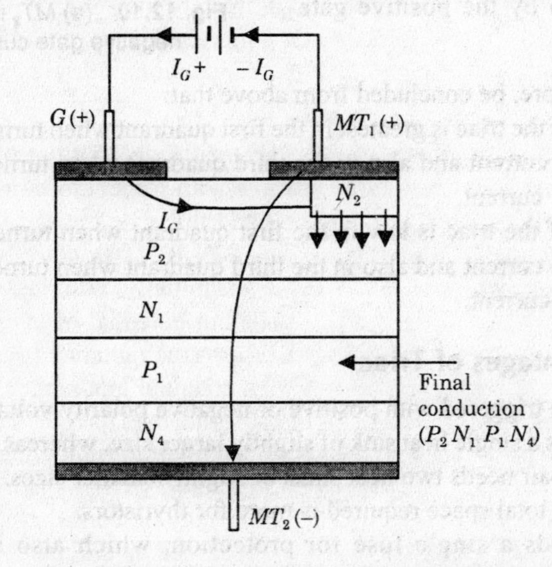


**Fig. 12.10** $MT_2$ negative, positive gate current

The external gate current $I_G$ forward biases $P_2N_2$ junction. Layer $N_2$ injects electrons into $P_2$ layer as shown by dotted arrows and are collected by the junction $P_2N_1$. The electrons from $N_2$ collected by $P_2N_1$. The holes injected from $P_2$, diffuse through $N_1$ and arrive in $P_1$. Hence, a positive space charge builds up in the $P_1$ region. More electrons from $N_4$ diffuse into $P_1$ to neutralize the positive space charge. These Electrons arrive at the junction $J_2$. They produce a negative space charge in the $N_1$ region which results in more holes being injected form $P_2$ into $N_1$. This regenerative process continues until the structure $P_2N_1P_1N_4$ completely turns on and conducts the current which is limited by the external load. As the triac is turned on by remote gate $N_2$ the device is less sensitive in 3rd quadrant with positive gate current.

*(iv) $MT_2$ is negative and also negative gate current (Mode 4):* A cross sectional view of the structure is shown in Fig 12.10(a). In this mode of operation $N_3$ acts as a remote gate. The external gate current $I_G$ forward biases $P_2N_3$ junction and electrons are injected as shown by the dotted arrows. These electrons from $N_3$ collected by $P_2N_1$ cause an increase of current across $P_1N_1$. The structure $P_2N_1$ $P_1N_4$ turns on by the regeneration. The device will turn on due to the increased current in layer $N_1$. The device is more sensitive in this mode compared with the turn on by the positive gate current.

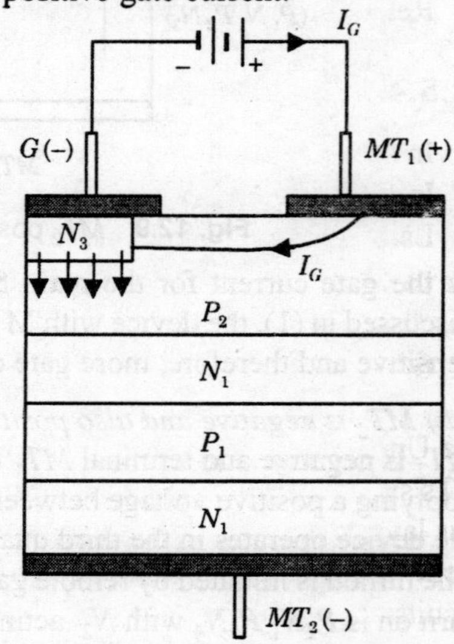


**Fig. 12.10** (a) $MT_2$ negative, negative gate current

It can, therefore, be concluded from above that:

(i) Sensitivity of the triac is greatest in the first quadrant when turned on with positive gate current and also in the third quadrant when turned on with negative gate current.

(ii) Sensitivity of the triac is low in the first quadrant when turned on with negative gate current and also in the third quadrant when turned on with positive gate current.

### 12.5.2 Advantages of Triac

1. Triacs can be triggered with positive or negative polarity voltages.
2. A Triac needs a single heat sink of slightly larger size, whereas anti parallel thyristor pair needs two heat sinks of slightly smaller sizes, but due to the clearance total space required is more for thyristors.
3. A Triac needs a single fuse for protection, which also simplifies construction.

4. In some d.c. applications, SCR is required to be connected with a parallel diode to protect against reverse voltage, whereas a Triac used may work without a diode as safe breakdown in either direction is possible

### 12.5.3 Disadvantes of Triac

1. Triacs have low *dv*/*dt* rating compared to SCRs.
2. SCRs are available in larger rating compared to Triacs.
3. Since a Triac can be triggered in either direction, a trigger circuit with Triac needs careful consideration.
4. Reliability of Triacs is less than of SCRs.

### 12.5.4 Applications

1. In speed controlling of single phase ac series or universal motors.
2. In food mixers and portable drills.
3. Lamp dimming and in heating control.
4. In zero voltage switched ac relay.

## 12.6 UNIJUNCTION TRANSISTOR

The Unijunction Transistor (UJT) is a three terminal, single junction device. UJTs switching voltage can be easily varied by the circuit designer. Like the four layer diode the UJT is always operated as a switch and finds most frequent applications in oscillators, timing circuits and SCR/TRIAC trigger circuits.

### 12.6.1 Basic Operation

A typical UJT structure consists of a lightly doped *N*-type silicon bar provided with ohmic contacts at each end. The two end connections are called base-1 ($B_1$) and base-2 ($B_2$). A small heavily doped p-region is alloyed into one side of the bar closer to $B_2$. This P-region is the UJT emitter (*E*) and forms a P-N junction with the bar.

An interbase resistance ($R_B$) exists between $B_1$ and $B_2$. It is typically between 4KΩ and 10KΩ and can easily be measured with an ohmeter with the emitter open. $R_{BB}$ is essentially the resistance of the *N*-type bar. This interbase resistance can be broken up into two resistances, the resistance from $B_1$ to emitter ($R_{B1}$) and resistance from $B_2$ to emitter ($RB_2$). Since the emitter is closer to $B_2$, the value of $R_{B1}$ is greater than $R_{B2}$.

The UJT's circuit symbol and its equivalent circuit are shown in Fig 12.12. The diode represents the P-N junction between the emitter and the base bar point. The arrow through $R_{B1}$ indicates that it is variable since during normal operation it may typically range from 4kΩ down to 10Ω.

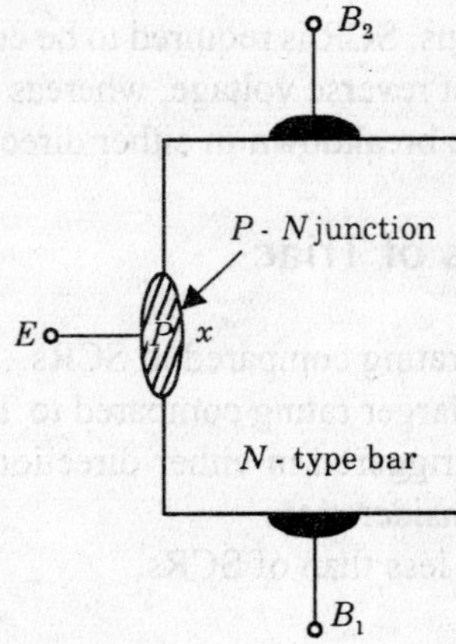


**Fig. 12.11** Basic UJT structure

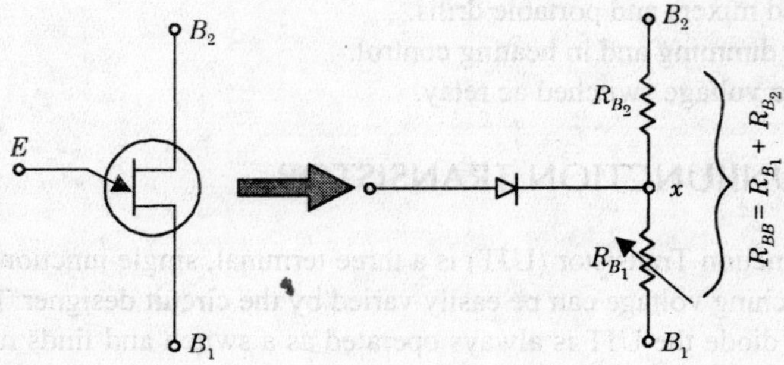


**Fig. 12.12** UJT symbol and equivalent circuit

## 12.6.2 Circuit Operation

The UJT operation can be stated as follows :

(a) When the emitter diode is reverse biased, only a very small emitter current flows. Under this condition, $R_{B1}$ is at its normal high value. This is UJTs "OFF" state.

(b) When the emitter diode becomes forward biased $R_{B1}$ drops to a very low value so that the total resistance between $E$ and $B_1$ becomes very low, allowing emitter current to flow readily. This is the "ON" state.

The UJT is normally operated with both $B_2$ and E biased positive relative to $B_1$ as shown in Fig 12.13 (a). $B_1$ is always the UJT reference terminal and all voltages are measured relative to $B_1$. The $V_{BB}$ source is generally fixed and provides a constant voltage from $B_2$ to $B_1$. The VEE source is generally a variable voltage and is considered the input to the circuit. The UJT's $V_E$-$I_E$ curve is shown in Fig 12.13(b).

### *The "Off" State*

When a voltage $V_{BB}$ is applied across the two base terminals $B_1$ and $B_2$ the potential of point $x$ with respect to $B_1$ is given by

$$V_x = \frac{V_{BB}}{RB_1 + RB_{k2}} .* RB_1 = \eta V_{BB}$$

where η(eta) = $\frac{R_{B1}}{R_{B1} + R_{B2}}$ is called the intrinsic stand off ratio. Typical values of are 0.51 to 0.82.

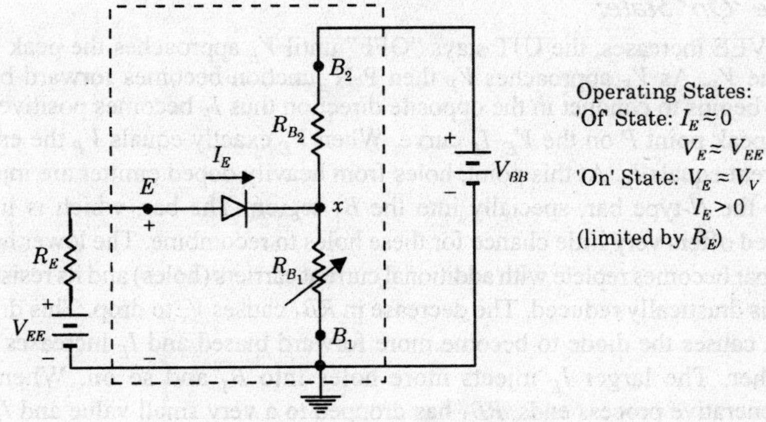


**Fig. 12.13 (a)** Equivalent circuit ofr UJT analysis

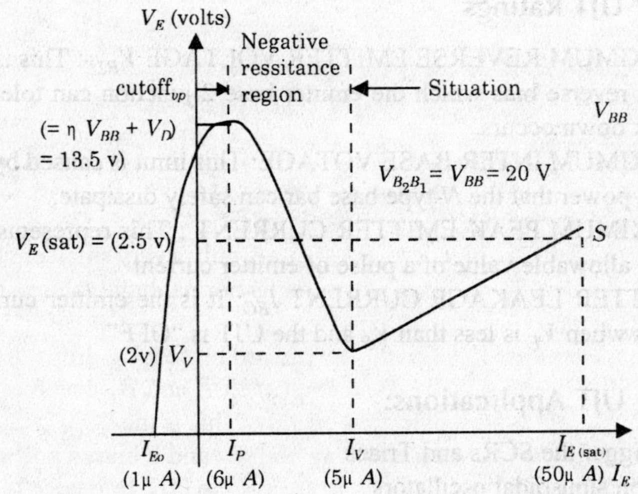


**Fig. 12.13 (b)** Typical UJT V-I characteristic curve

The $V_{EE}$ source is applied to the emitter which is the P-side. Thus the emitter diode will be reverse biased as long as $V_{EE}$ is less than $V_x$. This is "OFF" state and is shown on the $V_E$-$I_E$ curve as being a very low current region. In the "OFF" the UJT has a very high resistance between $E$ and $B_1$ and

$I_E$ is usually a negligible reverse leakage current. With no $I_E$, the drop across $R_E$ is zero and the emitter voltage equals the source voltage.

The UJT "OFF" state, as shown on the $V_E - I_E$ curve, actually extends to the point where the emitter voltage exceeds $V_x$ by the diode threshold voltage($V_d$), which is needed to produce forward current through the diode. The emitter voltage and this point $p$ is called the peak point voltage $V_p$ and is given by $V_p = V_x + V_D = \eta V_{BB} + V_D$ where $V_D$ is typically 0.5v.

### *The 'On' State:*

As VEE increases, the UJT stays "OFF" until $V_E$ approaches the peak point value $V_P$. As $V_E$ approaches $V_P$ then P-N junction becomes forward biased and begins to conduct in the opposite direction thus $I_E$ becomes positive near the peak point $P$ on the $V_E$–$I_E$ curve. When $V_E$ exactly equals $V_P$ the emitter current equals $I_P$. At this point, holes from heavily doped emitter are injected into the *N*-type bar, specially into the $B_1$ region. The bar, which is lightly doped offers very little chance for these holes to recombine. The lower half of the bar becomes replete with additional current carriers (holes) and its resistance *RB* is drastically reduced. The decrease in $RB_1$ causes $V_x$ to drop. This drop in turn causes the diode to become more forward biased and $I_E$ increases even further. The larger $I_E$ injects more holes into $B_1$ and so on. When this regenerative process ends, $RB_1$ has dropped to a very small value and $I_E$ can become very large limited mainly by external resistance $R_E$.

## 12.6.3 UJT Ratings

(a) MAXIMUM REVERSE EMITTER VOLTAGE $V_{B2E}$: This is the maximum reverse bias which the emitter base 2 junction can tolerate before break down occurs.

(b) MAXIMUM INTER BASE VOTAGE: This limit is caused by the maximum power that the *N*-type base bar can safely dissipate.

(c) MAXIMUM PEAK EMITTER CURRENT : This represents the maximum allowable value of a pulse of emitter current

(d) EMITTER LEAKAGE CURRENT $I_{EO}$: It is the emitter current which flows when $V_E$ is less than $V_P$ and the UJT is "OFF".

## 12.6.4 UJT Applications:

1. To trigger the SCRs and Triacs
2. As non sinusoidal oscillators
3. In saw tooth generators
4. Phase control and timing circuits.

### *UJT Relaxation Oscillator:*

Since the UJT exhibits negative resistance characteristics it can be used as a relaxation oscillator. The Unijunction Transistor is a highly efficient switch i.e., its switching time is in the range of nano seconds. The relaxation oscillator circuit diagram, its equivalent circuit and voltage wave forms are shown in the Fig. 12.14.

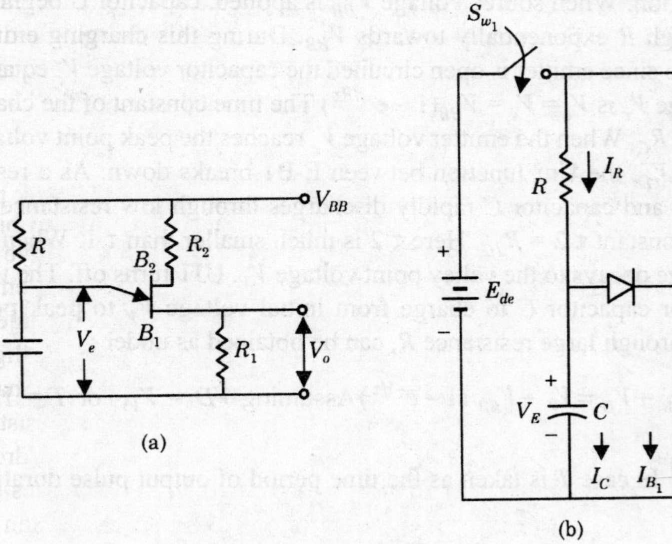


**Fig. 12.14** (a) UJT oscillator (b) Its equivalent circuit

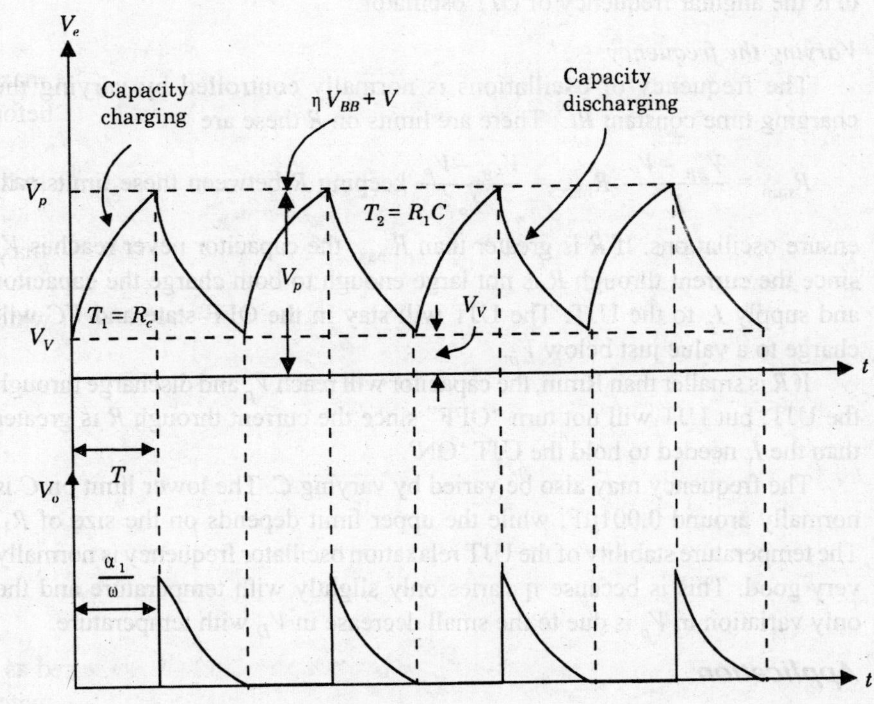


**Fig. 12.14** (c) Voltage waveforms

The External resistances $R_1$ and $R_2$ are small in comparision with the internal resistance $RB_1$ and $RB_2$ of UJT bases the charging resistance $R$ should be such that its load line intersects the device characteristics only in the negative resistance region. When source voltage $V_{BB}$ is applied, capacitor $C$ begins to change through $R$ exponentially towards $V_{BB}$. During this charging emitter current is zero since emitter is open circuited the capacitor voltage $V_c$ equal to emitter votlage $V_c$ is $V_c = V_e = V_{BB}(1 - e^{-t/Rc})$ The time constant of the charge circuit is $\mu_1 = R_C$. When the emitter voltage $V_e$ reaches the peak point voltage, $V_p = \eta V_{BB} + V_D$, the Uni Junction between E-B1 breaks down. As a result, UJT turns on and capacitor $C$ rapidly discharges through low resistance $R1$ with a time constant $\tau\ 2 = R_{IC}$. Here $\tau\ 2$ is much smaller than $\tau\ 1$. When the emitter voltage decays to the valley point voltage $V_V$. UJT turns off. The time $T$ required for capacitor $C$ to charge from initial voltage $V_V$ to peak point voltage $V_P$, through large resistance $R$, can be obtained as under :

$V_p = \eta V_{BB} + V_D = V_V + V_{BB}\ (1 - e^{-1/\tau})$ Assuming $VD = V_V$, or $T = 1/f =$ $RC \ln\left(\frac{1}{1-n}\right)$ In case $T$ is taken as the time period of output pulse duration, then the value of fixing angle $\alpha 1$ is given by $\alpha 1 = \omega T = \omega RC \ln \frac{1}{1-n}$ where $\omega$ is the angular frequency of UJT oscillator.

*Varying the frequency:*

The frequency of oscillations is normally controlled by varying the charging time constant $RC$. There are limits on $R$ these are

$R_{min} = \frac{V_{BB} - V_V}{I_V}$ $R_{max} = \frac{V_{BB} - V_P}{I_P}$ keeping $R$ between these limits will ensure oscillations. If $R$ is greater than $R_{max}$, the capacitor never reaches $V_p$ since the current through $R$ is not large enough to both charge the capacitor and supply $I_p$ to the UJT. The UJT will stay in the OFF state and $VC$ will charge to a value just below $V_p$.

It $R$ is smaller than Rmin, the capacitor will reach $V_p$ and discharge through the UJT, but UJT will not turn "OFF" since the current through $R$ is greater than the $I_v$ needed to hold the UJT 'ON'.

The frequency may also be varied by varying $C$. The lower limit on $C$ is normally around 0.001μF, while the upper limit depends on the size of $R_1$. The temperature stability of the UJT relaxation oscillator frequency is normally very good. This is because $\eta$ varies only slightly with temperature and the only variation in $V_p$ is due to the small decrease in $V_D$ with temperature.

## *Application*

Mainly used for SCR triggering

## 12.7 SOLVED PROBLEMS

**1. For an SCR, the gate-cathode characteristics has a straight line slope of 130. For trigger source voltage of 15V and allowable gate dissipation of 0.5 watts, calculate the gate source resistance.**

**Solution:**

Given $V_g I_g = 0.5\text{W}$

And $\dfrac{v_g}{I_g} = 130$

Therefore $130 I_g^2 = 0.5$

$$I_g = \sqrt{\frac{0.5}{130}} = 0.062 = 63\text{mA}$$

Therefore gate voltage, $V_g = 130 \times 62 \times 1 - 3$ and 8.06V

For the gate circuit $Es = I_g R_s + V_g$

$$15 = 0.062 R_s + 8.06$$

Therefore $R_s = \dfrac{15 - 8.06}{0.062} = 111.94\ \Omega$

**2. Latching current of a thyristor circuit shown in FIG is 50mA. The duration of the firing pulse is 50µs. will the thyristor get fired?**

**Solution:**

When SCR is triggered the current will rise exponentially in the inductive circuit.

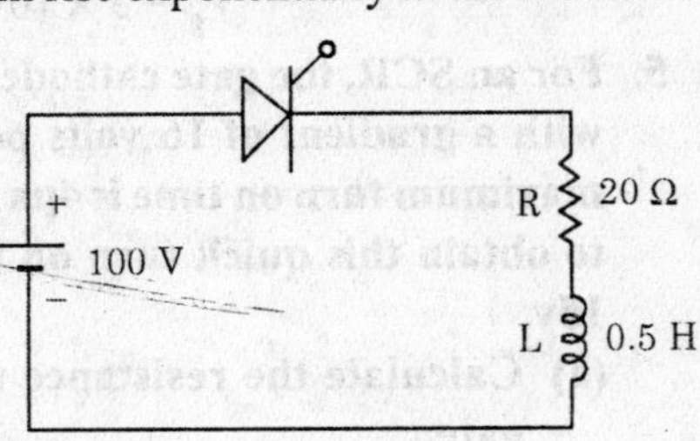


Therefore $i(t) = \dfrac{v}{R}\left(1 - e^{-t/\tau}\right)$ Where

$\tau = \dfrac{L}{R} = \dfrac{0.5}{20} = 0.025$ sec $i(t) = \dfrac{100}{20}\left(1 - e^{-t/0.025}\right)$

Therefore at $t = 50\mu\text{s}$ $i(50\mu\text{s}) = 5\left(1 - e^{-50\times10^{-6}/0.025}\right) = 9.99\text{mA}$

Since the calculated circuit value is less than the given latching current value of SCR, it will not get fired.

**3. If the latching current in the circuit shown in Fig is 4mA, obtain the minimum width of the gating pulse required to properly turn on the SCR**

**Solution:**

The circuit equation is $V = L\frac{di}{dt}$ where '$i$' is the latching current and $t$ is the pulse width

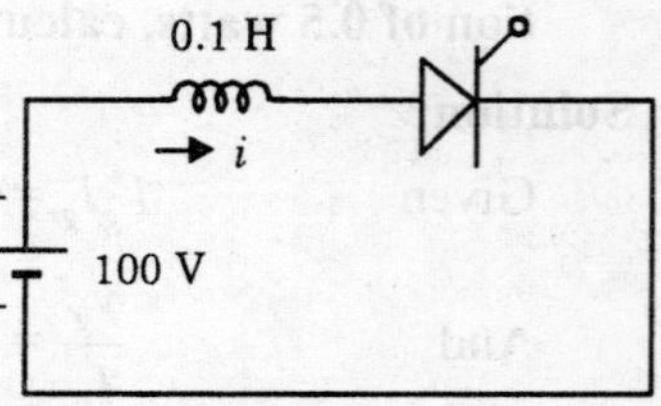


Therefore $dt = \frac{L}{V}$ integrating both

sides $t = \frac{L}{V}i$

$$t_{min} = \frac{0.1}{100} \times 4 \times 10^{-3} \quad t_{min} = 4\mu s$$

**4. If the $V_g - I_g$ characteristics of an SCR is assumed to be a straight line passing through the origin with a gradient of $3 \times 10^3$ calculate the required gate source resistance.**
**Given $E_{gs}$ = 10V and allowable $P_g$ = 0.012 Ω**

**Solution:** The allowable $P_g$ = 0.012 watt

Therefore $\quad V_g I_g = 0.012$

Also $\quad \text{gradient} = \frac{v_g}{I_g} = 3 \times 10^3$

Therefore $\quad V_g = 10^3 \times I_g$

$$3 \times 10^3 \times I_g \times I_g = 0.012$$

$$I_g = 2\text{mA}$$

$$V_g = 3 \times 10^3 \times 2 \times 10^{-3} = 6\text{v}.$$

**5. For an SCR, the gate cathode characteristic is given by a straight line with a gradient of 16 volts per amp passing through the origin, the maximum turn on time is 4μs and the minimum gate current required to obtain this quick turn on is 500 mA. If the gate source voltage is 15v.**

**(a) Calculate the resistance to be connected in series with the SCR gate.**

**(b) Compute the gate power dissipation, given that the pulse width is equal to the turn on time and the average gate power dissipation is 0.3W. Also, compute the maximum triggering frequency that will be possible when pulse firing is used.**

**Solution:**

(a) Given $\quad I_{gmin} = 500\text{mA} = 0.5\text{A}$

$$\frac{V_g}{I_g} = 16\text{v/A}$$

$V_g = 16 \times 0.5 = 8\text{v}$ from fig

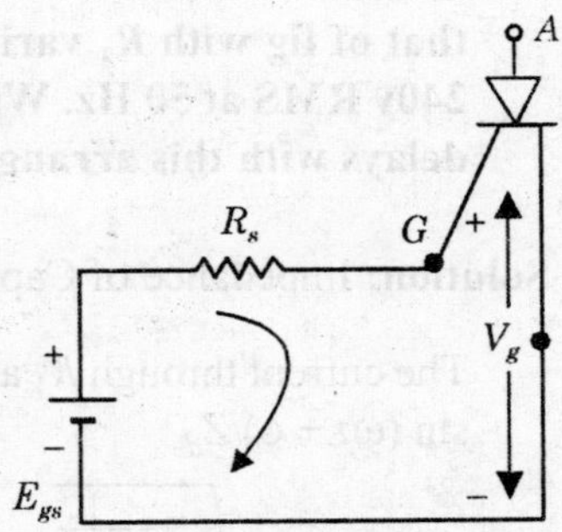


$$R_s = \frac{E_{gs} - V_g}{I_g} = \frac{15-8}{0.5} = 14\Omega$$

(b) power dissipation $P_g = V_g I_g = 8 \times 0.5$
= 4w

$$\text{Now } P_{gmax} = \frac{P_{gav}}{f \,.\, tab} \quad 4 = \frac{0.3\times10^6}{f\times4}$$

$$F = 18.75 \text{ KHz}$$

**6. The capacitance of reverse biased junction $J_2$ in a thyristor is $C_{J2}$ = 20 pF and can be assumed to be independent of the off state voltage. The limiting value of the charging current to turn on the thyristor is 16mA. Determine the critical value of $\frac{dy}{dt}$**

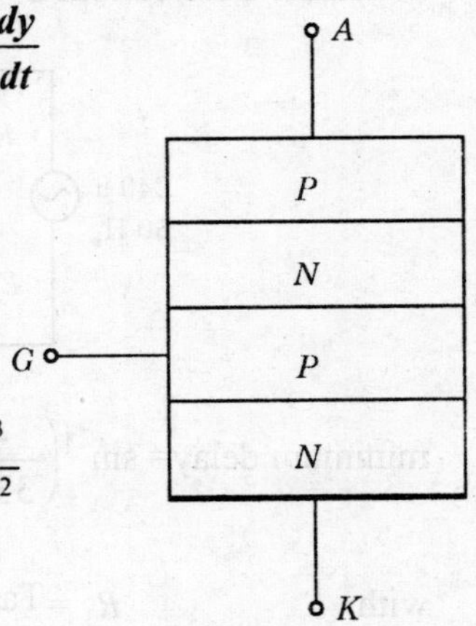


**Solution:**

$$C_{j2} = 20\text{pF}$$

$$i_{j2} = 16\text{mA}$$

$$\text{since } \frac{dCJ_2}{dt} = 0$$

$$\text{The critical value of } \frac{dv}{dt} = \frac{i_{j2}}{c_{j2}} = \frac{16\times10^{-3}}{20\times10^{-12}}$$

= 800v/μs

**7. An SCR has half cycle surge current rating of 3000 A for 50Hz supply. Calculate its one cycle and sub-cycle surge current rating and $I^2t$ rating**

**Solution:**

Let $I$ and $Isb$ be the one cycle and sub cycle surge current raings of the SCR respectively. Then equating the energies involved in them, we get

$$i^2T = i_{sb}^2.t$$

$$i^2 \times \frac{1}{100} = (3000)^2 \times \frac{1}{200}$$

$$I = \frac{200}{\sqrt{2}} = 2121.32\text{A}$$

$$I^2t \text{ rating} = I_{\text{rms}}^2 \times \frac{1}{2f} = \left(\frac{3000}{\sqrt{2}}\right)^2 \times \frac{1}{100} = 45000\ Amp^2 \text{ sec}$$

**8. A Diac with a breakdown voltge of 40V is used in a circuit such as that of fig with $R_1$ variable from 1kΩ to 25KΩ, C = 470nF, and E = 240v RMS at 50 Hz. What will be the maximum and minimum firing delays with this arrangement.**

**Solution:** Impedance of Capacitor $= \dfrac{1}{\omega c} = 6773\Omega$

The current through $R_1$ and when the Diac is not conducting is $I_d = 240\sqrt{2}$ sin $(\omega t + \phi)/Z_d$

Where $Z_d = \sqrt{R_1^{2} + \frac{1}{\omega^2 c^2}}$ $\phi = Tan^{-1}\left(\dfrac{1}{\omega RC}\right)$ with $R_1 = 1000\Omega$, $Z_d = 6846\Omega$.

The voltage across the capacitor is given by $V_c = I_d Z_c$

$$V_c = 335.8 \sin(\omega t - 8.40)$$

When the Diac conducts $Vc = 40$V.

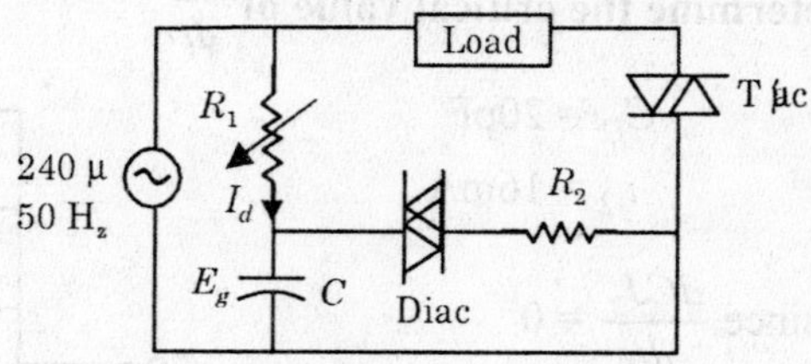


$$\text{minimum delay} = \sin^{-1}\left(\frac{40}{335.8}\right) + 8.40 = 15.24°$$

with $\qquad R_1 = \text{Tan}^{-1}\left(\dfrac{1}{\omega RC}\right)$

with $\qquad R_1 = 25\text{k}\Omega,\ Z_d = 25{,}901\Omega$

The voltage across the capacitor is $I_d - Z_c$ as before $V_c = 8.76$ sin $(\omega t - 74.84)$ When the Diac conducts $V_c = 40$/v Hence, maximum delay =

$$\sin^{-1}\left(\frac{40}{88.6}\right) + 74.84 = 101.6°$$

**9. If $R_E$ = 1kΩ and $I_V$ = 5mA, determine the value of $V_{EE}$ which will cause the UJT to turn 'OFF"**

**Solution:**

At the valley point $V_E = V_V = 2$v and $I_E + I_V = 5$mA

$$V_{EE} = I_E R_E + V_E = 7\text{v}.$$

is the value of $V_{EE}$ below which the UJT will switch back to the "OFF" state.

**10. Derive the expression for periodic time $T = Rc\left(\frac{1}{1-\eta}\right)$ of the UJT relaxation oscillator.**

**Solution:**

Voltage across the capacitor is given by $V_P = V_{BB}\,(1 - e^{-t/Rc})$

When $V_p = \eta V_{BB} + V_o$ the capacitor will discharge through $R_1$

$$\eta V_{BB} + V_D = V_{BB}\,(1 - e^{-t/Rc})$$

$$e^{-t/Rc} = 1 - \eta$$

$$e^{t/Rc} = \frac{1}{1-\eta} \qquad \frac{t}{Rc} = \log_e\left[\frac{1}{1-\eta}\right]$$

$$t = RC\log_e\left(\frac{1}{1-\eta}\right)$$

$$\therefore \text{ here } t = T \quad T = RC\log\left(\frac{1}{1-\eta}\right)$$

## 12.8 OBJECTIVE TYPE QUESTIONS

1. In a thyristor anode current is made up of
   (a) electrons only (b) electrons or holes
   (c) electrons and holes (d) holes only
   **Ans:** (c)
2. A thyristor, when triggered, will change from forward blocking state to conduction state if its anode to cathode voltage is equal to
   (a) peak repetitive off state forward voltge
   (b) peak working off state forward voltage
   (c) peak working off state reverse voltage
   (d) peak non-repetitive off state forward voltage
   **Ans:** (b)
3. In a thyristor, holding current is
   (a) more than latching current (b) less than $I_L$
   (c) equal to $I_L$ (d) very small
   **Ans:** (b)
4. For normal SCRs, turn on time is
   (a) less than turn off time $t_2$ (b) more than $t_2$
   (c) equal to $t_2$ (d) half to $t_2$
   **Ans:** (a)

5. In a thyristor, ratio of latching current to holding current is
   (a) 0.4 (b) 1.0
   (c) 2.5 (d) 6.0
   **Ans:** (c)
6. A thyristor can be termed as
   (a) DC switch (b) AC switch
   (c) either *a* or *b* (d) square wave switch
   **Ans:** (a)
7. Turn on time of an SCR can be reduced by using a
   (a) rectangular pulse of high amplitude and narrow width
   (b) rectangular pulse of low amplitude and wide width
   (c) triangular pulse (d) trapezoidal pulse
   **Ans:** (a)
8. For an SCR, *dv/dt* protection is achieved through the use of
   (a) *RL* in series with SCR (b) *RC* across SCR
   (c) *L* in series with SCR (d) *RC* in series with SCR
   **Ans:** (b)
9. For an SCR, *di/dt* protection is achieved through the use of
   (a) *R* in series with SCR (b) *RL* in series with SCR
   (c) *L* in series with SCR (d) *L* across SCR
   **Ans:** (c)
10. The function of snubber circuit connected across an SCR is to
    (a) suppress (*dv/dt*) (b) increase *dv/dt*
    (c) decrease *dv/dt* (d) keep transient over voltage at a constant value
    **Ans:** (a)
11. A forward voltage can be applied to an SCR after its
    (a) anode current reduces to zero (b) gate recovery time
    (c) reverse recovery time (d) anode voltage reduces to zero
    **Ans:** (b)
12. If an UJT, with $V_{BB}$ as the voltage across two base terminals the emitte potential at peak point is given by
    (a) $\eta\ VBB$ (b) $\eta V_o$
    (c) $\eta V_{BB} + V_D$ (d) $\eta V_D + V_{BB}$
    **Ans:** (c)
13. An UJT exhibits negative resistance region
    (a) before the peak point (b) between peak and valley poin
    (c) after the valley point (d) both a and c
    **Ans:** (b)
14. In an UJT maximum value of charging resistance is associated with
    (a) peak point (b) valley point
    (c) any point between peak and valley point
    (d) after the valley point
    **Ans:** (a)

15. When an UJT is used for triggering an SCR, the wave shape of the voltage obtained from the UJT circuit is a
(a) sine wave (b) saw tooth wave
(c) trapezoidal wave (d) square wave
**Ans:** (b)

16. In synchronized UJT triggering of an SCR voltage $V_c$ across capacitor reaches UJT threshold voltage thrice in each half cycle so that there are three firing pulses during each half cycle. The firing angle of the SCR can be controlled
(a) once in each half cycle (b) thrice in each half cycle
(c) twice in each half cycle (d) turn off time
**Ans:** (a)

17. A resistor connected across the gate and cathode of an SCR increases its
(a) *dv/dt* rating (b) holding current
(c) noise immunity (d) turn off time
**Ans:** (a), (b), (c)

18. A triac can be used only in
(a) inverter (b) rectifier
(c) multi quadrant chopper (d) cyclo convertor
**Ans:** (c)

19. Which of the following does not cause permanent damage of an SCR
(a) high current (b) high rate of rise of current
(c) high temperature rise (d) high rate of rise of voltage
**Ans:** (a)

20. Diac break over voltage is nearly
(a) 30v (b) 300v
(c) 100v (d) 200v
**Ans:** (a)

21. If a diode connected in anti parallel with thyristor, then
(a) both turn off power loss and turn off time decreases
(b) turn off power loss decreases but turn off time increases
(c) turn off power loss increases but turn off time decreases
(d) none of the above
**Ans:** (b)

22. Which semiconductor power device out of the following is not a current triggered device
(a) thyristor (b) G.T.O.
(c) Triac (d) MOSFET
**Ans:** (d)

23. In a thyristor, the magnitude of anode current will
(a) increase if gate current is increased
(b) decrease if gate current is decreased
(c) increase if gate current is decreased
(d) not change with any variation in gate current
**Ans:** (d)

**24.** A silicon controlled rectifier is a
(a) unijunction transistor (b) device with three junctions
(c) device with four junctions (d) none of the above
**Ans:** (b)

**25.** A thyristor is basically
(a) a PNPN device (b) a combination of diac and triac
(c) a set of SCRs (d) a set of SCR, diac and a triac
**Ans:** (a)

**26.** A triac is a
(a) 2 terminal switch (b) 2 terminal bilateral switch
(c) 3 terminal unilateral switch (d) 3 terminal bidirectional switch
**Ans:** (d)

**27.** A triac
(a) conducts when not triggered
(b) conducts when not triggered in both directions
(c) conducts when triggered in one direction
(d) none of the above
**Ans:** (b)

**28.** The thyristor is turned off when the anode current falls below
(a) forward current (b) latching current
(c) holding current (d) break over current
**Ans:** (b)

**29.** The VI characteristics of UJT is
(a) similar to CE with a linear and saturation region
(b) similar to FET with a linear and pinch off region
(c) similar to tunnel diode in some respects
(d) similar to pn junction diode.
**Ans:** (c)

**30.** If firing angle in a SCR rectifier is decreased output is
(a) increased (b) maximum
(c) decreased (d) unaffected
**Ans:** (a)

**31.** A SCR is a …………..switch
(a) one directional (b) two directional
(c) three directional (d) four directional
**Ans:** (a)

**32.** Comparing a triac and SCR
(a) both are unidirectional devices
(b) triac requires more current for turn on than SCR at a particular voltage
(c) a triac has less time for turn off than SCR
(d) both are bi directional devices.
**Ans:** (b), (c)

**33.** Each diode is 3ϕ half wave diode rectifier conducts for
(a) 30° (b) 60°
(c) 90° (d) 120°
**Ans:** (d)

**34.** UJT when used for triggering an SCR has wave form

(a) sine wave (b) square wave

(c) saw tooth wave (d) trapezoidal

**Ans:** (c)

**35.** Inverter converts

(a) DC to AC (b) AC to AC

(c) DC to AC (d) AU

**Ans:** (a)

**36.** In a single phase semi converter for continuous conduction each SCR conducts for

(a) $\alpha$ (b) $\pi$

(c) $\alpha + \pi$ (d) $\pi - \alpha$

**Ans:** (d)

**37.** In a single phase semi conductor, for discontinuous conduction and extinction angle $\beta < p$ Each SCR conducts for

(a) $\pi - \alpha$ (b) $\beta - \pi$

(c) $\alpha$ (d) $\beta$

**Ans:** (b)

**38.** In a 1$\phi$ semi converter with discontinuous conduction and extinction angle $\beta > \pi$ free wheeling diode conducts for

(a) $\alpha$ (b) $\beta - \pi$

(c) $\pi + \alpha$ (d) $\beta$

**Ans:** (b)

**39.** In a 1$\phi$ full converter resistive load and for a firing angle $\alpha$, the load current is zero and non zero, respectively for

(a) $\alpha, \pi - \alpha$ (b) $\pi - \alpha, \alpha$

(c) $\alpha, \pi + \alpha$ (d) $\alpha, \pi$

**Ans:** (a)

**40.** Each diode of a 3$\phi$, 6 pulse bridge diode rectifier conducts for

(a) 60° (b) 120°

(c) 180° (d) 90°

**Ans:** (b)

## 12.9 EXERCISE PROBLEMS

1. **For an SCR, the gate cathode characteristic is given by a straight line with a gradient of 20volts per ampere passing through origin. The maximum turn-on time is 4μs and the minimum gate current required to quick turn on is 400mA. If the gate source voltage is 15V, calculate the resistance to be connected in series and the gate power dissipation. Given that pulse width is equal to the turn-on time and the average power dissipation is 0.2w, compute the Maximum triggering frequency that will possible when pulse firing is used.**

**[Ans: 17.5Ω, 15.625KHz]**

2. **The equivalent capacitance of the depletion layer of reversed biased junction of an SCR is 30ϕF, fixed with a *dv*/*dt* of 150v/μs. Calculate the capacitive current flowing through the junction. [Ans : $Ic$ = 4.5mA]**
3. **A thyristor is triggered by a train of pulses of frequency 4KHz and of duty cycle 0.2. (a) compute the gate pulse width (b) if the allowable average gate power is 1W, find the maximum allowable gate power drive. [Ans: (a) 50μs (b) $P_{gmax}$ =5W]**
4. **A thyristor is rated to carry full load current with an allowable case temperature of 100°C, for maximum allowable junction temperature of 125°C and thermal resistance between case and ambient as 0.5°C/W. Find the sink temperature for an ambient temperature of 40°C. Take thermal resistance between sink and ambient as 0.4°C/w. [Ans. 88°C]**
5. **A UJT has the following parameters. $\eta = 0.66$, $V_D = 0.7V$ $I_V = 4mA$, $V_V = 1V$, $I_P = 10\mu A$, $V_{BB} = 20V$**
   **(a) assuming the UJT is initially "off" to what value must $V_{EE}$ be raised to turn on the UJT?**
   **(b) If $R_E = 1K\Omega$ to what value must be $V_{EE}$ be reduced before the UJT turns "off" [Ans: (a) 13.92V (b) 5v]**
6. **A relaxation oscillator using an UJT is to be designed for triggering an SCR. The UJT has the following data : $\eta = 0.7$. $I_p = 0.5mA$, $V_P = 15V$, $V_V = 0.8V$, $I_V = 2mA$, $R_{BB} = 6k\Omega$ Normal leakage current with emitter open = 3mA. The firing frequency is 1.5KHz. For $C = 0.05\mu F$, compute the values of charging resistor and the external resistors connected in the base circuits. Take forward voltage drop of E-$B_1$ junction zero. [Ans: 11.074KΩ, 476.66Ω, 666.67Ω]**
7. **Estimate the minimum and maximum values of charging resistor in the UJT oscillator circuit for manual trigger angle control of α between 20° and 160° for 50Hz supply. Take $c = 0.4\mu F$, $\eta = 0.7$ [Ans: 2.30KΩ, 18.457KΩ]**

## 12.10 LAB EXPERIMENTS

### Experiment No. 1

### *1. Phase full Converter*

**AIM:** To calculate the output average voltage for different firing angles

**Apparatus Required:**

1. Thyristor modules - 4nos
2. Resistor 100W/5A - 1no
3. CRO - 1no
4. Voltmeter 0-100Mctype - 1no
5. Triggering module - 1no

**Circuit Diagram:**

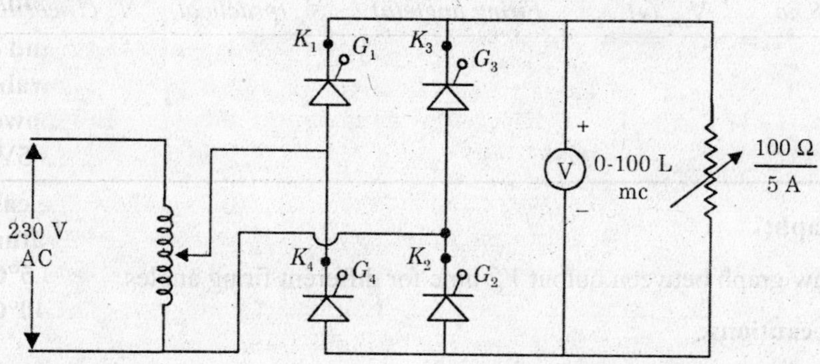


**Procedure:**

1. Connect the circuit diagram properly
2. Give the gate signals $K_1G_1$ and $K_2G_2$, $K_3G_3$ and $K_4G_4$ are in phase from triggering module
3. Connect the CRO across the o/p
4. Apply AC voltage through dimmerstat varying slowly.
5. Note down the voltmeter reading and CRO wave forms for different values of firing angle
6. Tabulate all the values

**Calculation:**

FOR *R*-load

$$V_o = \frac{1}{\pi}\int_{\alpha}^{\pi} V_m \sin\theta\, d\theta$$

$$= \left(\frac{1}{\pi} - v_m \cos\theta\right)_{\alpha}^{\pi}$$

$$= \frac{-v_m}{\pi}(-1 - \cos\alpha)$$

$$= \frac{v_m}{\pi}(1 + \cos\alpha)$$

FOR *R-L* load

$$V_o = \frac{1}{\pi}\int_{\alpha}^{\pi+\alpha} v_m \sin\theta\, d\theta$$

$$= \frac{v_m}{\pi}(-\cos\theta)_{\alpha}^{\pi+\alpha}$$

$$V_o = \frac{2v_m}{\pi}\cos\alpha \text{ where } V_m = \sqrt{2}\, V_{rms}$$

**Tabular Form:**

| *S.no* | $V_{rms}$*(v)* | *Firing angle(a)* | $V_o$ *(practical)* | $V_o$ *(Theoritical)* |
|---|---|---|---|---|
| | | | | |

**Graph:**

Draw graph between output $V_s$. time for different firing angles.

**Precautions:**

1. Connections should be tight
2. Apply AC voltages through variac only
3. Give correct sequence of gate pulses for four modules.

# ❮13❯

# CATHODE RAY OSCILLOSCOPE

## 13.1 INTRODUCTION

Cathode Ray Oscilloscope (CRO) is laboratory equipment used for display, measurement and analysis of waveforms. These are very fast *X-Y* plotters displaying an input signal versus another signal or time. CROs operate on voltage. It is possible to convert current, strain acceleration, pressure and other physical quantities in to voltages.

### *Operation of CRO*

For an operation as an oscilloscope the electron beam is deflected horizontally by a sweep voltage, and vertically by the voltage to be measured. While the electron beam is moved across the face of CRT by the horizontal sweep signal, the input signal deflects the beam vertically, resulting in a display of the input signal wave form. One sweep of the beam across the face of the tube, followed by a blank period during which the beam is turned off while being returned to the stating point across the tube face, constitutes one sweep of the

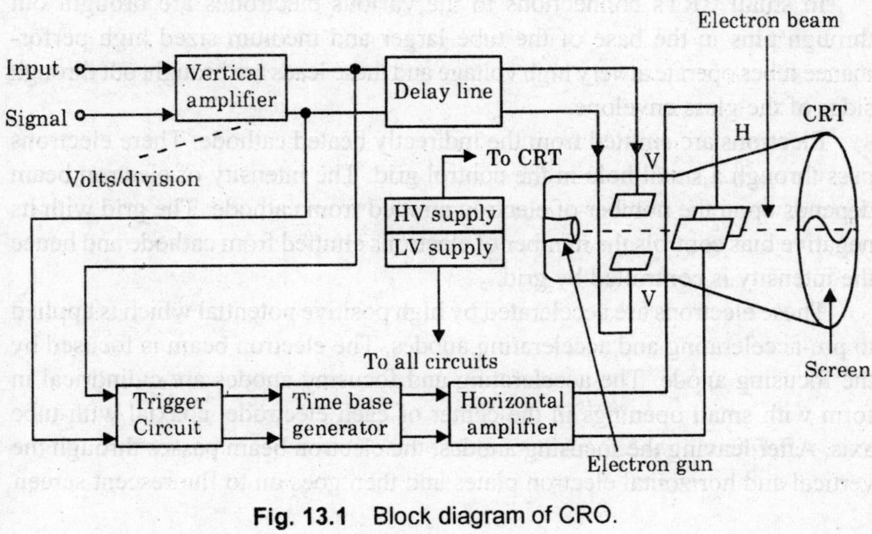


**Fig. 13.1** Block diagram of CRO.

beam. A steady display is obtained when the beam repeatedly sweeps across the tube with exactly the same image each sweep. This requires a synchronization starting the same point in a repetitive wave form cycle.

If the signal is properly synchronized, the display will be stationary. In the absence sync the picture will appear to drift or move horizontally across the screen.

CRO consists of a Cathode Ray Tube(CRT) and some circuit to operate CRT.

CRT consists of electron gun assembly, deflection plate assembly, fluorescent screen and glass envelope.

## 13.2 FUNCTION OF CRT

The electron gun assembly produces a sharply focused beam of electrons, which are accelerated to high velocity. These focused beam of electrons striker the fluorescent screen with sufficient energy to cause a luminous spot on screen. After leaving the electron gun the electron beam passes through two pairs of electrostatic deflection plates. Due to voltage applied to these plates, the first pair of plate plates which are connected horizontally moves the beam vertically up and down and the second pair of plates which are connected vertically, moves the beam horizontally from one side to another. These two movements are independent of each other and the beam may be positioned anywhere on the screen. The working parts of a CRT enclosed in an evaluated glass envelope so that emitted electrons are able to move about freely from one end of tube to another.

*(a) Electron Gun:* The electron Gun emits electrons and forms them into a beam consisting of heater, cathode, grid, pre-accelerating anode, focusing anode, and an accelerating anode.

In small CRTs connections to the various electrodes are brought out through pins in the base of the tube larger and medium sized high performance tubes operate at very high voltage and these leads are brought out through sides of the glass envelope.

Electrons are emitted from the indirectly heated cathode. There electrons pass through a small hole in the control grid. The intensity of electron beam depends upon the number of electron emitted from cathode. The grid with its negative bias controls the number of electrons emitted from cathode and hence the intensity is controlled by grid.

These electrons are accelerated by high positive potential which is applied to pre-accelerating and accelerating anodes. The electron beam is focused by the focusing anode. The accelerating and focusing anodes are cylindrical in form with small openings in the center of each electrode, coaxial with tube axis. After leaving the focusing anodes, the electron beam passes through the vertical and horizontal electron plates and then goes on to fluorescent screen

The electron beam can be focusing by electrostatic focusing and electromagnetic focusing.

*(b) Deflection plates:* The electron beam passes through two pairs of deflection plates. One pair of plate is mounted horizontally and produces an electric field in vertical plane. This pair produces a vertical deflection and is called vertical deflection plates or *Y* plates. The other pair of plates is mounted vertically and produces horizontal deflection and these are called horizontal deflection plates or *X* plates. The plates are fixed so as to allow the beam to pass through them without striking the plates.

*(c) Fluorescent screen:* The screen material on the inner surface of a CRT is called phosphor. The material absorbs the kinetic energy the bombarding electrons and re-emits it in the form of a bright spot. The bombarding electrons, striking the screen, release secondary emission electrons. These secondary electrons are collected by an aqueous solution of graphite called "Aquadog" which is connected to second anode. Collection of secondary electrons is necessary to keep the screen in a state of electrical equilibrium.

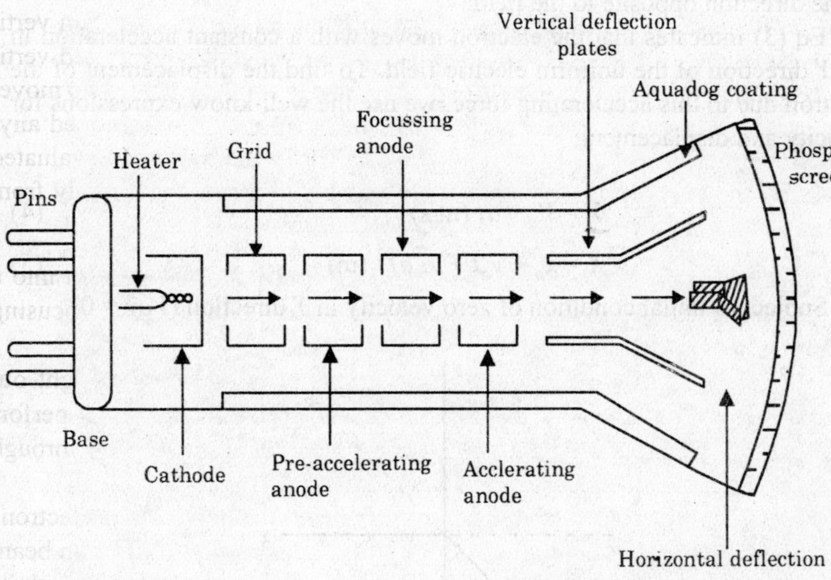


**Fig. 13.2** Internal structure of CRT

## 13.3 MOTION OF CHARGED PARTICLE IN ELECTRIC FIELD

Let us consider the motion of a charged particle in an electric field. The electric field intensity which is equal to negative of the voltage gradient, is defined as the force (in Newton) acting per unit positive charge (in coulombs), and has the same direction as that of the force.

$$\varepsilon = -dv/dx = f/q \quad \ldots(1)$$

In other words, the force $f$ acting on a positive charge $q$ is given by

$$f = q\,\varepsilon = ma = mdv/dt \quad \ldots(2)$$

where $\varepsilon$ = electric field intensity

$m$ = mass in kg

$a$ = acceleration m/sec$^2$

$v$ = velocity, m/sec

The solution of this equation, subject to appropriate initial conditions, gives the path of the particle resulting from the action of the electric forces. If the magnitude of the charge on the electron is $e$, the force on an electron in the field is $f$. Force on $e^-$ acting in $Y$-direction is

$$f = -eE_y \quad \ldots(3)$$

(by Newton's 2[nd] law of motion). The minus sign denotes that the force is in the direction opposite to the field.

Eq (3) indicates that the electron moves with a constant acceleration in the $Y$ direction of the uniform electric field. To find the displacement of the electron due to this accelerating force, we use the well-know expressions for velocity and displacement:

$$V = V_o + at \text{ (m/s)} \quad \ldots(4)$$

$$X = x_o + v_o t + \tfrac{1}{2} at^2 \text{ (m)} \quad \ldots(5)$$

Subject to initial condition of zero velocity in $Y$ direction ($Voy = 0$)

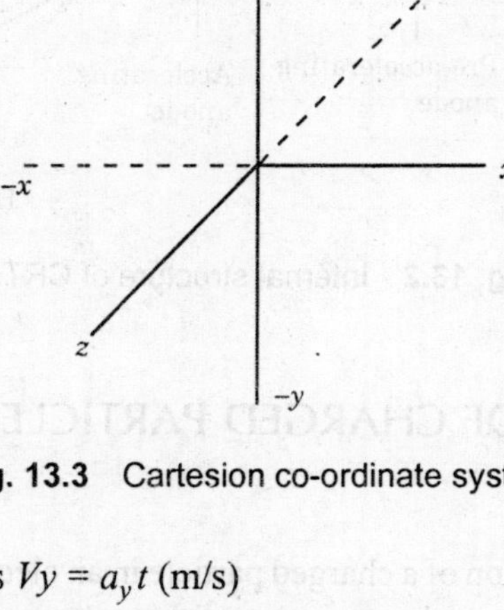


**Fig. 13.3** Cartesion co-ordinate system

eq (4) yields $Vy = a_y t$ (m/s) ...(6)

which, after substituting of eq (3), result is

$$Vy = -eE_y\, t/m \text{ (m/s)} \qquad \text{...(7)}$$

The displacement of the electrons in *y*-direction follows from eq (5) which yields applying the initial conditions of zero displacement ($Y_0 = 0$) and zero velocity ($V_{oy} = 0$)

$$y = \frac{1}{2} a_y t^2 \text{ (m)} \qquad \text{...(8)}$$

Which, after substitution in eq (3) results in

$$y = \frac{-e\, E_y\, t^2}{2\text{m}} \text{ (m)} \qquad \text{...(9)}$$

The *x* distance, traveled by the electron in the time interval *t*, depends on the initial velocity *Vox* and we can write again using equation (5)

$$Vx = Vox + a_x t$$

$$X = Xo + V_{ox} + 1/2\, a_x t^2 \text{ (m)} \qquad \text{...(10)}$$

which, after applying the initial conditions for *X* direction ($X_o = 0$ and $a_x = 0$) becomes

$$X = vox\, t\ t = x/vox \text{ (s)} \qquad \text{...(11)}$$

It is to be emphasized that, if the acceleration of the particle is not constant but depends upon the time, equation (10) are no longer valid. Under these circumstances the motion is determined by integrating the equation

$$dV_x/dt = ax \text{ and } dx/dt = Vx.$$

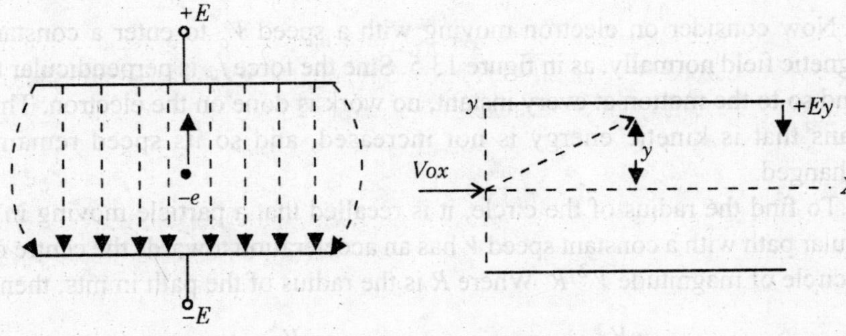


**Fig. 13.4 (a)** Force on electron in an uniform electric field. **Fig.13.4 (b)** Path of moving electron in an uniform Electric field

## 13.4 MOTION OF CHARGED PARTICLE IN THE MAGNETIC FIELD

When a charged particle moves in a magnetic field, it experiences a force whose magnitude is proportional to

(a) the magnetic flux density *B*

(b) the amount of charge on the particle $e$

(c) the component of the velocity of the particle perpendicular to the direction of the magnetic field

$$\therefore \qquad f_m = \mathrm{eBv} \qquad \ldots(1)$$

if the particle is at rest, $f_m = 0$ and the particle remains at rest. If the initial velocity of the particle is along the lines of the magnetic flux, there is no force on the particle according to the rule associated with the equation (1)

Hence a particle whose initial velocity has no component normal to a uniform magnetic field will continue to move with constant speed along the lines of flux.

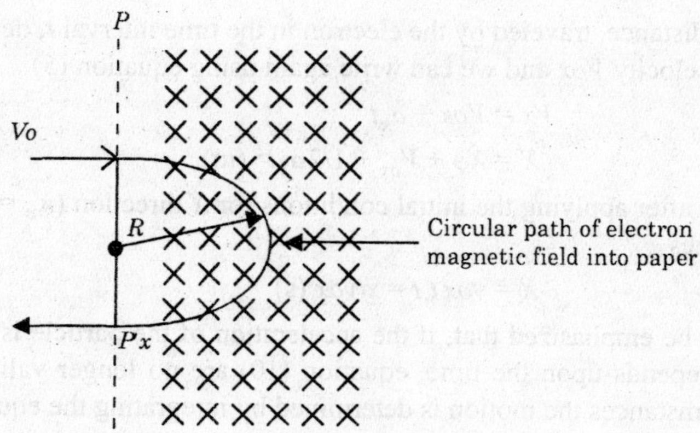


**Fig. 13.5** Circular motion of an electron in a transverse magnetic field

Now consider on electron moving with a speed $V_o$ to enter a constant magnetic field normally, as in figure 13.5. Sine the force $f_m$ is perpendicular to $V$ and so to the motion at every instant, no work is done on the electron. This means that is kinetic energy is not increased, and so its speed remains unchanged.

To find the radius of the circle, it is recalled that a particle moving in a circular path with a constant speed $V$ has an acceleration towards the centre of the circle of magnitude $V^2/R$. Where $R$ is the radius of the path in mts, then

$$\frac{mV^2}{R} = \mathrm{e}BV \text{ for which } R = \frac{mV}{e\mathrm{B}}.$$

The corresponding angular velocity in rad/sec is given by

$$\omega = \frac{V}{R} = \frac{eB}{m}.$$

The time in sec for one complete revolution, called the period is $T = \dfrac{2\pi}{\varpi}$ $= \dfrac{2\pi\, m}{e\,B}.$

For an electron, this reduces to $T = \dfrac{3.57 \times 10^{-11}}{B}$.

$e/B$ is an weber per square meter.

As the radius of the path is directly preportional to the speed of the particle, faster moving particles will travel larger circle in the same time that a slower particle moves in its smaller circle.

This theory is the basic operation of numerous devices, for example, the Cyclotron and magnetic focusing apparatus.

## 13.5 ELECTROSTATIC FOCUSING

In this technique of focussing of the electron beam the CRT is provided with an accelerating electrode and first anode and second anode which provide an electron lens system for focussing the beam into a fine spot on the fluorescent screen.

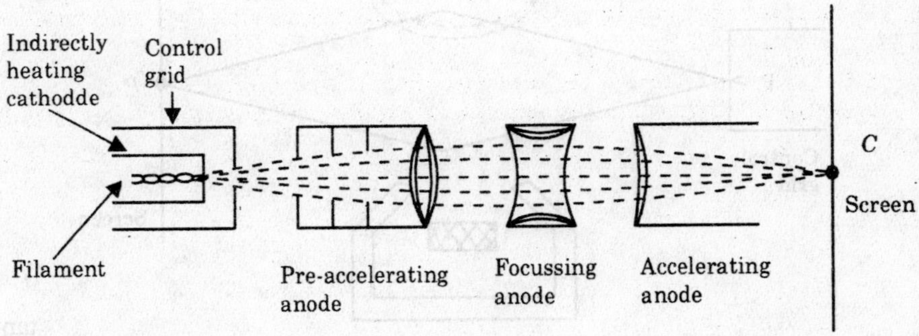


**Fig. 13.6** Electronic focusing system of a CRT.

The inside of the glass wall of the tube between the final anode and the screen are usually coated with a conducting layer of graphite particles, termed as aquadag, which is connector electrically to the second anode. Both the anodes are kept highly positive with respect to the cathode, the potential of the first anode being considerably lowers than that of the second anode. The second anode has a narrow aperture than first anode so as to provide well-defined beam emerging from it. Divergent electron tends to converge into a narrow beam, and this beam tends to pass through the hole at the centre of the electrode. However, the high velocity electrons may not remain in the narrow beam, as they are all similarly charged and hence repel one another. They require to be brought into sharp focus, so that they strike against the screen at a sharp, clearly defined spot. By using focusing electrodes. Thus focussing of the electron beam is achieved

## 13.6 MAGNETIC FOCUSING

In some of the CRTs the final focusing of the electrons beam is achieved both of the magnetic fields, produced either by a permanent magnet or by current carrying coil of wire, the axis of, which is same as that of the beam. The coil is so placed as to surround the electron beam as shown in the figure.

A strong magnetic field is set up, and under the impact of this fields, the electron emerging out of the aperture at the centre of the control grid get attracted towards the axis of the focussing coil.

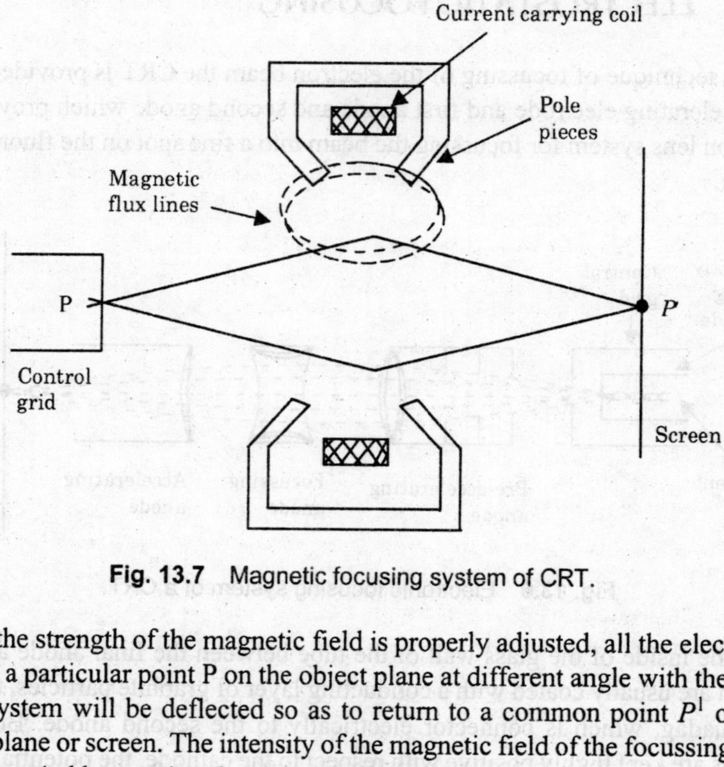


**Fig. 13.7** Magnetic focusing system of CRT.

In the strength of the magnetic field is properly adjusted, all the electrons leaving a particular point P on the object plane at different angle with the axis of he system will be deflected so as to return to a common point $P^1$ on an image plane or screen. The intensity of the magnetic field of the focussing coil may be varied by varying the strength of the current.

## 13.7 ELECTRIC FIELD DEFLECTION SENSITIVITY

A pair of vertical deflection plates of length $l_d$ and having separation of $d$ are shown in figure 1.8. let constant potential $V_d$ be applied between the deflection plates. An electron, which has been accelerated to a high velocity $Vox$ by a constant accelerating potential $Va$, enters the electric field of the deflection plates. Assume that the initial position of the electron is at the origin and the its velocities in $Y$ and $Z$-directions are zero. The velocity $V_{ox}$ is related to the potential $V_a$ of the final anode by equation (1)

$$V_{ox} = \sqrt{\frac{2e\,v_a}{m}} \qquad \ldots(1)$$

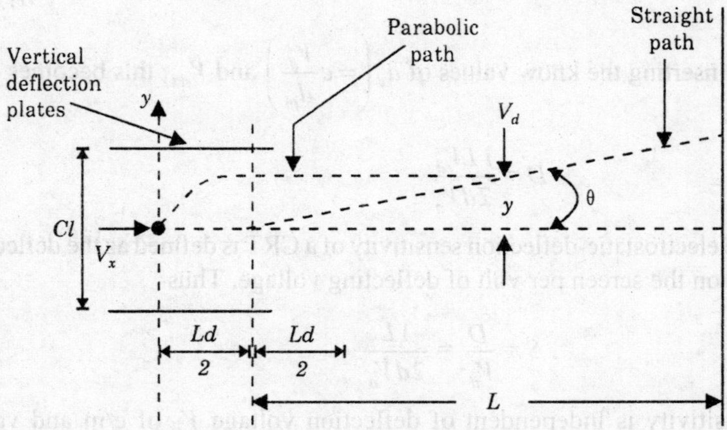


**Fig. 13.8** Deflection of cathode ray beam.

Since no field exist in the region from the anode to the point $O$, the electron will move with a constant velocity $V_{ox}$ in a straight-line path. In the region between the plates the electron will move in the parabolic path given by $Y = \frac{1}{2}\left(\frac{a_y}{V_{ox}}\right)x^2$.

The path is straight line from point $M$ at the edge of the plates to the point $P^1$, since this region is field-free. The straight-line path in the region from the deflecting plates to the screen is, tangent to the parabola at the point $M$. The slope of the line at this point, and so at every point between $M$ and $P^1$ is

$$\text{Tan}\,\theta = \frac{dy}{dx}\Big/ x = 1 = \frac{a_y l}{(V_{ox})^2} \qquad \ldots(2)$$

The equation of the straight line $MP^1$ is

$$Y = \frac{a_y l}{(V_{ox})^2}\left(x - \frac{1}{2}\right) \qquad \ldots(3)$$

Since $\qquad x = l$ and $y = \frac{1}{2}\left(\frac{a_y l^2}{(V_{OX})^2}\right)$ the point $M$

When $y = 0$, $x = l/2$ which indicates that when the straight line $MP^1$ is extended backward, it will intersect the tube axis at the point $O^1$, the center point of the plates.

Regardless of the applied potentials $V_a$ and $V_d$, the electrons appears to emerge form this "cathode" and move in a straight line to the point $P^1$

At poin $P^1$, $y = D$ and $x = L + \frac{1}{2}l$ equation (3) Reduces to $D = \frac{a_y l L}{(V_{OX})^2}$

By inserting the know values of $a_y \left(= e\frac{V_d}{d_m}\right)$ and $V_{ox}$, this becomes

$$D = \frac{i\,L V_d}{2 d V_a}$$

The electrostatic-deflection sensitivity of a CRT is defined as the deflection (in mts) on the screen per volt of deflecting voltage. Thus

$$S = \frac{D}{V_d} = \frac{1L}{2dV_a}$$

Sensitivity is independent of deflection voltage $V_d$ of e/m and varies inversely with accelerating potential $V_a$.

## 13.8 MAGNETIC FIELD DEFLECTION SENSITIVITY

In an electron with an initial velocity $V_{ox}$ enters perpendicularly into a uniform magnetic field of flux density $B$, it is deflected in a circular path, the reduces of which is given by

$$R = \frac{mV}{eB} \quad \text{...(1)}$$

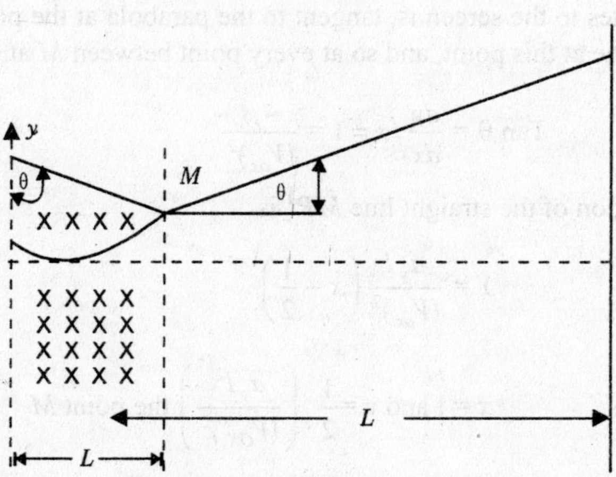


**Fig. 13.9** Magnetic /in a CRT.

The magnetic field is taken as pointing out of the paper, and beam is deflected upward. It is assumed that magnetic field intensity $B$ is uniform in the restricted region shown and is zero outside this area. The electron experiences a force eBv in this uniform magnetic field. Where $V$ is the speed.

The path OM will be the arc of a circle whose centre is at $Q$. The speed of the particles will remain constant and equal to

$$V = V_{ox} = \sqrt{\frac{zeV_a}{m}} \qquad \ldots(2)$$

The angle $\phi$ is equal to the length of the arc OM divided by $R$, the radius of the circle. If we assume a small angle of deflection then

$$\phi \approx l/R \text{ (in radians)} \qquad \ldots(3)$$

where $$R = \frac{mV}{eB}$$

in most practical cases, $L$ is very mush larger than $l$, so that little error will be made in assuming that straight line $MP^1$, if projected backward, will pass through the centre $0^1$ of the region of the magnetic field. Then

$$D \approx L \tan \phi \text{ L} \approx \phi \qquad \ldots(4)$$

By equation (1), (2), equation (4) can be written as

$$D \approx L\phi = Ll/R = \frac{lLeB}{m_{va}} = lLB/\sqrt{V_a}$$

The deflection per unit magnetic field intensity, $D/B$ is given by

$S_m \equiv D/B = Ll/\sqrt{V_a}\sqrt{\dfrac{e}{2m}}$ is called the magnetic-deflection sensitivity of the tube.

## 13.9 SPECIAL PURPOSE OSCILLOSCOPES

There are different types of oscilloscopes are used in different purposes

*(a) Multiple Beam Oscilloscopes:* are used in comparison of one signal with another when multiple beams are appeared at a time.

Normally multiple beam oscilloscopes are enclosed in a single tube. Several beams producing systems each with its vertical pair of plates with common time base each vertical pair has its own amplifiers.

*(b) Double beam Oscilloscopes:* In the name it self there must be two electron guns with in the same circuit in double beam oscilloscope. The electron beams of $X$ and $Y$ channels are completely independent of each other. The out put from it being divided in to two independent controllable beams.

*(c) Multiple Trace Oscilloscopes:* It is different from double beam oscilloscope, in Multiple trace oscilloscopes uses single electron gun and produces

multiple beams, when *Y* deflection plates switches from one to another input signal, it means *Y* channel is time shared by many signals.

*(d) Sampling Oscilloscopes: are:* Used for the frequency range of 50 to 300MHz depends on manufacture, these are commonly used for continuous display.

The sampling techniques transform the input signal in to low frequency domain where conventional low frequency circuit is then capable of producing a highly effective display.

*(e) Impulse Waveform Oscilloscopes:* Some at high voltages there may be occurs transient non period phenomena for investigation of these non period phenomena the oscilloscopes which are used is Impulse wave form Oscilloscopes circuits used in these type are different, where in the plates are mounted on the sides.

Photo graphic records of display can be obtained by suing these types. At very high speed up to $50 \times 10^6$ because a very bright display is obtained on account of the high voltage and the high beam current which exist for a very short duration.

*(f) Scanning Oscilloscopes:* One of the most useful Oscilloscopes for information storage purpose is Scanning (Storage) Oscilloscopes. Generally these are used in Mechanical and Medical fields.

## 13.10 APPLICATIONS OF CRO

The oscilloscope is a very versatile instrument whose use is limited only by the skill of the operator. CRO is used as test-equipment in a laboratory to study the waveforms that is measuring the amplitude, frequency, phase and the time period of a voltage or current.

*1. Study of waveforms:* To study the waveform of an alternating voltage, it is applied to the Y-input terminal.

An internally generated saw-tooth time base voltage is applied to the X-deflection plates. The size of the figure displayed on the screen may be adjusted suitably by adjusting the gain controls.

*2. Measurement of voltages:* To measure a dc voltage, it is applied between a pair of deflection plates. The deflection of the spot on the screen is measure. Then the amount of deflection multiplied by the deflection sensitivity gives the value of the dc voltage applied.

To measure an ac voltage, it is applied between a pair of deflection plates, and then the length of the straight line traced on the screen is measure. Knowing the deflection sensitively, $V_{p-p}$ of applied voltage is of sinusoidal nature, its $r_{ms}$ value is evidently $\dfrac{1}{2\sqrt{2}}$ times the $V_{p-p}$.

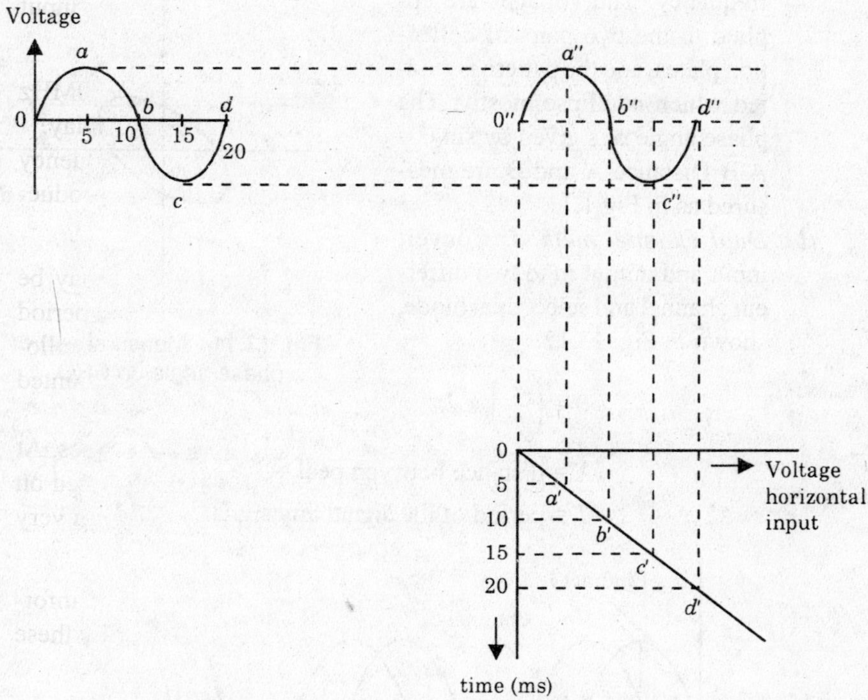


**Fig. 13.10** Display of waveform on CRO of a sinusoidal voltage.

*3. Measurement of current:* To measure current, it is passed through a know suitable resistance and the potential developed across it is measured as has been explained glove. The current may then be calculated.

*4. Measurement of Frequency:* To measure the frequency of a signals, it is applied to one set of deflection plates and across the other pair of deflection plates, an alternating voltage at some frequency obtained from a variable frequency oscillator is applied. The frequency of this voltage is varied until a suitable stationary at points where horizontal and vertical axes touch the pattern at one or more points, acting as tangent to a horizontal and a vertical line. The unknown frequency is where $f_H$ frequency of output voltage of variable

$$f = \left( \frac{\text{Number of points of vertical tan gency}}{\text{Number of point of horizontal tan gency}} \right) f_H$$

frequency oscillator, and it is known.

*5. Measurement of Periodic Time:* Periodic time (or time period) of an alternating voltage is the reciprocal of its frequency or $T = 1/f$

*6. Measurement of phase angle:*

(a) *X-Y mode method:* A CRO may be used to determine the phase angle between two alternating voltages where have the same amplitude and frequency. The voltages are applied to the two pairs of deflection plates, and the pattern is studied which is ellipse mostly. The phase angle $\phi$ is given by $\sin\theta = A/B$ Distance A and B are measured as in Fig 1.11

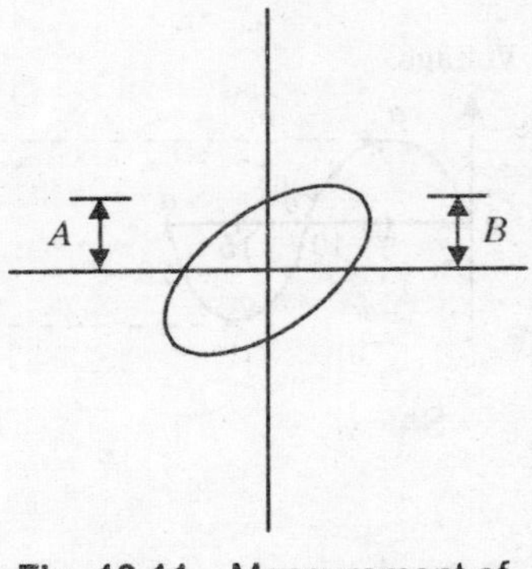


**Fig. 13.11** Measurement of phase angle on CRO.

(b) *Dual channel method:* Convert input and output in to two different channel and select dual mode, shown in Fig. 13.12.

$$\theta = \left(\frac{x}{T}\right) \times 2\pi$$

$X$ = distance between peaks

$T$ = period of the signal any signal.

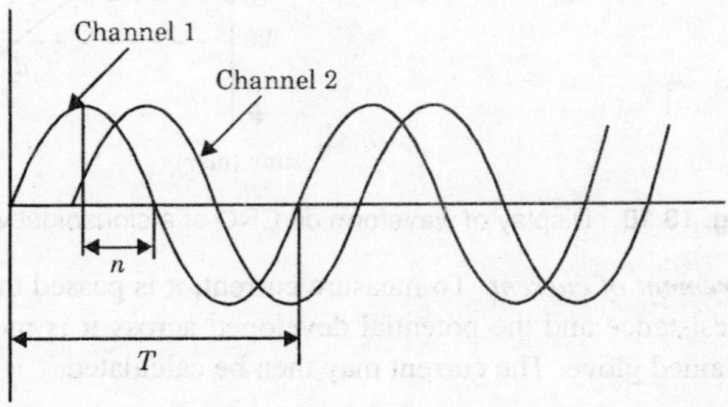


**Fig 13.12** Measurement of dual channel method

## 13.11 SOLVED PROBLEMS

**1. In a CRT, $3 \times 10^{17}$ electrons are accelerated through a potential difference of 10,000V over a distance of 40mm per minute. Calculate the average power supplied to the beam of electrons.**

**Solution:**

Total energy supplied by the source in one minute,

$$W = 3 \times 10^{17} \times 1.6 \times 10^{-19} \times 10000 = 4.8 \times 10^{2}J = 480J$$

Average power supplied to the beam = 480/60 = 8W.

**2. A sine wave voltage is displayed on a CRO. Its vertical amplifier sensitivity is set at 5V/cm and the time base selector switch is set at a sweep speed of 50 μs/cm. The displayed sine wave has a peak-to peak**

**amplitude of 5.4 cm and its two complete cycles are accommodated over 8.4cm of horizontal axis. Determine the r.m.s value and the frequency of the input voltage. If the voltage $V_{m1}$, cos ω *t* and $V_{m2}$ sin ω *t* are applied respectively to the horizontal and vertical deflecting plates of an oscilloscope, prove that the electron beam will trace an ellipse on the screen.**

**Solution:**

Peak-to-Peak amplitude = 5.4 × 5V= 27V.

Hence $\text{rms value} = \frac{27}{2\sqrt{2}} = 9.54\text{V}$

$$1 \text{ cycle takes} = \frac{8.4}{2} = 4.2 \text{ cm} = 4.2 \times 50\mu\text{s/cycle} = 210\mu\text{s}$$

Hence $f = \frac{1}{T} = \frac{1}{210 \times 10^{-6}} = 4.76\text{KHz}$

$$X = V_{m1} \cos \omega t$$

$$Y = V_{m2} \sin \omega t$$

cos $\omega t =$ and $\sin \omega t = \frac{Y}{V_{m2}}$

Squaring and adding, we get

$$\frac{X^2}{V_{m1}^2} + \frac{Y^2}{V_{m1}^2} = 1$$

This is the equation of an ellipse and hence proved.

3. **(a) An electron is emitted from a thermionic cathode with a negligible initial velocity and is accelerated by a potential of 1000V. Calculate the final velocity of the particle.**

   **(b) Repeat the problem for the case of a deuterium ion (heavy ion-atomic weight 2.01) that has been introduced into the electric field with an initial velocity of $10^5$m/sec.**

**Solution:**

The potential difference $V$ (in volts) of point $x$ with respect to point $x_o$ is given by

$$V = \frac{1}{2e} m\left(V_x^2 - V_{OX}\right)^2 \qquad \ldots(1)$$

Then energy $eV$ is

$$eV = \frac{1}{2} m\left(V_x^2 - V_{OX}\right)^2 \quad \ldots(2)$$

Since initial velocity is negligible, so

$$eV = \frac{1}{2} m V_X^2$$

$$\text{Final velocity} = V_x^2 = \frac{2eV}{m}$$

$$V_X = \left(\frac{2eV}{m}\right)^{1/2} = 5.93 \times 10^5\, V^{1/2} = 5.93 \times 10^5 (1000)^{1/2}$$

$$= 1.88 \times 10^7 \text{ m/sec}$$

Since from equation (2)

$$eV = \frac{1}{2} m\left(V_x^2 - V_{OX}^2\right)$$

or

$$V_X^2 = V_{OX}^2 + \frac{2eV}{m}$$

$$V_X^2 = (10)^5 + 2\,\frac{1.6 \times 10^{-19} \times 10^3}{2.01 \times 1.66 \times 10^{-27}} = 10.6 \times 10^{10}$$

$$V_X = 3.26 \times 10^5 \text{m/sec}$$

**4. What transverse magnetic field acting over the entire length of a CRT must be applied to cause a deflection of 3 cm on a screen that is 15 cm away from the anode if the accelerating voltage is 2000V?**

**Solution:**

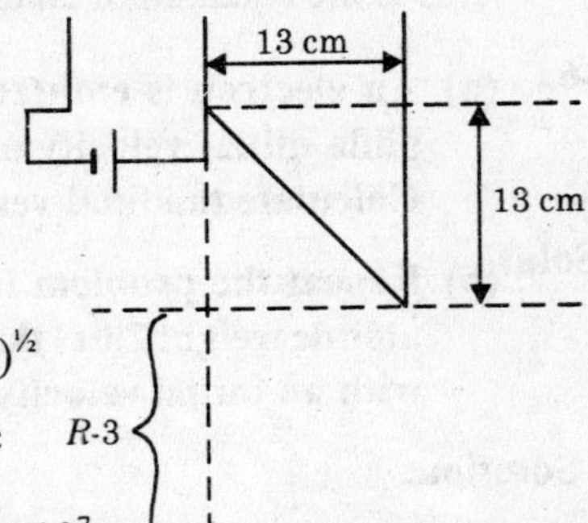

Fig. 13p2

$$R^2 = (15)^2 + (R - 3)^2$$

$$R = 39 \text{ cm}$$

Equation gives: $V_{OX} = 5.93 \times 10^5\, V^{1/2}$

$$= 5.93 \times 105 (2000)^{1/2}$$

$$= 2.65 \times 10^7 \text{ m/sec}$$

From equation $\quad B = \dfrac{V_{ox}}{\frac{e}{m}R} = \dfrac{2.65 \times 10^7}{1.76 \times 10^{11} \times 0.39}$

$$= 3.84 \times 10^{-4} \text{ wb/m}^2 = 3.84 \text{ gauss}$$

**5. The accelerating voltage of a CRT is 2000V. A sinusoidal voltage is applied to a set of deflecting plates. The axial length of the plates is 2 cm.**

**(a) What is the maximum frequency of this voltage if the electrons are not to remain in the region between the plates for more than one-half cycle?**

**(b) For what fraction of a cycle does the electrons remain in the region between the plates if the frequency is 60 Hz?**

**Solution:**

$$V = 5.93 \times 10^5 (2000) = 26.5 \times 10^6 \text{ m/sec}$$

$t = \dfrac{l}{V} = \dfrac{2 \times 10^{-2}}{26.5 \times 10^6} = 7.54 \times 10^{-10}$ sec is the time the electron is in the region between the plates.

If the frequency is $f$, then the time for one-half a cycle is $\dfrac{1}{2f}$

$$7.54 \times 10^{-10} = \frac{1}{2f}$$

or $$f_{\max} = \frac{10^{10}}{2 \times 7.54} = 6.63 \times 10^8 \text{ Hz}$$

(b) If $f = 60$Hz then one cycle is $\dfrac{1}{60}$ sec

$$\frac{t}{1/60} = 60t = (60)(7.54 \times 10^{-10}) = 4.524 \times 10^{-18}$$

**6. An electron starts at rest at the origin of the field configuration shown. The plane determined by *B* and *E* is chosen as the *XY* plane. Describe the motion of the particle.**

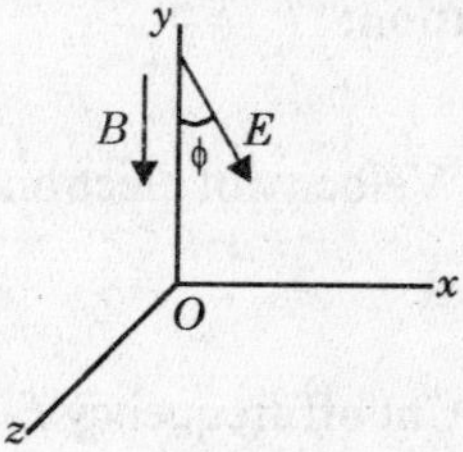


**Solution:**

$$\varepsilon_x = \varepsilon \sin \phi$$

$$\varepsilon_y = \varepsilon \cos \phi$$

Due to $B$ and $\varepsilon_x$ the motion is a common cycloid in the $XZ$ plane as given by

$$X = Q(1 - \cos \theta),\ Z = Q(\theta - \sin \theta)$$

The motion along $Y$ is given by $y = \dfrac{a_y t^2}{2} = \dfrac{e\varepsilon \cos \phi}{2m} t^2$

The path might be called a cycloidal helix of variable pitch.

**7. Calculate the maximum velocity of the beam of electrons in a CRT having a cathode anode voltage of 800V. Assume that the electrons to leave the cathode with zero velocity. Charge of electron = 1.6 × $10^{-19}$C and mass of electron = 9.1 × $10^{-31}$kg.**

**Solution:**

Velocity of electron is $V_{OX} = \sqrt{\dfrac{2eE_a}{m}} = \sqrt{\dfrac{2 \times 1.6 \times 10^{-19} \times 800}{9.1 \times 10^{-31}}} =$ $16.8 \times 10^6$ m/s

**8. An electrically deflected CRT has a final anode voltage of 2000v and parallel deflecting plates 1.5 cm long and 5mm apart. If the screen is 50cm from the centre of deflecting plates find (a) beam speed (b) the deflection sensitivity of the tube and (c) the deflection factor of the tube.**

**Solution:**

$$\text{Velocity of beam } V_{OX} = \sqrt{\frac{2 \times 1.6 \times 10^{-19} \times 2000}{9.1 \times 10^{-31}}}$$

$$V_{OX} = 26.5 \times 106 \text{ m/s}$$

Deflection sensitivity, $\delta = \dfrac{LId}{2dE_a} = \dfrac{0.5 \times 1.5 \times 10^{-2}}{2 \times 5 \times 10^{-3} \times 2000}$ m/V = 0.375 mm/V

Deflection factor $G$ = 1/S= 1/0.375 = 2.66V/mm

**9. Calculate the velocity of the electron beam in an oscilloscope if the voltage applied to its vertical deflection plates is 2000V. Also calculate the cut off frequency if the maximum transit time is ¼ of a cycle. The length of horizontal plates is 50mm.**

**Solution:**

$$\text{Velocity of electron beam } V_{OX} = \sqrt{\frac{2 \times 1.6 \times 10^{-19} \times 2000}{9.1 \times 10^{-31}}} = 26.5 \times 10^6 \text{ m/s}$$

$$\text{Cut off frequency } f_C = \frac{V_{ox}}{4l} = \frac{26.5 \times 10^6}{4 \times 50 \times 10^{-3}} = 132.6 \text{ MHz}$$

**10. Voltage $E_1$ is applied to the horizontal input and voltage $E_2$ is applied to the vertical input of a CRO. $E_1$ and $E_2$ have the same frequency. The trace is an ellipse. The slope of the major axis is positive. The**

**maximum vertical value is 2.5 divisions and the point where the ellipse crosses the vertical axis is 1.25 divisions. The ellipse is symmetrical about the horizontal and vertical axis. Determine the possible phase angles of $E_2$ with respect to $E_1$.**

**Solution:**

$$\sin\phi = \frac{Y_1}{Y_2} = \frac{1.25}{2.5} = 0.5$$

$$\phi = \sin^{-1}(0.5)$$

$$\phi = 30°$$

Thus possible phase angles are 30° or 330°

## 13.12 OBJECTIVE TYPE QUESTIONS

1. A pulse having a rise time a 40 nsec is displayed an a CRO of 12 MHz bandwidth. The rise time of the pulse as observed on the CRO would be approximately equal to 50 ns the input impedance of a CRO is nearly.
   (a) Zero (b) around 10Ω
   (c) Around 100Ω (d) around 1MΩ
   **Ans:** (d)
2. In CRT aquadag Carries
   (a) Aqueous solution of graphite (b) Sweep voltage
   (c) Secondary emission electrons (d) none of the above
   **Ans:** (a)
3. Two sinusoidal signals having the same amplitude and frequency are applied to the $X$ and $Y$ inputs of a CRO. The observed Lissajons figure is a straight line. The phase shift between the two signals would be
   (a) Zero (b) 90·degrees
   (c) Either Zero or 180 degrees
   (d) Either 90 degrees or 270 degrees.
   **Ans:** (c)
4. The Calibration signal available from a CRO is of
   (a) Square wave shape (b) sawtooth wave shape
   (c) Sinusoidal wave shape (d) Any of the above wave shapes
   **Ans:** (a)
5. If the retrace is visible an the CRT display, then the trouble may be that
   (a) The intensity is too high
   (b) the blanking control is not set properly
   (c) there is loss of SYNC signal
   (d) the fly back time of the time base saw tooth is not zero.
   **Ans:** (a)

**6.** To prevent loading of the circuit under test, the input impedance of the oscilloscope must
(a) Below (b) be high
(c) Appear inductive (d) appear capacitive
**Ans:** (b)

**7.** The purpose of the INT/EXT switch in a CRO is to
(a) Select the input to SYNC control
(b) Provide an internal signal to the vertical input
(c) Select input to the horizontal terminals
(d) None of the above
**Ans:** (c)

**8.** To the *Y*-input of a CRO a signal defined by 10 sin 100t is applied. To the *X*-input, the signal 10 cos 100t is fed. The gain for both *x*-channel and *y*-channel is the same. The screen shows.
(a) sinusoidal signal (b) A straight wave
(c) An ellipse (d) a circle
**Ans:** (d)

**9.** A CRO uses
(a) Electromagnetic focussing. (b) Electro-static focussing
(c) both focussing techniques (d) no focussing technique
**Ans:** (b)

**10.** A CRO can display
(a) A.C. signals (b) D.C. signals
(c) both A. C. and D.C. signals (d) time-invariant signals
**Ans:** (c)

**11.** Which meter is suitable for the measurement of 10 mv at 50 mHz?
(a) moving-iron voltmeter (b) VTVM
(c) electrostatic voltmeter (d) C.R.O
**Ans:** (d)

**12.** The input impedance of CRO is
(a) Around1 mΩ (b) zero
(c) Around 1000Ω (d) none of these
**Ans:** (a)

**13.** A CRO cannot be used for the measurement of
(a) Voltage (b) current
(c) Frequency (d) power
**Ans:** (d)

**14.** Phosphor coating for CRO tubes is provided on the
(a) Inside surface (b) outside surface
(c) Both sides of the surface (d) none of these
**Ans:** (a)

**15.** A delay line is used in high speed CRO to introduce time delay in
(a) Vertical channel (b) horizontal channel
(c) in the cathode z axis of CRT (d) none of these
**Ans:** (d)

**16.** Deflection sensitivity of a CRT is
(a) directly proportional
(b) inversely proportional
(c) does not depend on the distance between the deflecting plates and screen
(d) none
**Ans:** (a)

**17.** The picture on an oscilloscope screen is produced by
(a) A electron beam (b) a moving wave
(c) A T-V type camera (d) an intensity control
**Ans:** (a)

**18.** The oscilloscope is used to check what elements of a circuit?
(a) Voltage current and resistance
(b) voltage current and power
(c) frequency, phase and waveshape
(d) frequency, power and waveshape
**Ans:** (c)

**19.** When two frequencies are fed to $X$ and $Y$ plates of a CRO, the resultant pattern is called
(a) Field pattern (b) power pattern
(c) Lissajous pattern frequency pattern
**Ans:** (c)

**20.** CRO can be used
(a) To measure the phase difference between two waves
(b) To measure the phase of a single wave
(c) As a waveform generator
(d) As an amplifier.
**Ans:** (a)

**21.** In CRO the time base signal is
(a) Sawtooth wave (b) squarewave
(c) circular wave (d) sine wave
**Ans:** (a)

**22.** The Lissajous pattern observed on the screen of a CRO is a straight line inclined at an angle of 45 to the $X$-axis if the voltage applied to the $X$-plate is $z \sin z$ than the voltage applied to the $Y$-plates will be
(a) $2 \sin wt$ (b) $2 \sin (wt + 45°)$
(c) $2 \sin (wt - 45°)$ (c) $2\sqrt{2} \sin (wt + 45°)$
**Ans:** (a)

**23.** A CRO uses _________ focusing and _________ deflection.
(a) electro magnetic, electro magnetic
(b) electro magnetic, electro static
(c) electro static, electro static
(d) MASER, LASER

**24.** The deflection of electron beam on reducing pre accelerating anode voltage to half and making deflecting plate voltage double with initial electron beam on CRT decrease as 5mm is
(a) 5mm (b) 10mm
(c) 20 mm (d) 40mm
**Ans:** (c)

**25.** Vertical amplifier in a CRO is designed for
(a) constant gain bandwidth product (b) high gain
(c) large bandwidth (d) none
**Ans:** (a)

**26.** Deflection sensitivity of a CRT with length of deflection plate as 2 cm, distance between them being 1 cm,accelerating voltage as 500 v and distance between screen and centre of deflection plates as 15 cm.
(a) 0.01 cm/V (b) 0.02 cm/V
(c) 0.03 cm/V (d) 0.04 cm/V
**Ans:** (c)

**27.** The deflection sensitivity of a CRT varies inversely as the
(a) length of the deflection plates
(b) distance of screen from deflection plates
(c) deflection voltage
(d) separation between Y-plates
**Ans:** (b)

**28.** The signal to be observed on the screen of a CRO is applied across its
(a) *X*-Plates (b) *Y*-Plates
(c) accelerating anodes (d) focusing anodes
**Ans:** (b)

**29.** In a CRO spot deflection is related to the deflecting voltage and deflection sensitivity as
(a) deflection sensitivity/deflection voltage
(b) deflecting voltage/ deflection sensitivity
(c) deflecting voltage/ deflection sensitivity
(d) none of the above
**Ans:** (c)

**30.** Lissajous patterns obtained on a CRO screen can be used to determine
(a) Phase shift (b) Voltage Amplitude
(c) Amplitude Distortion (d) None
**Ans:** (a)

## 13.13 CONVENTIONAL QUESTIONS

1. Show the Electro static focusing of a CRT and explain about it.
2. Draw the block diagram of CRO and explain function of CRT.
3. What is electrostatic deflection sensitivity and magnetic field intensity?
4. Explain about horizontal and vertical deflection plates, what is their function?

## 13.14 EXERCISE PROBLEMS

1. **In a CRT the distance between the deflecting plates is 1.0 cm, the length of the deflecting plates is 4.5 cm and the distance of the screen from the center of the deflecting plates is 33 cm. If the accelerating voltage supply is 300 volts, calculate deflecting sensitivity of the tube.**

**Answer: 2.48 mm/V**

2. **An electro statically deflected CRT has planes parallel deflecting plates which are 2.5cm long and 0.5 cm apart, and the distance from their centre to the screen is 20 cm.The electron beam is accelerated by a p.d of 2500V and is projected centrally between the plates. Calculate the deflection voltage required to cause the beam to strike a deflecting voltage and find the corresponding deflection of the screen.**

**Answer: 200V; 4 cm**

3. **Voltage $E_1$ is applied to the horizontal input and $E_2$ to the vertical input of a CRO. $E_1$ and $E_2$, have same frequency. The trace on the screen is an ellipse. The slope of major axis is negative. The maximum vertical value is 3 divisions and the point where the ellipse crosses the vertical axis is 2.6 divisions. The ellipse is symmetrical about horizontal and vertical axis. Determine the possible phase angle of $E_1$ with respect to $E_1$.**

**Answer: 120° or 210°**

4. **A Lissajous pattern on an oscilloscope is stationary and has 5 horizontal tangencies and 2 vertical tangencies. The frequency of horizontal input is 1000Hz. determine the frequency of vertical input.**

**Answer: 2500Hz.**

5. **(a) The distance between the plates of a plane-parallel capacitor is 1cm. An e- starts at rest at negative plate. If a direct voltage of 1000v is applied, how ng will it take the negative to reach the positive plate.**

   **(b) If a 60Hz sinusoidal voltage of peak value 1000v is applies, how long will the time of transit be? Assume that the e- is released with zero velocity at the instant of time when the applied voltage is passing through zero.**

**Hint: expand the sine function into a power series.**

## 13.15 LAB EXPERIMENT

### *Study of CRO*

**AIM:** To measure the frequency, phase and sensitivity by using CRO

**Equipment:** CRO, Signal Generator, bread board, connecting wires etc.

**Theory:**

The principle of formation of electron beam and its deflection had been neglected for many years, and it was after the year 1925 that the cathode ray oscilloscope gained a place as a practical measuring device. Today Cathode Ray Oscilloscope (CRO) is used for a number of purposes such as measurement of current, voltage etc; measurement of frequency and phase; observations of waveforms; recreation of television images; as indicators in Radar for visual representation of target data; in industrial measurements etc.

A CRO consists of the following main constituents:

Cathode ray tube,

Time base circuits,

Power supplies and Deflection voltage amplifiers.

Cathode ray tube is an electronic device that produces a visual representation of electrical effects. Its chief advantages is that it produces the visual representation directly with extremely high speed because of the high velocity of electrons. The essential components of a cathode ray tube are the electron gun, deflecting device and fluorescent screen.

Time base may be defined as a circuit for causing the deflection of the spot in the horizontal or vertical or sometime circular direction to vary in a known manner, usually linearly with time. In the most common form, the deflection is proportional to time this deflection is along the *X*-axis or base line of coordinate system; hence the name time base. The waveform of this base is of the shape of saw tooth and hence this voltage is often called saw tooth voltage.

The voltage for a general purpose CRO is of the order of 1000 to 2000 volts. For special uses such as in Radar and T.V. much higher voltages are required.

Cathode Ray Oscilloscope is used for a variety of purposes. Some of them are given below.

**1.** For measurement of voltage and current (Direct or Indirect)

Direct voltage to be measured is applied between a pair of deflection plates and the deflection of the spot is observed. Then the amount of deflection multiplied by the deflection sensitivity gives the value of direct voltage applied.

To measure an alternating voltage of sinusoidal waveform, it is applied between a pair of deflection plates and the length of the straight line produced on the screen may be measured.

# APPENDICES

# Appendix A

### Physical Constants

| *Quantity* | *Symbol* | *Value* |
|---|---|---|
| Boltzmann's constant | $k$ | $1.38066 \times 10^{-23}$ J/K |
| Elementary charge | $q$ | $1.60218 \times 10^{-19}$ C |
| Electron rest mass | $m_e$ | $9.1095 \times 10^{-31}$ kg |
| Electron volt | eV | 1 eV = $1.60218 \times 10^{-19}$ J |
| Permittivity of free space | $\epsilon_0$ | $8.85418 \times 10^{-14}$ F/cm |
| | | $8.854 \times 10^{-12}$ F/m |
| Planck's constant | $h$ | $6.62617 \times 10^{-34}$ J-sec |
| Speed of light in vacuum | $c$ | $3.0 \times 10^{10}$ cm/sec = $3 \times 10^{8}$ m/sec |
| Thermal voltage at 300 K | $kT/q$ | 0.0259 V |

# Appendix B

### Conversion Factors and Prefixes

| *Unit* | *Symbol* | *Conversion* |
|---|---|---|
| *Angstrom unit* | Å | *1Å* = $10^{-10}$ *m* = $10^{-8}$ *cm* = $10^{-4}$ *μm* |
| *Angular frequency* | $\omega$ | $\omega = 2\pi f$ *rps (radians/sec)* |
| *Frequency* | $f$ | $f = \omega/2\pi$ *Hz (cyles/sec)* |
| *Micron, micrometer* | *μm* | $10^{-6}$ *m* = $10^{-4}$ *cm* = $10^{-3}$ *mm* |
| *Mil* | *mil* | $10^{-3}$ *in.* = 25.4 *μm* |
| *Temperature, Celsius* | °C | °C = K – 273.15° |
| femto | f | $\times 10^{-15}$ |
| pico | p | $\times 10^{-12}$ |
| nano | n | $\times 10^{-9}$ |
| micro | μ | $\times 10^{-6}$ |
| milli | m | $\times 10^{-3}$ |
| kilo | k | $\times 10^{3}$ |
| mega | M | $\times 10^{6}$ |
| giga | G | $\times 10^{9}$ |
| tera | T | $\times 10^{12}$ |

# Appendix C

**Useful Properties of Crystalline Silicon, Germanium and Gallium Arsenide**

| *Property (at 300 K)* | *Silicon* | *Germanium* | *Gallium Arsenide (GaAs)* |
|---|---|---|---|
| Atomic number | 14 | 32 | Gallium 31<br>Arsenic 33 |
| Atoms/cm$^3$ | $5 \times 10^{22}$ | $4.41 \times 10^{22}$ | $4.42 \times 10^{22}$ |
| Relative dielectric constant, $\in_r$ | 11.8 | 15.8 | 13.1 |
| Energy gap, $E_g$ (eV) | 1.12 | 0.66 | 1.42 |
| Electron mobility $\mu_n$ (cm$^2$/V-sec) | 1500 | 3900 | 8500 |
| Hole mobility, $\mu_p$ (cm$^2$/V-sec) | 480 | 1900 | 400 |
| Nominal $n_i = p_i$ (number/cm$^3$) | $1.5 \times 10^{10}$ | $2.4 \times 10^{13}$ | $1.8 \times 10^6$ |
| Melting point, °C | 1420 | 936 | 1238 |

# Appendix D

## PN Junction Diode

| Parameters / Type | $V_R$ (max) (V) | $I_R$ (max) (mA) | Continuous $V_F$ (V) | Continuous $I_F$ (mA) | Peak $V_F$ (V) | Peak $I_F$ (A) | Reverse recovery (ns) | Capacitance (10v) (pF) | Class | Comments |
|---|---|---|---|---|---|---|---|---|---|---|
| IN4002 | 100 | 50 | 0.9 | 1000 | 2.3 | 25 | 3500 | 15 | 1-amp rect | Indus std; 7-member family Silicon |
| IN4007 | 1000 | 50 | 0.9 | 1000 | 2.3 | 25 | 5000 | 10 | | Silicon |
| OA 79 | 30 | 1.5 to 150 | 1.2 to 3.8 | 35 | 1.4 to 4.0 | 100 | – | – | Detector Circuits | Germanium |
| BY 126 | 650 | 10 | – | – | 1.5 | 5 | – | – | Television receivers | Silicon |
| BY 127 | 1250 | 10 | – | – | 1.5 | 5 | – | – | Television receivers | Silicon |
| DR-25 | 25 | 200 | – | – | 1000 (mv) | 250 | – | – | Low power rectifier | Germanium |
| DS-10 | 10 | 500 | – | – | 22.5 | 20 | – | – | Stabilizing element | Germanium |
| IN4148 | 75 | 0.025 | 1 | 10 | 1 | 200 | 4 | 4 | Small Signal | Silicon |
| IN5404 | 400 | 5 | – | – | 1.1 | 3 | – | – | GP rectifier | Silicon |
| IN5408 | 1000 | 5 | – | 3 | 1.1 | 3 | – | – | GP rectifier | Silicon |

# Appendix E(a)

**Zener Diode**

| *Type* \ *Parameter* | *Volt Vz @ IZT (Volt)* | *Watts* | *Test Current IZT (mA)* |
|---|---|---|---|
| IN4728 | 3.3 | 1 | – |
| IN4732 | 4.7 | 1 | 53 |
| IN4734 | 5.6 | 1 | 45 |
| IN4736 | 6.8 | 1 | 37 |
| IN4740 | 10 | 1 | 25 |
| IN4742 | 12 | 1 | 21 |
| IN4744 | 15 | 1 | 17 |
| IN4747 | 20 | 1 | 12.5 |
| IN4749 | 24 | 1 | 10.5 |
| IN4751 | 30 | 1 | 8.5 |
| IN750 | 4.7 | 0.4 | 20 |
| IN752 | 5.6 | 0.4 | 20 |
| IN754 | 6.8 | 0.4 | 18.5 |
| IN755 | 7.5 | 0.4 | 16.5 |
| IN758 | 10 | 0.4 | 14.0 |
| IN759 | 12 | 0.4 | 11.5 |
| IN965 | 15 | 0.4 | 9.5 |
| IN968 | 20 | 0.4 | 7.0 |
| IN970 | 24 | 0.4 | 5.6 |
| IN972 | 30 | 0.4 | 5.3 |

# Appendix E(b)

**Varactor Diode**

| Parameter / Type | Reverse breakdown voltage (min) (volts) | Reverse leakage current (max) (nA) | Operating temperature range °C | Nominal capacitance pF | Minimum Q (figure of merit) | Tuning ratio Min. | Tuning ratio Max. |
|---|---|---|---|---|---|---|---|
| ZC830B (SMT) | 25 | 20 | –55 °C to + 150 °C | 10 | 300 | 4.5 | 60 |
| SOD 323 (SMT) | 30 | 20 at $T_A$ = 25 °C | –55 °C to + 125 °C | – | – | – | – |
| SOD 123 (SMT) | 30 | 10 at $T_A$ = 25 °C | – 55 °C to + 125 °C | 19.5 | – | – | – |
| BB 139 | 30 | 50 | –55 °C to + 150 °C | 6.3 | 150 | – | – |

# Appendix F

**Tunnel Diode**

| Parameter / Type | Maximum reverse voltage (volts) | Maximum forward current (mA) | Maximum dissipation at 25 °C (mW) | Maximum reverse leakage current at 10V (nA) | Series inductance (nH) | Q at 2V dc | Applications |
|---|---|---|---|---|---|---|---|
| MV1403 | 12 | 250 | 400 | 10 | 6 | 200 | AM broadcast band, general A.F.C. and tuning applications in lower RF frequencies |
| MV1600 | 20 | 250 | 400 | 100 | 4 | – | AFC applications in Radio, TV and general electronic tuning. |

# Appendix G

**Photo Diode**

| Parameter | Light Current | | | $V_{(BR)R}$ | Dark Current | | Response Time |
|---|---|---|---|---|---|---|---|
| Type | μA typ | @$V_R$ volts | H W/cm² | Volts (min) | nA (max) | @ volts | ns Typ |
| MRD 500 | 9.0 | 20 | 5.0 | 100 | 2.0 | 20 | 1.0 |
| MRD 510 | 2.0 | 20 | 5.0 | 100 | 2.0 | 20 | 1.0 |
| MRD 721 | 4.0 | 20 | 5.0 | 100 | 10 | 20 | 1.0 |

# Appendix H(a)

**BJT-NPN Small Signal Transistor**

| Type \ Parameter | $I_C$ (max) (mA) | $P_D$ (max) (mW) | $V_{CEO}$ (max) (volts) | $V_{CBO}$ (max) (volts) | $H_{fe}$(min-max) @ $I_C$(mA) | $V_{CE}$ | $F_T$@ MHz | Complement | Applications |
|---|---|---|---|---|---|---|---|---|---|
| BC107 | 100 | 300 | 45 | 50 | 110–450@2 | 5 | 300 | BC177 | Audio driver |
| BC108 | 100 | 300 | 20 | 30 | 110–800@2 | 5 | 300 | BC178 | General purpose |
| BC109 | 100 | 300 | 20 | 30 | 200–800@2 | 5 | 300 | BC179 | Low noise audio |
| BC547 | 100 | 625 | 45 | 50 | 110–800@2 | 5 | 300 | BC557 | Amplifier |
| BC548 | 100 | 625 | 30 | 30 | 110–800@2 | 5 | 300 | BC558 | Amplifier |
| BC549 | 100 | 625 | 30 | 30 | 110–800@2 | 5 | 250 | BC559 | Low noise audio |
| 2N2369A | 200 | 360 | 15 | 40 | 20(min)@100 | 1 | 500(min) | – | High speed switch |
| 2N3904 | 200 | 350 | 40 | 60 | 100–300@10 | 1 | 300(min) | 2N3906 | Low level Amp. |
| 2N4401 | 600 | 350 | 40 | 60 | 100–300@150 | 2 | 250(max) | 2N4403 | General purpose |
| 2N3053 | 700 | 5.0W | 40 | 60 | 50–250@150 | 10 | 100 | – | General purpose |
| 2N2222A | 800 | 500 | 40 | 75 | 100–300@150 | 10 | 300 | – | High speed switch |
| BFY50 | 1000 | 2800 | 35 | 80 | 30(min)@150 | 10 | 60(min) | – | General Purpose |
| BUY82 | 10000 | 30W | 60 | 150 | 40(min)@1.5A | 5 | 60 | – | High power switch |
| 2N3055 | 15A | 115W | 60 | 70 | 20–70@4A | 1.1 | 0.8 | BDY 20 | O/P-SW |
| 2N916 |  | 360 | 25 | 45 | 50–200@10 | 0.5 | 300 | 2N2222A |  |
| 2N2369 |  | 360 |  | 40 | 40–120@10 | 0.35 | 500 | – |  |

(*Contd.*)

(*Contd.* Appendix H(a))

| Type \ *Parameter* | $I_C$ *(max)* *(mA)* | $P_D$ *(max)* *(mW)* | $V_{CEO}$ *(max)* *(volts)* | $V_{CBO}$ *(max)* *(volts)* | $H_{fe}$*(min-max)* @ $I_C$*(mA)* | $V_{CE}$ | $F_T$@ *MHz* | *Complement* | *Applications* |
|---|---|---|---|---|---|---|---|---|---|
| 2N3040 | | 360 | 30 | 40 | 40–160@150 | 0.20 | 50 | 2N3040 | |
| BF184 | 30 | 145 | 20 | 30 | 75 to 750 | 10v | 300 | – | For IF amplifier |
| BF185 | 30 | 145 | 20 | 30 | 67 | 10v | 220 | – | Low noise AM and FM applications |
| BF195 | 30 | 250 | 20 | 30 | 67 | 10v | 200 | – | |
| SL100 | 500 | 800 | 50 | 60 | 50–280 | 7v | – | SK100 | AM for receivers Class B push pull stage |
| PT4 | 2 Amps | 4W | 20 | 32 | 80–320 | 10v | 3 | PT6 | Amplifier and Radio receivers |
| AC176 | 1 Amp | 155mW | 32 | 32 | 83 | – | Mc/S | AC128 | Radio receivers, Tape recording |
| BF115 | 30 | 145mW | 30 | 50 | 45–165 | – | 230 | – | Gen. Broadcast and television |

# Appendix H(b)

**BJT-PNP Small Signal Transistor**

| Parameter / Type | $V_{CE}$ (volts) | $V_{CB}$ (volts) | $I_C$(mA) | $V_{ces}$ | @$I_C$ | $H_{fe}$ | @ $I_C$(mA) | $F_T$ | @ $I_{CMHz}$(mA) | P to t (mW) | Use | Comparable Types |
|---|---|---|---|---|---|---|---|---|---|---|---|---|
| BC157 | –45 | –50 | –100 | –0.25 | 10 | 75–260 | 2 | 150 | 10 | 300 | S.S.Amp | BC177, BC212, BC307 |
| BC158 | –25 | –30 | –100 | 0.25 | 10 | 75–500 | 2 | 150 | 10 | 300 | S.S.Amp | BC175, BC308 |
| BC159 | –20 | –25 | –100 | –0.25 | 10 | 125–500 | 2 | 150 | 10 | 300 | S.S.Amp | BC179 BC309 |
| BC557 | –45 | –50 | –100 | – | | 1175–300 | 2 | 150 | – | 500 | 4p. small sig. | BC157 DS557 |
| BC558 | –30 | –30 | –100 | – | | 75 | 2 | 150 | – | 500 | 4p. small sig. | BC158 DS558 |
| AF115 | –32 | –32 | –10 | – | | 150 | | 75 | | 75 | RF. Amp, mixer oscillator in S.W. receivers | AF125 AF200 |
| 2N2904 | –40 | –60 | –0.6A | – | | 20 – 40 | | 200 | | 0.6W | Switching & driving applications | – |
| AD162 | –20 | –32 | –2A | –1v | | 50 – 300 | | 1.5 | | 6W | Audio matched pair | – |
| BC177 | –45 | –50 | –100 | –5v | | 175–500 | | 200 | | 300mW | Audio driver | BC107 |

# Appendix I(a)

**N-Channel JFET (Absolute Maximum Rating at 25°C)**

| Type \ Parameter | Gate Source voltage $V_{GS}$ volts | Drain-Gate voltage $V_{DG}$ (volts) | Drain-Source voltage $V_{DS}$ (volts) | Forward Gate current $I_{GF}$ (mA) | Device Dissipation $P_D$ (mW) | Storage Temperature Range (°C) $T_{stg}$ | Common uses | Features |
|---|---|---|---|---|---|---|---|---|
| BFW10 | –30 | –30 | ± 30 | 10 | 300 | – 65° to 200°C | UHF amplifiers | Low Capacitance High Trans-conductor |
| BFW11 | –30 | –30 | ± 30 | 10 | 300 | – 65° to 200°C | UHF amplifiers | Low Capacitance High Trans-conductor |

# Appendix I(b)

**P-Channel JFET (Absolute Maximum Rating at 25°C)**

| *Parameter* / *Type* | *Gate Source voltage* $V_{GS}$ *volts* | *Drain-Gate voltage* $V_{DG}$ *(volts)* | *Drain-Source voltage* $V_{DS}$ *(volts)* | *Forward Gate current* $I_{GF}$ *(mA)* | *Device Dissipation* $P_D$ *(mW)* | *Storage Temperature Range (°C)* $T_{stg}$ | *Common uses* | *Features* |
|---|---|---|---|---|---|---|---|---|
| E174 | 30 | 30 | ± 30 | 10 | 350 | –55 °C to + 150 °C | Analog switches choppers commutators | Low cost Low on resistance Fast switch-ing speed |
| 2N5018 | 30 | 30 | ± 30 | 10 | 300 | – 65°C to +200°C | Digital switch, sample and hold multiplexers | Low on resistance, High speed switch |

# Appendix J(a)

**Power MOSFET**

| *Parameter Type* | $V_{(BR)}DSS$ *Volts mini.* | $V_{DS}$ *(ohms) max.* | $I_D$ *(Amps)* | $I_D$ *Continuous (Amps) max.* | $P_D$ $T_C = 25°C$ *watts* |
|---|---|---|---|---|---|
| MTM6N55 | 550 | 1.2 | 3 | 6.0 | 150 |
| 2N6762 | 500 | 1.5 | 3 | 4.5 | 75 |
| 2N6760 | 400 | 1 | 3.5 | 5.5 | 75 |
| 2N6758 | 200 | 0.4 | 6 | 9 | 75 |
| 2N6757 | 150 | 0.6 | 5 | 8 | 75 |

# Appendix J(b)

**Small Signal MOSFET**

| *Parameter Type* | $V_{(BR)}DSS$ *Volts mini.* | $V_{DS}$ *(ohms) max.* | $I_D$ *(Amps)* | $I_D$ *Continuous (Amps) max.* | $P_D$ $T_C = 25°C$ *watts* |
|---|---|---|---|---|---|
| BS107 | 200 | 14 | 0.2 | 0.25 | 0.6 |
| BS170 | 200 | 5 | 0.2 | 0.50 | 0.6 |
| 2N6661 | 90 | 4 | 1 | 2 | 6.25 |

# Appendix K

**Uni Junction Transistor (Absolute Maximum Rating at 25°C)**

| *Parameter* / *Type* | *Emitter-base two reverse voltage $V_{EB2}$ (v)* | *Inter-base voltage $V_{BB}$ (v)* | *Continuous emitter current $I_E$ (mA)* | *Peak-emitter current $I_P$ (A)* | *Continuous device dissipation at (or below) 25°C (mW)* | *Storage temperature range* | *Lead temperature 1/16 inch from the case for 10 seconds* |
|---|---|---|---|---|---|---|---|
| 2N2646 | –30 | 35 | 50 | 2 | 300 | – 65 to 150°C | 260°C |
| 2N2647 | –30 | 35 | 50 | 2 | 300 | – 65 to 150°C | 260°C |
| MU10 | 30 | 35 | 50 | 1.0 | 300 | – 65 to 150°C | – |